Security Analysis and Portfolio Management

Falguni H. Pandya

'Curriculum Reference Material Provided By BSE Institute Ltd.'

JAICO PUBLISHING HOUSE
Ahmedabad Bangalore Bhopal Bhubaneswar Chennai
Delhi Hyderabad Kolkata Lucknow Mumbai

Published by Jaico Publishing House
A-2 Jash Chambers, 7-A Sir Phirozshah Mehta Road
Fort, Mumbai - 400 001
jaicopub@jaicobooks.com
www.jaicobooks.com

© Falguni H. Pandya

SECURITY ANALYSIS AND PORTFOLIO MANAGEMENT
ISBN 978-81-8495-410-4

First Jaico Impression: 2013

No part of this book may be reproduced or utilized in
any form or by any means, electronic or
mechanical including photocopying, recording or by any
information storage and retrieval system,
without permission in writing from the publishers.

Printed by
Pashupati Printers
1/429/16, Gali No. 1, Friends Colony
Industrial Area, G. T. Road, Shahdara, Delhi - 95

Dedicated to students

PREFACE

When I sat down to write this book, I had certain thoughts and ideas which guided me throughout to include or exclude certain aspects. Say, if I wanted to include something, in what better way could the reader know this? And how would he/she interpret or relate it in actual decision making? Also, the content must be relevant to the present circumstances. The objective of any teacher and subject is to make students to think, learn, relate and apply whatever they have learned to actual real life world.

While interacting with students as a faculty of this subject and other management subjects I have come across several queries and demands from them. Few of them are,

Does the real world exactly work like this?

Shouldn't we study this theory or concept in terms of Indian context and with real data and facts?

Can't the same theory/concept/model be explained or conveyed in simple, easy to understand manner?

Keeping these questions in mind, this book has attempted to provide a blend of sound theoretical knowledge of investment world and practical and empirical works to prove it in Indian context, starting from basics of investment, fundamentals of market to portfolio management. In depth and easy to understand coverage has also been provided on capital market. *Pause for thought* included at the end of each topic gives a quick and easy way to remember it. To ignite readers' mind to think further in the given topic, *check yourself* has been included at the end of certain topics wherever it was found essential. As it has been rightly said that any theory/concept should be supported/proved by empirical work, I have tried to relate each and every theory by empirically testing it with real market data. Often we have heard that securities or market should not be judged considering their short term behaviour; all the theories have been tested by taking last 10 to 12 years' data. *Assignment questions* and *cases* given at the end of the chapter are eye-catching, empirical, challenging and thought-provoking. *Suggested further reading for empirical work* given at the end of the chapters provides an idea to conduct empirical work for the further enhancement and testing of the concept in present time period.

This book is aimed at post-graduate students of management and commerce and carries a student-friendly pedagogical approach and an attempt to demystify the difficult topics. The book is divided into seven parts spread over 23 chapters.

PART 1: Indian Stock Market: An Overview
PART 2: Portfolio Theory
PART 3: Developments in the Capital Market Theory
PART 4: Fixed Income Securities
PART 5: Fundamental Analysis (E-I-C Framework)
PART 6: Technical Analysis
PART 7: Portfolio Management

Chapters 1, 2 and 3 cover the basics of investment, different investment alternatives of Indian market, and the fundamentals and functioning of the stock market.

Different aspects of security analysis such as risk, return, alpha, beta, systematic, unsystematic risk and construction of the portfolio are covered in Chapters 4 and 6. Chapter 5 thoroughly discusses construction of the portfolio and portfolio opportunity set. Chapter 7 discusses how investors' reward to volatility ratio is influenced by considering lending and borrowing at risk-free rate and constructing portfolio with it. An extension of Chapter 7, Chapter 8 discusses capital allocation line and construction of the optimum portfolio with the help of indifference curve.

The next three chapters exclusively deal with developments in capital market theory, capital asset pricing model and arbitrage pricing theory. Different forms and theory of market efficiency has been dealt with in the chapter on Market Efficiency.

In Chapters 12 to 14 fixed income securities related to valuation of bonds, term structure of interest rate and various techniques of bond portfolio management are covered.

Economic analysis, industry analysis, and company analysis and equity valuation have been covered in Part 5—Fundamental Analysis (E-I-C Framework), Chapters 15 to 18. As there are two approaches for valuation of security, namely technical analysis and E-I-C framework, the latter gives an insight to readers to relate certain consequences occurring to economy, industry, company specific to stock market. Chapter 18 on equity valuation discusses discounted cash flow approach to find out the intrinsic value of equity share.

The other approach for equity valuation is with the help of charts—called technical analysis. Chapter 19 exclusively deals with various methods and techniques adopted by chartists to take decisions such as when to buy/hold/sell the stock.

As the ultimate goal of investors is to construct and manage the portfolio by applying all theories, concepts and tools to enhance their return and minimize risk, Chapters 20 to 23 deal with portfolio management by applying Markowitz and Sharpe models. Chapter 22 discusses formation of the efficient set and finding out the optimal portfolio. Various techniques to evaluate the portfolio are discussed in Chapter 23.

I shall be extremely grateful to receive constructive suggestions and feedback from readers for further betterment of this book.

—**F.H. Pandya**

ACKNOWLEDGEMENTS

My first and foremost gratitude to the Lord All Mighty, because of His blessings this mammoth task became possible. I am grateful to all my students whose constructive queries and questions have made me write this book. I would like to express my very great appreciation to all the students for their help and smoothening out technical matters such as plotting of graphs and others. I wish to record my sincere thanks to Jaico Publishing House and Soumen Mukherjee, Senior Commissioning Editor, for putting trust in me and being a constant source of encouragement. I am also thankful to Theresa Chakravarty and Sushmita Mukherjee for their editorial support.

While writing this book, I have referred many books and web-based materials. These sources helped me to frame the theory constructively and application oriented. I acknowledge all the authors whose books, research papers I have referred.

I owe special thanks to my mother Smt. Bhavna H. Pandya and my father Shree H.L. Pandya; my brother Tarak Pandya and my sister-in-law Smt. Arti Pandya for their love and support.

CONTENTS

PREFACE v
ACKNOWLEDGEMENTS vii

PART 1
INDIAN STOCK MARKET: AN OVERVIEW

1. **UNDERSTANDING INVESTMENTS** 3-10
   1.1 Introduction 3
       1.1.1 Investment 4
       1.1.2 Start Investing Early 5
       1.1.3 Invest with a Long-Term Goal 5
       1.1.4 Buy Securities at Discount 6
   1.2 Investment Objectives 6
   1.3 Types of Investors 8
   1.4 Investment, Speculation and Gambling 9
   Summary 10
   Key Concepts 10
   Review Questions 10

2. **INVESTMENT ALTERNATIVES** 11-40
   2.1 Introduction 11
       2.1.1 Negotiable Instruments 11
       2.1.2 Variable Income Securities 12
       2.1.3 Equity Shares 13
       2.1.4 Fixed Income Securities 13
       2.1.5 Bonds 13
       2.1.6 Debentures 14
       2.1.7 Preference Shares 14
       2.1.8 Treasury Bills 15
       2.1.9 Commercial Paper 15

	2.1.10	Certificate of Deposit	16
	2.1.11	Kisan Vikas Patra (KVP)	17
2.2	Non-Negotiable Securities	17
	2.2.1	Bank Deposits	18
	2.2.2	Post Office Schemes	16
	2.2.3	Non-Banking Financial Corporation (NBFC)	18
	2.2.4	Tax Sheltered Instruments	19
	2.2.5	Public Provident Fund (PPF)	19
	2.2.6	National Savings Certificate (NSC)	21
	2.2.7	National Savings Schemes (NSSs)	22
	2.2.8	Rajiv Gandhi Equity Savings Schemes (RGESS)	22
	2.2.9	Life Insurance	23
2.3	Mutual Funds	24
2.4	Real Assets	26
	2.4.1	Gold	26
	2.4.2	Silver	27
2.5	Real Estate	29
2.6	Pension Plan	29
2.7	Foreign Currency Securities	30
	2.7.1	American Depository Receipts	30
	2.7.2	Global Depository Receipts	31
	2.7.3	External Commercial Borrowings	31
	2.7.4	Foreign Currency Convertible Bonds	34
	Summary	35
	Key Concepts	35
	Case Study	36
	Appendices	36

3. STOCK MARKET INDICES   41-68

3.1	Introduction	41
3.2	Market	42
	3.2.1	Uses of Stock Market Indices	42
	3.2.2	Benefits of Listing	43
	3.2.3	Factors to be Considered While Constructing the Market Indices	43
	3.2.4	Sensex Scrips Selection Criteria	48
3.3	Market Capitalization	49
	3.3.1	Free Float Methodology	50
3.4	Maintenance of Sensex and Index Closure Algorithm	55
3.5	Adjustments	56
	3.5.1	Adjustment for Bonus Issue	56
	3.5.2	Adjustment for Rights Issue	56
	3.5.3	Adjustment for New Issue	57

3.6	Impact Cost		57
3.7	Sensex		59
3.8	S&P CNX Nifty		60
	3.8.1 CNX Small Cap Index	60	
	3.8.2 CNX Mid Cap	61	
	3.8.3 S&P CNX 500	61	
3.9	Total Return Index—Calculation Methodology		61
3.10	Tracking Error		62
	Summary		62
	Key Concepts		64
	Review Questions		64
	Appendices		65

PART 2
PORTFOLIO THEORY

4. MEASURING RISK AND RETURN — 71-102

4.1	Introduction		71
4.2	The Basis of Investment Decisions: Return		71
	4.2.1 Return on a Single Asset	72	
	4.2.2 Annual Rate of Return	74	
	4.2.3 Average Rate of Return	75	
	4.2.4 Holding Period Return (HPR)	75	
	4.2.5 Annual Compound Rate of Return	76	
	4.2.6 Compound Annual Growth Rate (CAGR)	77	
	4.2.7 Limitations in the Methods for Calculating Return	78	
4.3	The Basis of Investment Decisions: Risk		79
	4.3.1 Calculation of Risk	79	
4.4	Calculation of the Expected Rate of Return by Using Probabilities		81
	4.4.1 Calculation of Risk for the Expected Rate of Return	82	
	4.4.2 Points to be Considered While Using Probabilities	83	
4.5	Concepts of Risk		85
	Summary		87
	Key Concepts		88
	Review Questions		88
	Assignment Questions		88
	Illustrations		88
	Problems		96
	Case Study		98

5. INTRODUCTION TO PORTFOLIO THEORY   103-157

- 5.1 Introduction   103
  - 5.1.1 Basis of the Portfolio Theory: Diversification Reduces the Risk   104
  - 5.1.2 Portfolio Return: Two Assets Case   105
  - 5.1.3 Portfolio Risk: Two Assets Case   106
  - 5.1.4 Covariance   108
  - 5.1.5 Correlation Coefficient   109
- 5.2 Estimated Return-Risk: Two Assets Case   111
  - 5.2.1 Variance and Standard Deviation: Two-Asset Portfolio   113
- 5.3 Optimum Portfolio   114
  - 5.3.1 Portfolio Risk and Correlation between Assets   115
  - 5.3.2 Notion of Dominance   117
  - 5.3.3 Coefficient of Variation (CV)   118
  - 5.3.4 Calculation of Portfolio Risk by Assigning Probabilities   119
- 5.4 Portfolio Risk-Return Analysis: Two Assets Case   122
- 5.5 Minimum Variance Portfolio   125
  - 5.5.1 Perfect Negative Correlation   125
  - 5.5.2 Perfect Positive Correlation   127
  - 5.5.3 Zero Correlation   129
  - 5.5.4 Power of Diversification when Correlation is Zero   130
- 5.6 Construction of the Portfolio with Three Securities   136
- Summary   141
- Key Concepts   142
- Review Questions   142
- Illustrations   143
- Problems   149
- Case Study   153

6. BETA AND RISK ESTIMATION   158-194

- 6.1 Introduction   158
  - 6.1.1 Portfolio Risk for a Portfolio of 'N' Securities   159
- 6.2 Risk Diversification   160
  - 6.2.1 Systematic Risk   160
  - 6.2.2 Unsystematic Risk   161
  - 6.2.3 Total Risk   162
- 6.3 How to Measure the Systematic Risk?   163
  - 6.3.1 Calculating Beta   164
  - 6.3.2 Accounting Beta   175
  - 6.3.3 Determinants of Beta   175
  - 6.3.4 Asset Beta and Equity Beta   178

	6.4	The Market Model	179
		6.4.1 Random Error	180
		6.4.2 Actual Returns	182
		Summary	184
		Key Concepts	185
		Review Questions	185
		Assignment Questions	185
		Illustrations	185
		Problems	188
		Case Study: 1	190
		Case Study: 2	193
7.	**RISK-FREE LENDING AND BORROWING**		**195-219**
	7.1	Introduction	195
		7.1.1 What is Meant by a Risk-Free Asset?	195
		7.1.2 Feasible Set and Efficient Set	196
		7.1.3 Risk-Free Lending	198
		7.1.4 Constructing a Portfolio of Risk-Free Asset and Risky Asset	198
		7.1.5 Investment in Risk-Free Asset and Risky Portfolio	201
		7.1.6 Portfolios: All Possible Combinations of the Risk-Free Asset, Utilizing All Available Risky Assets	203
		7.1.7 Selection of Optimal Portfolio (Risk-Free Lending) with Indifference Curves	204
	7.2	Constructing the Portfolio by Borrowing at the Risk-Free Rate	206
		7.2.1 Extending Leverage to the Risky Portfolio	210
		7.2.2 Portfolios: All Possible Combinations of the Risk-Free Asset with All Available Risky Assets, Utilizing Risk-Free Borrowing	211
	7.3	Efficient Set and Risk-Free Lending and Borrowing	212
		7.3.1 Analyzing the Effects of Risk-Free Lending and Borrowing on the Efficient Set	213
		Summary	214
		Key Concepts	215
		Review Questions	215
		Illustrations	215
		Problems	218
8.	**RISK AVERSION AND CAPITAL ALLOCATION**		**220-240**
	8.1	Introduction	220
		8.1.1 Utility Values	221
	8.2	Allocation of Funds to Risk-Free Security and Risky Portfolio	224
		8.2.1 Portfolio of One Risky Portfolio and One Risk-Free Asset	226

8.3	Capital Allocation Line with Risk-Free Borrowing		228
	8.3.1 Risk Aversion and Asset Allocation	231	
8.4	Risk, Return and Reward-to-Volatility Ratio of the Optimum Portfolio		234
	8.4.1 Selection of the Optimal Portfolio with the Help of Indifference Curves	234	
	8.4.2 Finding the Optimal Portfolio by Using Indifference Curves	236	
	Summary		238
	Key Concepts		239
	Problems		239

PART 3
DEVELOPMENTS IN THE CAPITAL MARKET THEORY

9.	**CAPITAL ASSET PRICING MODEL**		**243-261**
9.1	Introduction		243
	9.1.1 The Capital Asset Pricing Model (CAPM): Assumptions	244	
9.2	Characteristics Line		245
	9.2.1 The Capital Market Line (CML)	247	
	9.2.2 The Separation Principle	248	
	9.2.3 The Market Portfolio	248	
	9.2.4 Risk-Return and Efficient Portfolio	249	
9.3	The Security Market Line (SML)		250
	9.3.1 Beta and SML	253	
9.4	Implications of CAPM		254
	9.4.1 Limitation of the CAPM	255	
	Summary		256
	Key Concepts		256
	Review Questions		256
	Case Study		257
10.	**ARBITRAGE PRICING THEORY**		**262-271**
10.1	Introduction		262
	10.1.1 Arbitrage Pricing Theory (APT)	263	
	10.1.2 APT and Law of One Price	263	
	10.1.3 Comparative Study of APT and CAPM	264	
10.2	Well-Diversified Portfolio		266
	10.2.1 Systematic Risk and Expected Return on Portfolios	267	
	10.2.2 Systematic Risk and Expected Return on an Individual Security	269	
	Summary		269
	Key Concepts		270
	Review Questions		270

11. MARKET EFFICIENCY   272–301

11.1 Introduction   272
    11.1.1 The Efficient Market Hypothesis (EMH)   273

11.2 EMH in Other Countries   274

11.3 Random Walk Theory   275

11.4 Forms of Market Efficiency   276
    11.4.1 Tests of Market Efficiency   277
    11.4.2 Weak Form of Efficient Market   278
    11.4.3 Semi-Strong Form of Efficient Market   284
    11.4.4 Price-Earnings Ratio   286
    11.4.5 Price-to-Book Ratio   289

11.5 Strong Form of Efficient Market   292

11.6 Critique of EMH   292

Summary   293

Key Concepts   293

Review Questions   293

Assignment Questions   293

Illustrations   294

Appendix A   296

Appendix B   299

PART 4
FIXED INCOME SECURITIES

12. BOND ANALYSIS   305–342

12.1 Introduction   305

12.2 Basics of Bonds   305

12.3 Types of Bonds   307
    12.3.1 Novel Bonds   311

12.4 Difference between a Bond and a Debenture   312

12.5 Accrued Interest and Quoted Bond Prices   312
    12.5.1 Bond Values   313
    12.5.2 Bonds with Maturity   313
    12.5.3 Bond Values with Semi-Annual Interest   316
    12.5.4 Value of the Bond with Principal Amortization   317
    12.5.5 Yield to Maturity (YTM)   318
    12.5.6 YTM and Realized Yield   321
    12.5.7 Horizon Analysis   322
    12.5.8 Bond Prices over Time   324

12.6 YTM versus Holding Period Return (HPR)   325

12.7 Zero Coupon Bonds ... 326
12.8 After-Tax Returns ... 327
  12.8.1 Tax Treatment for Coupon Bearing Bonds ... 327
12.9 Current Yield ... 328
  12.9.1 Yield to Call (YTC) ... 329
12.10 How Coupon Rate, Required Yield and Price Move Together? ... 330
  12.10.1 Maturity of the Bond and Interest Rate Risk ... 332
  12.10.2 Interest Rate Sensitivity and Maturity of the Bonds ... 334
12.11 Default Risk and Credit Rating ... 335
Summary ... 336
Key Concepts ... 337
Review Questions ... 337
Illustrations ... 337
Problems ... 340
Appendix ... 341

13. THE TERM STRUCTURE OF INTEREST RATES ... 343-362
13.1 Introduction ... 343
13.2 Yield to Maturity (YTM) ... 343
  13.2.1 Spot Rates ... 346
  13.2.2 Discount Factors ... 347
  13.2.3 Forward Rates ... 348
  13.2.4 Forward Rates and Discount Factors ... 349
13.3 Yield Curve ... 350
  13.3.1 Types of Yield Curves ... 352
  13.3.2 The Credit Spread ... 354
13.4 Term Structure Theories ... 355
Summary ... 359
Key Concepts ... 360
Review Questions ... 360
Illustrations ... 360
Problems ... 361

14. BOND PORTFOLIO MANAGEMENT ... 363-399
14.1 Introduction ... 363
14.2 Bond Pricing Theorems ... 364
  14.2.1 Convexity ... 369
  14.2.2 Duration ... 370
  14.2.3 Features that Affect the Duration ... 373
  14.2.4 Application of Duration ... 373

	14.2.5 Duration for Zero Coupon Bonds	374
	14.2.6 Duration for Coupon Bearing Bonds	375
	14.2.7 Macaulay Duration	376
	14.2.8 Modified Duration	377
	14.2.9 Relationship between Convexity and Duration	378
14.3	Bond Portfolio Management	380
	14.3.1 Passive Bond Management Strategies	380
	14.3.2 Active Bond Management Strategies	381
14.4	Valuation Analysis	382
	14.4.1 Credit Analysis	382
	14.4.2 Swaps	382
14.5	Immunization	385
	14.5.1 Issues with Immunization	388
	14.5.2 Contingent Immunization	389
14.6	Horizon Analysis	390
	Summary	391
	Key Concepts	392
	Review Questions	392
	Illustrations	392
	Problems	397

PART 5
FUNDAMENTAL ANALYSIS (E-I-C FRAMEWORK)

15. ECONOMIC ANALYSIS 403-420

15.1	Introduction	403
	15.1.1 The Global Economic Environment: an Overview	404
15.2	Assessing the Indian Economy	406
	15.2.1 India's Economic Performance Post 1990-91	406
	15.2.2 Present Real Economy	407
	15.2.3 Agriculture	408
	15.2.4 Index of Industrial Production (IIP)	409
	15.2.5 Infrastructure	410
	15.2.6 Service Sector	411
	15.2.7 Savings and Capital Formation	412
	15.2.8 Fiscal Policy	413
	15.2.9 Business Cycles	413
	15.2.10 Monsoon	414
	15.2.11 Budget Deficit	415
	15.2.12 Sentiment	415

xviii   Contents

Summary		415
Key Concepts		416
Assignment Questions		416
Appendix		416

16. INDUSTRY ANALYSIS   421-432

16.1	Introduction		421
	16.1.1 The Industry Life Cycle	421	
	16.1.2 An Assessment of the Industry Life Cycle	424	
16.2	Industry Structure and Performance		425
	16.2.1 Michael Porter's Five Forces	425	
16.3	Industry Analysis		428
16.4	Factors Affecting Industry Performance		429
	Summary		431
	Key Concepts		431
	Assignment Questions		431

17. COMPANY ANALYSIS   433-458

17.1	Introduction		433
	17.1.1 Growth Companies and Growth Stocks	434	
	17.1.2 Defensive Companies and Defensive Stocks	435	
	17.1.3 Cyclical Companies and Cyclical Stocks	436	
	17.1.4 Speculative Companies and Speculative Stocks	436	
	17.1.5 Value Stocks	436	
17.2	Company Analysis and Financial Information		436
	17.2.1 Company Analysis of Reliance Industries Limited	437	
17.3	DuPont Analysis		443
	17.3.1 Ratio Analyses	444	
	17.3.2 Debt Equity Ratio	444	
	17.3.3 Interest Coverage Ratio	445	
	17.3.4 Inventory Turnover	445	
	17.3.5 Debtors Turnover	446	
	17.3.6 Fixed Assets Turnover	446	
	17.3.7 Return on Assets (ROA)	447	
	17.3.8 Return on Capital Employed	447	
	17.3.9 Return on Net Worth	448	
	17.3.10 Enterprise Multiple	448	
	17.3.11 Current Ratio	449	
	17.3.12 Price-Earnings Ratio	449	
	17.3.13 Dividend Yield	450	
	17.3.14 Earnings per Share (EPS)	450	
	17.3.15 Tobin's q	451	

	17.4	Leverage Analysis		451
		17.4.1 Financial Leverage	452	
		17.4.2 Estimating Earnings per Share	452	
	17.5	Capital Structure of RIL		452
		17.5.1 Management of RIL	453	
		17.5.2 Shareholding Patterns of RIL	454	
		17.5.3 Collaborations with Other Companies	455	
		17.5.4 The Competitive Edge of the Company	455	
		17.5.5 Overall Significance of RIL in Indian Economy	456	
		17.5.6 Rating to RIL	456	
		17.5.7 Risk and RIL	456	
		17.5.8 Future Scenario of RIL	456	
		Summary		457
		Key Concepts		457
		Review Questions		457
		Assignment Questions		457
18.	**EQUITY VALUATION**			**459–486**
	18.1	Introduction		459
		18.1.1 Valuation of Ordinary Share	459	
		18.1.2 Intrinsic Value versus Market Price	460	
		18.1.3 Single Period Valuation Model	460	
		18.1.4 Multi-Period Valuation Model	462	
		18.1.5 Zero Growth Model	465	
	18.2	Growth in Dividends		465
		18.2.1 Constant Growth Model	465	
		18.2.2 Supernormal Growth and Normal Growth	466	
	18.3	What Determines Growth?		468
		18.3.1 Non-Payment of Dividends by Firms	470	
	18.4	Earning Capitalization		471
		18.4.1 Cost of Equity Capital	472	
		18.4.2 Stock Prices, Earnings and Dividends	472	
		18.4.3 Value of Growth Opportunities	474	
	18.5	Discounted Cash Flow Valuation Approach		476
	18.6	Sensitivity Analysis		480
		Summary		481
		Key Concepts		482
		Review Questions		482
		Assignment Questions		482
		Appendix		482

PART 6
TECHNICAL ANALYSIS

19. TECHNICAL ANALYSIS — **489-530**

- 19.1 Introduction — 489
  - 19.1.1 History of Technical Analysis and Dow Theory — 490
- 19.2 Trend and Trend Lines — 492
  - 19.2.1 Market Movements — 492
  - 19.2.2 Primary Movements — 492
  - 19.2.3 Secondary Movements — 493
  - 19.2.4 Daily Fluctuations — 494
- 19.3 Technical Analysis versus Fundamental Analysis — 494
  - 19.3.1 Market Breadth Theory — 495
  - 19.3.2 Types of Charts — 498
  - 19.3.3 Support and Resistance — 501
  - 19.3.4 Chart Patterns — 503
- 19.4 Technical Analysis Indicators — 509
  - 19.4.1 Moving Averages — 509
  - 19.4.2 Simple Moving Averages — 510
  - 19.4.3 Weighted Moving Averages — 512
  - 19.4.4 Exponential Moving Averages — 514
  - 19.4.5 Triangular Moving Averages — 517
  - 19.4.6 Variable Moving Averages — 517
  - 19.4.7 Long-Term Moving Averages — 517
- 19.5 Relative Strength Index (RSI) — 518
- 19.6 Gap — 521
  - 19.6.1 Types of Gaps — 522
- Summary — 523
- Key Concepts — 523
- Review Questions — 524
- Appendix — 524

PART 7
PORTFOLIO MANAGEMENT

20. MARKOWITZ PORTFOLIO THEORY — **533-563**

- 20.1 Introduction — 533
  - 20.1.1 Modern Portfolio Theory — 533
  - 20.1.2 Theoretical Framework for Portfolio Selection Model — 534
  - 20.1.3 Construction of Efficient Portfolio as per the Markowitz Model — 538
  - 20.1.4 Passive Portfolio — 539
  - 20.1.5 Active Portfolio — 552

	20.2	Markowitz Optimization Model		552
		20.2.1 Evaluation of Portfolio	556	
		Summary		557
		Key Concepts		557
		Review Questions		557
		Assignment Questions		557
		Problems		557
		Case Study		559
		Appendix		561

21. SHARPE'S SINGLE INDEX MODEL — 564-591

	21.1	Introduction		564
	21.2	Sharpe's Single Index Model		565
		21.2.1 Components of Risk: Systematic Risk and Unsystematic Risk	569	
		21.2.2 Sharpe's Optimal Portfolio	570	
		21.2.3 Construction of Sharpe's Optimal Portfolio	570	
		21.2.4 Sharpe's Optimal Portfolio: Illustration	572	
		21.2.5 Constructing an Optimal Portfolio by Sharpe's Index Model of Nifty 50	575	
		21.2.6 Optimum Portfolio with Short Sales	584	
		Summary		587
		Key Concepts		587
		Review Question		587
		Assignment Questions		587
		Illustration		588
		Problems		589
		Case Study		590

22. PORTFOLIO SELECTION — 592-612

	22.1	Introduction		592
	22.2	The Theory of Indifference Curves		592
		22.2.1 Selection of Indifference Curves	595	
	22.3	The Efficient Set		597
		22.3.1 The Feasible Set	597	
		22.3.2 The Efficient Set and the Feasible Set	598	
		22.3.3 Feasible Set and Indifference Curves	599	
	22.4	Deriving the Location of the Efficient Set		601
		22.4.1 Optimal Portfolio	606	
		Summary		607

	Key Concepts	607
	Review Questions	608
	Case Study	608
	Appendix	611

23. PORTFOLIO PERFORMANCE EVALUATION 613-648

- 23.1 Introduction — 613
  - 23.1.1 Measuring Portfolio Performance: the Conventional Way — 613
  - 23.1.2 Performance Measurement by Adjusting Risk — 616
  - 23.1.3 Measuring Performance of Portfolios — 618
- 23.2 Beta of the Portfolio — 619
  - 23.2.1 Security Market Line (SML) of a Portfolio (Ex-Post) — 621
  - 23.2.2 Alpha — 622
  - 23.2.3 Interpretation of Alpha — 623
  - 23.2.4 Standard Deviation of Random Error Term — 625
- 23.3 Treynor's Performance Index: Reward-to-Volatility Ratio — 627
  - 23.3.1 Sharpe's Measure: Reward-to-Variability Ratio — 629
  - 23.3.2 Comparison of Treynor's Method and Sharpe's Method — 631
  - 23.3.3 Issues in Using Risk-Adjusted Performance Measures — 631
- 23.4 Jenson's Differential Return Measure — 632
- 23.5 Market Time and Selection of Portfolio — 635
- 23.6 A Comparative Study of All Three Measures — 636
- Summary — 638
- Key Concepts — 638
- Review Question — 638
- Assignment Questions — 638
- Illustrations — 639
- Problems — 643
- Case Study — 645
- Appendix — 646

FACTOR TABLES 649-664

Z-SCORE TABLES 665-666

INDEX 667-694

PART 1
INDIAN STOCK MARKET: AN OVERVIEW

1
UNDERSTANDING INVESTMENTS

> **LEARNING OBJECTIVES**
>
> The purpose of this chapter is to enable you to understand:
> • What is an investment.
> • The three golden rules of investment.
> • Why do we invest.
> • What is meant by return and risk.
> • How is the rate of return calculated.
> • How is risk of an investment assessed and evaluated.
> • What are the parameters to be considered while choosing from the different investment alternatives.
> • The relationship between investment, speculation and gambling.

1.1 INTRODUCTION

This book endeavors to tackle a very significant aspect of our day-to-day life. It deals with our money and how we maximize the output of our hard-earned money by optimizing its use. One way to do this is by investing the money in a judicious way. But how do we do this? It is easier said than done.

Furthermore, the terms, 'security analyses' and 'portfolio management' are likely to arouse interest with regard to their implications. These we will gradually discuss as the book progresses. This chapter holds an idea of what an investment actually is and the purpose(s) behind the same. Obviously various intricacies are encountered, and thus are tackled, as the learning objectives suggest.

Chapter 1 lays the foundation for an unambiguous assimilation of the complex matters, involved in handling of money in a proper way. A proper foundation for the understanding is important for ensuring a proper decision, as far as our financial investments are concerned. The objective here is to help you understand the investment field and reach sound investment decisions. This means keeping our money aside in such a way that it grows. The amount that returns to us should ideally be more than what we had invested.

We invest money for its growth, but then why do we seek this growth? Well it is primarily for the following reasons:

— The average life expectancy has increased. Thus, more money is required for sustenance now than before, with the increment in years being lived, directly translating to the money it demands.
— Medical expenses are higher than before. Same is applicable to education as well as to the cost of all essentials for daily living. Cost of living in general has increased and is ever on the rise, continually.
— So it is prudent to save money. The more we save now, more secure will be our future.
— This saving is done by wisely investing, so as to not merely saving the money, but seeing an increment in the saved money. That is wise investment decision. By investing wisely we can have a better standard of living, overall.

1.1.1 Investment

Though most of you are currently spending money, but not earning, however, soon you too will start earning. Many a times it is found that the current income falls short of our requirements. At the same time, it is also true that there are instances when we have more money than we want to spend. This mismatch forces us to either borrow money to meet the immediate demands or to save and thus accrue long term benefits on our income.

When the current income is more than the expenditure, various options are available to save this extra amount, instead of keeping it as an idle fund, which has no growth. These options differ in terms of risk, return, liquidity (each term will be addressed in depth and detail, subsequently). And analyses of these differences, is a major determinant of our investment decisions. Sometimes we prefer to sacrifice our wants to have a larger amount of fund available in the future. This fund is actually an incremented amount over that saved; vide what we call the process of investment. Similarly, when our spending exceeds the income, we are forced to borrow to bridge this gap[1]. This deficit could arise due to the following reasons:

— Health expenditures increasing, with failing health in old-age.
— Some unprecedented and unanticipated situation befalls the family.
— Last but not the least, careless spending during a phase in life.

Whatever be the reason for the shortfall, essential is that we save the money in a way to increase the saved money, which we have been referring to as investment.

There are other reasons too which leads us to make investments. We wish to protect our assets from tax and inflation.

Investment is the employment of funds to one or more assets, which are then held over a period of time to generate income, in the form of capital appreciation. An investment is always evaluated by two parameters: time and risk. We have already discussed above that we sacrifice current wants and save in order to get higher returns in future. Yet this lends an element of

---

[1] Borrowing will be discussed at other points of text (in Chapter 7—Risk-Free Lending and Borrowing), but the major emphasis of the text is on savings and investment.

uncertainty to the actual return on our savings, as the future is always uncertain. An element of risk persists always. This aspect of investment is referred to as the risk factor. But all of us do undertake some degree of risk, while investing, in order to gain higher benefits in the times to come.

Various classifications are possible for investments. But they are broadly classified as:

— Financial assets.
— Real assets.

Throughout this book, though, investment refers to financial assets, particularly to marketable securities. Financial assets are paper or electronic claims on some issuer, such as: government, commercial banks, corporations, etc. On the other hand real assets are physical assets, like gold, silver, antiques, diamond, real estate, etc.

Investment means making more money from the available funds, in an effort towards increasing money (wealth). Thus, the income earned from our investment in the form of, say, capital appreciation and/or interest/dividend (discussed later) increases our wealth. There are three golden rules for investments.

1.1.2 Start Investing Early

Many of us feel that the right time to begin investing is only when one has been earning for few years, instead of beginning immediately after one starts to earn. However, it is not true. It is imperative to save by reducing expenses and investing these savings, right from the beginning. You may ask why? The reason is the compound interest that savings enjoys, over a longer period of time.

Let us assume that at the age of 15, someone starts saving Rs.100 p.a. from his/her pocket money and invests in the safest zone (in terms of default risk), for example, in a savings scheme of post office, which provides 8% interest, Rs.100 becomes[2] Rs.2715.2 after 15 years, i.e., when he/she is 30. If, this so called small amount of Rs.100 had not been invested and had been kept in the house, it would have been Rs.1500 only after fifteen years. This is the most basic example of savings. On the other hand, if someone takes moderate[3] risk and invests[4] with rational decision in stock market (does not speculate), can make his/her money grow much more than Rs.1500 or Rs.2715, after 15 years. Hence, the sooner we start investing the better is the return we get. The other reason we need to begin investing early is to combat inflation. If we assume that the current inflation rate is 10% and invest Rs.100, at the rate of 10%, it grows to Rs.110 in one year. If we postpone our decision to invest by one year, the investment would cost Rs.110 to invest.

1.1.3 Invest with a Long-Term Goal

We should have a well defined investment plan to get the maximum benefits out of our investments. One component of such a plan is to invest over a longer period of time. Long term investment plans help with: retirement planning, housing loan, expenditure on the education of

---

[2] Rs.100 × [$(1.08)^{15}$ − 1/0.08] = Rs. 100 (27.152) = Rs. 2715.2
[3] We will address what we mean by moderate, high and low risk in this chapter and coming chapters also.
[4] The relationship between investment, speculation and gambling will be addressed too.

children, etc. Long term investments generate more returns by way of capital appreciation. According to the investment gurus, investment in market and other market related securities, such as mutual funds, for a long time period provides a whopping return, even when the market fluctuates. In fact, when market goes down, it is not a time to panic but to explore the investment opportunities (details to follow in subsequent chapters).

1.1.4 Buy Securities at Discount

Buying securities at discount, to their intrinsic value, means those securities which are under-priced. As an investor (and more specifically as a student learning about investments) our task is to find out those securities which are under-priced. Such securities not only provide higher return but also carry less risk. As when the price of such securities falls, their return is less affected. Buying securities at discount is also referred to as margin of safety. Benjamin Graham and David Dodd were the ones to coin this term.

> **Pause for thought**: An investment is a process of saving money by which money is not only saved, but it incurs growth as well.

1.2 INVESTMENT OBJECTIVES

The prime objective of an investment is to increase the return and reduce the risk. Investment decisions are based upon the parameters like liquidity, risk factor and hedge against inflation. These features are the determinants of the return, obtained from an investment.

Return

All investment decisions are categorized based upon the expected return from them. Returns expected from securities consist of two parts: Current income and capital appreciation. Capital appreciation is the difference between the closing price (selling price) and opening price (purchasing price), of the security. The dividend or the interest accrued from the given security reflects as the current income or current yield of the security. Mathematically, rate of return is presented as,

$$\text{Rate of return} = \frac{\text{Dividend (or Interest)}}{\text{Opening Price}} \times 100 + \frac{\text{Closing Price (Sale Price)} - \text{Opening Price (Purchase Price)}}{\text{Opening Price}} \times 100$$

Return from the particular assets/securities also depends on the expectations held by the investors. As already stated above, longer is the holding period of the investment, higher is the expectation of the investors as they have kept aside their funds for a longer period.

Risk

We know that there isn't a free lunch, either in economics or in finance. Hence return does not come without an element of risk. Risk is inherent in any investment. Theoretically, higher is the risk, higher is the return and vice versa. Higher return is expected from the securities/assets with high risk, to compensate the investors who hold such securities/assets, willing to bear the risk. Risk in an investment arises from many reasons, such as delay in repayment, loss of invested amount (capital loss), to name a couple of them. Investors estimate the risk of any investment based upon its past performance, the promoter's track record, maturity period, etc. Also, longer the duration of the investment greater is the risk, with a longer exposure to the market fluctuations, inflation and other uncertainty related to issuer of a security etc. Risk also varies with the kind of securities/assets selected for an investment. For example, equity shares (dealt in detail, later) are riskier than the debt securities like debentures and bonds. Also, shares differ in terms of risk level depending upon the issuing company.

Growth

Equity shares, MFs (mutual funds), ETFs (exchange traded funds) have provided compound annual growth rate (CAGR) of more than 15% in the last five years[5]. Compared to these instruments, bonds and debentures provide a return of around 7-8% p.a. ULIPs (unit linked insurance plans) also provide good return but only after few years have elapsed, from the date of the investment. Investment in real estate is highly profitable as it is a big money-spinner. Everyone is aware of the possibilities from investment in real estate.

Liquidity

An investment in a particular asset is considered to be liquid if it is easily saleable, without incurring much loss, in terms of both money and time. In other words, an asset or security is considered to be liquid if entire portion of the investment is converted to cash without much loss of time. Investments like fixed deposits in bank; savings schemes offered by post office; national savings certificates; etc., are not tradable in the market. Compared to all these instruments, investment options like equity shares[6], MFs, ETFs, debentures[7] are marketable as frequent buying and selling is possible of such securities. In case of ULIPs, surrender charges are substantial; hence scores low, in terms of liquidity. Investment in real estate is liquid only if at the right time buyers are available, with at least fair prices.

> **Pause for thought:** An asset that is convertible into cash without loss of time and money is referred to as a liquid asset. The ease and profitability of the conversion decides the liquidity of the asset.

Safety

We know that investment alternatives differ in terms of return, risk, liquidity and most important, safety (that is, the level of risk). Investments in government securities, such as government bonds, Treasury Bills and deposits in public sector banks are considered to be safer in terms of

— Default risk.
— Assurance of return, compared to investment in private sectors such as equity shares, debentures, deposits with NBFC (non-banking financial companies), etc.

For the safety of the given investment, it must come under the legal and regulatory framework. If any investment alternative is under the legal framework, it is easy to claim for any defaults or

---

[5] Based upon data from www.bajajcapital.com, www.bseindia.com and others.

[6] Equity shares traded on recognized stock exchanges.

[7] Traded on a stock exchange.

place one's grievances. However, despite legal and regulatory back-up, securities differ in terms of safety.

> **Pause for thought:** Safety is an index, inversely related to the risk factor.

Hedge against inflation

If the return of any security is lesser than the inflation, then loss is incurred in real terms. It is preferred that the investment opted for be safe; and it should provide a protection against inflation as well. However, most of the investment alternatives, discussed above, are not good hedge against inflation. It has been found that growth stocks are better hedge against inflation, through their capital appreciation.

Expenses

Investment alternatives should be evaluated in terms of expenses as well. For example, MFs are more expensive (2% brokerage charges) as compared to ETFs (0.5% charges). Investment in ULIPs is also expensive in the initial years. Equity shares, chosen at the right time and at right price, are fairly priced.

1.3 TYPES OF INVESTORS

Investors differ in terms of their risk bearing capacity, and thus are classified, in the financial market as:

— Aggressive and moderately aggressive: Those who love taking risks comprise this category; and even if they do not love risks, they are at least not averse to it..
— Conservatively aggressive and conservative: Depending upon the risk bearing capacity an investor could be moderately conservative. And again, could be purely conservative having no propensity to take risks whatsoever.

The risk bearing capacity of investors depends upon several factors; like income, age, number of family members and the general expenditure pattern. Apart from these there could be other personal factors; time and macroeconomic factors which too play their roles. An aggressive investor bears higher risk for the expectation of higher returns while an investor averse (conservative) to risk opts for those investment alternatives which promise secured return (at least in nominal terms) and less variations with the market. Moderately conservatives could be also referred to as neutral, at times, with respect to their approach towards market risks.

It is assumed that investors, usually with high income, have high risk bearing capacity. Furthermore, Investors are also classified as Individuals or institutions. Institutional investors are organizations, with the objective to invest in the market. Mutual funds, insurance companies, banks, non-banking companies, investment companies, etc., fall in the category of institutional investors. They have large surplus of funds. Individual investors are large in numbers, but they are fairly less in terms of their investment volumes. Also, institutional investors have professionals who conduct extensive analyses of the various securities/investment alternatives available in the market.

1.4 INVESTMENT, SPECULATION AND GAMBLING

Investment

Investment is employment of funds in securities, for capital appreciation, so as to earn higher returns thus. When a person decides to invest, he/she expects capital appreciation for his/her funds. However, these expected higher returns in the future are matter of uncertainty, depending upon various macro-economic, industrial, company-specific factors. The two most noteworthy attributes of an investment are: (i) time and (ii) risk. In layman's terms, even the purchase of a flat or a house, for personal use, is called an investment. However, in finance, it is not considered an investment as it involves sacrifice of consumption, in the present, without earning a return for the same. In financial terms, investment means allocation of funds, to assets, to earn higher income over a period of time. As per economists, investment is an addition to the country's net capital stock. Capital stock consists of goods and services. An addition to capital stock over the years means an increase in the production of other goods and services such as buildings, equipments, etc., as it is a part of a cyclic process.

Speculation

Investment and speculation, both involve purchase and sale of securities with the objective of earning return. However, speculation and investment differ in terms of risk bearing capacity of the investors and expected returns and duration of the transaction. An investor plays rationally by taking comparatively lower risk for the given/expected return. A speculator though, bears higher risk, hoping for higher returns. The prime concern of the speculator is to earn a return, and not the safety of his/her principal amount. Thus he/she undertakes frequent buying and selling of securities, without the actual intention of owning an investment. For speculators, capital gain is more important and he/she aims to achieve profit from the price changes, incurred by the securities. An investor tries to select the securities/assets for income, as well as capital gain. A speculator trades frequently, hence the holding period of his/her securities is very short. On the other hand, investment is a long term activity with a longer holding period.

Speculating is much more risky, than that involved in investing, as a speculator decides to buy/sell the securities based upon the market's expectation and price fluctuations. Speculation is purely market dependent. Compared to this, the investor is concerned with the intrinsic value of the security. Thus having assessed this, before investing in it, the investor expects a fair rate of return on a consistent basis for longer holding period.

In the stock market, speculators are broadly classified into two main categories: bulls and bears. A bull buys shares, in the expectation that the market will rise and hence rates of shares/securities too will; and that they will sell at a price higher than the purchase price. During a bullish trend, there is an upward movement in the market, with share prices too going up, as the demand is there. A bear sells the shares at a relatively higher price and will buy them later, at a relatively lower price. A bear expects a downward trend in the market and thus in shares as well. Hence, the bearish trend results in the fall of the price of the securities and market, due to the selling tendencies.

Speculator gives a momentum to the market or we can say that due to their presence, market is 'alive'. Never is the market allowed to be at rest, given the frequent buying and selling. For the healthy performance of the market, investments and speculative activities, both, are required.

Gambling

Compared to investment and speculation, gambling is haphazard and an unscientific activity. Gambling involves very high risk and high return as compared to speculating activity. It also involves an element of heightened excitement. Examples of gambling are horse races, card games, lotteries, etc., to name just a few of the gambling activities. Speculator calculates expected return, based on the market movement; while gambling is only about betting and hasty trading. The other notable difference between a speculator and gambler is that speculator bears higher risk for the expectation of higher return but does not bear continuous losses. While there are the strong chances that a gambler may lose his/her entire wealth in the process. But then one cannot expect a gambler to be guided by any logic and hence, gambling cannot be anything other than haphazard and unscientific!

SUMMARY

✓ An investment is evaluated mainly by two parameters: time and risk.

✓ There are three golden rules of investment: (i) start investing early; (ii) invest for a long time period and (iii) buy securities at discount.

✓ The main objective of the investor is to increase the return and reduce the risk. Investors also consider safety, liquidity, growth, etc., while making their investment decisions.

✓ Investment activity is classified into three categories: investment, speculation and gambling.

✓ Speculation and investment differs in terms of risk bearing capacity, expectation of returns and duration of the holding period.

✓ Gambling is haphazard and an unscientific activity. It involves very high risk and high return.

KEY CONCEPTS

Investment	Safety	Growth
Speculation	Security	Dividend
Gambling	Assets	Liquidity
Return	Stock	Expenses
Risk	Interest Income	Inflation

REVIEW QUESTIONS

1. Differentiate between: a. Investment and speculation and b. Investment and gambling.
2. What are the objectives of investors while investing in different securities?

2
INVESTMENT ALTERNATIVES

LEARNING OBJECTIVES

The purpose of this chapter is to enable you to understand:
- The key features of different investment alternatives.
- Their comparative study.
- Evaluation of the benefits of each alternative.

2.1 INTRODUCTION

Chapter 1 introduced us to the concept of investment and the requirements for the same. It is for the rational investment decisions to be arrived that we need to know the available investment alternatives. A comparative and detailed study of each would enable us to choose, depending on what our preferences are and how we wish to proceed. Exactly this forms the objective of this chapter.

Since there are varied alternatives available in which we can invest our funds and hence we wish to understand the options, it is desirable that they are classified into categories. The classification systematizes the study and lends enhanced clarity to our understanding. These options are also referred to as the instruments as indeed they are so: the tools for enhancing the growth of our funds.

2.1.1 Negotiable Instruments

It is a signed document which promises to pay the bearer a sum of money at a future date on demand and is transferable. Negotiable instruments are conditional orders—or commitments—to pay, and include cheques, drafts, bearer bonds, some certificate of deposits, promissory notes and bank notes (currency)[1].

---

[1] http://www.businessdictionary.com/definition/negotiable-instrument.html#ixzz25TPY6mDs

There are three main attributes of negotiable instruments:
- An asset (and that includes property), which is the subject to the instrument passes from the transferor to transferee by just delivering and/or endorsement of the instrument.
- A transferee who has not noticed any defect in the title of the transferor can accept the instrument in good faith. For value he/she obtains an indefeasible title and may sue on the instrument in his/her name.
- There is no need to give notice of the transfer to the party liable in the instrument.

The negotiable instruments have the following additional characteristics:
- Possessions: The owner or possessor of negotiable instrument not only enjoys possession of the instrument but right to property also. If it is a bearer instrument, property can be transferred by just delivering to the transferee, while in case of an order instrument endorsement and delivery are required for the transfer of the property.
- Title: The transferee of a negotiable instrument is known as a holder in due course. A bonafide transferee, for value, is not affected by any defect of title on the part of the transferor or any of the previous holders of the instrument.
- Right: The negotiable instrument can be transferred any number of times till maturity. Also the transferee of the negotiable instrument can sue in his own name in case of dishonor.
- Presumptions: It is presumed that for all negotiable instruments considerations have been paid under it.
- Prompt payment: It enables the holder to expect prompt payment because a dishonor means the ruin of the credit of all persons who are party to the instrument.

Negotiable instruments are recognized by statute and custom. Bills of exchange, promissory notes and cheques are negotiable instruments as per statute; while negotiable instruments like: hundis, share warrants, dividend warrants, banker's draft, circular notes and bearer debentures are classified as per the usage or custom.

Under negotiable instruments there are two types of securities. They are variable income securities and fixed income securities. Only equity shares come under the type of variable income security while bonds, debentures, preference shares, treasury bills, commercial papers, certificate of deposits, Kisan Vikas Patra, etc., come under the fixed income securities.

2.1.2 Variable Income Securities

The common stock is called variable income security as the rate of return on common stock is not fixed and changes as per the market dynamics.

> **Pause for thought:** The company is not obligated to pay fixed dividend and fixed price at the time of maturity.

2.1.3 Equity Shares

Equity shares are type of variable income security, given the fact that for an equity share the company is not bound to pay fixed dividend or price after maturity. Equity shares have a number of derivatives. As is its category, so is the result: the return on the equity shares is variable. It is affected by a number of factors (to be learnt in detail in the chapter on market efficiency). In the early 1990s, investing in the equity shares was preferred by the retail investors. But after incurring heavy losses in 2000 and in 2008-2009, they have become skeptical about it. Equity shares are also referred to as common stocks or ordinary shares.

There is a notable difference though between these two words: stock and share. The term share means, a share capital of the company divided into number of smaller units; while stock is referred to in terms of money[2]. Compared to bonds and other instruments, equity shares give high return accompanied by a corresponding high risk. The stock exchanges, where equity shares are traded, measure the financial health of the economy.

> **Pause for thought:** Equity shares give variable but high returns, and are accompanied by high risks.

2.1.4 Fixed Income Securities

Payment of fixed income securities are known in advance and it does not change as per the change in underlying factors such as interest rate. This type of instrument provides fixed periodic payment and eventual return of principal at maturity. Even though they offer guaranteed return their return is lower than other investment options.

An investment in a security that provides a return in the form of fixed periodic payments and the eventual return of principal at maturity is known as a fixed income security.

Bonds, debentures, preference shares, public provident fund, national savings certificate, national savings schemes, Kisan Vikas Patra, deposits with NBFCs are fixed income securities.

> **Pause for thought:** Unlike variable income securities these have to pay a fixed amount periodically as dividends, interests etc., along with the principal, to be returned at the time of maturity.

2.1.5 Bonds

A bond is a debt investment in which an investor loans money to an entity (corporate or governmental) that borrows the funds for a defined period of time at a fixed interest rate. Bonds are commonly referred to as fixed-income securities and are one of the three main asset classes, along with stocks and cash equivalents.

Bonds are issued by the RBI on behalf of government or public sector undertakings. It offers a promised cash flow on coupon payments till maturity of the bond, along with the principal. The prices of the bonds are inversely related to the interest rate. So when interest rates fall, the price rises and so does the yield of the bond. ICICI and IDBI have issued various types of bonds, like deep discount bonds, zero coupon bonds, etc. Deep discount bonds were issued for the first time in India, in January 1992, by IDBI. These bonds were issued for a price of Rs. 2700, at face value of Rs. 100,000 for a maturity period of 25 years. Thus it implies that the bond offered an attractive interest rate of Rs. 2700 = Rs.$100,000/(1 + r)^{25}$, i.e., 15.5%.

---

[2] Throughout this text, terms stock, share, scrip, etc., will be used interchangeably.

> **Pause for thought:** Bonds are debt investments in which the investor loans money to an entity that borrows it for a definite time period, at a fixed rate of interest.

2.1.6 Debentures

Fixed income securities, like bonds, issued by the private (corporate) sector are known as debentures. Like bonds they too offer coupon payments till the maturity period, along with keeping the principal assured, and paid at maturity. They are issued at discount, premium or at par value. Corporate houses, like ABB Ltd, Arvind Mills, and Ashok Leyland, have issued debentures.

Debt market in India is not as much developed as in foreign countries. However, compared to the initial phase of this millennium, India has notably become an active debt market. Debentures are long-term securities as their maturity period ranges from five to fifteen years. The interest received is taxable. So the tax rate reduces the net return accordingly. They are rated by credit rating agencies and a good rating indicates reasonable assurance of interest along with the principal. However as fundamental of the company changes, its rating may be revised to BBB from AAA; so one needs to keep a watch on it. The secondary market for debentures is not that developed like foreign countries. Hence, investment is not very liquid.

Debentures are of two types:

— Convertible.
— Non-convertible.

Convertible debentures: It is type of loan issued by a company which can be converted into a stock, under certain circumstances. The company issues such convertible debentures by offering lower interest rate, compared to non-convertible debentures (where there is no option to convert debentures into a stock). This instrument is used by the company for financing the asset to enable the growth of their business. However, debentures are not secured as in case of bankruptcy the debentures would be paid after fulfilling obligation of other fixed income holdings.

Non-convertible debentures (NCD): As equity market has become volatile and on the other hand interest rates are rising; avenues for safer and regular investment options are in demand. Presently, non-convertible debenture is such an option. Companies like Shriram City Union Finance, Mannapuram Finance, Muthoot Finance and IIFL have recently come up with an NCD at very attractive rate.

> **Pause for thought:** They too are fixed income securities, like bonds, but are issued by the private sector.

2.1.7 Preference Shares

Preference shares are characterized by their hybrid nature, as some of the features resemble the equity shares, while some resemble debt. As in bonds, a preference shareholder too receives fixed dividend.

The Companies Act section 85(1) defines preference shares as those shares which carry preferential rights, as the rate of preference dividend is fixed and also repayment of capital—in case of winding up of the company. Also the dividend on this share must be paid before any dividend is paid to ordinary shares. It may happen that the board of directors decides not to pay dividend to both preference share and equity shareholders. However, in case dividend has to be paid it must be first paid to the preference shareholders and then to the ordinary (equity) shareholders. There are number of companies who have raised funds through issuance of preference shares, for example, Siemens, JSW ISPAT Steel Ltd., Sujana Metals, C. Mahendra Expo etc.

Preference shares are of two types:
— Redeemable.
— Irredeemable.

Redeemable preference shares are those preference shares which can be redeemed on or after a fixed period of time, as per the terms at issuance or after giving a notice of redemption to the preference shareholders.

Irredeemable preference shares are those which can not be redeemed till the life time of the company.

Convertible preference shares are the ones which give the preference shareholders the right to convert their holding into ordinary shares within a specified period of time.

In case of non-convertible preference shares, the shareholders have no such right to convert the same into ordinary shares.

Also, preference shares with convertible option are an attractive investment option for the investor as they offer to convert preference shares into equity shares for the specified period.

> **Pause for thought:** A fixed income security, preference shares are unique given their nature, which is a hybrid of equity and debt shares.

2.1.8 Treasury Bills

It is a short term money market instrument, used by the government of India to fill up its short term deficits. In India, the RBI issues treasury bills (T-bills) on behalf of the government. Usually corporate and commercial banks invest in T-bills when they have short-term surplus. Thus T-bills have short-term maturities: 14 days, 91 days, 182 days, etc. Given their small holding periods, they are highly liquid investments and are as good as cash. Their high liquidity is also attributed to their zero default risk. T-bills are issued for a minimum amount of Rs.25,000 and in its multiples, subsequently.

> **Pause for thought:** It is a very short-term money market instrument, highly liquid; used by the government to combat short-term deficits and purchased by corporate and commercial banks as investments of their short-term surplus.

2.1.9 Commercial Paper

Commercial paper is a short-term money market instrument, available in India since 1990s. Though in the foreign countries, issuance and use of commercial paper started way back in early 1985. Its use in India began, manifesting the market reforms that started during this time. Commercial paper in India is issued in the form of promissory notes. It is used by large corporate houses as a short-term debt instrument for borrowing short-term funds from the money market. The commercial paper has become an effective instrument for these corporate companies to avail the short-term funds, from the money market, within the shortest possible time. This thus helps in avoiding the hassles of direct negotiation with the commercial banks for availing the short-term loans.

In Indian money market the commercial papers are issued by:
— Leasing and finance companies.
— Manufacturing companies.
— Financial institutions.

Herein, the difference between finance companies and financial institutions needs to be clarified, otherwise their mention (as above), as separate entities, might create confusion.

Financial institutions are institutions, which provide financial services for its clients or members. They provide their services as intermediaries and are regulated by the government. There are three main types of financial institutions: depository institutions, contractual institutions and investment institutions.

Finance companies in a simple term mean a company which forwards loans to clients. Unlike banks, finance companies do not receive deposits but obtain its financing from banks, institutions and other money market sources. There are three categories of finance companies: consumer finance companies, sales finance companies and commercial finance companies.

> **Pause for thought:** This tool is used by corporate sector as short-term instrument for borrowing short-term funds from the money market.

2.1.10 Certificate of Deposit

Certificate of deposits are bearer instruments and are negotiable. Usually it is issued by commercial banks and financial institutions. They are like deposits with a fixed maturity, for example, the fixed deposits (FDs). However, the latter is non-negotiable and non-tradable.

It was introduced in June 1989. Initially only the regional rural banks were allowed to issue these certificates. But later, in 1992, financial institutions were allowed to, with a specific limit for the certificates. They are issued at discount or face value.

Development financial institutions (DFIs) cater to the requirement of medium to long-term financing. Industrial Finance Corporation of India (IFCI) was the first DFI which was established to extend long-term finance to industry. After that several DFIs were established in the public and private sectors. They can be categorized into:

— Term lending institutions, such as EXIM Bank (Export-Import Bank of India), TFCI (Tourism Finance Corporation of India) etc.
— Refinance institutions, such as NABARD (National Bank for Agricultural and Rural Development), SIDBI (Small Industries Development Bank of India) and NHB (National Housing Bank) etc.

> **Pause for thought:** These certificates are like FDs, having a fixed maturity but are negotiable, bearer instruments.

2.1.11 Kisan Vikas Patra (KVP)

Kisan Vikas Patra (KVP) is a safe and long-term investment option, backed by the Government of India. It provides interest rates similar to bonds, which is at present 8.41%, compounded half-yearly. A KVP is sold at face value at maturity, which is printed on the certificate. Money doubles at the end of the specified time period of eight years and seven months. At the same time, encashment is possible only after two and half years. Income tax benefits are not available under the KVP scheme. And hence income from interest is taxable. However, the deposits are exempt from wealth tax, as well as from tax deduction at source (TDS), at the time of withdrawal.

The name of the scheme creates an illusion that it is meant only for the farmers, which is not true as anyone can invest in KVP. It can be purchased by an individual or jointly. A minor too can be a holder of KVP, but jointly with parent or guardian. Hindu undivided families are not eligible to purchase KVP. The minimum investment allowed in KVP is Rs. 100. Certificates are available in denominations accordingly of Rs. 100, Rs. 500, Rs. 1,000, Rs. 5,000, Rs. 10,000 and Rs. 50,000.

As is with all schemes, KVPs too have advantages and disadvantages, both.

Advantages
— KVP can be pledged as security against a loan from banks or government institutions.
— It is very flexible with the lower limit of investment being Rs.500 and the upper limit is not fixed. It solely depends on the investor.

Disadvantages
— No tax benefit: Compared to PPF and NSC it doesn't provide any tax benefits.
— Low return: Its return, 8.41%, is very low, compared to other investment options.
— Low liquidity: It takes 8 years and 7 months to double the invested amount. Encashment is possible only after two and half years; yet it turns out to be a costly affair with respect to the yield.

2.2 NON-NEGOTIABLE SECURITIES

In simple terms, non-negotiable instruments are documents which can not be exchanged for cash, for example, a crossed cheque. Such instruments cannot be bought, sold, exchanged or transferred. In short, they are such instruments which are not open to negotiation, as the terms of such contract are non-negotiable[3].

Examples of non-negotiable instruments are: money orders, deposit receipts, dock warrants and postal orders. Bank deposits, post office schemes, and various tax sheltered instruments, such as: public provident fund, national savings certificate, national savings schemes, etc., come under the non-negotiable securities.

> **Pause for thought:** The term non-negotiable is two-dimensional. It could pertain to a fixed price, which under no circumstances can be adjusted. And it could also apply to non-transference of the holding of the fund, from the original investor.

---

[3] http://www.investorwords.com/10423/non_negotiable_instrument.html#ixzz25TNuCCWz

2.2.1 Bank Deposits

Bank deposits can be in the form of current account, savings account or other type of bank accounts at a banking institution, which offers interest rate on it and can be withdrawn after some stipulated time period. Investors can deposit their funds in the banks under the account types:

— Savings account.
— Current account.
— Fixed deposit account.

The rate of interest in savings account is regulated by the Reserve Bank of India (RBI). The amount invested in current account doesn't earn any interest. The fixed deposit account offers higher interest rates, but the invested money gets blocked for a fixed time period.

A bank fixed deposit (FD) is an investment alternative where the interest rate is guaranteed not to change over the nominated term. Thus the worth of the investment at the end of the maturity is assured. It is also known as term deposits. FDs offer higher rate of interest than savings account. Some banks may offer additional services to FD holders, such as, providing loan against the FD certificate at a competent rate. In case of premature withdrawal, the bank may charge penalty from the customer.

Bank deposits in public sector banks are highly liquid (except fixed deposits) and safest form of investment.

> **Pause for thought:** Bank deposits are safest forms of investment, yet the account type does matter, as it determines the growth of the invested amount.

2.2.2 Post Office Schemes

Post office usually has small saving schemes for the public, designed to provide safe and attractive investment options. Through these small saving schemes government can mobilize resources for development. Post office in India operates through such schemes through approximately 1.54 lakh post offices in India. The Postal department operates the post office saving schemes through post office savings bank in India, on behalf of Ministry of Finance, Government of India. It offers a number of saving schemes, like the savings account schemes, recurring deposit schemes, time deposit schemes, public provident fund schemes, monthly income schemes, national savings certificates, Kisan Vikas Patra and senior citizen savings schemes.

These schemes have been enlisted in Appendix-2.1.

2.2.3 Non-Banking Financial Corporation (NBFC)

Non-banking financial corporations (NBFCs), engaged in financial activities, are part of Indian financial system—providing a range of financial services. NBFCs are incorporated under the Companies Act, 1956. They are classified into two broad categories:

— NBFCs accepting public deposit (NBFC-D).
— NBFCs that do not accept/hold public deposit (NBFC-ND).

Residuary non-banking companies (RNBCs) are another category of NBFCs whose principal business is acceptance of deposits and investing in approved securities.

Types of NBFCs registered with the RBI are:
— Equipment leasing company.
— Hire-purchase company.
— Loan company.
— Investment company.

The above classifications were reclassified on December 6, 2006, as follows:
— Asset finance company (AFC).
— Investment company (IC).
— Loan company (LC).

NBFCs, excluding RNBCs, cannot offer a rate of interest on deposits more than that approved by the RBI from time to time (at present it is 12.5%). It can accept public deposits for a period of 12 months to 60 months. Also it can offer gifts/incentives to solicit deposits from the public. NBFCs, including RNBCs, can accept deposits only against issue or proper receipt. If NBFCs fail to repay the deposits or the interest accrued thereon in accordance with terms and conditions of acceptance of such deposits, redressal of grievance is possible through the regional branch of the Company Law Board at Chennai/Delhi/Kolkata/Mumbai.

List of NBFCs permitted to accept public deposits as on May 31, 2012
— Arman Financial Services Ltd.
— Ceejay Finance Ltd.
— Chinmay Finlease Pvt. Ltd.
— Ishan Finlease Ltd.
— Jaylakshmi Credit Company Ltd.

> **Pause for thought:** Besides the banking sector, there are non-banking financial companies providing varied range of financial services to the public.

2.2.4 Tax Sheltered Instruments

Tax sheltered instruments allows the investors to reduce tax and defer tax payments while one saves and invests. They basically provide a shelter against taxes. In other words, it is a legal method of minimizing or decreasing an investor's taxable income and thus tax liability. There are number of tax sheltered plans, which can be employed in different ways at different stages of life. Post office savings account, post office time deposit account, public provident fund, national savings certificates are some of the tax sheltered plans which provide tax rebates to the investor.

> **Pause for thought:** These investments enable the investors to avoid—and not evade—taxes, as they provide legal investment options to minimize the taxable income.

2.2.5 Public Provident Fund (PPF)

Public provident fund (PPF) is a savings-cum-tax-saving instrument in India. It also serves as a retirement-planning tool for many—mainly those who do not have any structured pension plan.

PPF account can be opened in designated post offices, State Bank of India branches and branches of some select nationalized banks. ICICI Bank was the first private sector bank to be authorized to open PPF account.

The current interest rate, effective from April 1, 2012 is 8.8% p.a. (compounded annually).

An interest rate of 8.80% p.a. (compounded annually) is credited to the PPF account at the end of each financial year. A minimum of Rs.500, with additional investment in multiples of Rs.5, amounting to a maximum of Rs.1,00,000, can be deposited each year in PPF account. Tax benefits, under section 80C, are applicable to the amount invested and interest is tax free under section 80L. At the same time the entire amount at maturity, including the interest accrued and the principal, enjoys tax exemption. Furthermore, PPF investments are free from wealth tax too. Deposits in a PPF account qualify for a deduction under section 80C.

A PPF account can be opened and operated individually or jointly by more than two holders. A minor too can have a PPF account, jointly held with parent(s) or guardian. The tenure of the investment is 15 years, from the date of initial investment. It is followed with a block of 5 years up to a maximum of 30 years, inclusive of the first 15 years. In other words, once a PPF account matures after 15 years, the investor has the option of either continuing with the account for another 5 years or can opt for closure of the account. Investors can avail loan against their PPF account. But loans can be taken only after the second year and till the sixth year. A maximum of 25%, of the balance at the end of the second year, is sanctioned as loan. Such withdrawals though, have to be repaid within 2 years. Rate of interest charged on the loan is 2% more than the current rate of interest on PPF. The second loan can be availed, within the third and sixth year, but only if the first one has been repaid fully. Furthermore, it is to be noted that once the investor is eligible for withdrawals, he/she is no longer eligible for loans. Inactive accounts, or accounts that have been discontinued, do not permit sanction of loans.

The table below shows interest rate on PPF over time[4].

Time period	Interest rate
01.04.1986 to 14.01.2000	12%
15.01.2000 to 28.02.2001	11%
01.03.2001 to 28.02.2002	9.5%
01.03.2002 to 28.02.2003	9%
01.03.2003 to 30.11.2011	8%
01.12.2011 to 31.03.2012	8.6%
01.04.2012 onwards	8.8%

Advantages

— Lowest risk: It is a government-backed scheme and thus without any default risk.
— Tax rebate on the money invested: Investments are eligible for a 20% tax rebate, under section 88.

---

[4] http://en.wikipedia.org/wiki/Public_Provident_Fund_(India)

- Good return: Though rate of interest is 8.8% p.a., but it is compounded annually. This, along with tax rebate, leads to an actually realized return which is more than 8.8%.
- No tax on interest earned: The interest earned (8.8% p.a.) is totally exempt from tax, under section 10 (11) of the Income Tax Act.
- Flexible: It is a flexible mode of investment, ranging from Rs.500 to Rs.1,00,000 p.a. Investors can also invest an amount payable in 12 installments. These installments and mode of payments need not be identical.
- Exemption from wealth tax: The entire amount that accumulates over a period of time is exempt from wealth tax.
- Legal immunity: If an investor defaults on any loan repayment or is declared bankrupt, the amount in PPF account cannot be contested for, by the courts.

Disadvantages

- Interest rate risk: At the time of inception the interest rates on PPF was 12% p.a. Subsequently, it dropped to 11%, 9.5% and currently stands at 8.8%. The interest rates are regulated by the government and investors have to bear these changes in interest rate, and thus the risk involved.
- Lengthy lock-in period: Though the lock-in period is said to be 15 years, but it actually turns out to be 16 years since the last contribution is made in the sixteenth financial year.
- Interest calculated on the lowest balance: Interest is calculated on the lowest balance, between the fifth day and the last day of the month, in March.
- Lack of liquidity: Unlike mutual funds or shares, investors cannot trade on it (however, one can avail loan on it). Thus it is not liquid in nature. At the most, the investor can make partial withdrawals, but that too only after the investment is in the sixth financial year.

Pause for thought: Public provident fund (PPF) is a savings-cum-tax-saving instrument and serves as a retirement planning too for those who do not have a structured pension plan. Its biggest advantage is complete tax exemption of the entire amount at maturity, and that includes the interest accrued too.

2.2.6 National Savings Certificate (NSC)

National savings certificate is a long-term investment option and very safe too. As the name suggests, it is a scheme backed by the government. It earns an interest rate of 8% p.a. compounded half-yearly. It is issued by the Department of Post, Government of India and available at all post offices across the country. It is specially designed for government employees, businessmen and other salaried people who are income tax payees. The scheme avails of reductions in tax liability as per the provisions of the section 80C Income Tax Act, 1961. This works towards the growth of the investment, over and above the interest, which compounds half-yearly.

The duration of an NSC scheme is of 6 years. It is issued in denominations of Rs. 100, Rs. 500, Rs. 1,000, Rs. 5,000 and Rs. 10,000 for a maturity period of 6 years. There are no restrictions on the maximum investment that can be made in NSCs. Also, the investor can take a loan against the NSC by pledging it to the RBI, a scheduled bank, a co-operative society, a corporation, a government company or a housing finance company approved by the National Housing Bank. But the sanction of the loan requires the permission of the concerned post master. Though premature encashment is normally not permissible, sub-rule (1) of rule 16 makes it possible after the investment has completed three years.

Advantages

- No default risk: As it is backed by the government it is free from risk of default.
- Tax benefits: Deposits in NSC, up to Rs.1 lakh can avail of deduction under section 80C of the Income Tax Act.
- Transferability: NSCs can be transferred from one person to another through the post office on the payment of a prescribed fee. Thus it is a negotiable instrument.

Disadvantages

- Low return: It provides low return compared to other forms of investment.
- Low liquidity: As the blockage period is normally 6 years, it provides comparatively less liquidity.

> **Pause for thought:** NSCs provide an interest rate of 8% p.a., compounded half-yearly and are a form of a safe, non-negotiable instrument.

2.2.7 National Savings Schemes (NSSs)

These are tax saving instruments and combine growth in money and cuts in tax liability, albeit at a lower rate. They have the backing of the government of India and hence, are risk-free investments. So, any ratings by commercial rating agencies are not required by them. Tax rebates are offered under section 88 of Income Tax Act, 1961. Furthermore, they offer 9% interest rate p.a., compounded annually, and have a maturity period of four years. However, the investor can extend the duration of NSS after four years, if one desires so. Premature redemption is permitted only in case of death of the investor. The interest accrued can be withdrawn at any point, i.e., before maturity of the scheme but principal can be withdrawn only at maturity.

Advantages

- Investment in an NSS can begin with Rs.100 and there is no prescribed upper limit.
- Investor can avail rebate on both interest accrued, as well as the principal. Income from interest, up to Rs.9000, is exempted from tax under section 88 of Income Tax Act, 1961. Also, the income from interest is not subject to TDS.

Disadvantages

- One can open only one account in a year.
- Investor can not open account under the name of his/her spouse.

> **Pause for thought:** These are government-backed schemes—hence risk-free—focusing on growth of money (as is the primary objective of all investment options), with cuts in tax liability.

2.2.8 Rajiv Gandhi Equity Savings Schemes (RGESS)

Rajiv Gandhi Equity Saving scheme was introduced in the budget (2012-13) this year by the Finance Minister. This is first of its kind scheme in India which allows the retail investor to invest up to Rs. 50,000 directly into equity shares and avail tax benefit on 50% of investment made directly into equity shares. It offers tax benefit for new investors, investing up to Rs. 50,000. Those investors whose annual income is below Rs.10 lakhs are eligible to invest. The scheme is intended to encourage the flow of savings and improve the depth of the domestic capital market. It aims to promote equity culture in India and is expected to widen the retail investor base in the Indian securities market.

Salient features of the scheme are as follows:

— Criteria: It is open to the new investors, identified on the basis of their PAN. It is for those who have opened the Demat account but have not made any transactions in equity and/or in derivatives till the date of notification of this scheme and all those account holders other than the first account holder who wish to open a fresh account.

— Under the scheme, those stocks listed under the BSE 100 or CNX 100 or those of public sector undertakings, which are: Navratnas (BHEL, HPCL, NMDC, Power Finance and Shipping Corporation, besides others), Maharatnas (Coal India, IOC, ONGC, SAIL and NTPC), and Miniratnas (MOIL, Engineer India, MRPL and MMTC, besides others), would be eligible.

— Also, exchange traded fund, mutual funds that have RGESS eligible securities underlying, and are listed and traded in the stock exchanges and settled through a depository mechanism, have also been brought under RGESS.

— The total lock-in period for investments under the scheme is three years including an initial blanket lock-in period of one year, commencing from the date of last purchase of securities under RGESS.

— After the first year investors will be allowed to trade in the securities, in furtherance of the goal of promoting an equity culture and as a provision to protect them from adverse market movements or stock specific risk as well as to give them avenues to realize profits.

Such a scheme being launched for the first time, and given its specifics, the initial reaction that it has met with, is of criticism. But then it requires some time to prove itself, before being summarily rejected—as only time will tell of its efficacy or otherwise.

2.2.9 Life Insurance

The objective of insurance is to provide coverage for the eventuality of death. So it is long-term in nature.

LIC (Life Insurance Corporation) is the largest insurance group and investment company in India, with 100% stake of the government of India. There are 23 private players in the insurance sector; most of them have joint ventures with foreign players. It can be defined as a legal contract between insurer and the insured payee. As per the contract, the insurer promises to pay fixed amount of money on the occurrence of certain incidents, while the other party, called the insured payee, agrees to pay a fixed sum known as premium. The premium can be paid regularly in installments or as a lump sum.

The Indian insurance industry has a total of 49 companies, including life as well as non-life (i.e., general) insurance companies.

> **Pause for thought:** Life insurance schemes insures against the uncertainty of life; and certain events and eventualities in a life full of uncertainties.

2.3 MUTUAL FUNDS

The name suggests that these are funds which are mutually dependent on the investments, made by others too, in that fund. And indeed it is so.

A mutual fund is a trust which pools savings of a number of investors who share a common financial goal. The money collected from investors is invested in capital market instruments, such as shares, bonds, debentures and other securities. The income from this investment, and capital realized from it, is shared by its unit holders in proportion to the number of units held by them. However, investors consider investment in mutual fund very risky. Through mutual funds, investors can invest in a capital market in a professionally managed diversified basket of securities at a relatively lower cost. Mutual funds are run by asset management companies (AMC). AMCs earn by charging service fees from their clients. An AMC invests its clients' pooled fund in securities that match its declared financial objectives.

Thus a mutual fund is a type of professionally-managed collective investment scheme that pools money from many investors to purchase securities. While there is no legal definition of mutual fund, the term is most commonly applied only to those collective investment schemes that are: regulated, available to the general public and open-ended in nature.

In simple terms, these are the investment tools which pool funds from investors in the form of units to invest in market and other securities, on behalf of the investors. It is thus an indirect way of investing in stock market by investors who cannot directly study the market and invest on their own. It is a fact that a well managed mutual fund generates greater return than the market. In the past, mutual funds like Principal PNB, SBI Magnum, etc., have provided very good returns.

India was introduced to mutual funds for the first time in 1963 by the launching of Unit Trust of India (UTI) by the government of India. Till 1987 UTI enjoyed monopoly and after that, under the regime of liberalization, privatization and globalization, a host of other government controlled financial companies came up with their mutual funds. The market opened for private sector in 1993. The Kothari Pioneer (now merged with Franklin Templeton) was the first private sector mutual fund.

Around two decades have passed, thus, for mutual funds in India and have reached asset under management (AUM), equaling Rs.7,81,71,152 lakhs—less than 10% of households have invested in mutual funds[5]. Asset under management (AUM) is a market value of assets that an investment company manages on behalf of investors. It can increase/decrease due to both capital appreciation/losses and new inflow/outflow of money.

Top five AMCs as per their profit for the financial year 2011-12 are Reliance AMC, HDFC AMC, ICICI Prudential AMC, Birla Sun Life AMC and UTI AMC[6] as shown in the Table 2.1.

There are two types of mutual funds, with respect to their maturity and are mentioned below as follows:

— Closed-ended: These funds are open for a specific time period and have a fixed number of units. Close-ended schemes are traded on the stock exchanges, with their prices quoted at either premium or discount.

— Open-ended: These types of mutual funds provide with an option open to buy and sell the units continuously. They thus do not have any maturity period and so are not traded on the

---

[5] Association of Mutual Funds, India.
[6] Business Today, April 1, 2012.

Table 2.1: Top 10 Asset Management Companies (AUM in Rs.)

1	Reliance Mutual Fund	10206621.91
2	HDFC Mutual Fund	8788309.11
3	ICICI Prudential Mutual Fund	6584087.84
4	UTI Mutual Fund	6538724.42
5	Birla Sun Life Mutual Fund	5768946.91
6	SBI Mutual Fund	4149785.56
7	Franklin Templeton Mutual Fund	3944260.39
8	DSP BlackRock Mutual Fund	2766779.46
9	Kotak Mahindra Mutual Fund	2756536.86
10	Tata Mutual Fund	2085484.83

stock exchanges. The repurchase price of the fund is determined on the basis of its NAV (net assets value). The open-ended schemes are open to anytime liquidation and thus equivalent to cash.

$$\text{Net asset value (NAV)} = \frac{\text{Market value of assets minus liabilities}}{\text{Shares outstanding}}$$

Example: A mutual fund company is assumed to have a portfolio of securities worth Rs.100 crores, with outstanding shares worth 5 crores. It owes a total of Rs.10 crores in the form of rent, wages and other miscellaneous expenses, which thus form its liabilities. The firm's NAV is calculated as,

$$\text{NAV} = \frac{\text{Rs.100 crore} - \text{Rs.10 crore}}{5 \text{ crore}} = \text{Rs.18}$$

As there are two types of mutual funds with respect to maturity, there are two types of funds, with respect to the potential of growth for the investment. These types are known as mutual funds with:

— Growth option.
— Dividend option.

Growth option of mutual fund generates only capital gain. It doesn't pay any dividends. On the other hand, choosing to opt for the dividend option of a mutual fund implies that the investor earns cash regularly, in terms of the dividend payments. Each option has its merit as well as demerit. Choosing a growth fund means the growth is dependent only on the capital gain, on which thus the NAV depends. In dividend option though the investor earns regularly, but the NAV of the fund goes down, as dividend is continuously being paid.

Along with growth and dividend schemes other schemes offered by mutual funds are: balanced schemes, money market schemes, tax savings schemes, index schemes, etc.

> **Pause for thought:** These are funds which are mutually dependent on the investments, made by others too, in that fund.

2.4 REAL ASSETS

Physical or identifiable assets such as gold, land, equipment, patents, etc. They are the opposites of a financial asset. They tend to be most desirable during periods of high inflation, as is in the present scenario.

2.4.1 Gold

Demand of gold for the purpose of investment, has surpassed its demand for jewellery, since 2004. Advantages of investing in gold have been realized repeatedly, as compared to other investment options. The recommended range of investment varies from 15 to 20% of the allocation of the total portfolio. Gold can be invested in the form of jewellery, coins, bars, gold exchanged traded funds (ETFs), gold options and futures, gold mutual funds, gold certificates, etc.

Advantages of having gold in a portfolio are:

— Gold has low or negative correlation with most of the other classes.
— Portfolio, with some percentage allocated to gold, improves the consistency of performance of the portfolio during boom as well as during recession.
— The price of gold and thus returns from investments in it, are not linked to the performance of economy, industry and company.
— All the above points indicate that gold is independent of the macroeconomic factors, hence its unparalleled importance in a portfolio.

(Source: www.goldprice.org)

Figure 2.1: Price of gold for the period 2007 to 2011

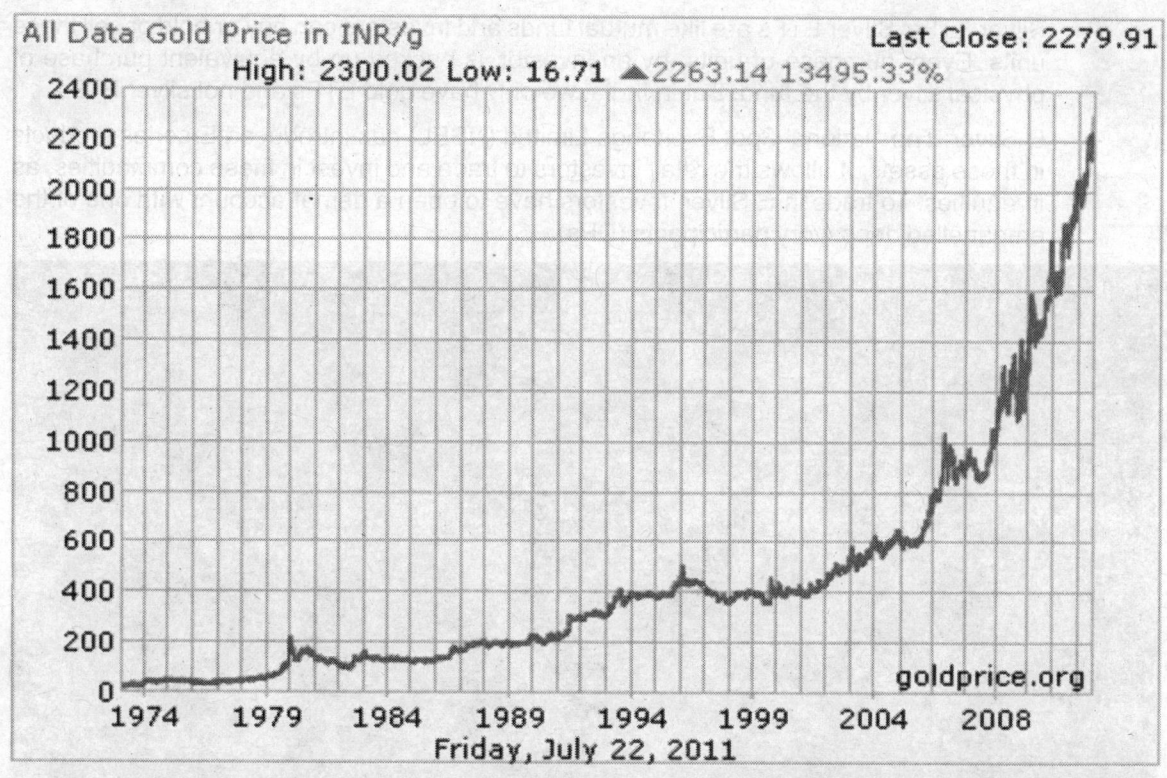

(Source: www.goldprice.org)

Figure 2.2: Price of gold for the period 1974 to 2008

2.4.2 Silver

Silver is not only often referred to as poor man's gold, but in the present financial environment, has become a viable option for investment as well. In the last one year, the price of silver has shot up from Rs.26,000 to Rs.70,000 (May, 2011) per kilogram. The large scale use of silver has increased in industry and otherwise. As a result, silver futures trade on worldwide exchanges, such as COMEX, which acts as a world reference for silver prices in the US; and National Commodity Exchange (NCDEX) and Multi Commodity Exchange (MCX) in India. Silver is used in photography, water purification, solar energy, batteries, electronics, medicine, etc. Gold and silver used in jewellery can be recycled.

Apart from the conventional applications, newer ones are emerging too. Silver has found its way, as a tradable commodity thus, apart from the prior utilities, which were restricted to jewellery, silver coins and bars. It is traded as:

— Silver futures: They offer an opportunity for investors adept at correctly anticipating the changes in price. Annually, only about 1% of silver futures contracts actually result in delivery because traders usually offset their positions before the contract matures. The difference between the initial purchase price and the price at the time of offsetting the transaction determines the profit or loss.

- Silver ETFs: Silver ETFs are like mutual funds and investors can buy or hold or sell these units. Every purchase of units, by an investor, is backed up by equivalent purchase of physical silver by the fund. But in India, we only have gold ETFs and not silver ETFs.
- E-Silver: The National Spot Exchange Limited (NSEL) has introduced E-series products in these assets. It allows the retail investors to trade and invest in these commodities, as in equities. To trade in E-Silver, investors have to open a demat account with one of the empanelled depository participants (DPs).

(Source: www.goldprice.org)

Figure 2.3: Price of the silver commodity from June 2010 to May 2011

Table 2.2: Price of Gold and Silver for the Indian Retail Investor

Year	10 gms of gold	1 kg of silver
2007	10700	19200
2008	11438	22500
2009	14508	21100
2010	16901	28200
2011	22832	71100
2012	29170	56300

Advantages of investing in silver are:
— Relatively less expensive, compared to gold.
— Easy to store and transport.
— Instant convertibility into cash.
— Internationally negotiable.

Disadvantages of the same:
— Must be stored securely.
— Yields no interest.

> **Pause for thought:** Real assets are physically identifiable assets and are indeed valuable, given the value they impart to the portfolio to which they are added.

2.5 REAL ESTATE

Real estate industry in India reached its prime during this time period, as it opened its gates for foreign investors also. It has a huge demand from almost every sector: educational, housing, hospitality, retail, manufacturing, healthcare, etc. But the major problem with investing in real estate is its very high upfront commitments. Furthermore, it cannot be liquidated as easily as can be shares and other investments. The rental yield from commercial property is 9 to 12%, while the yield from residential property is a meager 3-4%. Also, the demand for office space in India is likely to rise to almost 200 million square feet, over the next five years[7]. FDI is encouraged in the sectors: development of hotels, travels and tourism industry—that is the hospitality industry—township development, development of commercial real estates, special economic zones (SEZs), constructing educational institutions and recreational sites. All place their stake in real estates, as for the developments of infrastructure real estate is indispensable.

> **Pause for thought:** The demand for real estate is all-pervasive as no sector can come into existence without it: be it the housing, educational, hospitality, healthcare or the purely commercial sector. The infrastructural essentiality leads to the indispensability of real estate; and as is the demand, so is its growth.

2.6 PENSION PLAN

Pension is a kind of arrangement to provide people, who are no longer in service, with a regular income. It could be called compensation, or an appreciation for their service, once they are, superannuated from their profession. Pension plans are set up by employers, insurance companies, and other groups like employer associations or trade unions. Pension plans are in the form of guaranteed lifetime annuity, which thus reduces the risk pertaining to the uncertainty of life. Simply put, pension can be defined as the payments a person receives upon retirement, usually under pre-determined legal and/or contractual terms.

> **Pause for thought:** Pension is the analogue of salary, for a superannuated person. Though these sums do not equate, but it definitely is a reprieve, given that it serves as a steady source of sustenance.

---

[7] http://www.joneslanglasalleblog.com/realestatecompass/real-estate/2011/06/how-to-invest-in-commercial-real-estate

2.7 FOREIGN CURRENCY SECURITIES

There are quite a few securities which deal in foreign currencies. We know it is difficult for the Indian companies (and other companies of the developing economy) to raise funds from the capital market of a developed country. An indirect way of raising equity capital from the foreign capital market is through issuance of deposit receipts like American depository receipts and global depository receipts.

Deposit receipts are kind of negotiable securities that represent securities of companies, which enable domestic investors to buy securities of foreign companies without the accompanying risk or inconveniencies of cross-border and cross-currency transactions.

They have their unique features and thus utilities, which incites the following discussion.

2.7.1 American Depository Receipts

An American depository receipt (ADR) is the unit of the stocks of foreign companies traded, in the stock market of the United States. Each ADR represents one or more stock (it could be even a fraction of stock of the foreign companies, i.e., from the US point of view). Simply put, it is an excellent way to buy shares in a foreign company, while realizing any dividends and capital gain in foreign currency (US dollar). ADRs are either listed on NYSE, AMEX, NASDAQ or OTC. Investors who are holding an ADR have a right to obtain the foreign stock it represents. Often, the price of an ADR is very close to the price of the stock in the domestic market and is adjusted for the ratio of ADRs to foreign company shares. To issue ADRs, company has to issue its shares to reputed international financial institutions in the US, which acts as a depository or transfer agent. The depository collects the dividends from the issuing Indian company and then transfers the same to the depository holders in the US. The equities issued via the ADR route, by the Indian corporate, are shown in the table below.

Table 2.3 (A): Indian ADR Trading in the US

ADR issue	Symbol	Industry	Exchange
DR. REDDY'S LABORATORIES LTD.	RDY	Pharmaceutical	NYSE
HDFC BANK LTD.	HDB	Banks	NYSE
ICICI BANK LTD.	IBN	Banks	NYSE
INFOSYS TECHNOLOGIES LIMITED	INFY	Technology services	NASDAQ
MAHANAGAR TELEPHONE NIGAM LIMITED	MTE	Fixed line comm.	NYSE
REDIFF.COM INDIA LTD	REDF	Technology services	NASDAQ
SATYAM COMPUTER SERVICES LIMITED	SAY	Technology services	NYSE
SIFY LTD.	SIFY	Technology services	NASDAQ
VIDESH SANCHAR NIGAM LIMITED	VSL	Fixed line comm.	NYSE
WIPRO LTD.	WIT	Technology services	NYSE

Table 2.3 (B): Indian ADR trading in the US with Price and Number of Shares

Company	ADR Price (US$)	Change	Issue Price (US$)	Local Price (Rs)	Prem/(DISC) To Local	Total Share (m)
Dr. Reddy's (RDY)	30.4	0.4%	10.0	1,676.0	1.4%	169.3
HDFC Bank (HDB)	33.5	–0.1%	59.4	592.0	4.4%	2,349.4
ICICI Bank (IBN)	33.1	0.5%	11.0	879.6	5.0%	1,151.8
Infosystech (INFY)	42.2	–0.3%	17.0	2,338.5	0.9%	574.2
MTNL	1.4	0.0%	7.5	37.7	0.2%	630.0
Patnicomputers (PTI)	18.3	–0.1%	20.3	515.8	–0.9%	137.8
Rediff.com (REDF)	2.8	0.1%	12.0	NM	NM	NM
Satyam Comp (SAY)	34.7	–0.0%	9.7	96.1	908.6%	684.7
Satyaminfoway (SIFY)	2.1	0.0%	0.4	NM	NM	NM
Sterlite Ind. (SLT)	7.0	–0.1%	13.4	93.2	4.4%	3,361.2
Tata Comm. (TCL)	8.0	0.1%	0.0	224.9	–0.8%	285.0
Tata Motors (TTM)	20.9	–0.2%	0.0	228.7	410.4%	3,338.6
Wipro (WIT)	7.8	0.0%	41.2	361.5	–27.5%	2,454.4

(Source: http://www.equitymaster.com/stockquotes/adr.asp)

2.7.2 Global Depository Receipts

Global depository receipts (GDR) allow an Indian company, as well as that from any other country to raise the fund from UK and get listed and traded on the London Stock Exchange and Luxemburg Stock Exchange. Reliance was the first Indian company to issue GDR in May 1992, followed by Grasim in November 1992. GDRs are issued by an international bank and are subject to the capital markets worldwide. Like ADR, price of GDRs also are very close to the values of the related shares.

> **Pause for thought:** The foreign currency securities are like exporting a company, as commodity in the foreign capital market, to be traded on the respective financial stock exchange.

2.7.3 External Commercial Borrowings

External commercial borrowings (ECB) are commercial loans in the form of bank's loan, buyer's credit, supplier's credit, floating rate and fixed rate bonds. These are availed from non-resident lenders with average minimum maturity of three years. ECBs are issued by Indian companies and expressed in foreign currency. The principal and interest of such loans are payable in foreign currency.

Table 2.4: Indian GDR

GDR companies # Euro convertible bond **adjusted for bonus	The comprehensive GDR listing				
	Industry segregation	Date of GDR Issue (US$)	Size of GDR Issue (US$ m)	Shares per GDR	GDR issue price** (US$)
Arvind Mills	Textiles	03-02-94	125.00	1.0	9.78
Ashok Leyland	Autos	20-03-95	137.77	3.0	12.79
Bajaj Auto	Autos	27-10-94	110.00	1.0	16.89
Ballarpur Ind.#	Paper	27-05-94	35.00	1.0	8.77
Bombay Dye	Textiles	16-11-93	50.00	1.0	9.20
BSES Ltd	Power	04-03-96	125.00	3.0	14.40
Century Textiles	Diversified	21-09-94	100.00	2.0	254.00
CESC	Power	14-04-94	125.00	1.0	10.67
Core Parent	Pharma	21-06-94	70.00	1.0	12.60
Crompton Greaves	Electrical	02-07-96	50.00	1.0	7.56
DCW	Diversified	19-05-94	25.00	5.0	13.55
Dr. Reddy's	Pharma	18-07-94	48.00	1.0	11.16m
E. I. Hotels	Hotels	07-10-94	40.00	1.0	9.30
EID Parry	Fertilizer	07-07-94	40.00	1.0	8.39
Finolex Cab	Cables	19-07-94	55.00	1.0	16.60
Flex Industries	Packaging	30-11-95	30.00	2.0	8.05
G.E. Shipping	Shipping	17-02-94	100.00	5.0	15.94
G.N.F.C	Fertilizer	06-10-94	61.11	5.0	12.75
GAIL	Oil & Refineries	04-11-99	22.50	6.0	9.67
Garden Silk	Textiles	04-03-94	45.00	5.0	26.28
Grasim (1st)	Diversified	25-11-92	90.00	1.0	12.98
Grasim (2nd)	Diversified	09-06-94	100.00	1.0	20.50
Guj Ambuja #	Cement	26-11-93	80.00	1.0	5.95
Himachal Futuri	Telecomm.	02-08-95	50.00	4.0	9.30
Hindalco (1st)	Aluminium	22-07-93	72.00	1.0	10.73
Hindalco (2nd)	Aluminium	08-07-94	100.00	1.0	16.00
Hindustan Dev.	Diversified	21-09-94	76.00	1.0	2.05
India Cements	Cement	11-10-94	90.00	1.0	4.23
Indian Alum.	Aluminium	22-02-94	60.00	1.0	6.77
Indian Hotels	Hotels	28-04-95	86.25	1.0	16.60
Indian Rayon	Diversified	25-01-94	125.00	1.0	15.01
Indo Gulf	Fertilizer	18-01-94	100.00	1.0	4.51
Indo Rama	Textiles	21-03-96	50.00	10.0	11.37

INVESTMENT ALTERNATIVES

ICICI	Finance	02-08-96	230.00	5.0	11.50
ICICI (ADR)	Finance	22-09-99	315	5.0	9.80
Infosys	IT	11-03-99	70.38	0.5	34
IPCL	Petrochemicals	08-12-94	85.00	3.0	13.87
ITC	Cigarettes	13-10-93	68.85	1.0	7.65
J.K. Corp	Diversified	17-10-94	55.00	1.0	8.00
Jain Irrig	Plastics	25-02-94	30.00	1.0	11.13
JCT Ltd.	Textiles	29-07-94	45.00	10.0	16.96
Kesoram Ind	Diversified	31-07-96V	30.00	1.0	1.60
L & T (1st)	Diversified	18-11-94	150.00	2.0	16.70
L & T (2nd)	Diversified	01-03-96	135.00	2.0	15.35
Mahindra & Mahindra	Autos	30-11-93	74.75	1.0	4.46
MTNL	Telecom	04-12-97	418.53	2.0	11.958
NEPC Micon	Diversified	07-11-94	47.70	1.0	3.18
Nippon Denro#	Steel	03-03-94	125.00	10.0	21.36
Oriental Hotels	Hotels	14-12-94	30.00	1.5	12.75
Ranbaxy Labs	Pharma	29-06-94	100.00	1.0	19.38
Raymond Woolen	Textile	09-11-94	60.00	2.0	10.61
Reliance	Diversified	27-05-92	150.00	2.0	16.35
Reliance (2nd)	Diversified	15-02-94	300.00	2.0	23.50
Reliance Petroleum	Diversified	18-10-99	100	15.0	23.0
S.A.I.L.	Steel	07-03-96	125.00	15.0	12.97
Satyam Infoway	IT	19-10-99	75.00	1.0	18.0
S.I.E.L.	Diversified	14-10-94	40.00	3.0	14.64
Sanghi Poly	Textiles	28-07-94	50.00	5.0	9.56
SIV Ind	Textiles	01-08-94	45.00	1.0	6.37
SPIC	Fertilizer	28-09-93	65.00	5.0	11.15
SBI	Banking	03-10-96	369.95	2.0	14.15
Sterlite India#	Diversified	22-12-93	100.00	1.0	17.86
Tata Electric	Power	22-02-94	65.00	100.0	710.00
Telco (1st)	Autos	15-07-94	115.00	1.0	8.75
Telco (2nd)	Autos	06-08-96	200.00	1.0	14.25
Tube Invest	Cycles & Acc.	20-05-94	45.60	1.0	6.58
United Phos.	Pesticides	25-02-94	55.00	1.0	20.50
Usha Beltron	Cables	06-10-94	35.00	1.0	10.70
Videocon Int.	Electronics	26-01-94	90.00	1.0	8.10
VSNL	Telecomm.	24-03-97	527.00	0.5	13.93
Wockhardt	Pharma	25-02-94	75.00	1.0	14.35

ECBs are accessed by two routes:
— Automatic route.
— Approval route.

In India, ECBs for real estate sector, industrial sector and especially for the infrastructure sector are by the automatic route. The automatic route does not require the approval of the government. Hence these issuances are independent of the RBI. Financial institutions, which deal exclusively in infrastructure or export finance such as IDFC, IL&FS, power finance corporations and Exim bank, can raise ECB, but via the approval route. Corporate, registered under the company's act, such as banks, financial institutions, housing finance companies and NBFCs are eligible to raise ECB. On the other hand, individuals, trusts and non-profit making organizations are not eligible to raise ECB. Recently, special economic zones (SEZs) have been permitted to raise funds through ECB. Borrowers can raise ECB from internationally recognized sources, viz., international banks, international capital markets, multinational financial institutions, etc. The maximum amount of ECB, which can be raised by the corporate, is USD 500 million or equivalent during a financial year.

> **Pause for thought:** ECB is a commercial loan, issued by an Indian company but expressed in foreign currency.

2.7.4 Foreign Currency Convertible Bonds

Foreign currency convertible bonds (FCCBs) are optionally convertible bonds, issued in currencies other than the Indian Rupees. A convertible bond is a hybrid of debt and equity instruments. It is similar to bonds as it involves regular coupon payments, along with payment of the principal. But such bonds provide the option to the holders, of converting the bond into shares at maturity. Below is the list of euro convertible bonds, issued as FCCBs, by some of the Indian companies.

Company	Month of Issuance	Amt. ($m) Rate (US $)	Coupon	Shares per ECB	Conversion Date
Essar Gujarat	Jul-93	75	5.5	54.53	Jul-98
Reliance Ind.	Oct-93	140	3.5	10.86	Oct-99
TISCO	Feb-94	100	2.25	10.78	Feb-00
ICICI	Feb-94	200	2.5	1.43	Feb-00
Ballarpur Ind.	May-94	35	4	11.41	Aug-99
SPIC	Jul-94	67	2	28.17	Jul-99
Mah& Mah	Aug-94	100	5	8.38	Aug-01
Reliance Petro	Aug-94	125	7.84	Converted to GDRs	Aug-01

INVESTMENT ALTERNATIVES

GlobaTele-systems	Oct-96	48	1.75	500	Aug-03
IPCL	Mar-97	175	NA	At a price of Rs. 466 per share	Mar-02
GACL	Jan-01	100 mn	1	At a price 28% above GACL's share price at BSE	Mar-02

Pause for thought: These are optionally convertible bonds, issued in foreign currency.

SUMMARY

✓ There are number of instruments available in the market and they are classified as negotiable and non-negotiable instruments. Equity shares are negotiable variable security, while bonds and debentures are negotiable fixed income securities.

✓ Treasury bills, commercial paper and certificate of deposits are called money market securities.

✓ PPF is like a post office savings schemes with an early withdrawal facility. PPF and NSC provide tax exemption to their investors.

✓ Real estate has become one of the most attractive investment vehicles in recent times.

✓ Mutual fund is a portfolio of diversified securities, available in small units for the investment purpose.

✓ Indian corporate now has access to the foreign capital market, in terms of: ADR, GDR, FCCB and ECB.

KEY CONCEPTS

Equity Shares	Preference Shares	Certificate of Deposits
Bonds	Foreign Currency Convertible Bonds	Bank Deposits
Debentures	External Commercial Borrowings	Real Estate
Mutual Funds	Global Depository Receipts	Treasury Bills
NAV	American Depository Receipts	Commercial Paper
Public Provident Funds	Post Office Savings Schemes	Gold
National Savings Certificates	Kisan Vikas Patra	Silver

CASE STUDY

Ms. Dhara Shukla is an architect in Ahmedabad. She has been recently employed and her annual income is around Rs.10,00,000. She has accumulated savings of around Rs. 14,00,000. All her funds have been parked in savings account of a nationalized bank, where she is getting 3.5% interest p.a. She has not invested her funds anywhere else, except in tax saving investments. An agent, dealing in LIC, recently visited her office and tried to convince her to invest in the Jeevan Anand Policy and Money Back Plan of LIC. At the same time her colleague, Mr. Sharma, is advising her to invest her funds in the stock market. Mr. Sharma, as per his calculations, thinks it is the right time to invest in the stock market. The rationale behind this conclusion is the anticipated phase of boom in Indian Economy. He also feels that it will be one of the best economies for FII to invest their fund. Another colleague of Ms. Dhara, Mrs. Jagannathan, on the other hand opines that investing in stock market is akin to gambling. According to her, one must invest only in gold, silver or in fixed deposits as they are very safe investment options. Her boss observed that given the sky rocketing prices of real estate, one must go for it. But Mr. Sharma told Ms. Dhara that this bubble in the real estate might burst. Mr. Sharma is hence against investing in the real estate market at such high prices, as he also believes that as she would have to wait for a long period to get a reasonable return. Accountant of the company, where she works, strongly believes that investing in the mutual funds is highly profitable. And last but not the least, her father advises her to invest in PPF and/or various other schemes of post office.

With so many advisers and as many ideas, Ms. Dhara finds herself in an unprecedented puzzling situation. She herself has no idea of returns and other features of the various investment alternatives that are available. As a finance student, solve her queries looking at the current financial condition of the economy, in the following manner.

1. Analyze all the investment alternatives, in terms of: risk, return, liquidity, comparative benefits and disadvantages.
2. Explain the whole concept of 'risk' to her.
3. Suggest to her the best investment tool, by empirically working on various instruments.

APPENDICES

Appendix-2.1: Post Office Savings Schemes

Post Office Savings Account	4.0% p.a., on individual/joint accounts.	Minimum INR 50/-.	Cheque facility available. Interest, tax free.
5-Year Post Office Recurring Deposit Account	On maturity INR 10/- account fetches INR 738.62/-. Can be continued for another 5 years on year-to-year basis.	Minimum INR 10/-, per month, or any amount in multiples of INR 5/-. No maximum limit.	One withdrawal up to 50% of the balance allowed after one year. Full maturity value allowed on R.D. Accounts restricted to that of INR 50/- denomination in case of death of depositor, subject to fulfillment of certain conditions. 6 and 12 months advance deposits earn rebate.

Post Office Time Deposit Account	Interest payable annually but calculated quarterly. Period Rate 1 yr. a/c 7.70% 2 yr. a/c 7.80% 3 yr. a/c 8.00% 5 yr. a/c 8.30%	Minimum INR 200/- and in multiples thereof. No maximum limit.	Account may be opened by an individual. The investment under this scheme qualifies for benefit under Section 80C of the IT Act, 1961 w.e.f 1.4.2007.
Post Office Monthly Income Account Scheme	8.2% p.a., w.e.f. 01.12.2011	In multiples of INR 1500/-. Maximum INR 4.5 lakhs, in single account and INR 9 lakhs in joint account	Maturity period is 5 years. Can be prematurely encashed after one year, with certain conditions. Bonus is not admissible on maturity with respect to MIS accounts opened on or after 01.12.2011.
15 year PPF Account	8.8% p.a., w.e.f. 01.04.2012	Minimum INR. 500/-. Maximum INR. 1,00,000/- in a financial year. Deposits can be made in lump sum or in 12 installments.	Deposits qualify for deduction from income under Sec. 80C of the IT Act. Interest is completely tax-free. Withdrawal is permissible every year from the 7th financial year. Loan facility is available from the third financial year. No attachment under court decree order.
National Savings Certificate (VIII issue)	INR. 100/- grows INR. 150.90 after 5 years	Minimum INR. 100/- No maximum limit is there for investments in NSC. It is available in denominations of INR. 100/-, 500/-, 1000/-, 5000/- and 10,000/-.	A single holder type certificate A single holder type certificate can be purchased by an adult for himself or on behalf of a minor or can be gifted to a minor. Deposits qualify for tax rebate under Sec. 80C of the IT Act. The interest accrues annually, but deemed to be reinvested, will also qualify for deduction under section 80C of the IT Act.
National Savings Certificate (IX issue)	INR. 100/- grows to INR 234.35 after 10 years.	Minimum INR. 100/- No maximum limit is applicable. It is available in denominations of INR. 100/-, 500/-, 1000/-, 5000/- and 10,000/-.	A single holder type certificate can be purchased by an adult for himself or on behalf of a minor or to a minor. Interest on these certificates shall be liable to tax under the IT Act, 1961 (43 of 1961, on the basis of annual accrual specified in rule15; but no tax shall be deducted at the time of payment of discharge value).

Senior Citizen Saving Scheme	9% p.a., payable from the date of deposit of 31st March/30th September/31st December in the first instance and thereafter. Interest shall be payable on 31st March, 30th June, 30th September and 31st December.	There shall be only one deposit in the account in multiples of INR 1000/-, maximum not exceeding Rs. 15 lakhs.	Maturity period is 5 years. A depositor may operate more than one account in individual capacity, or jointly with spouse. Age should be 60 years or more, and 55 years or more. But it should be less than 60 years for the person who has retired or otherwise, on the date of opening of account, subject to the condition that the account is opened within one month of the receipt of retirement benefits. Premature closure is allowed after one year, on deduction of 1.5% interest; and after 2 years, with deductions at 1% interest. TDS is deducted at source, on interest, if the interest amount is more than INR 10,000/- p.a. The investment under this scheme qualifies for the benefits under section 80C of the IT Act, 1961 w.ef 1.4.2007.	

(Source: http://www.indiapost.gov.in/netscape/Banking.html)

Appendix-2.2: Comparison of Different Government Schemes

Scheme name	Returns	Min./Max. amount (Rs.)	Liquidity	Tax benefits
National Savings Certificate	8.0%	100/no limit	No premature withdrawal.	u/s 88 u/s 80L
Public Provident Fund	8.8%	500/1,00,000	Maturity is 15 years; loan available after 3rd year, up to max of 25% of balance at the end of the preceding year. Part withdrawal allowed after 7 years.	u/s 88 u/s 10
Kisan Vikas Patra	Money doubles in 8 years and 7 months	100/no limit	Premature withdrawals allowed.	NIL
Post Office Monthly Income Scheme	8.0%	1,000/3,00,000	No withdrawal before 1 year and on withdrawals between 1 to 3 years; 5% of principle is deducted No bonus is offered in such cases.	u/s 80L

INVESTMENT ALTERNATIVES

Post Office Savings Deposit*	3.5%	20/100000 **	Withdrawal anytime without notice.	NIL
Post Office Time Deposit***	6.25 to 7.50%	50/no limit	No interest is paid if withdrawn between 6 months to 1 year. Penal interest of 2% is deducted if withdrawn after 1 year from the date of deposit.	u/s 80L
5-year Post Office Recurring Deposit	Maturity value of Rs.10 Deposited Rs.728.90 (deposit to be made every month)	10/no limit	Amount can be withdrawn after three years at interest rate calculated as per rules.	u/s 80L

* Returns of individual/joint and group accounts.
** Maximum amount for joint account is Rs. 2,00,000 and no limit on institutional accounts.
*** Deposit schemes with duration of 1, 2, 3 and 5 years are available.

Appendix-2.3: Some Examples of NBFCs

Schemes	Ratings	Minimum amount (Rs.)	Interest payable	Interest rate (% p.a.) 180 days 1 year 2 years 3 years
Jaiprakash Associates Ltd.		20,000	Cumulative	11.50 11.75 12.25 12.50
Jaiprakash Associates Ltd.		20,000	Non-cumulative	11.50 11.75 12.25 12.50
Alembic Ltd.	CRISIL : P1+	50,000	Cumulative	0 9.50 9.00 9.00
Alembic Ltd.	CRISIL : P1+	50,000	Non-cumulative	0 9.50 9.00 9.00
Mahindra Finance Ltd.	CRISIL : FAAA	10,000	Cumulative	0 9.25 10.00 10.25

LIC Housing	CRISIL : FAAA Finance	10,000	Cumulative	0 9.00 9.25 9.50
PNB Housing	CRISIL : FAA+	10,000	Non-cumulative	0 9.50 9.50 9.75

REFERENCES

1. http://www.mutualfundsindia.com/
2. http://www.moneycontrol.com/mutualfundindia/
3. http://www.indiainfoline.com/MutualFunds/
4. http://www.amfiindia.com/
5. http://www.equitymaster.com
6. http://www.stocksabroad.com

3
STOCK MARKET INDICES

LEARNING OBJECTIVES
The purpose of this chapter is to enable you to understand:
- What is meant by the term 'market'.
- The different factors involved in constructing the market indices.
- Functioning of the different market indices.
- What is market capitalization.
- Computational procedures of these indices.
- The importance of impact cost.
- Tracking error.

3.1 INTRODUCTION

We come across the terms market, rally, downturn, Sensex, Nifty, sentiments, fundamentals, etc., daily, in newspapers and on television. These terms figure even in our conversation with people. Well, we discuss these aspects but very little do we actually know about what we are discussing!

This chapter intends to dispel the confusion, and ignorance, that shrouds our understanding, pertaining to the matters of stock market.

This chapter on stock market indices hence deals with the fundamentals of market and their functioning. Thus in this chapter we look forward to the details, and understanding, of how the stock market functions. The basics of the market pertain to the stock indices. It is of utmost importance to know what these indices are; how they are computed and how the securities are admitted to the top 30 and 50 for BSE Sensex and Nifty 50 respectively. But before these make their way into the respective indices, it is imperative to know the difference between BSE Sensex and Nifty 50. As then only we would know the parameter(s) of admittance into either of them, for the securities to be traded later.

What is actually meant by the fundamental term, 'market', seeks discussion primarily, hence.

3.2 MARKET

So very often we come across the questions, "How is the market today?" and "What is likely to happen to the market in near future?" The questions are very natural. For an investor who holds the portfolios of different individual stocks, it is cumbersome to follow the performance of the same individually and then to determine the composite performance of the portfolio. People investing in stock market want to know how the overall market will move in order to make an estimate of the performance of their investments.

With more than 8000 companies listed on the BSE and more than 3000 on NSE, it is not possible to keep a track of each so as to assess the whether the market is going upward or downward. The indices like Sensex, Nifty and others represent the market and reflect the overall market movement. The general notion is, when the market is high, the individual stocks too enjoy a rise in their price, and vice-versa. And this notion is based on the observation that stocks indeed move with the aggregate (overall) market.

Investors and analysts usually view and analyze the market indices like BSE 30 (Sensex), BSE 200, Dollex, NSE 50, Nifty Junior, RBI Indices, Financial Express Indices, etc. To track the sector-wise performance, investors usually refer to indices like BSE Reality Index, Bankex, BSE Tech., etc.

> **Pause for thought:** Market index is an index, a reflection, of the state of the market and hence, of economy.

3.2.1 Uses of Stock Market Indices

The basic application of the market indices is to compute risk and return of the index. These are then used as benchmark to judge the performance of individual securities or portfolios. An efficient portfolio manager tries to outperform the market and in this endeavor a benchmark, a standard reference, acts as the facilitator. Often, the stock market analysts, asset management companies and others refer to these indices to examine the factors that influence the simultaneous movements of all securities, in the market. The significance and utilities of market indices are summarized as:

— As the market reflects each and every input from economy, industry, company and politics, it acts as a progress report of a nation's economy.
— It serves as a benchmark, evaluating the performance of mutual fund managers and other market professionals.
— Since they mirror the behavior of stock market they are used successfully to assess the overall trend of the market.
— To calculate the systematic risk of the security, indices are used as a proxy.
— It is used by technical analysts or chartists to predict the future performance of a particular stock, by studying the past performance of the indices.
— To earn return at par with the market, indices are used by the investors to allocate the funds to different securities and sectors.
— With the help of indices, index funds[1] and futures are created.

---

[1] We will discuss about index funds subsequently.

> **Pause for thought:** Study of the market enables the assessment of the present trend, with respect to the past, to form an idea of the same, for the future, before an investment is made.

3.2.2 Benefits of Listing

A list systematizes the study, whatever is the paradigm of the list. Thus the same applies to the securities enlisted on a stock exchange. The benefits are many and are enlisted as follows:

— Listing of a security on a designated stock exchange provides it a visibility in the market through which corporate/entrepreneurs can raise capital to finance new project or can get fund for expansion, diversification, etc.
— An initial listing of a security raises the potential of the corresponding company to increase its capital through various routes, such as: preferential issue, rights issue, qualified institutional placements and ADRs/GDRs/FCCBs. It also helps in attracting a diverse group of professionals and institutional investors.
— Listing of the security protects the interest of the investors, as it allows independent evaluation of the company by the market. It further ensures a better and timely disclosure of important information to the investor, pertaining to the investments.
— It provides a continuing liquidity to the shareholders.
— It provides an easy exit route to private investors as well as liquidity to ESOP (employee stock option plan) holding employees.
— It acts as a premier marketplace for the company as it raises the public profile of the company—among investors, suppliers, financial institutions and media. Chances are more for a listed company to figure in an analyst's report. Also, the listing may pave the way for its inclusion in other indices of the stock exchanges.

> **Pause for thought:** The listing of a security works in the similar manner as an advertisement does for a product.

3.2.3 Factors to be Considered While Constructing the Market Indices

Market indices reflect the overall picture of the economy. So, care has to be taken while selecting securities for it. Indices are framed in a way which represents the total population of the market. To understand this, we take the example of Bombay Stock Exchange (BSE) where more than 8000 companies are listed. Hence, the total population of BSE is 8000 companies. Index should be framed in such a way that only a small group of securities, with their movement, represent the overall performance of all 8000 companies. The factors, that have to be kept in mind while constructing the market indices, are:

1. *The sample*

The size of the sample, its breadth[2], sectors and companies included in the sample to construct the indices, all are important. A judiciously selected small size of the sample reflects

---

[2] As per the chartist, it is the strength of the market according to the number of stocks, that advance or decline in a particular day. It is a technique used to gauge the direction of the overall market, by analyzing the number of companies advancing, compared to those declining. Positive market breadth occurs when more companies are moving higher than lower, and it is used to suggest that the bulls are in control of the momentum. Conversely, a disproportionate number of declining securities is used to confirm bearish momentum. This will be addressed in detail in Chapter 19-Technical Analysis.

compelling sign of the movement of the total population. But a large-biased sample is pointless. If index is constructed by including only large scale company—such index is not good representative of market. Similarly, an index constituted of a large number of companies, with majority of them skewed in terms of sector, size and other factors is not a good index of the performance of the market.

Costs incurred to construct the index, by taking a sample too large in size, sometimes outweighs its benefits. Also samples are selected in such a way that they represent each segment of the population.

We now take a look at the sample size of the different indices. The Sensex has 30 scrips like the DJIA (Dow Jones Industrial Average) of the USA; and Nikkie (Tokyo Stock Exchange) has 225 scrips. Nifty 50 has 50 scrips. Other comparatively less popular induces, like RBI Index, has 338 scrips; BSE National has 100 scrips; CRISIL has 500 scrips and Business Line has 250 scrips.

Many a times it is observed that some particular scrip in the sample loses the market interest. Its traded volume falls drastically or some new scrip attracts the investors with its performance. In such a case, such scrips are substituted. That is why, during the bear trend of the economy in 1996, with more than 60% scrips of the Sensex inactive, Sensex was drastically reconstructed, by replacing these non-performing securities. Table 3.1 shows the revision of the Sensex from 2005 to 2010. The third column shows the scrips that are substituted and the fifth column shows the scrips that substitute.

Table 3.1: History of Replacements in Sensex

Date	Scrip code	Scrips replaced	Scrip code	Scrips included
6-06-05	500104	Hindustan Petroleum Corp Ltd.	532555	National Thermal Power Corporation Ltd.
	505537	Zee Telefilms Ltd.	532540	Tata Consultancy Services Ltd.
12-06-06	500400	Tata Power Ltd.	532712	Reliance Communication Ltd.
9-07-07	500182	Hero Honda Motors Ltd.	500520	Mahindra & Mahindra Ltd.
19-11-07	500124	Dr. Reddy's Laboratories Ltd.	532868	DLF Ltd.
14-03-08	500490	Bajaj Auto Ltd.	532532	Jaiprakash Associates Ltd.
28-07-08	500425	Ambuja Cements Ltd.	500900	Sterlite Industries Ltd.
	500087	Cipla Ltd.	500400	Tata Power Co. Ltd.
12-01-09	500376	Satyam Computers Ltd.	524715	Sun Pharmaceutical Industries Ltd.
29-06-09	500359	Ranbaxy Laboratories Ltd.	500182	Hero Honda Motors Ltd.
3-05-10	524715	Sun Pharmaceutical Industries Ltd.	500087	Cipla Ltd.
26-05-10	500300	Grasim Industries Ltd.	532286	Jindal Steel & Power Ltd.
6-12-10	500410	ACC Ltd.	532977	Bajaj Auto Ltd.

(Source: www.bseindia.com)

Stock Market Indices

As the table shows, the exclusion and inclusion of scrips is found to be variable. Thus the scrip which is excluded is found to be reintroduced later and vice versa, as exemplified by Sun Pharmaceutical Industries Limited and Cipla Limited.

The BSE index committee meets every quarter to discuss index related issues. The replacement of any scrip of Sensex 30 is announced six weeks before the actual revision in the index is made, with respect to the security which replaces and the one replaced.

Similarly, the Table 3.2 enlists the incoming and outgoing scrips of S&P, CNX Nifty 50.

Table 3.2: List of Incoming and Outgoing Scrips of S&P, CNX Nifty 50

Date of inclusion	Securities included	Securities excluded
10-10-11	COALINDIA	RELCAPITAL
25-03-11	GRASIM	SUZLON
1-10-10	SESAGOA	UNITECH
1-10-10	DRREDDY	IDEA
1-10-10	BAJAJ-AUTO	ABB
8-04-10	KOTAKBANK	GRASIM
22-10-09	JPASSOCIAT	TATACOMM
22-10-09	IDFC	NATIONALUM
17-06-09	JINDALSTEL	RPL
27-03-09	AXISBANK	ZEEL
12-01-09	RELCAPITAL	SATYAMCOMP
10-09-08	RPOWER	DR.REDDY
14-03-08	DLF	GLAXO
14-03-08	POWERGRID	BAJAJAUTO
12-12-07	IDEA	MTNL
12-12-07	CAIRN	HINDPETRO
5-10-07	UNITECH	IPCL
24-09-07	NTPC	DABUR
4-04-07	RPL	JETAIRWAYS
4-04-07	STER	ORIENTBANK
1-09-06	RCOM	TATATEA
27-06-06	SUZLON	SCI
27-06-06	SIEMENS	TATACHEM
26-09-05	JETAIRWAYS	COLGATE
25-02-05	TCS	INDHOTEL

(Source: www.nseindia.com)

Pause for thought: Composition of the sample plays a huge role.

2. *The indices can be constructed by the following three methods:*

(a) Price-weighted index: A price-weighted index is calculated by adding the current prices of the stocks in the sample (used in the construction of the index) and dividing the sum by the total number of stocks. In this method, the stock with higher price dominates the index. This is exemplified by the following hypothetical situation.

An index is assumed to be composed of only two stocks, A and B, priced at Rs.10 and Rs.100 respectively. So, stock B is weighted nine times higher than stock A, with respect to the price.

$$\text{Price-weighted index value} = \frac{\text{Sum of stock prices}}{\text{Number of stocks after stock split}}$$

$$= \frac{10 + 100}{2}$$

$$= 55$$

In other words, we can say that the index is composed of 90% of B and 10% of A. With B dominating, changes in the value of A will hardly affect the index value. Dow Jones Industrial Average (DJIA) is a price-weighted average of 30 actively traded blue chip stocks.

Pause for thought: Price-weighted index is actually an average price of the stocks present in the sample.

(b) Market value-weighted index: The market value weighted index is calculated by multiplying the number of outstanding shares with the current market price. It is called market value weighted index because market value (n × p; where 'n' is the number of outstanding shares and 'p', their price) of the share acts as a weight. The scrips with heavy market capitalization govern the market rather than the scrips with high prices. In other words, the weight of the share dominates, not the one with the high price but with relatively high market capitalization. So the dominant shares are the heavy weights of the market!

The following example shows how market value-weighted index is calculated. It also shows how a price-weighted series and a market-value-weighted series adjust for stock splits.

Given a four security series and a 2-for-1 split for security A and a 3-for-1 split for security B, the divisor would change from 4 to 2.8 for a price-weighted series. Price of the stock A is Rs.20, before the split; so the stock A is divided into two stocks of Rs.10 each. Stock B is divided into three stocks of Rs.10 each (as before split price was Rs.30 per stock).

Table 3.3: Index Calculations in the Case of Stock Split (Price-weighted Series)

Stock	Price before split	Price after split
A	20	10
B	30	10
C	20	20
D	30	30
Total	100/4 = 25	70/X = 25 or X = 2.8

The price-weighted series adjusts for a stock split by deriving a new divisor. Thus is ensured the retention of the same value for the series, as is in absence of a split. The adjustment for a value-weighted series, due to a stock split, is automatic. The decrease in stock price is offset by an increase in the number of outstanding shares.

Let us take the same example to understand how stock split is taken care for by market-value-weighted method. As it is evident that in the market-value-weighted method price as well as the number of shares, both, are taken into account, number of share rises after stock split while price of that stock falls. Here, for stock A, there are 1,000,000 shares outstanding in the market and price per share before split is Rs.20. The market value is Rs.20,000,000 (Rs.20 × 1,000,000). As the stock split ratio is 2:1 for stock A, after the stock splits the price of the stock A becomes Rs.10 for each stock and number of stock increases to 2,000,000 in the market, resulting in the same market value of Rs.20,000,000 (Rs.10 × 2,000,000). Similar is the case for stock B.

Table 3.4: Index Before Split (Market-value-weighted Method)

Stock	Price/Share (Rs.)	Number of shares	Market value (Rs.)
A	20	1,000,000	20,000,000
B	30	500,000	15,000,000
C	20	2,000,000	40,000,000
D	30	3,500,000	105,000,000
Total			180,000,000

Rs.180,000,000 base value is set, equal to an index value of 100.

From Table 3.4 it can be concluded that the base value of the stock in the past, when stocks were not split, was Rs.180,000,000.

Table 3.5: Index After Splits

Stock	Price/Share (Rs.)	Number of shares	Market value (Rs.)
A	10	2,000,000	20,000,000
B	10	1,500,000	15,000,000
C	20	2,000,000	40,000,000
D	30	3,500,000	105,000,000
Total			180,000,000

After the stock splits, price of the stock decreases depending upon the stock split rate, but market value rises resulting in the same base value of Rs.180,000,000.

New index value = (Current market value/Base value) × Beginning index value
= (180,000,000/180,000,000) × 100
= 100

The value ascertained is precisely what one would expect—since there has been no change in prices other than the split.

> **Pause for thought:** Market value-weighted index gives the weight of the shares in the sample. Heavier is the weight, dominant is the share, irrespective of its current price.

(c) **An un-weighted index:** It is commonly known as equally weighted index. Thus is evident that all stocks carry equal weights. And because of this the market capitalization does not influence the movement of the index. In other words, as stocks are equally weighted, performance of one does not drastically impact the overall performance of the index. Rather changes in the index are dependent on the percentage change in the average price of the stocks. Economics Times Index is composed of 72 stocks and is based on the un-weighted index method. The calculation utilizes the simple arithmetic or geometric average.

> **Pause for thought:** This index is composed of stocks of equal weights. The change in the index is effected by the percentage change in the average price of the stocks.

3. Base year

The base year also plays an important role in the formation of an index. A base year is the year used for comparing the level of a particular economic index. It is the first year, in the series of years, in an economic or financial index. Any year can be chosen as a base year, but typically recent years are chosen. New, more up-to-date base years are periodically introduced to keep a particular index updated.

A base year is normally set to an arbitrary level of 100 so that percentage changes (rise or fall) can be easily depicted. For example, to find that rate of inflation (or any other economic index) between 2005 and 2010, one would make calculations using 2005 as the base year.

If the gap between the base year of one index and that of other indices is too large the comparison of the indices leads to biased judgment. With the gap increasing, the factors affecting the indices too undergo major changes. This causes a loss in parity in the parameters used for the comparison. For the construction of an ideal index the base year should be free from major economic upheavals. Too close a base year fails to compare the movement of the index with respect to the past data. On the other hand, when the base year is far apart, it fails to reflect the current movement. The base year of Sensex is 1978-79 while that of Nifty 50 is 1995.

> **Pause for thought:** For comparing the level of a particular index, ideally the years that are neither too recent nor too old, are chosen.

3.2.4 Sensex Scrips Selection Criteria

There are certain criteria for being selected as scrip on the Sensex. What follows is a discussion on the same.

1. Equities of companies, listed on the BSE, are considered eligible for inclusion in the index[3].

---

[3] Companies in the Z group, listed mutual funds, scrips suspended on the last day of the month prior to review date and scrips objected to by the surveillance department are not allowed inclusion in the index.

2. The scrip should be at least three months old at BSE. Exception is made for scrip, only one month into the exchange, if its average free float market capitalization ranks in the top 10 companies of BSE. And even such minimum history is not required in cases of merger, de-merger, amalgamation, etc.
3. The scrip must have been traded on each and every trading day during the last three months at BSE. In cases, such as of scrip suspension, exception may be allowed.
4. Only those companies, who have reported revenue in the last four quarters from their core activity, are considered eligible.
5. In accordance with the first four criteria, the top 75 companies, based on free float market capitalization, taking an average of three months, are selected. Other companies in the top 75, based on full market capitalization by taking average of three months, too, are selected.
6. The companies that are thus screened out, as per the fifth step, are ranked in coherence with their absolute turnover.
7. Any company, short listed according to the above step, with its cumulative turnover more than 98%, is excluded till the remaining list has more than 30 scrips.
8. The companies that are sorted thus, are further sorted, by free float market capitalization. Any company, within this filtered sample of scrips, with its weight less than 0.50%, is excluded.
9. The remaining companies are then sorted on the basis of sector and then ranked in the descending order with respect to free float market capitalization.
10. Scrips are selected in such a way that they maintain the weightage of sectors in the index, in the perspective of the overall market.
11. According to the norms of the BSE index committee an acceptable track record is a prerequisite for all companies to be included in the index.

3.3 MARKET CAPITALIZATION

Market capitalization is calculated by multiplying a company's outstanding shares by the current market price of one share. It is also referred to as 'market cap'. As opposed to sales or total asset figures, the term market capitalization is used by the investment community to determine the size or worth of the company.

Example: A company, XYZ, is assumed to have 1,00,000 outstanding shares, with a market value of Rs.100 for each share.

The company's market capitalization = (1,00,000 × Rs. 100) = Rs. 100,00,000.

The stocks of large, medium and small companies are referred to as large cap, mid cap and small cap, respectively. There is no consensus among the investment pundits on what is the exact criterion for this categorization. We only have an approximation, according to which the category of a company is dependent on its worth in the market. It is shown as follows.

Categorization: an approximation, based on market worth

— Large cap: above Rs. 10,000 crore.
— Mid-cap: Rs. 2000 to Rs. 10,000 crore.
— Small cap: up to Rs. 2,000 crore.

Table 3.6 shows the market cap of few of the companies of BSE Sensex, as on November 29, 2011.

Table 3.6: Market cap of selected scrips

Company name	Industry	Last price	Market cap (Rs. in crores)
Bajaj Auto	Auto: 2 and 3 wheelers	1,647.00	47,658.75
Bharti Airtel	Telecommunications: Service	373.40	141,799.77
BHEL	Engineering: Heavy	283.30	69,340.51
Cipla	Pharmaceuticals	326.45	26,211.37

(Source: www.bseindia.com)

BSE classifies companies according to their market capitalization using 80-15-5 method.

Categorization: based on the 80-15-5 method

The principles of this method are:

— The groups of companies which are responsible for 80% of the total market capitalization are deemed as large cap companies.

— Mid cap companies are those which contribute approximately 15% of the total market capitalization.

— The remaining are the small cap companies, contributing 5% to the total market capitalization.

Thus, the large cap, medium cap and small cap companies are those which contribute 80%, 15% and 5% to the total market capitalization, vide the 80-15-5 rule.

> **Pause for thought:** Market capitalization, frequently referred to as 'market cap', is the product of a company's outstanding shares and current price of a share. Depending upon the contribution of a group of companies to the total market capitalization, these are termed large, mid and small cap companies.

3.3.1 Free Float Methodology

The preceding section was devoted to discussion on market capitalization, their different categories and the parameters that determine the categorization. But it is essential to know how these assessments of companies, with respect to the category to which they belong, are carried out. And that requires a calculation of the market cap of a particular company. This is based on the free float method for market capitalization. The obvious question then is what is meant by the free float methodology?

A certain number of shares of a company are held by different types of investors, which include governments, founders and directors of the company, FDI, etc. These shares are called locked-in shares. The rest of the shares are floated in the open market, free to be traded by anyone. These are called free float shares. The calculation of market capitalization requires a prior knowledge of the number of free floats.

Given the importance of these shares, criteria are laid to ascertain which type of shares cannot be freely floated in the market for trading in the open market. Thus the following shares are the locked-in shares, and hence not free floats.

— Shares held by founders and directors and acquirers with an element of control on the market.
— Shares held by government as a promoter or acquirer.
— Those held by FDI.
— Shared held as strategic stakes by corporate bodies or individuals.
— Shares which allow cross holding-these are held by group of companies/associates.
— Shares held by employee welfare trust.
— Locked-in shares—which are not sold in the open market in normal course.

Based on the quarterly report submitted by the company, with details of its share holdings by the different shareholders, BSE decides the free float factor of the company. Total market capitalization of a company is adjusted with this free float factor to arrive at the free float market capitalization. Once free float factor is determined, it is rounded off to higher multiples of 5 and each company is classified into one of 20 bands given in the Table 3.7. For example, a free float factor of 0.65 means that only 65% of the market capitalization of the company would be considered for index calculation. When the free float factor of the company is multiplied with the market capitalization, the free float market capitalization is obtained. This is the value of the shares of the company in the open market. All BSE indices, except BSE PSU index, have adopted the free float methodology.

Table 3.7: Free Float Bands

% Free float	Free float factor	% Free float	Free float factor
>0 - 5%	0.05	>50 - 55%	0.55
>5 - 10%	0.10	>55 - 60%	0.60
>10 - 15%	0.15	>60 - 65%	0.65
>15 - 20%	0.20	>65 - 70%	0.70
>20 - 25%	0.25	>70 - 75%	0.75
>25 - 30%	0.30	>75 - 80%	0.80
>30 - 35%	0.35	>80 - 85%	0.85
>35 - 40%	0.40	>85 - 90%	0.90
>40 - 45%	0.45	>90 - 95%	0.95
>45 - 50%	0.50	>95 - 100%	1.00

(Source: www.bseindia.com)

The Table 3.8 shows the free float factor for 30 scrips of BSE.

Table 3.8: Free Float Factor, BSE

Sr. No.	Name	Sector	Free float factor	Weight in index (%)
1	Bajaj Auto	Transport equipments	0.55	0.77
2	Bhel	Capital goods	0.35	3.26
3	Bharti Airtel	Telecom	0.35	3
4	DLF Universal Limited	Housing	0.25	1.02
5	Grasim Industries	Diversified	0.75	1.5
6	HDFC	Finance	0.9	5.21
7	HDFC Bank	Finance	0.85	5.03
8	Hero Honda Motors.	Transport equipments	0.5	1.43
9	Hindalco Industries	Metal, metal products and mining	0.7	1.75
10	Hindustan Lever Ltd.	FMCG	0.5	2.08
11	ICICI Bank	Finance	1	7.86
12	Infosys	Information technology	0.85	10.26
13	ITC Limited	FMCG	0.7	4.99
14	Jaiprakash Associates	Housing	0.55	1.25
15	Larson & Turbro	Capital goods	0.9	6.85
16	Mahindra & Mahindra	Transport equipments	0.75	1.71
17	Maruti Suzuki	Transport equipments	0.5	1.71
18	NTPC	Power	0.15	2.03
19	ONGC	Oil and Gas	0.2	3.87
20	Reliance Communication	Telecom	0.35	0.92
21	Reliance Industries	Oil and Gas	0.5	12.94
22	Reliance Infrastructure	Power	0.65	1.19
23	State Bank of India	Finance	0.45	4.57
24	Sterlite Industries	Metal, metal products and mining	0.45	2.39
25	Sun Pharmaceutical	Healthcare	0.4	1.03
26	Tata Consultancy Services	Information technology	0.25	3.61
27	Tata Motors	Transport equipments	0.55	1.66
28	Tata Power	Power	0.7	1.63
29	Tata Steel	Metal, metal products and mining	0.7	2.88
30	Wipro	Information technology	0.2	1.61

(Source: www.bseindia.com)

From the above table it is apparent that ICICI has the highest free float factor of 1. This indicates that all the shares issued by the company are available in an open market for trading. On the other hand, ONGC and Wipro have a free float factor of 0.2. Thus the majority of their shares are locked-in. The fifth column represents the weight of the particular scrip in the index. Reliance Industries has the highest weight of 12.94% of the total index, followed by Infosys which has 10.26%; while Bajaj Auto has the lowest weight, 0.77%, in the index.

Table 3.9: Free Float Factor and Weightage at S&P CNX Nifty

Sr.	Symbol of the security	Free float market capitalization, Oct. 2011 (Rs. crores)	Weightage (%)	Beta	R^2	Volatility (%)	Monthly return	Avg. impact cost Oct. 2011 (%)
1	ACC	11152	0.69	0.58	0.46	1.48	8.59	0.08
2	AMBUJACEM	11673	0.72	0.78	0.45	1.85	4.16	0.1
3	AXISBANK	30045	1.86	1.39	0.75	2.84	17.28	0.08
4	BAJAJ-AUTO	23215	1.43	0.76	0.54	1.8	13.85	0.08
5	BHEL	25108	1.55	0.85	0.6	2.09	-0.66	0.08
6	BPCL	8045	0.5	0.53	0.38	1.88	-8.38	0.08
7	BHARTIARTL	47177	2.92	0.65	0.46	2.02	2.85	0.08
8	CAIRN	10859	0.67	0.77	0.53	1.77	10.22	0.08
9	CIPLA	14990	0.93	0.6	0.48	1.02	3.89	0.09
10	COALINDIA	20970	1.3	0.5	0.31	2.2	-1.43	0.07
11	DLF	8787	0.54	1.44	0.65	3.77	20.62	0.08
12	DRREDDY	21061	1.3	0.59	0.51	1.51	14.42	0.08
13	GAIL	18996	1.17	0.54	0.44	1.4	1.12	0.08
14	GRASIM	15744	0.97	0.67	0.54	2.01	8.18	0.09
15	HCLTECH	10905	0.67	1.16	0.67	2.99	10.72	0.08
16	HDFCBANK	87861	5.43	1.01	0.75	1.71	7.44	0.09
17	HEROMOTOCO	20816	1.29	0.46	0.24	1.23	11.31	0.05
18	HINDALCO	17485	1.08	1.43	0.7	3.76	9.68	0.07
19	HINDUNILVR	38549	2.38	0.46	0.38	2.18	12.46	0.06
20	HDFC	91392	5.65	1.08	0.73	2.01	8.57	0.08
21	ITC	114016	7.05	0.7	0.59	1.33	9.67	0.06
22	ICICIBANK	107284	6.63	1.4	0.82	3.06	10.97	0.07
23	INFY	138731	8.57	0.99	0.68	2.27	16.22	0.05
24	IDFC	15659	0.97	1.43	0.73	2.51	21	0.08

25	JPASSOCIAT	8755	0.54	1.82	0.73	2.85	10.41	0.08
26	JINDALSTEL	21872	1.35	1.21	0.73	3.89	18.57	0.08
27	KOTAKBANK	18940	1.17	1.15	0.71	2.25	14.82	0.1
28	LT	75832	4.69	1.12	0.71	2.5	7.12	0.07
29	M&M	39922	2.47	1.1	0.65	1.83	6.78	0.07
30	MARUTI	14887	0.92	0.68	0.5	2.03	4.41	0.07
31	NTPC	22910	1.42	0.74	0.59	1.61	9.07	0.07
32	ONGC	37455	2.31	0.55	0.4	1.88	3.58	0.07
33	POWERGRID	14844	0.92	0.55	0.54	1.13	7.7	0.06
34	PNB	12990	0.8	0.87	0.62	1.77	4.47	0.08
35	RANBAXY	7667	0.47	0.71	0.46	1.32	-2.21	0.08
36	RCOM	5296	0.33	1.44	0.56	2.08	10.83	0.09
37	RELIANCE	148021	9.15	1.1	0.76	2.38	11.34	0.07
38	RELINFRA	6374	0.39	1.29	0.53	2.64	22.88	0.08
39	RPOWER	5245	0.32	1.13	0.6	1.63	22.36	0.08
40	SESAGOA	8086	0.5	0.98	0.52	2.68	6.72	0.08
41	SIEMENS	7273	0.45	0.56	0.4	1.46	3.43	0.09
42	SBIN	49143	3.04	1.18	0.71	2.46	2.4	0.06
43	SAIL	6572	0.41	1.2	0.67	2.75	11.75	0.07
44	STER	17945	1.11	1.4	0.73	3.73	17.1	0.09
45	SUNPHARMA	18955	1.17	0.64	0.46	1.78	9.2	0.07
46	TCS	56617	3.5	1.04	0.67	2.46	6.95	0.07
47	TATAMOTORS	34807	2.15	1.62	0.73	3.95	29.2	0.08
48	TATAPOWER	16256	1	0.63	0.5	1.87	3.82	0.08
49	TATASTEEL	32138	1.99	1.22	0.75	2.81	22.34	0.06
50	WIPRO	18653	1.15	0.95	0.68	2.39	11.02	0.09
		1617975	100					0.07

(Source: www.nseindia.com)

The third column presents the market capitalization of Nifty 50 stocks in crores and the fourth column shows the weight of each security in the index. For example, free float market capitalization of ACC security is Rs. 11152 crore and the total market cap of the index is Rs. 1617975 crores. So, the weightage of the ACC stock is Rs. 11152/Rs. 1617975 = 0.69%. Impact cost, in the last column, is the weighted average impact cost and with respect to the data in Table 3.9, it has been calculated for a portfolio of Rs. 50 lakhs.

The free float market capitalization is useful for the various advantages it has.

Advantages of free float methodology

— It makes the index more broad-based by including more companies, as the governing companies of the index. Thus a larger number of companies determine the movement of the index. It reflects the market trend more rationally by including only those shares which are available for trading.

— It is an industry based proven practice. Hence all major index providers like MSCI, FTSE, S&P and STOXX use this method. NASDAQ-100 is also based on free float methodology.

— It enhances the flexibility of the index by including any stock from universe of the index. The index improves in terms of market and sector coverage. In a full market capitalization methodology, companies with large market capitalization, but with low free float factor, distorts the index by unjustifiably influencing the index movement. But, as under the free float methodology, only free float market capitalization of each company is considered, it even allows closely held companies to be included in the index. At the same time it prevents their unwarranted influence on the index movement.

— It acts as a benchmark for both active and passive investors.

> **Pause for thought:** The free float shares are those which are open to free trading in the market, by all. The free float method calculates the market capitalization of the company in a particular index. The product of the free float factor and market capitalization gives the free float market capitalization of the company and this is the value of its shares in the open market. Free float factor is the percentage, of the market capitalization of the company, considered for index calculation.

3.4 MAINTENANCE OF SENSEX AND INDEX CLOSURE ALGORITHM

During the trading hours, index is calculated and disseminated on real time basis. This is automatically based on the trading on 30 scrips of Sensex. The BSE index cell maintains the index with the broad index policy framework, as decided by the BSE index committee. The committee comprises of BSE governing body, market participants, fund managers, capital market experts, etc. The committee makes sure that Sensex and all other indices judiciously balance the frequent adjustments in the index, based upon corporate action and its historical continuity. It is also important for the committee to update the base year average. It ensures that the replacement of stocks in index, additional issues of capital by the corporate and other actions by the corporate, like issuance of rights issue, stock split, etc. does not disturb the historical value of the index. In other words, the committee works for the immunity of the index towards the various adjustments made by the corporate.

The closing value of Sensex, on all trading days, is calculated by taking the weighted average of trades on all 30 scrips of the Sensex, in the last 30 minutes of the trading session. If particular scrip of Sensex 30 does not trade in the last 30 minutes, then the last price at which it is traded is considered for calculating the closing value of the index. If any particular scrip does not trade at all on a given day, then its closing price on the day it last traded comes in for calculation of the index. This index closure algorithm prevents any manipulation in the market.

> **Pause for thought:** Maintenance of the index ensures immunity of the index to varied fluctuations and the index closure algorithm, with its transparent methodology ensures prevention of manipulation in the market.

3.5 ADJUSTMENTS

Certain adjustments are necessitated when the company brings forth changes in its existing set-up. These changes, that we intend to concentrate upon in this section, come in the form of bonus, rights and new issues. As these issues differ, so does the required adjustment. Hence to determine these adjustments, knowledge of bonus, rights and new issues is essential.

> **Pause for thought:** With adjustments, in terms of offerings of issues to the share holders, adjustment in the market capitalization of the company is necessitated.

3.5.1 Adjustment for Bonus Issue

Bonus issues are offered as free additional shares to existing shareholders. A company may decide to distribute further shares as an alternative to increasing the dividend payout. Bonus issues are also known as a 'scrip issue' or 'capitalization issue'. These shares could also be considered as a reward for, and acknowledgement of the loyalty of the shareholders, towards the company.

When a sample company of the index issues bonus shares, the market capitalization of the company does not undergo any change. So, no adjustment in the base market capitalization is required; only the number of shares in the formula is updated.

> **Pause for thought:** Bonus shares are free additional shares offered to the shareholders and they do not lead to any adjustments in the base market capitalization of the company.

3.5.2 Adjustment for Rights Issue

Companies, from time to time, issue rights to the existing shareholders to buy a proportional number of additional securities at a given price (usually at a discount), within a fixed period. These additional securities, since are bought under the purview of the rights issued for the same, are called the rights issue. Rights are often transferable, allowing the holder to sell them in the open market.

When a sample company of the index issues right shares, the free float market capitalization of the company is increased by the number of additional shares issued, based on the theoretical, i.e., ex-right[4] price. Ex-right price means shares of stock that are trading but no longer have rights attached because they have either expired, or have been transferred to another investor or have

---

[4] Shares which trade without rights attached. This term is used to describe a stock that trades without giving the stockholder the privilege to receive rights to buy shares of a new stock issue—because new shares are sold at price below the market price to rights holders. So stock trading ex-rights is worth less than the same stock with rights attached. A stock trading ex-rights is indicated in stock transaction tables in newspapers by the symbol x near the volume column. The theoretical ex-rights price is based on the company's market capitalization and the number of shares outstanding. For example, if a new rights offering gives buyers the rights to purchase 25% more shares than there are currently outstanding, the market price of the stock will theoretically be 25% less in the future than it is today (assuming that 100% of the new rights will be exercised by the holders)—without the rights to buy a company's stock at discount from the prevailing market price, which was distributed until a particular date. Typically, after that date, the rights trade separately from the stock itself.

been already exercised. In other words, the rights originally assigned to the stockholder, are, for whatever reason, no longer valid or no longer applicable to the stock. Hence an adjustment is required. So a proportionate adjustment is made to the base market capitalization by the formula,

New base market capitalization

$$= \text{Old base market capitalization} \times \frac{\text{New market capitalization}}{\text{Old market capitalization}}$$

It can be understood by the following hypothetical example. A company, PQR, is assumed to issue rights issue which increases the market capitalization of the company by Rs.100 crore. Its old base market capitalization is Rs.1000 crore. The aggregate market capitalization, of all shares included in the index, before the rights issue is offered, is Rs.2000 crore.

Then the new base market capitalization

$$= \text{Rs. } 1000 \times \frac{(\text{Rs. } 2000 + \text{Rs. } 100)}{\text{Rs. } 2000}$$

$$= \text{Rs. } 1050$$

Till further adjustments are called forth, due to corporate actions, Rs. 1050 is used as a base market capitalization.

> **Pause for thought:** Rights issue, offered to the share holders gives them the right to purchase further shares usually at discount. And these shares bring about an increase in the market cap of the company, necessitating an adjustment in the base market cap.

3.5.3 Adjustment for New Issue

New issue is a security that has been already registered and issued, but is being sold to the public for the first time in the stock market. New issues are sometimes referred to as primary shares or new offerings. Yet the term does not necessarily refer to newly issued stocks, although initial public offerings are most commonly known as new issues. Both debt and equity securities can be offered as new issues.

When convertible debentures are converted to new shares and offered thus as new issues,

— as during mergers and spin-offs;
— and the reduction in the number of shares due to buy-back of shares, corporate restructuring, etc., the base market capitalization adjustment is required, as in the case of rights issue, discussed above.

> **Pause for thought:** New issues are not necessarily newly issued, but they are offered to the public for the first time. Changes incurred in the market cap are similar to those by rights issue and hence the adjustment measure too is the same.

3.6 IMPACT COST

Impact cost is the cost of executing transaction at the stock exchanges. It has its significance, with one of the reasons being the dependence of the liquidity of a stock on it. Liquidity in the context of stock market is measured by the impact cost. Liquidity is inversely proportional to the transaction cost incurred in the liquidation. So higher is the transaction cost lower is the liquidity, and thus more facile is the convertibility into cash. The transaction costs do not include fixed costs like brokerage charges, depository charges, etc. Rather the transaction cost is the cost attributable to lack of market liquidity. Liquidity is facilitated by the presence of such buyers and sellers in the market who are constantly on the look-out for buying and selling opportunities. When the stock lacks liquidity, it is resistant to liquidation and has high transaction cost for buyers and sellers.

The electronic limit order book (ELOB), as available on NSE, is an ideal platform of market liquidity as it allows buying and selling from the available orders. Aided by the ELOB, when a buyer approaches the market with an intention of buying a particular stock, he can execute his buy order in the stock against such sell order which is already registered in the order book. Similar is the experience for the seller.

Example: Suppose we want to buy 4000 shares of a hypothetical company, X. As per the ELOB, on NSE terminal there is a buy order for 2000 shares of Rs. 100 and sell order, for 1000 shares, for Rs. 102.

The average price for buy and sell order = Rs. (100 + 102)/2 = Rs. 101.

Thus, the stocks of X can be sold or bought at Rs. 101. But, instead if we buy these stocks at an average cost of Rs. 103, the impact cost would be 2%.

It is 1% given the theoretical price of Rs.101. But the effective average acquisition cost is Rs. 103.

So the impact = $[(103 - 101)/101] \times 100 = 1.98\% = 2\%$.

It implies that we have incurred an impact cost of 2% for buying 1000 shares because of the liquidity condition of that stock. The more liquid a stock is, the lower its impact cost, as lower is the transaction cost. It must be remembered that impact cost varies with difference in transaction sizes and that in the outstanding orders. When a stock is not sufficiently liquid, a penal impact cost is applied.

As per the criterion set by the NSE, the stocks constituting S&P CNX Nifty should have an impact cost of less than 1.5%, for trades worth Rs.50 lakhs.

We consider another example for further clarity. This is an example of order book of stock at a given point of time.

Table 3.10: Order Book-1

Buy			Sell		
Sr. no.	Quantity	Price	Sr. no.	Quantity	Price
1	1000	3.50	5	2000	4.00
2	1000	3.40	6	1000	4.05
3	2000	3.40	7	500	4.20
4	1000	3.30	8	100	4.25

(Source: www.nseindia.com)

From Table 3.10 we can see that there are four buying and selling orders lying in this order book. Sr. no.1 is the best buy-sell deal for a particular stock and their difference (or bid-ask spread) is 0.50. If a person places a buy order of 100 shares, it would be matched against the best available sell order at Rs. 4. Thus he will buy 100 shares at Rs. 4. Similarly, if a person places sell order of 100 shares, it would be matched against the best available buy order of Rs. 3.50, which implies he will sell 100 shares at Rs. 3.50.

This spread is considered the transaction cost, which the market charges for the privilege of trading. The bid-ask spread does not allow for the arbitrage. It is evident from the above example that if the person buys and sells immediately, then he will incur a loss of 0.50.

Another example for the computation of impact cost follows, represented by the Table 3.11.

Table 3.11: Order Book-2

Buy quantity	Buy price	Sell quantity	Sell price
1000	98	1000	99
2000	97	1500	100
1000	96	1000	101

(Source: www.nseindia.com)

From the above table, the best buy deal = 99 + 98/2 = 98.5

Thus, for example, to buy 1500 shares, the sell price would be Rs. 99 for the first 1000 shares; and Rs. 100 for another 500. So, the actual buy price turns out to be,

Actual buy price = (1000 × 99) + (500 × 100)/1500 = 99.33

Impact cost = [(99.33 − 98.50)/98.50] × 100 = 0.84%

An index fund gives the same return as the index on which it is benchmarked. And a high impact cost results in a lower return of the index than the benchmark index. Hence, impact cost is very important for index fund managers.

> **Pause for thought:** Impact cost is the transaction cost of stocks. Higher is the transaction cost and thus the impact cost, lower is the liquidity of the stock.

3.7 SENSEX

Sensex came into being in 1986. It was computed by market value capitalization method of 30 large, financially established, companies across the key sectors. It is one of the oldest indices in the country. The base year for Sensex was taken as 1978-79. Today, it is a widely reported index in the national as well as international market, through print as well as electronic media. It has switched to free float market capitalization methodology since September 1, 2003. Since the early nineties, it has been witness to significant growth in the economy.

> **Pause for thought:** It is the oldest financial index in the country, comprised of 30 large and well established companies, bridging various sectors.

3.8 S&P CNX NIFTY

S&P CNX Nifty is a well-diversified index of 50 stocks, representing 24 sectors of the economy. It finds varied use in: benchmarking fund portfolios, index-based derivatives, structured products, ETFs and index funds. As on September 30, 2011, S&P CNX Nifty stocks represent approximately 63.55% of the total free float market capitalization, of the total stocks traded on NSE. It has been constructed after thorough economic and sector-wise research and is owned and managed by India Index Services and Products Ltd. (IISL). IISL is a joint venture of NSE and CRISIL, and India's first specialized company focusing on the index as a core product. IISL has a marketing and licensing agreement with Standard and Poor (S&P). There is a three-tier governance structure at NSE which comprises of board of directors of IISL, index policy committee and index maintenance sub-committee.

S&P CNX Nifty is the most attractive portfolio of all indices with 50 stocks which provide similar return. It resembles other portfolios with low risk. Being a very well-diversified portfolio it reflects the overall market conditions and has a higher risk-return ratio than any other leading indices. The construction of this index is based upon three criteria:

— Liquidity: Market impact cost is the best measure of liquidity of the stock. Moreover, S&P CNX Nifty has a criterion that for any stock to be included in the Nifty the impact cost has to be less than 0.5%, for trades of Rs.20 million.

— Floating stock: The companies aspiring to be included in the Nifty index must have a free float factor of at least 10%.

— Others: This pertains to a company coming out with an IPO. Such a company would be eligible for inclusion in the index only if it fulfills the criteria of impact cost, market capitalization and free float over a period of three months. It is calculated on real time basis on all days.

The base period for this index is the closing prices of November 3, 1995 and the value of the index has been set at 1000, with a base capital of Rs.2.06 trillion. Since June 26, 2009, S&P CNX Nifty is being computed using free float adjusted market capitalization method. From June 12, 2000, NSE has started trading in index futures. The futures contracts on NSE are based on S&P CNX Nifty. The trading on index options based on Nifty has started from June 4, 2001.

> **Pause for thought:** Nifty is a well-diversified portfolio of 50 stocks reflecting the overall market condition and has a higher risk-return ratio than all other leading indices of the country. Inclusion in the Nifty necessitates fulfillment of the criteria of liquidity and a minimum free float factor of 10%.

3.8.1 CNX Small Cap Index

CNX Small Cap Index consists of 100 tradable companies with small capitalization, listed on the exchange. The base date of this index is January 1, 2004 and base value is 1000. It reflects the behavior and performance of small scale companies. Like CNX S&P Nifty, it too is calculated by free float market capitalization method and it represents around 1.8% of the free float market capitalization of stocks listed on NSE (as on September 30, 2011).

> **Pause for thought:** It is an index of 100 companies with small capitalization and accounts for 1.8% of the total free float market capitalization of stocks listed on NSE, as on September 30, 2011.

3.8.2 CNX Mid Cap

CNX mid cap index reflects the movement and performance of the companies of medium capitalization in the market. Companies with medium market capitalization have always been considered an attractive investment segment, with high growth potential. The index represents about 11.98% of the free float market capitalization of the stocks listed on the NSE (as on September 30, 2011).

> **Pause for thought:** CNX mid cap index represent the performance of companies with medium capitalization and accounts for 11.98% of the free float market capitalization of stocks listed on NSE (as on September 30, 2011).

3.8.3 S&P CNX 500

The S&P CNX 500 represents about 94.95% of the free float market capitalization and about 93.64% of the total turnover of the NSE (as on September 30, 2011). It is a broad-based index and the 500 companies enlisted, are spread out into 72 sector indices. The beauty of this index is that industry weightages in the index represents the industry weighatges of the market. Thus if an IT sector has a 10% weightage in the universe of the stocks traded on NSE, the IT stocks would have an approximate representation of 10% on the index as well.

> **Pause for thought:** The 500 companies forming this index account for 94.95% of free float market cap and 93.64% of the total turnover of the NSE. Unique feature of this index is that industry weightages in the index represents the industry weightages of the market.

3.9 TOTAL RETURN INDEX—CALCULATION METHODOLOGY

For the exact picture of the index, with respect to its return, the total return index (TR index) is calculated.

Mere calculation of return from the index takes into account only the movement of prices. At the same time, the price indices do not consider the return from dividend payments of stocks constituting the index. The price index measures only capital gains measured due to price movements. So for a comprehensive idea of return from the index, dividend received from the index constituents stocks too has to be included in the index movement.

Total return index is an index to reflect the return from capital gain/loss in addition to dividend payment by constituent stocks of the index.

To calculate the total return index, the following data are required:
— Price index close.
— Price index return.
— Dividend payout in rupees.
— Index based capitalization on ex-dividend date.

$$\text{Indexed dividend} = \frac{\text{Dividend payout}}{\text{Base cap of index}} \times 1000$$

Indexed dividends are then reinvested in the index to give TR index.

TR index = [Previous total return index + (Previous total index × Index return)]
+ [Index dividends + (Indexed dividends × Index returns)]

Base, for both the price index close and TR index close will be the same. An investor in index stocks should benchmark investments against the total return index, instead of the price index to determine the actual returns vis-à-vis the index.

> **Pause for thought:** TR index gives the comprehensive return of the index, with both the capital gain/loss and dividend payouts of the constituent stocks considered.

3.10 TRACKING ERROR

An index fund is a mutual fund that invests in securities in the target index in the same proportion of securities, to achieve returns that are commensurate with that of target index. In other words, in index fund, an investment manager tries to replicate the investment results of the target index by holding all the securities of a target index. But, in practice rarely the return of the index funds are at par or near to the target index which it mimics. There are several factors causing this mismatch of the return on the index fund, with that of the target index. This mismatch, i.e., difference of the results is known as tracking error.

It is thus the annualized standard deviation of the difference in returns between the index fund and its target index. A low tracking error means less separation between the results from the index fund and the target index. It is always calculated against the total return on index portfolio, inclusive of the dividend. Tracking error arises due to the following reasons:

— Expenses like transaction costs, broker's commission, bid-ask spread, inflow and outflow of the fund, corporate actions, change of scrip in the index[5] and the level of cash that needs to be maintained for liquidation.

— Ideally, full corpus of the fund should be invested in the index. Yet this is not possible as fund managers have to keep some idle fund to meet obligations of redemption, dividend payments, etc. Further, when the fund receives dividend on the shares held by the investor, it must be invested immediately in the scrips of the portfolio of the benchmarked index. But if this reinvestment is not possible then the index fund ends up with more cash and its return is affected.

— Many times due to circuit filters, the index fund cannot be bought or sold. This results in the distortion of allocation of the fund.

— Due to corporate actions of: warrant conversion, rights issue, merger, change in the composition of index, bonus, forfeiture, preference shares, etc., the index fund has to realign its portfolio with the target index. This requires further buying and selling, which results in expenditure and affects the return. Moreover, at the time of corporate actions as mentioned above, the other share holders and the index end up by receiving more

---

[5] i.e., replacement of a scrip by another.

shares, but not the index funds. This is because these corporate actions come into effect from the ex-date as announced by the stock exchanges and usually there is a time gap between the ex-date and date on which the fund is actually credited with that benefit.
— Due to rounding-off of the number of shares for inclusion in the index fund, error arises.

But when there are errors, measures too exist for reduction of the same, if not for complete elimination.

Steps to reduce tracking error

— Use of index futures: Index fund managers can use futures contracts to keep their funds fully invested. The assets allocated to the futures contract generate the same return as that of index. Also it is relatively less expensive to enter and exit from the futures.
— The cash held by the fund for the liquidity purpose, and the dividend earned, can be invested in short-term money market. By doing so the fund earns return, as well as can maintain the cash required for liquidity.
— As per the scheme laid down by SEBI, the stocks held by the fund can be used for stock lending. This would enhance the return and reduce the tracking error.

Once we know what is meant by tracking error, what are the reasons behind and how this error can be reduced; automatically we are led to the calculation of the tracking error. Only when we have an estimate of this error can the available methods be applied accurately for its reduction.

Steps for the calculation of tracking error

1. The NAVs and TR index values, for each day, for the entire time period are required.
2. The percentage change in NAV and TR index for each day, with respect to the previous day, has to be calculated as,

$$\text{Percentage change in NAV} = \frac{\text{NAV as on date (t)} - \text{NAV as on date (t} - 1)}{\text{NAV as on date (t} - 1)}$$

3. The difference between the percentage change in the NAV and the percentage change in the TR index, each day, has to be calculated.
4. Standard deviation, of the difference obtained from day (1) to day (n) in step 3, is then calculated.
5. Finally, the annualized tracking error is calculated, as per the formula given below,

Annualized tracking error = Standard deviation (obtained in step 4) × ($\sqrt{250}$)

> **Pause for thought:** Tracking error is the error in tracking of the return on the index fund with respect to the target index. It is the annualized standard deviation of the difference in returns between index fund and its target index.

SUMMARY

✓ Market, in terms of finance and investment means stock market and it is very well represented by indices like BSE 30, Nifty 50, BSE 200, NSE small cap, etc.
✓ There are certain requirements, like, minimum issues capital, past track record, etc., for the securities to be listed on the exchange.

- ✓ NSE and BSE are computed on the basis of free float factor method.
- ✓ For listing on the exchanges, companies have to apply to the stock exchange and submit articles of association with drafts of prospects.
- ✓ Securities may be removed from the exchange in case of non-fulfillment of certain criteria.

KEY CONCEPTS

Market	NSE	Free Float Factor
Indices	BSE	Impact Cost
Listing	Price Weighted Index	Tracking Error
Delisting	Market weighted Index	

REVIEW QUESTIONS

1. What are the criteria to get listed on the stock exchange?
2. Write a short note on benefits of listing.
3. Under what circumstances are securities de-listed from the exchanges?
4. Explain the procedure of listing in detail.
5. What is an impact cost?
6. Explain: 'Tracking error'.

ILLUSTRATION

Q.1. You are given the following information on prices for stocks of the following firms:

Stock	Number of shares	Price (in Rs.)	
		T	T + 1
Ambuja Cements Ltd.	1,000,000	107	147
ICICI Bank Ltd.	10,000,000	885	1119
Infosys Technologies Ltd.	30,000,000	2636	3225

(a) Construct a price-weighted index for these three stocks; and compute the percentage change in the series for the period T to T + 1.

(b) Construct a market value-weighted index for these three stocks, and compute the percentage change in the series for the period T to T + 1.

(c) Discuss in brief, the difference in the results for the two stock indexes.

Ans:

(a) Price-weighted index: Price (in Rs.)

	Period	
	T	T + 1
Ambuja	107	147
ICICI	885	1119
Infosys	2636	3225
Sum	3628	4491
Divisor	3	3
Average	1209.3333	1497

Percentage change: (1497 − 1209.33)/1209.33 = 23.78%

(b) Market value-weighted index: Price (in Rs.)

	Period T		
Stock	Price/Share	Number of shares	Market value
Ambuja	107	1,000,000	107,000,000
ICICI	885	10,000,000	8,850,000,000
Infosys	2636	30,000,000	79,080,000,000
Total			88,037,000,000

	Period T + 1		
Stock	Price/Share	Number of shares	Market value
Ambuja	147	1,000,000	147,000,000
ICICI	1119	10,000,000	11,190,000,000
Infosys	3225	30,000,000	96,750,000,000
Total			108,087,000,000

Percentage change = (108,087− 88,037)/88,037 = 22.77%

APPENDICES

Appendix-3.1: Nifty Major Indices and their Value, as on October 9, 2012

Index	Current	% change	Open	High	Low	Prev. closing
Major indices						
S&P CNX NIFTY	5,676.00	-1.23	5,751.85	5,751.85	5,666.20	5,746.95
CNX NIFTY JUNIOR	11,136.60	-0.75	11,221.95	11,280.95	11,109.80	11,221.00
INDIA VIX	17.17	2.32	16.78	17.59	16.17	16.78
CNX 100	5,567.70	-1.16	5,637.45	5,637.45	5,559.20	5,633.30

S&P CNX DEFTY	3,756.35	-2.22	3,825.70	3,825.70	3,748.45	3,841.75
S&P CNX 500	4,499.85	-1.06	4,550.65	4,550.65	4,493.35	4,547.90
CNX MIDCAP	7,885.90	-0.61	7,934.50	7,980.95	7,875.55	7,934.40
NIFTY MIDCAP 50	2,255.90	-0.86	2,275.45	2,288.20	2,251.35	2,275.55
CNX SMALLCAP	3,499.20	-0.33	3,513.30	3,536.65	3,487.00	3,510.95
CNX 200	2,870.20	-1.11	2,904.50	2,904.50	2,865.80	2,902.55
NIFTY DIVIDEND	67.24	0.00	67.24	67.24	67.24	67.24
Sector-wise indices						
BANK NIFTY	11,362.20	-1.30	11,530.65	11,530.65	11,342.85	11,511.40
CNX AUTO	4,355.90	-1.16	4,409.95	4,415.45	4,349.40	4,406.95
CNX COMMODITIES	2,492.15	-1.30	2,523.75	2,523.75	2,486.95	2,524.95
CNX CONSUMPTION	2,108.95	-0.45	2,117.80	2,125.60	2,103.45	2,118.40
CNX DIVIDEND OPPT	1,633.90	-0.66	1,645.25	1,648.95	1,631.65	1,644.80
CNX ENERGY	8,003.95	-2.49	8,201.70	8,201.70	7,980.35	8,208.65
CNX FINANCE	4,682.05	-1.06	4,745.95	4,745.95	4,673.15	4,732.35
CNX FMCG	14,418.25	-0.01	14,408.10	14,501.40	14,362.75	14,419.25
CNX INFRA	2,534.95	-1.66	2,574.20	2,574.20	2,529.00	2,577.65
CNX IT	6,207.95	-1.34	6,298.90	6,324.00	6,192.30	6,292.45
CNX MEDIA	1,570.10	-1.55	1,597.15	1,603.85	1,565.35	1,594.80
CNX METAL	2,759.70	-1.11	2,788.80	2,806.55	2,753.60	2,790.75
CNX MNC	5,792.70	-0.78	5,830.75	5,845.15	5,781.90	5,838.45
CNX PHARMA	5,595.55	1.15	5,550.40	5,624.75	5,536.15	5,532.10
CNX PSE	3,004.40	-1.02	3,040.55	3,040.75	2,996.90	3,035.25
CNX PSU BANK	3,340.35	-2.31	3,419.40	3,419.40	3,332.00	3,419.20
CNX REALTY	250.80	-3.78	258.70	259.50	249.70	260.65
CNX SERVICE	6,725.85	-0.97	6,804.35	6,804.35	6,714.35	6,791.60

(Source: http://www.nseindia.com/live_market/dynaContent/live_watch/live_index_watch.htm)

Appendix-3.2: BSE Major Indices and their Value, as on October 9, 2012

Category/Index	Open	High	Low	Current value	Previous closing	Change (pts.)	Change (%)
Broad							
SENSEX	18969.19	18969.19	18684.40	18708.98	18938.46	-229.48	-1.21
MIDCAP	6683.58	6723.47	6638.48	6649.38	6678.77	-29.39	-0.44
SMLCAP	7150.28	7198.79	7120.67	7134.07	7145.71	-11.64	-0.16

BSE-100	5766.34	5768.31	5685.44	5693.03	5760.36	-67.33	-1.17
BSE-200	2331.41	2331.41	2301.98	2305.05	2330.78	-25.73	-1.10
BSE-500	7281.30	7282.04	7194.53	7204.03	7279.23	-75.20	-1.03
Thematic							
SHARIAH 50	1232.06	1234.53	1221.00	1222.65	1232.66	-10.01	-0.81
BSE-GREENEX	1580.10	1581.39	1561.23	1563.30	1582.06	-18.76	-1.19
Investment Strategy							
BSE IPO	1656.92	1676.38	1646.14	1657.56	1658.73	-1.17	-0.07
DOLLEX-30	3002.62	3002.62	2939.79	2943.38	3002.50	-59.12	-1.97
DOLLEX-100	1151.04	1151.04	1127.15	1128.56	1150.73	-22.17	-1.93
DOLLEX-200	749.55	749.55	734.41	735.39	749.35	-13.96	-1.86
Sectoral							
HC	7437.85	7562.89	7425.47	7516.01	7427.15	88.86	1.20
FMCG	5632.37	5673.11	5616.33	5638.14	5639.69	-1.55	-0.03
TECk	3417.91	3428.39	3374.40	3382.38	3413.88	-31.50	-0.92
METAL	10601.46	10679.83	10471.45	10498.75	10606.38	-107.63	-1.01
PSU	7535.96	7537.27	7433.87	7446.28	7527.71	-81.43	-1.08
BANKEX	13221.32	13221.32	13030.85	13051.05	13212.11	-161.06	-1.22
AUTO	10506.18	10519.26	10346.29	10360.86	10492.90	-132.04	-1.26
POWER	2082.59	2088.17	2055.23	2058.90	2087.67	-28.77	-1.38
IT	5917.42	5940.57	5811.20	5827.99	5910.93	-82.94	-1.40
CD	7168.28	7251.99	7024.04	7049.16	7160.59	-111.43	-1.56
CG	11312.49	11312.49	11009.74	11032.78	11339.51	-306.73	-2.70
OIL&GAS	8842.04	8846.82	8582.12	8606.89	8852.23	-245.34	-2.77
REALTY	1930.56	1943.51	1873.74	1881.40	1949.58	-68.18	-3.50
Volatility Index			08 Oct 12				
REALVOL-1MTH	--	--	--	12.96	11.25	1.71	15.20
REALVOL-2MTH	--	--	--	12.96	11.25	1.71	15.20
REALVOL-3MTH	--	--	--	12.98	12.82	0.16	1.25

(Source: http://www.bseindia.com/indices/indexwatch.aspx?expandable=0)

Appendix-3.3: Major Indices Worldwide

Indices	Base year	Sample	Calculation method	Base value
FTSC	January 3,1984	100	Market capitalization weighted index	1000
STOXX	December 31,1991	50	Market capitalization weighted index	1000
HANG SEN	July 31,1964	100	Market capital weighted index	100
NIKKEI	January 2,1968	225	Average price weighted	100
NASDAQ	January 31, 1985	100	Market capital weighted index	250
MSCI	December 31,1987	---	Market capital weighted index	100

Appendix-3.4: Value of the Worldwide Major Indices, as on October 9, 2012

Index	Last	Change	%	High	Low
STI	3081.10	4.45	0.14%	3082.39	3072.82
Hangseng	21039.67	215.11	1.03%	21060.15	20926.83
Nikkei225	8815.74	-47.56	-0.54%	8833.53	8799.76
SSE	2089.35	14.93	0.72%	2094.01	2081.59
KLCI	1661.28	1.06	0.06%	1661.28	1658.04
SET	1304.71	-6.64	-0.51%	1310.43	1300.51
FTSE100	5841.74	-29.28	-0.5%	5870.52	5818.76
DAX	7291.21	-106.66	-1.44%	7341.28	7286.24
CAC	3417.86	-39.18	-1.13%	3429.86	3404.97
Dow	13583.65	-26.50	-0.19%	13610.38	13552.09
NASDAQ	3112.35	-23.84	-0.76%	3125.49	3107.57
S&P500	1455.88	-5.05	-0.35%	1460.93	1453.10
Dow_Futures*	13534.00	33.00	0.24%	13535.00	13496.00
NASDAQ_Futures*	2784.50	7.00	0.25%	2785.50	2776.00
S&P500_Futures*	1453.25	3.50	0.24%	1453.75	1448.75
Gold_Futures**	1780.50	4.80	0.27%	1781.40	1775.80
Silver_Futures**	34.21	0.19	0.56%	34.26	34.00
Brent_Crude_Oil_Futures**	90.18	0.85	0.95%	90.30	89.58
Natural_Gas_Futures**	3.42	0.02	0.59%	3.42	3.41

(Source: www.liveindices.com)

PART 2
PORTFOLIO THEORY

PART 2

PORTFOLIO THEORY

4
MEASURING RISK AND RETURN

> **LEARNING OBJECTIVES**
> The purpose of this chapter is to enable you to understand:
> - How is the rate of return calculated by different methods.
> - How to calculate the expected rate of return.
> - The calculation of risk.
> - The risk-return relationship, which helps with investment decisions.

4.1 INTRODUCTION

In the earlier chapters we have discussed the different types of securities available to the investors and how these enable the investors to meet their investment objectives. The discussions have revolved primarily around the relative returns generated by these securities. But given that it is trading in the stock market we are concerned with, each security comes with an inherent insecurity—and for free! This insecurity is the risk involved in stock market trading.

As each security has a unique rate of return, similar it is with the risk. And since we cannot do away with the inherent risk quotient of a security, we need to have a clear idea of the risk-return relationships. This would enable us to weigh out the pros and cons with respect to the expected return and the unavoidable risk. For that an estimation of return, risk and their relationship is called for. Hence this chapter concentrates on investment options based on return and risk individually, and then sheds light on the risk involved for an expected return. As we are led to the potential risk for an expected return and vice-versa, our understanding of investment decision improves. Also improves thus our decisions.

4.2 THE BASIS OF INVESTMENT DECISIONS: RETURN

Return and risk are the elementary parameters that evaluate a security. And hence risk and return are the foundations of investment decision. But an investor is primarily concerned with the amount of return that an investment would generate. The interest aroused for a security is directly proportional to the rate of return. Concerns of risk follow subsequently. Hence here too we delve into the return first and then move to the risk inherent. Reverting to the return-based arousal of interest, of investors, methods of measuring return from varied securities and combination of securities are desired. And thus follows the discussion on the same.

4.2.1 Return on a Single Asset

When we have the option of assets to choose from, we are required to compare the relative returns before arriving at a decision. But when we have a single asset as an investment option, or we opt to invest in a single asset, all that we need to know is the return that this asset would generate.

We consider the example of Tata Motors, as the single asset, for the purpose of understanding here. It is one of the leading companies in automobile sector, with several thousand shareholders. Suppose we purchased 100 shares of the company in January 2010, at a market price of Rs. 789.9. The total investment at the beginning of the year = 100 × 789.9 = Rs. 78990. During the year company has declared dividend of Rs. 15 per share. So, total earnings from dividend = Rs. 15 × 100 = Rs. 1500.

At the end of the year the share price turns out to be Rs.1308.35. As the closing share price has increased, we have made a capital gain, which is calculated as,

Capital gain (loss) = (selling price − buying price) × 100
  = (Rs. 1308.35 − Rs. 789.9) × 100
  = Rs. 518.45 × 100
  = Rs. 51845

The total return is hence,

Total return = Dividend + Capital gain
  = Rs. 1500 + Rs. 51845
  = Rs. 53345

This return is actually unrealized if it is assumed that we continue to hold the share instead of selling the shares at the end of the year. Still, an investor must consider the unrealized capital gain as a part of the total return because had the investor so wanted he/she would have sold the shares and realized the capital gain (or loss, in this case though there is a capital gain).

If it is assumed that these shares are held by us for one year and sold only at the end of the year, the cash inflows would be the sum of the dividend and proceeds from the sale of shares.

Thus total cash flow, in this case = Dividend + Earnings from the sale of shares
  = Rs. 1500 + (Rs. 1308.35 × 100)
  = Rs. 1500 + Rs. 130835
  = Rs. 132335

It is equal to our investment at the beginning of the year and return
  = Rs. 78990 + Rs. 53345 = Rs. 132335.

Generally, return is measured in terms of percentage. In this case, the shares of Tata Motors have led to an earning of Rs. 53345, as total return, on an investment of Rs. 78990. The total return in terms of percentage, referred to as the rate of return, is calculated as,

$$\text{Return (in percentage)} = \frac{\text{Rs. } 53345 \times 100}{\text{Rs. } 78990}$$

$$= 67.43\%$$

Return, as discussed above, can also be calculated in terms of percentage, for each share. The return on each share too is referred to as the rate of return and calculated as follows:

Rate of return = Dividend yield + Capital gain yield

$$\therefore \quad R = \frac{Div_1}{P_0} + \frac{P_1 - P_0}{P_0}$$

where,

R = rate of return for a given year.
Div_1 = dividend per share for the given year.
P_0 = price of the share at the beginning of the year.
P_1 = price of the share at the end of the year.

Dividend yield is the percentage of dividend, in terms of price of the share at the beginning of the year. Capital gain (loss) is the difference between the share prices at the end and beginning of the year, divided by the share price at the beginning of the year.

Thus for Tata Motors, rate of return turns out to be,

$$R = \frac{Div_1}{P_0} + \frac{P_1 - P_0}{P_0}$$

$$= \frac{15 \times 100}{789.9} + \frac{(1308.35 - 789.9) \times 100}{789.9}$$

$$= 1.89 + 65.6$$

$$= 67.49\%$$

Thus the total return, in terms of percentage—calculated on the basis of total number of shares purchased, as well as in terms of each share—turns out to be the same, at 67.49%. To this dividend yield contributes 1.89% and capital gain, 65.6%.

The return on a share obviously depends largely on the changes in the share price. As the equity market shows wider fluctuations, investment in shares are rendered risky. But equity shares also provide a reasonably good return compared to the other investment alternatives.

> **Pause for thought:** Total return is the sum of the dividend and the earnings from the sale of shares and is generally measured in terms of percentage. These earnings which could lead to gain in the capital or loss—referred to as the capital gain or capital loss. Capital is gained when shares are sold at a higher price than the price at which they were bought, while when the reverse happens, one incurs capital loss.

4.2.2 Annual Rate of Return

The annualized rate of return is actually the rate of return for a period less than one year. The estimation of the annual rate of return is thus actually a mathematical extrapolation.

With extrapolation thus being the norm we compute the rate of return of a share of Punjab National Bank, for a period of more than one year. Table 4.1 below gives the annual rates of return and dividend per share.

Table 4.1: Punjab National Bank's Annual Rates of Return

Year	Market price	Capital gain/loss (%)	Dividend	Dividend yield (%)	Return (%)
1	2	3	4	5	6 (5+3)
2002	55.21		3		
2003	154.35	179.56	3.5	6.34	185.90
2004	317.75	105.86	4	2.59	108.45
2005	433.55	36.44	6	1.89	38.33
2006	464.05	7.03	6	1.38	8.42
2007	564.21	21.58	10	2.15	23.74
2008	560.95	-0.58	13	2.30	1.73
2009	680.00	21.22	20	3.57	24.79
2010	1091.73	60.55	22	3.24	63.78
Mean	480.20	53.96	9.72	2.93	56.89

It is thus evident that for the first year, i.e., 2003,

$$\text{Dividend yield} = \frac{Div_1}{P_0} \times 100 = \frac{Rs\ 3.5}{Rs\ 55.21} = 6.34\%$$

$$\text{The capital gain} = \frac{(Rs.\ 154.35 - Rs.\ 55.21)}{Rs.\ 55.21} \times 100 = 179.56\%$$

In a similar manner the dividend yield and capital gain (and loss, in the year 2008) are calculated. The annual rate of return, which turns out to be 56.89%, has contributions of 53.96% from capital gain (and loss) and 2.93% from the dividend yield. The above finding (from the table as well as the calculations) reflects the year 2003 as a very profitable year, as the annual rate of return is highest for the year. Not only it is highest, but it is a whopping 185.89% due to a massive jump in the share prices—from Rs. 55.21 in 2002 to Rs. 154.35 in 2003. The lowest return, obtained in 2008, due to fall in the prices, is understandable, given the recession that hit the global economy.

> **Pause for thought:** The annual rate of return is a mathematically extrapolated estimation of the rate of return for shares for one year, though actually the time period is not exactly one year.

4.2.3 Average Rate of Return

As the name suggests, average rate of return is the average of the annual rates of return of a share over the specified period of time. From the yearly returns, the average rate of return can be calculated.

$$\text{Average rate of return} = R = \frac{1}{n}\sum_{t=1}^{n} R_t$$

Thus it is calculated in the same manner as a simple average is calculated for any set of numbers; the numbers are added together into a single sum, and then the sum is divided by the count of the numbers in the set. For example, suppose an investment had returned the following annual returns over a period of five full years: 10%, 15%, 10%, 0% and 5%. To calculate the average return for the investment over this five-year period, the five annual returns would be added together and then divided by five to generate an annual average return of 8%.

We apply this theory to calculate the average rate of return for the PNB stock. The annual rates of return are available (Table 4.1) for the period: 2003 to 2010. The average rate of return in this case is thus a quotient of the summation of these annual rates of return divided by 8.

$$R_{average} = 1/n[\, R_1 + R_2 + \ldots + R_n\,]$$

where,

$R_{average}$ = average rate of return.

R_n = annual rate of return for the given year, 1 to n.

n = total time period.

Hence, the average rate of return for the share of PNB for the period 2003 to 2010 is,

$R_{average}$ = 1/8[185.89 + 108.45 + 38.33 + 8.42 + 23.74 + 1.726 + 24.79 + 63.78]

= 56.89%

> **Pause for thought:** The average rate of return is the arithmetic mean of the annual rates of returns of a share for the specified period of time.

4.2.4 Holding Period Return (HPR)

Holding period is the period for which the shares are held by the investors. This period could be the choice of the investor as he/she decides to hold a share for a particular period of time. But the rate of return for holding period is independent of the reason behind the specific period of time for which the shares are held, and not sold.

As an investor, many a times we tend to hold our investments for more than one year. This gives rise to the probability of earning a positive return one year, while it could be just the reverse in the succeeding year. And at the end of it all, it becomes important to calculate the net worth of the shares at the end of the holding period. It is cumulative return over the holding period which gives us the holding period return.

For further clarity on the issue, we consider a hypothetical investment in the share of State

Bank of India, in the year 2001. It is assumed to be held till 2011, with reinvestment of the dividends earned, in shares. The holding period in this case is 12 years. Table 4.2, below, shows the return on the shares of State Bank of India, for the holding period spanning 2001 to 2011.

Table 4.2: State Bank of India's Holding Period Return for the Period 2001 to 2011

Year	Return (%)	Year	Return (%)
2000	14.14	2006	36.94
2001	-31.88	2007	90.13
2002	54.45	2008	-45.89
2003	90.28	2009	75.32
2004	20.62	2010	24.10
2005	38.54	2011	-12.84

Now the return for the first year (here, the year is 2000) is 14.14%. So, it is 14.14/100 = 0.1414 and in a similar way can be calculated for other years.

$$HPR = [(1 + r_1) \times (1 + r_2) \times ... \times (1 + r_n)]$$

By putting the values in the above equation, the worth of our investment after 12 years is,

$= (1 + 0.1414) \times (1 - 0.3188) \times (1 + 0.5445) \times ... \times (1 - 0.1284)$

$= 1.1414 \times 0.6811 \times 1.5445 \times ... \times 0.8715$

= Rs. 10.2014 − 1

= Rs. 9.2014

This implies that an investment of Re. 1 in the share of State Bank of India in 2000, and held till 2011, has undergone a huge growth to become Rs. 9.2014, after the holding period of 12 years. And that is massive enhancement of 920.14% in the rate of return.

> **Pause for thought:** It is the total return that accumulates over the entire period of time that the shares are held.

4.2.5 Annual Compound Rate of Return

While the average rate of return is the arithmetic mean of annual returns over a period of time, annual compound rate of return is the geometric mean of annual returns. It is a measure of yearly return, compounded over the specified period of time the share is held. Thus the annual compound rate of return is equivalent to the holding period return.

Annual compound rate of return = $[(1 + r_1) \times (1 + r_2) \times ... \times (1 + r_n)]^{1/n} - 1$

By putting the values computed for HPR and as the number of years are 12, 1/12 root of the final value must be found out. With reference to Table 4.2, the annual compound rate of return is thus calculated as:

Annual compound rate of return = $[(1.1414 \times 0.6811 \times 1.5445 \times \ldots \times 0.8715)^{1/12} - 1] \times 100$
= $[1.2134 - 1] \times 100$
= 21.34%

Thus an investment of Re.1 in 2000, for 12 months, grows to Rs. 10.2014, courtesy 21.34% annual rate of return.

> **Pause for thought:** It is the geometric mean of the annual return reflecting the compounded yearly return over a specified period of time, becoming thus equivalent to the holding period return.

4.2.6 Compound Annual Growth Rate (CAGR)

Compound annual growth rate is the year-over-year growth rate of an investment, over a specified period of time.

It is calculated by taking the nth root of the total percentage growth rate, where 'n' is the number of years in the holding period considered. This can be written as follows:

CAGR = (Ending value/Beginning value)$^{1/n}$ − 1

CAGR, in reality, isn't the actual return. It is an imaginary number which describes the rate at which an investment would have grown if it grew at a steady rate. It represents the smoothed annualized gain an investor has earned over the investment time horizon.

For the purpose of a better understanding we consider an example, with the assumptions made guiding us to the corresponding CAGR. An investment is supposedly made in a stock of HUL in the year 2007. At that time its value was Rs. 213.9, changing through the years sequentially, till 2011, to Rs. 250.25, Rs. 264.75, Rs. 312.3 and Rs. 333.1 respectively.

Year	Price (Rs.)
2007	213.9
2008	250.25
2009	264.75
2010	312.3
2011	333.1

The CAGR value, in this case, with n = 5, is thus calculated as:

CAGR = (Ending value/Beginning value)$^{1/n}$ − 1
= (Rs. 333.1/ Rs. 213.9)$^{1/5}$ − 1
= (1.557)$^{1/5}$ − 1
= 1.09 − 1
= 0.09 = 9%

CAGR is built in the holding period return. It involves computing IRR[1].

> **Pause for thought:** CAGR is the year-over-year growth rate of an investment, over a period of 'n' years; and mathematically, the nth root of the total percentage growth rate.

4.2.7 Limitations in the Methods for Calculating Return

Any one of the methods discussed above can be used to calculate the return. Usually, the holding period return and simple annualized return are used frequently by the analysts. However, care must be taken with either of them, as they mislead quite often, such as magnifying the return when the holding period is large.

For example, Rs. 100 becomes Rs. 200 in 5 years, thereby reflecting 100% holding period return, while its annual return is 20% (100%/5). Similarly, Rs. 100, vide calculation, becomes Rs. 400 in 10 years, with the holding period return thus, 300% and its annual percentage, 30%. But it does not mean that the second option is better, that is more accurate, than the first one. Similar care should be taken while analyzing the average return of the security—an arithmetic mean. A hypothetical case of ABC Ltd. is considered with the assumption that the market price of ABC Ltd. increases from Rs. 100 to Rs. 200 in the first year.

$$\text{Its return for the first year} = \frac{(\text{Rs. 200} - \text{Rs. 100})}{\text{Rs. 100}} \times 100$$

$$= -100\%$$

The price of the security is assumed further to have decreased to Rs. 100 in the second year.

$$\text{The return in the second year} = \frac{(\text{Rs. 100} - \text{Rs. 200})}{\text{Rs. 100}} \times 100$$

$$= -100\%$$

So, the average return = [{100 − (−100)}/2]
= 100%

But fact of the matter is that when the price of a security is Rs. 100 at the beginning of the first year and again Rs. 100 at the end of the second year, it actually gives zero return.

Arithmetic mean preferred to CAGR

In an equity research field, CAGR is used to calculate the return. But, despite its mathematical accuracy and superiority, and at the same time, the limitations of arithmetic mean, the portfolio theory relies on arithmetic mean. The reasons behind the preference for arithmetic mean are:

— Measure of risk, the standard deviation, and its correlation with return (in portfolio theory) is ascertained from arithmetic mean.
— Compared to other methods, arithmetic mean represents a pattern which corresponds to the normal distribution in statistics.

---
[1] IRR means internal rate of return. It is used in capital budgeting techniques. IRR is a discount rate which makes the present value of all cash flows equivalent to zero. Generally, higher the IRR of the project, more desirable it is.

> **Pause for thought:** Any of the methods available can be used to calculate the return, but portfolio theory prefers the arithmetic mean, to CAGR, despite the accuracy of the latter and limitations of the former, as arithmetic mean is utilized in the measurement of risk and it produces a pattern in coherence with normal distribution in statistics.

4.3 THE BASIS OF INVESTMENT DECISIONS: RISK

As there is no free lunch, all return turn out to be accompanied by an inherent risk, as mentioned at the beginning of this chapter. We have to pay a price for a commodity. If the return is considered a commodity, the risk is the price one has to pay. It has been already mentioned that return and risk are directly proportional. Thus higher is the expected return, higher is the risk involved. It becomes imperative to calculate the risk too, to be able to compute it, as an investor assesses an investment option. Calculation of the risk, vis-à-vis the desired return, completes the process of a comprehensive evaluation of an investment option. So, calculation of risk is the content of discussion in this section.

4.3.1 Calculation of Risk

Table 4.2 above shows the variation of the annual rate of return for the stock of SBI. The range of variation is from 185.89% (in 2003 because of economic revival) to 1.72% (in 2008 due to the worldwide recession). These variations in the return are due to volatile nature of the stock and this volatility is termed as risk.

The risk of the stock is a measure of the deviation (also known as dispersion) from the average return. It is calculated by computing the variance or standard deviation. Standard deviation is the square root of variance. It provides information about the deviation of possible outcomes by measuring the distance of each outcome from the expected value. This deviation is the risk to be borne by the investors.

The following steps, as applied on the stock of PNB, are involved in the calculation of variance (and thus standard deviation).

1. The average rate of return on PNB's stock (as calculated in Table 4.1) is calculated first.
2. Then the yearly deviation of the rates of return are ascertained and squared, as $[R_1 - E(R)]^2$ and these values are summated.
   In this case, the average return for the stock of PNB is 56.89% and return for the year 2003 is 185.89%.
   So in 2003, the deviation = $(56.89 - 185.89)^2$ = 16641.82
   In a similar manner, the same is calculated for each year. Thus the sum of the squares of the deviations turns out to be 27215.25
3. Now this sum is divided by the number of periods, which is one less than the total period, to get the variance. It is to be remembered that the sum of the squares, of the deviations, are divided by $n - 1$ and not by 'n' because of the loss of degree of freedom. In case of the population data, the divisor is 'n'.

The term, degree of freedom, indicates how much freedom or independence there is within a group of numbers. The degrees of freedom have been limited by 1 and only $n - 1$ degrees of freedom remain. In the standard deviation formula, the numerator (square of the difference of return and mean return) is divided by $n - 1$, because the mean of the data has already been calculated which imposes one restriction on data set.

$$\text{Variance} = \sigma^2 = \frac{1}{n-1} \sum_{t=1}^{n} [R_t - E(R)]^2$$

$$= \frac{27215.25}{7}$$

$$= 3887.89$$

4. And finally the square root of the variance (σ^2), the standard deviation (σ), is calculated.

$$\text{Standard deviation} = \sqrt{\text{variance}}$$

$$\sigma = \sqrt{3887.89} = 62.35\%$$

The Table 4.3 below shows the calculation of standard deviation for the PNB stock with respect to the corresponding return.

Table 4.3 Risk and Return Calculation of PNB Stock

Year	Return, R (%)	$[R_t - E(R)]$	$[R_t - E(R)]^2$
2003	185.90	129.00	16641.82
2004	108.45	51.56	2658.70
2005	38.33	-18.56	344.48
2006	8.42	-48.47	2349.67
2007	23.74	-33.15	1099.11
2008	1.73	-55.17	3043.33
2009	24.79	-32.10	1030.66
2010	63.78	6.89	47.48
Average return	56.89		
Sum			27215.25
σ^2 (variance)			27215.25/7 =3887.89
σ (standard deviation)			0.6235 = 62.35%

The standard deviation of PNB's stock, 62.35%, shows a high degree of deviation from the average rate of return, 56.89%. As this return is too volatile, it is difficult to predict the future return of the stock from its past return. With change in market conditions the volatility too is impacted differently and the return too, thus is.

Pause for thought: Risk is the susceptibility of the asset prices, and thus of the return, to market fluctuations. A security, if thus immune to such fluctuations, involves zero risk. Risks are deviation from the average return and are calculated in terms of standard deviation, which measures the distance of deviation of the possible outcomes from their expected values.

4.4 CALCULATION OF THE EXPECTED RATE OF RETURN BY USING PROBABILITIES

One question that the above calculations could give rise to is, what would be the expected rate of return and the risk involved in the future. It is the performance in the future that we are interested, instead of that in the past or in the present. As we assume that the capital market is efficient and securities follow random walk hypothesis[2], it is difficult to estimate the future return from the past return. This difficulty is evident from the following illustration.

It is supposed that we intend to buy stocks of XYZ Co. whose current market price is Rs. 100 and dividend per share is Rs. 5. The holding period is assumed to be one year. It is difficult to forecast at what price the stock would be sold in the market at the end of the year. It is already known that the rate of return of a security consists of two parts: capital gain/loss and dividend yield. Yet both components depend upon various factors, viz., economic condition, company fundamentals and others.

Another assumption is that there are four likely stages of the economy and company fundamentals, with equal probability for all four possible outcomes. These four possible stages of the economy are: high growth, growth, static and recession. For these four stages the share prices are supposedly: Rs. 140, Rs. 120, Rs. 100 and Rs. 80; and dividend per share: Rs. 8, Rs. 7, Rs. 5 and Rs. 2 respectively. The possible four outcomes of the return are calculated and are as shown in Table 4.4, with the current price of the share being Rs. 100.

Table 4.4: Share Price of the Security Under the Four Possible Economic Stages

Economic stages 1	Share price (%) 2	Dividend 3	Dividend yield 4 (column3/Rs. 100)	Capital gain/loss (%) 5	Return 6 (4+5)
High Growth	140	8	8	40	48
Growth	120	7	7	20	27
Static	100	5	5	0	5
Recession	80	2	2	–20	–18

Here, dividend is calculated by following the formula:

Dividend yield = Dividend/P_0(beginning price) ×100

= 8/100 ×100 = 8%.

Capital gain/loss = [Ending price − Beginning price]/Beginning price × 100

= [140 − 100]/100 × 100 = 40%.

From the above results the return of XYZ Co. is anticipated to vary in the range of −18% (during recession) to 48% (in the high growth stage). Since it has been mentioned that all four stages are equally probable, each outcome has 25% probability. But from the theory of probability we know that the sum of the probabilities must always be equal to 1. By using the rates of return of four different economic stages and assigning equal probabilities, the expected rate of return turns to be as shown in Table 4.5.

---

[2] Discussed in Chapter 11, Market Efficiency.

Table 4.5: Expected Return, When Probability is Assigned

Economic stages 1	Return (%) R_i 2	Probability P_i 3	Expected rate of return (%) $R_i \times P_i$ 4 (2×3)
High Growth	28	0.25	12
Growth	27	0.25	6.75
Static	5	0.25	1.25
Recession	-18	0.25	4.5
		1.00	15.5

When equal probabilities are assigned to all four stages the expected rate of return is 15.5% for the XYZ Co. The assigning of probability depends upon the subjective estimation. In this case, each stage has been assigned equal probabilities of 0.25 (25%). However, an investor or a security analyst assigns probabilities based on the appraisal of past record. They consider such instances which have precedence, having occurred quite a number of times.

Thus, the expected return by assigning probabilities is formulated as:

$$E(R) = R_1 \times P_1 + R_2 \times P_2 + \ldots + R_n \times P_n$$

$$= \sum_{i=1}^{n} R_i P_i$$

where,

$E(R)$ = expected return.
R_i = return corresponding to the different economic stages.
P_i = probability assigned to an individual outcome.
n = total number of outcomes.

> **Pause for thought:** Expectation is linked to probability. Likewise the expected return is the summation of the product of probability and return, corresponding to the different economic stages.

4.4.1 Calculation of Risk for the Expected Rate of Return

The previous section has dealt with the calculation of expected return. And this section would provide an insight into how the risk is calculated from the expected rate of return. Almost identical steps, as above, are involved in the calculation of variance and standard deviation of security when probabilities are assigned. It involves calculation of the deviation from expected rate of return, which is then squared and multiplied with probability. Finally, summation of these products yields the risk.

The formula used to calculate the variance of the security with probability is,

$$\text{Variance} = \sigma^2 = [\{R_1 - E(R)\}^2 \times P_1] + [\{R_2 - E(R)\}^2 \times P_2] + \ldots + [\{R_n - E(R)\}^2 \times P_n]$$

The formula can be thus rewritten as,

$$\text{Variance} = \sigma^2 = \sum_{t=1}^{n}\left[R_n - E(R)\right]^2 \times P_n$$

For the stock of XYZ Co., the variance of return is calculated and tabulated, and shown in Table 4.6.

Table 4.6: Expected Risk of the Security When Probability is Assigned

Expected rate of return (%)	$[R_i - E(R)]$	$[R_i - E(R)]^2$	P_i	$[R_i - E(R)]^2 \times P_i$
12	-3.5	12.25	0.25	3.0625
6.75	-8.75	76.5625	0.25	19.14063
1.25	-14.25	203.0625	0.25	50.76563
4.5	-20	400	0.25	100
15.5			1.00	172.9688

The variance, $\sigma^2 = 172.9688$

Hence, standard deviation = $\sigma = \sqrt{172.9688} = 13.15\%$

Since the expected return, 15.5%, is more than the standard deviation, this stock can be considered as a sound investment option.

> **Pause for thought:** It is a product of deviation of the return from the expected value and probability of the outcome, aggregated over the entire period.

4.4.2 Points to be Considered While Using Probabilities

There are certain aspects that have to be considered while probabilities are being dealt with. In the previous example, we have incorporated the probability data on our own. In reality too there is no published and authentic information on probability. This deficiency can be overcome by the following methods.

Method 1

Actual results from the past, of comparable situation, can be taken as indicators as per the view of an analyst. Adjudging the correlation between the past and present scenarios, probabilities can be assigned.

For example, if in the past average profits of Rs. 100 on 5 out of 10 incidents have been realized, then the chances for the occurrence are, 5/10, i.e., 0.5 (50%).

Method 2

It is a more specific method, as return from normal distribution is calculated. From the normal distribution, one can estimate the probability of a range of possible outcomes.

Normal probability distribution and standard deviation

The normal probability distribution is the most common type of distribution used in stock market analysis. With enough observations available within a sample size, it is reasonable to make the assumption that returns follow a normally distributed pattern. However, these assumptions can be contradicted, disqualified and hence discarded. The normal probability distribution is neither skewed nor peaked. It is a smooth, symmetric, continuous bell-shaped curve as shown in Figure 4.1.

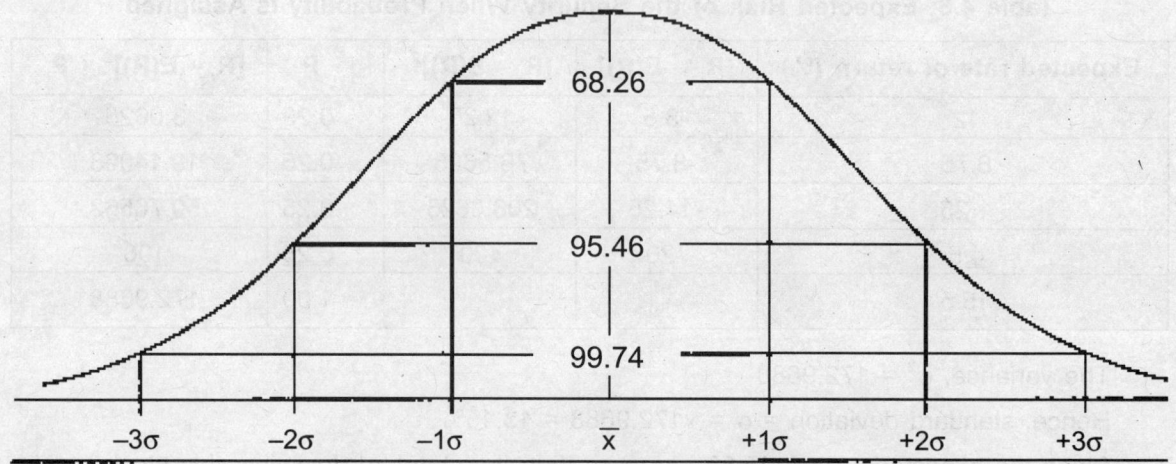

Figure 4.1: Normal probability distribution

Every normal probability distribution curve, regardless of its mean and standard deviation, confirms the following rule:

— About 68% of the area under the curve falls within 1 standard deviation of the mean.
— About 95% of the area under the curve falls within 2 standard deviations of the mean.
— About 99.7% of the area under the curve falls within 3 standard deviations of the mean.

Collectively these points are known as the empirical rule or *68/95/99.7 rule*. Thus, given a normal distribution, most outcomes are within 3 standard deviations of mean. Normal probability distribution is analyzed to understand the element of risk.

There are two very important aspects to understand from the figure:
— Total area under the curve is 1.
— The area is used to measure the probability.

The graph of the normal distribution depends on two factors:
— The mean.
— The standard deviation.

The mean of the distribution determines the location of the graph and standard deviation determines the height and width of the graph.

For example, in case of the stock of XYZ Co., as the expected return is 15.5% and the standard deviation is 13.15%, it could be said that there is a 68% chance the actual return will be within the range of 2.35% (15.5% − 13.15%) and 28.65% (15.5% + 13.15%). Similarly, there is a 95% chance of the actual return being in the range of −10.8% [15.5% − (13.15% * 2)] and 41.8% [15.5% + (13.15 * 2)].

To find out the area under normal curve for various standard deviations, the normal probability table, given at the end of the book, is used. The probability of occurrence can be read from the normal probability table. This table is the right tail of the distribution—which implies that probabilities of unknown quantity, greater than standard deviations from the expected value, are given in the table. The distribution values tabulated in the distribution table is a normal distribution with mean, zero, and standard deviation, 1. This is known as standard normal distribution. Normal distribution is an important concept in statistics and finance. However in practice, it is difficult to find a sample distribution which is normal (because of sampling error). It is only possible that data can be normally distributed by taking the return series for a very long period of time.

A normal distribution is intimately connected to Z-scores. The main idea is to standardize all the data that is given by using Z-scores (tables at the end of the text have been given in this context). These Z-scores can then be used to find the area (and thus the probability) under the normal curve. The computation, as shown below, of Z-scores gives the idea about computing probabilities.

$$Z = \frac{R - E(R)}{\sigma}$$

where,

R = the return which interest investors.
E(R) = the expected return.
σ = standard deviation (risk).

By taking the above example of XYZ Co.,

$$Z = \frac{0 - 15.5}{13.15}$$

$$= -1.178$$

The value, −1.178, indicates that a return of 0 is positioned 1.178 standard deviations, to the left of the expected value, of the probability distribution of possible returns. As per the normal distribution table, the probability of being less than 1.178 standard deviations from the expected value is 0.12. It implies that there is a 12% probability that the return of the asset will be zero or less.

4.5 CONCEPTS OF RISK

There are certain queries that arise with regards to the concept of risk. And since risk, along with return, is the major determinant of the investment decisions, it is imperative that the same are answered. Hence to the same this segment is dedicated.

Concept: Is standard deviation an expected measure?

Risk means deviation from the expected outcome. It includes both positive and negative deviations. If the probability distribution of possible outcomes is symmetrical, the standard deviation is an expected measure. But when the probability distribution departs from symmetry, the standard deviation too departs from the expected measure.

Concept: Is upside risk relevant?

The general mentality of investors is an aversion to risk. At the same time investors are willing to take risk to a certain degree, provided the returns are adequate. Usually risk is perceived as a downside risk, i.e., the risk of incurring loss. A gain is never deemed as a risk.

In the previous illustration the expected return of XYZ Co. is recorded as 15.5%. If there is further increase in the returns with respect to the average return, even with ups and downs in the market, the investors are not bothered. The upward movement is not considered a risk. So, if it moves to 20%, 28%, 31%, etc., investors would instead welcome the occurrence gladly! Only if there is a dip below the expected return of 15.5% it is perceived as risk, and hence a cause of concern. But, this is not an accurate assessment. The rationalized meaning of risk says that it includes both positive and negative deviation from anticipated levels. Thus, deviation in either direction should be considered as risk.

> **Pause for thought:** Both positive and negative deviations from the expected return are considered as risk. Other things remaining the same, securities with the lower risk should be preferred. And thus, automatically the stocks with positive risks are highly favorable!

Table 4.7: Risk-return of the Securities and Investment Decisions

Risk-return of the Securities (%)			
Year	ONGC	ITC	Kotak Bank
2002	90.68	−11.65	104.22
2003	127.52	22.87	131.39
2004	39.09	39.45	16.62
2005	29.14	−17.69	−3.54
2006	10.85	−80.98	2.92
2007	−0.76	12.14	177.04
2008	−8.59	5.27	−2.63
2009	−0.71	14.53	−34.19
2010	34.75	9.71	16.18
Return (%)	35.78	−0.71	45.34
Risk, σ (%)	45.75	34.57	73.06

As has been iterated repeatedly, returns come inevitably with risks. So the decision rests with the investors on how they wish to select the securities. This they do based upon their risk preferences. There are three types of investors:

- Risk-averse.
- Risk-lover.
- Risk-neutral.

Risk-averse investors choose to play safe. They opt for the security with lowest risk (standard deviation), for the given rates of return, from the available securities. In terms of risk, they choose the security with highest return, from the securities with equal level of risk. Risk-lover investor is willing take additional risk for an investment with relatively low expected return. For a risk-neutral investor risk doesn't decide the investment decisions; it is only the higher return which guides the decision. In this text we shall be discussing the decisions of all types of investors. But risk-averse investors draw more attention, as risk-averse mentality is a generality.

> **Pause for thought:** Investors belong to three categories, based on their aversion to risk (risk-averse investor); affinity for risk (risk-lover investor) and indifference to risk (risk-neutral investor), with higher return as the basis of the investment decisions.

SUMMARY

✓ Risk and return are the two fundamentals for the evaluation of securities.

✓ Return on a security consists of two parts: dividend yield and capital gain/loss.

✓ Arithmetic mean, holding period return, geometric mean and CAGR are the different methods for calculating return.

✓ The deviation from average rate of return is estimated by calculating variance and standard deviation.

$$\text{Variance} = \sigma^2 = \frac{1}{n-1} \sum_{t=1}^{n} [R_t - R]^2$$

✓ Standard deviation, σ, the square root of variance, is the risk involved in the return of the security.

✓ The expected rate of return is the sum of the possible rates of return multiplied with their respective probabilities.

$$E(R) = R_1 \times P_1 + R_2 \times P_2 + \ldots + R_n \times P_n$$

$$= \sum_{i=1}^{n} R_i P_i$$

✓ Investors have different risk preferences and based on this they are categorized as risk-averse, risk-lover and risk neutral.

SECURITY ANALYSIS AND PORTFOLIO MANAGEMENT

KEY CONCEPTS

Arithmetic Mean	Probability	Risk-Averse
Geometric Mean	Expected Rate Of Return	Risk-Lover
CAGR	Variance	Risk-Neutral
Holding Period Return	Standard Deviation	

REVIEW QUESTIONS

1. What is meant by return of a security? Explain the different methods that are used to calculate return and describe their limitations.
2. Define and explain risk of a security. Calculate the risk for the stock of Infosys by taking the share price data from www.bseindia.com for the period, 2001 to 2011.

ASSIGNMENT QUESTIONS

1. Calculate the holding period return and geometric mean for AXIS Bank, Bank of India, Bank of Baroda, ICICI Bank, HDFC Bank and Allahabad Bank by taking their share prices from BSE/NSE websites, for the period: 2000 to 2011. Compare these values and interpret them.
2. Calculate and compare return and risk of the following pairs of securities: (i) Infosys and TCS; (ii) Bank of India and HDFC Bank and (iii) Tata Steel and SAIL. Interpret the results. Prices for the period: 2002 to 2010 are to be taken.
3. Collect the prices of silver, gold and real estate (of your area) of last five years. Calculate their return and risk and compare them with securities of the market. What do you infer from your calculations?

ILLUSTRATIONS

Q.1. The return on securities, ACC and Hero Honda are given below.

Probability	ACC (%)	HERO HONDA (%)
0.5	1.94	5.10
0.4	2.74	74.92
0.1	3.37	52.59

Select the security of your preference on the basis of return and risk.

Ans:

	Return			
Probability (P_i)	ACC (R_i)	HERO HONDA (R_i)	ACC	HERO HONDA
1	2	3	4 (1 × 2)	5 (1 × 3)
0.5	1.94	5.10	0.97	2.55
0.4	2.74	74.92	1.10	29.97
0.1	3.37	52.59	0.34	5.26
			2.41	37.78

Risk							
ACC				HERO HONDA			
R_i	P_i	$[R_i - E(R_i)]$	$[R_i - E(R_i)]^2 \times P_i$	R_i	P_i	$[R_i - E(R_i)]$	$[R_i - E(R_i)]^2 \times P_i$
1.94	0.5	−6.11	18.66	5.10	0.5	−127.51	8129.42
2.74	0.4	−5.31	11.29	74.92	0.4	−57.69	1331.18
3.37	0.1	−4.69	2.20	52.59	0.1	−80.02	640.34
$E(R_i)$ = 8.05			Variance = 32.14	$E(R_i)$ = 132.61			Variance =10100.94
			S.D. = 5.67				S.D. = 100.50

Selection of the security depends on the individual investor's risk bearing capacity. However, in this case, even risk-averse investor will prefer to go for the ACC stock as return is almost at par with the risk-free government security. A risk-loving investor would prefer to go for the stock of Hero Honda, which is a high risk and high return stock.

Q.2. An investor is offered four stocks: Cipla, Gail, HCL and HDFC. An analyst has assigned the following probabilities to each stock, based upon their likely performance in the coming year. Their rates of return too are given below.

(a) Are all these stocks attractive investments with the given probabilities? Give reason(s) for your answer.

(b) Which stock would you prefer to buy and why?

PROBABILITY	CIPLA	PROB	GAIL	PROBABILITY	HCLTECH	PROB	HDFC
P_i	R_i	P_i	R_i	P_i	R_i	P_i	R_i
0.2	−45.73	0.15	56.02	0.20	−13.20	0.10	66.82
0.4	−9.32	0.35	−6.76	0.40	−52.44	0.25	−1.78
0.3	34.53	0.45	−12.85	0.30	12.07	0.40	−6.54
0.1	32.05	0.05	49.10	0.10	68.82	0.25	−10.45

Ans: Return

	Cipla			GAIL	
	Return			Return	
P_i	R_i	$P_i \times R_i$	P_i	R_i	$P_i \times R_i$
0.2	−45.73	−9.15	0.15	56.02	8.40
0.4	−9.32	−3.73	0.35	−6.76	−2.37
0.3	34.53	10.36	0.45	−12.85	−5.78
0.1	32.05	3.20	0.05	49.10	2.45
		$E(R_i) = 0.69$			$E(R_i) = 2.71$

	HCL Tech			HDFC	
	Return			Return	
P_i	R_i	$P_i \times R_i$	P_i	R_i	$P_i \times R_i$
0.20	−13.20	−2.64	−0.10	66.82	−6.68
0.40	−52.44	−20.97	0.25	−1.78	−0.44
0.30	12.07	3.62	0.40	−6.54	−2.62
0.10	68.82	6.88	0.25	−10.45	−2.61
		$E(R_i) = -13.11$			$E(R_i) = -12.36$

Variance and standard deviation (S.D.) of Cipla

P_i	R_i	$R_i \times P_i$	$[R_i - E(R_i)]$	$[R_i - E(R_i)]^2 \times P_i$
0.2	−45.73	−9.15	−9.84	19.36
0.4	−9.32	−3.73	−4.42	7.81
0.3	34.53	10.36	9.67	28.04
0.1	32.05	3.20	2.51	0.63
		$E(R_i) = 0.69$		Variance = 55.84
				S.D. = 7.47

Variance and standard deviation of GAIL

P_i	R_i	$R_i \times P_i$	$[R_i - E(R_i)]$	$[R_i - E(R_i)]^2 \times P_i$
0.15	56.02	8.40	5.69	4.86
0.35	−6.76	−2.37	−5.08	9.02
0.45	−12.85	−5.78	−8.49	32.46
0.05	49.10	2.45	−0.26	0.00
		$E(R_i) = 2.71$		Variance = 46.34
				S.D. = 6.81

Variance and standard deviation of HCL Tech.

P_i	R_i	$R_i \times P_i$	$[R_i - E(R_i)]$	$[R_i - E(R_i)]^2 \times P_i$
0.20	−13.20	−2.64	10.47	21.93
0.40	−52.44	−20.97	−7.86	24.73
0.30	12.07	3.62	16.73	84.01
0.10	68.82	6.88	19.99	39.97
		$E(R_i) = -13.11$		Variance = 170.64
				S.D. = 13.06

Variance and standard deviation of HDFC

P_i	R_i	$R_i \times P_i$	$[R_i - E(R_i)]$	$[R_i - E(R_i)]^2 \times P_i$
−0.10	66.82	−6.68	5.68	−3.22
0.25	−1.78	−0.44	11.91	35.48
0.40	−6.54	−2.62	9.74	37.95
0.25	−10.45	−2.61	9.75	23.74
		$E(R_i) = -12.36$		Variance = 93.96
				S.D. = 9.69

Summary table of return and risk of the four securities

Security	Return (%)	Risk (%)
CIPLA	0.69	7.47
GAIL	2.71	6.81
HCL Tech.	−13.11	13.06
HDFC	−12.36	9.69

From the above summary table we can say that GAIL should be selected.

Q.3. Nancy purchased the stocks of HUL, ICICI, ITC and JSW Steel with the expectation that all four stocks would provide very good return after a year. The purchase price and the closing price of each are given below. Find out the holding period return of all four shares.

Stock	Opening price	Closing price	Dividend yield
HUL	264.8	312.9	0.65
ICICI Bank	877	1145.1	0.12
ITC	253	174.65	0.1
JSW Steel	1020	1177.05	0.125

Ans:

Stock	Opening price	Closing price	Dividend yield
HUL	264.8	312.9	0.65
ICICI Bank	877	1145.1	0.12
ITC	253	174.65	0.1
JSW Steel	1020	1177.05	0.125

Holding period return is calculated by the formula

$$R = \frac{Div_1}{P_0} + \frac{P_1 - P_0}{P_0} \times 100$$

For the HUL stock,

$$R = 0.65 + \frac{(312.9 - 264.8)}{264.8} \times 100$$

$$= 0.65 + 0.181$$
$$= 0.8316$$
$$= 83.16$$

Similarly the holding period return (HPR) is calculated for other securities and tabulated as follows:

Stock	HPR (%)
HUL	83.16
ICICI Bank	42.57
ITC	−20.97
JSW Steel	27.90

Q.4. Devesh wants to purchase the stocks of the two companies, JP Associate and Kotak Bank. He estimates the return and probabilities of returns by analyzing the past records. Find out the expected return from the given details.

Probability P_i	Return JP Associate R_i	Return Kotak Bank R_i
0.3	86.48	2.92
0.15	73.39	177.03
0.15	-70.81	-2.63
0.2	-47.45	-34.19
0.2	-6.23	16.18

Ans:

Probability P_i	Return JP Associate R_i	$P_i \times R_i$	Probability P_i	Return Kotak Bank R_i	$P_i \times R_i$
0.3	86.48	25.94	0.3	2.92	0.88
0.15	73.39	11.01	0.15	177.03	26.55
0.15	-70.81	-10.62	0.15	-2.63	-0.39
0.2	-47.45	-9.49	0.2	-34.19	-6.84
0.2	-6.23	-1.25	0.2	16.18	3.24
		$E(R_i) =$ 15.60			$E(R_i) =$ 23.43

Q.5. Calculate the holding period return (HPR) and compound annual return (CAR) from the following data.

Year	Hero Honda Motors Opening price	Hero Honda Motors Closing price	Tata Chemicals Opening price	Tata Chemicals Closing price
2007	760	697.65	217.9	412.6
2008	698	805.1	414	164.6
2009	800	1,716.45	164.1	322.2
2010	1,739.00	1,986.10	322	393.85
2011	2,002.00	1,788.85	395	379.85

Ans:

HPR and CAR of Hero Honda Motors

Year	Hero Honda Motors			Tata Chemicals		
	Opening price	Closing price	Return (%)	Opening price	Closing price	Return (%)
2007	760	697.65	−8.20	217.9	412.6	89.35
2008	698	805.1	15.34	414	164.6	−60.24
2009	800	1,716.45	114.56	164.1	322.2	96.34
2010	1,739.00	1,986.10	14.21	322	393.85	22.31
2011	2,002.00	1,788.85	−10.65	395	379.85	−3.84
		HPR	2.32		HPR	1.74
		CAR	18		CAR	12

For Hero Honda:

HPR = [1 + (-0.082)] × (1 + 0.1534) × (1 + 1.1456) × (1 + 0.1421) × [1+ (-0.1065)] × (1+0.0232)
    = 0.918 × 1.1534 × 2.1456 × 1.1421 × 0.8935 × 1.0232
    = 2.32

CAR = (0.918 × 1.1534 × 2.1456 × 1.1421 × 0.8935 × 1.0232)1/5
    = 1.18 - 1
    = 0.18 (18%)

In a similar manner, for Tata Chemicals: HPR = 1.74 and CAR = 12%

Q.6. The details of IDFC's share prices and dividend from 2005 to 2010, are as follows. Calculate the dividend yield, capital gain, total return and risk of the IDFC.

	IDFC	
Year	Price (Rs.)	Dividend (Rs.)
2005	65.30	1
2006	69.69	1
2007	152.26	1
2008	137.98	1.2
2009	111.20	1.2
2010	174.24	1.5

Ans: Return of IDFC:

Year	IDFC Price (Rs.)	IDFC Dividend (Rs.)	Capital gain (%)	Dividend yield (%)	Total return (%)	[R – E(R)]	[R – E(R)]²
1	2	3	4	5	6	7	8
2005	65.30	1					
2006	69.69	1	6.72	1.53	8.25	–23.57	555.38
2007	152.26	1	118.49	1.43	119.93	88.11	7763.61
2008	137.98	1.2	–9.38	0.79	–8.60	–40.41	1633.15
2009	111.20	1.2	–19.41	0.87	–18.54	–50.35	2535.41
2010	174.24	1.5	56.69	1.35	58.04	26.22	687.51
Mean			30.62	1.19	31.82		Sum = 13175.06
						Variance	3293.77
						Standard deviation	57.39%

$$\text{Capital gain (for the year 2006)} = \frac{P_1 - P_0}{P_0}$$

$$= \frac{69.6875 - 65.3}{65.3} \times 100$$

$$= 6.72\%$$

$$\text{Dividend yield for 2006} = \frac{Div_1 \times 100}{P_0}$$

$$= \frac{1}{65.3} \times 100$$

$$= 1.53\%$$

Total return = Dividend yield + Capital gain
= 1.53% + 6.72%
= 8.25%

Calculations for each year are carried out in a similar manner. Columns 4 and 5 show the yearly dividend yield and capital gain respectively.

The average capital gain and dividend yield are 30.62% and 1.19% respectively.

The total return for the year 2006 = Dividend yield + Capital gain
= 6.72% + 1.53% = 8.25%.

The average capital gain from 2006 to 2010 is 31.82%.

Risk of IDFC:

Column 7 shows the difference of individual return and average return for each year.

For the year 2006 this difference = 8.25% - 31.82% = -23.57%.

Column 8 holds the squared values of column 7, which for the year 2006 is, 555.38. By repeating this procedure for other years, the subsequent summation of the values of column 8 turns out to be Rs. 13175.06

Variance = 13175.06/4 = 3293.77

Standard deviation = $(3293.77)^{1/2}$ = 57.39%

PROBLEMS

Q.1. On April 1, 2009 Ms. Aarna purchased 100 shares of ICICI Bank Ltd. for Rs. 877 per share and sold the same at Rs. 1145.1, on March 31, 2010. During the holding period Ms. Aarna received Rs. 12, per share, as dividend. Calculate Ms. Aarna's capital gain, dividend yield and total return.

Q.2. From the details given below for the corresponding stocks, calculate their HPR and CAR.

Year	HUL		Godrej Industries		Mahindra & Mahindra	
	Opening price	Closing price	Opening price	Closing price	Opening price	Closing price
2007	218	213.9	178.25	430.85	912	860.8
2008	214.2	250.25	437	68.55	862	274.85
2009	251.2	264.75	69.25	184.4	279	1,080.80
2010	265.95	312.3	185	191.55	1,095.00	777.55
2011	313.85	333.1	191.55	224.8	792	701.95

Q.3. The following table contains the share prices and dividends of Maruti for the period: 2003 to 2010. Calculate its dividend yield, capital gain, total return and risk.

Year	Price (Rs.)	Dividend (Rs.)
2003	270.50	1.5
2004	434.93	1.5
2005	544.23	2
2006	796.63	3.5
2007	974.13	4.5
2008	752.05	5
2009	1080.18	3.5
2010	1425.04	6

MEASURING RISK AND RETURN 97

Q.4. The table below contains the probabilities of the securities mentioned therein. Calculate the risk and return of these securities. Which security would you select?

Probability	ACC A	Cipla B	Sesa Goa C	Wipro D
0.1	8.62	−22.13	32.12	2.48
0.1	48.37	45.71	738.46	5.67
0.1	37.74	−76.31	70.27	−57.12
0.1	57.28	38.56	−2.19	−38.45
0.1	101.78	−43.66	38.65	30.29
0.1	−6.78	−16.10	167.97	−13.54
0.1	−53.83	−13.07	−97.76	−55.26
0.1	81.58	83.39	377.78	187.88
0.1	23.63	9.12	−20.27	−29.73
0.1	−9.11	−12.43	−12.72	−15.73

Q.5. Given the uncertainty that looms large over the global economy for the coming year, estimate from the following probabilities, the rate of return for XYZ Steel so that it ranges between −10% and +30%. Also, calculate the expected return for XYZ Steel.

Probability	Possible returns
0.13	−0.10
0.18	0.10
0.10	0.15
0.08	0.35
0.12	0.20
0.09	0.30
0.15	0.09
0.15	0.17

Q.6. An asset has the following possible returns, with the corresponding probabilities associated with it.

Possible returns (%)	24	19	10	12	0	−25	−8
Probabilities	0.10	0.10	0.20	0.30	0.10	0.10	0.10

Calculate the expected rate of return and standard deviation of the rate of return.

Q.7. Malhotra and Sons are extremely risk-averse. Hence, they will choose the least risky alternative. Calculate risk and return of the securities given below from the data of last 10 years (2001 to 2010) and then answer following queries:
  (a) Which is least risky, in terms of standard deviation?
  (b) Which is least risky in terms of coefficient of variation?
  (c) Which is a preferred measure of risk for the above project?

Stock	Return (%)	Risk
SBI		
Reliance		
Tata Steel		
Tata Motors		
Hindustan Lever		

CASE STUDY

The dilemma faced by Mr. Devershi Gupta over the investment decisions

Mr. Devershi Gupta, having completed B.Pharm, is employed at one of the pharmaceutical companies. He is happy with his chosen career and his financial status. He lives at Gurgaon with his wife, two kids and parents. His father, Mr. Bharat Bhai worked with one of the public sector banks for close to 35 years, in various capacities and retired as a branch manager. At present he draws a healthy amount for his pension and enjoys the benefits from gratuity, PF, etc. that he received at retirement. He has also saved quite a bit even while in service. Having a sound knowledge of the stock market he reviews the market and the economic condition periodically. He is worried with the current unstable economic and political scenarios. In addition, the corporate environment too is a cause of concern. With the ever increasing cost of living and with uncertainties in life, he is worried about the times to come. Medical expenses and education too are becoming expensive, to add to the woes of rapidly increasing cost of living. And it being impossible to estimate to what extent this rise will continue he frequently advises his son Devershi to plan for the future. Mr. Bharat Bhai concludes that it would be difficult for Devershi to meet ends for his family in the future, since in present times neither the job is guaranteed nor does it offer pension benefits, while the expenses are on the rise concurrently. So he approached an investment agent asked him to suggest appropriate plans for his son and his family.

Investment agent, Mr. Ramachandran, advised him to invest in the dream plan of India Insurance Company. The details of the plan, as provided by him are: premium of Rs. 75,907 p.a., payable till the investor is 51 years of age; a high risk coverage of Rs. 25,08,000 when one invests at the age of 30, which grows to Rs. 49,68,000 when the investor is 52. He states that in the year 2033 when Devershi attains 52 years of age, he will start receiving tax-free income annually, till he is 75. This payback (income) begins with Rs. 1,57,753, followed by an approximate increase of 5.00% every year, to counter the increase in inflation. There is a provision of risk coverage as well during this period. In case of death during this period, a lump sum corresponding to the prevailing risk coverage will be paid to the nominee. No premiums are payable after the deferment period, that is, after 51 years of age. In case of any emergencies, this Magic Plan has the provision

Measuring Risk and Return

of loan against the insurance policy. The loan is available only after the investment is 2 years old and 3 yearly premiums have been paid. Mr. Ramachandran has prepared the pension plan exclusively for Mr. Gupta. See the following details of the plan and help Mr. Gupta to take right decision.

- Premiums are available for exemption under Sec. 80 CCE of income tax act up to Rs. 1,00,000 p.a.
- Loan is calculated on the basis of current surrender value rates.
- The risk coverage of Rs. 2,400,000,00 will continue for lifetime.
- The effective yield in the above proposal turns out to be 8.56% (calculated according to the IRR method).
- IRR does not consider the death benefit after age 75.
- The net annuity is increasing every year at the rate of 5%, to take care of the inflation.

Quotation ref. no.: 39
Quotation date: 25/08/2011
Proposer's name: Mr. Devershi Gupta
Proposer's age: 30 (nearest birthday)
Sum proposed: 2400000
Yearly premium: 75,907
Sec. 80 CCE investment limit.: 100000
Sec. 80 CCE tax rebate: 30.60%

Benefits during deferment period

Year	Age	Normal	Accident	Yearly premium	Tax saved	Net premium	Loan available
2011	30	2508000	3008000	75907	23229	52678	0
2012	31	2616000	3116000	75907	23229	52678	0
2013	32	2724000	3224000	75907	23229	52678	30500
2014	33	2832000	3332000	75907	23229	52678	77000
2015	34	2940000	3440000	75907	23229	52678	110500
2016	35	3048000	3548000	75907	23229	52678	148250
2017	36	3156000	3656000	75907	23229	52678	191250
2018	37	3264000	3764000	75907	23229	52678	239750
2019	38	3372000	3872000	75907	23229	52678	294000
2020	39	3480000	3980000	75907	23229	52678	355250
2021	40	3588000	4088000	75907	23229	52678	424500
2022	41	3696000	4196000	75907	23229	52678	500750
2023	42	3804000	4304000	75907	23229	52678	587250
2024	43	3912000	4412000	75907	23229	52678	682250
2025	44	4044000	4544000	75907	23229	52678	787000

2026	45	4164000	4664000	75907	23229	52678	903250
2027	46	4284000	4784000	75907	23229	52678	1031250
2028	47	4404000	4904000	75907	23229	52678	1171000
2029	48	4524000	5024000	75907	23229	52678	1330500
2030	49	4656000	5156000	75907	23229	52678	1506000
2031	50	4788000	5288000	75907	23229	52678	1702500
2032	51	4968000	5468000	75907	23229	52678	1919250
				1669954	511038	1158916	

Risk coverage

Year	Age	Normal	Accident	Yearly premium	Tax saved	Net premium	Desired income	Amt. received	Used for prem. payment	Net receivable	Loan available
2033	52	5125500	5625500	70963	21716	49247	100000	207000	49247	157753	1982000
2034	53	5282000	5782000	66277	20282	45995	105000	218500	45995	172505	2041000
2035	54	5455500	5955500	61833	18922	42911	110250	231000	42911	188089	2098250
2036	55	5600000	6100000	57587	17623	39964	115763	245500	39964	205536	2151500
2037	56	5734500	6234500	53545	16386	37159	121551	260000	37159	222841	2199000
2038	57	5838000	6338000	49687	15205	34482	127628	275500	34482	241018	2242500
2039	58	5910500	6410500	45999	14076	31923	134010	291000	31923	259077	2279750
2040	29	6000000	6500000	42471	12996	29475	140710	306500	29475	277025	2311250
2041	60	6142500	6642500	39089	11961	27128	147746	325000	27128	297872	2336000
2042	61	6236000	6736000	35843	10968	24875	155133	349500	24875	324625	2355750
2043	62	6345500	6845500	32723	10013	22710	162889	374000	22710	351290	2364500
2044	63	6276000	6776000	29724	9095	20629	171034	403500	20629	382871	2366750
2045	64	6167500	6667500	26832	8210	18622	179586	423000	18622	404378	2359500
2046	65	6070000	6570000	24041	7356	16685	188565	442500	16685	425815	2339250
2047	66	5923500	6423500	21347	6532	14815	197993	467000	14815	452185	2309750
2048	67	5768000	6268000	18746	5736	13010	207893	491500	13010	478490	2265750
2049	68	5553500	6053500	16227	4965	11262	218287	521000	11262	509738	2213000
2050	69	5280000	5780000	13786	4218	9568	229202	550500	9568	540932	2146750
2051	70	4822500	4822500	11417	3493	7924	240662	580000	7924	572076	2060500
2052	71	4356000	4356000	9016	2758	6258	252695	584500	6258	578242	1961250
2053	72	3880500	3880500	6678	2043	4635	265330	589000	4635	584365	1835000
2054	73	3396000	3396000	4399	1346	3053	278596	593500	3053	590447	1689750
2055	74	2902500	2902500	2173	665	1508	292526	598000	1508	596492	1511750
2056	75	2400000	2400000	0	0	0	307152	602500	0	602500	1302000
				740403				9930000	513838	9416162	

Risk coverage–continued

Year	Age	Normal	Accident	Cash value	Loan available
2057	76	2400000	2400000	1483680	1338000
2058	77	2400000	2400000	1517760	1368000
2059	78	2400000	2400000	1550880	1398000
2060	79	2400000	2400000	1583520	1428000
2061	80	2400000	2400000	1615200	1452000
2062	81	2400000	2400000	1645920	1482000
2063	82	2400000	2400000	1675920	1506000
2064	83	2400000	2400000	1704960	1536000
2065	84	2400000	2400000	1733040	1560000
2066	85	2400000	2400000	1760400	1584000
2067	86	2400000	2400000	1786560	1608000
2068	87	2400000	2400000	1812000	1632000
2069	88	2400000	2400000	1836480	1650000
2070	89	2400000	2400000	1860960	1674000
2071	90	2400000	2400000	1884480	1698000
2072	91	2400000	2400000	1908480	1716000
2073	92	2400000	2400000	1933240	1740000
2074	93	2400000	2400000	1956720	1764000
2075	94	2400000	2400000	1987920	1788000
2076	95	2400000	2400000	2015280	1812000
2077	96	2400000	2400000	2067120	1860000
2078	97	2400000	2400000	2117760	1908000
2079	98	2400000	2400000	2234400	2010000
2080	99	2400000	2400000	0	0
2081	100	2400000	2400000	0	0

				Agent's copy				Premium				
Sr. No.	Plan/Tm/ PPT	Sum	DAB sum	Interim bonus rate	Bonus rate	Assu step rate	FAB	SSS	Mly.	Qly.	Hly.	Yly.
1	149/22/22	100000	0	45	45	0.00	80	428	447	1275	2511	4944
2	149/23/23	100000	0	45	45	0.00	150	403	424	1209	2380	4686
3	149/24/24	100000	0	45	45	0.00	230	382	402	1146	2257	4444
4	149/25/25	100000	0	45	45	0.00	330	365	384	1095	2156	4246
5	149/26/26	100000	0	45	45	0.00	430	347	365	1042	2053	4042
6	149/27/27	100000	0	45	45	0.00	540	330	349	995	1959	3858
7	149/28/28	100000	0	45	45	0.00	650	317	333	951	1873	3688
8	149/29/29	100000	0	45	45	0.00	760	303	319	910	1792	3528
9	149/30/30	100000	0	45	45	0.00	900	291	306	872	1718	3382
10	149/31/31	100000	0	45	45	0.00	1100	279	294	837	1649	3246
11	149/32/32	100000	0	45	45	0.00	1300	268	282	805	1585	3120
12	149/33/33	100000	0	45	45	0.00	1550	258	271	774	1524	2999
13	149/34/34	100000	0	45	45	0.00	1700	249	262	746	1469	2892
14	149/35/35	100000	0	45	45	0.00	1850	240	252	720	1418	2791
15	149/36/36	100000	0	45	45	0.00	2050	232	244	695	1368	2694
16	149/37/37	100000	0	45	45	0.00	2250	224	235	671	1322	2601
17	149/38/38	100000	0	45	45	0.00	2500	217	228	650	1280	2519
18	149/39/39	100000	0	45	45	0.00	2750	210	221	630	1240	2441
19	149/40/40	100000	0	45	45	0.00	3000	204	214	611	1203	2369
20	149/41/41	100000	100000	45	45	0.00	3000	206	217	619	1219	2401
21	149/42/42	100000	100000	45	45	0.00	3000	201	211	602	1187	2338
22	149/43/43	100000	100000	45	45	0.00	3000	196	206	587	1157	2279
23	149/44/44	100000	100000	45	45	0.00	3000	191	201	574	1130	2226
24	149/45/45	100000	100000	45	45	0.00	3000	187	196	560	1103	2173
		2400000	500000					6527	6863	19576	38553	75907

REFERENCES

1. Pandey I M (2010), *Financial Management*, 10th edition, Vikas Publication, Delhi.
2. Chandra Prasanna (2008), *Financial Management—Theory and Practice*, 7th edition, Tata McGraw Hill, Delhi.
3. Reilly Frank K. and Brown Kennith C. (2006), *Investment Analysis and Portfolio Management*, 8th edition, Cengage Learning India, New Delhi.
4. Fischer E. Donald and Jordan J. Ronald (2009), *Security Analysis and Portfolio Management*, 6th edition, Pearson Education, Delhi.

5
INTRODUCTION TO PORTFOLIO THEORY

> **LEARNING OBJECTIVES**
>
> The purpose of this chapter is to enable you to understand:
> - What is meant by a portfolio.
> - Risk and return of a portfolio, as formulated by Markowitz.
> - Magical effect of covariance and correlation coefficient on the risk of the portfolio, as compared to individual securities.
> - Formation of efficient set and its implications for investment decisions.

5.1 INTRODUCTION

Portfolio is a bunch of securities. And when we deal with investments (our own or that of an investor, in the capacity of a portfolio manager) in stock market we actually deal with a portfolio of investment, instead of an individual security. So it is imperative that we know in detail about portfolios and how they are constructed, so as to yield the best possible results. Hence this chapter introduces us to the theories involved, to be applied to the play of the portfolios in the stock market. Specifically, Markowitz theory is taken up for discussion.

The bunch of securities, that a portfolio is, could be a combination stocks, bonds and other money market instruments. Portfolio is thus a diversification of investments because the investments are made in diverse instruments. It is a spread of securities in which one invests. The objective behind investing in a portfolio is accessing the advantage it carries! The advantage being the fact, that when one invests in multiple securities, instead of a single, one reduces the risk on returns. The return of the portfolio is not dependent on the risk involved in an individual security. Hence, performance of a single security doesn't govern the outcome of a portfolio. Investing in portfolios enables one to obtain optimum return with minimum risk, compared to investment in individual securities. In other words, it can be said that by investing in a portfolio one is spared from the disadvantages of putting all the eggs in the same basket!

Chapter 4 discussed and analyzed the expected return and risk—the two components needed to be understood to arrive at an investment decision. These two parameters are required to analyze a portfolio as well, which is nothing but a mixture of securities. The aspects that apply to the components (the individual securities) also apply to the whole (the portfolio). The portfolio theory is based on the assumption that investors are risk-averse—the reason they opt for portfolios, which reduces the risk through diversification. The theory also assumes that returns are normally distributed. Therefore analysis of expected return and standard deviation analysis forms the basis of construction of a portfolio.

5.1.1 Basis of the Portfolio Theory: Diversification Reduces the Risk

The essence of portfolio is diversification as a portfolio is composed of diverse securities. Thus diversification of investment means investing in more than one security. But the very concept of portfolio theory is conceived by a defensive strategy. Diversification, generally, aims at reducing risk, instead of enhancing the return.

The nature of diversification and hence the constitution of the portfolio is modified on the basis of the needs and risk preferences of the investor. By constructing the portfolio solely with bonds, financial risk can be minimized. Though, the only problem with bonds in the portfolio is that they are bad insurance against inflation. In comparison, shares provide better protection but are prone to financial risks. One can also construct a portfolio of short and long-term fixed income securities. Short-term fixed income securities offer more risks to the income; while long-term fixed income securities offer more risks to principal.

Each has its merits as well as demerits, rendering the construction of a well-diversified portfolio a demanding and balancing act! For the purpose, the investors can adopt the following guidelines:

— Selection of the industry.
— Selection of the companies in the chosen industry.
— Determining the proportion of each security in the portfolio.

Investors should select the industry as per his/her investment objectives, because each industry can be matched as per the goals of the investors. The sales of some industries, viz., automobile and steel, tend to move in tandem with the business cycle. While the FMCG sector enjoys almost constant sales throughout the year, housing sectors move counter-cyclically. For the regular flow of income, such industries should be selected which resist the trade cycles. Once the sectors (industries) have been selected, investors should select one or two companies from each sector. The selection of companies from different sectors should depend upon some specific factors: growth, yield, expected earnings, potential of the management, R&D expenditure, price-earnings ratio, dividends, etc. After the companies have been selected thus, next step is to determine the number of shares of each company one must invest in. The different numbers, of different stocks, from different companies—and in turn from different industries—provide enough diversification to reduce the risk of the portfolio.

> *Check yourself*
> Compare the returns of last ten years, for at least 4 companies from each sector, such as: FMCG, IT, Steel, Pharmaceutical, Oil, etc. Observe their pattern of returns over this period and interpret it.

Pause for thought: Portfolio is a bunch of diverse securities and the basis of portfolio theory is thus diversification, which is a defensive strategy as diversification primarily looks to reduce the risk, instead of enhancing the return.

5.1.2 Portfolio Return: Two Assets Case

Since a portfolio is comprised of more than one security, the return of the portfolio is related to the returns of the individual securities. It is the sum of the weighted average returns of individual securities in the portfolio. The weights of the securities correspond to the proportion of investment in each of them respectively.

As an illustration, we consider a portfolio of two assets: Reliance Capital and ONGC, denoted as A and B respectively, in Table 5.1 below. Columns 2 and 3 represent the return of these two securities, calculated from their capital gain/loss and dividend yield. As economic scenarios vary each year, so do the possible outcomes of the two assets. It can also be observed that returns of the two securities do not move parallel to each other.

Table 5.1: Return of Reliance Capital and ONGC

Year	Reliance Capital (%)	ONGC (%)
	A	B
1	2	3
2002	−23.41	85.71
2003	69.07	121.78
2004	44.78	37.02
2005	121.67	26.62
2006	67.32	8.61
2007	220.71	−2.18
2008	0.19	−10.09
2009	−57.41	−2.37
2010	11.82	32.99
Average return	50.53	33.12

The portfolio of A and B is assumed to be composed of 50% weight of both the assets. When the expected rate of return and the respective weights of the securities in the portfolio are known, this method is the most simple and direct method for calculating the expected rate of return of a portfolio.

The expected rate of return of the portfolio is formulated as:

$E(R_P)$ = (Weight of security A × expected return on security A)
 + (Weight of security B × expected return on security B)

$$= [W \times E(R_A)] + [(1-W) \times E(R_B)] \quad (1)$$
$$= (0.5 \times 50.53\%) + (0.5 \times 33.12\%)$$
$$= 25.26 + 16.56$$
$$= 41.82\%$$

where,

W = proportion of investment in Reliance Capital (A).
(1-W) = the rest, invested in ONGC (B).
$E(R_A)$ = expected return on the scrip of Reliance Capital.
$E(R_B)$ = expected return on the scrip of ONGC.
$E(R_P)$ = expected return on the portfolio.

From Table 5.1 it is evident that the return of Reliance Capital is much better than that of ONGC. We know that the return of portfolio depends on the returns and proportion of the individual securities. In this case, Reliance Capital contributes more to the return of the portfolio, given its higher return, though the weights of both Reliance Capital and ONGC are same in the portfolio. Hence a rational investor will choose to increase the investment in Reliance Capital and at the same time can reduce proportion of investment in ONGC. In this way, one can change the expected rate of return, of a portfolio, by changing the proportion of investment in the constituting assets. If we assume that the investor invests 80% of the available fund in Reliance Capital and 20% in ONGC, then in this case, portfolio return would be:

$$E(Rp) = (0.8 \times 50.53\%) + (0.2 \times 33.12\%)$$
$$= 40.42 + 6.62$$
$$= 47.04\%$$

Thus, as the proportion of investment is changed to 80 : 20, the return of the portfolio increases by almost 6%, compared to what it was, with equi-proportional investment in Reliance Capital and ONGC.

> **Pause for thought:** Return of a portfolio is the weighted average return of the individual securities, weights being in proportion to the amount invested in these securities.

5.1.3 Portfolio Risk: Two Assets Case

As the expected return on a portfolio depends on that of the constituent securities and their proportion, it also depends on the risk inherent in them. Returns on securities are accompanied by risks as an integral part.

But when we talk of the risk involved in a bunch of securities, i.e., a portfolio, vis-à-vis that of an individual security, another parameter comes into the picture. We know that standard deviation is the measure of risk, and it is the square root of the variance. Thus variance too is a measure of risk. In a portfolio each security will have its variance dependent on that of the other. Risk is interdependent and hence, for the risk of a portfolio, the concept of covariance comes into play, alongside variance. Covariance is actually the variance, in company of the other!

For the risk of the portfolio we consider the same two assets, as we did for return on a portfolio: Reliance Capital and ONGC. The calculations involved and the results obtained are as shown in Table 5.2.

Table 5.2: Risk of Reliance Capital and ONGC
Standard deviation and covariance of portfolio of two securities: Reliance Capital and ONGC for the period, 2002-2010

Year	Reliance Capital			ONGC			Covariance
	Return	$(R_t - R)$	$(R_t - R)^2$	Return	$(R_t - R)$	$(R_t - R)^2$	$(R_t - R_{\text{Reliance Capital}})$ $\times (R_t - R_{\text{ONGC}})$
1	2	3	4	5	6	7	8 (3 × 6)
2002	−23.41	−73.94	5467.23	85.71	52.59	2765.87	−3888.66
2003	69.07	18.55	343.99	121.78	88.66	7860.31	1644.36
2004	44.78	−5.75	33.02	37.02	3.90	15.20	−22.40
2005	121.67	71.14	5061.55	26.62	−6.50	42.22	−462.30
2006	67.32	16.80	282.07	8.61	−24.51	600.58	−411.59
2007	220.71	170.18	28962.45	−2.18	−35.31	1246.50	−6008.46
2008	0.19	−50.33	2533.45	−10.09	−43.21	1867.16	2174.93
2009	−57.41	−107.94	11650.61	−2.37	−35.49	1259.79	3831.10
2010	11.82	−38.71	1498.60	32.99	−0.13	0.02	5.17
	50.53%		Total summation = 55832.97	33.12%		Total summation = 15657.65	Total = −3137.86
n − 1			8			8	8
			$\sigma^2 =$ 6979.12			$\sigma^2 =$ 1957.21	Cov = −392.23
			$\sigma = 83.54\%$			$\sigma = 44.24\%$	

In the above table, column 2 shows return of Reliance Capital from year 2002 to 2010. Column 3 is the difference of the yearly return and average return, of Reliance Capital. For example, in 2002, $(R_t - R) = (-23.41\% - 50.53\%) = -73.94\%$. Column 4 shows the square of the values in column 3. Summation of the values in column 4 is 55832.97. The sum is divided by $n - 1$ (i.e., 8) and not n (i.e., the total number of years, 9, in the period of evaluation). This reduction in the divisor by 1 is because one degree of freedom has been lost.

Thus, the variance of Reliance Capital is,

$$\text{Variance} = \sigma^2 = \frac{1}{n-1} \sum_{t=1}^{n} (R_t - R)^2 \tag{2}$$

$$= \frac{55832.97}{8} = 6979.12$$

Standard deviation = √variance

So, standard deviation = √6979.12 = 0.8354 = 83.54%

Similarly, the risk (standard deviation) of ONGC is calculated and it turns out to be 44.24%.

The last column in the above Table 5.2 is the product of difference of yearly return and average return of Reliance Capital and ONGC respectively. This product is actually a product of the deviation of each security from their expected returns. And with respect to Table 5.2, it is the product of columns 3 and 6. The summation of this column is −3137.86.

$$= \frac{\Sigma (R_t - R_{\text{Reliance Capital}}) \times (R_t - R_{\text{ONGC}})}{n-1}$$

Note: In the formula of covariance, $n-1$ and not n is used in the denominator. This is because of one less degree of freedom. It ranges from $-\infty$ to $+\infty$. The covariance of a variable with itself is its variance.

5.1.4 Covariance

Covariance of returns on two assets measures their co-movement. It is an absolute measure of the extent to which two assets move together over time. Covariance between two securities, A and B, is calculated by the following formula,

$$= \frac{\Sigma [R_A - E(R_A)][R_B - E(R_B)]}{n-1} \tag{3}$$

When it is required to assign the probability, the covariance between two stocks can be calculated as:

$$\text{Cov}_{AB} = \sum_{i=1}^{n} \Sigma [R_A - E(R_A)][R_B - E(R_B)] \times P_i \tag{4}$$

where,

Cov_{AB} = covariance of returns on securities A and B.
R_A = return on security A.
R_B = return on security B.
$E(R_A)$ = expected return of security A.
$E(R_B)$ = expected return of security B.
P_i = probability of occurrence, of the different stages of the economy.

Following steps are involved in the calculation of covariance between two assets.

— The expected returns on two assets are calculated first.
— It is followed by the calculation of deviation of their possible returns, from the average returns.
— These deviations are multiplied.
— The products from the third step are summated and multiplied with the corresponding probability[1].

---

[1] Probability is assigned when we need to estimate the return and risk of the security. For past data we do not need to multiply probability as they have already occurred.

Three types of covariance can arise between two securities. Taking A and B as the two securities, the types are enumerated as follows:

1. *Positive covariance*

In this case, the returns on A and B could be above or below their respective average returns, simultaneously. Both instances are referred to as positive covariance, with the movement of the returns being in the same direction.

2. *Negative covariance*

When the return of A is above its average return and that of B is below, and vice-versa, it shows a movement in opposite direction, with respect to the returns. Such a movement of returns, in presence of one another is called a negative covariance.

3. *Zero covariance*

There are instances when returns of securities A and B do not represent any relationship. This implies that their variances are not interdependent and hence their covariance is zero. Though, in reality, covariance may be non-zero due to randomness, whereby negative and positive terms do not cancel out each other exactly.

In the example considered here, covariance between the securities A (Reliance Capital) and B (ONGC) is −392.23. Thus it is a negative covariance, corresponding to the second situation above.

> **Pause for thought:** The risk of a portfolio is a measure of the interdependent risks of the assets therein, known as covariance. The calculation of covariance, of a portfolio, differs from that of an individual security, for which it is the square root of the variance. Covariance is actually the variance of the assets in company of the other, in a portfolio.

5.1.5 Correlation Coefficient

Correlation coefficient is a measure of the degree of linear relationship between two variables; by which is meant the two securities whose degree of correlation is sought.

In the example under consideration, the two securities which are being correlated are A and B. We have already seen that the covariance of two securities is a measure of the deviation of the two, when in association. Thus the covariance is dependent on how the two securities correlate with each other. Hence, the formula of covariance can also be written as,

Cov_{AB} = Standard deviation of A × Standard deviation of B × Correlation of A and B

Or, $Cov_{AB} = \sigma_A \sigma_B Cor_{AB}$ (5)

From this equation, correlation between securities A and B is formulated as,

$$Cor_{AB} = \frac{Cov_{AB}}{\sigma_A \sigma_B} \quad (6)$$

i.e., Correlation (A,B) = $\dfrac{\text{Covariance (A,B)}}{\text{Standard deviation of A} \times \text{Standard deviation of B}}$

$$= \frac{-392.23}{83.54\% \times 44.24\%}$$

$$= \frac{-392.23}{3695.886}$$

$$= -0.1061$$

When the probability distribution comes into the picture, correlation coefficient is formulated as:

$$Cor_{AB} = \frac{\Sigma[R_A - E(R_A)][R_B - E(R_B)]}{\sigma_A \sigma_B} \times P_i \qquad (7)$$

Vide Equation (6) it is clear that for calculating correlation coefficient of two securities:
— The standard deviations of the two are to be ascertained.
— This is followed by the calculation of their covariance.

Types of correlation coefficient

Like covariance, the correlation coefficient too can be positive, negative or zero. As standard deviations are always positive, the correlation coefficient depends on the sign of the covariance. It always ranges between −1.0 to +1.0. A correlation coefficient of +1.0 implies a perfectly positive correlation while a correlation coefficient of −1.0 is for a perfectly negative correlation. If two securities are not at all related to each other, the correlation coefficient between two securities will be zero.

Advantages of correlation over covariance

— The covariance ranges from −∞ to +∞, so it is difficult to interpret and correlate it with other group of two securities.
— Correlation coefficient is convenient to interpret as it always ranges from −1 to +1. Hence, it is a more convenient measure than covariance.
— Portfolio return depends upon the proportion of individual securities invested in a portfolio. Portfolio risk depends on the correlation between two securities. It is always desirable to include two securities with negative correlation with each other. It reduces the risk significantly.

> **Check yourself**
> Take two stocks from NSE 50 or BSE Sensex whose correlation coefficient is negative. Why do most of the stocks have positive correlation with each other?

> **Pause for thought:** Correlation coefficient is the extent to which the two securities correlate.

Further on portfolio risk

Securities when combined to form a portfolio the risk of the portfolio is found to be less than the weighted average risks of the individual securities. The reason behind this lowering of risk is the fact that the risk in a portfolio depends not only on the probable deviation of the returns of individual securities. The risk is also dependent upon the mutual impact the securities have on one another. Their inter-relationship has a major say, which we have come to know as correlation coefficient. Furthermore, covariance too has its effect. So the simple weighted average method is deficient in estimating the risk of a portfolio, even though it succeeds with the returns of a portfolio. This lowering of risk in a portfolio constituted of diverse securities, as compared to the individual securities, is the boon of diversification.

No theory can be understood comprehensively in absence of an appropriate illustration. Hence each segment of the text has been coming up with the requisite example. And the same follows here too, with a hypothetical portfolio, comprised of three securities: A, B and C being considered. In this case, we have different three deviations (one for each) from average returns and three different covariance and correlation coefficient: Cov_{AB}, Cov_{AC}, Cov_{BC} and Cor_{AB}, Cor_{AC}, Cor_{BC} respectively. These all come into the picture when the risk of the portfolio is estimated.

Since the ongoing discussion has been involving the portfolio of Reliance Capital (A) and ONGC (B), we revert to the same for the risk calculation of a two asset portfolio.

As already mentioned above, the risk of a portfolio is measured by the relationship between the securities that constitute the portfolio. And these relationships are of two types: covariance and coefficient of correlation. Though the question does arise as to why would one invest in both the funds, when investing in only Reliance Capital generates 50.53% return? But then the risk involved in a single investment, with no option which can counteract the risk, tilts the balance in the favor of investing in multiple assets (the very essence of portfolio theory). The range of return on this security varies from –57.41% to 220.71%. It is this very probability of negative return which is eliminated when the fund is invested in both the assets. From the comparison of the pattern of return of these two securities, it is evident that in the year 2002 when the return of Reliance Capital was –23.41%, ONGC returned an earning of 85.71%. On the other hand, in the subsequent years, movements of these two returns have been observed to be almost opposite to each other.

> **Pause for thought:** Negative correlation coefficient/covariance of securities lower the risk of a portfolio. Hence the risk of a portfolio cannot be measured by the weighted average method.

5.2 ESTIMATED RETURN-RISK: TWO ASSETS CASE

From the above example, we have seen that the return of ONGC (33.12%) is much less than that of portfolio returns, 41.82% (when invested in equal proportion in Reliance Capital and ONGC). Moreover, the scrip of ONGC shows greater volatility than that of Reliance Capital. On the other hand, at some point of time, return can be –57.41% if entire fund is invested Reliance Capital. Thus has been reiterated that investing in a single security is risky. We have already discussed how the risk of an individual security is calculated. And now in this segment we delve into the method for calculating the risk of the portfolio.

But prior to the risk calculation of a portfolio of two securities Reliance Capital and ONGC, we consider the following example.

Table 5.3: Return of Securities with Probability Distribution

State of the economy	Probability	Return (%) Security A	Return (%) Security B
Boom	0.50	25%	0
Recession	0.50	0	25%

The expected rate of return on security A:

$E(R_A) = (0.50 \times 25) + (0.50 \times 0)$
$= 12.5\%$

The variance of A is,

$\sigma^2_A = 0.50(25 - 12.5)^2 + 0.50(0 - 12.5)^2$
$= 78.125 + 78.125$
$= 156.25$

Standard deviation of A is,

$\sigma_A = \sqrt{156.25}$
$= 0.125 = 12.5\%$

Similarly, the expected return for the security B is, 12.5%; the variance is 156.25% and the standard deviation is 12.5%.

Here, thus both the securities are equally profitable and equally risky as they have the same return, variance and standard deviation. If this be the case, how will construction of such a portfolio reduce the risk for a given level of return?

Furthermore, the return of a portfolio, equally composed of A and B, would be:

$E(R_P) = (0.5 \times 12.5) + (0.5 \times 12.5)$
$= 12.5\%$

Hence, the question is obvious that with the identical return for the individual security, what is the use of constructing the portfolio? This is answered by the complete elimination of risk. When there is a boom in the economy, security A would earn 25% and B, zero. So the portfolio return will be,

$E(R_P) = (0.5 \times 25) + (0.5 \times 0)$
$= 12.5\%$

And during recession, there would be zero earnings from A, but B would earn 25%. This leads to the same return of the portfolio:

$E(R_P) = (0.5 \times 0) + (0.5 \times 25)$
$= 12.5\%$

This indicates that the investor is assured of a certain guaranteed return if they invested in both A and B, instead of investing the entire amount in either A or B. Diversification of funds is thus assurance of a certain amount of guaranteed return.

Note: In real life, it is impossible to eliminate the risk completely. Moreover, it is difficult to find two such assets, as above, which move in perfectly opposite direction, with respect to their returns.

Pause for thought: The risk of a portfolio is lowered by diversification.

5.2.1 Variance and Standard Deviation: Two-Asset Portfolio

We have discussed in the previous section the indispensability of diversification for reduction in the risk of the portfolio. In this section we shall have a detailed discussion on variance and standard deviation, the measures of risk of individual securities, applied to a portfolio. For the purpose we resort to the two asset case of Reliance Capital and ONGC. The previous section has made us aware that the variance of a two asset portfolio is not the weighted average of the variances of assets. So how can the variance of a two asset portfolio be calculated? Well, it is made possible by the following equation:

$$\sigma^2_P = \sigma^2_A W^2_A + \sigma^2_B W^2_B + 2W_A W_B Cov_{AB} \tag{8}$$

Substituting the value of Cov_{AB} from Equation (5), Equation (8) becomes,

$$\sigma^2_P = \sigma^2_A W^2_A + \sigma^2_B W^2_B + 2W_A W_B \sigma_A \sigma_B Cor_{AB} \tag{9}$$

The following inferences are drawn from Equations (8) and (9) for variance of a portfolio:
— Variance of the portfolio includes proportionate variances of the individual securities.
— It also includes the covariance of the individual securities.
— Since the covariance of the securities depends on the correlation between the securities in a portfolio, the variance of the portfolio too depends on them.
— Thus for a negative correlation, the risk of the portfolio would be less than the weighted average risk of the securities, as then Equation (9) becomes:

$$\sigma^2_P = \sigma^2_A W^2_A + \sigma^2_B W^2_B - [X],$$ where X is a negative value of correlation and $\sigma^2_A W^2_A + \sigma^2_B W^2_B$ is the weighted average risk of securities.

Thus the formula for variance of a portfolio has been derived. The inferences drawn from it are found to corroborate the theoretical aspects of variance, which we discussed in the early part of this section. Now comes the turn for the calculation of standard deviation of the portfolio. And we know that standard deviation is the square root of variance.

Equation (9) is substituted, with the values for the parameters therein, with those of Reliance Capital (A) and ONGC (B), from Table 5.2,

$$\sigma^2_P = \sigma^2_A W^2_A + \sigma^2_B W^2_B + 2W_A W_B \sigma_A \sigma_B Cor_{AB}$$
$$= (6979.12 \times 0.25) + (1957.20 \times 0.25)$$
$$\quad + [2 \times 0.5 \times 0.5 \times 83.54 \times 44.24 \times (-0.106)]$$
$$= 2037.97$$
$$\sigma_P = 0.4514 = 45.14\%$$

This value is cross-checked by computing the data in Equation (8), which in terms of covariance, calculates variance,

$$\sigma^2_P = \sigma^2_A W^2_A + \sigma^2_B W^2_B + 2W_A W_B \text{Cov}_{AB}$$
$$= (6979.12 \times 0.25) + (1957.20 \times 0.25) + [2 \times 0.5 \times 0.5 \times (-392.23)]$$
$$= 2037.97$$
$$\sigma_P = 0.4514 = 45.14\%$$

The inferences drawn from the calculation of standard deviation of a portfolio of Reliance Capital and ONGC, with equal proportion (50 : 50) of each in the portfolio, are:

— Hence, irrespective of whether the standard deviation is calculated with respect to covariance or correlation coefficient it remains the same for a given portfolio.
— The interpretation of the standard deviation of the portfolio is same as that of the individual securities. As computed above (with reference to Equation (1)), the expected return of the portfolio is 41.82% and the risk is 45.14%.
— The return could thus vary between –3.32% (41.82 – 45.14) and 86.96% (41.82 + 45.14) within one standard deviation from the mean.

When the proportion invested in these securities is changed to 80:20, in favor of Reliance Capital, the standard deviation too is found to vary as:

$$\sigma^2_P = \sigma^2_A W^2_A + \sigma^2_B W^2_B + 2W_A W_B \text{Cov}_{AB}$$
$$= (6979.12 \times 0.64) + (1957.20 \times 0.04) + [2 \times 0.8 \times 0.2 \times 83.54 \times 44.24 \times (-0.106)]$$
$$= 4419.41$$
$$\sigma_P = 0.6648 = 66.48\%$$

Thus when the ratio of the risky security, Reliance Capital increases to 80%, from 50%,

— The risk of the portfolio increases because proportion of risky security Reliance Capital increases in the portfolio.
— The return of the portfolio too increases to 47.01% (with reference to Equation (1)).
— Once again is evidenced an increase in risk with an increment in return. But then this is natural. There is nothing called free lunch—*neither in the stock market nor in life.*

> **Pause for thought:** The risk of a portfolio is measured in terms of the variance and standard deviation of the assets. With an increase in the proportion of the risky security, return of the portfolio increases, but the risk too does.

5.3 OPTIMUM PORTFOLIO

Selecting the securities and constructing a portfolio which has the right balance of return and risk is a task indeed. Not only are the risk and return of individual securities the determinants of the same, for a portfolio, their relative proportion too exercise their weight in net worth of the portfolio. The intent is to bring down the risk to the minimum for the maximum possible return, with optimum weights of the assets therein. When this is attained we have an optimum portfolio.

In the above illustration, a portfolio is assumed to contain equal proportion (50:50) of securities, A and B. At this weight, the portfolio risk has been found to be 45.14%. Obviously one is inclined to know whether the risk can be reduced further with a variation in the weights of the securities. Whether there is an ideal ratio for the relative weights, that too one wishes to ascertain.

The answers to these questions lie in the optimum or minimum variance portfolio. However, all investors do not endeavor for the minimum variance portfolio, with their differing preferences for risk and hence risk-return ratio. So such a portfolio is subject to the preferences of the specific investor.

But then we are interested in the minimum variance portfolio. And for that we need to estimate the optimum weights of securities A and B. The formula for calculating optimum weight of securities is,

$$W^* = \frac{\sigma_B^2 - Cov_{AB}}{\sigma_A^2 + \sigma_B^2 - 2Cov_{AB}} \qquad (10)$$

where,

W^* = optimum proportion of investment in security A.
$1 - W^*$ = optimum proportion of investment in security B.

In this case, from Table 5.2,

$$W^* = \frac{1957.20 - (-392.23)}{6979.12 + 1957.20 - 2(-392.23)}$$

$$= \frac{2349.43}{9720.78}$$

$$= 0.2416$$

So, the optimum weight of B is $1 - 0.2416 = 0.7584$

With this changed proportions of A (0.2416) and B (0.7584), the portfolio variance becomes,

$$\sigma_P^2 = \sigma_A^2 W_A^2 + \sigma_B^2 W_B^2 + 2W_A W_B \sigma_A \sigma_B Cor_{AB}$$
$$= [6979.12 \times (0.2416)^2] + [1957.20 \times (0.7584)^2]$$
$$\qquad + [2 \times 0.2416 \times 0.7584 \times 83.54 \times 44.24 \times (-0.106)]$$
$$= 1389.36$$

$\sigma_P = 0.3727 = 37.27\%$

Thus with weights of the assets changing from 50:50 to 24.16:75.84 (converted to percentage weights), the risk is brought down considerably. And this is understandable too, as the proportion of the less risky asset, of ONGC, has been raised significantly. Any other combination of A and B, by weight, will result in higher variance or standard deviation. Hence, this distribution by weight, of assets, is the optimum involving the minimum possible risk in the portfolio.

> **Pause for thought:** Optimum portfolio is the one with minimum risk, constructed with the optimum proportion of its securities.

5.3.1 Portfolio Risk and Correlation between Assets

We have already learnt that risk of the portfolio is not the weighted average risks (standard deviations multiplied with corresponding weight) of the assets in the portfolio. It is less than that owing to the diversification. We shall now prove this theory, mathematically.

When the weight of the securities A and B, is 50:50, the standard deviation has turned out to be 45.14%. We are interested in calculating the weighted standard deviation, which is the weighted average standard deviations of A and B; and prove that it is not equal to the standard deviation of the portfolio for the same weights of A and B.

Thus, weighted standard deviation = $(\sigma_A \times W_A) + (\sigma_B \times W_B)$

$$= (83.54 \times 0.50) + (44.24 \times 0.50)$$
$$= 0.6389$$
$$= 63.89\%$$

But the actual standard deviation of the portfolio, 45.14%, is much less.

Hence is proved and reiterated the following facts:

— The standard deviation of the portfolio is not the weight average standard deviations of the securities; is much less.
— Thus, investing funds in more than one security reduces portfolio risk.
— This happens because of diversification. However, the extent of diversification depends on the correlation between returns on securities. In this example, the correlation coefficient is –0.106. That is, returns of the two securities A and B are negatively correlated. This has to a great extent contributed in reducing the risk of the portfolio.

The question that is automatically triggered at this point is, what is the impact of a positive correlation between the two securities, on the risk of the portfolio? To know the answer we consider two correlation coefficients: +0.30 and +1.0.

When correlation coefficient is +0.30

The standard deviation of the portfolio is,

$$\sigma^2_P = \sigma^2_A W^2_A + \sigma^2_B W^2_B + 2W_A W_B \sigma_A \sigma_B Cor_{AB}$$
$$= (6979.12 \times 0.25) + (1957.20 \times 0.25) + [2 \times 0.5 \times 0.5 \times 83.54 \times 44.24 \times (+0.30)]$$
$$= 2788.46$$

$\sigma_P = 0.5280 = 52.80\%$

The portfolio risk (52.80%), even with a hypothetical positive correlation, is lower than the weighted average standard deviation of individual securities (63.89%).

When correlation coefficient is +1

The standard deviation of the portfolio is,

$$\sigma^2_P = \sigma^2_A W^2_A + \sigma^2_B W^2_B + 2W_A W_B \sigma_A \sigma_B Cor_{AB}$$
$$= (6979.12 \times 0.25) + (1957.20 \times 0.25) + [2 \times 0.5 \times 0.5 \times 83.54 \times 44.24 \times (+1.0)]$$
$$= 21.94 + 25.04 + 46.8$$
$$= 4082.02$$

$\sigma_P = 0.6389 = 63.89\%$

This is the same as the weighted average standard deviation of the individual securities! From this result the following conclusions are drawn:

Introduction to Portfolio Theory

- The standard deviation of a portfolio is equal to the weighted average standard deviation of the assets *only* when the correlation coefficient is +1.
- This further implies that when the securities are in perfect positive correlation (+1) there is no reduction of risk of the portfolio.
- Thus with perfect positive correlation of securities advantages of diversification are non-existent.
- Diversification of a portfolio reduces the risk of the portfolio *only* when the securities show a very low positive correlation or a negative correlation.

Yet at the same time, it is to be remembered that in reality perfectly negative correlation (−1) between the securities, is an impossibility. As the securities do have a tendency of moving together to some extent, and so risk cannot be eliminated completely.

> **Pause for thought:** Portfolio risk is a function of the proportion of, and correlation between, the individual securities, as well as of covariance. It is the weighted average of the standard deviation of the securities only when the correlation coefficient is +1. Otherwise, it is less than the weighted average.

5.3.2 Notion of Dominance

We have had a detailed discussion on the parameters: risk and return, for both, individual securities and a bunch of them, that is, portfolios. Furthermore, discussion on the concepts of covariance and correlation aids in the understanding of the risk of a portfolio and how it differs from that of the individual securities. Armed with these theories we are in a position to apply the same and hence should be able to construct a portfolio accordingly.

But then there are practical difficulties. It is not possible for one to track and examine the movement of all stocks. At the same time it is imperative to know which stocks can be included, and which cannot be, in the portfolio. Before we can assess such stocks it is essential that we consider the concept of dominance.

For the purpose, a hypothetical example is used. Thus, an investment in A Ltd. is said to dominate that in B Ltd., when no rational investor opts for B Ltd. if investment in A Ltd. is possible. In such a case, stock of B Ltd. is termed an inefficient stock, hence a dominated stock, compared to that of A Ltd.

But then what are the conditions which cause one stock to dominate over the other(s)? Well these are enumerated as the rules of dominance, below.

Rules of dominance

Rule 1: Stock A dominates stock B when stock A gives the higher return for the same risk.

Rule 2: In terms of risk, stock A dominates B when A carries a lower risk for the same return.

> **Pause for thought:** Portfolios are constructed with dominant stocks: those with higher return for the same level of risk or those with lower risk, amongst the securities with the same return.

5.3.3 Coefficient of Variation (CV)

Selecting the assets, while constructing an optimum portfolio, on the basis of solely their risk-return parameters, is not always easy. At times these values are found to overlap in a way to complicate the selection procedure. Thus, when there are two securities: one with higher return for a higher risk, and another with a lower return for a lower risk, one doesn't always choose the asset with the higher risk-return values. Standard deviation is a measure of how widely dispersed the possible outcomes are from the expected values. Yet, one cannot compare the standard deviation of cash flows of different projects if they have different expected values.

Coefficient of variation (CV) is the parameter which helps in the comparative assessment of assets in such instances. It is a statistical measure of the dispersion of data points in a data series around the mean. It is calculated as follows:

$$\text{Coefficient of variation} = \frac{\text{Standard deviation}}{\text{Expected return}}$$

The coefficient of variation represents the ratio of the standard deviation to the mean, and it is a useful statistic for comparing the degree of variation from one data series to another, even if the means are drastically different from each other.

The coefficient of variation allows one to determine how much volatility (risk) one is assuming in comparison to the amount of return one can expect from the investment. In other words, the lower the ratio of standard deviation to mean return, the better is the risk-return trade-off. It is to be noted that if the expected return in the denominator of the calculation is negative or zero, the ratio, that CV is, will not make any sense.

Hence, according to CV, one with lower CV should be preferred as it carries a lower risk for unit return. It thus translates the standard deviation of different probability distributions, so that they can be compared. It can be expressed as:

$$CV = \frac{\sigma}{R} \times 100 \qquad (11)$$

where,

σ = standard deviation.

R = mean of return.

The Table 5.4 below shows the return, variance and standard deviation of Sun Pharma and HDFC Bank. From these data their CV is calculated.

Table 5.4: Coefficient of Variation

	Sun Pharma	HDFC Bank
Return	15.19	25.06
Variance	430.08	1512.17
Standard deviation	20.74	38.89

The coefficient of variation of Sun Pharma = $\dfrac{\text{Standard deviation of Sun Pharma}}{\text{Return of Sun Pharma}}$

$$= \dfrac{20.74}{15.19}$$

$$= 1.365$$

Similarly, CV of HDFC Bank = $\dfrac{38.89}{25.06}$

$$= 1.551$$

Thus, in terms of volatility (and hence, risk) Sun Pharma is a better choice than HDFC Bank. The higher is the CV the greater will be the dispersion in the variable; and lower is the CV, better is the risk-return trade-off.

Note of caution

Since additional return for an additional risk is a matter of personal preference, CV should not be followed blindly. Many times CV is also represented by multiplying with 100. When the expected return in the denominator is zero or negative, it does not make any sense. According to the experts it is interesting to use CV and r^2 together. Both, CV and r^2, are unit-less measures and are indicative of model fit. However, both define model fits in different ways. r^2 measures the variability, explained by the market for a given security; while CV measures the relative closeness of the predictions to the actual values.

As it is unit-less it allows comparison of coefficient of variation. This is not possible in case of standard deviation and return. The standard deviation of two variables—while both measure dispersion in their respective variables—cannot be compared to each other in a meaningful way to determine which variable has greater dispersion, because they may vary greatly in their units and the return about which they occur.

To use an analogy, for an earning of additional Rs.10,00,000 one may be willing to jump from the tenth floor of a multi-storied building, whereas another person might do that just for Rs.1,00,000.

> **Pause for thought:** CV is the ratio of the standard deviation to the mean and enables the comparison of the degree of variation from one data series to another, even if means are drastically different from each other.

5.3.4 Calculation of Portfolio Risk by Assigning Probabilities

After CV, we bring in the probability factor, to make the calculation of portfolio risk further comprehensive. For the purpose we assume that the security analyst has estimated the return of two scrips: BPCL and ABB Ltd., for the coming year, depending upon their macroeconomic factors and other estimation[2]. Security analysts assign equal probabilities to all possible outcomes. I to V (see Table 5.5) indicate different stages of the economy.

---

[2] In fact, it is the actual return provided by two scrips, BPCL and ABB, for the period 2006 to 2010. To understand the calculation of portfolio return and risk with assigning probabilities, the above return of two scrips has been taken, as a result of the estimation.

Table 5.5: Portfolio Risk by Assigning Probabilities

Economic stage	Probability	Return (%)			
		BPCL (petroleum)	ABB Ltd (power)	BPCL: Return × P	ABB Ltd.: Return × P
I	0.2	–22.31	93.29	–4.46	18.66
II	0.2	54.90	–59.36	10.98	–11.87
III	0.2	–28.18	–69.99	–5.64	–14.00
IV	0.2	68.98	69.04	13.80	13.81
V	0.2	3.60	3.75	0.72	0.75
				15.40	7.35

The expected rate of return of BPCL is,

$E(R_{BPCL}) = [0.2 \times (-22.31)] + (0.2 \times 54.90) + [0.2 \times (-28.18)] + (0.2 \times 68.98) + (0.2 \times 3.60)$
$= 15.40\%$

Table 5.6: Estimated Risk of the Portfolio with Assigned Probabilities

P	BPCL (%)			ABB (%)			$[(R_t - R_{BPCL}) \times (R_t - R_{ABB})] \times P$
	Return	$(R_t - R)$	$(R_t - R)^2 \times P$	Return	$(R_t - R)$	$(R_t - R)^2 \times P$	
1	2	3	4	5	6	7	8
0.2	–4.46	–19.86	78.89	18.66	11.31	25.59	–44.93
0.2	10.98	–4.42	3.90	–11.87	–19.22	73.85	16.98
0.2	–5.64	–21.03	88.48	–14.00	–21.34	91.11	89.79
0.2	13.80	–1.60	0.51	13.81	6.46	8.35	–2.07
0.2	0.72	–14.68	43.10	0.75	–6.60	8.70	19.36
	E(R) = 15.40		Var = 214.89 σ = 14.66	E(R) = 7.35		Var = 207.61 σ = 14.41	Cov = 79.12

The variance of the scrip of BPCL is,

$\sigma^2_{BPCL} = [0.2 \times (-22.31 - 15.4)^2] + [0.2 \times (54.90 - 15.4)^2] + [0.2 \times (-28.18 - 15.4)^2]$
$\qquad + [0.2 \times (68.98 - 15.4)^2] + [0.2 \times (3.60 - 15.4)^2]$
$= 214.89$

Standard deviation is,

$\sigma_{BPCL} = \sqrt{214.89}$
$= 0.1466 = 14.66\%$

In a similar manner, for ABB Ltd. the expected rate of return and standard deviation turns out to be:

$$E(R_{ABB}) = 7.35\%$$
$$\sigma_{ABB} = \sqrt{207.61}$$
$$= 0.1441 = 14.41\%$$

Thus, the expected return of both the securities is 15.40% and 7.35% respectively. If a portfolio is constructed with equal proportion of the two, the portfolio return would be:

$$E(R_P) = [W \times E(R_{BPCL})] + [(1 - W) \times E(R_{ABB})]$$
$$E(R_P) = (0.5 \times 15.40\%) + (0.5 \times 7.35\%)$$
$$= 11.37\%$$

Next we calculate the covariance of such a portfolio, vide Equation (4), as the probabilities have been assigned.

$$Cov_{AB} = \sum_{i=1}^{n} \Sigma [R_A - E(R_A)][R_B - E(R_B)] \times P_i$$

where,

Cov_{AB} = covariance of returns on securities A and B.
R_A = return on security A.
R_B = return on security B.
$E(R_A)$ = expected return of A.
$E(R_B)$ = expected return of B.
P_i = probability of occurrence of different stages of the economy.

The last column (column 8) in the Table 5.6 is the product of columns 1, 3 and 6. The summation of all values of column 8 gives the value of covariance. Thus, covariance of the portfolio under consideration is,

$$Cov_{(BPCL, ABB)} = (-)44.93 + 16.98 + 89.79 + (-)2.07 + 19.36$$
$$= 79.12$$

Based on the probability distribution, correlation coefficient can be ascertained, vide Equation (7) as:

$$Cor_{AB} = \frac{\Sigma[R_A - E(R_A)][R_B - E(R_B)] \times P_i}{\sigma_A \sigma_B}$$

$$Cor_{(BPCL, ABB)} = \frac{79.12}{14.66\% \times 14.41\%}$$

$$= 0.374$$

The risk of the portfolio comprising two securities, BPCL and ABB, is,

$$\sigma^2_P = \sigma^2_A W^2_A + \sigma^2_B W^2_B + 2W_A W_B Covar_{AB}$$
$$= \sigma^2_A W^2_A + \sigma^2_B W^2_B + 2W_A W_B \sigma_A \sigma_B Cor_{AB}$$

$$= (0.25 \times 214.89) + (0.25 \times 207.61) + (2 \times 0.5 \times 0.5 \times 14.66 \times 14.41 \times 0.374)$$
$$= 145.19$$
$$\sigma_p = \sqrt{145.19}$$
$$= 12.04\%$$

> **Pause for thought:** The risk of the portfolio, of BPCL and ABB, when probabilities are assigned, are found to be lower than the risk of individual securities and thus the portfolio can be considered to have benefited from the diversification.

5.4 PORTFOLIO RISK-RETURN ANALYSIS: TWO ASSETS CASE

Till now, the constructions of portfolios have been basically based on naïve diversification of securities. By naïve diversification is meant a rough and, more or less, instinctive common sense division of a portfolio, without bothering with sophisticated mathematical models. At worst, say some pundits, this approach can make portfolios very risky. Then again, some recent research indicates that this kind of informed, but informally logical division is just as effective as those fancy, optimizing models.

So now, we aim towards creating efficient portfolios utilizing some definite mathematical models. In this endeavor a portfolio of risky securities, but with lowest possible risk at the given level of expected return, is being constructed, with stocks of Tata Coffee and ACC.

But prior to that, we recall the fact that portfolio return depends on the proportion of wealth invested in two assets. *While portfolio risk depends on both correlation and proportion of assets constructing the portfolio, portfolio return is never ever affected by the correlation between the return of the two assets.*

We know that correlation coefficient always varies between +1.0 and −1.0. When the correlation coefficient is +1.0, returns of two securities always vary together in the same direction. Benefits of diversification are not realized as portfolio risk becomes equivalent to the weighted average risk of the securities. When correlation coefficient is −1.0, returns of two securities move in the opposite direction, and risk can be eliminated completely. Though yes, perfectly negative correlation is impossible in reality. But a negative correlation, and a small positive correlation, brings about the reduction in risk of the portfolio than the weighted average risk.

As has been mentioned at the beginning of the section, we analyze the risk-return parameters of a portfolio composed of the two securities, Tata Coffee and ACC.

Introduction to Portfolio Theory

Table 5.7: Return on the Scrip of Tata Coffee

Year	Opening price	Closing price	Return (x)	x – x'	(x – x')²
2001	114	56	–50.88	–84.69	7171.66
2002	56.8	68.65	20.86	–12.95	167.59
2003	67.4	148.5	120.33	86.52	7485.36
2004	150.5	260.1	72.82	39.02	1522.21
2005	264.7	331.2	25.12	–8.69	75.44
2006	335.9	300.65	–10.49	–44.30	1962.72
2007	304.9	311.6	2.20	–31.61	999.26
2008	312	154.4	–50.51	–84.32	7110.07
2009	158.5	397.5	150.79	116.98	13684.37
2010	404.9	501.95	23.97	–9.84	96.82
2011	510	855.2	67.69	33.88	1147.71
		Average return	33.80%		
					σ^2 = 4142.32
					σ = 64.36%

Table 5.8: Return on the Scrip of ACC

Year	Opening price	Closing price	Return (x)	x – x'	(x – x')²
2001	160	151.80	–5.12	–30.96	958.33
2002	152	165.10	8.62	–17.21	296.31
2003	165.5	245.55	48.37	22.54	507.90
2004	245.9	338.70	37.74	11.91	141.78
2005	339.65	534.20	57.28	31.45	988.95
2006	538	1085.55	101.78	75.94	5767.36
2007	1099	1024.50	–6.78	–32.61	1063.47
2008	1035	477.90	–53.83	–79.66	6345.41
2009	479.95	871.50	81.58	55.75	3108.00
2010	870	1075.60	23.63	–2.20	4.84
2011	1076	977.95	–9.11	–34.94	1221.11
		Average return	25.83%		σ^2 = 2040.34
					σ = 45.17%

Thus, these two securities, Tata Coffee and ACC, have the following characteristics:

Table 5.9: Summary Statistics of ACC and Tata Coffee

	ACC	Tata Coffee
Average return (%)	25.83%	33.80%
σ^2	2040.34	4142.32
σ (%)	45.17%	64.36%

To access the efficient portfolio and its mean-variance criterion, seven possible correlations are assumed between the returns of ACC and Tata Coffee. It is evident from the above table that the stock of Tata Coffee has a higher risk-return profile than that of ACC. If we invest 100% of fund in security Tata Coffee, return is 33.80% and its risk is 64.36%. On the other hand, if we invest the entire fund in ACC, a significantly lower risk-return profile (45.17% and 25.83%) is obtained.

Table 5.10: Portfolio Risk Assuming Different Correlation Coefficients

ACC	Tata Coffee	Return	Portfolio risk — Portfolio standard deviation for given correlation						
	Proportion		–1	1	0	–0.5	0.5	–0.25	0.25
1	0	25.83	45.17	45.17	45.17	45.17	45.17	45.17	45.17
0.9	0.1	26.63	34.22	47.09	41.16	37.85	44.22	39.54	42.72
0.8	0.2	27.43	23.26	49.01	38.36	31.72	44.01	35.20	41.28
0.7	0.3	28.22	12.31	50.93	37.05	27.61	44.53	32.67	40.96
0.6	0.4	29.02	1.36	52.85	37.38	26.45	45.77	32.38	41.79
0.5	0.5	29.82	9.60	54.77	39.31	28.62	47.67	34.38	43.69
0.4	0.6	30.62	20.55	56.68	42.63	33.47	50.15	38.33	46.55
0.3	0.7	31.42	31.50	58.60	47.05	40.04	53.14	43.68	50.19
0.2	0.8	32.21	42.45	60.52	52.28	47.62	56.55	50.00	54.45
0.1	0.9	33.01	53.41	62.44	58.10	55.80	60.31	56.96	59.22
0	1	33.81	64.36	64.36	64.36	64.36	64.36	64.36	64.36
0.6699	0.3301	**28.47**	9.01	51.51	**36.97**	26.91	44.83	32.34	41.09
0.8208	0.1791	27.26	25.55	48.60	38.83	32.86	43.99	35.97	41.49
0.5876	0.4123	29.12	**0.01**						

Thus, under the circumstances when different proportions (columns 1 and 2) of the securities are assumed to form the portfolio, with seven different correlations between them their risk and return are found to move in a very surprising manner. We would use Equation (1) to calculate return and Equation (9) to calculate portfolio risk, by taking different correlation values in the range of ±1.0. We can use Equation (10) to calculate minimum variance portfolio. Under different scenarios of correlation, Equation (9) can be simplified.

> **Pause for thought:** The return of a portfolio is independent of the correlation between securities, while the risk is not. Risk of a portfolio is lowered under negative correlation or a slightly positive correlation.

5.5 MINIMUM VARIANCE PORTFOLIO

Minimum variance portfolio is comprised of stocks with the lowest volatilities. Hence it is least sensitive to risk. This portfolio makes use of diversification to achieve the resultant risk level, which is lower than the individual risk level of the each of the stocks it contains. And we already know the part played by the correlation, between the return of securities, in determining the risk of the portfolio.

So in this section we shall discuss, in detail, how the different types of correlation are utilized in the construction of the minimum variance portfolio.

5.5.1 Perfect Negative Correlation

We begin our discussion with perfect negative correlation, of –1, given that negative correlation reduces the risk of the portfolio. It is almost impossible to find two securities with perfectly negative correlation of –1.0. Rarely is such a situation created, with securities in perfect negative correlation brought together. Columns 3 and 4, in Table 5.10, show the consequences of risk and return of the portfolio of two securities (here, Tata Coffee and ACC), when they have perfect negative correlation of –1. From the values in columns 3 and 4 it is apparent when proportion of the comparatively risky security, Tata Coffee, increases from 0 to 1, return increases,

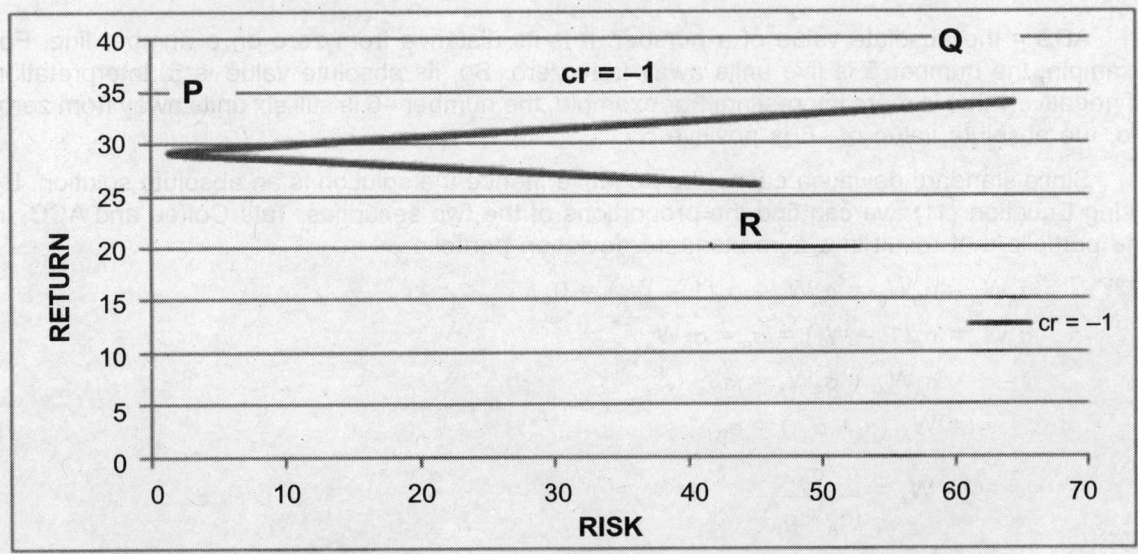

Figure 5.1: Risk-return ratio, when correlation = –1.0

and portfolio risk decreases till a certain level (in this case, till the proportion of Tata Coffee and ACC are 40 and 60% respectively). After this point, the risk starts rising. When 10% of the fund is invested in Tata Coffee and 90% in ACC, the standard deviation of the portfolio is 34.21%. It is to be remembered that the portfolio risk is lower than that of the individual security even if we invest 100% of the fund in ACC—a low risk security—whose risk is 45.17%. When Tata Coffee and ACC are present in the proportion of 40% and 60% respectively, return and risk of the portfolio are 29.02% and 1.356% respectively. This can be shown by extremely skewed line on left hand side in Figure 5.1.

In the above figure, point R represents risk-return of ACC while point Q indicates that of Tata Coffee. Point P indicates the point where risk is almost zero, by investing 60% and 40% in ACC and Tata Coffee respectively. From the above figure it can be concluded that it is always better to invest anywhere on line PQ, rather than on PR, as all the portfolios (or different combinations, by weight, of Tata Coffee and ACC) on line PQ dominates those on line PR. The reason behind this is the fact that for majority of the combinations of Tata Coffee and ACC, return is more for the same level of risk on the line PQ—compared to that on the line PR. Thus, portfolio on line PQ dominates that of PR.

The calculation for the minimum variance portfolio, when correlation is -1.0, is carried out as follows.

When correlation is -1.0,

$$\sigma^2_P = \sigma^2_A W^2_A + \sigma^2_B W^2_B + 2W_A W_B \sigma_A \sigma_B Cor_{AB}$$

Since correlation is -1, the above equation becomes.

$$\sigma^2_P = \sqrt{\sigma^2_A W^2_A + \sigma^2_B W^2_B - 2W_A W_B \sigma_A \sigma_B}$$

Or, $\sigma_P = \sqrt{\sigma^2_A W^2_A + \sigma^2_B W^2_B - 2W_A W_B \sigma_A \sigma_B}$ \hfill (12)

$$= ABS[\sigma_A W_A - \sigma_B W_B]$$

where,

ABS = the absolute value of a number. It is its distance from zero on a number line. For example, the number 5 is five units away from zero. So, its absolute value is 5. Interpretation of negative value is more interesting. For example, the number -6 is still six units away from zero. So, the absolute value of -6 is positive 6.

Since standard deviation cannot be negative, hence the solution is an absolute solution. By using Equation (11), we can find the proportions of the two securities, Tata Coffee and ACC, in the portfolio that result in a zero-standard deviation portfolio.

$$\sigma_A W_A - \sigma_B W_B = \sigma_A W_A - \sigma_B(1 - W_A) = 0$$
$$\sigma_A W_A = \sigma_B(1 - W_A) = \sigma_B - \sigma_B W_A$$
$$= \sigma_A W_A + \sigma_B W_A = \sigma_B$$
$$= W_A (\sigma_A + \sigma_B) = \sigma_B$$
$$= W_A = \frac{\sigma_B}{(\sigma_A + \sigma_B)}$$

Thus for above mentioned case of Tata Coffee and ACC, their proportion—in a minimum variance portfolio, when their correlation is –1, should be:

$$W_{\text{Tata Coffee}} = \frac{45.17}{45.17 + 64.36}$$

$$= \frac{45.17}{09.53}$$

$$= 0.4123$$

And the weight of ACC would be, $W_{ACC} = 1 - 0.4123 = 0.5876$

Hence, to have a zero standard deviation portfolio, i.e., minimum variance portfolio, 41.23% of the fund should be invested in Tata Coffee and the remaining 58.76% in ACC. This utilizes the maximum benefit of diversification when returns of the two securities have perfectly negative correlation. When we look at the last row and fourth column of Table 5.10, we find an almost negligible risk of 0.01%, with the proportion of ACC and Tata Coffee being 58.76% and 41.23% respectively.

From the above discussion the following conclusions can be drawn:

— When perfect negative correlation is present between the securities of a portfolio, there is an increase in the return, and decrease in the risk, when the proportion of the risky asset increases, but only till a certain level.
— After that the risk starts increasing.
— This point, till which the risk decreases and thus is the minimum possible for the portfolio, gives us the proportion of the assets required to form the minimum variance portfolio, with correlation coefficient at –1.
— This proportion of risky asset to less risky asset, in this case for Tata Coffee (the risky asset) and ACC, is 40 : 60.

Pause for thought: Minimum variance portfolio is the one with minimum risk, utilizing the benefits of diversification to the maximum.

5.5.2 Perfect Positive Correlation

As is finding a perfectly negative correlation a rarity, same is with finding two securities having a perfectly positive correlation with each other. Columns 3 and 5, in table 5.10, show that with an increase in the proportion of Tata Coffee (a security with high risk-return profile) and decrease in that of ACC (a security with low risk-return profile), the return and risk, both, of the portfolio increases. The Figure 5.2 depicts the risk-return combination of these securities when correlation coefficient is +1.0.

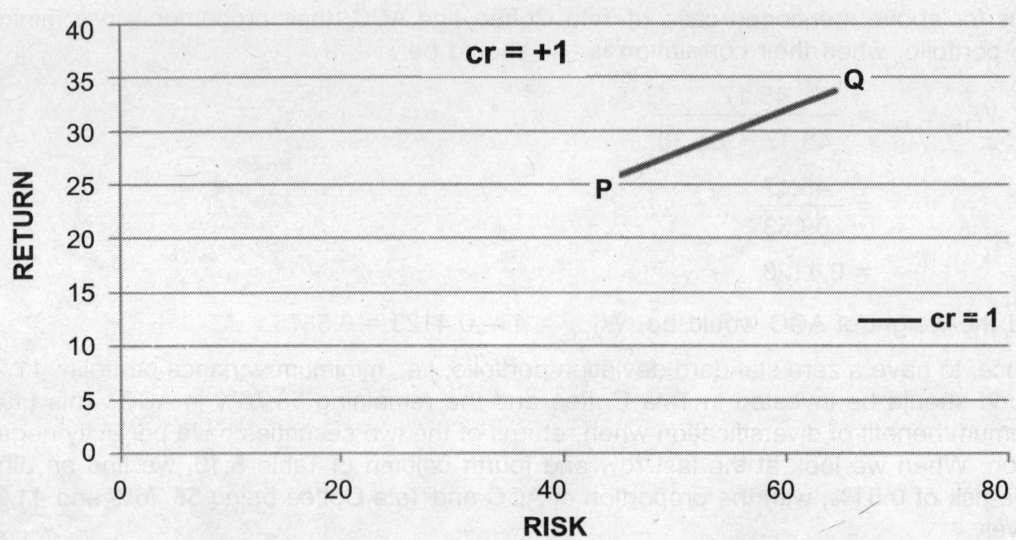

Figure 5.2: Risk-return ratio, when correlation= +1.0

In the above figure point P indicates investment in ACC and Q shows that in Tata Coffee. From Figure 5.2, we can see that return and risk of the portfolio exhibit linear relationship. Thus, higher is the return, higher the risk and vice versa. The selection of the portfolio depends upon the risk preference of the investor. An extremely risk-averse investor may choose to invest the entire fund in ACC; while a risk-lover might opt to invest fully in the stock of Tata Coffee only.

We calculate the portfolio risk using Equation (9):

$$\sigma^2_P = \sigma^2_A W^2_A + \sigma^2_B W^2_B + 2 W_A W_B \sigma_A \sigma_B Cor_{AB}$$

Since in this case correlation is +1.0, the above equation can be rewritten as,

$$\sigma^2_P = \sigma^2_A W^2_A + \sigma^2_B W^2_B + 2 W_A W_B \sigma_A \sigma_B$$

Or, $\sigma^2_P = (\sigma_A W_A + \sigma_B W_B)^2$ $\qquad [\because (a+b)^2 = a^2 + b^2 + 2ab]$

$\therefore \quad \sigma_P = \sigma_A W_A + \sigma_B W_B$

Thus these calculations lead to the conclusions, which corroborate our earlier learning of situation that arises out of a +1 correlation coefficient. They are as follows:

— When the securities shows perfect positive correlation the standard deviation of the returns of the portfolio is the weighted average of the standard deviation of individual securities.
— In other words, portfolio risk is equal to the weighted average risk of the individual securities.
— It further implies that benefits of diversification are not experienced at all, with zero reduction in risk of the portfolio, as compared to the individual risks of the securities.

Pause for thought: With a perfectly positive correlation between the securities the risk and return of the portfolio shows a linear relationship, with all advantages of diversification lost.

5.5.3 Zero Correlation

When returns of two securities are completely independent of each other, they do not correlate at all. This is a state of zero correlation between the return of the two securities. We have seen how negative and positive correlations, and perfect ones at that, affect the diversification of the portfolio. And this case of zero correlation would be all the more interesting as securities are together, yet not impacting one another. So how can they impact the diversification of the portfolio? In other words, what is the risk-status of the portfolio?

From columns 3 and 6 in Table 5.10, the return of the two securities is observed to increase, as the proportion of Tata Coffee increases and that of ACC decreases. On the other hand, portfolio risk decreases initially, but only up to a certain point, after which it starts rising. In fact the same trend was observed with a perfectly negative correlation. Though yes, the proportion of the securities at which the portfolio behaves as a minimum-variance portfolio, with its risk being minimum at 37.05%, varies. In this case, the minimum variance is observed when the proportions invested in ACC and Tata Coffee is 70% and 30%, respectively.

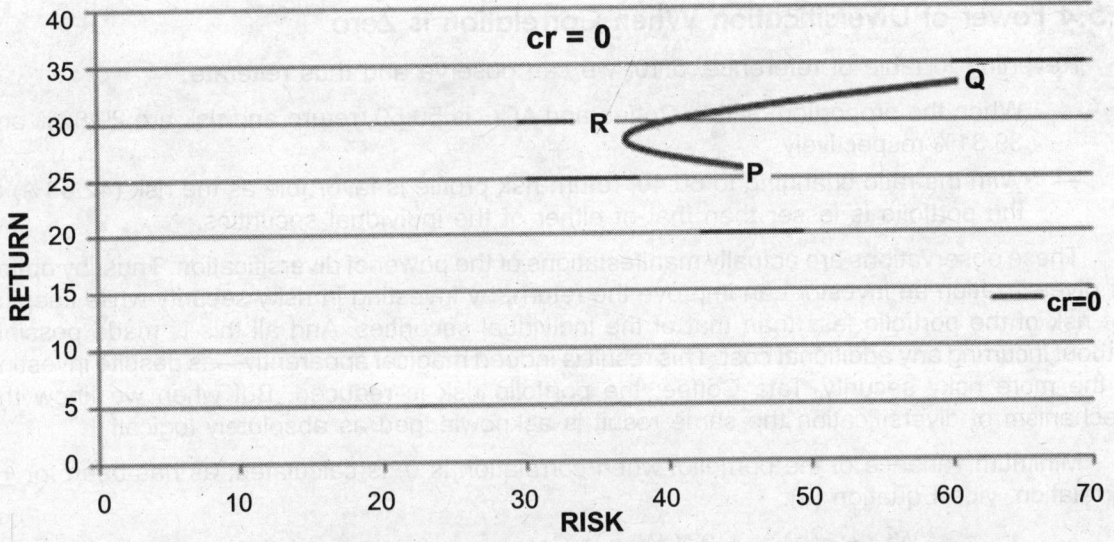

Figure 5.3: Risk-return ratio, when correlation = 0

From Figure 5.3, we can see that point P on the curve PQ represents a portfolio entirely consisting of ACC (where return is 25.83% and risk is 45.17%), while point Q represents the portfolio consisting of only Tata Coffee (return: 33.80% and risk: 64.36%). Unlike the case of perfectly negative (−1.0) correlations, in this case no combination of the two securities are observed which can result in zero standard deviation. So there is no possibility of constructing risk-less portfolio. Point R, on the downward sloping part of curve PQ, represents the minimum variance portfolio and it dominates any portfolio on PQ. While moving from R to Q, the different combinations of two securities have higher return as well as high risk.

From the figure it is thus concluded:

— When there is zero correlation between securities, with an increase in the proportion of risky security, return increases but the risk decreases initially.

- After the risk has reduced to a certain level, touched its minimum under the given condition, it begins to rise.
- This point of minimum risk corresponds to specific proportion of the securities invested in the portfolio.
- Thus at this stage the portfolio behaves as the minimum variance portfolio.
- The pattern followed—initial reduction of the risk, till a level, followed by a rise in it—is similar to that shown with −1 correlation. But the weights of the assets involved at this minimum risk, differs for the two cases. Also differs, the magnitude of the minimum risk when correlation is −1 from that when correlation is 0.
- With zero correlation, minimum variance is attained with quite high proportion of investment in the less risky asset, compared to that in risky asset.

Pause for thought: Zero correlation between securities is complete independence of the securities from one another, in a portfolio. The risk-return relationship is non-linear.

5.5.4 Power of Diversification When Correlation is Zero

Reverting to table of reference, 5.10, we can observe and thus reiterate:

- When the proportion of Tata Coffee and ACC is 50:50, return and risk are 29.82% and 39.31% respectively.
- With the ratio changing to 60:40, return-risk profile is favorable as the risk (42.63%) of the portfolio is lesser than that of either of the individual securities.

These observations are actually manifestations of the power of diversification. Thus, by opting for diversification an investor can improve the return, by investing in risky security while keeping the risk of the portfolio less than that of the individual securities. And all this is made possible without incurring any additional cost. This result is indeed magical apparently—as despite investing in the more risky security, Tata Coffee, the portfolio risk is reduced. But when we know the mechanism of diversification the same result is acknowledged as absolutely logical!

Minimum variance of the portfolio, when correlation is 0, is calculated, as has been for ±1 correlation, vide Equation (9):

$$\sigma^2_P = \sigma^2_A W^2_A + \sigma^2_B W^2_B + 2W_A W_B \sigma_A \sigma_B Cor_{AB}$$

Here as correlation is 0, the above equation becomes

$$\sigma_P = \sqrt{\sigma^2_A W^2_A + \sigma^2_B W^2_B}$$

Equation (10),

$$W^* = \frac{\sigma^2_B - Cov_{AB}}{\sigma^2_A + \sigma^2_B - 2Cov_{AB}}$$

for the calculation of the optimum weights of the minimum variance portfolio can be utilized here. We already know that,

$$Cov_{AB} = Cor_{AB} \sigma_A \sigma_B$$

With correlation being 0, Equation (10), for minimum variance, simplifies to,

$$W_A = \frac{\sigma_B^2}{\sigma_A^2 + \sigma_B^2}$$

∴ For Tata Coffee, from the data in Table 5.10, the optimum weight for the minimum variance of the portfolio of Tata Coffee and ACC, is

$$W_{Tata\ Coffee} = \frac{(64.3608)^2}{(45.1701)^2 + (64.3608)^2}$$

$$= \frac{4142.3125}{4142.3125 + 2040.33}$$

$$= 0.6699 \simeq 0.67$$

∴ $W_{ACC} = 1 - 0.6699$

$$= 0.3301 \simeq 0.33$$

Thus by investing 66.99%, i.e., almost 67%, in ACC and the remaining 33.01%, in Tata Coffee, we can construct a minimum variance portfolio. The risk is 36.97%—the minimum possible for the portfolio—and the return at this risk is, 28.47%. This is the risk-return profile for the minimum variance portfolio of Tata Coffee and ACC, when the correlation is zero.

However, it is not necessary that the minimum variance portfolio will be the same for all investors. It is fully decided by the risk preference of the investor concerned.

> **Pause for thought:** The power of diversification is very much visible with zero and negative correlation, while it is completely absent with perfectly positive correlation between securities.

We are now armed with understanding of minimum variance of portfolios, as the correlation changes from +1 to −1, through 0. We have found that advantages of diversification are lost with a +1 correlation. So, we now proceed to consider cases of minimum variance portfolio with positive correlations, but less than +1.

Positive correlations of +0.5 and +0.25

As discussed above, in reality, two securities whose correlation is exactly +1.0 are rarely found. But those with lesser values are easily accessible. And hence are selected, +0.5 and +0.25, as positive correlations and the minimum variance portfolios studied under these conditions. They are depicted in the following Figures: 5.4 and 5.5 respectively.

Figure 5.4 shows the various risk-return combinations of ACC and Tata Coffee when correlation is +0.5. The curve formed implies a possibility of diversification benefit. At zero correlation, point P in the graph represents 100% investment in ACC and at point Q, 100% investment in Tata Coffee. From Table 5.11, we can observe that till ACC and Tata Coffee are in the proportion of 80% and 20% respectively, risk decreases. Thereof, it rises. Column 5 in this table shows the computation of the risk-return ratio, with respect to the individual security

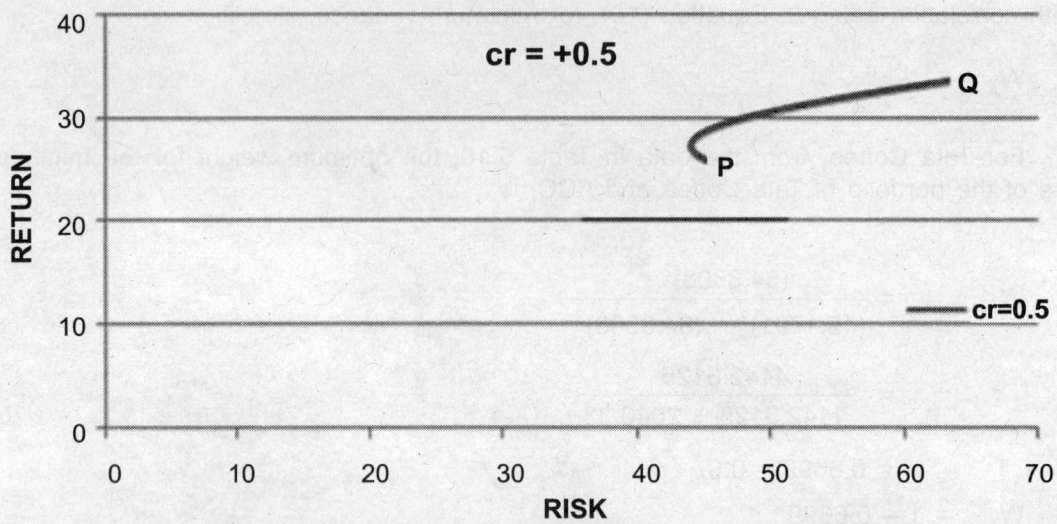

Figure 5.4: Risk-return, when correlation = +0.5

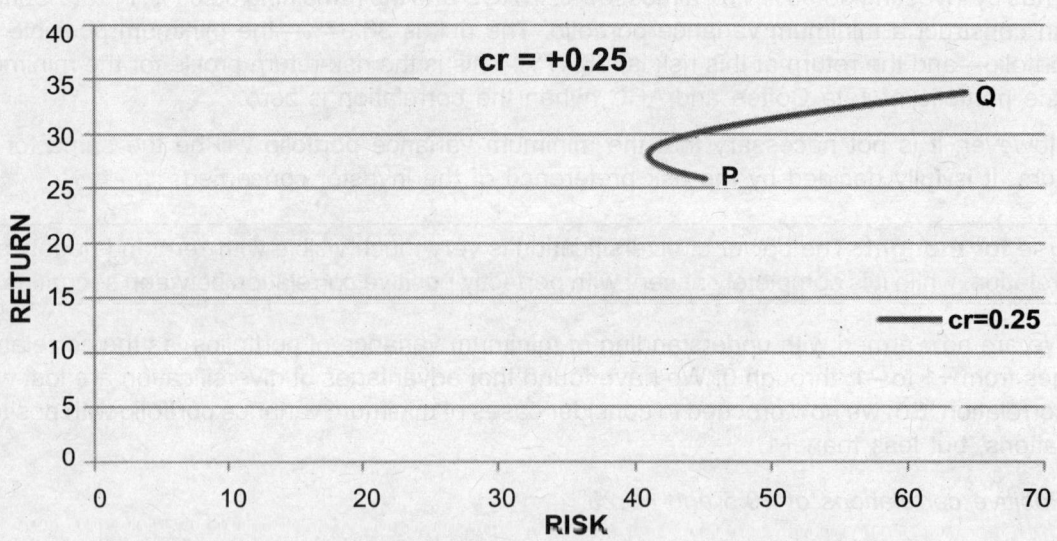

Figure 5.5: Risk-return, when correlation is +0.25

either: ACC or Tata Coffee. If 90% of the fund is invested in ACC and 10% in Tata Coffee, the expected return is 26.63% and risk, 44.22%. Comparing this return and risk with that of ACC, a gain is observed, with an increase of 3.09% [(26.63 − 25.83)/25.83] in return. At the same time, risk decreases by −2.10% [(44.22-45.17)/45.17)]. Thus the incremental return-risk ratio is −1.47 (3.09/−2.10). This can be interpreted as: for one unit of increase in return, the risk decreases by −1.47 times. In a similar way, incremental return-risk can be calculated for other weights of this portfolio. (The investment proportion of 50:50 in both the stocks is to be omitted, as has been discussed already).

Table 5.11: Summary Table of Portfolio Return and Risk When Correlation is +0.5

Proportions		Return	Portfolio risk at Cor = +0.5	Return ratio with respect to individual security	Risk ratio with respect to individual security	Incremental return-risk ratio
ACC	Tata Coffee					
1	0	25.83	45.17			
0.9	0.1	26.63	44.22	3.09	−2.10	−1.47
0.8	0.2	27.43	44.01	6.18	−2.57	−2.40
0.7	0.3	28.22	44.53	9.26	−1.41	−6.56
0.6	0.4	29.02	45.77	12.35	1.33	9.28
0.5	0.5	29.82	47.67			
0.4	0.6	30.62	50.15	10.42	28.33	0.37
0.3	0.7	31.42	53.14	7.62	21.12	0.36
0.2	0.8	32.21	56.55	4.95	13.81	0.36
0.1	0.9	33.01	60.31	2.42	6.72	0.36
0	1	33.81	64.36			

Thus when correlation is +0.5, return-risk ratio can improve through diversification.

Minimum variance portfolio: the optimum weights when correlation is +0.5

By computing the values in the following equation, we get:

$$W_{ACC} = \frac{\sigma_B^2 - \sigma_A \sigma_B Cor_{AB}}{\sigma_A^2 + \sigma_B^2 - 2\sigma_A \sigma_B Cor_{AB}}$$

$$= 0.8208$$

$$\therefore W_{Tata\ Coffee} = 1 - 0.8208 = 0.1792$$

So, at correlation of +0.5, for a minimum variance portfolio of ACC and Tata Coffee, the proportions of investments are, 0.8208 and 0.1792, respectively. These weights lead to return-risk profile of the portfolio as 27.26% and 43.99% respectively.

134 SECURITY ANALYSIS AND PORTFOLIO MANAGEMENT

> **Pause for thought:** Though +1 correlation doesn't lead to reduction in the risk of portfolio, a +0.5 value does reduce the risk, with advantages of diversification enjoyed thus.

We consider another case when an investor thinks of investing his entire fund in Tata Coffee. In this case, his expected return and risk would be 33.81% and 64.36% respectively. Following it, if the proportion of investment is changed to 40% and 60%, in ACC and Tata Coffee respectively, the expected return and risk change to 30.62% and 50.15% respectively. Thus compared to the exclusive investment in Tata Coffee the diversification has caused the return to decrease by 10.42%. But more significant is the reduction in risk by 28.33%, with incremental return-risk ratio as 0.37. From this observation it can be interpreted that while moving from too risky stock of Tata Coffee to portfolio with the weight of 40:60 in ACC and Tata Coffee, for one unit of fall in risk, return decreases just by 0.37 times. And this is quite appreciable.

> **Pause for thought:** More significant, than reduction in return and risk percentages, is the reduction in incremental risk of a portfolio, which is the reduction in risk for one unit fall in the return of the portfolio. The incremental risk gives a correct assessment of changes in risk, vis-à-vis return. As it reduces, it indicates that risk has not incremented, but reduced, for a decrease of one unit in return.

Table 5.12: Summary Table of Portfolio Return and Risk When Correlation is +0.25

Proportions		Return	Portfolio risk at Cor = +0.5	Return ratio with respect to individual security	Risk ratio with respect to individual security	Incremental return-risk ratio
ACC	Tata Coffee					
1	0	25.83	45.17			
0.9	0.1	26.63	42.72	3.10	−5.42	−0.57
0.8	0.2	27.43	41.28	6.19	−8.61	−0.72
0.7	0.3	28.22	40.96	9.25	−9.32	−0.99
0.6	0.4	29.02	41.79	12.35	−7.48	−1.65
0.5	0.5	29.82	43.69			
0.4	0.6	30.62	46.55	10.12	38.26	0.27
0.3	0.7	31.42	50.19	7.61	28.23	0.27
0.2	0.8	32.21	54.45	4.97	18.20	0.27
0.1	0.9	33.01	59.22	2.42	8.68	0.28
0	1	33.81	64.36			

Figure 5.5, above, shows the risk and return of various combinations of ACC and Tata Coffee, when correlation is +0.25. The curve formed in the above case implies a possibility of benefits from diversification slightly more than that when correlation was +0.5. Like the zero correlation case, point P in the above graph represents 100% investment in ACC stock and at point Q, 100%

investment in Tata Coffee. From the above Table 5.12, we can find that till the proportion of ACC and Tata Coffee is 70% and 30% respectively, risk decreases and thereof it rises. Column 5 in the above table shows the computation of the risk-return ratio with respect to the individual security—either ACC or Tata Coffee. It can be interpreted (in a similar way when cor = 0.5) that when 90% of the fund is invested in ACC and 10% in Tata Coffee, compared to 100% investment in ACC, return increases by 3.10% while risk falls by 5.42% and the incremental return-risk ratio is −0.57. It means for a one unit of increase in return, risk falls by 0.57 times. For a proportion of 60:40 in ACC and Tata Coffee respectively, for a one unit of rise in return, risk falls by 1.65 times. Comparing these return and risk, generated and involved, with respect to 100% investment in Tata Coffee, return-risk ratio remains almost constant, at 0.27. For example, by investing 40% in ACC and 60% in Tata Coffee, return decreases from 33.81% to 30.62% (10.42); and risk also decreases from 64.36% to 46.55% (38.26). A value of 0.27 indicates that for a one unit fall in risk, return decreases by 0.27 times only.

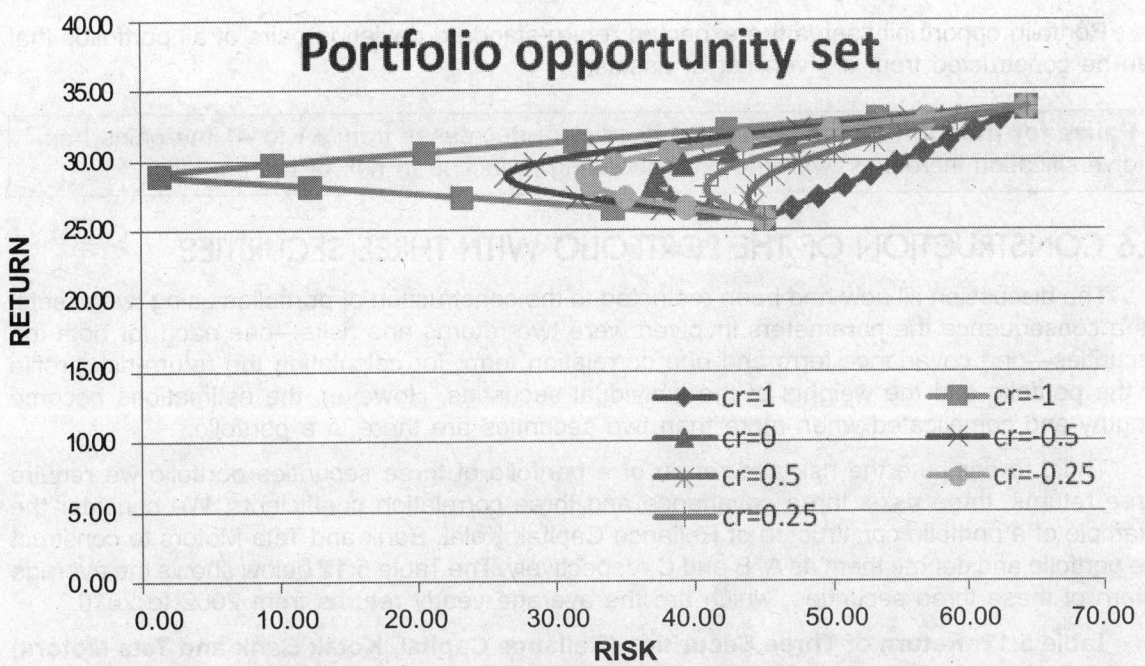

Figure 5.6: Efficient portfolio and Mean-variance criterion
(Investment Opportunity Set: Two Asset Case)

Table 5.10 and Figure 5.6 represent the portfolio opportunity set of two securities ACC and Tata Coffee. Portfolio opportunity set means the expected return and standard deviation of all pairs of assets that can be constructed from a given set of assets. Here, the portfolio opportunity set is constructed by taking six different correlations and different weight of the two securities, ACC and Tata Coffee. The given portfolio opportunity set allows the investor to choose the portfolio configuration that match his level of risk tolerance. It is also known as feasible set of portfolios. The outermost line on the extreme left hand side shows the portfolio opportunity set for correlation = −1. It is called a portfolio opportunity set as it represents all possible return-risk combinations of portfolio, constructed by two securities. The other inward curved lines, and lines on the right hand side, show the portfolio opportunity set for other values of the correlation coefficient. The straight line on the extreme right hand side represents the return-risk profile of the portfolio, when correlation coefficient is +1. It clearly indicates that there is no benefit of diversification when correlation coefficient is +1. The benefits of diversification increase when the correlation coefficient decreases from +1 and ultimately reaches −1. At correlation coefficient of −1, an investor gets perfect hedging opportunity and maximum reduction of risks. As we move from the right to the left hand side, we actually move towards north-west region increasingly. Portfolios to the north-east region provide higher rate of return but at the cost of higher risk. The trade-off among these various combinations of return and risk depends upon the investor's personal preferences. Investors with high degree of risk aversion move towards the south-west region of efficient set where return-risk is comparatively lower. We will discuss this issue with further elaboration in Chapter 20—Markowitz Portfolio Theory. From the above Figure 5.6 we can see that the investors have to choose their preferred combination of given assets, depending upon their risk-return trade-off with the correlation ranging within ±1.

Portfolio opportunity set is the expected return-standard deviation pairs of all portfolios that can be constructed from a given set of assets.

> **Pause for thought:** As the correlation coefficient decreases from +1 to −1 the gains from diversification increases, with the corresponding reduction in risk of the portfolio.

5.6 CONSTRUCTION OF THE PORTFOLIO WITH THREE SECURITIES

The discussion till now had been restricted to the construction of portfolios using two assets. As a consequence the parameters involved were two returns and risks—one each for both the securities—one covariance term and one correlation term, for calculating the return-risk profile of the portfolio and the weights of the individual securities. However, the estimations become lengthy and complicated when more than two securities are there in a portfolio.

Thus, to compute the risk and return of a portfolio of three securities portfolio we require three returns, three risks, three covariance and three correlation coefficients. We consider the example of a portfolio constructed of Reliance Capital, Kotak Bank and Tata Motors to construct the portfolio and denote them as A, B and C respectively. The Table 5.12 below shows the average return of these three securities, which are the average yearly returns from 2002 to 2010.

Table 5.12: Return of Three Securities (Reliance Capital, Kotak Bank and Tata Motors)

Year	Return (%)		
	A	B	C
2002	−23.41	97.53	48.81
2003	69.07	129.66	127.51
2004	44.78	15.76	50.06
2005	121.67	−3.92	21.91
2006	67.32	2.72	41.97
2007	220.71	176.81	1.40

Introduction to Portfolio Theory

2008	0.19	−2.71	−42.28
2009	−57.41	−34.28	1.60
2010	11.82	16.03	118.85
Average return	**50.53**	**44.18**	**41.09**

The average returns are observed to be 50.53%, 44.18% and 41.09% for Reliance Capital, Kotak Bank and Tata Motors respectively.

The calculation of risk of a portfolio, involves the covariance and correlation coefficient of two securities at a time. Hence the standard deviation—the measure of risk—is estimated by taking pairs of securities at a time. We begin with the pair of Reliance Capital and Kotak Bank and calculate their covariance, correlation coefficient and standard deviation.

Table 5.13: Covariance, Correlation and Standard Deviation of Reliance Capital (A) and Kotak Bank (B)

Year	A			B			Cov_{AB}
	Return (%)	$[R_t - E(R)]$	$[R_t - E(R)]^2$	Return (%)	$[R_t - E(R)]$	$[R_t - E(R)]^2$	$[R_t - E(R_{Reliance\ Capital})] \times [R_t - E(R_{Kotak\ Bank})]$
2002	−23.41	−73.94	5467.23	97.53	53.36	2846.84	−3945.16
2003	69.07	18.55	343.99	129.66	85.48	7306.79	1585.40
2004	44.78	−5.75	33.02	15.76	−28.42	807.58	163.30
2005	121.67	71.14	5061.55	−3.92	−48.10	2313.88	−3422.25
2006	67.32	16.80	282.07	2.72	−41.45	1718.51	−696.24
2007	220.71	170.18	28962.45	176.81	132.64	17592.58	22572.64
2008	0.19	−50.33	2533.45	−2.71	−46.89	2198.77	2360.18
2009	−57.41	−107.94	11650.61	−34.28	−78.46	6155.49	8468.48
2010	11.82	−38.71	1498.60	16.03	−28.15	792.36	1089.70
	50.53		55832.97	44.18		41732.81	28176.06
			8.00			8.00	8.00
			Var = 6979.12 σ = 83.54%			Var = 5216.60 σ = 72.23% $\sigma_A \times \sigma_B$ = 6033.84	Cov = 3522.01 Cor = $Cov_{AB}/\sigma_A \times \sigma_B$ = 3522.01/6033.84 = 0.584

Note: Covariance or correlation for security A to B or B to A is same. Hence if the correlation between Reliance Capital and Kotak Bank is 0.584, it implies the same for Kotak Bank and Reliance Capital. The order of reference doesn't matter.

From the above Table 5.13 the data obtained is:

Standard deviation$_{(Reliance\ Capital)}$ = 83.54%

Standard deviation$_{(Kotak\ Bank)}$ = 72.23%

Covariance of the two = 3522.01
Correlation between the two = 0.584

Next comes up the pair of Kotak Bank and Tata Motors, for similar calculations; and the same are recorded in the Table 5.14.

Table 5.14: Covariance, Correlation and Standard Deviation of Kotak Bank (B) and Tata Motors (C)

Year	B			C			Cov_{BC}
	Return (%)	$[R_t - E(R)]$	$[R_t - E(R)]^2$	Return (%)	$[R_t - E(R)]$	$[R_t - E(R)]^2$	$[R_t - E(R_{Kotak\ Bank})]$ × $[R_t - E(R_{Tata\ Motors})]$
2002	97.53	53.36	2846.84	48.81	7.72	59.57	411.82
2003	129.66	85.48	7306.79	127.51	86.42	7468.25	7387.08
2004	15.76	−28.42	807.58	50.06	8.97	80.40	−254.81
2005	−3.92	−48.10	2313.88	21.91	−19.19	368.08	922.87
2006	2.72	−41.45	1718.51	41.97	0.87	0.77	−36.27
2007	176.81	132.64	17592.58	1.40	−39.69	1575.45	−5264.61
2008	−2.71	−46.89	2198.77	−42.28	−83.37	6950.45	3909.28
2009	−34.28	−78.46	6155.49	1.60	−39.49	1559.60	3098.40
2010	16.03	−28.15	792.36	118.85	77.76	6046.54	−2188.85
	44.18		41732.81	41.09		24109.10	7984.91
			8.00			8.00	8.00
			Var = 5216.60 σ = 72.23%			Var = 3013.64 σ = 54.90% $\sigma_B \times \sigma_C$ = 72.23 × 54.90 = 3964.96	Cov = 998.11 Cor = $Cov_{BC}/\sigma_B \times \sigma_C$ = 998.11/3964.96 = 0.252

From the above calculation is obtained:

Standard deviation$_{(Kotak\ Bank)}$ = 72.23%
Standard deviation$_{(Tata\ Motors)}$ = 54.90%
Covariance of the two = 998.1
Correlation between the two − 0.252

The correlation coefficient between Kotak Bank and Tata Motors is less than that of Reliance Capital and Kotak Bank. Thus, the risk of the portfolio constructed with Kotak Bank and Tata Motors will be less than that of a portfolio of Reliance capital and Kotak Bank, as correlation and reduction in risk are inversely related. Correlation between the *return* on securities and *reduction in risk* show *inverse variation*. Greater is the positive correlation lesser is the reduction of risk. While greater is the negative correlation higher is the reduction in risk. That is why higher is the negative correlation lower is the risk, while higher is the positive correlation higher is the risk.

> *Check yourself*
> Calculate the risk of two portfolios: portfolio 1 comprising of Reliance Capital and Kotak Bank and portfolio 2, of Kotak Bank and Tata Motors. Compare the risk of the two portfolios and interpret the result obtained.

We are now left with the pair of securities, Tata Motors and Reliance Capital. Table 5.15 below represents the requisite calculations.

Table 5.15: Covariance, Correlation and Standard Deviation of Tata Motors (C) and Reliance Capital (A)

| Year | C | | | A | | | Cov_{CA} |
	Return (%)	$[R_t - E(R)]$	$[R_t - E(R)]^2$	Return (%)	$[R_t - E(R)]$	$[R_t - E(R)]^2$	$[R_t - E(R_{Tata\ Motors})]$ × $[R_t - E(R_{Reliance\ Capital})]$
2002	48.81	7.72	59.57	−23.41	−73.94	5467.23	−570.71
2003	127.51	86.42	7468.25	69.07	18.55	343.99	1602.82
2004	50.06	8.97	80.40	44.78	−5.75	33.02	−51.53
2005	21.91	−19.19	368.08	121.67	71.14	5061.55	−1364.94
2006	41.97	0.87	0.77	67.32	16.80	282.07	14.70
2007	1.40	−39.69	1575.45	220.71	170.18	28962.45	−6754.91
2008	−42.28	−83.37	6950.45	0.19	−50.33	2533.45	4196.26
2009	1.60	−39.49	1559.60	−57.41	−107.94	11650.61	4262.66
2010	118.85	77.76	6046.54	11.82	−38.71	1498.60	−3010.21
	41.09		24109.10	50.53		55832.97	−1675.86
			8.00			8.00	8.00
			Var = 3013.64 σ = 54.90%			Var = 6979.12 σ = 83.54% $\sigma_C \times \sigma_A$ = 54.90 × 83.54 = 4586.12	−209.48 Cor = $Cov_{CA}/\sigma_C \times \sigma_A$ = −209.48/4586.12 = −0.045

The above calculation leads us to the following results:

Standard deviation$_{(Tata\ Motors)}$ = 54.90%

Standard deviation$_{(Reliance\ Capital)}$ = 83.54%

Covariance of the two = −209.48

Correlation between the two = −0.045

We know that standard deviation cannot be negative. Furthermore, correlation coefficient is negative only when covariance is negative, which is the case between the two securities of Tata Motors and Reliance Capital. With the correlation coefficient negative, a portfolio formed of these two will have a lower risk than that constructed with securities having positive correlation. Thus, presence of these two securities in the portfolio is highly favorable.

> *Check yourself*
>
> Calculate the portfolio risk of the given securities: Tata Motors and Reliance Capital and compare this risk with those of the earlier two portfolios: 1 and 2.

Table 5.16: Summary Chart of Return, Risk (Standard Deviation) and Correlation of Securities A, B and C

	A Reliance Capital	B Kotak Bank	C Tata Motors
Return (%)	50.53	44.18	41.09
Variance	6979.12	5216.6	3013.64
Risk (%)	83.54	72.23	54.89
	AB	BC	CA
Covariance	3522.01	998.11	−209.48
Correlation coefficient	0.5837	0.2517	−0.0456

Note: When the number of stocks increases in a portfolio, the number of covariance and correlation terms increase notably. For example, for two stocks we need 3 terms (2 for variances and 1 for covariance/correlation. When number of securities are 3 in a portfolio, we need 9 terms [3 for variances and $3 \times (3-1) = 6$ for covariance]. Generalizing it, we can say that for the portfolio of n stocks we need n variances and $[n \times (n-1)]$ for covariance/correlation. Here for portfolio of three stocks, namely A, B and C we need three covariance/correlation AB, BC and CA. Similarly, when we have portfolio of four securities (A, B, C and D), what we need is four variances, and six covariance AB, BC, CA, CD, DA, BD.

Calculation of the parameters, for the portfolio of three securities

The calculations have been recorded in the Tables: 5.13, 5.14 and 5.15 and the results have been summarized in Table 5.16. Now we carry out the calculations explicitly. For that all three securities are assumed to be in equal proportion.

The expected return of the portfolio is the weighted average returns on each security and thus is calculated as:

$$E(R_P) = W_A \times E(R_A) + W_B \times E(R_B) + W_C \times E(R_C)$$
$$= (0.33 \times 50.53\%) + (0.33 \times 44.18\%) + (0.33 \times 41.09)$$
$$= 44.81\%$$

The standard deviation (measure of risk) of a portfolio, we already know, is not the weighted average of the standard deviation of the individual securities (only when correlation is +1, it is the weighted average). It depends on the covariance between the securities and thus on the correlation too, as covariance and correlation are related as $Cov_{xy} = Cor_{xy}\sigma_x\sigma_y$ (where x and y are two securities of a portfolio). In this case we calculate the standard deviation of the portfolio considering the values of correlation. Hence, the formula used is the one (equation 9) in terms of correlation, as follows:

$$\sigma^2_P = \sigma^2_A W^2_A + \sigma^2_B W^2_B + \sigma^2_C W^2_C + 2W_A W_B \sigma_A \sigma_B Cor_{AB}$$
$$+ 2W_B W_C \sigma_B \sigma_C Cor_{BC} + 2W_C W_A \sigma_C \sigma_A Cor_{CA}$$

$$= [6979.12 \times (0.33)^2] + [5216.6 \times (0.33)^2] + [3013.64 \times (0.33)^2]$$
$$+ [2 \times 0.33 \times 0.33 \times 83.54 \times 72.23 \times 0.5837]$$
$$+ [2 \times 0.33 \times 0.33 \times 72.23 \times 54.89 \times 0.2517]$$
$$+ [2 \times 0.33 \times 0.33 \times 54.89 \times 83.54 \times (-0.0456)]$$

$$= 2595.16$$
$$\therefore \sigma_P = 0.5094 = 50.94\%$$

> **Check yourself**
> Calculate and compare the return and risk of four portfolios: 1. Reliance Capital and Kotak Bank; 2. Kotak Bank and Tata Motors; 3. Tata Motors and Reliance Capital; and 4. Reliance Capital, Kotak Bank and Tata Motors. What is your conclusion?

> **Pause for thought:** With the increase in the number of securities diversification increases and when securities having negative correlation are more in the portfolio, benefits of diversification too are higher, with greater reduction in the risk of the portfolio.

SUMMARY

- ✓ Risk and return are the basic parameters of evaluating securities.
- ✓ The expected rate of return is the average rate of return, which may deviate from the possible outcomes.
- ✓ Variance and standard deviation are the measures of risk, of the expected returns on a security.
- ✓ Portfolio is a combination of two or more than two securities. The expected return of a portfolio is sum of the weighted average return of the securities in a portfolio.
- ✓ Portfolio risk is less than the sum of the weighted average risk of all securities in a portfolio, except when correlation = +1. And when two securities have perfectly negative correlation, i.e., correlation = −1, the portfolio risk becomes zero.
- ✓ Minimum variance portfolio is the one having the minimum possible risk. This is also called an optimum portfolio; and the weights at which the risk of the portfolio is minimum, are the optimum weights of the securities.
- ✓ The minimum variance, that is, the minimum risk, of the portfolio is dependent upon the correlation between the securities and their relative weights.
- ✓ Correlation between the return on securities and reduction of risk show inverse variation. Greater is positive correlation lesser is the reduction of risk. While greater is the negative correlation higher is the reduction in risk. That is why higher is the negative correlation lower is the risk, while higher is the positive correlation higher is the risk.

KEY CONCEPTS

Portfolio Risk	Diversification	Coefficient of Variation
Variance	Limits to Diversification	Expected Rate of Return
Standard Deviation	Incremental Return-Risk Ratio	Portfolio Return
Covariance	Minimum Variance Portfolio	Probability
Correlation Coefficient	Portfolio Opportunity Set	Mean Variance Criterion

REVIEW QUESTIONS

1. Explain with example how diversification reduces the risk of an investment.
2. Why do most investors prefer to hold a diversified portfolio of securities instead of investing their wealth in a single asset? Support your answer utilizing data from the market.
3. How are the concepts of diversification and correlation related?
4. When two securities are in perfectly positive correlation, how does the risk of the portfolio differ from the risk when they are in perfectly negative correlation?
5. How would you interpret the portfolio risk with the help of correlation coefficient?
6. What is meant by an optimal portfolio?
7. Explain the power of diversification even when correlation coefficient is not −1.
8. Explain what is meant by the return-risk ratio. What role does this ratio play in the construction of a portfolio?
9. Explain: "A portfolio's expected return is equal to the weighted average return of its component securities, but its risk is not equal to the weighted average risk of the component securities." Also explain the circumstances under which the portfolio risk is equal to the weighted average risk of its component securities.
10. Explain the relationship between covariance and correlation. Why correlation coefficient is a preferred estimate of risk?

ASSIGNMENT QUESTION

Construct the portfolio return and risk of BSE Sensex 30 scrips. Calculate return and risk of this portfolio by varying the weights of scrips and select the portfolio with highest return-risk ratio. Follow it up by selecting on your own, 30 or less than 30 or more than 30 scrips from BSE. Criterion of selection is that these scrips should not be a part of any index: either Nifty 50 or Sensex. Also, ensure that these scrips chosen by you cover almost all the sectors of the economy. Now calculate the return and risk of the portfolio by varying the weights as above.

ILLUSTRATIONS

Q.1. Consider the following data of Infosys, Zydus Wellness and Gold price:

Year	Zydus Wellness (%)	Infosys (%)	Gold price (Rs.)	Gold return (%)
2004	357.27	-62.73	6522	
2005	126.89	42.77	7553	15.81
2006	-36.34	-25.32	9356	23.87
2007	79.48	-21.12	10134	8.32
2008	-45.91	-36.41	12571	24.05
2009	268.88	131.58	17973	42.97
2010	113.68	32.19	20553	14.35
2011	10.26	-19.52	26364	28.27

Calculate the return, risk and correlation of these three assets and interpret your results.

Ans: From the table in Q.1 it can be said that during recession (year 2008), when both the securities have given negative return, gold has given a positive return of 24.05%. The risk and return of these three securities, as calculated are tabulated below.

Return

Year	Zydus Wellness (%)	Infosys (%)	Gold return (%)
2004	357.27	-62.73	
2005	126.89	42.77	15.81
2006	-36.34	-25.32	23.87
2007	79.48	-21.12	8.32
2008	-45.91	-36.41	24.05
2009	268.88	131.58	42.97
2010	113.68	32.19	14.35
2011	-10.26	-19.52	28.27
Return	70.92	14.88	22.52

It is evident that Zydus Wellness has given the highest return of 70.92%, while Infosys has the lowest yield of 14.88%. The return on gold has been 22.52%.

Variance, Standard Deviation and Correlation Coefficient of Gold and Zydus Wellness

Year	Zydus Wellness (%)	$[R_t - E(R)]$	$[R_t - E(R)]^2$	Gold Return (%)	$[R_t - E(R)]$	$[R_t - E(R)]^2$	$[R_t - E(R_{Zydus\ Wellness})]$ $[R_t - E(R_{Gold})]$
2004	357.27						
2005	126.89	55.97	3132.96	15.81	-6.71	45.06	-375.71
2006	-36.34	-107.26	11504.09	23.87	1.35	1.83	-144.90
2007	79.48	8.56	73.32	8.32	-14.20	201.78	-121.63
2008	-45.91	-116.83	13648.58	24.05	1.53	2.33	-178.44
2009	268.88	197.96	39189.29	42.97	20.45	418.27	4048.65
2010	113.68	42.76	1828.66	14.35	-8.17	66.68	-349.18
2011	-10.26	-81.18	6589.73	28.27	5.75	33.10	-467.00
Return	70.92		75966.64	22.52		769.03	2411.78
			6			6	6
			Var = 12661.11 S.D. = 112.52			Var = 128.17 S.D. = 11.32	Covar = 401.96

Variance and standard deviation of these three securities

	Stock	Variance	Standard deviation
A	Zydus Wellness	12661.11	112.52
B	Infosys	3570.41	59.75
C	Gold	128.17	11.32

Calculation of correlation between Zydus Wellness and Gold:

$$Cor_{AB} = \frac{Covariance}{SD_A \times SD_B}$$

$$= \frac{401.96}{111.52 \times 11.32}$$

$$= 0.32$$

Similarly the correlation between all possible pairs of securities are calculated and recorded as follows:

Stock		Correlation
Zydus Wellness and Infosys	AB	0.95
Infosys and Gold	BC	0.55
Gold and Zydus Wellness	CA	0.32

Calculation of the portfolio return and risk by taking equal weight of all three securities:

$E(R_P) = W_A \times E(R_A) + W_B \times E(R_B) + W_C \times E(R_C)$

$= (0.33 \times 70.92\%) + (0.33 \times 14.88\%) + (0.33 \times 22.52\%)$

$= 35.74\%$

$\sigma^2_P = \sigma^2_A W^2_A + \sigma^2_B W^2_B + \sigma^2_C W^2_C + 2W_A W_B \sigma_A \sigma_B Cor_{AB}$
$\quad\quad\quad\quad\quad\quad\quad\quad\quad\quad\quad\quad\quad + 2W_B W_C \sigma_B \sigma_C Cor_{BC} + 2W_C W_A \sigma_C \sigma_A Cor_{CA}$

$= 3670.74$

$\therefore \sigma_P = \sqrt{(3670.74)}$

$= 0.6059 = 60.59\%$

Q.2. Consider the following three securities: Tata Power, Mahindra & Mahindra and Neyvelli Lignite. From the available returns, for the period 2000-2011, calculate return and risk of each of the three securities. Also, construct the portfolio by taking equal weights of these securities. Calculate return and risk of the constructed portfolio.

Year	Tata Power	Mahindra & Mahindra	Neyvelli Lignite
		Return (%)	
2000	32.48	−66.32	−31.66
2000	0.00	−69.31	−4.52
2001	30.77	−46.53	52.99
2001	−0.46	−31.35	10.00
2002	−7.69	25.22	121.43
2003	180.27	244.14	179.23
2004	23.67	38.90	10.79
2005	10.32	−6.87	6.38
2006	28.55	76.92	−29.39
2007	163.12	−5.61	350.96
2008	−49.12	−68.11	−74.31
2009	83.48	287.38	128.70
2010	−1.11	−28.99	−13.56
2011	−92.43	1.78	−44.22

Ans:

Return on these three securities

Year	Tata Power	Mahindra & Mahindra Return (%)	Neyvelli Lignite
2000	32.48	−66.32	−31.66
2000	0.00	−69.31	−4.52
2001	30.77	−46.53	52.99
2001	−0.46	−31.35	10.00
2002	−7.69	25.22	121.43
2003	180.27	244.14	179.23
2004	23.67	38.90	10.79
2005	10.32	−6.87	6.38
2006	28.55	76.92	−29.39
2007	163.12	−5.61	350.96
2008	−49.12	−68.11	−74.31
2009	83.48	287.38	128.70
2010	−1.11	−28.99	−13.56
2011	−92.43	1.78	−44.22
Total	401.85	351.26	662.82
Average	28.70	25.09	47.34

Correlation, Variance and Standard Deviation of the Three Securities

Year 1	Tata Power 2	$[R_t - E(R)]$ 3	Mahindra & Mahindra 4	$[R_t - E(R)]$ 5	$[R_t - E(R)] \times [R_t - E(R)]$ 6 (3 × 5)
2000	32.48	3.78	−66.32	−91.41	−345.19
2000	0.00	−28.70	−69.31	−94.40	2709.70
2001	30.77	2.07	−46.53	−71.62	−147.96
2001	−0.46	−29.16	−31.35	−56.44	1645.75
2002	−7.69	−36.39	25.22	0.13	−4.82
2003	180.27	151.56	244.14	219.05	33200.21
2004	23.67	−5.03	38.90	13.81	−69.53
2005	10.32	−18.39	−6.87	−31.96	587.57
2006	28.55	−0.15	76.92	51.83	−7.78
2007	163.12	134.41	−5.61	−30.70	−4126.97

Introduction to Portfolio Theory

2008	-49.12	-77.83	-68.11	-93.20	7253.93
2009	83.48	54.78	287.38	262.29	14368.10
2010	-1.11	-29.81	-28.99	-54.08	1612.21
2011	-92.43	-121.13	1.78	-23.31	2823.56
Total	401.85		351.26		59498.77
	28.70		25.09		Cov = 4576.83

Variance and Standard Deviation of all Three Securities

	Stock	Variance	Standard deviation
A	Tata Power	5310.70	72.87
B	Mahindra & Mahindra	12258.45	110.71
C	Neyvelli Lignite	12910.78	113.62

Calculation of correlation between Tata Motors and Mahindra & Mahindra:

$$Cor_{AB} = \frac{Covariance}{SD_A \times SD_B}$$

$$= \frac{4576.83}{72.87 \times 110.71}$$

$$= 0.56$$

The correlation between all possible pairs of these three securities

Stock		Correlation
Tata Power and Mahindra & Mahindra	AB	0.56
Mahindra & Mahindra and Neyvelli Lignite	BC	0.42
Tata Power and Neyvelli Lignite	CA	0.82

Calculation of the portfolio return and risk, by taking equal weight of all three securities:

$E(R_P) = W_A \times E(R_A) + W_B \times E(R_B) + W_C \times E(R_C)$

$= (0.33 \times 28.70\%) + (0.33 \times 25.09\%) + (0.33 \times 47.34)$

$= 33.37\%$

$\sigma^2_P = \sigma^2_A W^2_A + \sigma^2_B W^2_B + \sigma^2_C W^2_C + 2W_A W_B \sigma_A \sigma_B Cor_{AB}$
$\qquad\qquad\qquad\qquad\qquad\qquad + 2W_B W_C \sigma_B \sigma_C Cor_{BC} + 2W_C W_A \sigma_C \sigma_A Cor_{CA}$

$= 6932.18$

$\therefore \quad \sigma_P = \sqrt{6932.18}$

$= 0.8326 = 83.26\%$

148   Security Analysis and Portfolio Management

Q.3. Construct the efficient set by taking the return of Zydus Wellness and Infosys. Construct further, the efficient set by taking correlation coefficients: –1, 1, 0, 05, –0.5, 0.25, –0.25.

Year	Zydus Wellness Return (%)	Infosys Return (%)
2002	–60.78	17.08
2003	207.38	16.84
2004	357.27	–62.73
2005	126.89	42.77
2006	–36.34	–25.32
2007	79.48	–21.12
2008	–45.91	–36.41
2009	268.88	131.58
2010	113.68	32.19
2011	–10.26	–19.52

Ans:

	Zydus Wellness	Infosys
Average rate of return (%)	100.03	7.54
Variance	18545.96	2691.53
Standard deviation (σ)	136.18	51.88
Covariance	1808.24	
Correlation	0.26	

INFOSYS	ZYDUS	Return	Correlation						
			–1.00	1.00	0.00	–0.50	0.50	–0.25	0.25
1.00	0.00	100.03	136.18	136.18	136.18	136.18	136.18	136.18	136.18
0.90	0.10	90.78	117.38	127.75	122.67	120.06	125.24	121.37	123.96
0.80	0.20	81.53	98.57	119.32	109.44	104.15	114.49	106.83	111.99
0.70	0.30	72.28	79.76	110.89	96.59	88.58	103.99	92.67	100.36
0.60	0.40	63.03	60.96	102.46	84.30	73.56	93.82	79.12	89.19
0.50	0.50	53.78	42.15	94.03	72.87	59.52	84.12	66.53	78.69
0.40	0.60	44.53	23.35	85.60	62.74	47.34	75.05	55.57	69.17
0.30	0.70	35.28	4.54	77.17	54.66	38.79	66.87	47.39	61.07

0.20	0.80	26.03	14.27	68.74	49.64	36.52	59.96	43.58	55.04
0.10	0.90	16.78	33.07	60.31	48.64	41.59	54.79	45.25	51.80
0.00	1.00	7.54	51.88	51.88	51.88	51.88	51.88	51.88	51.88

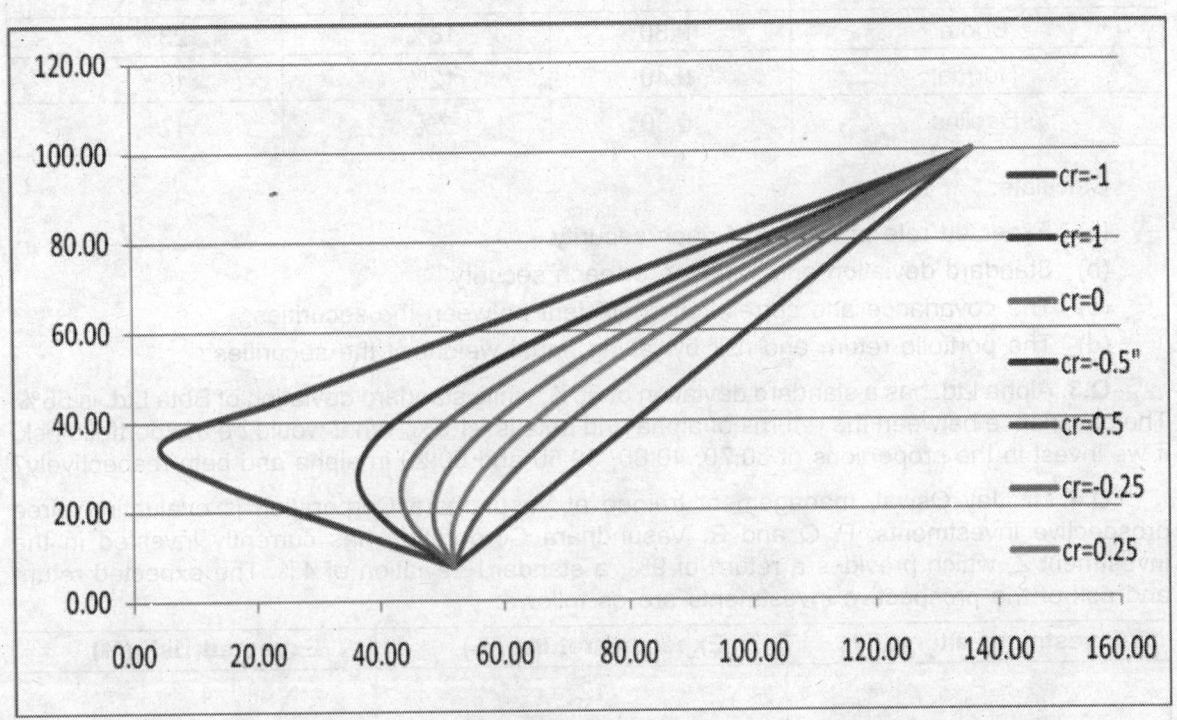

PROBLEMS

Q.1. A portfolio consists of three securities: A, B and C. These securities have the following risk, return and correlation coefficient.

Stock	Expected return (%)	Standard deviation (%)
A	27	32
B	23	27
C	20	25

Correlation coefficient

AB	BC	AC
−0.5	0.6	0.4

Find out the risk and return of the portfolio if all three securities have equal weights in the portfolio.

Q.2. Consider the following parameters of two companies, X and Y, in three different stages of the economy.

State of the economy	Probability	Stock X (%)	Stock Y (%)
Boom	0.30	18%	23%
Normal	0.40	12%	19%
Decline	0.30	7%	17%

Calculate:

(a) Expected rate of return, of each security.
(b) Standard deviation and variance of each security.
(c) The covariance and correlation coefficient between the securities.
(d) The portfolio return and risk by taking equal weight of the securities.

Q.3. Alpha Ltd. has a standard deviation of 39%, while standard deviation of Beta Ltd. is 56%. The covariance between the returns of alpha and beta is −1.9%. What would be the portfolio risk, if we invest in the proportions of 30:70, 40:60, 50:50 and 80:20 in alpha and beta respectively?

Q.4. Mr. Jay Oswal, management trainee at Vasundhara Corporation is evaluating three prospective investments: P, Q and R. Vasundhara Corporation has currently invested in the investment Z, which provides a return of 9%, a standard deviation of 4%. The expected return and risk of the prospective investments are as follows:

Investment alternative	Expected return (%)	Expected risk (%)
P	12	4
Q	10	5
R	9	5

Find out which investment would Mr. Oswal opt for if he is a:

(a) Risk-averse investor.
(b) Risk-loving investor.
(c) Risk-neutral investor.

Q.5. Hardik has estimated the following joint probability distribution of returns for investments in the PQR and ABC stocks.

Probability	PQR	ABC
0.25	−13	20
0.20	11	23
0.35	30	18
0.20	25	12

Calculate the covariance and correlation coefficient between the two securities.

Q.6. From the following data of gold and the securities: NTPC, L&T and Hindalco, calculate their covariance and correlation and interpret your results.

Year	Gold price (Rs.)	NTPC	L&T	Hindalco
2004	6522	83.5875	663.8875	1289.425
2005	7553	97.825	1396.038	796.4375
2006	9356	122.975	1857.975	177.2625
2007	10134	200.25	2919.85	187.8375
2008	12571	209.3375	2509.188	131.7
2009	17973	205.7125	1187	103.25
2010	20553	213.075	1816.213	196.5625

Q.7. Albert inherited the securities, shown below, on his uncle's death.

Type of security	No.	Annual coupon %	Maturity period (years)	Yield
Bond A (Rs.1000)	20	8	5	?
Bond B (Rs.1000)	20	11	8	?
Preference share A (Rs.100)	100	13	*	14
Preference share B (Rs.100)	100	15	*	14

* Likelihood of being called at a premium over par.

Calculate the current value of Albert's inherited portfolio.

Q.8. Select two companies, one from the software sector and the other belonging to the power sector, and tabulate their return over the last twelve months and calculate the following:

(a) Expected rate of return for each stock.
(b) Standard deviation of return for each stock.
(c) The covariance between the rates of return.
(d) The correlation coefficient between the rates of return.

What level of correlation did you expect? How does your expectations compare with the correlation obtained? Would these two stocks lead to a well–diversified portfolio? Give reasons for your answer.

Q.9. Repeat the above problem, 8, by taking the data of last 10 years, for the sectors: (i) Banking and FMCG; (ii) Power and Software; (iii) Steel and Cement; (iv) Textile and Petrochemicals. Also prepare a table of variance–covariance matrix.

Q.10. Calculate the monthly percentage changes, over the last five years, of the following four markets by ascertaining the following:

	Sensex	Nikkie	Hang Seng	Dow Jones
1				
60				

(a) Expected monthly rate of return for each market.
(b) Standard deviation for each series.
(c) Covariance between the rates of return, for the above indices with each other.
(d) The correlation coefficient for the above indices.
(e) Using the answers from (a) to (d), calculate the expected return and standard deviation of a portfolio containing equal parts of: (i) Sensex and Hang Seng; (ii) Sensex and Dow Jones and (iii) Sensex and Nikkie.

Q.11. Take two scrips, one each from two different sectors, and calculate:

(a) Their average return of last five years.
(b) Their variance and standard deviation.
(c) Minimum variance for a portfolio of above two securities.
(d) The minimum risk portfolio, when the correlation coefficient of above two securities is –1.0.

Q.12. Take two scrips each from the sectors: automobile and power. This means now you have four scrips with you. Take the data of last ten years of all four and calculate return and risk of each. Also, calculate the correlation between two scrips: of same sector and of different sectors.

Q.13. Take two scrips: one from the IT sector and the other from pharmaceutical sector.

(a) Calculate their return and risk, computing the data of last 10 years.
(b) Calculate the respective portfolio return and risk if you are planning to invest in the IT and pharmaceutical sectors in the proportions of 60:40 and 40:60.
(c) Assuming that you have sold partially your holdings in the IT stock, and replaced it with a power sector scrip, calculate the revised portfolio's return and risk, with the distribution of weights being in the ratio of 60:40 and 40:60.

Q.14. You are holding a stock, P, with a standard deviation of 28%. You wish to buy a new stock, Q, with a standard deviation of 40%. You will hold these two stocks in a portfolio, with 50% of your money invested in each. Correlation coefficient of stock (P, Q) is –0.30. Your friend advises against this, stating such addition would result in a riskier portfolio than just holding P alone. Is he right? Give reasons for your answer.

Q.15. Two companies, X Ltd. and Y Ltd., have standard deviations of 35% and 57% respectively. The covariance between the returns of X and Y is –1.5%.

(a) Calculate the portfolio risks if you invest in a proportion of 30:70 and 70:30.
(b) Had covariance been +1.5%, what would have been your portfolio risk?

Q.16. Calculate return, risk and correlation coefficient of the securities: Tata Coffee, ACC and Sesa Goa, computing the data of last five years and fill up the table below.

Company	Return	S.D.	Correlation coefficient		
			Tata Coffee–ACC	Tata Coffee–Sesa Goa	ACC–Sesa Goa
Tata Coffee					XX
ACC				XX	
Sesa Goa			XX		

What is the expected return and standard deviation of a portfolio composed of equi-proportional investments in each?

CASE STUDY

Mr. Rishabh Jain is a Branch Manager at one of the credit rating agencies. He holds an M.Com degree in accountancy and has 8 years of experience with different credit rating agencies. He was sent for one year PGP executive program at one of the leading B–schools of India. There he learnt about the mechanisms of the market and factors determining the output of an investment. Being commerce major, he developed more interest in financial management and the allied subjects. From the one year executive program that he attended, he also learnt that a skilled portfolio manager can outperform any mutual fund. In the past, his investments in mutual funds had been for tax saving purposes. But he is not at all happy with their performances. He believes it is better to construct the portfolio on our own and then reconstruct it periodically to avail better returns, instead of buying a mutual fund to invest in the market. Mr. Jain spent considerable time to watch the movement of particular scrip before including it in his portfolio. He read the market related news to get an insight of the market and on the securities to select. At last he decided that it is better to invest only in the top 30 scrips of SENSEX constituents or 50 scrips of Nifty. He studied and calculated the performance of top 50 scrips of Nifty and selected the top 10 scrips on the basis of high return. At the same time he chose the top 10 scrips on the basis of low risk. He wants to construct the two portfolios, composed of high return securities and low risk securities respectively. Construct the two portfolios with equal weights of the constituents in each. Which portfolio Mr. Jain should select? Assist Mr. Jain by computing both the risk and return portfolios.

High return				Low risk			
Sr. no.	Scrip	Return (%)	Risk (%)	Sr. no.	Scrip	Return (%)	Risk (%)
1	AXISBANK	57.7	52.37	1	BPCL	21.24	20.43
2	BHARTIARTL	46.6	67.03	2	CAIRN	17.3	17.45
3	BHEL	43.61	44.88	3	HDFCBANK	30.73	24.84
4	JSWSTEEL	46.24	90.43	4	HINDUUNILVR	6.95	14.14
5	KOTAKBANK	44.17	72.23	5	IDEA	–16.76	19.68
6	PNB	53.98	61.09	6	NTPC	18.68	23.86
7	RELCAPITAL	50.53	83.54	7	POWERGRID	–4.23	8.97
8	SAIL	67.1	101.14	8	SBIN	35.3	24.17
9	TATAMOTORS	41.1	54.9	9	SUNPHARMA	10.23	16.56
10	UNITECH	37	92.57	10	WIPRO	–9.22	25.58

Covariance Matrix Table 1

	ABB	AXIS	BHARTI	BHEL	GAIL	HDFCBANK	ICICIBANK
ABB							
AXISBANK	1895.64						
BHARTIARTL	2397.40	1427.96					
BHEL	2330.57	1531.54	1898.08				
GAIL	1282.69	1980.04	957.69	1093.14			
HDFCBANK	906.38	783.65	598.98	581.84	387.38		
ICICIBANK	1788.70	1677.19	1168.97	1289.13	1198.77	757.47	
IDFC	578.88	578.88	1039.82	222.17	1374.48	1065.63	1373.09
JSWSTEEL	300.58	2530.34	1356.69	2.07	2087.00	1497.30	1871.29
KOTAKBANK	321.47	1927.80	1443.47	345.35	2137.15	374.67	990.74
L&T	2221.73	1405.82	1500.69	1339.89	815.66	1089.94	1637.44
M&M	1982.52	2041.85	1637.16	1706.89	1792.64	485.78	1337.54
ONGC	1135.95	1071.40	769.92	908.17	1450.87	−27.25	634.51
PNB	1935.36	2248.95	1443.82	1703.48	2400.15	268.79	1335.56
RELCAPITAL	1580.89	2228.51	2569.91	1197.75	1165.80	1351.64	1841.15
SAIL	2170.64	4165.31	2225.91	2128.83	4015.28	735.65	2332.90
SBIN	952.35	1046.49	670.04	675.56	832.71	426.55	804.19
SIEMENS	3351.23	2528.20	1719.17	2549.89	2166.90	763.48	2066.78
TATAMOTORS	1919.60	1704.87	286.28	1292.03	1726.59	512.55	1320.56
TATAPOWER	797.49	1515.53	1264.17	722.44	1165.56	536.19	964.36
UNITECH	3736.45	1561.42	3800.13	2740.41	956.65	884.24	1785.73

Covariance Matrix Table 2

	IDFC	JSW STEEL	KOTAK BANK	LT	M&M	ONGC	PNB
ABB							
AXISBANK							
BHARTIARTL							
BHEL							
GAIL							
HDFCBANK							
ICICIBANK							
IDFC							
JSWSTEEL	4111.82						
KOTAKBANK	3554.24	5622.87					

L&T	1773.52	2516.96	1273.60				
M&M	451.37	599.68	1005.21	430.24			
ONGC	199.33	235.32	1303.79	574.11	1308.55		
PNB	449.56	714.09	1622.30	484.75	2767.54	2204.95	
RELCAPITAL	4210.67	6380.83	3130.67	3428.46	735.20	−348.65	36.86
SAIL	3034.60	4752.05	5046.36	1247.96	3622.21	2545.38	4470.99
SBIN	1057.74	1493.79	976.28	932.33	764.99	465.46	823.47
SIEMENS	314.18	132.29	479.00	2729.26	2589.73	2142.22	3453.56
TATAMOTORS	775.73	919.09	887.21	1038.36	1820.08	1622.33	2455.39
TATAPOWER	1729.59	2699.44	1698.58	780.15	1156.63	337.27	1152.24
UNITECH	316.17	132.15	−558.15	3828.11	1937.82	1425.88	2486.78

Covariance Matrix Table 3

	REL CAPITAL	SAIL	SBIN	SIEMENS	TATA MOTORS	TATA POWER	UNITECH
ABB							
AXISBANK							
BHARTIARTL							
BHEL							
GAIL							
HDFCBANK							
ICICIBANK							
IDFC							
JSWSTEEL							
KOTAKBANK							
L&T							
M&M							
ONGC							
PNB							
RELCAPITAL							
SAIL	3532.54						
SBIN	1183.03	1673.10					
SIEMENS	985.48	3580.44	1070.67				
TATAMOTORS	−186.21	2641.24	824.45	2797.18			
TATAPOWER	2094.93	2761.95	640.26	861.73	571.65		
UNITECH	1777.28	1026.37	737.56	5002.63	1499.09	598.10	

SUGGESTED FURTHER READING FOR EMPIRICAL WORK

1. Feinstein, C.D., and Mukund N. (1993), "Reformulation of a Mean–Absolute Deviation Portfolio Optimization Model", *Management Science*, Vol. 39, No.12.
2. Parkhe, A. (1991), "International Portfolio Analysis: A New Model", *MIR: Management International Review*, Vol. 31, No.4.
3. Perold, A.F. (1984), "Large–Scale Portfolio Optimization", *Management Science*, Vol. 30, No.10.
4. Lee, S., and Chang, K. (1995), "Mean–Variance–Instability Portfolio Analysis: A Case of Taiwan's Stock Market", *Management Science*, Vol. 41, No.7.
5. Lim, A.E.B., and Zhou, X.Y. (2002), "Mean–Variance Portfolio Selection with Random Parameters in a Complete Market", *Mathematics of Operations Research*, Vol. 27, No.1.
6. Bird, R., and Tippett, M. (1986), "Naive Diversification and Portfolio Risk–A Note", *Management Science*, Vol. 32, No.2.
7. Hui, T., Kwan, E.K., and Lee, C. (1993), "Optimal Portfolio Diversification: Empirical Bayes versus Classical Approach", *The Journal of the Operational Research Society*, Vol. 44, No.11.
8. Jorion, P. (2003), "Portfolio Optimization with Tracking–Error Constraints", *Financial Analysts Journal*, Vol. 59, No.5.
9. Finkelshtain, I., and Chalfant, J.A. (1993), "Portfolio Choices in the Presence of Other Risks", *Management Science*, Vol. 39, No.8.
10. Scherer, B. (2002), "Portfolio Resampling: Review and Critique", *Financial Analysts Journal*, Vol. 58, No.6.
11. Simaan, Y. (1993), "Portfolio Selection and Asset Pricing–Three–Parameter Framework", *Management Science*, Vol. 39, No.5.
12. Devinney, T.M., and Stewart, D.W. (1988), "Rethinking the Product Portfolio: A Generalized Investment Model", *Management Science*, Vol. 34, No.9.
13. Goldfarb, D., and Iyengar, G. (2003), "Robust Portfolio Selection Problems", *Mathematics of Operations Research*, Vol. 28, No.1.

REFERENCES

1. http://www.investorwords.com/18466/portfolio_opportunity_set.html
2. http://financial-dictionary.thefreedictionary.com/Portfolio+Opportunity+Set
3. http://en.wikipedia.org/wiki/Efficient_frontier
4. http://people.stern.nyu.edu/lpederse/courses/c150002/08pf_2risky.pdf
5. http://www.josemarin.com/2009IEportmanag/slides/04%20Modern%20Portfolio%20Theory.pdf
6. http://www.dur.ac.uk/t.i.renstrom/teaching/IMEF/Lect_6.pdf
7. http://www.actuarialoutpost.com/actuarial_discussion_forum/archive/index.php/t-24304.html
8. http://www.zenwealth.com/BusinessFinanceOnline/RR/Diversification.html

9. http://www.ulb.ac.be/cours/solvay/farber/DESG/3%20Agatha%20Solution.pdf
10. http://www.investopedia.com/terms/p/portfolio-variance.asp#axzz2E4qQ3tva
11. http://en.wikipedia.org/wiki/Modern_portfolio_theory
12. http://www.investorwords.com/7442/portfolio_variance.html
13. http://www.public.iastate.edu/~shanyang/FS/Pennacchi23
14. http://sma.epfl.ch/~eisenbra/OptInFinance/Slides/Oct-14.pdf
15. http://www.uam.es/personal_pdi/economicas/bdeblas/teaching/ucd/ecn134/lectures/mv_review.pdf
16. http://www.yorku.ca/eprisman/PortEssHtml/chp2-4.html
17. http://mit.econ.au.dk/vip_htm/akoch/ec3314_l3.pdf
18. http://www.airxcell.com/doc/userGuide/portfolio_optimTheory.html

6
BETA AND RISK ESTIMATION

LEARNING OBJECTIVES

The purpose of this chapter is to enable you to understand:

- How is the total risk of the portfolio resolved into two components: systematic and unsystematic.
- Estimation of beta, alpha, correlation coefficient and coefficient of determination.
- Formation of the characteristics line, as a regression fit of market return and security return.
- The market model.

6.1 INTRODUCTION

In the previous two chapters we discussed the risk and return of both individual securities, as well as the portfolios constructed of a bunch of securities. The correlation between the securities, studied in detail, has made it evident that risk quotient of the portfolio is major determinant of the assets in a portfolio. Thus the portfolio risk becomes dependent on the risks of the individual assets. Though it is not a weighted average (exception is perfect positive correlation between the assets), still risk of each has its weight on the net risk of the portfolio. Risk of a portfolio, we know now is measured in terms of covariance or correlation between the returns on the assets. As the risks on the returns of different securities correlate amongst each other, they impact the overall risk of the portfolio.

So this chapter concentrates on the various aspects of risk, and on what it depends. And the parameter on what it depends decides its types. Thus has been observed that there are two components of risk:

- Systematic.
- Unsystematic.

And here, in this chapter we look forward to resolve the total risk into its components. This would enable assessment of the modification required in the constitution of a portfolio. These modifications enhance the efficiency of the portfolio.

6.1.1 Portfolio Risk for a Portfolio of 'N' Securities

Prior to this chapter discussions on risk have centered on its measurement. But this chapter intends to approach risk at its core level—the concept that risk is—and thus access its essence. The previous chapter showed that while individual securities have their risks measured in terms of standard deviation that of a portfolio required further parameters. These were found to be correlation and covariance and accordingly equations were formulated [Chapter 5, Equations (8) and (9), respectively], in addition to the weighted average return on securities.

Now we express the portfolio risk as the sum of the variances (square of standard deviation) of individual securities and their covariance with each other. Thus, for a portfolio comprised of 'N' securities (where 'N' is an integer), the variance of the portfolio taking equal weight of all securities, is expressed as:

Portfolio variance = $N[1/N^2]$ × average variance + $N(N-1)[1/N^2]$ × average covariance (1)

i.e., $\sigma^2_P = [1/N]$ × average variance + $[1 - 1/N]$ × average covariance (2)

When 'N' is large, Equation (2) thus reduces to:

$$\sigma^2_P = \text{average covariance} \quad (3)$$

Thus, Equation (2), it can be re-written as,

$$\sigma^2_P = 1/N\ \sigma^2 + N - 1/N\ \text{Cov} \quad (4)$$

How the derivation is arrived at is an obvious question. For that we need to understand the formula for variance of portfolio with two assets.

$$\sigma^2_P = \sigma^2_1 w^2_1 + \sigma^2_2 w^2_2 + 2w_1 w_2 \text{Cov}_{12} \quad (5)$$

This can be generalized into (where i is not equal to j)

$$\sigma^2_P = \sum_{i=1} \sigma^2_i w^2_i + \sum_{j=1} w_i w_j \text{Cov}_{ij} \quad (6)$$

So, the portfolios with 'N' assets, there will be 'N' terms in the form of $\sigma^2_i w^2_i$ and $N(N-1)$ terms in the form of $w_i w_j \text{Cov}_{ij}$.

Similarly, the covariance formula for a portfolio of three assets is:

$$\sigma^2_P = \sigma^2_1 w^2_1 + \sigma^2_2 w^2_2 + \sigma^2_3 w^2_3 + 2w_1 w_2 \text{Cov}_{12} + 2w_1 w_3 \text{Cov}_{13} + 2w_2 w_3 \text{Cov}_{23} \quad (7)$$

From Equation (7) we can see that there are 3 $\sigma^2_i w^2_i$ terms of variance, and 6 terms in the form of $w_i w_j \text{Cov}_{ij}$.

In a similar manner, when there are four assets in a portfolio there are 4 variance terms and 12 covariance terms.

As the portfolio is equally weighted and the weight of each security is 1/N, the formula becomes,

$$\sigma^2_P = N \times [(1/N)^2\ \sigma^2] + N(N-1) \times [1/N\ 1/N\ \text{Cov}] \quad (8)$$

Equation (7) is the outcome of substituting each asset's weight by 1/N, each asset's variance with average variance, and each covariance with average covariance. By simple multiplication Equation (7) becomes:

$$\sigma^2_P = 1/N\sigma^2 + N - 1/N\ \text{Cov} \quad (9)$$

It is evident that in a well-diversified portfolio, when the number of scrips increases in a portfolio, the value of 1/N renders the first term inconsequential. This implies that variances of individual securities become negligible. But the second term does not become entirely negligible. Though the variances are found to be insignificant, their relationship with that of other securities—the covariance—has a sustained impact. Hence, covariance of securities with each other always has an influence on the variance of the portfolio.

It is concluded thereby that with an increase in the number of scrips in a portfolio, the average covariance between the securities become the measure of the variance of the portfolio. In other words, with a higher degree of diversification, the risk of the portfolio is equal to the average covariance of the securities. Obviously this implies an appreciable reduction in risk, which is the characteristic, as well as utility, of diversification. And as the number of scrips increases in the portfolio, so does diversification, accompanied by further reductions in the portfolio risk.

We are now aware that securities might have a positive or negative covariance with each other, depending on their movement with other securities, either in the same direction or in the opposite. And we also know that when their correlation decreases from +1 to −1, reduction in risk of the portfolio increases. Thus higher is the number of such negatively correlated scrips, lower will be the risk of the portfolio.

> **Pause for thought:** When diversification is high, lower is the risk of the portfolio as it becomes equal to the average covariance only, of the securities in the portfolio.

6.2 RISK DIVERSIFICATION

We now know that the risk of a portfolio is reduced by increasing the diversification. But then increasing the number of scrips at random, in the portfolio, will not result in the desired reduction in risk. Since risk of the portfolio is dependent upon the covariance and correlation between the scrips, these additions have to be based on the nature of the risk of individual scrips. Furthermore, even in presence of a large number ('N') of scrips, with the average variances of scrips becoming negligible, the risk is still not completely eliminated. The risk due to the average covariance remains [Equation (3)], which thus does not allow the portfolio a complete freedom from risk. Only a reduction in the total risk of the portfolio is permissible and so, possible.

Thus automatically we are led to a conclusion, that the total risk of the portfolio involves a component which is independent of the impact of diversification. This part of the risk hence doesn't undergo reduction. As we have already noted above that the total risk is composed of two parts, systematic and unsystematic, now the question that arises is which of these is resistant to diversification.

> **Pause for thought:** Risk of a portfolio can be reduced, via diversification, but cannot be completely eliminated, as one component of the total risk is irreducible.

6.2.1 Systematic Risk

A natural progression of the preceding discussion is towards the identification of these components of risk which are resistant and receptive to diversification, respectively. Since it is the resistant component which retains, at least a residual risk in the portfolio, we choose to begin our discussion with the same. And through its study we look forward to know why it is resistant to diversification.

Systematic risk is that component of the risk which is irreducible and hence doesn't allow complete elimination of risk from a portfolio. It is hence also termed as the undiversifiable risk or market risk. This type of risk arises because of unavoidable situations and their equally unavoidable impacts. These include macroeconomic events like recession, government policies, political factors, natural calamities etc., which inevitably influence the market, and hence the scrips. Systematic risk envelopes the entire market and none of the scrips can escape from it because of the susceptibility of securities to market fluctuations. No matter how efficient a portfolio is, constructed judiciously with the potentially best possible scrip for the portfolio, the systematic risk is sustained, refusing diversification.

Some of the factors responsible for systematic risks are:
- Changes made in the industrial policies by the government.
- Removal of tax exemption for certain industries of the economy.
- Changes in the interest rates through the periodic change in CRR[1] and SLR[2]..
- Government's effort to reduce massive fiscal deficit.
- Foreign policy of the government.

It is thus bound by the systems—the macroeconomic factors—of the market and hence aptly termed systematic risk!

Check yourself

Find out the impact on retail FDI, of the announcement by RBI to reveal from time to time: the actual GDP for the current year and the actual fiscal deficit, which is in fact huge. Also find out the response of retail FDI to the periodic changes in the interest rate made by the RBI. Collect all information and interpret their impact on the market. See how Sensex and Nifty have reacted to this announcement, for disclosure of the said figures.

Check yourself

Collect the opening, high, low and closing price data of at least 10 securities from each segment of the market: large cap, medium cap and small cap, for the period 2006 to 2011. What is your observation of the prices of all these securities in the year 2008 and 2011? Also, consult and compare the data of Sensex, on the prices of these securities and interpret your result.

Pause for thought: It is the undiversifiable, and thus irreducible component of the total risk, arising out of the inescapable macroeconomic factors pervading the market.

6.2.2 Unsystematic Risk

We now come to that component of the risk which allows diversification and utilizes the advantages of the same. Since it responds to diversification it allows itself to be reduced, and thus the risk of the portfolio is reduced.

This reducible component of risk, susceptible to diversification is thus the diversifiable risk as opposed to the undiversifiable risk. Hence it is commonly referred to as the unsystematic risk. It is also known as unique risk because of the fact that complete elimination of the unsystematic risk is permissible and possible. One can eliminate this risk through an efficient and large scale diversification of the securities in a portfolio.

---

[1] Credit reserve ratio.
[2] Statutory liquidity ratio

But then just as the systematic risk comes into effect because of certain factors, there must be reasons which give rise to the unsystematic risk. Logically concluded, whatever be the factor(s) it allows the risk to be free from the systems prevalent in the market, hence unsystematic. They must be rendering the risk to be non-responsive to the factors which bring forth the systematic risk—the market risks, dependent on the macroeconomic causes, as mentioned above.

So what are these unique factors which lead to this unique risk?

Well, it arises out of the unique uncertainty inherent in individual scrips. And this very element of uncertainty, in one scrip, can be annulled by the unique uncertainty of another scrip, when added to the portfolio. This contradiction between uncertainties, followed by elimination of the risk can be understood as follows.

A portfolio is assumed to be constructed with 20 securities from different sectors. When problems involving: the union, export orders, inability to import required raw materials, R&D, resignation of experts, etc., are assumed for one or more than one securities of the portfolio, it does not imply that the overall portfolio return will be zero or negative. Why? Well, it is simply the uncertainties which cancel each other. Thus, if one or other security is not able to perform well due to any (or many) reason(s), at the same time some another security may perform very well due to some unexpected good tidings, in the form of:

- An early approval of patent.
- Rise in profit due to operational excellence.
- Signing of a deal with another company—national or international—and still earning expected return from the portfolio.

The issues of uncertainty are not an issue of the entire economy. Rather it is unique to one or two companies of the economy. Thus uncertainty that a security will not perform well is completely negated by the uncertainties which lead to exceptionally good and unexpected performance of another security. These uncertainties make a mockery of the systems prevalent in the market, as the unsystematic risk is found to prevail.

> **Pause for thought:** Unsystematic risk of a security is the market independent, diversifiable risk, causing the reduction in risk of a portfolio.

6.2.3 Total Risk

Total risk (the variance) of the security having been resolved into its components: systematic risk and unsystematic risk, how and why these arise, too have been discussed above. Hence we now know why the total risk can never be zero. The systematic risk ensures the maintenance of a certain level of risk, despite the unsystematic risk being completely susceptible to diversification and reducible to zero. So now we proceed to interpret these in terms of Equations (2) and (3), derived in the beginning of this chapter.

Systematic risk is the covariance of the individual securities in a portfolio, which is maintained, throughout the process of diversification, as the average covariance. On the other hand, the difference between the variance and covariance is the unsystematic risk, representing the average variance, in Equation (1), which becomes negligible through diversification.

For an investor who holds a well-diversified portfolio, total risk is irrelevant as only the systematic risk, is the matter of concern, as it cannot be diversified away. It is just because of this reason market gives compensation for only the systematic risk of a security and not for unsystematic risk of the security. In other words, market compensates only for the market-dependent, undiversifiable risks, and not for the market-independent, diversifiable risks. And it is quite logical. An investor has to bear the systematic risk of the security, while it is in the investor's hand to reduce and eliminate the unsystematic risk. If one is judicious enough, one can choose the right type and right number of scrips and thus construct an efficient portfolio, which eliminates that risk which can be eliminated—the unsystematic risk.

The following Figure 6.1 shows the diversification of unsystematic risk.

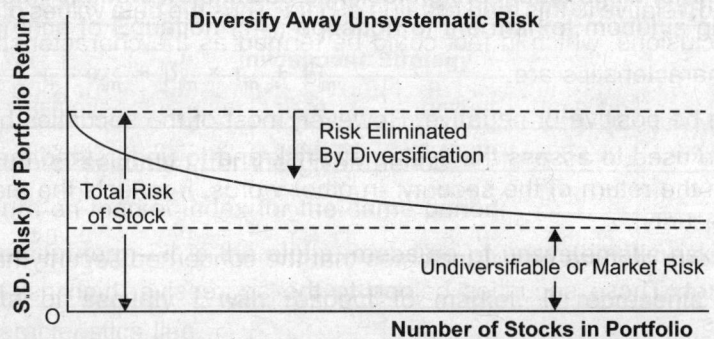

Figure 6.1: Systematic and unsystematic risk

From the figure is evidenced the increase in the reduction of diversifiable, unsystematic risk with an increase in the number of scrips in a portfolio. As the number increases, there is a rapid fall in the risk initially. Subsequently the decrease in risk is gradual and after a certain level is reached the risk is stabilized with no further reduction. It could be the point where the risk of the portfolio attains the average covariance of the scrips [Equation (3)]. Thus the figure too corroborates what we have been discussing—that diversification reduces substantially the unique risk of the portfolio.

As far as the market dependent systematic risk is concerned, the figure validates its resistance to diversification. It is thus observed to be constant, irrespective of the extent of diversification, which is typified by the gradual increase in the number of scrips, represented by the X-axis. This constancy of the systematic risk symbolizes averaging of market risk, by diversification. As discussed above this risk arises from the macroeconomic factors and affects all the scrips traded in the market. Thus diversification gives an averaged view, of the market risk, with no reduction of the market risk possible via diversification.

In India, it has been found that a portfolio comprised of around 40 scrips has its unsystematic risk[3] completely eliminated.

> **Pause for thought:** The total risk of the portfolio depends on the investor to the extent of choosing the right type and right number of scrips to reduce and eliminate the diversifiable risk, as the market dependent risk, the systematic risk, rejects diversification—and reduction.

6.3 HOW TO MEASURE THE SYSTEMATIC RISK?

Each measurable parameter has a measure for its estimation. For example, standard deviation is a measure of the risk of a security and is denoted by σ. Similarly, systematic risk too has a measure.

---

[3] Gupta, L C (1981), "Rate of Returns on Equities: The Indian Experience", Oxford.

Beta (β) is the measure of the undiversifiable, systematic, market risk. Since beta measures the market risk, hence it reflects, as it measures, the response of the price of securities to market forces. In fact beta shows direct variation with the fluctuations in the prices of a security. That is, when the prices are more sensitive and susceptible to changes in the market, higher is the value of beta, of that security. So higher is the beta, higher will be the market compensation for the systematic risk of the concerned security.

The beta of market, Sensex and Nifty, is always considered as 1.00 and betas of the other securities are viewed, relative to this market value of beta. Thus the beta values of different securities lead to certain conclusions, which in fact could be termed as the characteristics of beta. These conclusions and characteristics are:

- Beta can be positive or negative. However, most of the securities have positive beta.
- Betas are used to assess the systematic risk and to understand the impact of market return on the return of the security. In other words, it reflects the market susceptibility of the security.
- A beta value of more than 1 indicates that the concerned security has higher risk than the market. These securities belong to the aggressive, high risk-return category of securities.
- When the beta value of a security is less than 1, it represents a conservative security having lesser risk than the market.
- Last but not the least, a security with negative beta indicates that the return of such securities move opposite to that of market. Hence such securities are desirable during recession!
- As opposed to this, when the market is in a phase of growth or even if it is a case of anticipated growth, it is desirable to hold securities with positive beta.

Pause for thought: Beta is the measure of the market risk, directly varying with the susceptibility of the security to the market fluctuations. It is also an index of the risk of the security, with respect to the market risk.

6.3.1 Calculating Beta

As beta is an index of the risk on the return of a security, which is dependent on the market returns, beta is calculated by relating the returns of a security with the returns for the market.

When we revert to Equation (3), the variance of the portfolio is found to be equal to the average covariance of the securities, when the number of securities is high in the portfolio.

$$\sigma^2_P = \text{average covariance}$$

And this risk we know is because of the systematic, undiversifiable component of the total risk. So, the ratio of average covariance of the securities and the variance of the portfolio would logically be the measure of the systematic risk, beta, of the market.

This very logic applies to the calculation of beta for a security. But the parameters of the ratio change, in keeping with the fact that in this case, it is a single security whose risk with respect to the market risk is to be ascertained.

Thus the systematic risk, beta, of a security is measured as the ratio of covariance between returns of the security and the market and the variance of the market. It is formulated as:

BETA AND RISK ESTIMATION

$$\beta_i = \frac{Cov_{im}}{\sigma_m^2} \tag{10}$$

Or, $\quad \beta_i = \dfrac{\sigma_{im}}{\sigma_m^2}$

Where,

β_i = systematic risk of security, i.

$Cov_{im} = \sigma_{im}$ = covariance between return on security, i, and the market return.

σ_m^2 = variance of the market.

Table 6.1 Calculation of beta of Larsen and Toubro (L&T)

No.	Month	Market Return X (%)	L&T Return Y (%)	[R(x) − E{R(x)}]	[R(Y) − E{R(Y)}]	[R(x) − E(R(x))] × [R(Y) − E{R(Y)}]	[R(x) − E{R(x)}]²
1	Aug–06	8.96	9.14	7.96	7.47	59.43858	63.30768
2	Sep–06	6.45	−47.52	5.45	−49.19	−268.274	29.74061
3	Oct–06	3.91	3.37	2.91	1.70	4.960063	8.495089
4	Nov–06	5.42	4.31	4.42	2.64	11.6762	19.5154
5	Dec–06	0.42	4.64	−0.58	2.97	−1.72667	0.338194
6	Jan–07	1.90	13.39	0.90	11.72	10.59961	0.818307
7	Feb–07	−8.40	−7.03	−9.40	−8.70	81.75144	88.30744
8	Mar–07	0.45	8.09	−0.55	6.42	−3.53055	0.302503
9	Apr–07	8.28	6.09	7.28	4.42	32.19296	52.97688
10	May–07	3.98	16.88	2.98	15.21	45.35224	8.888641
11	Jun–07	0.28	8.72	−0.72	7.05	−5.0957	0.52287
12	Jul–07	5.90	19.02	4.90	17.35	84.97147	23.98551
13	Aug–07	−0.17	2.06	−1.16	0.39	−0.45689	1.355172
14	Sep–07	12.27	6.14	11.27	4.47	50.33549	126.9433
15	Oct–07	14.29	54.35	13.30	52.68	700.3934	176.7704
16	Nov–07	−3.81	−3.98	−4.81	−5.65	27.14611	23.12494
17	Dec–07	3.79	−0.17	2.79	−1.84	−5.12596	7.766069
18	Jan–08	−13.17	−12.18	−14.17	−13.85	196.253	200.7063
19	Feb–08	−1.36	−4.78	−2.36	−6.45	15.19886	5.551417
20	Mar–08	−9.19	−13.58	−10.19	−15.25	155.3192	103.7936
21	Apr–08	9.61	−1.53	8.61	−3.20	−27.5505	74.15087
22	May–08	−6.52	−1.64	−7.52	−3.31	24.85237	56.49785
23	Jun–08	−18.86	−27.40	−19.86	−29.06	577.298	394.5282

24	Jul–08	6.50	18.36	5.50	16.69	91.76274	30.22858
25	Aug–08	3.56	0.77	2.56	–0.90	–2.2923	6.546326
26	Sep–08	–10.77	–5.31	–11.77	–6.98	82.12033	138.5423
27	Oct–08	–24.75	–35.46	–25.74	–37.13	955.8716	662.7835
28	Nov–08	–10.94	–12.94	–11.94	–14.61	174.3654	142.467
29	Dec–08	5.29	6.08	4.29	4.41	18.9256	18.38466
30	Jan–09	–3.05	–11.31	–4.05	–12.97	52.50186	16.37607
31	Feb–09	–4.80	–12.15	–5.80	–13.82	80.17553	33.67448
32	Mar–09	10.79	12.30	9.79	10.63	104.0694	95.89795
33	Apr–09	17.01	29.35	16.01	27.68	443.078	256.2792
34	May–09	25.70	57.05	24.70	55.38	1367.903	610.0618
35	Jun–09	–1.71	10.44	–2.71	8.78	–23.7977	7.354259
36	Jul–09	8.02	–4.52	7.02	–6.19	–43.5044	49.3471
37	Aug–09	–0.18	3.23	–1.18	1.57	–1.84336	1.387087
38	Sep–09	9.15	6.60	8.15	4.93	40.18807	66.42892
39	Oct–09	–7.51	–6.55	–8.50	–8.22	69.89178	72.31816
40	Nov–09	6.87	3.03	5.87	1.36	7.982917	34.43625
41	Dec–09	3.05	3.79	2.05	2.13	4.368314	4.219813
42	Jan–10	–6.38	–16.07	–7.38	–17.74	130.986	54.49932
43	Feb–10	0.55	9.95	–0.45	8.29	–3.69746	0.199117
44	Mar–10	6.63	2.61	5.63	0.94	5.293517	31.67672
45	Apr–10	0.02	–1.65	–0.98	–3.31	3.23891	0.955596
46	May–10	–3.38	1.79	–4.38	0.12	–0.52156	19.14509
47	Jun–10	4.47	10.73	3.48	9.06	31.49391	12.08183
48	Jul–10	1.07	0.12	0.07	–1.55	–0.10907	0.004944
49	Aug–10	0.33	0.36	–0.66	–1.31	0.871301	0.441598
50	Sep–10	11.33	12.35	10.33	10.68	110.2908	106.6867
51	Oct–10	–0.31	–1.12	–1.31	–2.79	3.637742	1.705128
52	Nov–10	–3.71	–3.85	–4.70	–5.52	25.97568	22.12915
53	Dec–10	5.01	1.49	4.01	–0.18	–0.72733	16.11913
54	Jan–11	–11.12	–17.53	–12.12	–19.20	232.7232	146.9423
55	Feb–11	–3.27	–7.39	–4.26	–9.06	38.63322	18.18618
56	Mar–11	8.14	7.01	7.14	5.34	38.09855	50.9368
57	Apr–11	–1.68	–4.12	–2.68	–5.78	15.49911	7.178775
58	May–11	–3.75	1.54	–4.75	–0.12	0.589371	22.54128
59	Jun–11	1.72	10.95	0.72	9.29	6.704651	0.521283
60	Jul–11	–2.41	–6.20	–3.41	–7.87	26.79009	11.59756
Total		59.91	100.10			5853.52	4238.67
Average		0.998	1.668				

The covariance between the market returns and that of the L&T security is calculated, by computing the data from the table above, in the formula below:

$$Cov_{im} = \sigma_{im} = \frac{\Sigma[R(X) - E\{R(X)\}] \times [R(Y) - E\{R(Y)\}]}{n} \quad (11)$$

$$= \frac{5853.52}{60} = 97.56$$

The market variance is,

$$\sigma_m^2 = \frac{\Sigma[R(x) - E\{R(x)\}]^2}{n} \quad (12)$$

$$= \frac{4238.67}{60}$$

$$= 70.64$$

The systematic risk is given by,

$$\beta_i = \frac{Cov_{im}}{\sigma_m^2}$$

$$\therefore \beta_{L\&T} = \frac{97.56}{70.64}$$

$$= 1.38$$

The systematic risk, hence, is 1.38, for L&T during the period: August 2006 to July 2011. As this value is more than 1, it indicates that the return of L&T is more volatile than the return on the market portfolio. So, if the return on the market portfolio rises (or falls) by 10%, the return on the L&T security is expected to rise (or fall) by 13.8% (1.38 × 10%). Similarly, if return on market portfolio or index falls by 5%, return on the security is expected to fall by 6.9% (1.38 × 5%). Beta can be calculated by taking yearly data. However, research in this area shows that for more accurate estimates, monthly data of at least five years should be taken.

Further on beta

- Beta has no upper and lower limit. There are some securities whose betas are found to be as high as 3 or 4—which indicates highly volatile stocks.
- Some securities have a zero beta. However, it does not mean that such securities are risk-free. Beta can be zero if correlation between security's return and that of market return is zero.
- Betas of same stock from different countries are not comparable as it is a result of regression of one stock against the market where it is listed.
- Stocks which are thought to be less affected by cycles have usually lower beta. Companies falling in FMCG, healthcare sector, etc., have a low beta. Also tech-stocks have usually higher beta.

> **Check yourself**
> Calculate beta of companies by taking their last five years monthly data (from January 2007 to December 2011). Check if you have received any negative beta. Also check if beta value is consistent across the sector or is varying as per the sector.

> **Pause for thought:** Beta is the ratio of covariance between the returns of the market and the security and the variance of the market return.

In this case, volatility of the L&T security is being assessed with respect to the beta value of 1, for the market portfolio. But what happens when the return on the market portfolio is zero? For that we need to be acquainted with another parameter, alpha (α). Alpha indicates the return of the security when the market return is zero. In other words, it is the difference between the expected return of the security and its equilibrium expected return.

A bit on alpha

Alpha measures the risk-adjusted return or the actual return the given security provides, in relation to the return one expects based upon that security's beta. It is evident from the above discussion that beta measures security's volatility in relation to the benchmark index. For example, here beta of L&T is 1.38; and if benchmark index (here, Sensex) gained 5%, it would be expected that L&T would gain 7% (5% ×1.38 = 6.9%). But if L&T actually increased its gain to say 8% (or in other words more than 7%), it would have a positive alpha. This generalization is frequently used by analysts while selecting the securities from the market for an investment purpose. Alpha refers to potential of the stock to gain value, based on the rate at which the company's earnings are growing and on other fundamental indicators.

Some conclusions, drawn with respect to different alpha values, are:

- If a stock is assigned alpha value of 1 by analysts, it is estimated that the given stock would have a 10% rise in a year when the market is flat. It is an investment strategy used by the analysts to look for the securities with positive alpha; as such securities are usually under-valued.
- Also, in an efficient market, the expected value of alpha should be zero and it is a tendency of all securities to give zero alpha value over a long time period. Alpha indicates how an investment has performed after accounting for the risk involved.
- Alpha value of less than zero indicates that the security has earned too little for its risk or is too risky for the given return.
- Zero value of alpha indicates security has earned return adequate to its risk.
- Alpha value greater than zero indicates the security has a return in excess of the reward for the assumed risk.

The following equation enables the determination of alpha.

$$\alpha_i = R_i - (\beta_i \times R_m) \tag{13}$$

Where,

α_i = alpha of the security, i.

R_i = return on security, i.

β_i = beta of the security, i.

R_m = return of the market.

Alpha is the risk-adjusted measure of the so called active return of a security or an investment (in case of a portfolio). It is the return in excess of the compensation, for the risk borne is usually used to assess managers' performance. It is mainly used to assess the performance of mutual funds. The excess return of a mutual fund or a portfolio, relative to the return of the benchmark index, is called fund's alpha[4]. Alpha is the Y-intercept and theoretically it must be zero. If it is not zero, it is yielding abnormal returns. Thus, alpha is an abnormal (given that market return is considered zero) rate of return of the security, in excess of that estimated by an equilibrium model like CAPM and APT (to be discussed later). Graphical representation has alpha as the intercept term, signifying the expected return on security (in this case, L&T), when the return on the market portfolio is zero.

For the given example of L&T security,

$$\therefore \quad \alpha_{L\&T} = R_{L\&T} - (\beta_{L\&T} \times R_m)$$
$$= 1.668 - [(1.38 \times 0.998)]$$
$$= 0.29$$

Being an aggressive stock (already concluded on the basis of a β value higher than 1), this value of $\alpha_{L\&T}$ can easily be interpreted as a return of 0.29 being generated by L&T, even when the market gives zero return. But this abnormal return on the security is due to unsystematic risk.

Thus, alpha is the measure of the unsystematic risk, the risk which is diversifiable, while beta is the measure of the systematic, undiversifiable risk, the reason behind the maintenance of a certain level of risk in a portfolio! Since the calculation of beta has led us to the concept of alpha, the cause of abnormal returns on security, the characteristics of alpha need to be paid attention. The significance of alpha and its varied values are:

- It is a measure of the unsystematic, diversifiable risk of a security.
- Hence, it is company-specific.
- Because of the randomness of a security, over a long period of time alpha becomes zero.
- Positive value of alpha indicates that the stock delivers more than its theoretical return, which means it is an under-priced stock and therefore should be bought.
- A negative value of alpha indicates that the actual return of the stock delivered is less than the theoretical return, hence is over-priced and should be avoided.

Check yourself

Calculate alpha values of at least 10 stocks of BSE Sensex or NSE Nifty by taking their last five years monthly data (from January 2007 to December 2011). Check how many stocks have positive alpha. Compare this with actual return of the stocks. What does your result show?

Pause for thought: Alpha is a measure of the unsystematic, diversifiable risk of a security.

Security characteristics line (SCL) is the regression line, which plots the performance of a particular security or a portfolio against market at a specific period of time. Security characteristics line is plotted on a graph where the Y-axis is the return on a security and X-axis the market return. The slope of the graph is the security's beta and intercept is alpha. The slope of the line is the

---
[4] Alpha will be further discussed in Chapter 23: Portfolio Performance Evaluation.

measure of the systematic risk, which determines the risk-return trade-off. So, as per this metric the more risk we take, the higher the returns we can expect to earn. However, it is to be noted that there is a considerable controversy about the use of beta as a measure of risk and return.

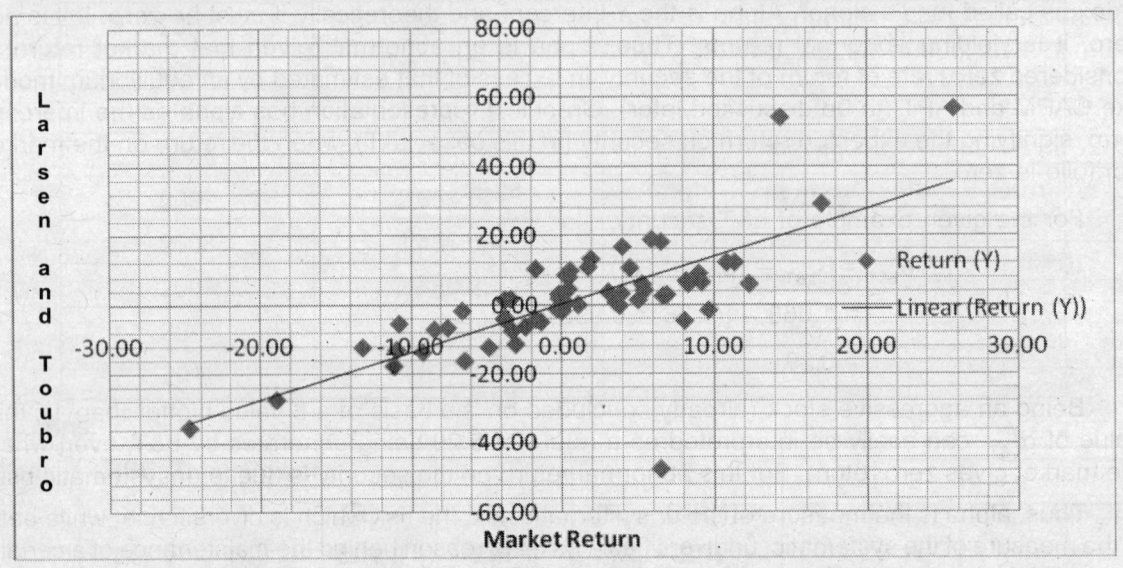

Figure 6.2: Characteristics line of L&T

Regression line is the line known as the line of best fit. It is an attempt to find the straight line, which best represents the plotted points of observable data on a graph. This line helps to understand the correlation between the data. Once we derive the equation for regression line, it can be used to predict possible future values, which are yet to be observed.

The above graph shows the market returns and contribution of L&T to the market returns and how it fits a regression line represented by the market model.

The market model is:

$$R_i = \alpha_i + \beta_i \times R_m + \epsilon_{im} \tag{14}$$

Where, ϵ_{im} = random error.

The regression line of the market model is called the characteristics line. It is called so because it is a characteristic of a given security. Regression is a statistical measure that attempts to determine the strength of the relationship between one dependent variable (usually denoted by the Y-axis) and a series of other changing variables, known as the independent variables.

The characteristics line for L&T is,

$$R_i = \alpha_i + \beta_i \times R_m + \epsilon_{im} = 0.29 + 1.38 \times R_m$$

It is thus evident that beta, and alpha, can be estimated by the regression equation.

Beta And Risk Estimation

Table 6.2 Calculation of β as per the Regression Method

No.	Month	Market Return, X (%)	L&T Return, Y (%)	X × Y	X^2	Y^2
1	Aug–06	8.96	9.14	81.84	80.19	83.51
2	Sep–06	6.45	–47.52	–306.63	41.63	2258.60
3	Oct–06	3.91	3.37	13.19	15.31	11.36
4	Nov–06	5.42	4.31	23.35	29.33	18.59
5	Dec–06	0.42	4.64	1.93	0.17	21.51
6	Jan–07	1.90	13.39	25.47	3.62	179.18
7	Feb–07	–8.40	–7.03	59.05	70.54	49.44
8	Mar–07	0.45	8.09	3.63	0.20	65.41
9	Apr–07	8.28	6.09	50.42	68.51	37.10
10	May–07	3.98	16.88	67.18	15.84	284.94
11	Jun–07	0.28	8.72	2.40	0.08	75.96
12	Jul–07	5.90	19.02	112.13	34.76	361.69
13	Aug–07	–0.17	2.06	–0.34	0.03	4.25
14	Sep–07	12.27	6.14	75.26	150.44	37.65
15	Oct–07	14.29	54.35	776.84	204.32	2953.63
16	Nov–07	–3.81	–3.98	15.15	14.52	15.81
17	Dec–07	3.79	–0.17	–0.65	14.33	0.03
18	Jan–08	–13.17	–12.18	160.45	173.41	148.46
19	Feb–08	–1.36	–4.78	6.49	1.84	22.87
20	Mar–08	–9.19	–13.58	124.77	84.45	184.34
21	Apr–08	9.61	–1.53	–14.71	92.34	2.34
22	May–08	–6.52	–1.64	10.68	42.49	2.68
23	Jun–08	–18.86	–27.40	516.81	355.86	750.54
24	Jul–08	6.50	18.36	119.27	42.20	337.03
25	Aug–08	3.56	0.77	2.75	12.65	0.60
26	Sep–08	–10.77	–5.31	57.18	116.03	28.18
27	Oct–08	–24.75	–35.46	877.52	612.37	1257.46
28	Nov–08	–10.94	–12.94	141.53	119.63	167.45
29	Dec–08	5.29	6.08	32.15	27.94	36.99
30	Jan–09	–3.05	–11.31	34.46	9.29	127.82
31	Feb–09	–4.80	–12.15	58.37	23.08	147.57

32	Mar–09	10.79	12.30	132.68	116.45	151.18
33	Apr–09	17.01	29.35	499.09	289.24	861.16
34	May–09	25.70	57.05	1466.07	660.38	3254.73
35	Jun–09	–1.71	10.44	–17.89	2.94	109.07
36	Jul–09	8.02	–4.52	–36.30	64.37	20.47
37	Aug–09	–0.18	3.23	–0.58	0.03	10.46
38	Sep–09	9.15	6.60	60.37	83.70	43.55
39	Oct–09	–7.51	–6.55	49.16	56.33	42.91
40	Nov–09	6.87	3.03	20.80	47.15	9.17
41	Dec–09	3.05	3.79	11.58	9.32	14.40
42	Jan–10	–6.38	–16.07	102.62	40.75	258.40
43	Feb–10	0.55	9.95	5.50	0.30	99.09
44	Mar–10	6.63	2.61	17.29	43.91	6.81
45	Apr–10	0.02	–1.65	–0.03	0.00	2.71
46	May–10	–3.38	1.79	–6.04	11.40	3.20
47	Jun–10	4.47	10.73	48.01	20.02	115.11
48	Jul–10	1.07	0.12	0.13	1.14	0.01
49	Aug–10	0.33	0.36	0.12	0.11	0.13
50	Sep–10	11.33	12.35	139.85	128.31	152.43
51	Oct–10	–0.31	–1.12	0.34	0.09	1.25
52	Nov–10	–3.71	–3.85	14.28	13.73	14.85
53	Dec–10	5.01	1.49	7.46	25.13	2.21
54	Jan–11	–11.12	–17.53	195.00	123.73	307.31
55	Feb–11	–3.27	–7.39	24.14	10.67	54.63
56	Mar–11	8.14	7.01	57.00	66.19	49.09
57	Apr–11	–1.68	–4.12	6.92	2.83	16.94
58	May–11	–3.75	1.54	–5.79	14.06	2.38
59	Jun–11	1.72	10.95	18.85	2.96	120.00
60	Jul–11	–2.41	–6.20	14.92	5.79	38.42
Total		59.91	100.10	5953.46	4298.48	15435.05
Average		0.998	1.668			

The values of beta and alpha, as represented by the regression Equation (15), can be calculated, using the following equations as well.

$$\beta = \frac{[n(\Sigma XY) - (\Sigma X)(\Sigma Y)]}{[n\Sigma X^2 - (\Sigma X)^2]} \tag{15}$$

Where,

X = market return.

Y = return on security.

n = time period.

$$\therefore \quad \beta_{L\&T} = \frac{[(60)(5953.46)] - [(59.91)(100.10)]}{[(60)(4298.48) - (59.91)^2]}$$

$$= \frac{357207.6 - 5996.99}{257908.8 - 3589.21}$$

$$= \frac{351210.61}{254319.59} = 1.38$$

$$\alpha_i = R_i - (b_i \times R_m)$$

$$\therefore \quad \alpha_{L\&T} = 1.668 - [(1.38 \times 0.998)]$$

$$= 0.29$$

Thus, irrespective of the method of calculation, the values of alpha and beta remain the same for a given security, for the given period of time, with respect to the return it generates.

This discussion is all about the risk of a security (and of the portfolio)—be it the systematic or the unsystematic component—symbolized by their respective measures, beta and alpha respectively. Therefore, reference to correlation coefficient too is natural. We have already discussed how correlation coefficients decide the risk of a portfolio. We are now also aware that the portfolio risk is maintained at a certain level by the systematic, undiversifiable risk. Hence, the correlation coefficient between the market return and that on the security is calculated by a formula that resembles that for beta [Equation (15)]. It is denoted by Cor_{im}.

$$\text{Coefficient of correlation} = Cor_{im} = \frac{[N(\Sigma XY) - (\Sigma X)(\Sigma Y)]}{[(N\Sigma Y^2) - (\Sigma Y)^2 \{N\Sigma X^2 - (\Sigma X)^2\}]^{1/2}} \tag{16}$$

$$\therefore \quad Cor_{(L\&T),\ market} = \frac{(60)(5953.46) - (59.91)(100.10)}{[\{(60)(15435.05) - (100.10)^2\}\{(60)(4298.48) - (59.91)^2\}]^{1/2}}$$

$$= \frac{351210.61}{482677.79}$$

$$= 0.7276 = 0.73$$

The square of correlation coefficient is called coefficient of determination, denoted by r^2.

$$r^2 = (Cor_{im})^2 \tag{17}$$

$$\therefore \quad r_{(L\&T),\ market}^2 = (0.73)^2$$
$$= 0.53$$

The value of coefficient of determination is the extent to which the return of a security is explained by the market return. In this case, a value of 0.53, for the coefficient of determination, implies that the market is able to explain only 53% of the return generated by the share of L&T.

> **Pause for thought:** As variance is the square of standard deviation, similarly, the coefficient of determination is the square of correlation coefficient! It is denoted by r^2 and is a measure of the extent to which the market is able to explain the return on a security. It is thus an estimate of the efficiency of the market, explaining the reason behind the return on a security.

Now that we have discussed quite in detail the components of the total risk—the systematic and unsystematic risks—we would like to put to use our learning by calculating the total risk. We have evaluated the measures of both components, in the form of the calculated values of beta and alpha for L&T. So we can calculate the total risk on the return of L&T.

> **Check yourself**
>
> Calculate the correlation coefficient of at least 10 securities of BSE Sensex or Nifty 50 by taking their last five years monthly data (from January 2007 to December 2011). Relate the correlation coefficient with alpha and beta? What does it indicate?

Total risk and systematic risk of L&T

$$\text{Total risk} = \text{Variance of L\&T}$$
$$= Var(\alpha + \beta \times R_m + \epsilon_{im}) \quad (18)$$

Variance of alpha is zero. As alpha is the measure of the diversifiable risk, which can be completely eliminated, the above equation can be rewritten as:

$$\text{Total risk} = \beta^2(L\&T) \times Var(R_m) + Var(\epsilon_{im}) \quad (19)$$

We know that the measure of risk is standard deviation, σ and variance is σ^2. Similarly, variance of beta (β) is β^2, as beta is the measure of risk.

The first component of this equation shows the systematic risk. For L&T,

$$\text{Systematic risk} = \text{coefficient of determination } (r^2) \quad (20)$$
$$= 0.53.$$

Thus systematic risk is 53% of the variance. The total risk of the market is considered as 1.

$$\therefore \quad \text{Unsystematic risk of L\&T} = 1 - r^2$$
$$= 1 - 0.53 = 0.47$$

Hence, the unsystematic risk of L&T is 47%.

> **Check yourself**
>
> Calculate the coefficient of determination of at least 10 securities of BSE Sensex or Nifty 50 by taking their last five years monthly data (from January 2007 to December 2011). Is it actually happening for these securities? Relate your answer with beta.

> **Pause for thought:** Systematic risk is explained by the term coefficient of determination, r^2, while unsystematic risk is explained by $1 - r^2$.

Market portfolio means portfolio of all securities that are available in the market. These include bonds, debentures, gold, real estate, etc. But, in practice we consider different indices as a market portfolio[5]. To compute the beta of any security, the data of market return and return on security is required. There are several indices and equity research firms which publish the values of beta, the scrips, from time to time. They differ in terms of: the period for which the data is collected and time interval between the successive data collection. However, the standard practice is to compute beta by taking monthly data of five years. The return should be total return—sum of the capital gain (or loss) and dividend yield. However, dividend yield may be omitted, computing beta simply on the basis of capital gain (or loss) of market and security.

6.3.2 Accounting Beta

Accounting beta too can be calculated. It is the sensitivity of the earnings of a company with respect to the aggregate of incomes of all companies in the economy. Accounting beta can also be calculated by running a regression by using the company's return on assets (ROA) against the ROA of the market benchmark such as BSE Sensex or Nifty 50. The accounting beta is the slope coefficient of regression. Accounting beta can be related to market beta. This relation leads to important conclusions on the sensitivity of the earnings, of companies, towards the business conditions. Thus it is a relative measure of the systematic risk and its susceptibility to the market conditions.

Furthermore, the value of beta depends also upon the time period, as we have seen in Equation (10). It does not remain stable over a longer period of time. Even if the companies are in the same sector or belong to the portfolios comprised of similar scrips, beta of a security is different for two different time intervals. There are several other factors too which determine the variation in the values of beta. These may be: changes in the technology used by the firm; change in the level of competition; shift in product portfolio; change in the operational equation due to government policies; impact of foreign policy; etc., to name a few. In the following section we shall be discussing on the parameters that determine beta.

> **Pause for thought:** Accounting beta is a measure of the systematic risk vis-à-vis its susceptibility to market conditions. It is the sensitivity of the returns of a company with respect to the market return.

6.3.3 Determinants of Beta

1. *Nature of business:* All companies in the market are affected by business cycles. So their incomes change in these different phases of business cycles. Usually, incomes rise in a growth phase, remain stable in the maturity phase and fall in the declining phase of the business cycles. For example, betas of IT and steel sectors are usually higher. So, with the higher risk content they will fluctuate with the business cycle more than the FMCG sector. Beta of FMCG sector is more stable, hence their earnings are least affected by the business cycles.

> **Pause for thought:** Companies with high beta are more susceptible to the fluctuation of the business cycles.

2. *Operating leverage:* We know that companies differ in their cost structures. Some of the companies in a same sector may have higher fixed costs and lower variable costs; while it might be the reverse for other companies. Operating leverage refers to the use of fixed costs. Degree

---
[5] These indices include only shares of companies.

of operating leverage means $\Delta EBIT^6/\Delta Sales$. Variable costs change with respect to change in sales, while fixed costs remain constant irrespective of the status of earnings. Companies with high operating leverage face greater fluctuations in their earnings during unfavorable situation. Hence such companies are more risky, as impact of the business cycles is more on such companies. As a consequence, companies with high operating leverage have high beta.

> **Pause for thought**: Operating leverage is the use of fixed costs, irrespective of the market conditions. Hence, with this inherent rigidity such companies cannot adopt situations to overcome unfavorable market conditions. Thus companies with high operating leverage have high beta.

3. *Financial leverage:* It refers to the use of debt funds in the capital structure and such firms are called levered firms. For such companies, as use of interest obligatory funds are higher, outflow of funds in terms of interest payments is fixed. This causes change in PAT[7] with changes in EBIT. It increases the financial risk of the company due to high fixed obligation (as with companies having high operating leverage). The matter worsens during recessions. Companies with high fixed obligation too have high beta.

> **Pause for thought**: Financial leverage refers to the use of debt funds in the capital structure. Such firms, called levered firms, too have high risk, and thus high beta because of high fixed obligations.

Table 6.3 Beta, r^2, volatility and returns of Sensex scrips for the period of one year, from November 2011 to October 2012

Scrip code	Company	Beta values	Co-efficient of determination (r^2)	Average daily volatility[8] (%)	Returns for 1 year (%)	Weightage (%) in Sensex as on 31/10/2011
532977	Bajaj Auto Ltd.	0.75	0.30	1.75	14.49%	1.72%
532454	Bharti Airtel Ltd.	0.66	0.23	1.76	20.17%	3.57%
500103	Bharat Heavy Electricals Ltd.	0.81	0.36	1.74	−35.02%	1.87%
500087	Cipla Ltd.	0.59	0.23	1.56	−16.38%	1.06%
533278	Coal India Ltd.	0.53	0.10	2.08	−2.91%	1.44%
532868	DLF Ltd.	1.41	0.42	2.78	−30.86%	0.71%
500010	Housing Development Finance Corporation Ltd.	1.04	0.55	1.79	0.01%	6.59%

---

[6] Earnings before Interest and taxes—it is also known as operating income.
[7] Profit after tax.
[8] Average daily volatility = standard deviation of daily returns, of individual stock prices, for the past one year.

500180	HDFC Bank Ltd.	0.98	0.56	1.67	7.34%	6.28%
500182	Hero Motor Corp. Ltd.	0.47	0.07	2.29	16.61%	1.49%
500696	Hindustan Unilever Ltd.	0.46	0.15	1.51	27.59%	2.78%
500440	Hindalco Industries Ltd.	1.43	0.50	2.57	−35.23%	1.26%
532174	ICICI Bank Ltd.	1.37	0.67	2.14	−19.90%	7.37%
500209	Infosys Ltd.	0.98	0.47	1.82	−3.18%	9.64%
500875	ITC Ltd.	0.69	0.36	1.48	24.54%	7.97%
532532	Jaiprakash Associates Ltd.	1.78	0.52	3.16	−35.84%	0.62%
532286	Jindal Steel & Power Ltd.	1.19	0.54	2.08	−19.27%	1.63%
500510	Larsen & Toubro Ltd.	1.10	0.51	1.96	−30.10%	5.34%
500520	Mahindra & Mahindra Ltd.	1.08	0.43	2.11	17.95%	2.91%
532500	Maruti Suzuki India Ltd.	0.68	0.25	1.72	−27.43%	1.12%
532555	NTPC Ltd.	0.75	0.39	1.53	−8.00%	2.03%
500312	Oil And Natural Gas Corporation Ltd.	0.57	0.17	1.75	−14.61%	3.27%
500325	Reliance Industries Ltd.	1.08	0.58	1.81	−19.90%	10.86%
500112	State Bank Of India	1.16	0.49	2.10	−39.49%	3.74%
500900	Sterlite Industries (India) Ltd.	1.39	0.55	2.39	−24.45%	1.32%
524715	Sun Pharmaceutical Industries Ltd.	0.62	0.21	1.72	19.42%	1.43%
500570	Tata Motors Ltd.	1.58	0.53	2.76	−14.42%	2.57%
500400	Tata Power Co. Ltd.	0.62	0.26	1.56	−28.19%	1.14%
500470	Tata Steel Ltd.	1.17	0.56	1.99	−18.14%	2.23%
532540	Tata Consultancy Services Ltd.	1.02	0.46	1.92	5.93%	4.49%
507685	Wipro Ltd.	0.95	0.46	1.77	−12.67%	1.55%
	Sensex	**1.00**		**1.27**	**−11.62%**	

(Source: www.bseindia.com)

From the above table we can say that Jaiprakash Associates has a highest beta of 1.78 and Hero Motor Corp. Ltd. has the lowest beta of 0.47.

6.3.4 Asset Beta and Equity Beta

Asset beta, as per the definition, reflects the beta of a company without debt. It is also referred to as un-levered beta (un-levered means without debt). For many companies it is beneficial to employ debt in their capital structure for financial gain. In such a case, with the use of asset beta, the evaluation of the volatility of a company's stock without debt is possible.

Usually asset beta takes account of the business risk while equity beta takes account of both business risk and financial risk. In other words, asset beta removes the effect of financial risk.

Moreover asset beta of the company is used to estimate equity beta for companies which are not publicly traded, and also for such projects which are unrelated to company's core business.

Equity beta means stock beta. Most commonly when the term beta is referred to, it means equity beta or stock beta.

As assets of any firm are financed by debt and equity, asset beta is the weighted average of the equity beta and debt beta.

$$\beta_A = \beta_E \left(\frac{\text{Equity}}{\text{Equity} + (1-t)\text{Debt}} \right) + \beta_D \left(\frac{\text{Debt}}{\text{Equity} + (1-t)\text{Debt}} \right) \tag{21}$$

Where,

β_A = asset beta (β of the net asset of the firm).

β_E = equity beta (β of equity funds).

β_D = debt beta (β of debt funds)

And, $(1-t)$ should be added with debt as debt component gets the advantage of tax deduction.

Asset β, by definition, reflects the β of a company without debt. It is sometimes referred to as unlevered β.

As debt funds are less expensive than equity capital, debt beta is lower than equity beta. But, in case of an unlevered company, which is actually financed by the equity capital only, the asset beta is equivalent to the equity beta.

Hence Equation (21), for asset beta, reduces to,

$$\beta_A = \beta_E \left(\frac{\text{Equity}}{\text{Equity} + (1-t)\text{Debt}} \right) \tag{22}$$

For a levered firm, proportion of equity fund is less than 1 because the total fund is comprised of both debt and equity resources. So, beta of the asset, which is being referred to as asset beta, is less than beta of equity; beta of equity can be defined as,

$$\beta_E = \beta_A \left(1 + \frac{(1-t)\text{Debt}}{\text{Equity}} \right) \tag{23}$$

The ratio on the right hand side of debt and equity shows the financial leverage. The above equation thus shows the linear relationship between equity beta and financial leverage. The equation also indicates that when proportion of debt increases in a company, equity beta increases.

> **Pause for thought:** Asset beta is the beta of a company without debt, while equity beta is the beta of an equity fund.

6.4 THE MARKET MODEL

The market model represents the relationship between return of security with the market. It has been already discussed [Equation (14)], though in brief, for the stock of L&T whereby the regression equation was utilized. And now we shall be considering the model again for the stock of L&T, but in detail. With reference to Equation (14), equation of the market model is given as follows:

$$r_i = \alpha_{im} + \beta_{im} \times r_m + \epsilon_{im} \qquad (24)$$

Where,

r_i = return of security i, for the given period.

r_m = return on market index for the same period.

α_{im} = intercept-term—it is the alpha, measure of unsystematic risk.

β_{im} = beta of security i with respect to market. It represents the slope of the characteristics line.

ϵ_{im} = random error term.

From the above equation, the relationship between the return of security i for a given time period and the market return over the same time period is very much evident. The market referred could be Sensex, Nifty or any broad-based market index. The equation shows a direct variation between the market returns and that of security. Hence, when the market shows upward trend, the return on the scrip being studied too is likely to increase, provided it has a positive beta. Beta always shows a positive correlation with the market. Thus it rises and falls with the market, and it is quite understandable given that beta is the market-risk—the undiversifiable risk.

A point to be noted, in the context of our analysis is that the value of the random error is assumed to be zero all through this discussion.

As mentioned above we consider the scrip of L&T, for a detailed discussion on the market model. Alpha and beta values of 0.29 and 1.38, respectively, have already been derived. By putting these values in the Equation (24) the market model of L&T, for the time period August 2006 to July 2011, is evaluated.

$$r_{L\&T} = 0.29\% + 1.38 \times r_m + \epsilon_{im}$$

When the value of market index, Sensex, is considered for the same time period, the market return turns out to be 14%. So r_m = 14%.

∴ r_m = 14%

So, return on L&T is expected to be

$$r_{L\&T} = 0.29\% + (1.38 \times 14\%) + 0$$

[random error assumed to be zero, as mentioned above]

$$= 0.29\% + 19.32 + 0$$

$$= 19.61\%$$

If the market (Sensex is the market index) return is assumed to have gone down to −9%, during the said period, the expected return for L&T is,

$$r_{L\&T} = 0.29 + [1.38 \times (-9)] + 0$$
$$= 0.29 - 12 + 0$$
$$= -12.13\%$$

Thus, when the market return is 14%, the return on L&T is 19.61%. But, when the market return is down to −9%, that of L&T too follows suit dipping to −12.13%.

> **Pause for thought:** The market model shows that for the given time period, all parameters of risk remaining the same and random error term being zero, the return on a scrip has a direct relationship with the market return.

6.4.1 Random Error

Random error term has been used in Equation (24), for the market model. And it has been subsequently assumed to be zero for L&T. But what is random error that we have to know. Well, the random error term is the insufficiency of the market model in explaining the return of particular scrip efficiently.

Thus, the projected returns, 19.61% and −12.13%, of L&T at market returns of 14% and −9% respectively are not the exact returns of L&T. The actual return at these values of market returns might vary significantly. And again the departure of the actual return, from that projected, could be small. Thus the return provided by the market model differs from the actual. And this difference arises due to randomness. This random error term is the measure of this randomness which causes this difference in returns. The standard deviation of the random error term is denoted by $\sigma \epsilon_{im}$.

For example, return on L&T is 19.61% as per the market model, when market return is 14%. However, in real life L&T stock may not rise to 19.61% when the market is providing 14% return. Instead L&T may provide return of, say 16.61% (16.61% is assumed for our simplicity, it can be any other number), the difference would be attributed to random error term (which is 3% here). Similarly, L&T stock gives return of −10% instead of −12.13% when market goes down to −9%. Then the difference of 2.13 is due to the random error term.

Random error term is viewed as a variable which is random in nature and has a probability distribution with a mean of zero. So, it can be viewed as having equal chances of occurrence on both the sides (up-side as well as down-side—that is return may move in either direction).

For simplicity let us assume that L&T has random error term with integer values which can range from −7% to 7% (instead of 3% or 2.13% as above).

For example, when the return on L&T moves from −12.13% to 19.61%, with market return rising from −9% to 14%, for enhancing the understanding the random error term of L&T is assumed to be in the range of −7% to 7%. This leads to possibility of 15 outcomes: −7, −6, −5, −4, −3, −2, −1, 0, 1, 2, 3, 4, 5, 6, 7. And all the 15 outcomes have equal probability of occurring. As the range of random error term is from −7 to +7, it means that the expected outcome is zero. So, the expected return of random error term is calculated as:

$$\{(-7) \times (1/15)\} + \{(-6) \times (1/15)\} + \ldots + \{(6) \times (1/15)\} + \{(7) \times (1/15)\} = 0$$

Each occurrence has been multiplied with its probability (which is 1/15 for each as total number of outcomes is 15, ranging from –7 to +7) of occurrence and as assumed, their total sum is taken as zero.

The variance of the random error is calculated as:

$[\{(-7-0)^2 \times (1/15)\} + \{(-6-0)^2 \times (1/15)\} + ... + \{(6-0)^2 \times (1/15)\} + \{(7-0)^2 \times (1/15)\}]$

$= [(49/15 + 36/15 + 25/15 + 16/15 + 9/15 + 4/15 + 1/15 + 0 + 1/15 + 4/15 + 9/15 + 16/15 + 25/15 + 36/15 + 49/15)]$

∴ Standard deviation of the random error term, $\sigma\epsilon_{im}$ = (18.66%)1/2

= 4.32%

The computation of risk (variance) involves subtraction of the average return from actual return [x – E(x)] and squaring of the difference. These values have then been summated to give the variance, whose square root leads to the standard deviation, 4.32%, for the random error term.

Figure 6.3 below is the graphical representation of the scrip of L&T, ignoring the random error term.

The market model equation for security of L&T, with random error term as zero, is,

$r_{L\&T} = 0.29 + (1.38 \times r_m)$

If the market provides an average return of 12% during the given time period (August 2006 to July 2011), the return provided by L&T is,

$r_{L\&T}$ = 0.29 + (1.38 × 12)

= 0.29 + 16.56

= 16.85%

It has been already seen that with a market return (during the same time period) of 14%, return of L&T is 19.61%.

These values when are plotted, we get the graph as follows, where the market return is plotted on X-axis and that of L&T on Y-axis. It is evident with positive values of alpha and beta, return on L&T goes up, when market return goes up.

Value of the slope (beta) is

ß = y₂ – y₁/x₂ – x₁

= (19.61 – 16.85)/(14 – 12)

= 1.38

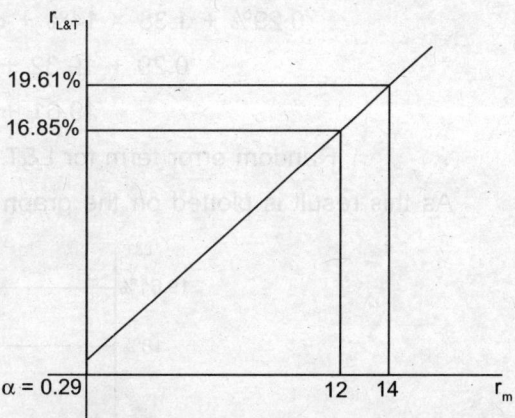

Figure 6.3: Return and risk of the stock of L&T as per market model

---

Check yourself

Calculate the return as per market model for Reliance Communication, whose beta is 1.54 and alpha is –1.91 for the time period: August 2006 to July 2011, when the market returns are 14% and 12% respectively. Plot the results on the graph and explain the relationship.

Beta

From the above graph, beta is derived as the difference of the return on security (Y-axis) as compared to that of the market (X-axis). In other words, it is the sensitivity of the return on security to that of the market index. The value of beta, 1.38, is same irrespective of whether it is derived through computation in equation (see appendix A of this chapter) or from the graph. Also, the positive value of beta indicates that if market goes up, return of security (in this case L&T) also goes up. When the return of Reliance Communication is calculated and plotted it will be seen that the slope of the Reliance Communication is higher than the slope of L&T. This implies a higher sensitivity of the scrip of Reliance Communication towards the market returns, compared to L&T.

Beta has been dealt with in further detail, in chapter 9 on CAPM.

> **Pause for thought:** Random error term is the measure of randomness which leads to the insufficiency of the market model in explaining efficiently the returns on a security and thus their departure in reality, from the projected value by the market model too remains unexplained.

6.4.2 Actual Returns

We have discussed above that the given market model equation does not explain the return on security exactly. At the same time this happens because random error term is assumed to be zero. We have seen how the return for L&T was derived to be 19.61% and –12.13% at the market returns of 14% and –9% respectively.

Suppose the actual return turns out to be 18% for L&T. Then the equation of the market model for the return on L&T becomes,

$$0.29\% + 1.38 \times 14\% + \sigma\epsilon_{im} = 18.00\%$$

$$0.29 + 19.32 + \epsilon_{im} = 18.00$$

$$19.61 + \epsilon_{im} = 18.00$$

∴ Random error term for L&T, $\epsilon_{im} = -1.61\%$

As this result is plotted on the graph we are led to Figure 6.4.

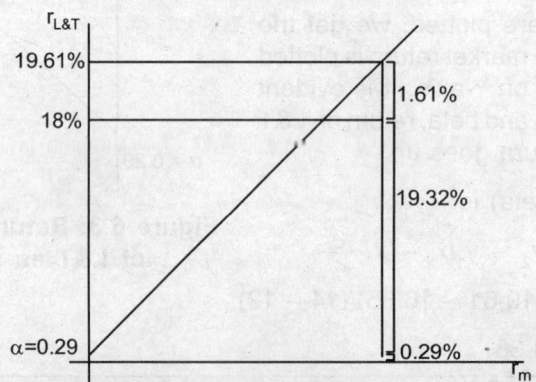

Figure 6.4: Alpha value for L&T

Where, –1.61% shows the difference between the actual return and that derived from the market model.

> **Pause for thought:** The actual return on a security can be projected by the market model only when the random error term is non-zero.

Further on Market Model

As per the market model, the total risk (variance) of any security is comprised of two parts:

- Market risk—the undiversifiable, systematic risk
- Unique risk—the diversifiable, unsystematic risk.

Thus variance is resolved into two parts, as per the market model.

$$\sigma_i^2 = \beta_i^2 \sigma_m^2 + \sigma\epsilon_{im}^2 \qquad (25)$$

Where,

σ_i^2 = variance of security, i.

β_i^2 = beta of security, i.

σ_m^2 = variance of the return of the market index.

$\sigma\epsilon_{im}^2$ = unique risk of security i and is the variance of the random error term.

We know that the return of a portfolio, which is a bunch of securities, is the weighted average return of the individual securities. Hence can be represented as,

$$r_p = \sum_{i=1}^{n} w_i r_i \qquad (26)$$

Where,

w_i = respective weights of the individual securities in a portfolio.

r_i = return of individual security in a portfolio.

r_p = return of the portfolio.

By putting the value of Equation (24) in Equation (26), we get:

$$r_p = \sum_{i=1}^{n} w_i(\alpha_{im} + \beta_{im} r_m + \epsilon_{im}) \qquad (27)$$

$$= \sum_{i=1}^{n} w_i \alpha_{im} + \sum_{i=1}^{n} (w_i \beta_{im}) r_m + \sum_{i=1}^{n} w_i \epsilon_{im}$$

$$= \alpha_{Pm} + \beta_{Pm} r_M + \epsilon_{Pm} \qquad (28)$$

Where,

$$\alpha_{Pm} = \sum_{i=1}^{n} w_i \alpha_{im} \qquad (29)$$

$$\beta_{Pm} = \sum_{i=1}^{n} w_i \beta_{im} \qquad (30)$$

$$\epsilon_{Pm} = \sum_{i=1}^{n} w_i \epsilon_{im} \qquad (31)$$

Equation (29) shows the intercept (alpha) of the portfolio and Equation (30) shows the slope (beta) of the portfolio. Alpha of the portfolio is nothing but the weighted average alphas of the individual securities. Similarly, beta of the portfolio is the weighted average betas of the individual securities in a portfolio.

Given the fact that beta is the sensitivity of the return on a security, with respect to the market return, beta is represented by:

$$\beta = \text{covariance } (i,m)/\sigma_m^2.$$

On the other hand, ϵ_{Pm} is the random error term of the portfolio, which is the weighted average of random error terms of individual securities, as are the portfolio return, alpha and beta, all weighted averages.

Equation (28) gives the return of portfolio as per the market model. The risk of the portfolio is derived from this equation as:

$$\sigma_P^2 = \beta_{Pm}^2 \sigma_m^2 + \sigma_{\epsilon im}^2 \qquad (32)$$

Where,

σ_P^2 = variance of the portfolio.

β_{Pm}^2 = measured as $\sum_{i=1}^{n} [w_i \beta_{im}]^2$ = systematic risk of the portfolio.

$\sigma_\epsilon^2 = \sum_{i=1}^{n} w_i^2 \sigma_{\epsilon im}$ = standard deviation of the random error term.

Thus, as per Equation (25) based on the market model, the total risk of the portfolio is comprised of two parts, just as is that of an individual security risk. As derived in the portfolio analysis, in Chapter 5, risk of the portfolio decreases when securities are added further to it. Addition of securities brings down the unique risk of the portfolio, while market risk may remain the same.

Pause for thought: Alpha, the measure of diversifiable risk, is represented as the intercept of the portfolio; and beta, the measure of undiversifiable risk and thus sensitivity to the market, is physically represented as the slope of the portfolio, vide the equation on the return of a portfolio, based on the market model. Total risk of a portfolio too has two components—undiversifiable and diversifiable—as have the individual securities.

SUMMARY

- For a portfolio with 'N' number of securities, the average variance of individual securities becomes negligible but covariance among the securities continues to have its impact. So, for a well-diversified portfolio, portfolio variance becomes equivalent to average covariance.
- Systematic risk arises due to macroeconomic factors. The systematic risk of the security shows the sensitivity of security's return towards the market returns. This sensitivity of

a security is known as its beta. Higher beta, indicates higher risk and vice versa. Systematic risk cannot be diversified.

- Unsystematic risk arises due to company specific factors and in a well-diversified portfolio it can be reduced or eliminated completely.
- Nature of business, operating leverage and financial leverage are some of the factors which affect beta the most.
- The relationship between the return on a security and return on a market index is known as a market model.
- The difference between the return estimated by the market model and the actual return is known as the random error term.
- In a market model, the slope measures the sensitivity of security's return to the market index.
- As per the market model, total risk = market risk + unique risk.

KEY CONCEPTS

Alpha	Market Portfolio	Portfolio Risk
Unsystematic Risk	Market Index	Covariance
Beta	Market Model	Correlation Coefficient
Systematic Risk	Diversification	Coefficient of Determination

REVIEW QUESTIONS

1. Does beta remain stable over time? What do you interpret from the values of alpha?
2. What are the factors which influence beta?

ASSIGNMENT QUESTIONS

1. Calculate beta of at least two or three companies from each sector by taking the monthly data of at least five years of the market index (Sensex or Nifty) and of the selected securities. Interpret your results obtained of alpha and beta. Now shortlist those stocks from which have as per your calculation: the highest beta, lowest beta and negative beta. Calculate risk and return of these stocks for the same time period. What do you conclude from these results? Does it prove the statement right: "Higher the beta, higher is the risk and higher is the return as well"?
2. Select two sectors: FMCG and Infrastructure. Calculate the beta of the companies of these sectors. Also calculate the beta for the sector from the given individual betas. Compare and analyze the betas of these two sectors.

ILLUSTRATIONS

Q.1. The table below shows the closing prices of Sensex and the scrip of Tata Power for the period 2001 to 2011. Calculate alpha and beta; and interpret your result.

Year	BSE (Rs.)	Tata Power (Rs.)
2001	341.25	119.55
2002	394.04	111.7
2003	766.31	313.9
2004	886.55	390.55
2005	1,186.23	435.75
2006	1,655.74	559.85
2007	2,656.52	1470.95
2008	1,156.59	748.35
2009	2,180.25	1377.95
2010	2,533.90	1365.7
2011	2,077.79	1021.1

Ans:

Year	BSE X (%)	Tata Power Y (%)	$[R_t - E(R_x)]$	$[R_t - E(R_y)]$	$[R_t - E(R_x)] \times [R_t - E(R_y)]$	$[R_t - E(R_x)]^2$	$[R_t - E(R_y)]^2$
1	2	3	4	5	6 (4*5)	7(4*4)	8(5*5)
2002	15.47	−6.57	−13.50	−47.62	643.03	182.33	2267.80
2003	94.48	181.02	65.50	139.97	9168.09	4290.58	19590.32
2004	15.69	24.42	−13.28	−16.64	220.96	176.41	276.77
2005	33.80	11.57	4.83	−29.48	−142.41	23.33	869.17
2006	39.58	28.48	10.61	−12.58	−133.39	112.52	158.14
2007	60.44	162.74	31.47	121.68	3829.47	990.39	14807.21
2008	−56.46	−49.12	−85.43	−90.18	7704.50	7299.11	8132.41
2009	88.51	84.13	59.53	43.08	2564.53	3544.31	1855.59
2010	16.22	−0.89	−12.75	−41.94	534.87	162.01	1759.31
2011	−18.00	−25.23	−46.97	−66.29	3113.73	2206.46	4394.05
	E(R) = 28.97	E(R) = 41.06			Sum = 27503.40	Sum = 18988.05	Sum = 54110.79
					Cov = 3055.93	Variance = 2109.78	Variance = 6012.31
						S.D.= 45.93	S.D.= 77.54

Return for the BSE for the year 2002 is calculated as $[(P1-P0)/P0] \times 100$ = (Rs.394.04–Rs.341.25)/Rs.341.25 × 100 = 15.47%. In a similar fashion, returns for the other years and

BETA AND RISK ESTIMATION

that for Tata Power are calculated. The average return of BSE from 2002 to 2011 is 28.97%. Tata Power's average return is 41.06%.

$$Cov_{im} = \sigma_{im} = \frac{\Sigma[R(x) - E\{R(x)\}] \times [R(Y) - E\{R(Y)\}]}{n}$$

$$= \frac{27503.40}{9}$$

$$= 3055.93$$

$$\sigma_m^2 = \frac{\Sigma[R(x) - E\{R(x)\}]^2}{n}$$

$$= \frac{189878.05}{9}$$

$$\beta_i = \frac{Cov_{im}}{\sigma_m^2}$$

$$= \frac{3055.93}{2109.78}$$

$$= 1.45$$

$$\alpha_i = R_i - (b_i \times R_m)$$

∴ In this case, alpha would be

$$= 41.06 - (1.45 \times 28.97)$$

$$= 41.06 - 42.00 = -0.9465$$

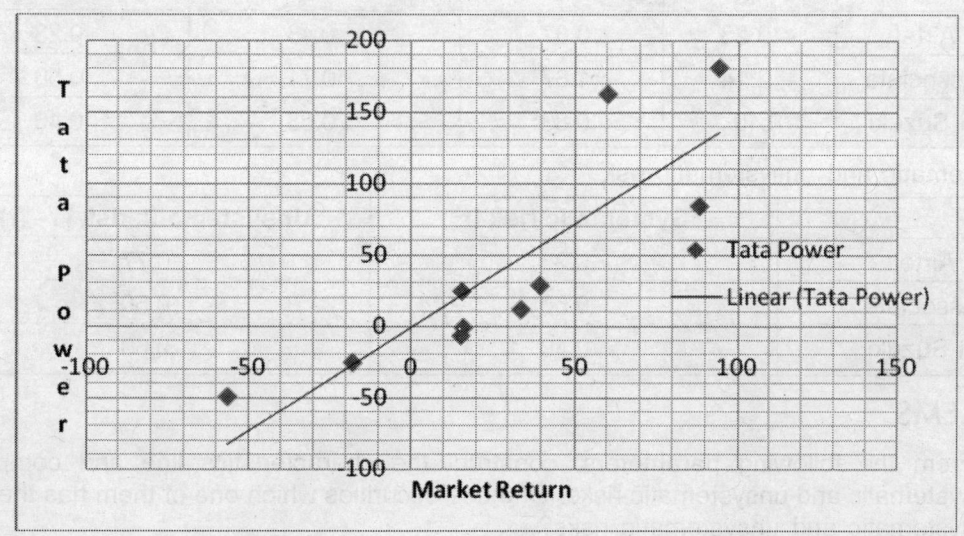

We know that beta of the market is 1. And we also know that higher is the beta, higher is the risk of the given stock. Here, for the given stock of Tata Power, beta is 1.45, which shows that stock is aggressive, being more sensitive compared to the market return. When the risk and return of Tata Power and market are compared it is found that Tata Power gives more return compared to market. But it also carries higher risk than the market. It is all because beta of Tata Power is 1.45, which is greater than that of the market. Alpha indicates the return of the security when the market return is zero. The stock being of aggressive nature, we can interpret that the return on Tata Power is −0.9465, when market gives zero return.

Q.2. Following are the characteristics lines of the securities Bharti Airtel, J.P. Associate and Maruti Suzuki. Find out the systematic risk of these securities and explain which asset is more risky and why? Calculate unsystematic risk as well of each asset. The given alpha, beta and correlation coefficient are for the time period: August 2006 to July 2011.

$$R_{Bharti\ Airtel} = \alpha_i + \beta_i \times R_m + \epsilon_{im} \times R_{Bharti\ Airtel} = (-0.23) + 0.67 \times R_m$$
$$R_{J.P.Associate} = \alpha_i + \beta_i \times R_m + \epsilon_{im} \times R_{J.P.Associate} = (-2.14) + 1.87 \times R_m$$
$$R_{Maruti\ Suzuki} = \alpha_i + \beta_i \times R_m + \epsilon_{im} \times R_{Maruti\ Suzuki} = (0.40) + 0.83 \times R_m$$

Stock	Correlation coefficient
Bharti Airtel	0.48
J.P. Associate	0.71
Maruti Suzuki	0.63

Ans: Systematic risk of J.P. Asscociate is highest as its beta is 1.87, while Bharti Airtel with a comparatively low beta indicates a lesser magnitude of the systematic risk.

Stock	Alpha (a)	Beta (b)	Correlation coefficient (r)	Coefficient of determination $(r)^2$
Bharti Airtel	− 0.23	0.67	0.48	0.23
J.P. Associate	− 2.14	1.87	0.71	0.50
Maruti Suzuki	0.40	0.83	0.63	0.40

Systematic and unsystematic risk

Stock	Systematic risk (r^2)	Unsystematic risk $[1-(r)^2]$
Bharti Airtel	0.23	0.77
J P Associate	0.50	0.50
Maruti Suzuki	0.40	0.60

PROBLEMS

Q.1 From the following parameters, construct the characteristics line and compute the systematic and unsystematic risks. Of these securities which one of them has the highest systematic and unsystematic risks?

BETA AND RISK ESTIMATION

Name of company	Alpha	Beta	Correlation coefficient	Coefficient of determination
ICICI Bank	1.15	1.19	0.78	0.61
Infosys	0.36	0.57	0.55	0.30
ONGC	-2.28	1.00	0.56	0.32

Q.2 Collect the monthly data of BHEL and the market index of last five years, *i.e.*, a of 60 months. Calculate α, β, correlation coefficient and coefficient of determination. Also interpret your results obtained for systematic and unsystematic risks.

Q.3 Calculate: β, a, correlation coefficient and coefficient of determination for the scrip of Ranbaxy for the period, 2002 to 2010.

Year	Sensex	Ranbaxy
2002	3.27	9.14
2003	71.89	27.41
2004	10.64	34.45
2005	36.37	-26.86
2006	39.82	-49.48
2007	54.77	0.81
2008	-51.78	-3.35
2009	75.52	-4.15
2010	17.25	48.13

Q.4 Consider the following data for the two companies, A and B:

Company	Beta	Standard deviation	Covariance with market
A	?	35	0.123
B	1.3	30	?

The expected return on the market index is 18% and the risk-free rate of interest is 8%. (You can lend and borrow at the risk-free rate).

(a) If the standard deviation of the market is 18%, what is the beta of A and covariance of B?

(b) Calculate the correlation coefficients between: the return on A and the market; and the return on B and the market return?

(c) How can you construct a portfolio of A and B that has the exactly same expected rate of return as the market?

(d) How can you form a portfolio 1, comprising of A and B, with 22% rate of return? What is the risk of the portfolio if the correlation between A and B is 0.5?

(e) How can you form a portfolio 2, which has the same expected return as the portfolio formed in part (d), but with a lower standard deviation? What is the lowest risk that you have to assume for this expected return?

(f) Now assume that there are two more scrips: P and Q, with 12 and 16% returns respectively and standard deviations of 12 and 20% respectively. How can you form a portfolio 3, comprising of P and Q that has a rate of return of 14% and a total standard deviation of 14%?

(g) How can you form (using risk free asset) a portfolio 4 that has the same risk as the portfolio formed in part (f), but has a higher expected return? (Assume portfolio 1 and 3 are efficient. Plot all the portfolios: 1, 2, 3 and 4 portfolios, in the graph.)

Q.5 Consider the rate of return on the security of the company, HUL, and the market portfolio for a period of 10 years.

(a) What is the beta of the stock of HUL?

(b) What is the characteristics line of the stock?

(c) Calculate beta using the regression formula.

(d) Resolve the total risk of HUL into its systematic and unsystematic components.

(e) Determine beta from the returns as plotted in the characteristics line.

Q.6 Calculate the beta of: ABB, Vijaya Bank, BASF and other two companies of your choice, taking the monthly data of last five years.

Q.7 Complete the missing values in the table by taking the data of last five years:

Security	Expected return	Standard deviation	Correlation with market portfolio	Beta
ACC				
Ambuja Cement				
Axis Bank				
Bharti Airtel				
BHEL				
Market Portfolio				
Risk-free Asset				

CASE STUDY: 1

Mr. Kashyap Mehta, having retired from his service, aspires to start trading in stock market. A youngster, Joy, residing in his neighborhood has inspired him. He has told Mr. Kashyap that now it is easy to trade in the market, sitting at home. Joy has also told that only a basic knowledge of the market and internet connection, are the only requirements for the purpose. But Mr. Mehta thought it was better to attend some seminar or a training program before he began trading in the market. So he attended one seminar on trading in the market. Mr. Mehta holds a bachelor's degree and a master's degree, in Psychology, from Bombay University and has a huge experience, of 36 years, in Pioneer Government School at Ulhasnagar. Due to the lack of a business background, Mr. Mehta was particularly interested in Investment Training Program. In this program, a session leader dealt with few terms like market, risk, return, alpha, beta, coefficient of correlation, coefficient of determination, diversification, etc.

Mr. Mehta could grasp these aspects, but not in totality. He had difficulty in grasping the details of the concepts and terminology used. So he decided to get acquainted with all of them lest his decisions went wrong and incurred losses. Therefore, before beginning to trade in the market he approached Joy. Joy provided some reading material, which contained short exercises and examples to help him familiarize with the concepts of: risk, return and other terminologies. Joy also provided him with the monthly data of return on some scrips and that of the market.

Month	Market	Hero Motor Corp.	Infosys	ICICI Bank	ONGC
Aug–06	8.955064	1.493589	8.963855	8.257713	3.480851
Sep–06	6.451947	8.343824	2.26342	19.4753	–3.69959
Oct–06	3.913085	–2.87091	13.72421	10.97857	–30.0339
Nov–06	5.416075	–2.53937	3.353557	12.15573	5.372861
Dec–06	0.416907	3.02027	1.840909	1.76	0.653633
Jan–07	1.903055	–5.56579	0.109277	5.793026	2.892938
Feb–07	–8.39875	–5.58312	–7.40048	–13.0721	–12.9007
Mar–07	0.448449	1.518744	–4.1619	1.438763	10.45912
Apr–07	8.276973	3.41124	2.4675	5.212637	5.057604
May–07	3.979834	4.621429	–7.68029	5.438898	–0.58696
Jun–07	0.275354	–5.63014	–0.29974	3.387446	–1.83351
Jul–07	5.895952	–2.65173	2.183463	–2.9267	0.43956
Aug–07	–0.16567	–2.53944	–5.59542	–4.24311	–5.76374
Sep–07	12.26536	12.84848	1.16	17.99667	11.38372
Oct–07	14.29395	–2.06818	–3.20526	18.23355	28.64948
Nov–07	–3.81039	–0.31724	–13.2477	–7.15909	–7.08333
Dec–07	3.785218	–4.13604	9.430693	4.440678	5.234043
Jan–08	–13.1686	–3.01576	–14.4539	–7.23482	–20.852
Feb–08	–1.35769	12.91728	2.10231	–6.75641	0.332012
Mar–08	–9.18946	–9.42257	–6.52614	–27.4244	–2.64385
Apr–08	9.609542	20.58115	20.94828	13.47097	3.547094
May–08	–6.51805	–12.8705	9.116499	–12.3137	–17.2919
Jun–08	–18.8643	–10.7451	–11.3113	–19.6173	–6.5711
Jul–08	6.496504	16.61594	–9.00052	0.769841	22.06495
Aug–08	3.55703	4.911392	12.73372	10.08197	3.363636
Sep–08	–10.7719	5.834348	–20.5938	–18.8083	0.538835
Oct–08	–24.7461	–14.48	–3.04211	–26.06	–35.7198
Nov–08	–10.9375	4.135241	–12.201	–15.3253	–1.17254

Dec–08	5.286185	1.27044	–14.0115	25.90564	–4.62143
Jan–09	–3.04828	9.61875	16.04444	–8.50549	–2.48889
Feb–09	–4.80452	6.316695	–4.77185	–19.78	4.719697
Mar–09	10.7912	15.00806	9.312309	3.404321	13.99123
Apr–09	17.00717	10.16279	13.6727	41.34615	11.00423
May–09	25.69788	11.18574	5.742574	51.19412	34.2275
Jun–09	–1.71342	2.118567	10.71028	–4.37086	–10.3277
Jul–09	8.023201	9.590444	16.15826	2.574324	9.137769
Aug–09	–0.1793	–6.41796	3.509709	–1.64042	1.320795
Sep–09	9.148845	9.701051	7.879241	19.84106	–1.96275
Oct–09	–7.50556	–5.95796	–4.15472	–12.7514	–3.5918
Nov–09	6.866692	11.02581	8.6082	10.80769	5.633865
Dec–09	3.05267	–1.35345	8.597332	0.887097	–2.27801
Jan–10	–6.38391	–10.368	–4.96163	–6.48649	–7.42424
Feb–10	0.552226	13.59936	5.327935	6.064477	–0.26339
Mar–10	6.626659	9.132022	–0.79287	7.637555	–2.26868
Apr–10	0.020906	–3.05598	4.433206	–0.15756	–4.08182
May–10	–3.37706	1.989474	–1.45903	–8.24868	10.95057
Jun–10	4.474344	5.184995	5.030132	–0.34682	10.58626
Jul–10	1.068762	–11.4007	–0.43377	5.907494	–5.14885
Aug–10	0.333923	–1.98031	–2.65732	6.465494	7.53012
Sep–10	11.32738	2.439429	12.33838	12.84045	4.281994
Oct–10	–0.30735	0.204082	–2.44415	3.71875	–7.96257
Nov–10	–3.70571	6.67027	2.053144	–3.59115	–5.43939
Dec–10	5.013315	0.817259	13.32237	–0.37859	3.059761
Jan–11	–11.1235	–18.5564	–9.64627	–11.5351	–8.99923
Feb–11	–3.26607	–11.5368	–4.14778	–4.89716	–77.3211
Mar–11	8.135453	7.199324	6.647446	13.19939	5.991962
Apr–11	–1.68087	6.853125	–9.89302	0.382883	6.151203
May–11	–3.74931	8.055394	–4.54235	–2.72739	–8.86731
Jun–11	1.720451	1.008607	4.058697	0.951238	–3.02655
Jul–11	–2.40707	–4.93617	–5.56997	–5.90715	–4.06109

TASKS:

1. Explain to Mr. Mehta all the terms which he has come across in the training session.
2. Calculate the return and risk of the scrips and market. Plot each scrip separately with the market return on the graph, and indicate which scrip shows the highest volatility and which one has the lowest. Relate these volatilities with beta of the scrips.
3. Plot the characteristic line for the given scrips for the period: August 2006 to July 2011. Interpret the values and the implications of alpha and beta for the given scrips.
4. Also explain to Mr. Mehta, in terms of statistical parameter and company basics, the relation of the scrips with the market, during the same period.
5. If market return goes up by 0.5 % in a month. How much return would you expect from the individual scrips?

CASE STUDY: 2

Valuegain is an investment firm, with its headquarters in Mumbai. Its regional offices are at Ahmedabad, Banglore, Chennai, Gurgaon and in Kolkata. Valuegain provides wealth management services to industries having a net worth of more than Rs.1 crore. The annual fee of the firm depends upon the performance of the actual portfolio, accompanied by 1.5%, which is a fixed amount. The firm was established by Mr. Rishi Chaitanya in 1981 and has performed notably, with a very good track record in the industry. The firm is comprised of experienced equity research analysts and portfolio managers, graduated from top B-schools of India, as its financial staff. And its staffs are its assets. The firm also has a very good infrastructure, in terms of IT and matter related to IT, such as software. His son and daughter, Mr. Kosh Chaitanya and Ms. Vidhi Chaitanya, assist him in his business. Both of them are MBA, Finance, from one of the top B-schools of the country. The firm tries to construct the portfolio and evaluate them periodically, on the basis of the theoretical fundamentals: risk, return, beta, alpha, systematic risk, unsystematic risk, diversification of the portfolio, etc. The company also spends an appreciable sum on sound E-I-C analysis (dealt with, in part 5, chapters: 15-18, of the book).

Mr. Hari Bhatt is an entrepreneur and has two plants for generic drugs at Gurgaon. His company is in the regulated drug market. Mr. Bhatt has risen to success and his acquired fortune is attributed to his foresight, and skill of identifying the nerve of the market. He recently visited the Gurgaon Branch of Valuegain firm and placed Rs.10 crores with the firm for investments on his behalf. Earlier, he had invested in the market through Vittanidhi firm. But with unsatisfactory returns he has withdrew his funds from Vittanidhi and has opted for Valuegain, having heard a lot about the efficient management of Valuegain and their services. Mr. Bhatt has asked the regional portfolio manager, Mr. Prince Thomas, to explain to him how they construct a portfolio for their clients. Mr. Prince Thomas has prepared the following list, with the relevant data for the period: August 2006 to July 2011, to explain the functioning of the market vis-à-vis the performance of the portfolio.

Name of company	Alpha	Beta	Correlation coefficient	Coefficient of determination
Sun Pharma	–0.22	0.65	0.41	0.17
Tata Steel	–0.10	1.67	0.80	0.64
Reliance Communication	–1.91	1.59	0.80	0.64

Infosys	0.36	0.57	0.55	0.30
ICICI Bank	0.21	1.45	0.88	0.77
Hero Motor Corp.	0.93	0.56	0.57	0.33
TCS	0.25	0.78	0.58	0.33
ONGC	−2.23	1	0.56	0.32
Mahindra & Mahindra	−0.32	0.94	0.61	0.38
HUL	0.34	0.28	0.31	0.10
Punjab National Bank	1.12	0.96	0.70	0.50

REFERENCES

1. www.investopedia.com

7
RISK-FREE LENDING AND BORROWING

> **LEARNING OBJECTIVES**
>
> The purpose of this chapter is to enable you to understand:
> • The impact of risk-free lending, on the efficient set of portfolios.
> • The impact of risk-free borrowing, on the efficient set of portfolios.

7.1 INTRODUCTION

The two chapters which precede, delved on the philosophies and the methodologies involved in the construction of a portfolio. These serve as the guiding principles for the investors when it comes to selecting the securities, and thus a portfolio. But these chapters were based on the assumption that the investors began with only a certain amount of fund (solely depending upon their capacity), as they were not allowed to borrow money to supplement their initial investments. The investors were further assumed to have opted for a specific holding period for their investments, at the end of which their capital either gained or incurred loss. The net result depended on the returns of the portfolio.

Yet through the entire discussions, these chapters have concentrated upon risky assets, which are inherently in the grips of uncertainty over their returns. None of the securities were shown to have a perfect negative correlation with each other. This chapter expands upon the learning from the previous chapters by incorporating in the portfolio, risk-free assets along with the risky assets. Herein, allowance for leverage, by borrowing at the risk-free rate too is being made.

So as the risk-free assets are accorded entry, it is essential to know the characteristics of risk-free assets.

7.1.1 What is Meant by a Risk-Free Asset?

A risk-free asset is the one whose theoretical return is completely free from risk. The definition of risk-free asset is slightly modified by Markowitz portfolio theory as this theory deals with investments having a single holding period. Since the risk involved is zero, the sum is assured, and not uncertain, at the end of the holding period. This also eliminates the possibilities of default. Thus, standard deviation for risk-free asset is zero, at least by nominal terms. In other words, covariance between the rate of return on the risk-free asset and the rate of return on risky asset is zero.

Also the covariance between the rate of return on the risk-free asset (x) and the rate of return on risky asset (y) is zero. It is because the return of risk-free asset is fixed over their investment horizon. As return is fixed (say 8% p.a.), and if the investor is holding for five years, the average return will be also fixed 8%. So, in case of risk-free asset $[x - E(x)]$ will be zero. In the case of risky security (for example take the stock of ONGC), return is varying over a time period and if we calculate its yearly return—it is not fixed but different for each year. In case of ONGC stock we will get some value as an average return and also for $[y - E(y)]$. We know that covariance $= [x - E(x)] \times [y - E(y)]/(n - 1)$. As $[x - E(x)] = 0$, the whole covariance term becomes zero. Also $Cov_{x,y} = Cor_{x,y} \times \sigma_x \times \sigma_y$. As $\sigma_x = 0$, the $Cov_{x,y} = 0$.

But for all corporate securities chances of default are very real. So, the securities issued by the corporations cannot be, and hence are not called, risk-free assets. Only a security issued by the government can be free from risk. However, it does not mean that all securities issued by the government too can be called a risk-free security.

The ongoing discussion notes that a risk-free asset is a kind of fixed income security with no possibility of default. But the fact remains that even a minimum amount of risk cannot be ruled out. That is an inherent aspect of security. Therefore, to take into account all the aspects of a risk-free asset the following considerations are to be paid attention to:

- Any fixed income security, even issued by the government cannot be called as risk-free security if its maturity period is greater than the holding period of the investor. We consider an example to enhance our understanding. It is supposed that an investor, whose holding period is one year, invests in a government security maturing in eight years. Such a security is called risky security because in this case an investor would have to sell it to get the cash after the completion of one year. It is highly probable that the interest would change in an unpredictable manner during this period. So, an investor cannot know what this security will be worth at the end of one year. Thus the presence of interest rate risk adds an uncertainty, not allowing the asset to be termed risk-free.

- Similarly, when the maturity period of a fixed-income asset issued by the government is less than that of the holding period of the investor, even then it cannot be called a risk-free security. To answer why it is so, the above example is slightly modified. Now the holding period remaining one year, maturity period is brought down from eight years to 91 days, for investments in T-bills. An investor gets the proceeds from investment in T-bills after 91 days, which would have to be reinvested in some other security as his holding period is one year. But an investor cannot know with certainty at what interest rates the proceeds from the Treasury Bills can be reinvested for the remainder of the holding period. This is called reinvestment risk. Thus, all the securities which have shorter maturity than the investor's holding period are not considered as risk-free security.

By considering the above two parameters: the interest rate risk and reinvestment risk, only those government securities are called risk-free security whose maturity matches with the investor's holding period.

> **Pause for thought:** It is an asset whose default risk and standard deviation is zero; and a certain sum is assured, at least in nominal terms, at the end of the holding period. Only the government securities, and that too when their maturity period and the holding period of the investor are identical, are considered risk-free securities.

7.1.2 Feasible Set and Efficient Set

Before proceeding further, let us discuss two basic terms: feasible set and efficient set.

Efficient set theory starts with construction of feasible set. Feasible set presents all portfolios that can be formed from group of 'N' securities. The efficient set can be located by applying efficient set theorem to the feasible set[1]. Efficient set can be selected with the help of indifference curves from almost an infinite number of portfolios available for an investment. As per the efficient set theorem an investor will choose a portfolio from the set of portfolios which:

- Offers maximum expected return for varying levels of risk.
- Offers minimum risk for varying levels of expected return.

Feasible set is also sometimes referred to as opportunity set. An opportunity set comprises of the expected return–standard deviation pairs of all portfolios that can be constructed from the given set of assets.

Selection of the efficient portfolio with the help of indifference curves demonstrates that all the portfolios in the efficient set are located on the 'northwest' boundary of the feasible set—often called the efficient frontier. Thus, portfolios is selected by simply plotting the investor's indifference curve on the same figure as the efficient set and then proceed to choose the portfolio which is farthest on the northwest zone. An empirical property of efficient set is that it is concave–however, the proof is beyond the scope of this book.

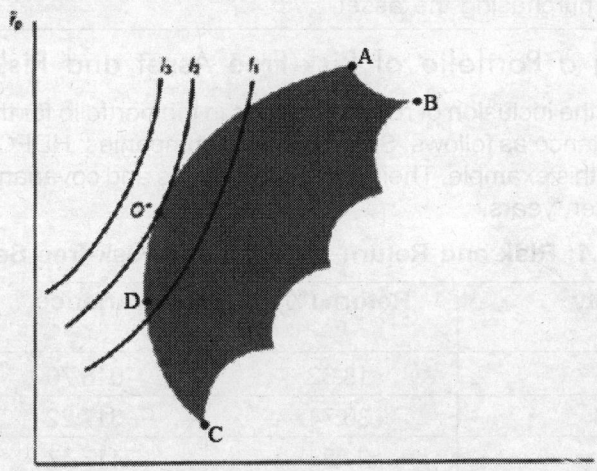

Figure 7.1: Feasible set and efficient set

The dark area in the above figure shows the feasible set. The feasible set shows all the possible combinations of 'N' securities with their risk and return. From the thus available 'N' portfolios (feasible set), efficient portfolios are selected by considering: maximum return for varying level of risk or minimum risk for varying levels of expected return. The efficient set is portfolios or any combination of risk-return lying on the north-western region—in the context of the figure above it is region between portfolio D and A (however more towards D). O* shows optimum portfolio with the help of indifference curve.

---

[1] This will be further discussed in Chapter 20—Markowitz Portfolio Theory and Chapter 22—Portfolio Selection.

> **Pause for thought:** Feasible set presents all portfolios that can be formed from group of 'N' securities. The efficient set can be located by applying efficient set theorem to the feasible set.

7.1.3 Risk-Free Lending

Risk-free lending has a unique attribute. The one who issues the risk-free asset is not considered the lender, rather the one who buys the asset, is!

Investment in a risk-free asset is referred to as risk-free lending. As an investor invests in such an asset the investor is actually lending the fund to the government by purchasing its security. It is a kind of loan—by the investor, to the government.

As already mentioned above, in this chapter the risk-free assets are being introduced in addition to the risky assets, in the portfolio. In doing so, the feasible set of the portfolio is expanded significantly with changes in their location (the efficient frontier) as well. A rational investor is concerned only with selecting a portfolio with the efficient set. Hence the changes brought about in an efficient set, with the addition of risk-free assets, seeks analyses and understanding.

It is to be noted that the terms 'risky security' or 'risky asset' referred to in this chapter, and throughout this book, is for any security of market, other than the security free from default risk—such as an equity stock.

> **Pause for thought:** When the government sells risk-free asset, it is actually lent as risk-free fund by the investor purchasing the asset.

7.1.4 Constructing a Portfolio of Risk-Free Asset and Risky Asset

Having mentioned the inclusion of risk-free assets in the portfolio for the purpose of discussion here, we analyze an instance as follows. Stocks of three companies: HDFC, HDFC Bank and BPCL are being considered in this example. Their returns, variances and covariance have been calculated from the data[2] of last ten years.

Table 7.1: Risk and Return of Risky and Risk-free Securities

Sl. No.	Security	Return (%)	Variance	Standard deviation (%)
1.	HDFC	18.32	918.70	30.31
2.	HDFC Bank	30.74	617.22	24.84
3.	BPCL	21.24	417.47	20.43
4.	Risk-free security	8%		

Table 7.2: Covariance of these three Securities

Stock	Covariance
HDFC and HDFC Bank	497.79
HDFC Bank and BPCL	-51.41
BPCL and HDFC	-326.70

Table 7.2 shows the covariance of risky securities.

---
[2] From the year 2001 to 2010.

As declared above we begin the construction of the portfolio of both risky and risk-free assets. We first begin construction of the portfolio by taking risk-free security (sr. no.4) and risky stock HDFC.

If W_1 = weight of the fund invested in HDFC

∴ $W_4 = 1 - W_1$ = weight of the fund in risk-free asset.

Table 7.3 shows the portfolio of HDFC and risk-free asset with different combinations, with respect to the varying proportion of each in the portfolio.

Table 7.3: Proportions of Risky Stock-HDFC, and Risk-free Security for the Construction of Portfolios

Weight	Portfolios					
	1	2	3	4	5	6
W_1 (HDFC)	0.00	0.20	0.40	0.60	0.80	1.00
W_4 (Risk-free security)	1.00	0.80	0.60	0.40	0.20	0.00

The risk-free return has been assumed to be 8% p.a. and will be denoted as r_f. The expected return and risk of the above six portfolios can be calculated. Yet at the same time this calculation is trivial for portfolios 1 and 6, with investments made solely in either of the two securities. Thus their expected returns are 8% and 18.32% respectively (refer to Table 7.1).

So we calculate the return of portfolio 2 as follows:

$$E(R_P) = (W_1 \times R_1) + (W_4 \times R_4) \quad (1)$$

Where,

W_1 = proportion of funds invested in risky stock HDFC.
W_4 = proportion of funds invested in risk-free asset.
R_1 = return of HDFC = 18.32%.
R_4 = return of risk-free security = 8% (as assumed).

∴
$$\begin{aligned} E(R_P) &= (W_1 \times R_1) + (W_4 \times R_4) \\ &= (0.20 \times 18.32\%) + (0.80 \times 8\%) \\ &= 10.064\% \end{aligned}$$

In a similar manner, returns of rest of the portfolios too can be calculated.

Risk of the portfolios 1 to 6 can be calculated, as exemplified by the calculation of risk of the portfolio of risky asset, HDFC and risk-free asset, as below:

$$\sigma_P = (\sigma_1^2 W_1^2 + \sigma_4^2 W_4^2 + 2 W_1 W_4 Cov_{14})^{1/2} \quad (2)$$

In terms of correlation, this equation becomes

$$\sigma_P = (\sigma_1^2 W_1^2 + \sigma_4^2 W_4^2 + 2 W_1 W_4 \sigma_1 \sigma_4 Cor_{14})^{1/2} \quad (3)$$

All six portfolios that have been constructed, there is one thing that is common—the presence of the risk-free asset, 4. Since its risk is zero, so is its covariance with all other securities. Hence, in the context of the portfolio constructed of 1 (HDFC) and 4, both the variance (square of standard deviation) of 4 and its covariance with 1 is zero. That is,

$$\sigma_4^2 = 0 \text{ and } Cov_{14} = 0$$

So, Equation (2) for risk of portfolio 2, can be reduced by substitution of these values to,

$$\sigma_P = (\sigma^2_1 W^2_1)^{1/2} \quad (4)$$
$$= 0.20 \times 30.31$$
$$= 6.062\%$$

Similarly, the risk of all six portfolios can be calculated. In fact this method enables calculation of the risk of any portfolio which is comprised of a risky and risk-free asset, when the data on their weights and standard deviation is available.

> **Pause for thought:** The covariance of a risk-free security with any risky security is always zero.

Table 7.4, below, shows the return and risk of the portfolios, 1 to 6.

Table 7.4 Risk and Return of the Portfolios, 1 to 6, Consisting of the Risky Security HDFC and the Risk-free Security, Present in different Proportions

Weight	Portfolios					
	1	2	3	4	5	6
W_1 (HDFC)	0.00	0.20	0.40	0.60	0.80	1.00
W_4 (Risk-free security)	1.00	0.80	0.60	0.40	0.20	0.00
Return (%)	8	10.06	12.13	14.19	16.25	18.32
Risk (%)	0	6.06	12.12	18.19	24.25	30.31

All six portfolios can be plotted, as in the Figure 7.2 below, with risk on the X-axis and return on the Y-axis. From the graph it is apparent that all the portfolios lie on a straight line, representing

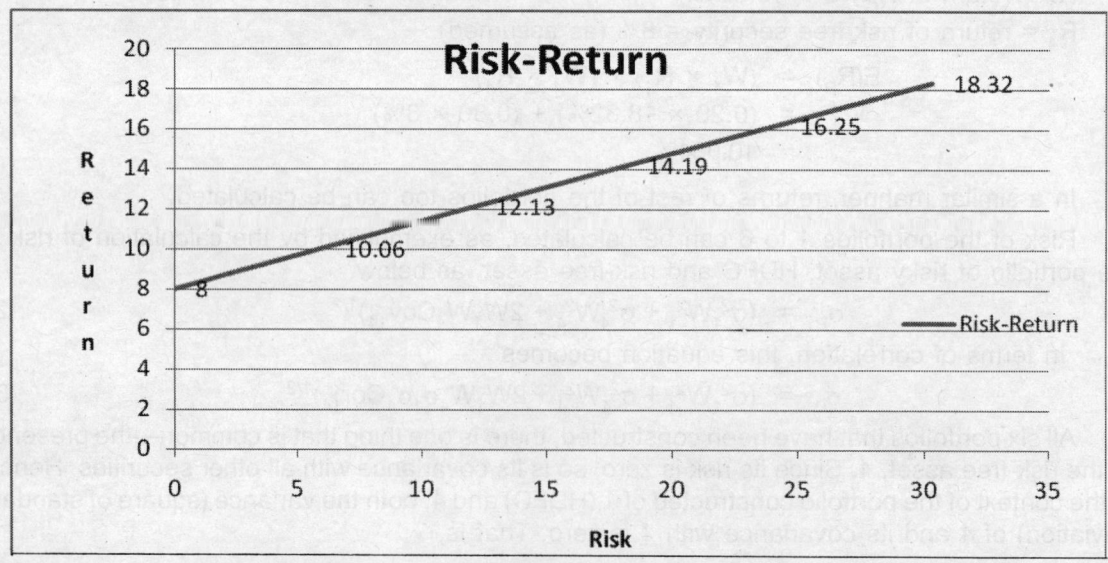

Figure 7.2: Risk and return of the portfolio of HDFC stock and risk-free security

the location of the risk-free asset and HDFC. Thus is implied that for portfolio of a risk-free security and risky stock, the return-risk profile can always be ascertained from their positions on the straight line. However, their location on the straight line depends on the proportion of the stocks invested in each security. Thus from the graph it is further concluded that for risk-free lending, with investments in a risky and a risk-free asset, the resultant straight line graph indicates that higher the proportion of the risky security, higher is the risk and return of the portfolio.

It is also known as portfolio characteristics in the expected return-standard deviation plane. From the Table 7.4 and Figure 7.2 risk-free assets appears on the vertical axis as an intercept because its standard deviation is zero. It can be concluded that on increasing the proportion of risky security HDFC in the portfolio, return and risk also increases.

The slope is $\quad S = (Y_2 - Y_1)/(X_2 - X_1)$ (5)

For example, taking the first two return and risk, at the proportion of 0:1 and 20:80 respectively,

$$S = (10.06 - 8)/(6.06 - 0) = 0.3399 = 0.34$$

Similarly, slope at the point when proportion invested is 80:20 and 1:0, is,

$$S = (18.32 - 16.25)/(30.31 - 24.25) = 2.07/6.06 = 0.34$$

It should be noted that this will remain the same at any other risk-return, taken at any other point on the straight line. S = 0.34 reflects extra return earned, per extra risk. It indicates that by increasing the proportion of risky security, HDFC, in the portfolio along with the risk-free security, return increases by 0.34% for a 1% increase in risk—and this ratio will remain constant at any other point on the straight line, in the figure 7.2. This straight line is called the capital allocation line (CAL) and it presents all risk-return combinations available to investors. In other words, CAL is a graph created by investors to measure the risk-return profile of risky and risk-free asset. The graph displays the return by taking on a certain level of risk. The slope of the CAL indicates incremental return per incremental risk. This slope is also named as reward-to-volatility ratio or return-to-risk ratio. It is also known as Sharpe's ratio and it is denoted by

$$\frac{E(R_p) - R_f}{\sigma_p} \quad (6)$$

where,

$E(R_p)$ = return of the portfolio.

R_f = risk-free rate on return of security.

σ_p = risk of the portfolio.

It is to be noted that Equations (5) and (6) result in similar answer and interpretation.

> **Pause for thought:** Risk-free lending is most suited for risk-averse investors, as it involves investing in risky as well as risk-free assets. For a portfolio comprised of one from each type the risk-return profile is a straight line with the position of risk and return depending on the proportions of the assets. Higher is the percentage of risky asset, higher is the risk and return of the portfolio.

7.1.5 Investment in Risk-Free Asset and Risky Portfolio

The preceding section delved on the portfolio of individual assets: combining risk-free with risky. But this section proceeds to discuss what happens to the given feasible set when a risky portfolio, instead of a single risky asset, is combined with a risk-free asset. Thus it is a combination of a risk-free security with a portfolio, which is considered as a unit of the main portfolio.

For the purpose of discussion, the risky securities considered are HDFC and BPCL. This type of combination requires construction of the portfolio of the risky assets first. It is assumed that the proportions of HDFC and BPCL are 20% and 80% respectively.

The return and risk of the portfolio of HDFC-BPCL is

$$R_{HDFC-BPCL} = (0.20 \times 18.32\%) + (0.80 \times 21.24\%)$$
$$= 20.66\%$$

And the risk is,

$$\sigma_{HDFC-BPCL} = (\sigma^2_{HDFC} W^2_{HDFC} + \sigma^2_{BPCL} W^2_{BPCL} + 2W_{HDFC} W_{BPCL} Cov_{HDFC,BPCL})^{1/2}$$
$$= [\{(918.7) \times (0.20 \times 0.20)\} + \{(417.47) \times (0.80 \times 0.80)\} + \{(-326.7) \times 2 \times 0.20 \times 0.80\}]^{1/2}$$
$$= 14.12\%$$

With this portfolio of HDFC-BPCL, the main portfolio has to be constructed, combining it with risk-free security. In this main portfolio, the portfolio of HDFC-BPCL is treated as one risky security. The return and weight of risk-free asset is again denoted, as above: R_4 and W_4, respectively.

Table 7.5: Risk and Return of the Portfolio Consisting of Portfolios of HDFC-BPCL and a Risk-free Security, in differing Proportions

	Portfolios					
	1	2	3	4	5	6
$W_{HDFC-BPCL}$	0.00	0.20	0.40	0.60	0.80	1.00
W_4	1.00	0.80	0.60	0.40	0.20	0.00
Return (%)	8	10.53	13.06	15.59	18.12	20.66
Risk (%)	0	2.82	5.65	8.48	11.30	14.12

These results when plotted, the graph obtained shows that even this portfolio lies on a straight line, connecting risk-free asset and $P_{HDFC-BPCL}$ (portfolio of HDFC-BPCL). The location of this combination obviously depends upon the proportion invested in HDFC-BPCL and risk-free asset.

When these two Figures 7.2 and 7.3 are compared, it is observed that results do not differ even when the single risky security is replaced by a portfolio of risky securities to form the main portfolio along with a risk-free asset. In both instances the resulting portfolio lies on the straight line, with the risk-return profile ascertainable from their position on the straight line. The position as usual depends on the ratio of investments in each.

Like Equations (5) and/or (6), the slope for a proportion of 40:60 and 60:40 as from Table 7.5 and Figure 7.3, is

$$S = (15.59 - 13.06)/(8.48 - 5.65) = 2.53/2.83 = 0.89$$

Similarly, for the other combination of 80:20 and 20:80, the slope is,

$$S = (18.12 - 10.53)/(11.30 - 2.82) = 7.59/8.48 = 0.89$$

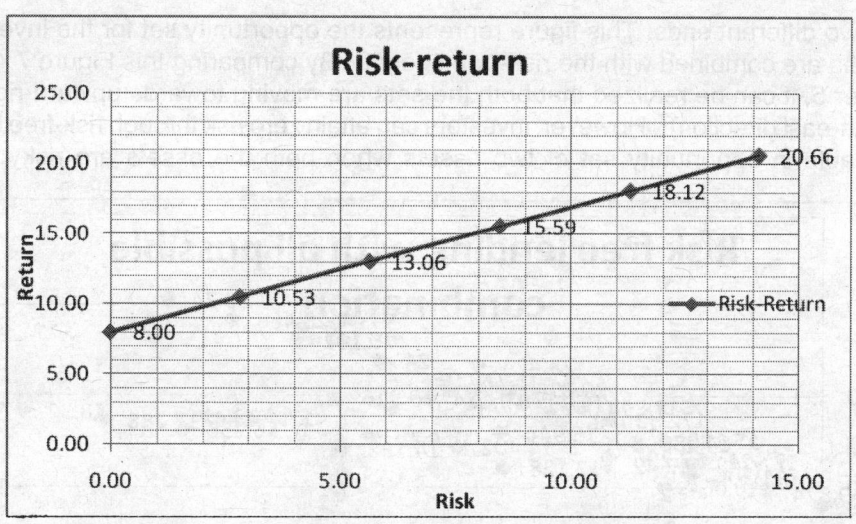

Figure 7.3: Risk and return of the portfolio consisting of a portfolio of risky securities HDFC-BPCL and a risk-free single security

The slope remains constant at 0.89 for all other combinations on CAL. From the above calculation it can be inferred that return to risk ratio (or slope) increases substantially as risky portfolio of two securities (HDFC-BPCL) improves in terms of its risk-return performance. The return and risk of this risky portfolio is, 20.66% and 14.12%, respectively—compared to HDFC taken as the only risky security, as shown in Table 7.4 and represented in Figure 7.2. Slope or reward-to-volatility ratio of 0.89 shows incremental return for incremental risk.

> **Pause for thought:** Even if the single risky security is replaced with a portfolio of risky securities, in a portfolio of risk-free asset and a risky security, the characteristics of the resultant portfolio remains the same, with a straight line graph maintained. The risk and return lie on this line, with their position on the line depending on the ratio of investments in each.

7.1.6 Portfolios: All Possible Combinations of the Risk-Free Asset, Utilizing All Available Risky Assets

The previous section has led to the impact on the feasible set when a portfolio of risky securities, instead of a single risky asset, combines with a risk-free asset to form the main portfolio. And in this section, all that we have learnt in the previous is being applied.

The opportunity set being considered are portfolios of all risky securities: HDFC, HDFC Bank and BPCL, in combination with the risk-free security in different proportions. The lowest line on the Y-axis shows the intercept. This represents the portfolios formed by combining-risk free and other risky stocks.

The Figure 7.4 below depicts the same result as presented by Figures 7.2 and 7.3. But it also shows how the feasible set changes significantly when all possible combinations of all three risky assets are considered, along with the risk-free asset. If characteristics line can be plotted it will be found to be in the same straight line as in Figures 7.2 and 7.3, and going in the upward direction to two different ends. This figure represents the opportunity set for the investor when all risky securities are combined with the risk-free security. By comparing this Figure 7.4, with Figure 5.6 of Chapter 5, it can be realized that both the sets are moving towards upward-right hand side (towards north-east direction)[3]. However, investors can attain zero risk through risk-free lending, while it is unattainable in opportunity set of two assets when both the assets are risky.

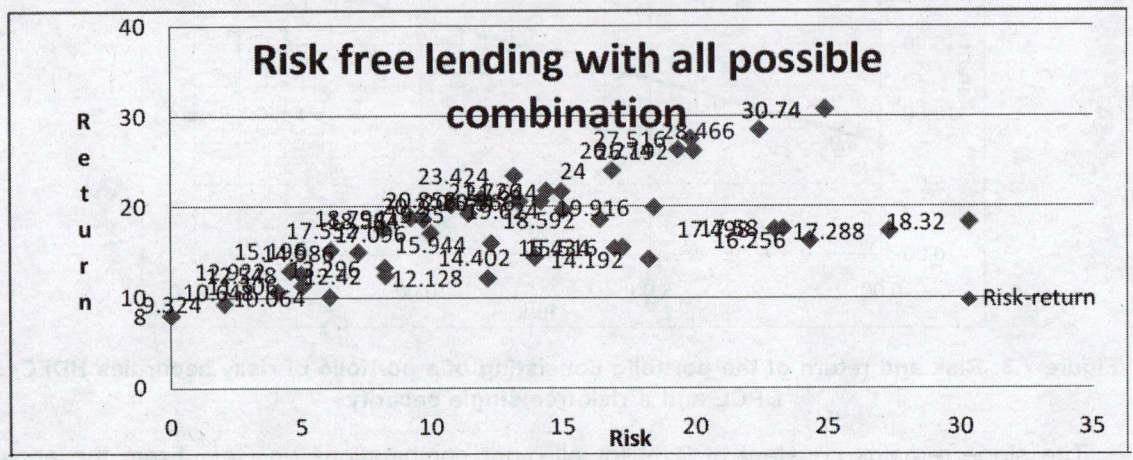

Figure 7.4: Risk-free lending with all combinations

> **Pause for thought:** When all possible combinations of the all available risky assets are used to construct a risk-free lending portfolio, with a risk-free asset, with varying proportions of all, the lowest line in the graph that is generated by plotting the risk-return values, is called the intercept. And this represents the feasible set composed of risky assets and risk-free asset.

7.1.7 Selection of Optimal Portfolio (Risk-Free Lending) with Indifference Curves

But out of these all probable combinations one has to select the optimal portfolio for risk-free lending. How would that be possible?

The feasible set having been already derived by combining all risky securities with risk-free asset, the selection of the optimal portfolio which is required is guided by the investor's choice. And we know that the investor's choice is guided by his risk preferences. This in turn is not only governed by the affinity or otherwise for risk, but also by risk bearing capacity for a given level of return. So the selection of the optimal portfolio, as usual will be decided by the type of investor, investing the funds. Thus there would be three different optimal portfolios, one each for: risk-averse, risk-lover and risk-neutral investor.

The panel A in the graph shown in the Figure 7.5, below, indicates that if the investor is averse to risk, he/she will select the optimal portfolio, P*. It is apparent that P* is lying on the lower part of the feasible set, and is on south-western part of the feasible set. This implies that as investor is risk-averse, he will select the portfolios with lower risk and lower return. P*, the optimum portfolio,

---

[3] This will be further discussed in Chapter 22—Portfolio Selection.

selected by the investor consists of risk-free security along with risky stocks. Panel B of the graph shown in the Figure 7.6, below, shows the risk-return characteristics of the selected portfolios P* by a risk-lover investor. It shows that the optimum portfolio selected by a risk-lover investor consists of only risky securities, lying on north-eastern part of the feasible set. This represents a high risk-return zone. The two graphs, which have been shown below, represent the indifference curves, generated by extrapolation of Figure 7.4.

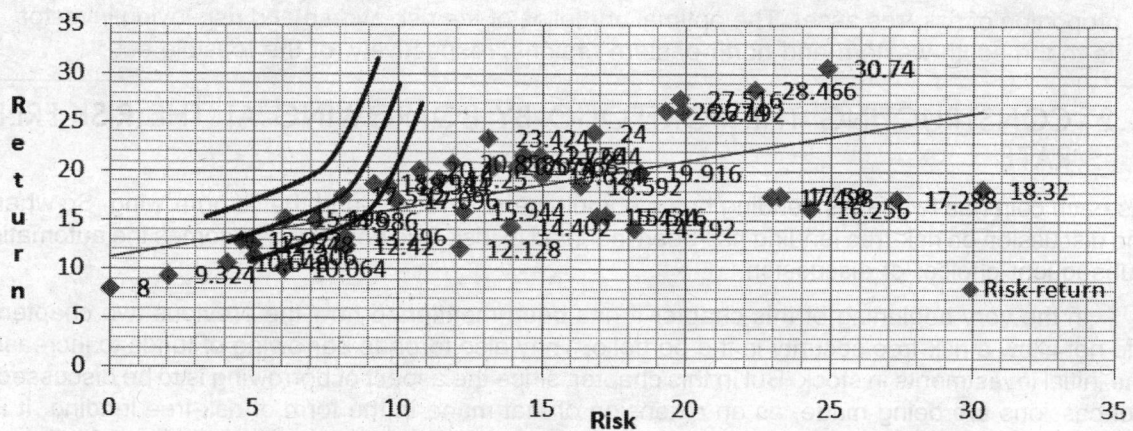

Figure 7.5: Risk-free lending and selection of the portfolio by risk-averse investor (Panel A)

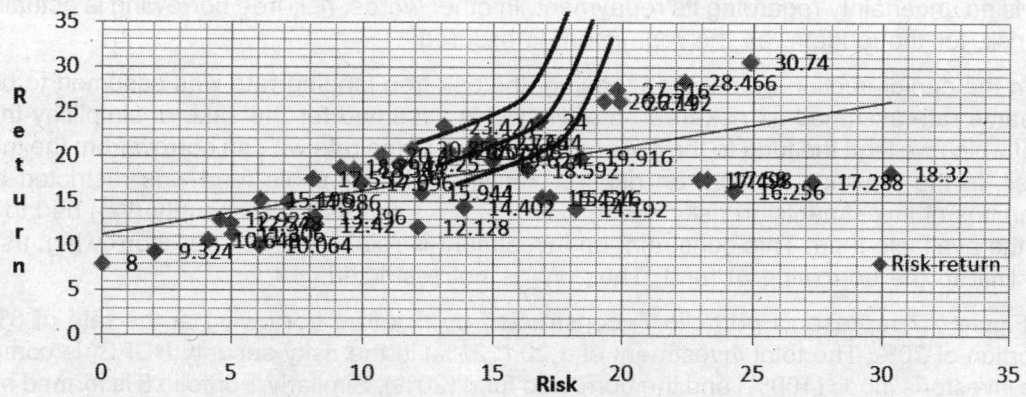

Figure 7.6: Risk-free lending and selection of the portfolio by risk-lover investor (Panel B)

From these two graphs the indifference curves can be termed as tangents to the linear efficient set. Figure 7.5 (panel A) shows the selection of the optimal portfolio, P*, by risk-averse investors. As such, investors prefer to play safe and the selected portfolio contains higher proportions of: less risky stocks or less risky portfolio and more of risk-free asset. Figure 7.6 (panel B) represents the selection of the risk-loving investors. Since these investors can bear high risk for high returns, their selection of the optimal portfolio lies to the north-eastern region of the above combination of the feasible set. Their optimal portfolio comprises of higher proportion of risky assets or portfolios, in combination with lower proportion of the risk-free asset.

> **Pause for thought:** Given the same set of risky assets and risk-free asset, the optimal portfolio of risk-averse investor contains higher proportions of less risky assets or portfolio, combined with a higher proportion of risk-free asset. For the risk-loving investor the optimal portfolio comprises of higher proportions of risky assets or portfolios, in combination with lower proportion of risk-free asset. The optimal portfolios of the risk-averse and risk-loving investor lie to the south-western and north-eastern regions, respectively, of the feasible set.

7.2 CONSTRUCTING THE PORTFOLIO BY BORROWING AT THE RISK-FREE RATE

As each coin has two faces, lending has a complementing facet—and that is borrowing. So when the discussion on risk-free lending has been indulged in, risk-free borrowing becomes the automatic subsequent choice, of discussion.

In the very beginning of this chapter it has been mentioned how the previous two chapters did not allow a risk-free security in the portfolio. They also forbade borrowing of funds to increase the initial investments in stock. But in this chapter, since the aspect of borrowing is to be discussed, concessions are being made, as an extension of that made in the form of risk-free lending. It is thus assumed that investors are allowed to borrow at the risk-free rate. This borrowed fund they invest, along with the seed money they possess, in the risky securities. In these circumstances, thus, there is no restriction on the amount that can be invested.

Furthermore, the assumption that investors are allowed to borrow at the risk-free rate implies there is no uncertainty regarding its repayment. In other words, risk-free borrowing is actually free from risk, for the lenders, as the repayment is assured!

In the earlier section on risk-free lending, the risk-free lending rate was assumed to be 8%. The same rate assumed as risk-free borrowing. It is assumed for the sake of simplicity that the rate at which we lend the fund to the government, at the same rate we can borrow from the market[4] as well. In the previous section, on risk-free lending, the investible fund was restricted as the proportions of investments: in risky security, HDFC (W_1) and risk-free security (W_4) had to come from the available fund. This constraint on investment is relaxed in risk-free borrowing, as there is no limit to the borrowing of fund. Thus, W_1 is not restricted.

Figure 7.7 represents portfolio 7, constructed by risk-free borrowing at the rate of 8% in a proportion of 20%. The total investment of 1.20 (120%) in the risky security HDFC, is composed of the investor's funds (100%) and the borrowed fund (20%). Similarly, portfolio 8 is formed by risk-free borrowing with the proportion of 40%, with the total investment of 1.40 (140%) in the HDFC stock. Other portfolios too are formed in the similar fashion. While proportions of the assets are assumed and computed it should be remembered that the sum of both assets, for example, W_1 and W_4, should be 1, as is in this case:

$$-0.20 + 1.20 = 1$$

---

[4] However, this assumption is not true in real life for investors like us. Only government can borrow at the risk-free rate, neither an individual nor a group of investors can borrow at this rate.

To analyze the impact of risk-free borrowing on the total risk and return of the portfolio and thus on the feasible set, portfolios are constructed, as is the case of risk-free lending. Likewise, table below, consisting of two assets: HDFC and risk-free security are considered. In all the portfolios: 7 to 12, the investor utilizes the borrowed fund as wells as own fund to invest in the risky stock of HDFC. These portfolios are different combinations of the stocks: risk-free and the risky, HDFC.

Table 7.6 Different Proportions of HDFC and the Risk-free Security

Weight	Portfolios					
	7	8	9	10	11	12
W_1 (HDFC)	0	1.20	1.40	1.60	1.80	2.00
W_4 (Risk-free security)	1	-0.20	-0.40	-0.60	-0.80	-1.00

The return and risk of the portfolios are calculated as in the case of risk free lending and the results have been tabulated as below. From this table, it can be stated that the return has increased, compared to the return with risk-free lending (Table 7.4). But as is the norm, risk too has increased substantially. Moreover, the risk increases with the increase in the extent of borrowing.

Table 7.7 Risk and Return of different Proportions of HDFC and the Risk-free Security

	Portfolios					
	7	8	9	10	11	12
W_1 (HDFC)	0	1.20	1.40	1.60	1.80	2.00
W_4 (Risk- free security)	1	-0.20	-0.40	-0.60	-0.80	-1.00
Return (%)	8	20.38	22.45	24.51	26.577	28.64
Risk %)	0	36.37	42.43	48.50	54.56	60.62

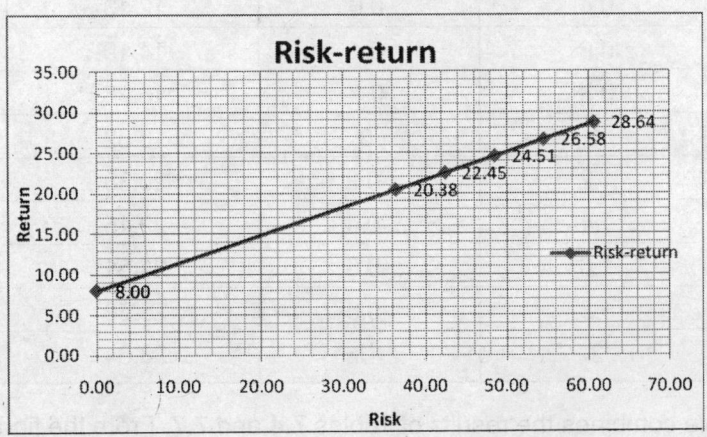

Figure 7.7: Risk-return profile of a portfolio of HDFC and risk-free security, at risk-free borrowing

With risk-free borrowing the portfolio constructed of risky security and risk-free security results in a comparatively higher return and high risk. Thus the effect of leverage (borrowed fund added to construct the portfolio) is incremental for both, risk and return. In other words, leverage raised the risk of the portfolio substantially along with the return of the portfolio. Since with increase in leverage, the risk increases, it is the preferred mode of investment for risk-loving, more adventurous investors.

From the Table 7.7 and Figure 7.7, it can be realized that CAL has moved towards the northeast due to risk-free borrowing.

Slope, at the proportion of 0:1 and 1.20:-0.20 is,

$$S = (20.38 - 8)/(36.37 - 0) = 12.38/36.37 = 0.34$$

Similarly, slope calculated at the other proportion of 1.60:-0.60 and 1.80:-0.80 is,

$$S = (26.577 - 24.51)/(54.56 - 48.50) = 2.067/6.06 = 0.34$$

This slope will remain same at any other proportion as well. Here, the slope, 0.34, is similar to that derived from Table 7.4 and Figure 7.2, where it was the case of risk-free lending. Thus, it can be concluded that leverage does not help to increase the slope or return-to-risk ratio. Even though the investor can borrow at the risk-free rate of 8% and can invest in risky security HDFC—which provides very good return of 18.32%—investor's return-to-volatility ratio remains the same. Thus, leverage does not help the investor to earn additional return for a given level of risk.

The table below is the comparative risk-return statistics of risk-free lending and risk-free borrowing, for hence the portfolios: 1 to 11.

Table 7.8 Summary of Risk-return of Portfolios at Risk-free Lending and Risk-free Borrowing

Portfolio	W_1	W_4	Return (%)	Risk (%)
1	0	1	8	0
2	0.2	0.8	10.06	6.06
3	0.4	0.6	12.13	12.12
4	0.6	0.4	14.19	18.19
5	0.8	0.2	16.25	24.25
6	1	0	18.32	30.31
7	1.2	-0.2	20.38	36.37
8	1.4	-0.4	22.45	42.43
9	1.6	-0.6	24.51	48.50
10	1.8	-0.8	26.58	54.56
11	2	-1	28.64	60.62

The above table combines the results of Tables 7.4 and 7.7. From the figure below (obtained by plotting the results of Table 7.8), it can be concluded that all the portfolios with risk-free lending: 1 to 6, and those with risk-free borrowing: 8 to 12, all lie on the same straight line. In other words, the portfolios resulting out of risk-free borrowing and risk-free lending, all lie on the same straight line. The difference is in their location on the straight line. Those from risk-free borrowing, having higher risk-return profile are located farthest on the straight line.

In this text, it is true that discussion on the characteristics of portfolios with risk-free lending and borrowing have revolved around a very limited range of stocks, and thus possibilities considered too have been limited. However, all that has been concluded is found to be true with other combinations of risk and return as well, of portfolios arising through investing in different proportions in risk-free and risky stocks.

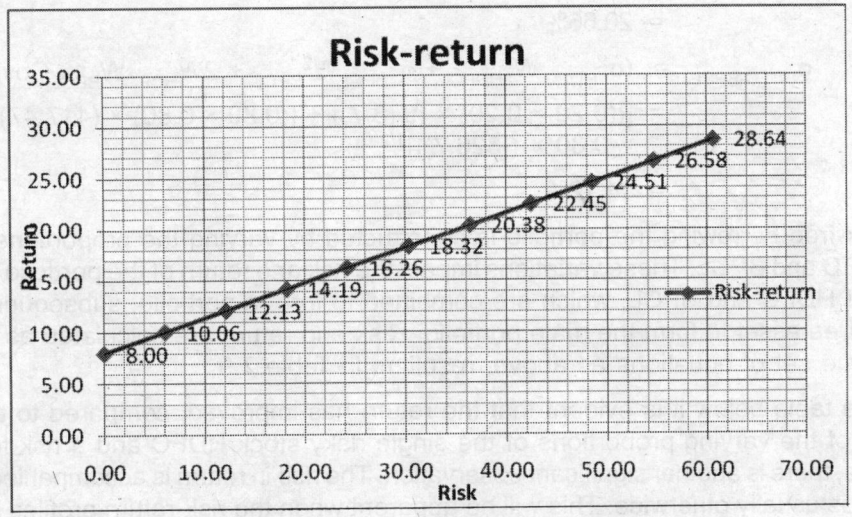

Figure 7.8: Risk-free lending and borrowing

Since risk-free lending has been accorded a more detailed analysis till now, as compared to the risk-free borrowing, the characteristics of risk-free borrowing, learnt in this section are summarized as follows:

- Risk-free borrowing means borrowing at the risk-free rate and investing one's own funds and borrowed fund in a risky security or portfolio. This is also known as leverage.
- Borrowing the fund and investing the same along with one's own funds, in a risky security or a portfolio, is an option practiced by risk-loving investors.
- As the leverage increases so does the return of the portfolio, but with a significant rise in the risk as well.
- So investors with high degree of risk aversion will engage in less borrowing and more lending, than a risk-loving investor.
- Irrespective of risk-free lending or borrowing, the resulting portfolio of a risky asset and a risk-free, all lie on the same straight line plotted as a graph of their combined risk-return profile. Only their positions differ on the straight line, with those from risk-free borrowing, having higher risk-return profile, lying farthest.

Pause for thought: Risk-free borrowing is completely free from risk, for the lenders, as the repayment of the borrowed fund is assured.

7.2.1 Extending Leverage to the Risky Portfolio

As the risk-free lending had been extended to include more than one risky asset in a portfolio, the same is carried out with risk-free borrowing. Leverage is thus extended to invest in two risky securities HDFC and BPCL. The risk and return of the portfolio is carried out, as has been earlier, in the case of risk-free lending.

The return portfolio, HDFC-BPCL, is

$$R_{HDFC-BPCL} = (0.20 \times 18.32\%) + (0.80 \times 21.24\%)$$
$$= 20.66\%$$

$$\sigma_{HDFC-BPCL} = (\sigma^2_{HDFC} W^2_{HDFC} + \sigma^2_{BPCL} W^2_{BPCL} + 2W_{HDFC}W_{BPCL}Cov_{HDFC,BPCL})^{1/2}$$
$$= [\{(0.20 \times 0.20) \times (918.7)\} + \{(0.80 \times 0.80) \times (417.47)\} + \{2 \times 0.20 \times 0.80 \times (-326.7)\}]^{1/2}$$
$$= 14.12\%$$

With risk-free borrowing the portfolio is constructed by varying the proportions of the risky assets of HDFC and BPCL. These variations impact the risk and return of the portfolio as is natural. The stocks of HDFC and BPCL, which are combined to form a portfolio, subsequently combine with the risk-free asset to form the main portfolio. Risk and return are calculated as in Table 7.7, using the same set of equations as above, resulting in Table 7.9.

From the table below it is evident that the return has improved, compared to the portfolios resulting out of the varying proportions of the single risky stock HDFC and a risk-free stock. In addition to this, there is another significant observation. The rise in return is accompanied by lowering of risk, which is usually otherwise. This will be apparent when the risk-return profiles in Tables 7.7 and 7.9 are compared.

Table 7.9 Risk and Return of a Portfolio of a Portfolio of HDFC-BPCL and Risk-free Security

	Portfolios					
	7	8	9	10	11	12
$W_{HDFC-BPCL}$	0	1.20	1.40	1.60	1.80	2.00
W_4	1	-0.20	-0.40	-0.60	-0.80	-1.00
Return (%)	8	23.19	25.72	28.25	30.78	33.31
Risk (%)	0	16.94	19.77	22.6	25.41	28.24

The Figure 7.9 is drawn by combining risk-free lending and borrowing and risky portfolio HDFC-BPCL with risk-free assets.

When leverage is used for a risky portfolio CAL extends more towards the north-east. The slope calculated at the proportion of 1.40:-0.40 and 1.60:-0.60 is,

$$S = (28.25 - 25.72)/(22.6 - 19.77) = 2.53/2.83 = 0.89$$

This is same as the slope derived from Table 7.5 and Figure 7.3 when portfolio of risky securities (HDFC-BPCL) and risk-free security was constructed. Thus, risk-free borrowing at 8% and investing the borrowed and own fund in risky securities (HDFC-BPCL), too results in the same slope, 0.89, indicating same incremental return per incremental risk.

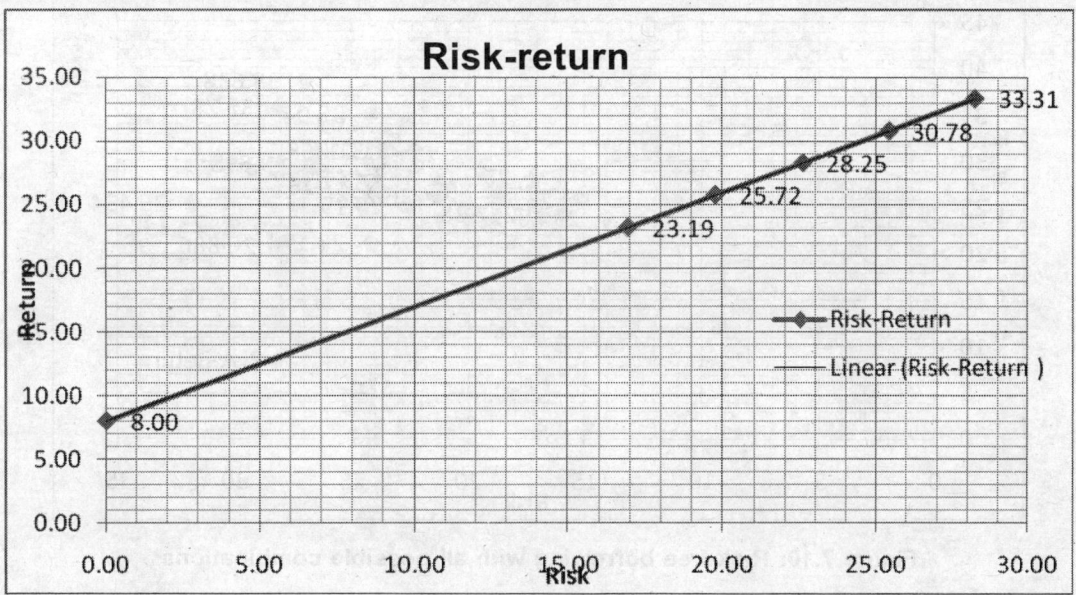

Figure 7.9: Portfolio of HDFC-BPCL and risk-free ssset, with risk-free borrowing

Pause for thought: When the leverage is extended to two risky assets, the return of the portfolio increases, but with a decrease in the risk of the portfolio, contrary to the usual observations of high return being accompanied by high risk.

7.2.2 Portfolios: All Possible Combinations of the Risk-Free Asset with All Available Risky Assets, Utilizing Risk-Free Borrowing

As in case of risk-free lending, here too portfolios with all possible combinations of the three risky securities and the risk-free security are constructed. The risky securities considered are same as before: HDFC, BPCL and HDFC Bank; and their different proportions used, leads to the different portfolios, as mentioned. How these combinations *affect* the formation of the efficient set as they change the risk-return profile of portfolios can be viewed in the figure below.

On comparing Figures 7.4 (risk-free lending) and 7.10 (risk-free borrowing), it is concluded that: with risk-free borrowing, the portfolios with varying proportions of three risky securities and risk-free asset, have shifted more towards the north-eastern region. This region we know represents the higher return-risk portfolios. In Figure 7.4, which represents risk-free lending, majority of the portfolios, are found to be lying on the north-southern region. This signifies comparatively low risk of the portfolios, but with low returns as well. Thus, while Figure 7.4 represents the selection preferred by risk-averse investors, Figure 7.10 is those for the risk takers.

Pause for thought: With increment in the risky securities, by risk-free borrowing, their all possible combinations with a risk-free asset leads to portfolios with higher returns, but accompanied by corresponding high risks too.

212 SECURITY ANALYSIS AND PORTFOLIO MANAGEMENT

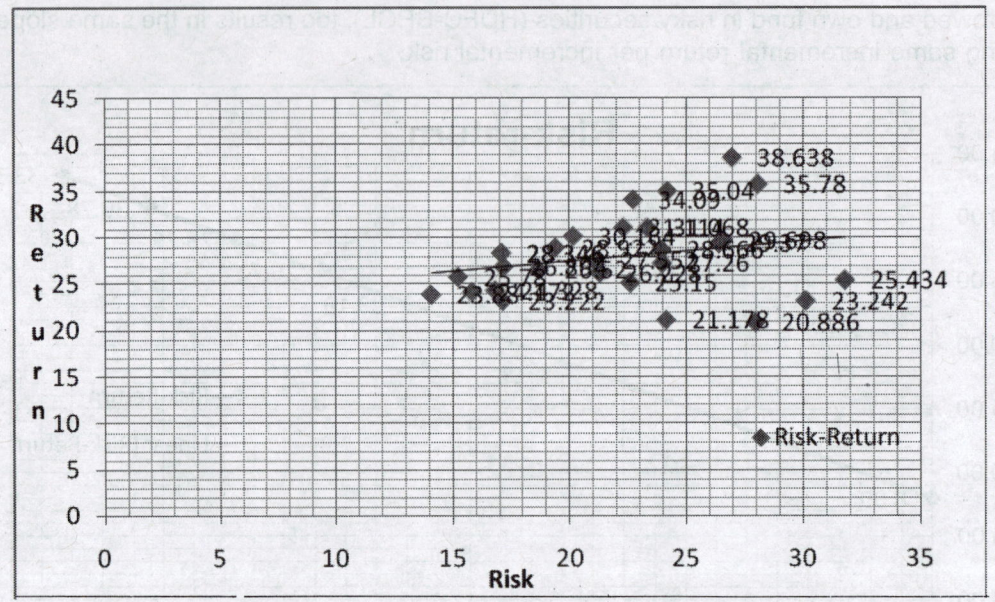

Figure 7.10: Risk-free borrowing with all possible combinations

7.3 EFFICIENT SET AND RISK-FREE LENDING AND BORROWING

The risk-free lending and borrowing and how the changes in the composition of the portfolios impact the efficient set, have been dealt with separately. But when one has to weigh out the options available, a comparative study of the efficient sets, from risk-free lending and borrowing comes in very handy. Hence that forms the context of discussion in this and the following segment.

The following figure plots all possible combinations of portfolios, with varying proportions of the constituents—under both risk-free lending, as well as borrowing.

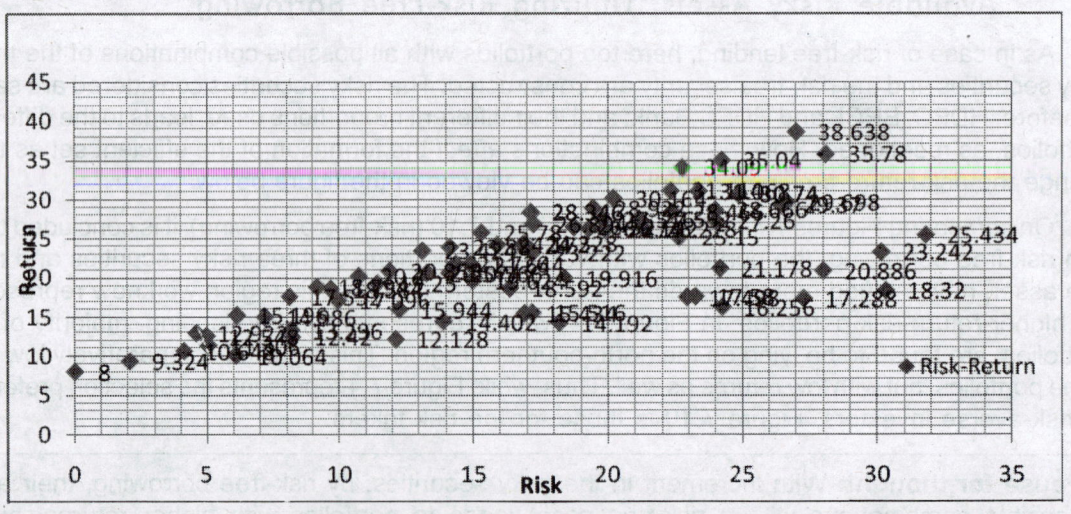

Figure 7.11: Risk-free lending and borrowing with all possible combinations

Risk-Free Lending and Borrowing 213

Figure 7.11 is thus a fusion of Figures 7.4 and 7.10. This figure shows, quite naturally, the majority of the portfolios to be lying in the north-west and north-east regions. The former corresponds to the risk-free lending efficient set of portfolios, while the latter is for the same, but with risk-free borrowing. Hence, the combined results once again lead to the same conclusion: selection of the portfolio from the available combinations depends upon the risk-return preferences of the investor. For the selection of the optimal portfolio, similar analysis can be applied, as discussed in Figures 7.6 and 7.7.

> **Pause for thought:** A fusion of all possible combinations of portfolios, of risky securities with risk-free asset, invested with risk-free lending and borrowing remain mutually exclusive. Those from risk-free lending lie on the north-western region, representing low risk-return profile; while those with risk-free borrowing lie on high risk-return, north-eastern, region.

7.3.1 Analyzing the Effects of Risk-Free Lending and Borrowing on the Efficient Set

We have already seen how the fusion of the combinations leads us to reinforce the conclusion that choice of portfolio is ultimately determined by the risk-return preferences of the investor. So now we shall be analyzing the selections preferred by the different categories of investors.

Figure 7.11 is generalized and when the indifference curve is plotted as tangent, it becomes evident which regions of the efficient set will be selected by the risk-averse and risk-loving investors. Figures 7.12 and 7.13, represent these regions of preference, as they show the selection of the optimal portfolios by risk-averse and risk-loving investors respectively.

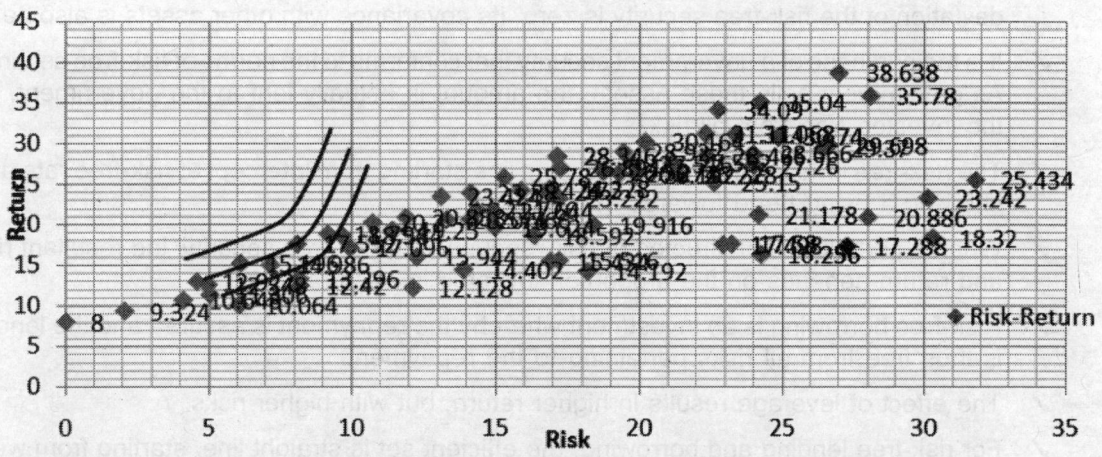

Figure 7.12: Risk-free lending and borrowing and selection of the portfolio by risk-averse investor

214 SECURITY ANALYSIS AND PORTFOLIO MANAGEMENT

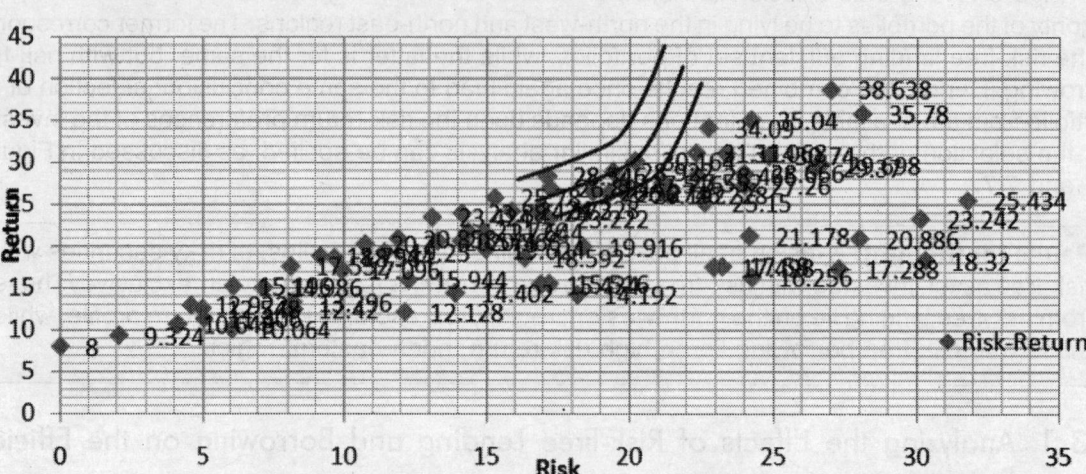

Figure 7.13: Risk-free lending and borrowing and selection of the portfolio by risk-loving investor

> **Pause for thought:** The optimal portfolio for the specific investor type is determined by plotting the indifference curve as a tangent to the efficient set.

SUMMARY

- ✓ The return of risk-free asset is assured. The chances of default risk being nil, the standard deviation of the risk-free security is zero. Its covariance with other assets is also zero.
- ✓ It is the purchase of a government security that conforms to the norms of risk-free security. As government sells these assets, the amount is actually lent to the government, by the investor, free from all risks.
- ✓ The risk-free lending graph is the straight line starting from intercept at risk-free rate and showing a rising trend towards the east.
- ✓ When a portfolio is constructed of risky security and risk-free security, the resultant risk and return depends on the proportion invested in each of them.
- ✓ Risk-free borrowing is an investment whereby the repayment is assured and the lender is thus free from all risks pertaining to the repayment.
- ✓ The effect of leverage results in higher return, but with higher risks
- ✓ For risk-free lending and borrowing, the efficient set is straight line, starting from west (from the risk-free rate point), and moving towards the north.
- ✓ The optimal portfolio is constructed by investing in risky portfolio, with either risk-free borrowing or lending, depending upon the choice of the investor.
- ✓ The optimal portfolio for the specific investor type is determined by plotting the indifference curve as a tangent to the efficient set.

KEY CONCEPTS

Risk-Free Asset	Risk-Free Lending	Interest Rate Risk
Risky Security	Risk-Free Borrowing	Reinvestment Risk
Risky Portfolio	Efficient Set	Corner Portfolio
Optimal Portfolio	Indifference Curves	

REVIEW QUESTIONS

1. Explain the terms: reinvestment risk and interest rate risk.
2. Why is the covariance between a risk-free asset and risky asset zero? Explain mathematically and intuitively.
3. Describe how the efficient set changes when investments with risk-free borrowing are included with those from risk-free lending. Corroborate the description with a corresponding graph.
4. Explain the impact of leverage on the risk-return profile of the portfolios comprised of:
   (a) A single risky asset and risk-free asset.
   (b) Portfolio of risky securities and a risk-free security.
5. When risk-free lending is allowed, what will be the effect on the risk and return of a portfolio and the efficient set:
   (a) Of a portfolio of a single risky asset and a risk-free asset?
   (b) Of a portfolio of risky assets and a risk-free asset?
6. How would the shape of the efficient set change, if risk-free borrowing is allowed but not risk-free lending? What will be the changes in the graph?

ILLUSTRATIONS

Q.1. Mr. Vijay owns a risky security of Infosys, whose average return has been 7.625% at a risk of 43.98% for the period: 2002 to 2011. Mr. Vijay invests in a 365 days T-Bill, which provides a return of 4% p.a.

(i) What is the portfolio return, if Mr. Vijay invests the following proportion in the risky stock Infosys and the remaining in the risk-free security?

   a. 0
   b. 0.25
   c. 0.50
   d. 0.75
   e. 1

(ii) Also calculate for the given security, if leverage is used and it is invested in the risky stock, Infosys.

(iii) Plot both results on the graph separately, then combine them and interpret the results.

Ans:

(i) Risk-free lending for Infosys and T-Bill:

The expected return on a portfolio invested in a risky security and risk-free security is given by,

$$R_P = (W_1 \times R_i) + (W_2 \times R_f)$$

$$\therefore W_1 + W_2 = 1$$

$$\therefore W_1 = 1 - W_2$$

$$R_P = (0 \times 7.625\%) + (1 \times 4\%)$$

$$= 4\%$$

Now, the risk of the portfolio:

$$\sigma_P = (\sigma_1^2 W_1^2 + \sigma_2^2 W_2^2 + 2W_1 W_2 \sigma_1 \sigma_2 Cov_{12})^{1/2}$$

For the risk-free security, T-bill, its variance (σ_2^2) and its covariance (Cov_{12}), with other risky stocks becomes zero. So, the above equation reduces to

$$\sigma_P = (\sigma_1^2 W_1^2)^{1/2}$$

$$= (2686.75 \times 0)^{1/2} \text{ [weight used for the risky stock is 0]}$$

$$= 0$$

Similarly, for the other weights, 0.25 and 0.75, in Infosys and in the risk-free asset, R_f, the return and risk are:

$$R_P = (0.25 \times 7.625\%) + (0.75 \times 4\%)$$

$$= 4.90\%$$

$$\sigma_P = (\sigma_1^2 W_1^2)^{1/2}$$

$$= (2686.75 \times 0.0625)^{1/2}$$

$$= 10.99\%$$

The return and risk for all four weights, with risk-free lending is,

Infosys	T-Bill	Return	Risk
Weights			
0	1	4	0
0.25	0.75	4.90625	10.997
0.5	0.5	5.8125	21.994
0.75	0.25	6.71875	32.991
1	0	7.625	43.988

RISK-FREE LENDING AND BORROWING

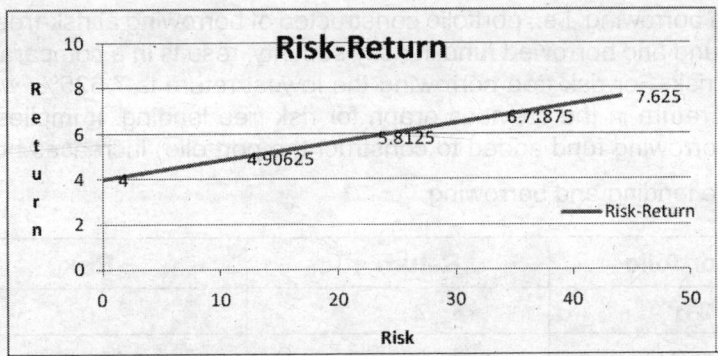

Figure: Risk-free Lending

From the figure above it can be said that for risk-free lending, i.e., when the portfolio is constructed of risky security and risk-free security, the resultant graph is a straight line, where higher the proportion of risky security, higher the return and hence, risk.

(ii) Risk-free borrowing for T-Bills at the rate of 4% and investing one's own fund and borrowed fund in Infosys, calculate the risk and return in a similar manner as shown above.

Risk-free borrowing at the rate of T-Bills:

Infosys Weights	T-Bills	Return	Risk
2	-1	11.25	87.976
1.75	-0.75	10.34375	76.979
1.5	-0.5	9.4375	65.982
1.25	-0.25	8.53125	54.985
1	0	7.625	43.988

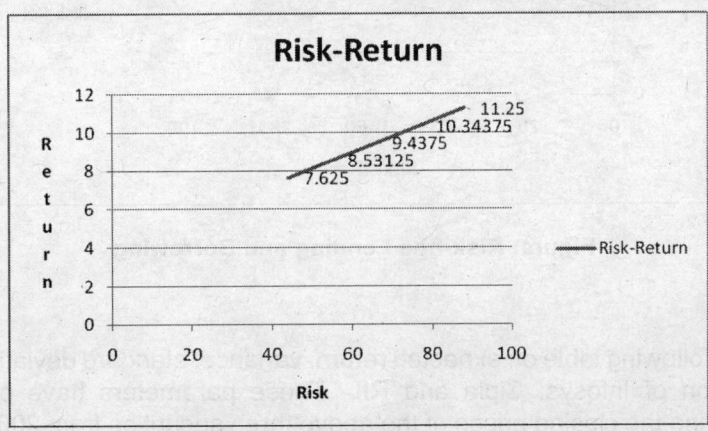

Figure: Risk-free Borrowing

For risk-free borrowing, i.e., portfolio constructed of borrowing at risk-free rate and investing one's own fund and borrowed fund in risky security, results in a comparatively higher return at a higher risk. For risk-free borrowing the lowest return is 7.625%, which is incidentally the highest return in the previous graph for risk-free lending. It implies thus the effect of leverage (borrowing fund added to construct the portfolio) increases both risk and return.

(iii) Risk-free lending and borrowing

Portfolio	Return	Risk
1	4	0
2	4.90625	10.997
3	5.8125	21.994
4	6.71875	32.991
5	7.625	43.988
6	11.25	87.976
7	10.34375	76.979
8	9.4375	65.982
9	8.53125	54.985
10	7.625	43.988

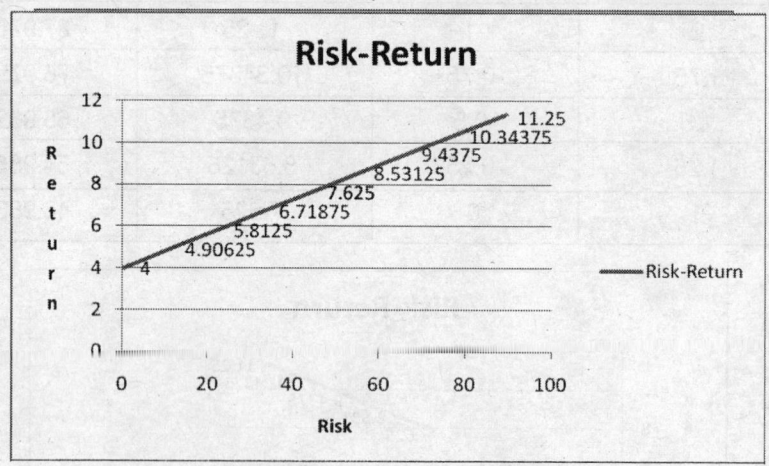

Figure: Risk-free Lending and Borrowing

PROBLEMS

1. See the following table of: expected return, variance, standard deviation, covariance and correlation of Infosys, Cipla and RIL. These parameters have been calculated by considering the closing prices of the above three securities from 2002 to 2011. Assume the risk-free rate of 8% for one year default free security.

	A	B	C
Return	7.625	-0.6925	23.4074
Risk	43.988	44.059	238.084
Variance	2686.753	1941.225	3043.194
	AB	AC	BC
Covariance	2029.89	6.395482	362.118
Correlation	1.047379	0.000611	0.034521

Where A = Infosys, B = Cipla and C = RIL.

(a) Calculate the risk-free lending and borrowing of all these three securities separately. Calculate their return and risk by taking weights of 0, 0.25, 0.5, 0.75 and 1 of each risky security with the risk-free asset.

(b) Construct the portfolio of Infosys and Cipla by taking 50% of each. (i) Now construct another portfolio, with this risky portfolio: (i) merging it with a risk-free security and (ii) borrowing at risk-free rate, investing borrowed fund, as well selves fund in risky portfolio of Infosys and Cipla security. Explain your answer by tabulating the results obtained with different proportions of the risky securities and plot your results on the graph. Use the same proportions as above. (iii) Also construct another portfolio of all three securities by borrowing and/or lending with risk-free asset in such a way that the total weight does not exceed 1.

2. Mr. Vikas Agarwal holds a risky portfolio, with standard deviation of 18%. Mr. Agarwal wants to invest in the following proportions: -0.20:1.20, 20:80, 50:50 and 40:60 in the risk-free asset and risky portfolio respectively. Find out the standard deviation of all the portfolios that Mr. Agarwal constructs by varying the proportions of the assets.

3. A portfolio with risky securities has an expected return of 22%. The risk-free rate of return is 8.56%. If the expected return is 26%, how would you construct the portfolio?

REFERENCES

1. http://www.d42.com/portfolio/theory/the-efficient-frontier-with-risk-free-lending-and-borrowing
2. http://www.docstoc.com/docs/3871973/12-Riskfree-Borrowing-and-Lending
3. http://en.wikipedia.org/wiki/File:CML_and_Risk-free_lending_and_borrowing.jpg
4. http://marriottschool.net/emp/boyer/410_10/other/CAL%20Steps.pdf
5. http://www.slidefinder.net/c/chapter_eight_riskfree_lending_and/investsab08/14095893

8
RISK AVERSION AND CAPITAL ALLOCATION

> **LEARNING OBJECTIVES**
>
> The purpose of this chapter is to enable you to understand:
> - What is a utility function.
> - Application of utility values for the selection of the portfolios with different degrees of risk aversion.
> - Derivation of the indifference curves.
> - Investment decisions across risk-free and risky portfolio.
> - Derivation of capital allocation line (CAL).

8.1 INTRODUCTION

The primary objective of investment is saving, subsequently leading to growth, of the hard earned money. And because of this, the primary cause of concern becomes the involvement of inevitable risk, when one chooses to invest in the stock market. The concern is compounded by the presence of too many options of compounding the invested fund! How to choose and which ones to choose, cannot be solely decided by the individual characteristics of the securities. It is their interdependence, their unique response to the presence of the other—apart from their response to the market—that have to be taken cognizance of. This has been reiterated, during the course of the text, accompanied by the discussions on these varied aspects and the ways to resolve the specific issues.

In line with these discussions, the previous chapter, on risk-free lending and borrowing, again reflected on how the investors are caught up in a dilemma. For investors, allocation of their funds to, and distribution of the same amongst, the risk-free asset and risky portfolio poses quite a bit of confusion and thus worries. A need for a standard parameter to rank the assets, individually, as well as in collaboration, in a portfolio, is felt. This is what we intend to do in this chapter.

The chapter concentrates on the portfolio theory for the purpose as it too focuses mainly on the risk quotient. The fundamental principle for investment in the stock market is avoidance of risk by the investors unless a commensurate return is offered, to bear the risk. It could be called a compensatory measure. And above all, the construction of the portfolio depends upon the personal choice of the investor with respect to: selection of risky security, risk-free security and their relative proportions.

The present chapter introduces the standard parameter for ranking, as mentioned above. It is called the utility function. This function allows the investor to assign the utility score to the functionality of the portfolio. The utility score depends upon the risk-return preferences of the investor and they can choose the portfolio with the ascertained highest value. The use of return, risk and utility function drives the investor towards the optimal allocation of their capital in the risky portfolio and risk-free asset. In other words, utility function enables the optimal distribution of capital amongst the risky portfolio and risk-free asset.

8.1.1 Utility Values

The discussions through the text have been repeatedly mentioning that various investment assets are categorized on the basis of their risk-return profile. Also, these securities find takers in the investors depending upon their preferences for specific risk-return profiles. Risk-averse investors thus prefer to invest either in risk-free security or in a risky security, but with positive risk premium.

It has also been mentioned in this chapter as the fundamental principle of the market, the high premium sought by the investments in risky assets. So higher risk premiums are demanded for the corresponding high risk quotient of the security, as generally the investors choose to play safe. They can be lured to invest in risky securities only when they are assured of a corresponding compensation, in terms of the said premium.

Coming to the allocation of the capital optimally, a guideline is required. But that would have to be based on the utility function. For that the utility function would have to be determined. That implies the guidelines for its estimation, as, first and foremost then, the utility function has to be calculated.

For the purpose of developing the capital allocation line (CAL), all feasible risk-return combinations of risk-free assets and risky portfolio are constructed as portfolios. The risky securities considered are: Sun Pharma, ICICI Bank and GAIL. The following Table 8.1 represents the return, risk and risk premium of these three risky securities, along with the risk-free asset, with the risk-free rate of return assumed to be 8%. Three portfolios result out of their feasible combinations (as mentioned above).

Table 8.1 Risk and Return of the Securities, Sun Pharma, ICICI Bank and GAIL

Security	Expected return, R_i (%)	Risk, σ (%)	Risk premium, $R_i - R_f$ (%)
Risk-free asset	8	0	0
Sun Pharma	11.17	16.55	3.17
ICICI Bank	33.43	39.33	25.43
GAIL	36.21	47.12	28.21

Investment in an asset becomes automatically more attractive when its expected return is higher, and is just the reverse when its risk is higher. But this trade-off between return and risk does not remain that straightforward, as the risk too increases with an increase in the return. And this is what usually happens, as has been observed in the preceding chapters. Thus is ushered in the concept of utility function. This enables the discerning of the comparative utility, translated in terms of the productivity—the return—in spite of high risks involved. With utility function scores can be assigned to the competing assets or portfolios, based on their expected returns and risks. With scores assigned, the assets (be it an individual security or a portfolio) are ranked. Higher is the score, higher is the rank. Based on their ranks, the investment decisions are ranked!

Higher utility scores are assigned to assets or portfolios with higher expected return; while those with lower expected return are ranked lower. In terms of risk, assets with lower risk are assigned higher utility values and those with higher risk get lower scores. The utility function is thus calculated as:

$$U = E(r) - \tfrac{1}{2}(A\sigma^2) \tag{1}$$

Where,

U = utility function.
A = index of the investor's risk aversion.
$\tfrac{1}{2}$ = a scaling convention.

The Table 8.2 below represents the utility scores for each asset, assigned by the investors.

For the purpose of illustration we consider the security, Sun Pharma, to calculate its utility score, when $A = 3$ as follows:

$$\begin{aligned} U &= E(r) - \tfrac{1}{2}(A\sigma^2) \\ &= 0.1117 - [\tfrac{1}{2} \times 3 \times (0.1655)^2] \\ &= 0.070615 \end{aligned}$$

This is value recorded in the third column of third row. To calculate utility function return and risk must be taken in decimal only.

Table 8.2 Utility Score of the Risk-free and Risky Securities

Investor's risk aversion (A)	Utility score of the assets			
	Risk-free asset	Sun Pharma	ICICI Bank	GAIL
1	0.08	0.098005	0.256958	0.251085
2	0.08	0.08431	0.179615	0.140071
3	0.08	0.070615	0.102273	0.029056
4	0.08	0.05692	0.02493	-0.08196
5	0.08	0.043224	-0.05241	-0.19297
6	0.08	0.029529	-0.12975	-0.30399

Out of the three assets, GAIL is the most risky security as its standard deviation is highest while Sun Pharma is the least risky security, with the lowest standard deviation. ICICI Bank is between these two, with respect to its standard deviation. So, without assigning utility score it can be stated that GAIL is preferred by risk-loving investors and Sun Pharma by risk-averse investor. Investors' risk aversion index (A) show risk aversion or preference of the investors. Higher value of A indicates that investors are more averse to risk, compared to when value of A is lower. Or in other words, lower value of A indicates investors are comparatively less risk-averse and are gradually moving towards the category of a risk-lover. Utility score of risk-free asset will remain 0.08, irrespective of the value of A.

Now we consider Table 8.2 and interpret the utility scores horizontally. When A = 1, the highest value or utility score is provided by ICICI Bank. This trend continues till A = 3. It implies that ICICI stock will be selected only by less risk-averse investors as value of A is less. The GAIL stock would be the second choice after ICICI Bank, even for less risk-averse investor (considering GAIL's utility score is less than ICICI Bank's). Till A = 3, risk-free asset and Sun Pharma's stock would be overlooked by risk-averse investors, as other two stocks provide better utility score. When A = 4 and more, Sun Pharma's utility score decreases and that of ICICI Bank and GAIL become negative. This shows that when value of A (risk-averse nature of the investors or degree of risk-aversion) increases, investors try to come in the safer zone. Thus, when value of A rises investors prefer to invest in risk-free security, compared to other securities whose utility score is much less than that of the risk-free asset.

Risk-averse Investor

The information that this table conveys for the risk-averse investors are:

- The utility score of risk-free assets is equivalent to their return as there is no risk, at least in nominal terms. Thus investors of all types would assign utility score of 0.08 to it as in the example above, return offered by risk-free asset is 8%[1].
- Till a given level of risk aversion, all three assets beat the risk-free asset. In this case, the level is 2 and below.
- Hence, a risky asset is desirable only if its utility score is higher than that of risk-free assets.
- Higher risk aversion points towards investors who discount risky assets by assigning lower utility scores. Thus, for the given degree of risk aversion (A), higher the risk of the assets lower is its utility score.

Thus a risk-averse investor will opt for assets with highest utility score while selecting the competing assets based on their risk-return trade-off. An asset with a utility score less than that of risk-free asset will be rejected. More importantly, this utility score of the risky assets can be interpreted as a certainty equivalent rate of return. This implies that utility score for risky assets can be considered as their assured returns.

Risk-neutral Investor

For the risk-neutral investor, interpretation of utility values differs. And that is obvious because for him the degree of risk aversion (A) is zero. So the risky assets would be judged purely on the

---

[1] It is because $U = E(r) - \frac{1}{2}(A\sigma^2) = 0.08 - (\frac{1}{2} \times 3 \times 0) = 0.08$.

basis of their rate of return. Risk is irrelevant for risk-neutral investor. Thus in this case, utility score is simply equivalent to its expected return.

Risk-loving Investor

A risk-loving investor is an aggressive investor, with degree of risk aversion even less than zero (A < 0). As they simply love to take risk with no concern for caution, their expectation is always of a higher return. So, such investors adjust the expected return upward, to confront the given asset's risk. Their utility score is more than that of risk-free assets even when A is lower. The Table 8.3, as shown below, gives the summary of the utility scores of following risky securities.

Table 8.3 Utility Scores for the Following Risky Securities (A = 2)

Security	Return (R_i)	Standard deviation (σ)	Utility score
ACC	0.2973	0.3462	0.177446
BHEL	0.436	0.4487	0.234668
Hero Honda	0.2926	0.3665	0.158278
Maruti	0.3015	0.2671	0.230158
NTPC	0.2093	0.2422	0.150639
ONGC	0.3577	0.4574	0.148485
RIL	0.2173	0.4373	0.026069

Here for the securities: Hero Honda, NTPC and ONGC, utility values are almost same; while similar is the case with the securities of BHEL and Maruti. Except for RIL, utility score of all other assets is substantially more than that of the risk-free asset.

A lot has been mentioned about the utility function and how it highlights the utility or otherwise of the assets. The variation in the approach towards the utility values, with difference in the investor type, too has been discussed. Yet amongst all, the two most striking features of the utility functions are:

- Utility score rises with an increase in expected return, but is lowered by increment in risk.
- The utility score of risk-free asset is equal to their return. So investors do not discount such asset.

> **Pause for thought:** Utility function enables the optimal distribution of capital amongst the risky portfolio and risk-free asset.

8.2 Allocation of Funds to Risk-Free Security and Risky Portfolio

Allocation of capital to different kind of assets is known as capital allocation decision. This decision is obviously guided by the risk-return characteristics of the assets and nature of the investor.

An investor intends to allocate the funds to assets that yield high return. As to the extent risk would be accepted is the investor's choice. But for the investor in general, assets with low risk are a favorite when investment decisions are taken. Thus, they are on the lookout for ways to even reduce the risk of a portfolio they already possess. Risk-averse investors can reduce the risk of the portfolio most conveniently by allocating the part of the funds to risk-free security and the rest to the risky portfolio.

How the capital allocation is done is analyzed by studying the example of the basic capital allocation between risk-free security (for example, treasury bills or government bonds) and risky portfolio. A risk-free security and a risky portfolio of an equity (E) and bond (B) are considered (which is issued by the private player). The risky portfolio, comprised of bonds and equity, is considered an asset as a whole. Thus the portfolio selected is that of a risk-free security and a risky portfolio (as a risky asset). Market value of the portfolio, at the time of investment is assumed to be Rs.1,00,000, with Rs.30,000 invested in risk-free security, such as government bonds. The remaining Rs.70,000, is invested in risky securities (of the risky portfolio) equally between the different equity shares and in long-term bonds. The weights of equities and long term bonds are thus in the ratio, 0.50:0.50 [as E = (35,000/70,000) = 0.5 and B = (35,000/70,000) = 0.5]. The weight (in rupees) of risky securities, with respect to the total weight is 70,000/1,00,000 = 0.70. That of the risk-free security is, 30,000/1,00,000 = 0.30. Furthermore, the proportion of the risky securities, in the risky portfolio has been assumed to be equal. So the weights of both, the equity shares and bonds, in the risky portfolio are, 0.35 (35,000/100,000 = 0.35) out of total investment of Rs.1,00,000 in the final portfolio. Thus, their ratio in the portfolio is 0.35:0.35. It is also assumed that the investor wants to maintain this proportion throughout the holding period.

Given the propensity for risk-aversion, it is natural to suppose that the holder of the portfolio wants to decrease the allocation of funds, in risky securities, from .70 to .55. The investment would thus reduce from Rs.70,000 to Rs.55,000, in risky securities. This implies the need to sell investments in risky securities worth Rs.15,000. The proceeds from the sale will be used to buy more of risk-free securities, worth Rs.15,000. Thus the proportion of risk-free securities is, 0.45 (45,000/1,00,000) and that of risky securities is, 0.55 (55,000/1,00,000), in the revised portfolio. In order to maintain the earlier proportion of 0.35:0.35, of the equity shares and bonds in the risky portfolio, fund allocation in both of them has to be reduced by Rs.5250 (15,000 × 0.35).

The earlier proportion was 0.50:0.50 in risky portfolio comprised of equity and bond. Now, as the investment in risky security is reduced from Rs.70,000 to Rs.55,000, an investment worth Rs.15,000 from risky portfolio would have to be sold and the proceeds would be poured in to invest in the risk-free security. Earlier with total investment of Rs.70,000 in risky portfolio, Rs.35,000 was invested in each asset (equity and bond). Now the total investment is Rs.50,000, from which Rs.25,000 has to be invested in each so as to maintain the proportion of investment, 0.50:0.50.

This can be achieved by another method. To maintain the same proportion of 0.50:0.50 in both the assets (equity and bond), investment worth, 0.50 × Rs.15,000 = Rs.7500 of equity and bond each, has to be sold. With the total investment down to Rs.50,000, from Rs. 70,000, for both bond and equity, the proportion becomes,

$$W_e = \frac{35,000 - 7500}{70,000 - 15000} = .50$$

$$W_b = \frac{35,000 - 7500}{70,000 - 1500} = .50$$

Where,

W_e = weight of investment in equity shares.
W_b = weight of investment in bonds.

As already mentioned, fund allocated to equities and bonds have been considered as an allocation in a single asset, their portfolio, instead of considering them as individual assets. The example has assumed a change in the fund allocation of the main (final) portfolio by transferring certain percentage of funds from risky securities to risk-free security. However, the proportion of each security in the risky portfolio has remained the same. So, the probability distribution of rate of return on the risky portfolio remains unchanged by the reallocation of the assets. But, the probability distribution of rate of return of the complete portfolio[2] has changed as the overall proportion of risk-free and risky assets has undergone a change.

> **Pause for thought:** Allocation of capital to different kind of assets is known as capital allocation decision. When fund allocation changes, overall rate of return of the main portfolio changes. But if the fund invested in the securities of the constituent portfolio remains unchanged, the change in the overall rate of return doesn't affect the rate of return of the constituent portfolio.

8.2.1 Portfolio of One Risky Portfolio and One Risk-Free Asset

Extending upon the discussions of the previous section, calculations of return and risk of a portfolio of a risky portfolio, with capital reallocations, is the focus of this section. An investor is assumed to hold the portfolio of two assets: one is risk-free, with the 8% risk-free rate of return (R_f). The other one is a risky portfolio of two securities, HDFC and BPCL, and its return and risk are 20.66% and 14.12% respectively[3].

The risk premium = Return of the risky portfolio − Risk-free rate of return
$$= E(r) - R_f = 20.66 - 8 = 12.66\%.$$

By investing a weight W in the risky portfolio, the weight in the risk-free asset is 1-W. The rate of return on the final portfolio is thus,

$$E(R) = [W \times E(r)] + (1 - W)R_f \qquad (2)$$

Where,

R = return of the complete portfolio.
W = weight of investment in the constituent risky portfolio.
r = return of the constituent risky portfolio.
R_f = risk-free rate of return.

The above equation can be rewritten as,

$$E(R) = [W \times E(r)] + (1 - W)R_f \qquad (3)$$
$$= R_f + W[E(r) - R_f]$$
$$= 8\% + W(20.66\% - 8\%)$$
$$= 8\% + 12.66\%W$$

The above observation makes it apparent that the base rate of return for any portfolio is the risk free-rate, which is the sum assured, on the portfolio. The portfolio is expected to earn a risk

---

[2] Portfolio of risk free security and risky security (here bond and equity).
[3] With the proportion to be invested: 80% and 20% in BPCL and HDFC respectively.

premium that depends on the risk premium of the risky portfolio, multiplied by the proportion of investment, W, in it. The net return of the portfolio is thus the sum of the risk-free rate of return and the risk-premium. As it is assumed that investors are risk-averse, they are ready to invest only when offered a positive risk premium. As the risk of the risk-free asset is zero, and the covariance and correlation between the rate of return of risky portfolio and the risk-free asset is zero, the risk (standard deviation) of the final portfolio is calculated as follows.

Thus, the variance (σ^2_P) of the two assets (1—risky security and 2—risk-free security) portfolio is given by,

$$\sigma^2_P = \sigma^2_1 W^2 + \sigma^2_2 (1-W)^2 + 2W(1-W)\sigma_1 \sigma_2 Cor_{12} \qquad (4)$$

Where,

W = proportion to be invested in risky assets.
$(1-W)$ = proportion to be invested in risk-free security.

Where, σ^2_1, σ^2_2 and Cor_{12} are the variance of the risky constituent portfolio, variance of the risk-free asset and correlation between the two, respectively. But in this case, risk of risk-free asset is zero and hence its covariance and correlation with the other asset too is zero.

That is, σ^2_2, σ_2 and Cor_{12} are all zero.

Hence the above equation reduces to,

$$\sigma^2_P = \sigma^2_1 W^2 \qquad (5)$$

Or, $\quad \sigma_P = W\sigma_1 \quad (\therefore W = \sigma_P/\sigma_1)$
$\quad\quad\quad = 14.12W$

If the investor invests 100% of his available fund in risky assets, then W=1. Thus the final portfolio R is equivalent to r. On the other hand, if only the risk-free asset is chosen, then R becomes equivalent to the risk-free portfolio, R_f. If the investor doesn't opt for these extreme measures of investing in a single asset, then the proportion of investment in risky portfolio and risk-free asset varies in the range of 0 to 1. The table shown below represents the risk and return of the final portfolio, by varying the proportions of risky portfolio and risk-free asset. Thus, as in Chapter 7, it is the example of risk-free lending as fund is invested in risk-free and risky securities and total investment does not exceed 1.

Table 8.4 Portfolio Composed of Risky Constituent Portfolio and Risk-free Security

	Portfolio						
	1	2	3	4	5	6	7
$W_{HDFC-BPCL}$	0.00	0.20	0.40	0.50	0.60	0.80	1.00
W_2	1.00	0.80	0.60	0.50	0.40	0.20	0.00
Return (%)	8	10.53	13.06	14.33	15.59	18.12	20.66
Risk (%)	0	2.82	5.65	7.06	8.48	11.30	14.12

These different combinations of risky portfolio and risk-free asset will lie on the straight line as shown in Figure 8.1, below.

The slope of this straight line is,

$$[E(r) - R_f]/\sigma_1 = 12.66/14.12 = 0.896.$$

It can be interpreted that by increasing the proportion of risky portfolio in this complete portfolio 0.896 for a 1 percent of risk. The return-risk trade-off, represented by the slope, is 0.896. This is the extra return earned, per extra risk, and also holds true for any other combinations of risky portfolio and risk free asset. This return-risk ratio is also called Sharpe's ratio or reward-to-volatility ratio (discussed in Chapter 21).

By rearranging Equation (3) we get,

$$E(R) = R_f + W[E(r) - R_f] \qquad (6)$$
$$= R_f + \sigma_P/\sigma_1[E(r) - R_f] \qquad (7)$$

With the inputs from the available data, Equation (6), for the return on complete portfolio, becomes,

$$E(R) = 8 + 12.66/14.12\sigma_P$$

∴ The slope of the final portfolio = $[E(r) - R_f]/\sigma_1$

And R_f serves as the intercept.

The straight line in the Figure 8.1 below is called the capital allocation line (CAL). CAL represents all possible risk-return combinations of the final portfolio R.

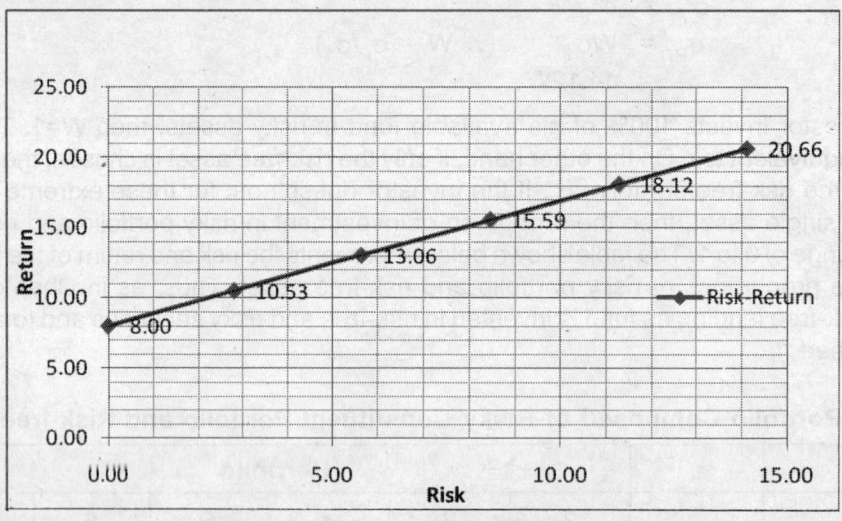

Figure 8.1: Capital allocation line

Pause for thought: CAL represents all possible risk-return combinations of the main portfolio, wherein assets present as portfolios are considered constituents of the main portfolio.

8.3 CAPITAL ALLOCATION LINE WITH RISK-FREE BORROWING

It is the variation in the capital allocation line, which is of interest now. CAL would be characteristic of the investment made, as it is about the relative allocation of the available capital to the components of the portfolio.

In this section we look forward to have an idea of the CAL when investments include risk-free borrowing. As above, the available fund for investment is assumed to be Rs.1,00,000. To it the investor adds Rs.25000, generated by risk-free borrowing. The total amount of Rs.1,25,000 is invested in risky portfolio. In other words, the effect of leverage on the distribution of the rate of return of the portfolio is being analyzed, and the corresponding CAL as well. This would lead us thus to the value of reward-to-volatility ratio (discussed in Chapter 21).

∴ The total amount invested, in this case, is Rs.1,25,000

∴ Proportion invested in the risky portfolio,

$$W = 125000/100000 = 1.25$$

And that in risk-free asset,

$$1 - W = 1 - 1.25 = -0.25$$

–0.25 represents the investment in risk-free asset through risk-free borrowing. Here the investor is assumed to borrow at the risk-free rate of 8%, to subsequently invest the borrowed fund, along with his own fund in the risky portfolio.

These values of W and 1-W, when substituted in Equation (6), the return obtained is,

$$E(R) = R_f + W[E(r) - R_f]$$
$$E(R) = 8\% + 1.25(12.66\%)$$
$$= 23.82\%$$

The risk of the investment would be,

$$\sigma_P = W\sigma_1$$
$$= 1.25 \times 14.12\%$$
$$= 17.65\%$$

∴ The slope of the portfolio = $[E(r) - R_f]/\sigma_1$ \hfill (8)
$$= (23.82\% - 8\%)/17.65\%$$
$$= 0.896$$

In the earlier example also, where the fund was invested in risk-free asset and risky security in different proportion, though total investment did not exceed 1, slope of the portfolio was 0.896. As per the theory discussed in Chapter 7, it falls under the purview of risk-free lending. In this example of leverage, or risk-free borrowing, investors can borrow as much as they want and can invest own fund and borrowed fund in risky portfolio or assets. However, the introduction of leverage helps only to increase return along with risk. The slope of the portfolio remains the same—0.896. This can be interpreted as before: for 1% rise in risk, return increases by 0.896 only. Thus, leverage does not help to increase return-risk ratio of the investment. This is applicable for government or only institutional borrowers who can borrow at the same risk-free rate of 8%. For common investors like us the borrowing rates are higher than the lending rates.

The conclusions that can be drawn from the calculation, and the Figure 8.2 are:
- Slope of the portfolio remains the same, at 0.896, irrespective of whether the investor lends at the risk-free rate or borrows at the risk-free rate.
- Risk of the final portfolio increases with leverage.

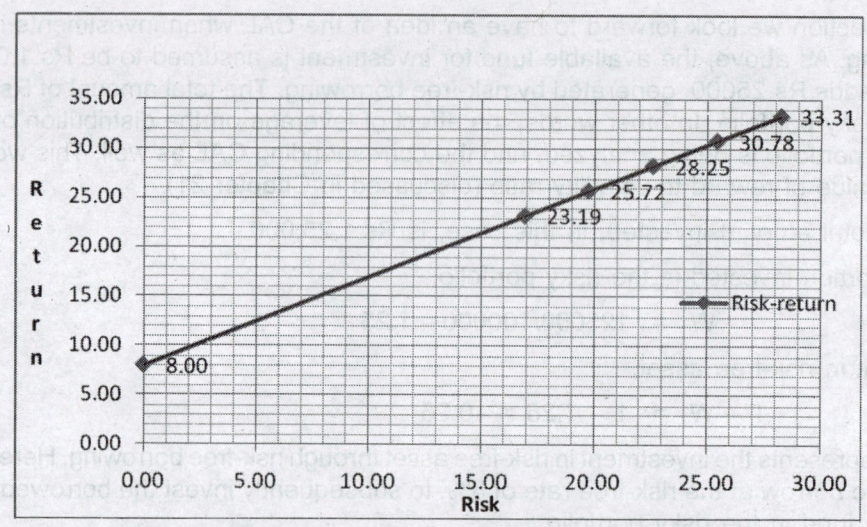

Figure 8.2: Portfolio composed of risk-free borrowing in risky assets (government borrowers)

Realistic borrowing

But in reality, this situation does not prevail as only government can borrow at the risk-free rate. The risk of the non-government borrower forces lenders to charge higher interest rate on loans. Hence, the non-government borrowers end up borrowing at a rate more than the risk-free rate. Under the realistic situation, borrowing rate is assumed to be 12%.

∴ The slope = $[E(r) - R_f]/\sigma_1$ = (20.66-12)/14.12 = 0.613

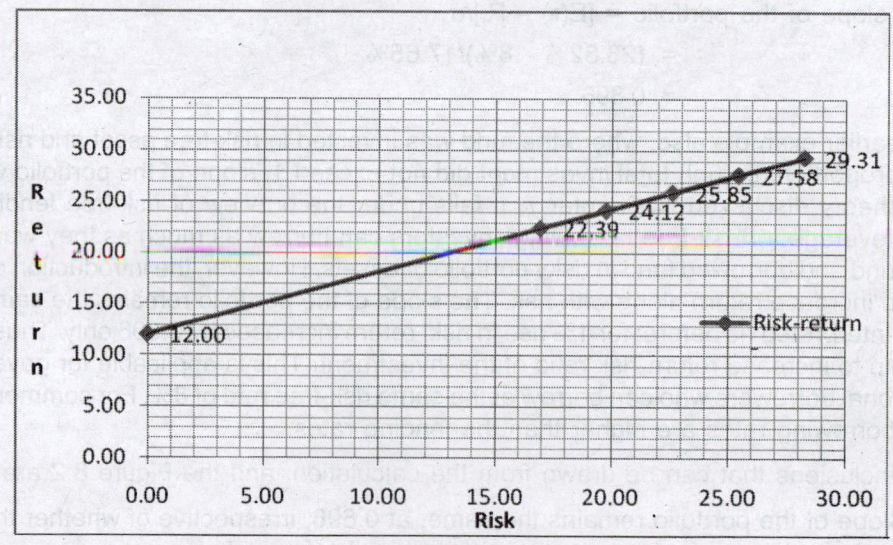

Figure 8.3: Portfolio composed of risk-free borrowing and risky assets (non-government borrowers)

This is a marked change from the earlier value of 0.896. We discussed earlier that slope was 0.896 in the case of risk-free lending and borrowing at the risk-free rate of 8%. But when the realistic risk-free borrowing rate, 12% is considered, the slope decreases from 0.896 to 0.613. The slope of 0.613 shows that for a 1% of rise in risk, return increases by 0.613 only. This shows that investors are receiving less reward or return for bearing the given level of risk. Thus, the investor's reward-to-volatility ratio decreases as borrowing rate is increased from 8% to 12%.

Conclusions drawn from the realistic borrowing are:

- Slope of the risky portfolio decreases. Obviously the steepness of the CAL decreases, as shown in the Figure 8.3.
- The slope changes from 0.896 to 0.613, with a corresponding change in the risk-free borrowing rate from 8% to 12%.

Borrowing at the risk-free rate in real life can be practiced if we have a margin account with the broker. By purchasing securities on margin (margin allows to purchase the securities up to 50% of its purchase value) we can have a benefit of leverage. Margin account means borrowing money from our broker (where we have a demat account, for example, India Infoline, Sharekhan, etc.) to buy stocks; and for that our investment is used as a collateral. It gives the investors purchasing power so more stocks can be purchased without paying for the same. It is a kind of loan and in that account is collateralized by stock and cash. However, if the value of the stock drops significantly, the account holder is required to deposit more cash or sell a portion of the stock. In other words, we are investing with the broker's money. It is a leverage which magnifies both return and risk.

> **Pause for thought:** Irrespective of risk-free lending or borrowing, the slope of CAL remains the same. But this is an ideal situation. In reality, when the risk-free rate is increased, the slope of the CAL is found to decrease.

8.3.1 Risk Aversion and Asset Allocation

Till now the discussion on CAL has been unidirectional. CAL has been developed by using all available risk-return combinations of risk-free asset and risky portfolio. But now the focus shifts to the selection of optimal portfolio. That is the CAL for the portfolio with best risk-return trade-off, from the set of feasible choices, will be developed.

In the example above, risky portfolio has been constructed by investing in BPCL and HDFC. With the assumption that investments in these stocks are in the proportion of 80% and 20% respectively, return and risk have been found to be 20.66 % and 14.12 % respectively. Investors may invest in different securities—and in different proportions—based on their return-risk profile. As discussed above, risk-free rate is assumed to be 8% and the final portfolio is constructed by investing in risky portfolio and risk-free asset. The return and risk of the final portfolio is calculated by using Equations (3) and (4).

The optimal portfolio can be calculated with help of utility function, using Equation (1). The table below indicates that an increase in the proportion of risky portfolio, W, increases the expected return, as well as the risk of the revised portfolio. Because of the increased return and risk, volatility also increases and then decreases. (Refer to Table 8.2, A = 5)

Table 8.5 Utility Function (A= 5)

W	E(R)	σ_P	U
0	0.08	0	0.08
0.1	0.09266	0.01412	0.092162
0.2	0.10532	0.02824	0.103326
0.3	0.11798	0.04236	0.113494
0.4	0.13064	0.05648	0.122665
0.5	0.1433	0.0706	0.130839
0.6	0.15596	0.08472	0.138016
0.7	0.16862	0.09884	0.144197
0.8	0.18128	0.11296	0.14938
0.9	0.19394	0.12708	0.153567
1	0.2066	0.1412	0.156756
1.1	0.21926	0.15532	0.158949
1.2	0.23192	0.16944	0.160145
1.3	**0.24458**	**0.18356**	**0.160344**
1.4	0.25724	0.19768	0.159547
1.5	0.2699	0.2118	0.157752
1.6	0.28256	0.22592	0.15496
1.7	0.29522	0.24004	0.151172
1.8	0.30788	0.25416	0.146387
1.9	0.32054	0.26828	0.140605
2.0	0.3332	0.2824	0.133826

Utility functions when plotted from table 8.5, results in a graph, as shown in Figure 8.4. The X-axis represents the proportion of risky portfolio and Y-axis, the corresponding utility function.

The implications of this graph are:

- Utility increases first and then decreases and it is highest when proportion of W is 1.3 (marked in 'bold', in Table 8.5).
- However, this is an approximation. The exact value of W can be obtained with the help of an equation (to be discussed later).
- When W is less than 1.3, investors prefer risk-free borrowing along with risky portfolio and are willing to bear more risk for the expected return.
- But when W is above 1.3, risk becomes so high that investors do not prefer to construct the portfolio with risk-free borrowing.

- When W is equal to 2 and more than 2, the risk rises faster than return and reduces utility significantly.

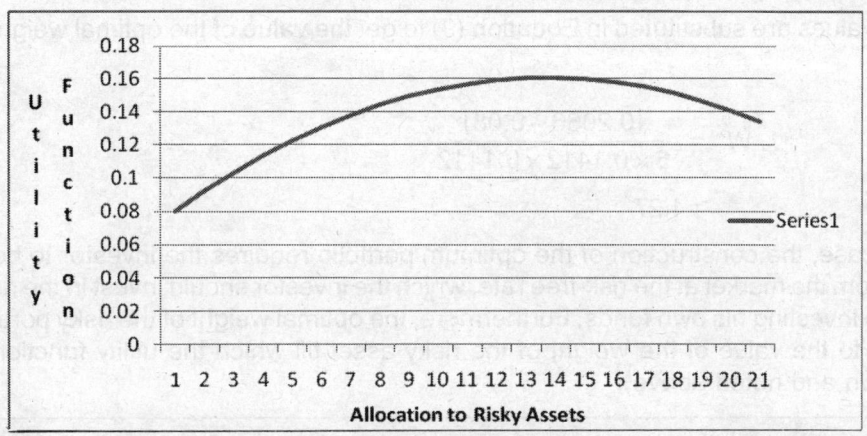

Figure 8.4: Utility function and allocation to risky assets

The equation below gives the optimal proportion of risky assets in a portfolio—in other words, weight of the risky asset in an optimal portfolio.

$$W^* = \frac{[E(r) - R_f]}{A\sigma_1^2} \tag{9}$$

It can also be rewritten as,

$$(W^*) \times \sigma_1^2 = \frac{[E(r) - R_f]}{A}$$

Where,

W^* = optimal proportion of the risky portfolio.
r = return on the risky portfolio.
R_f = rate of return of risk-free asset.
A = level of risk aversion.
σ^2 = variance (measure if risk) of the portfolio.

From the above equations it is apparent that, weight of risky asset in the optimal portfolio, W^*, is inversely proportional, to the level of risk aversion (A). At the same time, the variance of the risky portfolio is directly proportional to the risk premium offered by the risky assets. Which is obvious, as higher will be the risk, higher will be the risk premium sought and thus offered to lure the investors.

We already know from Table 8.4 that:

The return of the risky portfolio = 20.66%

The risk of the risky portfolio = 14.12%.

R_f = 8%

The degree of risk aversion, A, considered is 5.

These values are substituted in Equation (9) to get the value of the optimal weight of the risky asset.

$$W^* = \frac{[0.2066 - 0.08]}{5 \times 0.1412 \times 0.1412}$$

$$= 1.27$$

In this case, the construction of the optimum portfolio requires the investor to borrow 0.27% of the fund from the market at the risk-free rate, which the investor should invest in the risky portfolio, in addition to investing his own funds. Furthermore, the optimal weight of the risky portfolio is found to be closer to the value of the weight of the risky asset till which the utility function rises (W = 1.3, as shown and noted above).

> **Pause for thought:** The value of utility function for a risky asset is found to increase till a particular weight of the asset, beyond which the utility function decreases. This weight of the risky asset is invariably closer to its weight in the optimal portfolio. So it can be stated that till the optimal weight of the risky asset, its utility function rises. Or in other words, the utility function of a risky asset is maximum, at its optimum weight in a portfolio.

8.4 RISK, RETURN AND REWARD-TO-VOLATILITY RATIO OF THE OPTIMUM PORTFOLIO

The values of risk, return and W* when placed in Equation (9), yields the return and risk of the optimal portfolio as:

$$E(R) = 0.08 + [1.27 \times (0.2066 - 0.08)] = 24.07\%$$

$$\sigma_R = 1.27 \times 0.1412 = 17.93\%$$

The reward-to-volatility ratio of the optimum portfolio, i.e., the slope, is

$$[E(r) - R_f]/\sigma_1 = (0.2407 - 0.08)/0.1793 = 0.896$$

> **Pause for thought:** The slope of the CAL of the optimum portfolio is identical to that of the portfolio obtained with risk-free lending and borrowing.

8.4.1 Selection of the Optimal Portfolio with the Help of Indifference Curves

The risk, return and the optimal proportion of the risky asset have been calculated, for an optimal portfolio, utilizing Equation (9). But there is another method for determining these parameters. It is a graphical method, involving the curves, known as indifference curves.

It is assumed that the investor pours his entire fund in risk-free security, with an 8% interest rate on return and has zero risk. The assumption for the level of risk aversion is maintained at A = 5. These values are incorporated in Equation (1) for the utility function,

$$U = E(r) - \tfrac{1}{2}(A\sigma^2) = 0.08 - \tfrac{1}{2}(5 \times 0^2) = 0.08$$

Thus, the utility function is equal to the utility of the risk-free asset, which is actually the risk-free rate of interest. This is natural as the entire investment has been made in the risk-free asset.

Subsequently, the investor is assumed to construct the portfolio by combining the risk-free asset and the risky portfolio (as discussed in the earlier sections). But the intent is to maintain the same level of utility, 0.08, equivalent to the utility of the risk-free asset. We do know now that whenever a portfolio is constructed by combining a risk-free asset and a risky portfolio, return increases. Yet at the same time the risk also increases, while the utility may increase or decrease. Since in this case the assumption is for maintenance of the level of utility, irrespective of the proportions of the assets, equation is modified as:

$$U = E(r) - \tfrac{1}{2}(A\sigma^2)$$
$$E(r) = U + \tfrac{1}{2}(A\sigma^2)$$

It is assumed that the risk (σ) of the risky portfolio invested in is, 0.05. As the utility value is assumed to be kept constant, at 0.08, the expected return of the portfolio would be,

$$E(r) = 0.08 + \tfrac{1}{2}(5 \times 0.05^2) = 0.08625$$

In a similar manner, the expected return can be calculated for different levels of σ, with the utility value remaining constant at 0.08. This results in different combinations of expected return and risk with utility level of 0.08. The results thus obtained are shown in the Table 8.6 below. When all combinations of risk, return, along with the utility values (recorded in the table), are plotted graphically, indifference curves result.

Conversely, from the indifference curve, thus, the risk, return and utility values can be ascertained, as noted above. Similar method is applied when A = 3 and also for utility value of 0.12.

Table 8.6 Indifference Curves at Specific Utility and Risk Aversion Values

σ	U = 0.08		U = 0.12	
	A = 5	A = 3	A = 5	A = 3
0	0.08	0.08	0.12	0.12
0.05	0.08625	0.08375	0.12625	0.12375
0.1	0.105	0.095	0.145	0.135
0.15	0.13625	0.11375	0.17625	0.15375
0.2	0.18	0.14	0.22	0.18
0.25	0.23625	0.17375	0.27625	0.21375
0.3	0.305	0.215	0.345	0.255
0.35	0.38625	0.26375	0.42625	0.30375
0.4	0.48	0.32	0.52	0.36
0.45	0.58625	0.38375	0.62625	0.42375
0.5	0.705	0.455	0.745	0.495
0.55	0.83625	0.53375	0.87625	0.57375
0.6	0.98	0.62	1.02	0.66

The above table contains the risk-return combinations for two sets of utility values: 0.08 (risk-free interest rate (with government as the borrower), and 0.12 (risk-free interest rate for non-government borrowers). Even two levels of risk aversion too have been used: A=5 and A=3. These combinations of risk and return have been plotted with respect to two sets each, of utility and risk aversion values. Thus the two different indifference curves that result, as shown in Figure 8.5 below, have two different intercepts of 0.08 and 0.12 respectively.

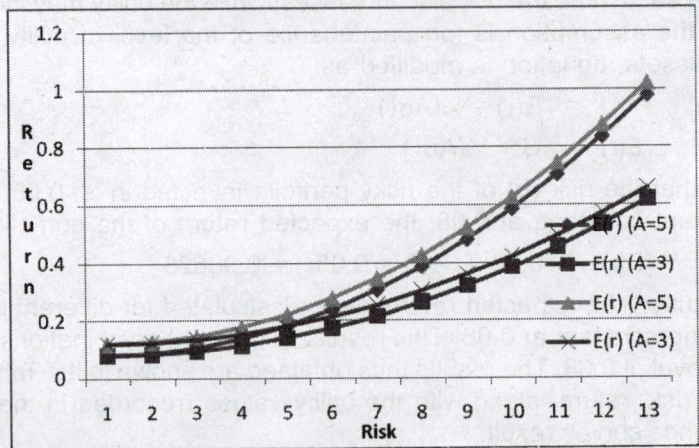

Figure 8.5: Indifference curves with specific utility and risk aversion

The conclusions that can be drawn from the table, as well as the graph are:
- Indifference curves with higher utility values and higher risk aversion have a higher expected return for a given level of risk.
- Hence, portfolios on the curve with higher utility offer higher return.
- Columns, 2 and 4, of the above table are represented by pair of the corresponding indifference curves which are steeper, indicating that risk-averse investor requires higher portfolio return for a given increase in risk.

> **Pause for thought:** The indifference curve represents the risk, return and utility function of assets. Hence these curves can be used to ascertain these parameters.

8.4.2 Finding the Optimal Portfolio by Using Indifference Curves

As discussed and derived in the previous section, the return and risk of the optimal portfolio is 24.07% and 17.93% respectively, with the corresponding utility value of 0.16038. Now that the indifference curve for a portfolio has been studied, the discussion is spontaneously guided to the indifference curve of an optimal portfolio. For that, the indifference curve, which is tangent to the CAL (derived in an earlier section), has to be found out from the available set of indifference curves. As steeper indifference curves correspond to higher level of utility, the rational tendency of an investor is to select a final portfolio lying on such indifference curves.

The Table 8.7 below represents calculations of indifference curves with different utility values: 0.14, 0.16, 0.16038 (utility of optimal portfolio has been derived from Figure 8.5), 0.18 and 0.2, at different levels of risk, when A = 5. The corresponding expected return is determined with the given range of risk, utility values and risk aversion, A = 5. And these returns are shown in Table 8.7 below.

Table 8.7 CAL and Indifference Curves

Risk	U = 0.14	U = 0.16	U = 0.16038	U = 0.18	U = 0.2	CAL
0	0.14	0.16	0.16038	0.18	0.2	0.08
0.02	0.141	0.161	0.16138	0.181	0.201	0.10915
0.04	0.144	0.164	0.16438	0.184	0.204	0.1383
0.06	0.149	0.169	0.16938	0.189	0.209	0.16745
0.08	0.156	0.176	0.17638	0.196	0.216	0.196601
0.1	0.165	0.185	0.18538	0.205	0.225	0.225751
0.12	0.176	0.196	0.19638	0.216	0.236	0.254901
0.14	0.189	0.209	0.20938	0.229	0.249	0.284051
0.16	0.204	0.224	0.22438	0.244	0.264	0.313201
0.1793	0.220371	0.240371	0.240751	0.260371	0.280371	0.341331
0.2	0.24	0.26	0.26038	0.28	0.3	0.371501
0.22	0.261	0.281	0.28138	0.301	0.321	0.400652
0.24	0.284	0.304	0.30438	0.324	0.344	0.429802
0.26	0.309	0.329	0.32938	0.349	0.369	0.458952
0.28	0.336	0.356	0.35638	0.376	0.396	0.488102
0.3	0.365	0.385	0.38538	0.405	0.425	0.517252
0.32	0.396	0.416	0.41638	0.436	0.456	0.546402
0.34	0.429	0.449	0.44938	0.469	0.489	0.575552
0.36	0.464	0.484	0.48438	0.504	0.524	0.604703

CAL is ascertained for different values of risk by using the following equation:

$$E(R) = R_f + \sigma_R/\sigma_r \, [E(r) - R_f]$$

Where,

$E(R)$ = return on the main (or final) portfolio.
$E(r)$ = return on the constituent risky portfolio.
R_f = risk-free rate of return.
σ_R = risk of the main portfolio.
σ_r = risk of the constituent risky portfolio.

If the values of the parameters in the equation are:

$E(r)$ = 20.66%; R_f = 8%; σ_R = 0 and σ_r = 14.12%

$E(R) = 8 + 0/14.12[20.66\% - 8\%]$

$= 0.08$

Five indifference curves and the CAL are plotted in the Figure 8.6 below.

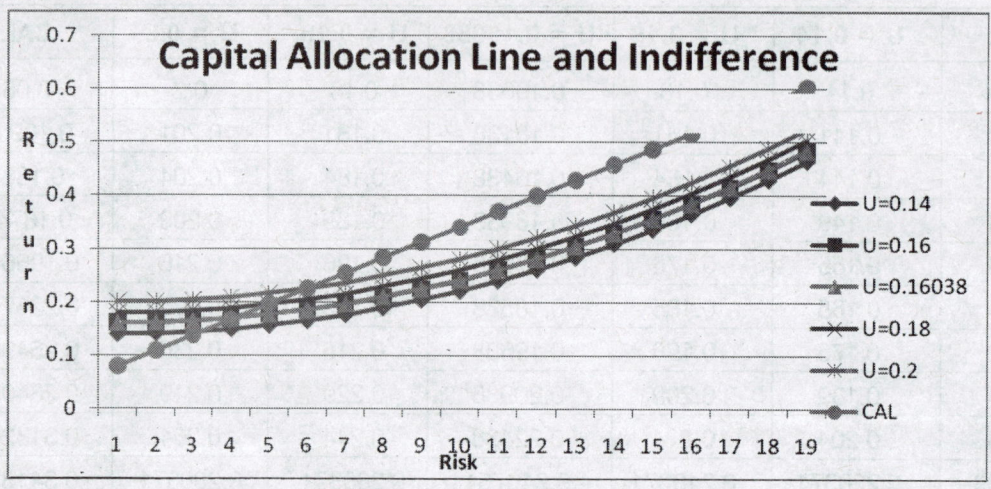

Figure 8.6: CAL and indifference curves

The figure leads to the conclusions:

- The indifference curve with U = 0.16038 is tangent to the CAL.
- This tangency point corresponds to the optimum portfolio, at which the utility is maximum.
- At this tangency point, return and risk are 24.07 and 17.93% respectively.
- The weight at this point is the optimal weight and its value, W = 1.27, is identical to that calculated earlier (in the section on 'risk aversion and asset allocation').
- Hence, for an optimum portfolio, even highly risk-averse investors are willing to take the advantage of leverage to invest in the risky portfolio.

Pause for thought: The indifference curve which is tangent to the CAL corresponds to the optimum portfolio and the point of tangency is the optimal weight of the risky asset in the complete portfolio—of risk-free asset and a risky constituent portfolio.

SUMMARY

✓ Selection of the portfolio depends upon the preferences of the investors, which in turn is dependent on the expected return and risk of the portfolio.
✓ Utility function is a measure of the utility of an asset which aids the investor in the selection process.
✓ Utility value is higher for those portfolios whose return is higher and lower for those portfolios whose risk is higher.
✓ For risk-averse investors value of the utility function is higher.

- ✓ For the risk-averse investor selection of the risky portfolio is decided by the certainty equivalent value of the portfolio.
- ✓ Risky portfolio is characterized and judged by the reward-to-volatility ratio. This is the slope for the capital allocation line (CAL).
- ✓ Constituents of a complete portfolio: risky assets and risk free security, all lie on the CAL line.
- ✓ For a leveraged portfolio, reward-to-volatility ratio falls and CAL is slightly moved towards the risky security.
- ✓ The degree of risk aversion is determined by slope of the indifference curve.

KEY CONCEPTS

Utility	Risk Averse	Risk-Free Borrowing
Risk	Degree Of Risk Aversion	The Optimal Portfolio
Return	Reward-To-Volatility Ratio	Capital Allocation Line
Risk-Free Asset	Certainty Equivalent Method	Indifference Curve

PROBLEM

As an investment manager, you are holding a risky portfolio whose expected rate of return is 25% and standard deviation is 32%. Assume that the risk free rate is 7%. Answer the following:

1. If Mr. Dev, your client, prefers to invest 50% in your portfolio and 50% in a risk-free security, what would be the return and risk of this portfolio?
2. What is the reward-to-volatility ratio of your portfolio and that of your client's?

SUGGESTED FURTHER READING FOR EMPIRICAL WORK

Nielsen, L.T., and Vassalou, M. (2006), "The Instantaneous Capital Market Line", *Economic Theory*, Vol. 28, No. 3.

REFERENCES

1. http://www.public.asu.edu/~kirkwood/DAStuff/decisiontrees/DecisionTreePrimer-2.pdf
2. http://en.wikipedia.org/wiki/Utility
3. http://www.econ.ucsb.edu/~tedb/Courses/Ec100C/VarianExpectedUtility.pdf
4. http://wiki.lesswrong.com/wiki/Utility_function
5. http://www.chastainskillman.com/downloads/articles/3Q10DecisionMaking.pdf
6. http://www.smartfolio.com/theory/details/portfolio_optimization/
7. http://en.wikipedia.org/wiki/Risk_aversion
8. http://www.econ.ubc.ca/discpapers/dp0520.pdf

9. http://dare.uva.nl/document/153
10. http://people.duke.edu/~charvey/Classes/ba350_1997/diverse/diverse.htm
11. http://www.ba.metu.edu.tr/~ba4814/slides/chapter%206.pdf
12. http://www.docstoc.com/docs/87219410/Risk-Aversion-and-Capital-Allocation-to-Risky-Assets-Answer-Key
13. http://www.hussmanfunds.com/pdf/mixdist.pdf
14. http://www.kellogg.northwestern.edu/faculty/papanikolaou/htm/finc460/ln/lecture1.pdf

PART 3

DEVELOPMENTS IN THE CAPITAL MARKET THEORY

9
CAPITAL ASSET PRICING MODEL

LEARNING OBJECTIVES

The purpose of this chapter is to enable you to understand:
- Capital market theory (CMT) developed from the portfolio theory.
- The capital market line (CML), which applies to the efficient portfolio.
- The security market line (SML), which applies to portfolios as well as individual securities.

9.1 INTRODUCTION

Till now theories have been discussed for construction of portfolios. They take into account the huge role played by the preferences of investors in this process. Importance of the presence of a risk-free security in the portfolio too has been acknowledged. In this chapter are discussed, capital market theory (CMT) and capital asset pricing model (CAPM). These two aid in the understanding and estimation of the required rate of return. CAPM is analyzed in detail as it is the best recognized model, used for the evaluation of risky securities. This is an equilibrium model, applied to predict the theoretical equilibrium prices of an asset. It uses Markowitz portfolio theory (MPT) and its principles for evaluating an asset.

The methods enabling identification of the optimal portfolio have been dealt with in the preceding chapters. At the same time it has been observed that optimal portfolios vary with type of the investor involved. The portfolio theories discussed in the earlier chapters provide guidelines to the investor on what should be done to select an optimal portfolio of risky securities. In this chapter will be discussed the risk-return characteristics of all risky securities in the portfolios to be held by all types of investors—either in a hypothetical, or in an ideal, situation. It would be a generalized analysis for all investor types, thus. Focus would be on how the market prices of these securities, and their return-risk trade-off, are affected by the optimal diversification of the risky securities which construct the portfolio.

The CAPM does just that. It explains the prices of the securities and their risk-return trade-off under the ideal situation, of market equilibrium. Thus CAPM is an equilibrium model. In other words, the capital market theory (CMT) explains how assets are priced in ideal world. CAPM establishes the relationship between the expected return of an asset with the market risk, beta, of that asset. CAPM and APT (discussed in the next chapter) are nothing but the models for evaluating the risky assets.

CMT is a generic term for the analysis of securities. By using one or the other mathematical model it tries to explain and predict the progression of the capital market. It is applied to seek the price of equity shares, in terms of the return sought by investors and the inherent risk involved. The capital asset pricing model (CAPM) is the most well known model of the CMT.

CAPM is one of the most widely used equilibrium model to assess the relationship between risk and returns expected from the prospective investment and hence plays a significant role in the selection of the optimal portfolios. The model proceeds on a framework to measure the related risk of the individual security and its risk-return trade-off. It thus assesses the risk premium that would be sought for a given return on a risky security. The theory is based on Markowitz portfolio theory (MPT), which states that each investor diversifies his portfolio; and based upon risk-return trade-off selects the location on efficient set. In other words, the optimal portfolio is decided on the basis of the risk-return trade-off.

9.1.1 The Capital Asset Pricing Model (CAPM): Assumptions

CAPM is based on MPT, but it actually begins from where MPT ends. It can be stated that CAPM works on lines of MPT. The theory has put forth a set of simple assumptions, free from the complexities of the real world to develop the framework. These assumptions are:

- All investors can borrow or lend money at the risk-free interest rate.
- All investors have the similar expectations of return, variance and covariance matrix of the securities held in the portfolio. Thus, based on the given risk-free interest rate, all investors locate the securities on the same efficient frontier set. This is also known as homogenous expectation, indicating the desire to hold the identical risky portfolios.
- Capital market works in equilibrium, i.e., is in perfect coherence.
- The price of a stock cannot be affected by the decision of any single investor to buy or sell shares of that stock.
- No income taxes are levied on the investors, causing them to be indifferent to both, capital gains and dividends.
- The holding period for investments is one year.
- There are no transaction costs.
- There is no inflation.

Given the over-simplified nature of the assumptions an obvious question arises as to how effective these would be, as they seem too unrealistic. But the fact is, despite the valid query, CAPM is able to explain the returns of risky assets through the very good analytical framework it has. So now the question shifts to how CAPM is so efficient in what it does, despite the unrealistic nature of its assumptions. As the assumptions are given a thorough attention it is found that some of the assumptions truly hold. For example, brokerage costs nowadays are very small; many institutional investors are exempted from tax. Furthermore, majority of the investors hold their investment for less than one year, during which the inflation is almost predicted.

CAPITAL ASSET PRICING MODEL 245

> **Pause for thought:** CAPM assesses the relationship between the expected return and risk of the prospective investment in an asset, under the ideal situation of market equilibrium.

9.2 CHARACTERISTICS LINE

As discussed in Chapter 6, risk has two components: systematic and unsystematic, of which the unsystematic risk can be eliminated through diversification. But the systematic risk is undiversifiable, and hence the market pays premium only for the systematic risk. In this section we consider the systematic risk and the risk-adjusted return (taking into account the risk premium offered) of individual securities.

This relationship between the risk, and the risk-adjusted return of a stock, is given by its characteristics line. Characteristics line is defined as: a line formed using regression analysis that summarizes a particular security or portfolio's systematic risk and rate of return. The rate of return is dependent on the standard deviation of the asset's returns and the slope of the characteristic line, which is represented by the beta (systematic risk) of the asset.

The Table 9.1 below shows the rate of return of the stock of ICICI and the market returns.

Table 9.1: Return of ICICI and the market

No.	Months	Market (%)	ICICI (%)	No.	Months	Market (%)	ICICI (%)
1	2	3	4	5	6	7	8
1	Aug–06	8.96	16.25	31	Feb–09	–4.80	–9.99
2	Sep–06	6.45	10.81	32	Mar–09	10.79	5.60
3	Oct–06	3.91	8.36	33	Apr–09	17.01	18.34
4	Nov–06	5.42	20.00	34	May–09	25.70	43.78
5	Dec–06	0.42	–5.18	35	Jun–09	–1.71	–7.09
6	Jan–07	1.90	–8.74	36	Jul–09	8.02	4.38
7	Feb–07	–8.40	–8.85	37	Aug–09	–0.18	–4.49
8	Mar–07	0.45	–4.44	38	Sep–09	9.15	24.76
9	Apr–07	8.28	15.29	39	Oct–09	–7.51	0.50
10	May–07	3.98	20.21	40	Nov–09	6.87	2.20
11	Jun–07	0.28	11.74	41	Dec–09	3.05	0.73
12	Jul–07	5.90	6.05	42	Jan–10	–6.38	–9.14
13	Aug–07	–0.17	–0.65	43	Feb–10	0.55	–3.38
14	Sep–07	12.27	20.82	44	Mar–10	6.63	4.47
15	Oct–07	14.29	4.24	45	Apr–10	0.02	10.21
16	Nov–07	–3.81	9.54	46	May–10	–3.38	–0.99
17	Dec–07	3.79	1.76	47	Jun–10	4.47	1.86
18	Jan–08	–13.17	–9.19	48	Jul–10	1.07	9.34

1	2	3	4	5	6	7	8
19	Feb–08	–1.36	–3.49	49	Aug–10	0.33	9.72
20	Mar–08	–9.19	–23.46	50	Sep–10	11.33	16.64
21	Apr–08	9.61	10.26	51	Oct–10	–0.31	–3.04
22	May–08	–6.52	–19.64	52	Nov–10	–3.71	–6.05
23	Jun–08	–18.86	–23.35	53	Dec–10	5.01	–6.24
24	Jul–08	6.50	26.32	54	Jan–11	–11.12	–6.68
25	Aug–08	3.56	0.54	55	Feb–11	–3.27	–0.75
26	Sep–08	–10.77	6.52	56	Mar–11	8.14	4.41
27	Oct–08	–24.75	–25.03	57	Apr–11	–1.68	1.21
28	Nov–08	–10.94	–5.90	58	May–11	–3.75	–18.27
29	Dec–08	5.29	17.65	59	Jun–11	1.72	4.24
30	Jan–09	–3.05	–10.99	60	Jul–11	–2.41	–3.22

As these values are plotted, the characteristics line for the stock of ICICI is obtained as shown in the Figure 9.1 below, showing the response of the stock relative to the market return.

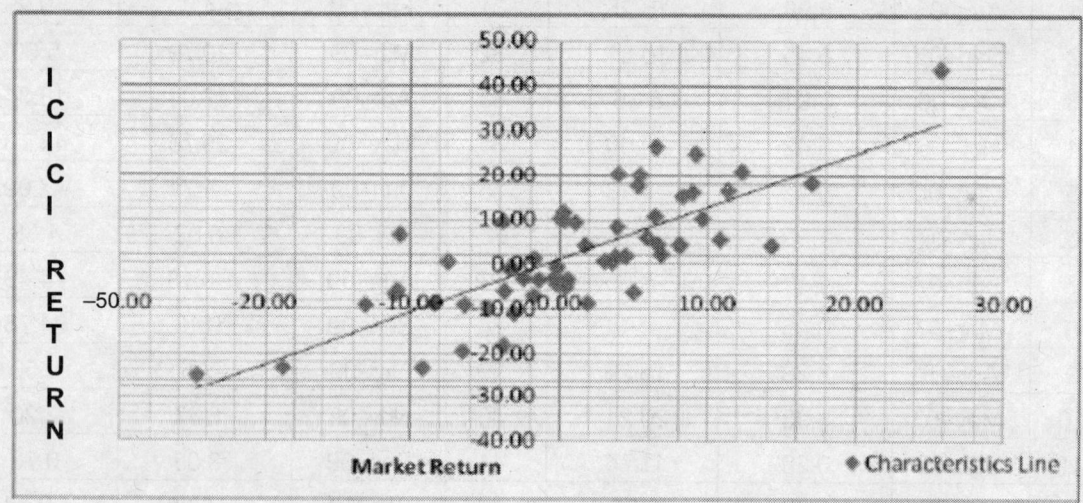

Figure 9.1: Characteristics Line of ICICI

The equation for the characteristics line is expressed as follows:

$$R_i = \alpha_i + \beta_i \times R_m + \epsilon_{iM}$$

Where,

R_i = return on security, i.

α_i = regression line intercept for the security, i.

β_i = beta of security, i.

R_m = return of the market.

ϵ_{iM} = random error term for the security, i.

Value of alpha (α), from the above equation of characteristics line, indicates whether the stock delivers the expected theoretical return or varies from it. A positive value of alpha indicates that the actual return is higher than that expected. This further signifies the stock to be under-priced and hence suitable for investing in. When that happens, the persistent buying of the stock raises the price of the stock and hence the return decreases. As the return drops, there is a gradual decrease in the purchase of the stock, and ultimately stops. Contrary to this, a negative value of alpha indicates the reverse. Thus, the actual return being less than that expected, the security is deemed over-priced. The investors sell such a stock. But if such stocks are sold by all investors the price of such stocks falls drastically rendering it attractive to the investors, as these can be bought at a very low price. Alpha helps the investor to determine whether the stock is over-priced or under-priced and thus aid in the portfolio construction.

The characteristics line for the ICICI is given by (with the corresponding values of alpha and beta being as indicated by the equation: 1.15 and 1.19 respectively), the equation as follows:

$$R_{ICICI} = 1.15 + 1.19 \times R_m + \epsilon_{ICICIM}$$

Beta (β) we know gives the slope of the characteristics line, as is a measure of the sensitivity of the security to the market returns. Values of alpha and beta together provide ample inputs on which of the stocks be invested in.

The stock of ICICI, having a positive value of alpha indicates that the stock is under-priced as it delivers more return than that theoretically expected. Value of beta too is more than 1(1.19), indicating that the stock is aggressive, compared to market. (These have been already dealt with in detail in Chapter 6).

> **Pause for thought:** It is a line characteristic of the security, correlating its return with its susceptibility to the market risk.

9.2.1 The Capital Market Line (CML)

The preceding discussion has been on the characteristic response, in terms of returns, of a security, to the market return, characterized by the characteristics line. And in this segment another line will be analyzed—the capital market line. It is an extension of the characteristic line as it deals with the characteristic responses of the portfolios. It concentrates on the optimum portfolio though.

The CML is a line used in the capital asset pricing model to illustrate the rates of return for efficient portfolios, depending on the risk-free rate of return and the level of risk (standard deviation) for a particular portfolio.

The CML is derived by drawing a tangent line from the intercept point on the efficient frontier to the point where the expected return equals the risk-free rate of return.

The CML is considered to be superior to the efficient frontier since it takes into account the inclusion of a risk-free asset in the portfolio. The capital asset pricing model (CAPM) demonstrates that the market portfolio is essentially the efficient frontier. This is achieved visually through the security market line (SML), which is discussed later in the chapter.

Obviously given the assumptions of the CAPM, discussion on the CML is called for. Since it assumes that all investors have homogenous expectations and capital market works in equilibrium, all investors face the same efficient set and same optimal portfolio. But though all investors possess the same efficient set, they may select different portfolios based upon their individual preferences on indifference curve, as has been mentioned in Chapter 7.

It is the optimal portfolio which becomes the focal point as per the assumptions. Hence a relation for the same is required and that is what is provided by the CML.

> **Pause for thought:** CML relates the rates of return for efficient portfolios depending on the risk-free rate of return and the level of risk (standard deviation) for a particular portfolio.

9.2.2 The Separation Principle

However, in Chapter 22, during portfolio selection it has been derived (while deriving the location of the efficient set) that the resultant portfolio consists of only risky securities in the proportion: 0.1275, 0.4347 and 0.4377 in HDFC, HDFC Bank and BPCL respectively. This indicates that optimal portfolio of portfolios comprised of only risky securities can be determined without the investor's risk-return preferences. Thus this separates the investor's impact from the selection process of an optimal portfolio, making the selection more of a generalization. This feature of CAPM is known as the separation principle.

The root of the separation principle lies in the property of linear efficient set, derived in Chapter 7 on risk-free lending and borrowing. It has been derived in Chapter 7 that irrespective of risk-free lending or borrowing, the resulting portfolio of a risky asset and a risk-free asset, all lie on the same straight line plotted as a graph of their combined risk-return profile. Only their positions differ on the straight line, with those from risk-free borrowing, having higher risk-return profile lying farthest. As per the CAPM, each investor will invest in the same linear efficient set with different combinations of risky security along with risk-free lending or borrowing. It means it is the portfolio of all risky securities held by individual investors, irrespective of whether it involves risk-free lending or borrowing.

Continuing with the earlier example of HDFC, HDFC Bank and BPCL and risk-free security at 8% rate of return, the derived optimal portfolio has these three securities in the proportion: 0.1275, 0.4347 and 0.4377 respectively. The return and risk of this optimal portfolio are 25% and 14.51% respectively.

> **Pause for thought:** The separation principle separates, as it excludes, the investor's risk-return preferences from the selection process of the optimal portfolio.

9.2.3 The Market Portfolio

The market portfolio represents the entire wealth of the economy. It is the portfolio of all risky securities held by individual investors, by canceling out lending or borrowing at the risk-free rate. The market portfolio is denoted by the symbol M.

It is defined as the theoretical bundle of investments that includes every type of asset available in the financial markets worldwide. Each asset is weighted in proportion to its total presence in the market. The expected return of a market portfolio is identical to the expected return of the market as a whole. Because a market portfolio is completely diversified, it is subject only to systematic risk (risk that affects the market as a whole) and not to the unsystematic risk (the risk inherent to a particular asset class).

Thus, theoretically the market portfolio includes the assets: financial (e.g. stocks, bonds, options, futures, etc.) and real (gold, silver, real estate, antique collection, etc.)[1], worldwide. The proportion of each stock in the market portfolio is equal to the price per assets times' number of assets outstanding, divided by the sum of the market value of all assets.

According to CAPM, each investor in trying to optimize his individual portfolio and arrives at the portfolio with weights equal to that of the market portfolio. In other words, in keeping with the assumptions of CAPM, it can be concluded that with the same type of factors and their extent and input (lists of data), all investors end up with the same composition of risky portfolio.

It can be further concluded, by extrapolation, that separation principle ensures that contribution from none of the risky security, in the optimal portfolio, is zero. Each of them must be present in some proportion. This is so because separation principle is independent of the risk-return trade-off.

For the purpose of enhancing the understanding of this principle, only three risky securities: HDFC, HDFC Bank and BPCL are assumed to be in the market. It is further assumed that one of the securities, HDFC Bank, doesn't figure in the optimal portfolios of any investor. When all investors avoid HDFC Bank's stock, its price falls and the stock becomes cheaper. This renders the stock of HDFC Bank more attractive, while the other two stocks become less attractive. Ultimately the price of the stock of HDFC Bank reaches a price which makes it eligible to be included in the optimal portfolio. This is actually a display of demand and supply principle. It necessitates price adjustments and thus assures the inclusion of all securities in the optimal portfolio and thus in the market portfolio.

Hence, CAPM implies that if all investors hold an identical risky portfolio, this is nothing but the market portfolio, M.

> **Pause for thought:** Market portfolio is a theoretical bundle of investments that includes every type of asset available in the world financial market. According to CAPM, market portfolio is the identical risky portfolio held by all investors.

9.2.4 Risk-Return and Efficient Portfolio

As has been discussed above, the CML determines the relationship between risk and return for efficient portfolios. The graphical representation of CML is as below, in Figure 9.2.

Where,

    M = market portfolio.

    R_f = risk-free rate of return.

X-axis and Y-axis represent risk (standard deviation, S.D.) and return, σ_P and R_P, of the market portfolio, respectively.

Efficient portfolios start at the intercept, R_f, having

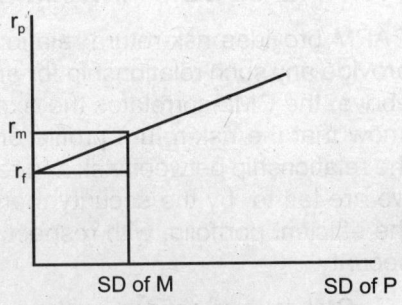

Figure 9.2: The CML

---

[1] However, some people just restrict M to common stocks only.

different combinations of risky securities, with risk-free lending and borrowing, reaching ultimately the composition of M. This linear efficient set of CAPM is known as CML. All portfolios with risk free-borrowing or lending, other than the market portfolio, are either below or lie near the CML.

The slope of the CML is equal to the difference of the expected return of market portfolio and risk-free asset divided by the difference of risk of the risky security and risk-free security.

$$\text{Slope of the CML} = \frac{R_M - R_f}{(\sigma_M - 0)} \qquad (1)$$

As the intercept of the CML is R_f, the straight line equation (for the CML, that is) is,

$$R_P = R_f + [(R_M - R_f)/\sigma_M]\sigma_P \qquad (2)$$

As derived in Chapter 22, on Portfolio Selection, the optimum portfolio consists of risky securities HDFC, HDFC Bank and BPCL in the proportions of 0.1275, 0.4347 and 0.4377 respectively. As the return and the risk of the portfolio are 25% and 14.51% respectively, and risk-free rate, R_f, is 8%, the CML becomes:

$$r_P = 8 + [(25 - 8)/14.51]\sigma_P$$
$$= 8 + 1.171\ \sigma_P$$

In this case, the risk-free rate 8% is the reward for waiting. 1.171 is the slope of the CML. It indicates that the return offered is $1.171\sigma_P$ for bearing 1 unit of risk. Thus CML is composed of two returns:

- The vertical intercept of CML is the risk-free interest rate of 8%, which represents the return obtained only because of having waited.
- Other part of the CML $[(R_M-R_f)/\sigma_M]\sigma_P$ is the return per unit of risk borne. Thus the market return compensates for both time and risk.

> **Pause for thought:** CML shows that the market return compensates for both time and risk.

9.3 THE SECURITY MARKET LINE (SML)

CAPM provides risk-return relationships only for the portfolios of risky securities, and does not provide any such relationship for an individual security. On the other hand, as has been discussed above, the CML correlates the expected return and standard deviation of efficient portfolios. We know that the risk-return profile of individual securities is less than that of a portfolio. But then, the relationship between risk and return of individual securities too has to be analyzed. That is what we are led to, by the security market line, SML. While CML correlates the capital generated by the efficient portfolio, with respect to the risk involved, SML does the same, but for an individual security.

SML is thus defined as the line that graphs the systematic risk (i.e., the market risk) versus return of the whole market at a certain time and shows all risky marketable securities.

But then this is what the characteristics line too is. So SML is also referred to as the characteristics line of a security.

The SML essentially graphs the results from the capital asset pricing model (CAPM) formula. The X-axis represents the risk (beta), and the Y-axis represents the expected return. The graph, in Figure 9.3 below, of SML is plotted by taking variance on X-axis and return of the security on Y-axis.

Since we are interested in establishing a risk-return relationship of individual securities, we proceed towards the same. But a slight modification is brought about in the equation of standard deviation for the market portfolio.

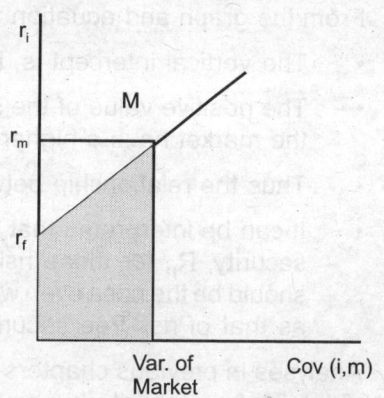

Figure 9.3: SML versus covariance

$$\sigma_M = [W_{1M}\Sigma W_{iM}\sigma_{1i} + W_{2M}\Sigma W_{iM}\sigma_{2i} + \ldots + W_{nM}\Sigma W_{nM}\sigma_{ni}]^{1/2} \quad (3)$$

Where,

$W_{1M}, W_{2M}\ldots,W_{nM}$ = weights invested in securities: 1, 2,….., n to construct the market portfolio.

$\Sigma W_{iM}\sigma_{1i} = \sigma_{iM}$ = covariance of security, i, with the market portfolio, M.

The covariance is the weighted average of the covariance of each security with security, i.

∴ Equation (3) reduces to the following form:

$$\sigma_M = [(W_{1M} \times \sigma_{1M}) + (W_{1M} \times \sigma_{2M}) + \ldots + (W_{nM} \times \sigma_{nM})]^{1/2} \quad (4)$$

Where,

σ_{1M} = covariance of security 1 with the market portfolio, M.

σ_{nM} = covariance of security, n, with the market portfolio, M.

Hence, standard deviation of the market portfolio is the summation of weight of securities multiplied by their corresponding covariance. In other words, standard deviation of the market portfolio is the product of the proportion of securities multiplied by the weighted average covariance of all securities in it. It implies thus securities with higher covariance should not be added in the portfolio as they raise the overall risk of the portfolio.

The fundamental principle of the market is, when risk is higher, return too must be high as a compensatory measure. Failing to do, the investors cannot be motivated to invest in such securities. So, securities with high covariance must provide higher expected return. If such securities fail to provide higher return, then they will just raise the risk of the market portfolio, without any contribution to the desired higher returns. Thus, in such cases if one wants to raise the expected return of the market portfolio relative to its standard deviation, such securities have to be discarded. And if that happens then the market portfolio no longer remains an optimal risky portfolio as security prices would be out of equilibrium.

In such a case, relationship between risk and return can be written as,

$$R_i = R_f + [(R_m - R_f)/\sigma^2_M]\sigma_{iM} \quad (5)$$

From the graph and equation the following conclusions are drawn:
- The vertical intercept is, R_f, and the slope is $[(R_M - R_f)/\sigma^2_M]$.
- The positive value of the slope indicates that the securities with higher covariance with the market have a higher expected return.
- Thus the relationship between covariance and expected return is called SML.
- It can be interpreted that at least theoretically expected return will be equal to risk-free security, R_f, for those risky securities which have zero covariance with the market. It should be the case even with those risky securities that have a positive standard deviation, as that of risk-free security is zero.

Analyses in previous chapters have led us to many risky securities whose return is less than that of the risk-free security, but having a high standard deviation. If this is the case (at $\sigma_{iM} < 0$) then as per the CAPM, such securities would reduce the risk of the market portfolio. On the other hand, those risky securities for whom $\sigma_{iM} = \sigma^2_M$, the expected return would be equal to that of the market portfolio. Also, they contribute only an average amount of risk to the total risk of the market portfolio.

The SML can be also expressed as,

$$r_i = r_f + [(r_m - r_f)/\sigma^2_m]\sigma_{im} \qquad (6)$$

Or, $\qquad r_i = r_f + \sigma_{im}/\sigma^2_m (r_m - r_f) \qquad (7)$

But, $\qquad \sigma_{iM}/\sigma^2_M = \beta$ of the security, i.

$\therefore \qquad R_i = R_f + \beta_i \cdot (R_M - R_f) \qquad (8)$

This equation and the graph below correlate the SML with beta.

The graph in Figure 9.3 has the same intercept, R_f, as that of the graph in Figure 9.4. But the slopes are different.

The slope of the graph in Figure 9.4 is,

$$\beta = (R_M - R_f)/(1-0) = R_M - R_f$$

Beta of the portfolio is the summation of the proportions of each security multiplied by their respective beta in the portfolio. Thus beta of the market portfolio is given by,

$$\beta_M = [W_1\beta_1 + W_2\beta_2 + ... + W_n\beta_n]$$

The positive value of slope, i.e., beta, indicates that a security with higher beta provides higher expected return. The expected return of the portfolio is the weighted average return of the securities in the portfolio. Hence as every security is plotted on the SML, it is the market portfolio that is plotted. So, both efficient as well as inefficient portfolios are plotted on the SML. Efficient portfolios plot on the CML and inefficient one below it.

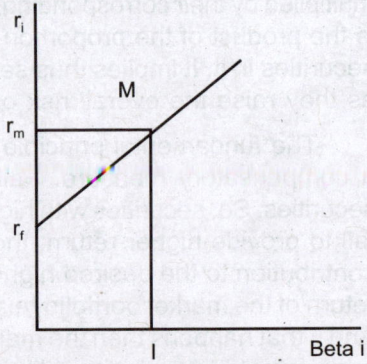

Figure 9.4: SML with beta

Pause for thought: A line that graphs the systematic, or market risk, versus return of the whole market at a certain time and shows all risky marketable securities is called the SML. It is also referred to as the characteristics line of the security.

9.3.1 Beta and SML

In Chapter 6, the systematic risk, beta, has been discussed at length. And here too it seeks discussion as CAPM assumes all investors to possess the market portfolio. Furthermore, all other portfolios are evaluated against this market portfolio. Obviously investors are concerned with the risk premium while adding the risky securities to such a portfolio. Higher is the risk quotient of individual stock, higher is the risk premium desired and provided. At the same time, when the portfolio is well-diversified, it is the total risk of the portfolio, and not that of the individual securities that matter to an investor. That too, the systematic risk draws the attention it being undiversifiable. Since as per the CAPM all investors hold the same portfolios of risky assets, i.e., the market portfolio, so the risk concerned is the covariance between individual security and market portfolio.

SML is the linear relationship between expected return and covariance of the security with the market portfolio. And as the risk that cannot be diversified becomes more significant in the context, beta, which is the measure of this risk, finds presence in SML, plotted against the return of the market portfolio. Hence, as shown above, in Figure 9.4, for a given amount of systematic risk (β), SML gives the required rate of return.

This becomes the utility of SML. When the required data is available the SML can be plotted. But when the SML is given, the required rate of return can be envisaged, for a given value of beta and vice-versa.

Certain inferences that are drawn from the values of beta are as follows:

- $\beta = 1$, for a security, indicates that the systematic risk is equal to the aggregate market risk. Hence, the required rate of return too, of the security, is equal to the rate of return of the market portfolio.
- $\beta > 1$, represents an aggressive security, as its systematic risk is greater than market risk and the required rate of return on the security is more than market return. A beta value higher than the market indicates a greater fluctuation of the return on security than the market return.
- Similarly, $\beta < 1$, represents conservative securities. As the systematic risk of the security is lesser than market risk, the required rate of return on the security too is less than the market return (because beta value lower than that of the market indicates lesser fluctuation of the return on security as compared to that of the market return).
- Security with negative beta (i.e., $\beta < 0$) indicates that the return of such securities move in a direction opposite to that of the market return. Such securities are considered to be good for reducing the risk of the portfolio. However, many times such stocks provide less return than the risk-free security. Furthermore, from the formula, $\beta = \sigma_{iM}/\sigma^2_M$, it is inferred that the market variance cannot be negative. Hence, the only possibility is that the covariance of the security with the market return is negative.

These discussions on beta and SML are further extended with the following examples.

EXAMPLES

Q.1. For the period, 2002 to 2010, the risk-free rate of return is 8% and market rate of return is 28.64%. Sensex is used as a proxy to calculate market return as it is practically impossible to calculate the return of the market portfolio. The beta values of Axis Bank and Bharti Airtel are 0.560 and 1.33 respectively. What are the required rates of return on these two stocks?

By using the CAPM formula, $R_i = R_f + \beta_i(R_M - R_f)$ the required rate of return is calculated as follows.

For Axis Bank:

$R_{Axis\ Bank}$ = 8% + 0.560(28.64% − 8%) = 19.55%

For Bharti Airtel:

$R_{Bharti\ Airtel}$ = 8% + 1.33(28.64% − 8%) = 35.45%

Thus, the stock of Bharti Airtel has a higher beta and a higher return.

Q.2. The return on the stock of DLF is to be calculated. Beta of the stock is ascertained as -0.266 from its prices for the period, 2007 to 2010. Return, on Nifty 50 taken as the market index, turns out (calculating the returns during this period) to be 13.66%. The risk-free return is assumed to be 8%.

∴ From the CAPM formula, the return on the stock of DLF is,

$$R_{DLF} = R_f + \beta_{DLF}(R_{Nifty\ 50} - R_f)$$
$$= 8\% + (-0.266) \times (13.66\% - 8\%)$$
$$= 6.5\%$$

Thus, the rate of return on the stock of DLF is less than the return on the risk-free security. It is because the beta of the DLF is -0.266; and as discussed above, securities with negative beta provides less return in normal time period.

Note: The second example represents a case of negative beta. Since it leads to a rate of return even lower than that of the return on the risk-free security, the question arises as to why should then one invest in such a stock. And it is answered by the fact that during a slump in the market though investing in risk-free security enables one to earn risk-free return, it cannot reduce the overall **risk** of the portfolio, as the correlation between risky asset and risk-free asset is zero and not negative. On the other hand, an addition of a stock with negative beta, to the portfolio, can reduce the overall risk of the substantially, even if the return is less than the risk-free return. This is so because a stock with negative beta has a negative correlation with other risky assets. Hence, as gold has negative correlation with stocks, it is always advisable to have a portfolio which is a blend of stock market and gold.

> **Pause for thought:** SML correlates the beta of a security with the return on the market portfolio, comprised of all risky securities.

9.4 IMPLICATIONS OF CAPM

Numbers of questions have been raised, on number of occasions, on the validity of the CAPM. And they have been answered too by the utilities of CAPM. Out of these, one of the most important is that it has given the concept of discount rate to find out the intrinsic value of the firm and thus of the equity share. This is used by various equity research firms and AMCs to derive the intrinsic value of shares. Had this has not been the case, the applications of Markowitz model and index model would have given inferior portfolios. The concept of risk and return as given by the CAPM finds many useful application as it is very easy to understand. Portfolio managers use these concepts to find out the required rate of return estimated for, and provided by, the security for the valuation of firms and securities; costs of capital measurement; investment risk analyses etc. It provides logical and quantitative approach for estimating risk.

The CAPM provides us with the theoretical required rate of return of a security. After calculating the expected rate of return, based on the current market price data (or other method) over a period of time, and then comparing it with the required rate of return, investors can take a decision regarding their investment(s).

The variations in the CAPM and what they imply are discussed as follows.

Application 1

CAPM<Expected return.

Decision: Buy

The stock is considered under-valued when the required rate of return, calculated as per the CAPM, is less than the expected return. It means the stock gives more return than what it should give. So, it should be bought.

Application 2

CAPM>Expected return

Decision: Sell

The stock is considered over-valued when the required rate of return is higher than the expected return. So, it gives less return than what is expected from it. Hence, it should be sold.

Application 3

CAPM = Expected return

Decision: Hold

The stock is considered rightly valued when the required return equals the expected return.

> **Pause for thought:** The rate of return of a security obtained from CAPM, vis-à-vis the expected return, provides with insight on whether to buy, sell or hold that security.

9.4.1 Limitation of the CAPM

There are certain limitations of CAPM. And it is quite natural, as rarely any concept is free from any limitation.

1. CAPM and rate of return: From the CAPM formula, it is evident that it has assumed alpha to be zero. But this can be true only in principle or in a hypothetical case, not in real life. It is true that because of the forces of buyers and suppliers security prices reach their fair value, and at this value alpha is zero. But if alpha is zero for all securities, security analysis won't be required. While CAPM is considered to be the best available model to predict the required rate of return of the security, the empirical test rejects the hypothesis that alpha values are zero at given level of significance. In real market, it has been found that securities with low beta have positive alpha; and those with high beta have negative alpha. It is essential for the investors to thoroughly investigate the security by applying fundamental analysis to their investment decisions. Moreover, empirical studies by researchers indicate that CAPM is an ex-ante model, i.e., data on expected prices are required for verification. Whereas, in practice, one has ex-post data (actual data) at disposal, for the above mentioned purpose (of verification). Thus this assumption of CAPM ($\alpha = 0$) reflects bias.

2. Market portfolio: In real life it is difficult to construct and estimate the return of the market portfolio as per the definition of CAPM. Instead we rely on indices such as CNX Nifty 50 or Sensex, as a proxy for market portfolio. Because of this data of the proxy market portfolio, hypothesis about alpha is rejected.

3. Unrealistic assumptions: CAPM is based on the number of assumptions which are far from reality. Along with assumptions of inflation rate and one year investment horizon, the assumption of equality of lending and borrowing rate is simply improbable.

4. Beta: As per CAPM, beta is a measure of the security's future risk. But we have to derive beta based on the past prices of the security and market portfolio. We can use this historical beta of security to measure the security's future risk, but only if it is stable during this time period. But most of the empirical studies indicate that beta is not stable over time. So, historical beta is a poor estimate for future risk of securities. Also, many times the risk of security is not accurately estimated by beta only.

SUMMARY

- ✓ Capital market theory based on efficient set, estimates the pricing of assets in the capital market.
- ✓ The CAPM is based on a set of assumptions, according which all investors hold the same efficient portfolios of risky assets.
- ✓ The portfolio of all risky securities held by the investors is known as market portfolio. Theoretically the market portfolio consists of both financial and real assets, each weighted in proportion to its market value relative to the market value of all securities.
- ✓ The CML represents the equilibrium relationship between the expected return and standard deviation of efficient portfolios.
- ✓ As per the CAPM, the risk of a security can be measured by its covariance with the market portfolio.
- ✓ The linear relationship between market covariance and expected return is known as the Security Market Line (SML).
- ✓ Beta is a measure of covariance relative to the variance of the market portfolio.

KEY CONCEPTS

Capital Market Theory	Separation Principle	Required Rate of Return
Capital Market Line	Market Model	Portfolio Risk
Capital Asset Pricing Model	Market Portfolio	Unique Risk
Security Market Line	Market Index	Market Risk
Characteristics Line	The Efficient Set	Covariance

REVIEW QUESTIONS

1. Describe the key assumptions underlying CAPM. Also explain to what extent it can be relaxed in a present time period.

2. Give a brief explanation of the capital market line (CML).
3. Distinguish between CML and SML (security market line).
4. Is the security plotted above SML a profitable investment?

CASE STUDY

Ms. Neelam Balan is very active as far as restructuring the portfolio of investment she holds is concerned, from time to time. She has heard it being said on various occasions that investors should invest in a market portfolio as it provides the highest of returns at the lowest of risk, compared to all other probable portfolios. Ms. Neelam believed in this saying firmly and till now her investment consists of only index funds. She has purchased number of index funds provided by different asset management companies. She has invested in ICICI index fund, which comprises of 50 stocks of BSE Sensex in the same proportion as they are present in BSE. An index fund has outperformed many actively managed funds and it also carries low management cost. But as market is yet to recover fully after the recession, Ms. Balan is thinking about changing her passive management strategy. So she now wants to invest actively after carefully checking the fundamentals of the companies. At the same time as she intends to start conservatively, finally she has screened out the following stocks for her investment purpose.

Infosys

Infosys Limited, formerly Infosys Technologies Limited, is a global technology services company, headquartered in Bangalore, India. It is the second largest IT exporter in India with 133,560 employees, as of March 2011. It has offices in 33 countries and development centers in India, China, Australia, UK, Canada, Brazil and Japan. Infosys was the only Indian company to win the Global MAKE (Most Admired Knowledge Enterprises) award continuously for three years (2003, 2004 and 2005). It has been inducted into the Global Hall of Fame for the same. Infosys will invest $100 million (Rs.440 crores) for a campus in Shanghai, with employee strength of 20,000, which it is establishing.

Sun Pharmaceutical

Sun Pharmaceutical (Sun Pharmaceutical Industries Limited) is an international pharmaceutical company based in Mumbai, India. Sun Pharmaceutical, often referred to as Sun Pharma, manufactures many generic and brand name drugs that are distributed in the United States, Europe, Asia and even to other parts of the world. A planned acquisition of Israeli, Taro Pharmaceuticals, which was initiated in March 2007 finally materialized in September 2010. Taro has a monopoly in dermatology and topical products, in addition to its products in the cardiovascular, neuro-psychiatric and anti-inflammatory categories.

ICICI

ICICI Bank is India's second largest bank with total assets of Rs.4,062.34 billion (US$ 91 billion), with huge profits accrued even after paying tax of Rs.51.51 billion (US$ 1,155 million), as on March 31, 2011. ICICI bank's equity shares are listed in India on Bombay Stock Exchange and the National Stock Exchange. Its American Depositary Receipts (ADRs) are listed on the New York Stock Exchange (NYSE).

The bank has a large network, comprising of 2,550 branches and 7,440 ATMs in India. Furthermore its network extends beyond India, to 19 countries, with branches in the United States, Singapore, Bahrain, Hong Kong, Sri Lanka, Qatar and Dubai International Finance Centre—to name some of the countries. It also has representative offices in the United Arab Emirates, China, South Africa, Bangladesh, Thailand, Malaysia and Indonesia. The bank currently has subsidiaries in the United Kingdom, Russia and Canada. The UK subsidiary has established branches in Belgium and Germany.

Suzlon

Suzlon Energy (BSE: 532667, NSE: SUZLON) is a global wind power company based in India. In terms of its share in the market, the company is the fifth largest wind turbine manufacturer in Asia (and the 8th largest, worldwide). In terms of net worth, it is the world's most valuable wind power company. But in terms of market value, the company is smaller than Vestas. Also, the companies, viz., GE, Gamesa Corporation Technology, Enercon and Siemens too are possibly larger than Suzlon. It is difficult to state with certainty, as the market value of these companies are harder to know given that they are not traded as independent entities. In January 2011, Suzlon received an order, worth $1.28 billion, for building 1000MW of wind energy projects, from the Indian branch of the Lord Swaraj Paul-owned Caparo Energy Ltd. In May 2011, Suzlon announced its return to profit after the financial crisis of 2008.

The table below shows the monthly returns of last five years of Infosys, Sun Pharma, ICICI, Suzlon and the market index, Sensex. Besides comparing the return and risk of these four stocks, Ms. Neelam also wants to compare the risk of these companies with that of the market. She wants to ensure that the expected return of her new portfolio will provide adequate compensation for the inclusion of any new risky asset.

Guide Ms. Balan, with your knowledge of the market and risk-return criterion involved.

MONTH	SENSEX	INFOSYS	SUNPHARMA	ICICI	SUZLON
Apr-06	6.168	5.705	-1.178	-0.296	-2.401
May-06	-14.088	-8.695	-8.472	-11.397	-24.556
Jun-06	1.306	4.324	-1.770	-10.569	5.752
Jul-06	1.195	-46.648	2.444	13.523	2.719
Aug-06	8.955	8.964	12.802	8.258	11.940
Sep-06	6.452	2.263	2.779	19.475	2.568
Oct-06	3.913	13.724	-2.645	10.979	5.779
Nov-06	5.416	3.354	12.268	12.156	9.786
Dec-06	0.417	1.841	-5.411	1.760	-10.354
Jan-07	1.903	0.109	4.340	5.793	-13.063
Feb-07	-8.399	-7.400	-9.938	-13.072	-11.211
Mar-07	0.448	-4.162	14.565	1.439	-4.120
Apr-07	8.277	2.468	-2.659	5.213	18.765

MONTH	SENSEX	INFOSYS	SUNPHARMA	ICICI	SUZLON
May-07	3.980	-7.680	1.772	5.439	7.206
Jun-07	0.275	-0.300	-9.629	3.387	17.602
Jul-07	5.896	2.183	-10.088	-2.927	-16.365
Aug-07	-0.166	-5.595	0.113	-4.243	-0.276
Sep-07	12.265	1.160	4.820	17.997	13.046
Oct-07	14.294	-3.205	9.244	18.234	38.162
Nov-07	-3.810	-13.248	3.245	-7.159	-5.203
Dec-07	3.785	9.431	10.493	4.441	1.401
Jan-08	-13.169	-14.454	-6.524	-7.235	-84.346
Feb-08	-1.358	2.102	8.009	-6.756	-10.727
Mar-08	-9.189	-6.526	0.951	-27.424	-4.493
Apr-08	9.610	20.948	18.206	13.471	6.906
May-08	-6.518	9.116	-4.304	-12.314	-4.397
Jun-08	-18.864	-11.311	-3.962	-19.617	-22.893
Jul-08	6.497	-9.001	1.446	0.770	3.148
Aug-08	3.557	12.734	5.328	10.082	0.230
Sep-08	-10.772	-20.594	0.538	-18.808	-29.839
Oct-08	-24.746	-3.042	-24.536	-26.060	-71.341
Nov-08	-10.938	-12.201	-5.906	-15.325	-11.383
Dec-08	5.286	-14.012	-0.023	25.906	48.157
Jan-09	-3.048	16.044	0.322	-8.505	-25.158
Feb-09	-4.805	-4.772	-5.510	-19.780	-12.796
Mar-09	10.791	9.312	10.792	3.404	6.000
Apr-09	17.007	13.673	15.827	41.346	48.368
May-09	25.698	5.743	-6.946	51.194	50.231
Jun-09	-1.713	10.710	-11.305	-4.371	4.274
Jul-09	8.023	16.158	5.486	2.574	-4.179
Aug-09	-0.179	3.510	-0.423	-1.640	-0.689
Sep-09	9.149	7.879	18.585	19.841	-2.707
Oct-09	-7.506	-4.155	-1.240	-12.751	-26.885
Nov-09	6.867	8.608	6.971	10.808	20.692

MONTH	SENSEX	INFOSYS	SUNPHARMA	ICICI	SUZLON
Dec-09	3.053	8.597	2.804	0.887	15.169
Jan-10	-6.384	-4.962	-4.457	-6.486	-15.987
Feb-10	0.552	5.328	7.590	6.064	-9.114
Mar-10	6.627	-0.793	15.458	7.638	-1.642
Apr-10	0.021	4.433	-12.645	-0.158	-4.236
May-10	-3.377	-1.459	5.588	-8.249	-18.993
Jun-10	4.474	5.030	7.379	-0.347	1.847
Jul-10	1.069	-0.434	-1.617	5.907	-1.739
Aug-10	0.334	-2.657	-0.599	6.465	-18.629
Sep-10	11.327	12.338	14.065	12.840	16.222
Oct-10	-0.307	-2.444	3.808	3.719	4.623
Nov-10	-3.706	2.053	-79.167	-3.591	-14.619
Dec-10	5.013	13.322	7.271	-0.379	14.690
Jan-11	-11.124	-9.646	-10.447	-11.535	-10.436
Feb-11	-3.266	-4.148	-5.446	-4.897	-6.325
Mar-11	8.135	6.647	3.116	13.199	-5.802
Apr-11	-1.681	-9.893	5.465	0.383	19.037

SUGGESTED FURTHER READING FOR EMPIRICAL WORK

1. Dowen, R.J., and Bauman, W.S. (1986), "A Fundamental Multifactor Asset Pricing Model", *Financial Analysts Journal*, Vol. 42, No. 4.

2. Feinstein, C.D., and Thapa, M.N. (1993), "A Reformulation of a Mean-Absolute Deviation Portfolio Optimization Model", *Management Science*, Vol. 39, No. 12.

3. Merton, R.C. (1973), "An Intertemporal Capital Asset Pricing Model", *Econometrica*, Vol. 41, No. 5.

4. Shefrin, H., and Statman, M. (1994), "Behavioral Capital Asset Pricing Theory", *The Journal of Financial and Quantitative Analysis*, Vol. 29, No. 3.

5. Mukherjee, D., and Metia, S. (2001), "Capital Asset Pricing Model When Data Is Skewed", *Sankhyâ: The Indian Journal of Statistics,* Series B (1960-2002), Vol. 63, No. 1.

6. Hodgson D.J., and Vorkink, K.P. (2003), "Efficient Estimation of Conditional Asset-Pricing Models", *Journal of Business & Economic Statistics*, Vol. 21, No. 2.

7. Hansen, L.P., and Singleton, K.J. (1996), "Efficient Estimation of Linear Asset-Pricing Models with Moving Average Errors", *Journal of Business & Economic Statistics*, Vol. 14, No. 1.

8. Drakos, K. (2002), "Estimating a Multifactor Model for the Greek Mutual Fund Market", *Russian and East European Finance and Trade*, Vol. 38, No. 3.
9. Markowitz, H.M. (1983), "Nonnegative or Not Nonnegative: A Question about CAPMs", *The Journal of Finance*, Vol. 38, No. 2.
10. Levy, H., and Samuelson, P.A. (1992), "The Capital Asset Pricing Model with Diverse Holding Periods", *Management Science*, Vol. 38, No. 11.
11. Stapleton, R. C., and Subrahmanyam, M.G. (1983), "The Market Model and Capital Asset Pricing Theory: A Note", *The Journal of Finance*, Vol. 38, No. 5.
12. Dempsey, M.J. (2002), "The Nature of Market Growth, Risk, and Return", *Financial Analysts Journal*, Vol. 58, No. 3.

REFERENCES

1. http://www.public.asu.edu/~kirkwood/DAStuff/decisiontrees/DecisionTreePrimer-2.pdf
2. http://en.wikipedia.org/wiki/Utility
3. http://www.econ.ucsb.edu/~tedb/Courses/Ec100C/VarianExpectedUtility.pdf
4. http://wiki.lesswrong.com/wiki/Utility_function
5. http://www.chastainskillman.com/downloads/articles/3Q10DecisionMaking.pdf
6. http://www.smartfolio.com/theory/details/portfolio_optimization/
7. http://en.wikipedia.org/wiki/Risk_aversion
8. http://www.econ.ubc.ca/discpapers/dp0520.pdf
9. http://dare.uva.nl/document/153
10. http://people.duke.edu/~charvey/Classes/ba350_1997/diverse/diverse.htm
11. http://www.ba.metu.edu.tr/~ba4814/slides/chapter%206.pdf
12. http://www.docstoc.com/docs/87219410/Risk-Aversion-and-Capital-Allocation-to-Risky-Assets-Answer-Key
13. http://www.hussmanfunds.com/pdf/mixdist.pdf
14. http://www.kellogg.northwestern.edu/faculty/papanikolaou/htm/finc460/ln/lecture1.pdf

10
ARBITRAGE PRICING THEORY

> **LEARNING OBJECTIVES**
>
> The purpose of this chapter is to enable you to understand:
> - What is meant by arbitrage pricing theory (APT).
> - No arbitrage argument.
> - The alternative theory of capital market for pricing of assets.

10.1 INTRODUCTION

CAPM has had to face a lot of criticism in the wake of its over-simplified assumptions. Another major reason for its criticism is its use of a single factor, β, in the estimation of the return of the portfolio. This chapter on arbitrage pricing theory (APT) deals with the other dimensions of the systematic risk. While the models based on beta as an index of return on securities are concerned with variations in beta with the market returns, those based on the multi-faceted systematic risk of return on securities take into account various macroeconomic factors. These factors include business cycle risk, interest rate risk, inflation risk, GNP, Forex reserves, IIP, etc., to name a few.

When multiple factors come into the picture, the risk premium too arises from exposure to multiple risk sources, each demanding their own risk premiums. Multiple factor models, studied with no arbitrage argument, give a relationship between risk and return. This relationship of the risk-return trade-off is called arbitrage pricing theory.

But before APT is discussed we need to know what is actually meant by the term arbitrage. The simultaneous purchase and sale of an asset in order to profit from a difference in the price is known as arbitrage. It is a trade that profits by exploiting price differences of identical or similar financial instruments, in different markets or in different forms. Arbitrage exists as a result of market inefficiencies. And it provides a mechanism to ensure prices do not deviate substantially from fair value for long periods of time. In other words, arbitrage is the practice of taking positive expected return, from over-valued or under-valued securities in the efficient market—without any incremental risk and zero additional investment.

In the context of APT, arbitrage consists of trading in two assets—with at least one being mis-priced. The arbitrageur earns the profit by selling the asset which is relatively expensive and uses the proceeds from the sale to buy the asset which is relatively cheaper. As per the APT, an asset or security is considered mis-priced, if its market price diverges or deviates from the equilibrium price or the price determined by the model.

10.1.1 Arbitrage Pricing Theory (APT)

As mentioned above CAPM, considers the single factor, β, the sole determinant of the return on a security or a portfolio. In other words, it is only the non-diversifiable risk of the portfolio which is significant for the purpose. So CAPM provides risk premium only for the undiversifiable, systematic risk. And this is what causes the deficiency in CAPM, which is overcome by the APT, developed by economist Stephen Ross in 1976, further evolved by others.

APT too follows the fundamental principle that return is related to risk. But it takes care of the lacuna in CAPM by extending the undiversifiable risk to include some of the macroeconomic factors too, as mentioned above. Furthermore, APT has fewer assumptions than CAPM.

> **Pause for thought:** In addition to β, APT adds further dimensions to the systematic risk of the portfolios, taking cognizance of various macroeconomic factors.

10.1.2 APT and Law of One Price[1]

The APT is based on the concept of arbitrage, i.e. law of one price, according to which no two identical investments can be sold at different prices, in the same market.

When they are not sold at one price (in different markets) there is a possibility of earning a profit, but without risk, by buying the product in a cheaper market and selling the same with some margin in another market. This process of random buying in one market would increase the demand and in turn, prices, in that market. On the other hand, the market in which it is sold will have an increased supply of the same, thereby reducing its price. This process continues until the price discrepancy disappears and the markets are in equilibrium.

According to the CMT, when markets are in equilibrium market prices are rational, ruling out the possibilities of arbitrage. If it is assumed that security prices allow for arbitrage, with thus identical securities selling at different prices in two markets, the resultant buying and selling soon enforces a restoration of equilibrium. As with CAPM, with APT too in this chapter, we will generalize the SML to understand in further detail the risk-return relationships.

The law of one price slightly differs with respect to investment management, as compared to the normal arbitrage opportunities. Herein, it implies that two financial products or portfolios (even if they are not identical) should cost the same if their return and risk is identical. This is so because the evaluation of the financial products is based only on risk and return. Thus, in APT, the law of one price means that any two financial products, or portfolios, having the same return-risk profile should sell for the same price. In case of any kind of deviation from this generalization profit can be realized.

---

[1] Two terms, 'arbitrage and 'arbitrageurs' are different. Arbitrageur is a professional and searches for the mis-priced securities at some specific corporate events like merger, take-over, etc. This activity is also referred to as risk-arbitrage to distinguish it from pure arbitrage.

> **Pause for thought:** Law of one price, according to APT, means any two identical assets should sell for the same price, in the same market.

10.1.3 Comparative Study of APT and CAPM

The points of similarities and dissimilarities in CAPM and APT have been noted above. And now a detailed study of the same is being endeavored in this segment.

Like CAPM, APT presumes a linear relationship between risk and return. But it doesn't accept beta as the sole measure of risk. This is the major difference between the two, with APT, as discussed above, considers various determinants for the performance of portfolios. In other words, it does not accept market risk as the only factor to determine risk of the security.

There are infinite numbers of security-specific influences (some of them have been mentioned in the 'introduction' to this chapter) for any given security, such as: inflation, production measures, investor's confidence, exchange rate, market indices etc. It is up to the investor to decide which influences are relevant to the assets being analyzed. After determining the expected rate of return from APT model, investor or an analyst can determine what the correct price of the asset by discounting the cash flow. The general idea behind APT is that two things can explain the return on a financial asset:

- Macroeconomic and security specific influences.
- The asset's sensitivity to those influences. This relationship can be explained in the form of linear regression below.

APT is represented mathematically as:

$$E(R_i) = R_f + \beta_1[E(R_1) - R_f] + \beta_2[E(R_2) - R_f] + \ldots + \beta_n[E(R_n) - R_f] \qquad (1)$$

Where, 1, 2, ..., n represents the different macroeconomic factors.

The assumptions of CAPM, retained by APT, are:

- The market is efficient and perfect, wherein all securities are marketable.
- All investors are rational and they have homogenous expectations, as they all have identical expectations: higher return for a higher risk.
- All investors hold well-diversified portfolio.

The assumptions of CAPM that are discarded by the APT are as follows:

- It does not accept that there are neither any transaction costs nor taxes.
- It disagrees with the fact that all investors can lend or borrow at only one and the same risk-free rate of return.
- It also refutes the claims of the CAPM of a single holding period, of one year, for all investors.

The assumptions the APT retains and those which it discards, from the CAPM, renders it more practical, with dependence thus on very few assumptions. However, CAPM too has its advantages. It is of a more general nature as it follows the SML concept more logically and in a straightforward manner. Since CAPM relies on only one undiversifiable risk factor, calculation of beta is easy, but the construction of a market portfolio is difficult. The market portfolio theory includes all types of assets, viz., equities, debt, gold, real estate, etc. On the other hand, the CAPM relies upon any of the indices (Nifty, Sensex, BSE 500, etc.) as a proxy to calculate the return on security. Given the inclusion of all assets in the portfolio but with a proxy measure of the return, the estimated return is not exact. Hence, in such a case, beta of the portfolio of several assets is not consistent with the beta of the market portfolio. This is serious dent to the assumption of CAPM that beta is the sole measure of the return of a portfolio.

Contrary to this, APT does not require construction of a market portfolio, but it necessitates the identification of the relevant macroeconomic factors. The biggest challenge, while applying APT, is to calculate whole set of beta values, as till date accurate calculation of beta values is a huge unsolved problem. One major reason behind this inaccuracy is the fact that there is no consensus among the experts on the macroeconomic factors to be considered. Actually, there cannot be common factors, applicable to all, as these different macroeconomic factors affect the different firms—and in turn, securities—differently. The hypothetical example that follows should enable the understanding of the effects, of these factors, as firm-specific.

Firm A is assumed to be a local manufacturer of bicycles, selling its products in the domestic market only. At the same time, firm B is a software company, exporting its products to Japan and European countries. Thus, firm A relies only on the domestic market for the raw materials as well as for selling the finished products. So it incurs the risk only of the domestic market. But firm B is exposed to the foreign exchange risk as it exports majority of its products, which is always higher than the risk of the domestic market. Even after applying hedging techniques to reduce the contra-effects of its exposure, firm B remains susceptible to foreign exchange risk, which is absent in case of firm A. Besides this, the other macroeconomic factors, mentioned above, affect both the firms differently. The net effect on the firms is a cumulative impact of all the factors, all of which have to be calculated for a comparative study of the status of the firms. The steps involved in this study are:

- The macroeconomic factors that affect the stocks of the firms included in the portfolio are identified first.
- Since the systematic risk is extended beyond a single β, to include beta values for other macroeconomic factors, these different values are called factor-β. For a company traded in the market, examples of factors are: for a change in its inflation; for a growth in GDP of the economy; for a term structure of the interest rate—to name three of them.
- The risk premium for each factor-beta has to be estimated. We already know that the risk premium is the difference between the expected return on the market for a given factor, and the risk-free rate of interest. It can be estimated as: $R_{interest\ rate} - R_f$ here the inflation being considered as the affecting factor.

This calculation is undertaken by considering a hypothetical situation, wherein four factors are assumed to be affecting the return of the stock. In this case, thus we would be having four beta values and the same number of risk premiums—for each factor-β. The factors considered here are: inflation; Forex rate; GDP and IIP. Hence, the corresponding risk-premiums are: $(R_{interest\ rate} - R_f)$; $(R_{Forex\ rate} - R_f)$; $(R_{GDP} - R_f)$ and $(R_{IIP} - R_f)$.

By calculating each factor-β, the expected return on the stocks of a company is re-adjusted accordingly. The adjusted net return can be represented as:

$$R_i = R_f + \beta_1(R_{interest\ rate} - R_f) + \beta_2(R_{Forex\ rate} - R_f) + \beta_3(R_{GDP} - R_f) + \beta_4(R_{IIP} - R_f) \qquad (2)$$

$$R_i = R_f + [\beta_1 \times (F_1 - \text{interest rate})] + [\beta_2 \times (F_2 - \text{Forex rate})]$$
$$+ [\beta_3(F_3 - \text{GDP})] + \beta_4(F_4 - \text{IIP}) \quad (3)$$

It can be also calculated by restructuring equation (2) as,

$$R_i - R_f = \beta_1(R_{\text{interest rate}} - R_f) + \beta_2(R_{\text{Forex rate}} - R_f) + \beta_3(R_{\text{GDP}} - R_f) + \beta_4(R_{\text{IIP}} - R_f) \quad (4)$$

Where,

R_f = rate of risk-free return.

$\beta_1, \beta_2, \beta_3, \beta_4$ = four different factor-β, for the four different macroeconomic factors considered.

Pause for thought: Net return of a security is decided by the different factor-beta values.

10.2 WELL-DIVERSIFIED PORTFOLIO

Armed with understanding of the factor-beta values and their involvement in the net return of a security (and the same can be applied to the portfolio), the same is applied in this section. Thus the risk of a portfolio, comprised of various securities, is formulated.

Though the factor-specific risks (betas) play a role, as per APT, in the overall impact, it is also true that the firm-specific (and the factor-specific unsystematic) risks are negligible, for a well-diversified portfolio. It is only the systematic risks that need to be addressed. Hence follows the following derivation, through the requisite assumptions.

A portfolio of 'n' securities is considered, with an assumed weight, W_i, and $\Sigma W_i = 1$. The rate of return of this portfolio can be calculated as,

$$R_P = E(R_P) + \beta_P F + e_P \quad (5)$$

Where,

β_P = weighted average beta of all securities in the given portfolio.

$E(R_P) = \Sigma W_i E(R_i)$ = weighted average return of 'n' securities in the portfolio.

$e_P = \Sigma W_i e_i$ = weighted average of the e_i of 'n' securities of a portfolio and is a unsystematic component of risk, unrelated to F. It is also called risky asset's idiosyncratic random shock with mean zero.

F = the macroeconomic factor under consideration.

The equation for variance of the portfolio is,

$$\sigma^2_P = \beta^2_P \sigma^2 F + \sigma^2(e_P) \quad (6)$$

Where,

$\beta^2_P \sigma^2 F$ = systematic component of variance of the portfolio.

$\sigma^2(e_P)$ = unsystematic component of variance of the portfolio.

Risk of the unsystematic component, $\sigma^2(e_P)$ is measured by:

$$\sigma^2(e_P) = \text{Variance}(\Sigma W_i e_i) = \Sigma W_i^2 \sigma^2(e_i) \quad (7)$$

Thus, the variance of the unsystematic risk of the portfolio is the weighted average of the unsystematic variance of the individual securities multiplied by the square of their respective weights.

If the portfolio is assumed to be equally weighted,

$$W_i = 1/n$$

∴ The unsystematic variance becomes,

$$\sigma^2(e_P) = \text{Variance}(\Sigma W_i e_i) = \Sigma(1/n)^2 \sigma^2(e_i) = 1/n \, \Sigma\sigma^2(e_i)/n = \frac{1 \times \sigma^2(e_i)}{n} \quad (8)$$

The conclusions led to, by the above equation, are:

- The unsystematic variance of the portfolio equals the average unsystematic variance of the securities, divided by the number of securities, 'n'.
- When 'n' is large, as is in a well-diversified portfolio, the unsystematic variance of the portfolio approaches zero[2]. Hence, APT too leads to the same result as led to by the other theories: for a well diversified portfolio, unsystematic risk becomes negligible.

This is the reason why large and well-diversified portfolios are constructed and managed by institutional investors.

Thus is implied, the expected value of e_P and also unsystematic risk $\sigma^2(e_P)$ is zero for a well-diversified portfolio.

∴ Equation (5) can be rewritten as:

$$R_P = E(R_P) + \beta_P F \quad (9)$$

> **Pause for thought:** The unsystematic risk of a portfolio, including the factor-specific risks as per the APT, is diversified away in a well-diversified portfolio, with increment in diversification with an increase in the number of securities in the portfolio.

10.2.1 Systematic Risk and Expected Return on Portfolios

Through the ensuing discussion it is absolutely clear that the unsystematic risk (factor-risk, as is considered by APT) is in the hands of the investor, as a well-diversified portfolio can eliminate such risk. It is the systematic risk, which the investors cannot diversify and thus reduce. As a result, investors are compensated only for systematic risk (the factor-specific risks). Since they evade diversification they are correlated with the expected return.

Hypothetical examples, as follows, are presumed to facilitate the understanding of the preceding discussion.

Portfolios with identical beta values

A well-diversified portfolio, P, is assumed, with its beta equal to 1 and its expected return, 20%. If there are no fluctuations in the macroeconomic factors in the country, then the systematic

---

[2] We have discussed that in an equally weighted portfolio unsystematic variance approaches zero, as number of securities rises in a portfolio. This is also true for a portfolio other than the equally weighted one.

risk factor is zero and the return of the portfolio is equivalent to its expected return (i.e., 20%) When the macroeconomic factors enhance the performance of the securities in a portfolio, the return of the portfolio exceeds its expected return (i.e., more than 20%, in this case). But if the macroeconomic variables are not in favor of the securities of the portfolio, the return of the portfolio is less than its expected return (i.e., less than 20%).

∴ The return of the hypothetical portfolio, vide Equation (9) is,

$$R_P = E(R_P) + \beta_P F$$
$$= 20\% + 1 \times F$$

where,

$E(R_P)$ = expected return of the portfolio.

β_P = beta of the portfolio = 1 (in this example).

F = the macroeconomic factor, F.

Another well-diversified portfolio, Q, is assumed, whose beta too is 1—identical to that of the portfolio P—and an expected return of 19%. And as with the portfolio P, only the undiversifiable risk is considered. The reason for these different portfolios being discussed here is the intent to know the impact of macroeconomic factors, on the return of portfolios, P and Q. This we are led to, through the assumption that irrespective of the macroeconomic factor involved, portfolio P gives a better return than portfolio Q. This difference in return, at the same level of risk (β =1), arises because of arbitrage opportunity in the market. To realize risk-free gain, the strategy should be to withdraw the invested amount from portfolio Q and invest in portfolio P. Following this rationale, if the total investment is Rs.100,000, then the risk-free payoff will be Rs.1000. This strategy generates risk-free profit of Rs.1000. Thus the condition for a no-arbitrage situation is that portfolios with equal beta values must have identical expected returns. If any market violates this rule, arbitrage would occur.

The return for portfolio P, vide Equation (9), with an investment of Rs.100,000, is,

$$R_P = [20\% + (1 \times F)] \times Rs.100,000$$

Similarly, for portfolio Q, the return is given by,

$$R_Q = E(R_Q) + \beta_Q F$$

For an investment of Rs.100, 000, the return becomes,

$$R_Q = [19\% + (1 \times F)] \times Rs.100,000$$

The difference between these two returns would give the risk-free payoff, which thus is,

Risk-free payoff = $[\{20\% + (1 \times F)\} \times Rs.10,000] - [\{19\% + (1 \times F)\} \times Rs.100,000]$
= 1% + Rs.100,000
= Rs.1000

Portfolios with different Beta Values

In the previous example, portfolios P and Q, both were assumed to have the same beta but different expected returns. Now, the arbitrage opportunities are looked into with the portfolios having different beta values. Hence are assumed: a risk-free security whose return is 8%; a well-diversified portfolio, R, whose beta is 0.5 and an expected return of 15%. Another portfolio, S, is constructed which is actually the weighted average portfolio of portfolio P and risk-free security.

∴ Beta of portfolio S,
$$S_\beta = (0.5 \times 1) + (0.5 \times 0) = 0.5$$
Return of portfolio S,
$$R_S = (0.5 \times 20\%) + (0.5 \times 8\%)$$
$$= (10\% + 4\%)$$
$$= 14\%$$

Thus, the expected return and systematic risk (the factor risk, as per the APT) of the portfolio R is 14% and 0.5 respectively. By comparing portfolios R and S we realize that both have same β, but different expected returns. Hence as with portfolios P and Q, a risk-free profit can be earned leading to arbitrage opportunity.

From the above example, it is observed that risk premium is proportional to the beta of the corresponding portfolio.

> **Pause for thought:** The risk premium has a direct variation with beta of the portfolio and thus gives different return for different portfolios.

10.2.2 Systematic Risk and Expected Return on an Individual Security

The above concept is applied to an individual security rather than a portfolio. A security, W, whose beta is 1, is considered. As it is an individual security it is prone to both systematic and unsystematic risk. In the earlier examples unsystematic (the non-factor risks) of portfolios were eliminated by investing in number of securities and only the systematic risk (the factor risks) were relevant. But in case of individual security, W, return is subject to firm-specific factors as well as market factors.

> **Pause for thought:** An individual security doesn't have the advantage of diversification, causing its return to be susceptible to both the firm-specific, as well as market factors.

The APT is a revolutionary model as it allows analyst to analyze the security and to find out whether it is over-valued or under-valued. It aids the construction of portfolios as it allows managers to test to what extent their portfolios are exposed to certain factors. APT is a more customized model than CAPM. However, it is difficult to identify which factors will affect the security—and in turn the portfolio's return. Moreover, it is subjective to determine the different factors and their extent. Also, it is extremely difficult to determine the minor or small effect of certain factors on the portfolio. However, at least approximation is desirable in the absence of exactness.

SUMMARY

- ✓ The APT is not based upon the market portfolio as CAPM and it utilizes fewer assumptions than CAPM.
- ✓ APT is based upon no-arbitrage argument.
- ✓ As per APT too, the return is determined by the systematic risk. But the total systematic risk, in this case, is dependent on the systematic risk brought forth by various macroeconomic factors. Hence it doesn't involve only one β, rather the number of beta values equal the number of factors involved.

- ✓ The various market factors that are deemed responsible for the return on a security, thus, are: interest rate, inflation rate, IIP, GDP, etc.
- ✓ However, these factors are different for different firms—as is their relative impacts—as the sensitivity of firms, to these factors differ.

KEY CONCEPTS

Arbitrage	CAPM	Beta
Arbitrage Pricing Theory	Market Portfolio	Factor Beta

REVIEW QUESTIONS

1. How does APT differ from CAPM? Explain.
2. Explain the variance of a well-diversified arbitrage portfolio.

SUGGESTED FURTHER READING FOR EMPIRICAL WORK

1. Shanken, J. (1982), "The Arbitrage Pricing Theory: Is it Testable?", *The Journal of Finance*, Vol. 37, No. 5.
2. Handa, P., and Linn, S.C. (1993), "Arbitrage Pricing with Estimation Risk", *The Journal of Financial and Quantitative Analysis*, Vol. 28, No. 1.
3. Arthur, L.M., Carter, C.A., and Abizadeh, F. (1988), "Arbitrage Pricing, Capital Asset Pricing, and Agricultural Assets", *American Journal of Agricultural Economics*, Vol. 70, No. 2.
4. Strasser, E. (2005), "Characterization of Arbitrage-Free Markets" *The Annals of Applied Probability*, Vol. 15, No. 1A.
5. Khan M.A., and Sun, Y. (2003), "Exact Arbitrage and Portfolio Analysis in Large Asset Markets" *Economic Theory*, Vol. 22, No. 3.
6. Reisman, H. (1992), "Intertemporal Arbitrage Pricing Theory" *The Review of Financial Studies*, Vol. 5, No. 1.
7. Gilles, C., and LeRoy, S.F. (1991), "On the Arbitrage Pricing Theory" *Economic Theory*, Vol. 1, No. 3.
8. Bekker, P., Dobbelstein, P., and Wansbeek, T. (1996), "The APT Model as Reduced-Rank Regression" *Journal of Business & Economic Statistics*, Vol. 14, No. 2.
9. Latham, M. (1989), "The Arbitrage Pricing Theory and Supershares Author" *The Journal of Finance*, Vol. 44, No. 2.
10. Kale, P., Dyer, J.H., and Singh, H. (2002), "Alliance Capability, Stock Market Response, and Long-Term Alliance Success: The Role of the Alliance Function", *Strategic Management Journal*, Vol. 23, No. 8.

REFERENCES

1. Shanken Jay (1982), "The Arbitrage Pricing Theory: Is it testable?, *The Journal of Finance*, Vol.37, No.5, pp.1129-1140.

2. Priesteley Richard (1995), "The Arbitrage Pricing Theory, Macroeconomic and Financial Factors and Expectations Generating Processes", *Journal of Banking and Finance*, Vol. 20, pp. 869-890.

3. Dhrymes J.Phoebus; Friend Irwin and Gultekin Bulent (1982), "A Critical Re-examination of the Empirical Evidence on the Arbitrage Pricing Theory", *Working Paper No.12-82*. The Wharton School, University of Pennsylvania.

4. http://www.scribd.com/doc/47893678/Arbitrage-Pricing-Theory

5. http://www.scribd.com/doc/39039405/Arbitrage-Pricing-Theory

6. http://www.scribd.com/doc/76774652/International-Arbitrage-Pricing-Theory

7. http://www.scribd.com/doc/91799018/Arbitrage-Pricing-Theory

8. http://www.scribd.com/doc/66241655/The-Arbitrage-Pricing-Theory

11
MARKET EFFICIENCY

> **LEARNING OBJECTIVES**
>
> The purpose of this chapter is to enable you to understand:
> - The efficient market hypothesis (EMH) and find out its impact on the different aspects of investments.
> - The discussion on, and study of, the three forms of EMH: weak, semi-strong and strong.
> - Some tests and evidences of EMH.
> - The market anomalies and identify them.

11.1 INTRODUCTION

The present chapter deals with the efficient market hypothesis (EMH) in detail, with the hypothesis being put to various tests as well. But first and foremost, it analyzes the implications of market efficiency to investors. Otherwise, the understanding lost to ignorance would find it to be not being utilized. The chapter also sheds light on how fast and accurate information, concerning the securities, is disseminated in financial markets as it extends its ambit of attention to different markets.

Though the EMH is studied with respect to the stock market only, it is applicable to the financial markets in entirety. Whether the market is efficient or not, has been a debatable issue for decades—for both, practitioners as well as academicians. Since for an efficient market, accurate information serve as a close ally, it has been observed that many traditional investment tactics fail.

The idea of efficient market triggered tremendous controversy, and it continues unabated through the intervening decades. Given the fact that jobs and reputation of market analysts and portfolio managers are at stake, they are averse to the EMH. Hence the ongoing controversy follows EMH. From the point of view of portfolio managers, accepting that the market is efficient would be extremely difficult. Because how would they then claim to be adding value to the portfolio of their huge clientele? On other hand, a person employed at the stock exchange has least interest of beating the market, and considers the market as truly efficient. Furthermore, beginners in the market find it easier to accept the market as highly efficient and difficult to beat at any point of time. At this juncture, even if some analyst or a well known person involved since long with the stock-market trading, refuses to accept this concept that does not reduce the credibility of EMH. In fact, when the available information is unable to distinguish between profitable investments from an unprofitable one, it signals an efficient market.

11.1.1 The Efficient Market Hypothesis (EMH)

Before getting into the details of EMH it is essential to know what is actually meant by an efficient market. Market where all pertinent information is available to all participants, simultaneously, and where prices respond immediately to available information, is called an efficient market. Stock markets are considered the best examples of efficient markets.

In other words, an efficient market is defined as one in which the prices of all securities quickly and fully reflect all available information. This definition assumes that investors incorporate all relevant data before arriving at a decision regarding their investments.

Since efficient market is the true representation of the market, the current stock price is the discounted estimate of the expected future cash flows and the risk involved in it. Accessing all available information becomes a prerequisite for any rational investor, before investing in a market. EMH renders information as the key to the determination of the prices of stocks.

The EMH is made up of the following assumptions with respect to the current price of the stock. According to it, the current price of the stock reflects the following:

— All known information that includes:
  - Past information (financial statements and announcements of the previous year).
  - The continuous flow of information (dividend, bonus share, stock split, mergers, takeovers, etc.).
— Conclusions based on personal judgment, belief, views from experts, etc. One such example is the belief that due to huge fiscal deficits, RBI as well as the Ministry of Finance might take some actions pertaining to credit, interest, tax rates etc. In such cases, prices react well in advance, much before the actual announcement is made or its implementation takes place.

Hence an efficient market can be described in yet another manner: a market is efficient if investors are unable to earn abnormal profits, as the present set of information is available to all investors in the market. And as security prices are deemed to be true reflection of the available information, the same are thus liable to used by all investors, without any favor accorded to any investor. It is the IT revolution which is responsible for the fast dissemination of information. This gift of technology was not available in the earlier days.

One thing to be noted is that, this concept of and reason behind, market efficiency does not mean the prices absorb or reflect all information. Rather it means that absorption or reflection of all information is unbiased. An efficient market is such a market where the market price of the security is an unbiased estimate of its intrinsic value. When the market is referred to as efficient it is not meant that market price of the security is equal to its intrinsic value at every point of time. According to the EMH, it means that the error in the market prices is unbiased. So, as per this theory market prices can deviate from the intrinsic value, i.e., price is not at equilibrium. This can happen for existing as well as new securities. Such deviations from intrinsic value are random and so it is not always possible to identify over or under-valued securities. It can be further inferred that any new price does not necessarily have to be a price in equilibrium with the market. The final equilibrium price materializes once the investors have fully reviewed all available information.

The ensuing discussion on efficient market having presented varied dimensions of the same, the following conclusions are drawn to characterize an efficient market.

— When the market, if formed by the large number of investors who are price takers, a single investor cannot influence the price of a security. It implies that when there are 'n' numbers of players in the market and because of their consistent and joint effort prices are always influenced—which is not possible for a single investor to influence the market even by buying/selling security in a large quantity.

— Market consists of a large number of rational, profit maximizing investors who are active in the market.

— Information is almost costless and commonly available to market participants almost at the same time.

— Information and announcements are random and hence independent of one another.

— Investors swiftly react to new information and this leads to adjustment in stock prices.

From the above conclusions absence of any exaggeration is evident. It is indeed true that there are a large number of individuals and institutions, constantly active in the market. They keep an uninterrupted vigil on the market to track all available information. This they do to arrive at the decision to buy or sell a stock, at the right time. Thus the price of the stock is the outcome of strong and consistent presence of buyers and suppliers. The available information is not actually costless—when brokerage and other charges are considered. However, it is almost negligible for institutions. And given the fact that this is an era of information and technology, the information cost is negligible for individuals as well.

> **Pause for thought:** Market, where all pertinent information is available to all participants simultaneously, and where prices respond immediately to available information, is called an efficient market.

11.2 EMH IN OTHER COUNTRIES

The market efficiency depends on various factors, over and above the general economy. As these factors differ for different countries, so do their market efficiency, and likewise the EMH as well.

Since the primary reason assumed for market efficiency is the easy availability of information to all investors, if this parameter varies, the efficient market too will be different. This is what is observed. Countries differ in terms of their market efficiency because of difference in the facilities—mainly pertaining to technology, which enhances or otherwise, the accessibility of information. Also there might be differences in terms of analysts and number of investors—individual and institutional, as well the general.

Usually large and developed countries differ significantly in this regard from the developing countries. The latter suffer from huge gaps in information. Thus it has been found that United States possesses comparatively higher market efficiency than other countries. In the 1990s, around 10% of the US mutual funds outperformed the market and more than 40% outperformed an emerging market index. As emerging countries are comparatively and significantly inefficient, the portfolio managers of developed countries can tap the mis-priced securities to beat such markets. A study by Copeland and Copeland has found that the US market has statistically one day lead over the other markets of Asia and Europe.

Pause for thought: Market efficiency is almost completely dependent upon the advancements made in technology in a given country, as on the technology, depends the accessibility of information of the market.

11.3 RANDOM WALK THEORY

The various characteristics of an efficient market have been mentioned above. Yet there is another very important trait that needs mention and discussion, and which thus follows in this section.

In an efficient market the available information is executed in a random manner by different institutions and individuals based upon their judgment. The reason behind the randomness is the absolute uncertainties involving and impacting the market. Some of the uncertainties pertain to the following queries:

— When a company will float an IPO?
— When it will make some significant announcements?
— When will currencies get devalued?
— When could war break out?
— When a country will suffer a huge fiscal deficit?
— When key personnel of a company might resign?
— Whether a deal between companies or countries will materialize or fall through?

Thus, the prices move in a random manner and the current equilibrium price is independent of the prices on the previous day.

The random walk theory was proposed by researchers on the basis of their empirical work on the behavior of market prices. The observation is that prices move independently and market absorbs the information quickly and efficiently. This theory has been named just because of the random movement of the prices of stock, free from one another and from past influences. Hence the current price is determined randomly. The only thing that can affect the prices is the flow of information. Since the information cannot be predicted with any certainty, the flow of information is independent, thus rendering the prices too independent. Based on the available information, the equilibrium price of a stock is determined by the demand and supply principle.

The random walk theory, though entails and advocates the random movement of prices in the market, still it has a basis, in the form of its assumptions.

Assumptions of random walk theory

— No individual investor or group of investors can influence the market by his/their action.
— Stock prices discount all information quickly.
— The flow of information is free and unbiased. All investors can access the same information and nobody has extra access to information; hence cannot influence.
— Prices move in a random fashion without undue pressures or manipulation.

The random walk hypothesis contradicts the belief of technical analysts that the present prices are the result of past trends and current prices discount all available information. Chartists believe that prices move in a predictable manner and history of the trend repeats itself.

> **Pause for thought:** Random walk theory is an aspect of EMH and states that there is a random movement in the prices of stock, completely independent of one another and from past influences, thus ruling out the possibilities of predicting the future trends in the market, based on the one prevalent in the present.

11.4 FORMS OF MARKET EFFICIENCY

Till now the discussions have been on the conditions a market requires to fulfill to be efficient. But as mentioned above the market efficiency of countries vary depending on the overall economy and various other factors. So a framework of EMH is developed and applied to assess the market efficiencies, leading to the relative efficiencies of markets. The framework working on a guideline estimates the extent to which the security prices rapidly and fully reflect available information. Depending on this market efficiencies are categorized. But all market forms are deemed to follow the random walk theory of EMH.

In 1970, Fama established three categories of efficient market, which have been applied since then for any discussion of the EMH. These three stages are as shown below, followed by discussions on them.

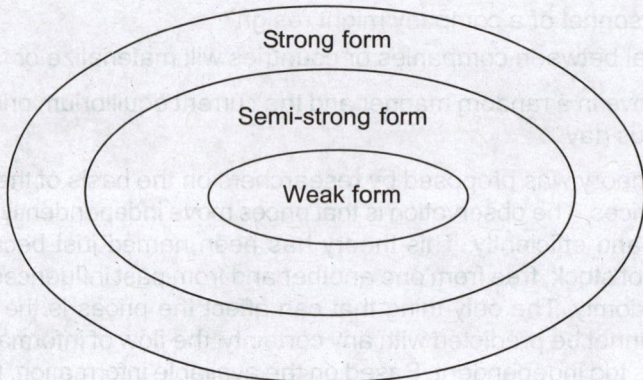

Figure 11.1: Forms of market efficiency

1. Weak form

A market is referred to as weakly efficient if the current price reflects only the past data of the market. Weak form of market efficiency claims that all past prices of a stock are reflected in the current stock price. This is against the theory of technical analyst who believes that it is easy to beat the market by identifying the trend of the security.

2. Semi-strong form

The semi-strong efficient market states that prices reflect all publicly available information. This form of the market also incorporates weak form of the EMH, as all publicly available information includes the past data as well. It can be thus elaborated that market efficiency includes not only known and past data, but all publicly available data and information. The latter includes: quarterly announcements; launching of new product(s); stock-splits; changes in key personnel; cancellation of deal with foreign partner(s); sudden approval of patent etc.

Thus, the semi-strong form focuses on the speed with which prices reflect all publicly available data and availability of public data as well. As it reflects all publicly available information, investors cannot earn abnormal profit on new information after it is announced. But if a delay occurs in conversion of the information into prices, and the investor identifies such a lag, he can exploit the same. If that happens the market reflects that it is not fully efficient.

3. *Strong form*

An efficient market which reflects all available information—public as well as private—is referred to as the strong form of efficient market. It is the highest form of an efficient market. The privately available information which this market form reflects includes information which is accessible only to corporate insiders. As per EMH, no one with such private data can make money in this form of the market. Also, no investor can earn abnormal profit for a reasonable period of time. However, such severe restrictions are mostly unaccepted. It goes without saying that strong form of EMH accounts for weak form and semi-strong form of the efficient markets as well.

Thus the market forms and their characteristics are:

— The current price reflects only the past data of the market, in a weakly efficient market.
— The semi-strong form of the market deals with speed with which prices reflect all publicly available data and focuses on the availability of public data as well, i.e., it encompasses the weak form as well.
— The strong form of efficient market encompasses both the weak and semi-strong forms of efficient market. And it reflects both the public as well as private data.

Pause for thought: The type and the extent to which the security prices rapidly and fully reflect available information decides the market efficiency of the market concerned. When there is a delay in the conversion of available information into prices and this delay is exploited by an investor to earn abnormal profits, the market loses its efficiency.

11.4.1 Tests of Market Efficiency

Once the forms of market efficiencies are theoretically known, the markets have to be tested to accord them the label corresponding to their efficiency. Hence markets are tested for their efficiency and the evidences they come up with ensures the assessment of the market efficiency.

There are several evidences of the random walk theory, which are empirical in nature. There are few tests which the markets, and hence the prices of the security, are subjected to, for an evidence whether the security prices follow, the random walk theory. That is, they seek to test if the current prices are in any way a function of the past prices. Similarly several empirical studies test the weak form of market efficiency. The evidence these studies look for is that no investor actually earns superior return on investment, using the information on the prices from the past.

Various empirical studies have been conducted in India and abroad, in the past and even today, to assess all three forms of market efficiency. Random walk theory too has been put to test. However, outcome of these studies are not in complete agreement with the EMH and their result varies with time. Some of the most important tests are discussed as follows.

11.4.2 Weak Form of Efficient Market

We begin with the tests for the weak form of efficient market.

1. *Filter test*

It is based on the principle of fixing the filter level varying from 0.5% to 5% and then examining both trends and their reversals. Filter tests are conducted by fixing a filter level, of 2% for example, and all trends and reversals in the market are examined in this respect. If the upward movement of the stock from its base price is of the size of the filter or more, the stock is purchased and held, until the fall in price is at least of the size of the filter, from the preceding high. In a similar manner, if the fall in the price from the base price is of the size of the filter, long position should be liquidated (by covering the short position) and stock should be sold short (by assuming a long position) until the price rises[1], from a preceding fall of the size of the filter or more. In other words, it implies that when the stock price reverses again at the filter point, short sale position is covered, by buying the share in the market.

The test and its analysis were conducted by Fama, Blame and Alexander. But they could not come up with anything conclusive. If the filter level is too low, the market fluctuations can easily capture it, but if the filter level is too large, then it is difficult to prove the hypothesis. Also, it has been observed that when filter level is small, market can easily attain it. But in such a case investors cannot profit much by using these filters, if transaction costs and other charges are taken into account.

Thus, it does not agree with the chartist's (technical analyst) view who believes that price and volume data of the past reflects all information of the market and through which trends and reversals can be predicted easily. The discussion also proves that it is not possible to estimate the current price from the price information of the market; indicating the weak form of market hypothesis. Fama and others, in their research have tried with different filter levels say 1%, 2%, 5% etc.

Table 11.1: Filter test for ABB Ltd.

Date	Closing price	At 0.05%	At 0.5%
1-12-03	544.9	-	-
2-12-03	569.45	Hold	Hold
3-12-03	622.6	Buy	Hold
4-12-03	603.95	Hold	Hold
5-12-03	593.25	Hold	Hold
8-12-03	597.25	Hold	Hold
9-12-03	608.4	Hold	Hold
10-12-03	611.8	Hold	Hold
11-12-03	610.1	Hold	Hold
12-12-03	605.45	Hold	Hold

---

[1] Long means to buy and short means to sell. Short sale means selling the security without owning or having it. In case of short sale, securities are sold 'now' and bought later on.

15-12-03	611	Hold	Hold
16-12-03	600.35	Hold	Hold
17-12-03	611.75	Hold	Hold
18-12-03	616.65	Hold	Hold
19-12-03	614.2	Hold	Hold
22-12-03	635.1	Buy	Hold
23-12-03	631.9	Hold	Hold
24-12-03	630.85	Hold	Hold
26-12-03	627.75	Hold	Hold
29-12-03	644.8	Hold	Hold
30-12-03	656.6	Hold	Hold
31-12-03	673.75	Hold	Hold

It is thus observed that the price fluctuates between Rs.544.9 to 673.75.

In this case, with the filter level is at 5%, it can be concluded that:

— If price rises from 544.9 to 572.15, it is a signal to buy and hold the shares of the company.
— But if prices go down from 673.75 to 640.06 the shares should be sold.

Pause for thought: A filter level for the market is fixed and the trends and reversals in market are assessed with respect to the same. This test comes up with evidences in favor of weak form of the efficient market.

2. *Serial correlation test*

Serial correlation is used by technical analysts to determine how well the past price of a security predicts the future price.

Because technical analysis is based entirely on a stock's price movement and the associated volume—rather than the company's fundamentals—finding and validating profitable patterns is an essential component of the success one will have using such methods.

It is also known as auto-correlation test, performed for the first time by Moore. Moore studied and measured the extent of correlation, between a series of prices of a security in the past, as is shown in Table 11.2 below. He conducted the study on the price changes during a week with price changes in the previous week, measuring the correlation coefficient (r) thereby. Very low correlation coefficient was obtained. This indicated that the price rise did not predict the fall in prices that followed; neither did a fall in the price predict the subsequent rise in the price. This unpredictability implies that the price changes over a week (or month or quarter) do not depend significantly on the price changes during the previous week (or previous month or previous quarter).

Similar test was conducted by Fama on the basis of daily prices, in 1965. For that he selected DJIA (Dow Jones Industrial Average) companies as sample stocks and studied them for five years. His research too showed the low correlation of the sample companies included in the study. Thus the studies by Moore and Fama indicate the same, that is, there is no significant relationship between price changes in successive periods, indicating the movement of prices to be independent, to a large extent.

As this test too leads to the fact that the price changes are independent of previous trends, EMH is validated.

Table 11.2: Serial Correlation Test for ONGC Security (Weekly Analysis)

Date	Previous week	Date	Current week
1-12-03	622.5	8-12-03	617.1
2-12-03	614.7	9-12-03	646.55
3-12-03	625.15	10-12-03	682.25
4-12-03	627	11-12-03	693.45
5-12-03	615.75	12-12-03	690.45

Correlation coefficient = 0.209 (as calculated)

The auto-correlation between prices on weekly basis is found to be insignificant. With the obtained result close to zero, the absence of any significant relationship between performances of previous week and the current week is implicit.

Table 11.3: Serial Correlation Test for ONGC Security (Monthly Analysis)

Date	Previous month	Date	Current month
3-11-03	609.7	1-12-03	622.5
4-11-03	625.85	2-12-03	614.7
5-11-03	639.7	3-12-03	625.15
6-11-03	639.35	4-12-03	627
7-11-03	641.1	5-12-03	615.75
10-11-03	658.7	8-12-03	617.1
11-11-03	664.95	9-12-03	646.55
12-11-03	659.9	10-12-03	682.25
13-11-03	639.8	11-12-03	693.45
14-11-03	623.1	12-12-03	690.45
15-11-03	625.3	15-12-03	686
17-11-03	630.9	16-12-03	675.35
18-11-03	617.95	17-12-03	675.65
19-11-03	611	18-12-03	712.1
20-11-03	603.45	19-12-03	748

21-11-03	606.6	22-12-03	759.6
24-11-03	606.55	23-12-03	738.6
25-11-03	606.45	24-12-03	731.85
27-11-03	604.55	26-12-03	736.65
28-11-03	617.4	29-12-03	748.9

Correlation coefficient = –0.644 (calculated)

The auto-correlation between prices on monthly basis is thus observed to be insignificant. As the correlation is found to be very far from -1, it implies that there is no relationship at all between the monthly prices. They are neither exactly inversely related nor do they show even an approximate inverse variation.

> **Pause for thought:** Serial correlation is used by technical analysts to determine how well the past price of a security predicts the future price. When the serial correlation test turns out to be negative, in the sense that the previous data do not correlate with the current data, the market efficiency is proved, and thus EMH too stands validated.

3. *Runs test*

Runs test is a statistical procedure that examines whether a string of data is occurring randomly given a specific distribution. It analyzes the occurrence of similar events that are separated by events that are different.

Fama through this test examined whether the price changes are likely to be followed by further price changes in the same direction. In other words, this test again tests whether a trend in the price change is followed and when the test turns out negative, the efficiency of the market and the EMH are validated.

This method requires a time series data on price changes of stocks. The test is conducted on this series to measure whether there is dependence among these series. The dependence or its absence is represented in terms of same (positive) sign and opposite (negative) sign respectively; and no change is marked as zero. 'Run' is a set of consecutive price changes in the same direction.

The following example of the hypothetical XYZ scrip should facilitate the understanding of the concept behind this test. The Table 11.4 below shows the changes in the prices of the scrip XYZ, over the last ten days. The second row shows such changes with the corresponding signs. The successive changes in the same direction is marked by the consecutive + (plus) sign; while – (minus) sign indicates a movement in the opposite (decline in the prices, in this case) direction and marked as 0 (zero) when there is no change.

Table 11.4 Runs test for hypothetical scrip XYZ with prices of consecutive ten days

Prices	10	10.8	11.8	11.8	13	12	12	12.5	14	13
Sign		+	+	0	+	–	0	+	+	–

From this test too is concluded that the previous day's price does not predict the price for today and today's price does not have any say on the price that will be, tomorrow. It is apparent that the prices do not move in a consistent and thus unpredictable manner. Thus is proved the market efficiency, validating the EMH, through this yet again proving the independence of prices.

There are two types of runs test:

— If the sample size for runs test is greater than 30, Z-test is applied.
— When the sample size is less than 30, t-distribution is applied.

Z-test, when sample size is greater than 30

$$Z = \frac{R - X}{\sigma} \qquad (1)$$

where,
R = number of runs.

$$X = \frac{2n_1n_2 + 1}{n_1 + n_2} \qquad (2)$$

$$\sigma^2 = \frac{2n_1n_2(2n_1n_2 - n_1 - n_2)}{(n_1 + n_2)^2 (n_1 + n_2 - 1)} \qquad (3)$$

where,

$n_1 + n_2$ = number of observations.
σ = standard deviation.
Z = standard normal variate.

t-distribution test, when sample size is less than 30

t-distribution is applied, as follows, when the sample size is less than 30:

$$S = \frac{[(n_1 - 1)s_1^2 + (n_2 - 1)s_2^2]^{1/2}}{n_1 + n_2 - 2} \qquad (4)$$

where,
s_1 and s_2 = standard deviations of the samples, with

$$s_1 = \frac{\sum [X - R(X)^2]}{n_1 - 1} \qquad (5a)$$

$$s_2 = \frac{\sum [Y - R(Y)^2]}{n_2 - 1} \qquad (5b)$$

t-distribution is defined as,

$$t = \frac{[R(X) - R(Y)] [n_1 n_2]^{1/2}}{S(n_1 + n_2)} \qquad (6)$$

Table 11.5: Runs Test for the Stock of Wipro

Date	Closing price	Sign	Runs	Date	Closing price	Sign	Runs
1–10–03	1242.35			14–11–03	1413.5	–	
3–10–03	1216.65	–	1	15–11–03	1419.2	+	18
6–10–03	1236.7	+	2	17–11–03	1440.55	+	
7–10–03	1231.85	–	3	18–11–03	1414.25	–	19
8–10–03	1219.2	–		19–11–03	1413.5	–	
9–10–03	1243	+	4	20–11–03	1400.2	–	
10–10–03	1348.45	+		21–11–03	1451.1	+	20
13–10–03	1371.15	+		24–11–03	1445.2	–	21
14–10–03	1330	–	5	25–11–03	1449.25	+	22
15–10–03	1338.9	+	6	27–11–03	1520.3	+	
16–10–03	1374.6	+		28–11–03	1538.9	+	
17–10–03	1420.8	+		1–12–03	1619.1	+	
20–10–03	1370.35	–	7	2–12–03	1565.2	–	23
21–10–03	1312.15	–		3–12–03	1586.1	+	24
22–10–03	1269.5	–		4–12–03	1569.65	–	25
23–10–03	1233.45	–		5–12–03	1506.7	–	
24–10–03	1287.5	+	8	8–12–03	1529.1	+	26
25–10–03	1284.1	–	9	9–12–03	1548.4	+	
27–10–03	1227.4	–		10–12–03	1599.15	+	
28–10–03	1257.65	+	10	11–12–03	1634.45	+	
29–10–03	1255.6	–	11	12–12–03	1607.2	–	27
30–10–03	1253.4	–		15–12–03	1668.5	+	28
31–10–03	1343.4	+	12	16–12–03	1687.2	+	
3–11–03	1433.65	+		17–12–03	1659.35	–	29
4–11–03	1452.55	+		18–12–03	1678.85	+	30
5–11–03	1424.6	–	13	19–12–03	1699.6	+	
6–11–03	1451.45	+	14	22–12–03	1675.8	–	31
7–11–03	1425.75	–	15	23–12–03	1654.45	–	
10–11–03	1419.7	–		24–12–03	1723.3	+	32
11–11–03	1446.6	+	16	26–12–03	1713.5	–	33
12–11–03	1453.9	+		29–12–03	1753.5	+	34
13–11–03	1419.95	–	17	30–12–03	1753	–	35

From the Table 11.5 it is observed that,

The number of runs, R = 35

$n_1 = 33$; where, $n_1 = (+)$ signs.

$n_2 = 30$; where, $n_2 = (-)$ signs.

$$\therefore \quad X = \frac{2 n_1 n_2}{n_1 + n_2} + 1 \qquad \text{[vide equation (2)]}$$

∴ By putting the values in the above equation,

X = 32.429

$$\sigma^2 = \frac{2n_1 n_2 (2n_1 n_2 - n_1 - n_2)}{(n_1 + n_2)^2 (n_1 + n_2 - 1)} \qquad \text{[vide equation (3)]}$$

∴ From the values available,

$\sigma^2 = 15.425$

Furthermore from Equation (1) Z can be calculated:

$$Z = \frac{R - X}{\sigma}$$

Substituting the values of R, X and σ,

Z = 0.655

The conclusions drawn from these results are:

— According to probability theory, 95 percent of the area under the normal curve lies within + or – 1.96 standard deviation of the mean. Since the calculated value, 0.655, is less than +1.96, the runs have occurred by chance.
— Results of the studies using runs test have suggested that the runs in the price series of stocks are not significantly different from the runs in the series of random numbers.

Pause for thought: Runs test is a statistical procedure that examines whether a string of data is occurring randomly given a specific distribution. It analyzes the occurrence of similar events that are separated by events that are different. The random occurrence is a proof of the independence of events from one another, thereby validating the EMH.

4. *Other tests*

Research conducted by Levy (1967), Jenson and Brington (1970) and by Osborne (1959, 1962) concluded that:

— Current price trends are independent of past price trends.
— No significant return can be earned based upon past prices and volume data.

11.4.3 Semi-Strong Form of Efficient Market

Having tested the EMH for weak form of efficient market, the discussion now moves to the tests that come up with evidences for the semi-strong form of the efficient market and thus validate it.

1. Event study tests

Study of the consequences of an event in the market, on the market returns is called the event study test. And in the stock market, even an announcement is an event. The market reacts at the time of specific announcements like:

— Quarterly report.
— Issue of bonus shares.
— Stock splits.
— Resignation of key personnel.
— Failure of a contract with foreign company.
— Cancellation of an export order.

These are some of the events that finds the market reacting. The event study examines the market reactions to such announcements and checks for any excess return. But the results from event studies are not clear. Some event studies have proved the semi-strong of the market, coming up with evidences of stock prices adjusting rapidly to all publicly available information. However, there are some event studies whose conclusions run contrary to the semi-strong form of the market.

> **Pause for thought:** Event study tests check upon the impact of varied events concerning the market, on the market returns. But the results from it are inconclusive as they are inconsistent.

2. Portfolio study: comparative study of large cap, mid cap and small cap companies

It examines the return earned by a portfolio of stocks, with respect to some characteristics, viz., low P/E ratio (discussed later), small market capitalization, P/B ratio (discussed later), etc. Like event studies, results of the portfolios studies too are not clear. Some portfolio studies have proved that it is not possible to earn superior return, through risk adjustments, by considering the above mentioned characteristics. But, there are instances when such studies have shown evidence that sometimes it is possible to earn superior returns. These ambiguities shown by the market are also known as market inefficiencies or market anomalies.

For a proper understanding of the portfolio study, the data of the market prices, for the last ten years (2002-2011), of 10 companies in each category (large, medium and small caps), are being considered. From these companies, portfolios of ten companies have been constructed by taking equal weights of each company. Thus, the Table 11.6 below shows the risk and return of ten portfolios in each category[2].

Table 11.6: Comparative Study of Large, Mid and Small Cap Companies

Company	Portfolio return (%)	Portfolio risk (%)	Coefficient of variation
Large Cap	25.433	48.01	1.88
Mid Cap	37.788	51.70	1.368
Small Cap	43.831	62.63	1.42

---

[2] Large cap, medium (mid) cap and small cap companies.

- Mid cap companies have given comparatively fair return with respect to the risk level.
- Small cap companies have come up with higher returns than both the large cap as well as mid cap companies. But its risk too is much higher than that of the large and mid cap companies.
- When the return and risk of mid cap companies is compared with that of large cap companies, for the almost same level of risk the mid cap companies yield better returns.

> **Pause for thought:** It examines the return generated by portfolios with respect to certain specific parameters, but the results are inconclusive as in the case of event study. At times it proves the semi-strong form of market efficiency while at times it provides contradictory evidences, with these inconsistencies thus termed market inefficiencies.

11.4.4 Price-Earnings Ratio

The portfolio study refers to the market returns in terms of price-earning (P/E) and price-to-book (P/B) ratios. But to correlate the return with its P/E ratio one has to know what is meant by the same, and it holds true for P/B ratio as well. In this section P/E ratio holds the attention of discussion.

It is a ratio which serves as a measure of the valuation of a company. The ratio of a company's current share price and its per-share earnings is known as its price-earnings ratio. It is represented as:

$$\frac{P}{E} = \frac{\text{Market value per share}}{\text{Earnings per share (EPS)}}$$

The importance of P/E ratios in selecting the stocks is observed repeatedly. However, at the same time P/E ratio is also found to be misleading many a times. This makes the selection of stocks on the basis of P/E value alone, difficult. But when P/E ratios are held as the sole criterion, the following steps are involved in the selection process.

Step 1: P/E ratios are collected over a period of time. In the example that follows, it is for the period 2002 to 2011. The ratios are divided into two groups. The first group consists of stocks with the low P/E ratios and the second groups consisting of stocks with high P/E ratios. Firms with negative price-earnings ratios are ignored.

Step 2: The return on each individual security is computed using data of market price for the same period. Similarly, the risk of each individual security is computed using the relevant data for the given period.

Step 3: Portfolios are constructed with stocks of low and high P/E ratios separately.

Step 4: Two types of portfolio thus constructed in the third step—one with low P/E ratio and the other one with high P/E ratio—undergo a comparative study in this step.

Companies with high P/E ratio

The data of market price from 2002-2011, of five companies with high P/E ratios, are considered. Risk and return are computed by taking the data of market price for the same time period (2002-2011). With these values thus collected, portfolio of these five scrips has been constructed by taking equal weights of each.

Table 11.7: Risk and Return of Companies with High P/E Ratio

Year	BOMBAY DYEING	ADANI ENTERPRISE	STERLING INTER	MMTC LTD.	AXIS CAPITAL
2002	3.670	-16.879	-43.548	491.667	-14.583
2003	232.412	171.024	100.743	45.070	-33.333
2004	53.522	-80.295	-55.649	72.758	162.857
2005	58.365	-24.729	-69.077	43.982	29.950
2006	104.906	283.600	184.087	315.364	58.672
2007	-2.157	399.630	62.627	1371.150	393.556
2008	-74.400	-74.985	53.623	-43.692	-79.631
2009	106.405	43.470	-28.309	79.040	77.632
2010	30.456	48.208	32.756	-96.632	1.111
2011	-34.562	-55.195	-61.548	-54.043	-43.415
Return (%)	47.862	69.385	17.570	222.466	55.281
Variance	7486.857	26829.609	7019.438	195111.593	18973.895
Risk (%)	86.527	163.797	83.782	441.714	137.746
Portfolio return	82.513%				
Portfolio risk	146.04%				

Companies with low P/E ratio

The data of the market prices of five companies, with low P/E ratio, are considered for the same time period (2002-2011), as above. Risk and return are computed similarly with the data of the market prices for the same time period. Subsequently, portfolio of these five scrips has been constructed by taking equal weights of each of these five securities.

Table 11.8: Risk and Return of Companies With Low P/E Ratio

Year	TCFC FINANCE	BPL LTD.	PRAKASH IND.	ROLTA	WELSPUN
2002	–20.635	–10.097	120.833	–19.088	–44.186
2003	37.808	4.025	162.500	20.770	168.493
2004	36.432	–12.625	44.585	–28.036	16.944
2005	67.600	–7.353	32.075	150.613	–24.320
2006	–6.744	122.995	49.378	23.537	–24.615
2007	236.750	22.487	844.755	179.180	103.207

2008	−85.460	−83.916	−85.779	−83.972	−66.576
2009	227.731	89.526	309.641	66.538	211.400
2010	−0.656	−15.026	−38.936	−20.972	23.913
2011	−49.695	−52.018	−76.537	−63.843	−47.681
Return (%)	44.313	5.800	136.252	22.473	31.658
Variance	11760.737	3735.250	76115.317	7541.088	9380.422
Risk (%)	108.447	61.117	275.890	86.839	96.853
Portfolio return	48.099%				
Portfolio risk	108.42%				

Table 11.9: Comparison of Return and Risk of Individual Securities, Based on their P/E Ratios

High P/E ratio security	BOMBAY DYEING	ADANI ENTERPRISE	STERLING INTER	MMTC LTD.	AXIS CAPITAL
Return (%)	47.862	69.385	17.570	222.466	55.281
Risk (%)	86.527	163.797	83.782	441.714	137.746
Coefficient of variation (CV), (σ/R)	1.807843	2.360698	4.768469	1.985535	2.491742
Low P/E ratio security	TCFC FINANCE	BPL LTD.	PRAKASH IND.	ROLTA	WELSPUN
Return (%)	44.313	5.800	136.252	22.473	31.658
Risk (%)	108.447	61.117	275.890	86.839	96.853
Coefficient of variation (CV), (σ/R)	2.447295	10.53741	2.024851	3.864148	3.059353

From the Table 11.9, which summarizes the combined results of companies with low and high P/E ratios, the following conclusions can be drawn:

— Return and risk of securities with high P/E ratio are more than those having low P/E value.
— As per CV, one with lower CV should be preferred as it carries a lower risk for a unit of return.
— Stocks having high P/E value have a comparatively lower CV, than the CV of stocks with low P/E stocks.
— P/E is inversely proportional to CV.

Now the risk and return of portfolios with high and low P/E ratios, corresponding to the companies with high and low P/E ratios that comprise them, are compared in the Table 11.10 below.

Table 11.10: Comparison of the Portfolios

Portfolio	Portfolio return (%)	Portfolio risk (%)	Coefficient of variation (CV) (σ/R)
High P/E ratio	82.513	146.04	1.70
Low P/E ratio	48.099	108.42	2.254

Analysts have claimed that portfolios comprised of stocks with low P/E are generally good bargains, compared to those with high P/E. But in the example used here, just the reverse is observed. Portfolios with low P/E stocks are shown as having yielded lower returns than the portfolio with high P/E stocks—though yes, its risk too is less. However, based upon coefficient of variation, the portfolio of high P/E stocks is better than the portfolio composed of low P/E stocks.

> **Pause for thought:** The ratio of a company's current share price and its per-share earnings is known as its price-earnings ratio. It serves as the measure of valuation, of a company.

11.4.5 Price-to-Book Ratio

Now that the parameter of P/E ratio has been dealt with, we come to another parameter on the basis of which the risk and return of portfolios are assessed, as mentioned in the portfolio study. It is the price-to-book ratio, denoted as P/B. If one had to define book-value in a single sentence, then it would be, as: the value at which an asset is carried on a balance sheet—in other words, the value as mentioned in the book, which is the balance sheet in this context.

Price-to-book ratio is current closing price of the stock and the latest quarter's book value per share. And book value is the difference between the total assets and the intangible assets, as well as liabilities. This ratio is a stock's market value with its book-value and is also known as price-equity ratio. It is calculated as:

$$\frac{P}{B} = \frac{\text{Stock price}}{\text{Total assets} - \text{Intangible assets and liabilities}}$$

A lower P/B ratio could mean that the stock is under-valued. However, it could also mean that something is fundamentally wrong with the company. As with most ratios, it has to be kept in mind that this too varies with the industry.

This ratio also gives some idea of whether one is paying too much for what would be left if the company went bankrupt immediately.

As the companies are categorized as per their P/E values, so they are on the basis of their P/B values too. Thus as the risk and return of stocks were computed on the basis of their P/E ratio above, the Table 11.11 below represents the computation of the same as per the P/B ratio of the given stocks. Furthermore, the risk and return of companies with high and low P/B values have been tabulated separately, as in the case of P/E ratio. Table 11.11 shows the risk and return of securities whose P/B ratios are high. Risk and return of individual securities have been calculated by taking the data of market prices for the last 10 years (2002 to 2011). Subsequent to that, portfolio has been constructed by taking equal weights of each security.

Companies with high P/B ratio

Table 11.11: Risk and Return of Companies with High P/B Ratio

Year	CIPLA	TATA POWER	INFOSYS	M&M	SAVERA LTD.
2002	–22.131	–7.686	17.083	25.222	–42.041
2003	45.713	180.268	16.835	244.140	67.470
2004	–76.307	23.670	–62.730	38.903	91.051
2005	38.563	10.316	42.770	–6.866	65.139
2006	–43.663	28.553	–25.317	76.924	83.313
2007	–16.101	163.116	–21.124	–5.614	51.240
2008	–13.070	–49.125	–36.414	–68.115	–74.783
2009	83.388	83.482	131.578	287.384	21.548
2010	9.115	–1.108	32.195	–28.991	2.506
2011	–13.635	–93.631	–19.830	–13.756	–28.896
Return (%)	–0.813	33.786	7.505	54.923	23.655
Variance	2160.197	7486.699	2992.439	13982.557	3302.454
Risk (%)	46.478	86.526	54.703	118.248	57.467
Portfolio return	23.81%				
Portfolio risk	55.35%				

Companies with low P/B ratio

Table 11.12 represents the risk and return, calculated with the market price data for the same period (2002 to 2011), of securities with high P/B ratios. The portfolio has been constructed by taking equal weights of each of these securities.

Table 11.12: Risk and Return of Companies with Low P/B Ratio

Year	RIL	L&T	BHEL	AIRTEL	R INFRA
2002	–3.029	10.762	22.847	–58.364	11.796
2003	91.000	146.771	191.925	347.234	130.551
2004	–6.515	85.283	50.371	102.918	1.835
2005	71.070	86.528	79.799	57.926	15.143
2006	42.185	–21.791	64.860	80.238	–14.374
2007	130.015	197.989	12.261	56.622	308.145
2008	–58.297	–81.522	–47.296	–29.198	–72.847

2009	−12.149	116.125	75.372	−54.314	96.051
2010	−3.268	16.552	−3.537	8.606	−27.017
2011	−34.755	−49.995	−89.742	−4.325	−59.947
Return (%)	21.626	50.670	35.686	50.734	38.934
Variance	3572.772	8146.907	5985.417	13969.453	12919.267
Risk (%)	59.773	90.260	77.365	118.192	113.663
Portfolio return	39.53%				
Portfolio risk	75.83%				

Table 11.13: Comparison of the Return and Risk of Individual Securities Based on their P/B Ratios

High P/B ratio security	CIPLA	TATA POWER	INFOSYS	M&M	SAVERA LTD.
Return	−0.813	33.786	7.505	54.923	23.655
Risk	46.478	86.526	54.703	118.248	57.467
Coefficient of variation (CV), (σ/R)	−57.1685	2.561002	7.288874	2.152978	2.429381
Low P/B ratio security	RIL	L&T	BHEL	AIRTEL	Reliance INFRA
Return	21.626	50.670	35.686	50.734	38.934
Risk	59.773	90.260	77.365	118.192	113.663
Coefficient of variation (CV), (σ/R)	2.763942	1.78133	2.167937	2.329641	2.919376

From the above table, which is a summary of the combined results of the securities with high and low P/B values, the following conclusions are drawn:

— Return of stocks with low P/B ratio is comparatively higher than those with high P/B ratio.
— However, the P/B ratio being inversely proportional to risk, stocks having low P/B ratio though have higher return, their risk too is higher, as compared to the stocks with high P/B. This again reiterates the fact that risk and return are directly related.
— On comparing the results on the basis of the coefficient of variation (CV), it is found that CV of stocks with low P/B ratio is lower than that of high P/B ratio stocks.
— Hence CV is directly proportional to P/B ratio.

After the risk and return of individual securities, with high and low P/B values have been analyzed, the same for the portfolios constructed with such securities, separately, are estimated and subsequently compared. The following Table 11.14 thus compares the risk and return of portfolios having high and low P/B value.

Table 11.14: Comparison of the Portfolios

Portfolio	Portfolio return (%)	Portfolio risk (%)	Coefficient of variation (CV) (σ/R)
High P/B ratio	23.81	55.35	2.32
Low P/B ratio	39.53	75.83	1.92

From Table 11.14 it is observed that the return of the portfolio with high P/B value is very low, as compared to that of the portfolio with low P/B value. But at the same time, its risk too is much lower. However, the overall result obtained favors the portfolio of low P/B ratio, as its performance, in terms of risk and return, is found to be much better than the portfolio having a high P/B ratio.

> **Pause for thought:** Price-to-book ratio is current closing price of the stock and the latest quarter's book-value per share.

11.5 STRONG FORM OF EFFICIENT MARKET

The strong form of EMH is extreme in nature. To test the strong form of market efficiency, researchers have analyzed the returns earned by the privileged group. It is that group which has special access to information. Researchers have found that corporate insiders and the professionals, who specialize in the trading in stock exchange, earn superior risk-adjusted return. Contrary to this, the mutual fund managers generally do not earn superior risk-adjusted returns.

> **Pause for thought:** It is the extreme form of EMH and can be tested only by analyzing the returns earned by the privileged group of investors who have special access to information. They earn superior risk-adjusted return as a consequence of the privileged information they access.

11.6 CRITIQUE OF EMH

This theory has posed a challenge to both the chartists, as well as the fundamentalists, with respect to the stock market. Since they do not agree with it, this disagreement has led to quite a bit of controversy questioning the validity of efficient market theory.

They have their reasons for criticizing the same. It has been noted that portfolio managers could not perform better based on this theory in real market. There is no clear cut evidence to test the validity of the theory for the strong form of efficient market. Similarly, semi-strong form too has less empirical evidences to prove it. Compared to strong and semi-strong forms, the weak form of the efficient market has proved to be slightly better. It is because of the fact that a perfect market does not exist and shares are not traded at their intrinsic value.

Moreover, many a time it has been found that sentiments and speculations force the trend, instead of the actual fundamentals of the stock. There are also no concrete evidences of any superior earning of return from any of the empirical methods studied. If weak form of EMH holds good, chartists find that they cannot earn superior return by applying its tools. Under the same conditions, even the fundamentalists too find that it is impossible to earn superior return unless the privileged information is accessed, which though is available to only a select group.

SUMMARY

— In the weak form of efficient market, the current prices of stocks reflect past performance of the market.

— In the semi-strong form of the efficient market all public information is reflected on security prices.

— The strong form of an efficient market reflects both private as well as public information in the prices of securities.

— The empirical evidences support the weak form. But the semi-strong and strong forms of efficient market get ambiguous response from the empirical studies.

KEY CONCEPTS

Market Efficiency	Efficient Market Hypothesis	Correlation coefficient
Weak Form	Random Walk Theory	Event
Semi-Strong Form	Past Information	Chartists
Strong Form	All Information	Fundamentalists

REVIEW QUESTIONS

1. Explain, "Stock prices are like random numbers."
2. State and explain the criticisms of EMH.
3. Critically examine whether the Indian stock market is a semi-strong efficient market or is strongly efficient.
4. Compare:
   (a) The weak form of efficient market and the semi-strong form.
   (b) The semi-strong form and the strong form of efficient market.
5. As per the random walk theory what has to be done by the chartists and fundamentalists to succeed in the market?

ASSIGNMENT QUESTIONS

1. Collect the news events and its impact on market price of Biocon stock. Collect this data for the period 2008 to 2011 and analyze its impact on the performance of stock periodically.
2. From the daily Economics Times, select the securities based on the: (i) high P/E ratio and (ii) low P/E ratio. Then take their daily prices over the past one month and compare it with the P/E ratio. Show your results. What your analysis indicates?

294 SECURITY ANALYSIS AND PORTFOLIO MANAGEMENT

3. Carry out the similar exercise for stocks with low and high P/B ratios.
4. Answer the questions, 2 and 3 again, by constructing the portfolios of 10 securities for each category of P/E and P/B ratios respectively and interpret your results.

ILLUSTRATIONS

Q.1. Perform the runs test on RIL security by taking the prices from October 1, 2003 to December 30, 2003.

Date	Closing price	Sign	Runs	Date	Closing price	Sign	Runs
1–10–03	434.65			14–11–03	464.35	–	
3–10–03	448.6	+	1	15–11–03	468.7	+	19
6–10–03	458.1	+		17–11–03	473.95	+	
7–10–03	451.65	–	2	18–11–03	465.75	–	20
8–10–03	456.8	+	3	19–11–03	460.5	–	
9–10–03	455.1	–	4	20–11–03	449.9	–	
10–10–03	470.6	+	5	21–11–03	460.5	+	21
13–10–03	481.3	+		24–11–03	455.4	–	22
14–10–03	466.85	–	6	25–11–03	467.3	+	23
15–10–03	480	+	7	27–11–03	475.3	+	
16–10–03	484.6	+		28–11–03	487.9	+	
17–10–03	489.1	+		1–12–03	491.6	+	
20–10–03	480.85	–	8	2–12–03	501.9	+	
21–10–03	467.9	–		3–12–03	496.3	–	24
22–10–03	470	+	9	4–12–03	508.25	+	25
23–10–03	457.4	–	10	5–12–03	492.85	–	26
24–10–03	471.65	+	11	8–12–03	480	–	
25–10–03	475.25	+		9–12–03	485.9	+	27
27–10–03	458.2	–	12	10–12–03	498.5	+	
28–10–03	465.5	+	13	11–12–03	491.8	–	28
29–10–03	473.45	+		12–12–03	490.8	–	
30–10–03	477.9	+		15–12–03	499.1	+	29
31–10–03	486.3	+		16–12–03	504.65	+	
3–11–03	498.55	+		17–12–03	501.7	–	30
4–11–03	490.05	–	14	18–12–03	506.35	+	31
5–11–03	488.6	–		19–12–03	520.4	+	

6–11–03	491.75	+	15	22–12–03	526.35	+	
7–11–03	481.05	–	16	23–12–03	523	–	32
10–11–03	482.25	+	17	24–12–03	528.95	+	
11–11–03	482.35	+		26–12–03	530.1	+	
12–11–03	483.2	+		29–12–03	536.75	+	
13–11–03	476.9	–	18	30–12–03	560.95	+	

Ans:

R = 32

$n_1 = 40$ where, $n_1 = $ (+) signs.

$n_2 = 23$ where, $n_2 = $ (–) signs.

$$X = \frac{2 n_1 n_2}{n_1 + n_2} + 1$$

∴ X = 30.206

$$\sigma^2 = \frac{2n_1 n_2 (2n_1 n_2 - n_1 - n_2)}{(n_1 + n_2)^2 (n_1 + n_2 - 1)}$$

∴ $\sigma^2 = 13.287$

$$Z = \frac{R - X}{\sigma}$$

∴ Z = 0.492

According to probability theory, 95% of the area under the normal curve lies within + 1.96 mean standard deviation. Since the calculated value, 0.492, is less than +1.96, the runs have occurred by chance. Results of the studies using runs test, suggest that the runs in the price series of stocks are not significantly different from the runs in the series of random numbers.

Q.2. Perform the filter test for Hero Motor Corp. with the help of the data for the period: December 1, 2003 to December 31, 2003.

Date	Closing price	At 0.05%	At 0.5%
1-12-03	397.4	Buy	Hold
2-12-03	409.75	Hold	Hold
3-12-03	403.35	Hold	Hold
4-12-03	390.2	Sell	Hold
5-12-03	380.8	Hold	Hold
8-12-03	384.45	Hold	Hold
9-12-03	397.6	Buy	Hold

10-12-03	396.8	Hold	Hold
11-12-03	399.7	Hold	Hold
12-12-03	395.55	Hold	Hold
15-12-03	397.4	Hold	Hold
16-12-03	387	Hold	Hold
17-12-03	389.3	Hold	Hold
18-12-03	397.7	Hold	Hold
19-12-03	412.05	Hold	Hold
22-12-03	408.35	Hold	Hold
23-12-03	417.9	Hold	Hold
24-12-03	451.3	Buy	Hold
26-12-03	462.15	Hold	Hold
29-12-03	461.75	Hold	Hold
30-12-03	452	Hold	Hold
31-12-03	448.85	Hold	Hold

Ans: Here the price fluctuates for ABB stock between Rs.397.4 to Rs.462.15. Filter is applied at the level of 0.05% and 0.5%.

— Price fluctuates between Rs.380.8 to Rs.462.15.
— When the filter level is at 5%, a rise in the price from 380.8 to 399.84 is a sign of an opportune moment to buy the share. On the other hand, if the price goes down from Rs.462.15 to Rs.439.04, it is a signal for the investor to sell the share.

APPENDIX A

January effect

January effect is a puzzling calendar anomaly. It has been observed that stock prices rise more in the month of January than in any other month of the year. The following tables show the January effect for Titan Industries and Mahindra & Mahindra Ltd., from 2006-07 to 2010-11. According to the researchers and analysts, there are several reasons behind it. However, all available explanations are partially capable of explaining the reason behind the same.

January effect for Titan Industries

2006-07		2007-08		2008-09		2009-10		2010-11	
Date	Closing price	Date	Closing price	Date	Closing price	Date	Closing price	Date	Closing price
15/12/06	759.3	17/12/07	1,390.30	15/12/08	902.4	15/12/09	1,289.75	15/12/10	3,416.00
18/12/06	749.8	18/12/07	1,459.65	16/12/08	923.75	16/12/09	1,275.15	16/12/10	3,407.45
19/12/06	737.7	19/12/07	1,501.80	17/12/08	914	17/12/09	1,323.75	20/12/10	3,387.15
20/12/06	743.25	20/12/07	1,484.70	18/12/08	955.95	18/12/09	1,333.95	21/12/10	3,411.60
21/12/06	783.05	24/12/07	1,513.90	19/12/08	984.85	21/12/09	1,375.95	22/12/10	3,392.80
22/12/06	781.25	26/12/07	1,531.40	22/12/08	1,010.20	22/12/09	1,371.40	23/12/10	3,335.25
26/12/06	789.35	27/12/07	1,478.85	23/12/08	932.65	23/12/09	1,374.45	24/12/10	3,466.75
27/12/06	807.7	28/12/07	1,533.00	24/12/08	940.65	24/12/09	1,415.70	27/12/10	3,477.35
28/12/06	798.95	*31/12/07*	*1,562.30*	26/12/08	898.6	29/12/09	1,433.90	28/12/10	3,464.50
29/12/06	*859.05*	*1/1/2008*	*1,544.95*	29/12/08	907.25	30/12/09	1,460.15	29/12/10	3,515.80
2/1/2007	*876.65*	*2/1/2008*	*1,572.95*	30/12/08	920.95	*31/12/09*	*1,422.05*	30/12/10	3,534.40
3/1/2007	*894.6*	*3/1/2008*	*1,533.55*	31/12/08	927.25	*4/1/2010*	*1,420.75*	*31/12/10*	*3,601.30*
4/1/2007	*889.9*	*4/1/2008*	*1,534.05*	*1/1/2009*	*940.5*	*5/1/2010*	*1,450.55*	*3/1/2011*	*3,682.40*
5/1/2007	*876.7*	*7/1/2008*	*1,666.60*	*2/1/2009*	*952.4*	*6/1/2010*	*1,474.20*	*4/1/2011*	*3,657.90*
8/1/2007	878.8	8/1/2008	1,601.55	*5/1/2009*	*958.8*	7/1/2010	1,509.80	*5/1/2011*	*3,640.25*
9/1/2007	858.2	9/1/2008	1,656.75	6/1/2009	924.95	8/1/2010	1,495.15	6/1/2011	3,574.00
######	850.2	######	1,558.45	7/1/2009	898.55	######	1,487.50	7/1/2011	3,415.15
######	882.05	######	1,568.25	9/1/2009	896.45	######	1,476.60	######	3,291.05
######	894.2	14/01/08	1,560.70	######	886.45	13/01/10	1,469.75	######	3,305.25
15/01/07	899.35	15/01/08	1,525.85	13/01/09	905.8	14/01/10	1,517.50	######	3,568.30
				14/01/09	937.95	15/01/10	1,515.55	13/01/11	3,415.80
				15/01/09	929.05			14/01/11	3,410.55

The above table shows the share price of Titan Industries from year 2006-07 to 2010-11. As the title of the table suggests—here it shows the one of the market anomaly—called the January effect. The January effect states that stock prices are usually higher in the month of January, every year, compared to other months of the year. Herein, without any calculation just the closing prices of Titan Industries are shown. For example, it can be seen that in every year (here 2006-07 to 2010-11), stock price of Titan is higher in the month of January than in any other month. Students can check it by comparing the stock prices in January with that of other months of the year. This is found in most of the countries of the world.

January effect for Mahindra & Mahindra Ltd.

2006-07		2007-08		2008-09		2009-10		2010-11	
Date	Closing price	Date	Closing price	Date	Closing price	Date	Closing price	Date	Closing price
15/12/06	808.25	17/12/07	773.6	15/12/08	303.2	15/12/09	1,017.40	15/12/10	753.15
18/12/06	813	18/12/07	770.65	16/12/08	300.2	16/12/09	1,046.45	16/12/10	732.6
19/12/06	793	19/12/07	777.3	17/12/08	303.95	17/12/09	1,056.50	20/12/10	745.8
20/12/06	815.25	20/12/07	785.45	18/12/08	308.15	18/12/09	1,054.20	21/12/10	753.8
21/12/06	848.4	24/12/07	823.55	19/12/08	321.2	21/12/09	1,020.50	22/12/10	757.55
22/12/06	870.5	26/12/07	833.55	22/12/08	306.6	22/12/09	1,009.85	23/12/10	751.5
26/12/06	878.8	27/12/07	827.9	23/12/08	290.25	23/12/09	1,040.55	24/12/10	760.75
27/12/06	884.1	28/12/07	834.4	24/12/08	278.45	24/12/09	1,061.85	27/12/10	758.4
28/12/06	888.15	*31/12/07*	*860.8*	26/12/08	265.5	29/12/09	1,058.80	28/12/10	763.9
29/12/06	*905.85*	*1/1/2008*	*864.85*	29/12/08	255.75	30/12/09	1,062.40	29/12/10	773.4
2/1/2007	*956.1*	*2/1/2008*	*860.05*	*30/12/08*	*270.45*	*31/12/09*	*1,080.80*	30/12/10	775.7
3/1/2007	*933.95*	*3/1/2008*	*835.7*	*31/12/08*	*274.85*	*4/1/2010*	*1,129.60*	*31/12/10*	*777.55*
4/1/2007	*925.75*	*4/1/2008*	*823.1*	*1/1/2009*	*282.65*	*5/1/2010*	*1,150.65*	*3/1/2011*	*787.05*
5/1/2007	*896.5*	7/1/2008	810.6	*2/1/2009*	*287.45*	*6/1/2010*	*1,178.15*	*4/1/2011*	*780.2*
8/1/2007	899.05	8/1/2008	830.1	*5/1/2009*	*296.5*	7/1/2010	1,152.95	*5/1/2011*	*771.05*
9/1/2007	890.3	9/1/2008	807.9	6/1/2009	317.95	8/1/2010	1,151.70	6/1/2011	769.9
######	874.3	######	803.15	7/1/2009	300.65	######	1,158.65	7/1/2011	738.6
######	912.35	######	774.75	9/1/2009	311.2	######	1,189.25	######	729.2
######	933.4	14/01/08	755.65	######	308.85	13/01/10	1,154.70	######	735.5
15/01/07	950.5	15/01/08	735.2	13/01/09	303.6	14/01/10	1,170.80	######	751.05
				14/01/09	319.95	15/01/10	1,155.25	13/01/11	738.1
				15/01/09	319.05			14/01/11	739.05

Similarly, the January effect was analyzed for Aban Offshore Ltd., BHEL, JSW Steel Ltd., Sesa Goa, Sun Pharma, Tata Motors and Reliance Infrastructure for the same time period, as above. The results obtained were similar.

APPENDIX B

Large Cap Companies

Year	ONGC	RIL	ITC	HDFC	ICICI PHARMA	SUN	DR. READY	WIPRO	GAIL	JINDAL STEEL
2002	153.478	−3.029	−1.514	−2.493	56.167	1.794	−3.117	2.476	11.429	121.204
2003	126.841	91	48.298	66.849	108.68	−1.105	57.813	5.668	267.986	77.507
2004	1.216	−6.515	31.771	43.329	23.707	−9.33	−40.324	−57.12	−12.164	42.742
2005	41.919	71.07	−89.279	35.527	55.982	23.132	12.471	−38.453	13.106	72.296
2006	−25.953	42.185	23.474	50.478	51.881	45.685	−17.728	30.291	−1.931	42.004
2007	40.831	130.015	18.212	61.477	38.628	24.066	−9.662	−13.538	105.05	576.619
2008	−46.537	−58.297	−19.127	−42.269	−63.696	−12.559	−36.119	−55.259	−62.409	−94.071
2009	74.452	−12.149	45.42	68.816	92.462	40.85	140.8	187.881	98.606	−23.484
2010	8.872	−3.268	−30.478	38.826	28.902	−68.488	45.838	−29.733	23.83	1.163
2011	−80.143	−34.755	14.505	−81.973	−40.624	0.986	−5.285	−18.943	−25.272	−37.061

Mid Cap Companies

Year	L&T	SATYAM	P&G	GSFC	BERGER PAINT	MRF	EICHER MOTOR	GODFREY PHILIPS	IPCA LAB	AVENTIS PHARMA
2002	10.762	18.964	−13.839	126.339	7.246	26.939	251.139	−16.000	126.868	−29.166
2003	146.771	31.150	16.208	89.189	128.937	152.874	180.824	28.500	244.588	136.405
2004	85.283	10.784	17.929	98.367	−77.599	6.380	3.416	19.023	38.952	90.044
2005	86.528	79.078	45.634	64.363	83.924	12.101	−8.020	164.792	−55.681	20.942
2006	−21.791	−34.663	−0.574	11.485	−35.943	54.802	55.729	−4.438	42.728	−19.548
2007	197.989	−7.582	−9.219	87.928	35.141	66.797	11.688	12.376	13.551	−15.411
2008	−81.522	−61.850	−3.596	−78.406	−47.288	−72.569	−42.683	−41.932	−46.489	−18.521
2009	116.125	−44.080	126.994	156.941	76.029	204.532	175.315	127.716	188.554	79.386
2010	16.552	−33.650	7.248	95.181	70.333	18.157	91.321	4.642	−66.881	14.747
2011	−49.995	−3.134	2.151	−10.535	−16.876	−3.833	18.976	21.176	−20.400	19.005
Return	50.670	−4.498	18.894	64.085	22.390	46.618	73.770	31.586	46.579	27.788
Variance	8146.907	1740.749	1730.143	4941.926	4500.411	6384.441	9546.908	4146.964	11494.745	3125.005
Risk	90.260	41.722	41.595	70.299	67.085	79.903	97.708	64.397	107.214	55.902

Small Cap Companies

Year	SANGHI IND.	BELLARY STEEL	TRENT LTD.	AARTI IND.	BALAJI FILM	BINANI IND.	CAN FIN HOMES	DL BANK	HINDU MOTORS	JMC PROJECTS
2002	32.432	74.074	139.648	83.923	−72.229	−39.667	17.982	13.072	115.054	4.054
2003	−23.618	89.600	62.018	260.413	16.628	103.056	89.474	73.011	79.426	55.462
2004	15.414	35.039	91.776	56.594	19.307	−13.562	7.086	10.127	22.632	103.276
2005	486.350	−91.127	54.461	−58.579	17.087	72.727	−11.111	−21.588	22.267	76.724
2006	43.043	39.394	−4.164	−80.093	−11.294	501.628	37.385	84.063	11.475	81.658
2007	−67.431	1076.042	−12.601	54.276	175.078	−31.135	21.884	98.165	77.213	159.046
2008	9.408	−82.110	−58.484	−34.177	−81.703	−85.655	−42.460	−55.159	−78.662	−87.768
2009	−18.413	51.152	174.439	56.398	−10.942	156.974	78.615	175.637	79.848	176.302
2010	−35.828	−30.000	7.708	29.212	−34.944	125.746	34.124	−13.508	1.667	20.581
2011	2.532	−35.034	−11.621	−26.308	−18.719	−60.444	−28.023	−66.316	−67.028	−56.308
Return	44.389	112.703	44.318	34.166	−0.173	72.967	20.496	29.751	26.389	53.303
Variance	25199.632	118547.848	5479.542	9452.718	5033.791	29829.848	1790.154	5821.489	4082.508	7286.309
Risk	158.744	344.308	74.024	97.225	70.949	172.713	42.310	76.299	63.895	85.360

SUGGESTED FURTHER READING FOR EMPIRICAL WORK

1. Maier, M.H. (2002), "A Critical Review of Learning from the Market: Integrating 'The Stock Market Game' across the Curriculum", *The Journal of Economic Education*, Vol. 33, No. 1.

2. French, K.R. (1988), "Crash-Testing the Efficient Market Hypothesis", *NBER Macroeconomics Annual*, Vol. 3.

3. Malkiel, B.G. (1989), "Is the Stock Market Efficient?", Science, *New Series*, Vol. 243, No. 4896.

4. Laffer, A.B., and Ranson, R.D. (1978), "Some Practical Applications of the Efficient-Market Concept", *Financial Management*, Vol. 7, No. 2.

5. Sarkar, N., and Mukhopadhyay, D. (2005), "Testing Predictability and Nonlinear Dependence in the Indian Stock Market", *Emerging Markets Finance & Trade*, Vol. 41, No. 6.

6. Keane, S.M. (1986), "The Efficient Market Hypothesis on Trial", *Financial Analysts Journal*, Vol. 42, No. 2.

7. Vasicek, O.A., and McQuown, J.A. (1972), "The Efficient Market Model", *Financial Analysts Journal*, Vol. 28, No. 5.

8. Dempsey, M.J. (2002), "The Nature of Market Growth, Risk and Return", *Financial Analysts Journal*, Vol. 58, No. 3.

REFERENCES

1. Malkiel G Burton (2003), "The Efficient Market Hypothesis and its crisis", *CEPS working paper no. 91*.

2. Cadsby Bram Charles (1992), "CAPM and the Calendar: Empirical anomalies and the Risk-return relationship", *Management Science*, Vol. 38, no.11, pp.1543-1561.

3. Avramov Doron and Chordia Tarun (2006), "Asset Pricing Models and Financial Market Anomalies", *The Review of Financial Studies*, Vol. 19, no.3 pp. 1001-1040.

4. Lundholm J Russell (1991), "What affects the efficiency of Market? Some answers from the laboratory", *The Accounting Review*, Vol. 66, No.3, pp.486-515.

5. Hadi M Mahdi (2006), "Review of Capital Market Efficiency: Some evidence from Jordanian markets", *International Research Journal of Finance and Economics*, issue 3, pp. 1-15.

6. Sarkar Nityananda and Mukhopadhyay (2005), "Testing Predictability and Non-linear Dependence in the Indian Stock Market", *Emerging Markets Finance and Trade*, Vol. 41, No. 6. pp. 7-44.

7. Ajayi A Richard, Mehdian Seyed and Perry J Mark (2004), "The day-of the week effect in Stock Returns: Further Evidence from Eastern European Emerging Markets", Vol. 40, No.4, pp. 53-62.

8. Ferson E. Wayne, Heuson Andrea and Su Tie (2005), "Weak –Form and Semi-Strong Form Return Predictability Revisited", *Management Science*, Vol. 51, No.10, pp. 1582-1592.

9. Ziemba T.W. and Hensel R. C. (1994), "Worldwide Security Market Anomalies", *Philosophical Transactions: Physical Sciences and Engineering*, Vol.347, No.1684, pp.495-509.

10. Zhang Frank X. (2006), "Information Uncertainty and Stock Returns", *The Journal of Finance*, Vol.61, No.1, pp.105-137.

11. Malkiel G. Burton (1989), "Is the Stock Market Efficient?", *Science, New Series*, Vol.243, No. 4896, pp. 1313-1318.

12. http://en.wikipedia.org/wiki/Efficient-market_hypothesis

13. http://www.investopedia.com/terms/m/marketefficiency.asp

14. http://www.investopedia.com/terms/e/efficientmarkethypothesis.asp

15. http://www.investorwords.com/1672/Efficient_Market_Theory.html

PART 4
FIXED INCOME SECURITIES

12
BOND ANALYSIS

> **LEARNING OBJECTIVES**
>
> The purpose of this chapter is to enable you to understand:
> - Types of bonds and their characteristics.
> - Innovations in bond market.
> - Pricing of the bonds.
> - Numerous measures of bond returns, such as yield to maturity (YTM), yield to call (YTC), realized compound rate of return.

12.1 INTRODUCTION

In chapter 2 we have had discussions on bonds and various other investment alternatives. Out of those, this chapter concentrates on the alternative of bonds, which are basically fixed income securities.

Bond is analyzed in this chapter as a basic debt security, and families of bond markets are dealt with. Hence this chapter begins with the analysis of debt securities. Debt securities are also called fixed income securities as they promise a fixed stream of income. It is easy to estimate the valuation of such securities, as the stream of income to be received by the bond holder is known well in advance. Also, the risk is at a minimum level, compared to stocks and other securities.

12.2 BASICS OF BONDS

Bonds are the long-term debt securities issued by governments[1], PSUs and private companies; to raise fund from the market. The biggest advantage of the bonds issued by the government is that they do not have any default risk[2]. The bonds issued by the public sector units (PSUs) too are usually secure. The bonds issued by the private sector are known as debentures.

---
[1] Actually, RBI issues on behalf of the government in India.
[2] However, there are evidences of the bond issued by the government, which defaulted during the Second World War.

Holders of the bonds receive periodic payments of interest called coupon payments till maturity. At the time of maturity they receive the last coupon payment along with face value of the bond. The bond indenture specifies the features of the issued bond. The coupon rate, maturity date and par value of the bond are part of the bond indenture, which is a contract between the issuer and the bond holder. After the issuance of the bonds, investors may buy or sell bonds in a secondary market where bond prices move in accordance with market forces of demand and supply.

Bonds[3] are characterized by the following features mainly:

- Face value: It is also called par value. A bond is usually issued at par values of Rs. 100 or Rs. 1000 or Rs. 10,000.
- Coupon rate or interest rate: It is expressed as a percentage of the bond's face value. It has thus a fixed value and is known to the investors, right at beginning when bonds or debentures are issued. Interest paid on bonds (or debentures) enjoys income tax deductions. The cost is levied on the issuer of the interest.
- Maturity date: The maturity date mentioned on the bonds (or debentures) shows the date on which it matures.
- Redemption value: The amount a bond holder (or debenture holder) receives on maturity is called the redemption (or maturity) value.
- The time left for maturity from the date the bond is issued is known as the remaining maturity.
- Market value: The bond (or debenture) may be traded on a stock exchange at a price, which is known as its market value.
- Callable bonds: Callable bonds are those bonds which can be redeemed before maturity. The call dates of such bonds at which they can be redeemed are printed on the certificate issued for the bonds. When the bonds are called—that is, when they are redeemed before maturity—the issuer sets the call price. The call price is usually sum of the face value of the bond and its interest accrued in one year. It is a bond which is redeemed by the issuer before its maturity. Usually premium is paid for such a bond. Hence, callable bonds can be defined as: *the bonds which are called-in, before maturity*! Price of the callable bond is always lower than the price of the straight bond because the call option adds value to an issuer.
- Yield to maturity (YTM): Yield to maturity means the discount rate which is equal to the discounted value of a bond's future cash flows (series of coupon + redemption value), to its current market price. Simply put, it is the yield, the return obtained at a specific rate of interest, at maturity; hence the amount generated only when the bond is held till maturity.
- Yield to call (YTC): Like YTM, it shows the discount rate which equals to the discounted value of future cash flows (series of coupon + call price), to its call price. Thus, YTC is the yield of the callable bond when it is called-in and redeemed, prematurely.

> **Pause for thought:** A bond is a fixed income security. Thus the return that would be received at maturity is known right at the time of purchasing the bond. There are bonds which can be redeemed prematurely, while others do not allow redemption before maturity.

---

[3] Throughout this text we will use the terms: bond and/or debenture interchangeably.

12.3 TYPES OF BONDS

There are different types of bonds available to investors to choose from and these bonds are discussed in detail, in this section.

1. Zero coupon bonds

Zero coupon bonds (ZCBs), also referred to as pure discount bonds, are issued at discount and redeemed at par. The usual face values of such bonds are: Rs. 100, Rs. 1000, Rs. 10, 000, etc. Neither any interest is paid nor any coupon payment made, before maturity. An advantage to the issuer of these bonds is that they do not have to pay any intermediate cash flows before maturity. The Indian government issued such securities in the nineties, but since then it has not.

NABARD issued ZCB on July 18, 2012 at a face value of Rs. 20,000 and at a price of Rs. 11,980; and it would be redeemed on January 1, 2019. So the yield[4] generated by the bond is,

$$20,000 = 11,980/(1 + r)^5$$
$$(1 + r)^5 = 20,000/11,980$$
$$= 1.6694$$
$$1 + r = (1.6694)^{1/5} = 1.1079$$
$$r = 1.1079 - 1 = 0.1079$$
$$= 10.79\%$$

> **Pause for thought:** They are issued at discount and redeemed at par, with no intermediate payments made before maturity.

2. Deep discount bonds

Bonds which are issued at large discount on their face value and mature at par are called deep discount bonds. Like zero coupon bonds, no intermediate payments (including interests) are to be paid by the issuer before redemption, at maturity. These bonds usually have maturity period between 20 to 25 years. At the same time, allows the issuer to exit, if the issuer so wishes, but only after a specified number of years from purchase of the bond.

ICICI bank has issued deep discount bonds in 1997. Ashirwad deep discount bond was issued at the face value of Rs. 2,00,000 and at a discounted price of Rs. 5200. It will be redeemed at the end of the twenty fifth year from the deemed date of allotment on July 15, 2021.

NABARD issued a deep discount bond at the face value of Rs. 9750 for a maturity value of Rs. 20,000 redeemable after 10 years. This bond is traded on the BSE.

> **Pause for thought:** These are issued at large discount on their face value and mature at par; and are similar to zero coupon bonds in some respect. Such bonds are long-termed, but allow the issuer to exit, before maturity, after a specific period.

3. Perpetual bonds

These bonds neither have any maturity date nor a maturity value. Perpetual bonds are also referred to as consoles. Since these have no maturity or terminal value, their value is simply the

---

[4] The calculation part will be discussed in this chapter later on.

discounted value of the infinite stream of interest that accrues. Such bonds were most common during the Second World War.

Tata Steel issued a perpetual bond, which has closed on July 18, 2012. It was issued at a minimum investment size of Rs. 11.42 lakhs.

Power Finance Corporation raised Rs. 2500 crore via perpetual bonds for capital adequacy purposes.

> **Pause for thought:** As the name suggests, these are sort of perpetuating—continuous—bonds, with no predetermined redemption value.

4. Fixed rate bonds

Those bonds whose coupon rates are fixed for the entire term of the bond are called fixed rate bonds. Most government bonds are issued as fixed rate bonds.

Example: 8.24%GS2018 was issued on April 22, 2008 for a tenure of 10 years, maturing on April 22, 2018. Coupon on this security are set and paid half-yearly at 4.12% (half-yearly payment rate being the half of the annual coupon rate of 8.24%), of the face value, on October 22 and April 22 of each year.

> **Pause for thought:** They have a fixed rate for the coupon payments for the entire term of the bond.

5. Floating rate bonds

Floating rate bonds are such securities which do not have a fixed coupon rate. The first coupon payment of such bonds (whether it is yearly or half yearly) is fixed or known in advance because it is derived from the past six months or one year; and the base rate for the past six months or one year is known well in advance. So holder and issuer of such bond can know their first coupon payment but can not predict thereafter. The first coupon rate is determined or set by taking the rate prevalent six months or one year prior. Then spread is added to the base rate. For most of the floating rate bonds issued by the Government of India, the base rate is the weighted average cut-off yield of the last three 364 days T-bills auctions, preceding the coupon reset date. The spread is decided through the auction. In India, floating rate bonds were first issued in September 1995. Issuers of such bonds face an uncertainty as they cannot block or limit their liabilities, when market rates are rising—unlike the fixed rate bonds. Also, if a firm's financial position weakens, the issuer may fall in the debt trap.

They are thus, just the reverse of the fixed rate bonds.

Example: A floating rate bond was issued on July 2, 2002 for a period of 15 years, thus maturing on July 2, 2017. The base rate of the bond for the coupon payments was fixed at 6.50%, which is the weighted average rate of implicit yield on 364-days T-bills during the preceding six auctions. In the auction, a cut-off spread (markup over the benchmark rate) of 34 basis points (0.34%) was decided. Hence, the coupon rate for the first six months was fixed at 6.84%.

> **Pause for thought:** Floating rate bonds are such securities which do not have a fixed coupon rate.

6. *Capital indexed bonds*

The principal of these bonds are linked to an accepted index of inflation with a purpose to protect the holder of the security from inflation[5]. A capital indexed bond, with the principal hedged against inflation, was issued for the first time in December 1997 and matured in the year 2002.

In December 1997, the Reserve Bank of India issued capital indexed bonds at a coupon rate of 6%, which matured in the year 2002.

> **Pause for thought:** Such bonds have their principal hedged against inflation through linking to an accepted index of inflation.

7. *Puttable bonds*

In callable bonds, issuers have the right to extend or buy back the bonds before maturity. Puttable bonds give the same right to bond holders. If the coupon rates on invested bonds are more than the prevailing market rate, bond holders would naturally want to extend the term of the bond. Opposite to it, when the rates are less than the market rates, investors prefer to redeem such bonds before maturity so that they reinvest the redeemed amount, but in some other investment option.

> **Pause for thought:** Puttable bonds allow the bond holders to extend their holdings in such bonds beyond, or sell before, maturity.

8. *Convertible bonds*

Such bonds provide an investor with the option to exchange each bond for a specified number of shares of the issuing company. At the time of issuance itself, the company specifies the conversion rate.

Example: A convertible bond is assumed to be issued at par value of Rs. 1000, convertible into 10 shares of the firm. It is natural to convert the bonds to shares when prices are high. However, such bonds have been found to provide lower coupon rate, with their YTM too lower, compared to non-convertible bonds.

Suzlon Energy, the world's fifth largest wind turbine maker has issued $200 million of zero coupon convertible bonds and another $20.8 million of bonds with 7.5% coupon.

> **Pause for thought:** These bonds are convertible into shares of the issuing company.

9. *Foreign bonds*

These are the bonds issued by one country and are sold in another country. It is akin to export of bonds! The denominations are in the currency of the country in which it is sold. For example, if a Chinese company issues bonds in India, denominated in Indian rupees, it is called foreign bonds.

---

[5] The government is currently working on a fresh issuance of Inflation Indexed Bonds wherein payment of both, the coupon and the principal on the bonds, will be linked to an Inflation Index (Wholesale Price Index, WPI). In the proposed structure, the principal will be indexed and the coupon will be calculated on the indexed principal. In order to provide the holders protection against actual inflation, the final WPI will be used for indexation.

Such bonds are identified by different names depending upon the country in which it is sold. A few examples of such bonds are:

Yankee bonds: US Dollar denominated foreign bonds sold in the USA.

Samurai bonds: Japanese Yen denominated foreign bonds sold in Japan.

Bulldog bonds: British Pound denominated foreign bonds sold in the UK.

Below are the examples of Yankee bonds issued by Indian companies.

Names	Issue year	Maturity year	Amount	Coupon rate
Reliance Ind.	1995	2005	$150 mn	8.15% US$
Reliance Ind.	1997	2027	$214 mn	NA
ICICI Ltd.	1997	2007	$150 mn	7.55% US$
PFC Ltd.	1999	2009	$100 mn	7.5% US$
Telco	1997	NA	$200 mn	Libor BP + 200
Reliance Ind.	1997	2097	$100 mn	NA
Tata Electric Co.	1997	2007	$150 mn	7.875%
Tata Electric Co.	1997	2017	$150 mn	8.5%

Pause for thought: These are so called because they are issued by one country but sold in another, in the currency of the country in which they are sold.

10. *Euro bonds*

Euro bonds are issued in the currency of the home country by the issuer (borrower), but are sold in different countries. Euro Yen bond, is an example of such bonds. It is Yen denominated bonds, issued by Japanese firms, but selling outside Japan. Another such bond is the Euro Sterling bond, which is a Pound denominated bond, selling outside the UK.

Thus, there is a basic difference between foreign bonds and Euro bonds. While the former is sold in the currency of the country in which it is sold and not in the currency of the issuing country, the latter sells in the currency of the issuing country, but outside the issuing country.

Examples of Euro bonds, issued by the Indian companies, are as given below.

Names	Date of issue	Amount	Date of maturity	Coupon rate
IDBI	June-89	$100 mn	June-96	10%
ONGC	Dce-88	$125 mn	Nov-93	9.75%
SBI	June-88	Yen 15 bn	June-93	5.25%
IDBI	March-87	DM 200 mn	Dec-94	6.375%
IDBI	Sep-88	DM 250 mn	Sep-95	6.625%
IDBI	Feb-86	DM 100 mn	Feb-93	7%
ONGC	2/1987	DM 150 mn	Feb-94	6.375%

> **Pause for thought:** Euro bonds are issued in the currency of the issuing country but sold in other countries.

12.3.1 Novel Bonds

Apart from the bond types mentioned in the preceding section there are certain bonds with certain novelties. Hence, they are clubbed together as novel bonds and form the core of discussion in the ensuing section.

1. Inverse floaters

These bonds are like floating rate bonds as their interest rates are not fixed (linked to some benchmark interest rate plus some basis above/below it). But coupon rate on these bonds falls when market interest rates rises; and when market rates falls, coupon rate on such bonds rise.

Royal Bank of Canada has offered the redeemable inverse floating rate bonds on July 30, 2010, which will expire on July 30, 2020. The payment of interest on the bonds are to be made quarterly on January 30, April 30, July 30 and October 30 of each year—commencing on October 30, 2010. It provides quarterly interest payment per annum, during the indicated year of their term, as follows:

Year	Interest rate	Year	Interest rate
1	3.00%	5	7.50% minus 3-Month LIBOR
2	4.50% minus 3-Month LIBOR	6	8.50% minus 3-Month LIBOR
3	5.50% minus 3-Month LIBOR	7-10	9.50% minus 3-Month LIBOR
4	6.50% minus 3-Month LIBOR		

> **Pause for thought:** These bonds are similar to floating rate bonds with no fixed rate of interest. Furthermore, their rates vary inversely with market rates; hence the name.

2. Asset-backed bonds

In asset-backed bonds, the income from a particular asset of a firm is used for coupon payments, in addition to the principal of the bond at maturity. It is like a loan backed by house, vehicles, fixed deposit or any other type of assets. It is obvious that the performance of such bonds is linked to the performance of the particular assets of the issuing company.

Example: Bonds issued by the Walt Disney firm, in which coupon rates were tied to the financial performance of its few specified films. China Development Bank has issued 10.2 billion Yuan ($1.6 billion) of asset-backed securities in 2008. It is backed by 49 loans from 43 borrowers, according to the information available.

> **Pause for thought:** In these bonds income from a particular asset of the issuing firm is used for the coupon payments at maturity, thus rendering the performance of such bonds dependent on the performance of the concerned assets.

3. Catastrophe bonds

These are special type of bonds, issued with specific purpose. It is a high yield debt instrument that is usually insurance-linked and meant to raise money in case of a catastrophe, such as hurricane, earthquake, etc. But it has a special feature—it places a condition that if the issuer (insurance or reinsurance companies) suffers a loss from a particular pre-defined catastrophe, then the issuer's obligation to pay interest and/or repay the principal is either deferred or completely waived.

The purpose is to compensate for the losses incurred during disasters (earth quake, tsunami, hurricane, cyclone etc). To attract the investors, coupon rates that are provided are much higher than those for the other (general) bonds. The level of disaster is determined by total incurred losses. The other criteria used for such assessment are: wind speed, magnitude of earthquake crossing a certain level on the Richter scale, etc. It is one of the effective ways to spread the risk of the issuing company's risk, related to some disaster, to number of participants in a market. However, when some disaster occurs, bond holder's coupon rate and final maturity payments are ceased.

India's Prime Minister, government officials and National Disaster Management Authority (NDMA) have discussed the issuance of catastrophe bonds.

Example: In Japan, the Oriental Land Company issued such bonds to mitigate the risk in earthquake, in 1999.

> **Pause for thought:** These are bonds issued as risk coverage, for uncertainties related to catastrophes—the natural disasters—and have higher coupon rates than general bonds.

12.4 DIFFERENCE BETWEEN A BOND AND A DEBENTURE

Bond means a long-term debt security issued by government—state governments or their undertakings, by development financial institutions, etc. But when the same is issued by some other entities, such as private companies (corporate houses), they are called debentures. The difference between bonds and debentures thus automatically lies in their functionality, registration and the stamp duty, which issuers have to pay. For issuance of debentures, stamp duty is decided by the states and it varies for each state. Debentures are charged with two types of stamp duties: issuance and transfer. An issuer has to pay the issuance stamp duty where (in the particular state) the principal mortgage is registered. Stamp duty on transfer is paid to the states in which the registered office of the company is located. Transfer stamp duties are usually very high. There is no transfer stamp duty on bonds and it is transferred by endorsement and delivery. Bonds are subject to stamp duty as per the Indian Stamp Act, 1899 (Central Act).

> **Pause for thought:** The long-term debt securities issued by the government or its undertakings are called bonds, while the same issued by the corporate is a debenture.

12.5 ACCRUED INTEREST AND QUOTED BOND PRICES

The bond prices which are reported in the financial newspapers or listed in the stock exchanges are not the actual prices that an investor has to pay for trading in a particular bond. The difference arises because the listed price does not include the interest that accrues between coupon payment dates. If a bond is purchased between two coupon payments, the buyer ought to pay the seller for accrued interest, the prorated share of the forthcoming interest payments.

An example will aid in the understanding of the concept, hence follows the same. A coupon rate is assumed to compound semi-annually at 10% and 90 days have passed since the last coupon payment[6]. The quoted price of the bond is Rs. 950. Calculate the invoice price and accrued interest on the bond.

$$\text{Accrued interest} = \frac{\text{Annual coupon payments}}{2} \times \frac{\text{Days elapsed since last coupon payment}}{\text{Days between two coupon payments}}$$

$$= \frac{100}{2} \times \frac{90}{182}$$

$$= \text{Rs. } 24.73$$

Invoice Price = Quoted price + Accrued interest

= Rs. 950 + Rs. 24.73

= Rs. 974.72

In the market, bonds are quoted at face value of Rs. 1000, and not at Rs. 1000 plus accrued interest. This is in practice because if a buyer buys a bond of 10% coupon payment one day before coupon payment, he would receive Rs. 1050 [(Rs. 1000) + (Rs. 100)/2] on the next day. Thus, it means the investor should be willing to pay a total price of Rs. 1050 for the bond.

The above discussion is further exemplified by the corporate bonds, as shown on next page.

> **Pause for thought:** The bond prices which are reported are not the actual prices that an investor has to pay for trading in a particular bond because the listed price does not include the interest that accrues between coupon payment dates.

12.5.1 Bond Values

The total cash flow (coupon payments + maturity value) of the bonds are known. Furthermore, its discount rates can be determined without much difficulty. Hence, it is easy to find out the present value of the bond. The discount rate depends upon the risks of the bond for other than government bonds. Though of course, it is easier to determine the cash flows of the bonds issued by the government as they are free from default risks. As the risk of the government and PSU issued bonds are less, cash flows of such bonds are discounted at lower discount rate, compared to the cash flows of debentures issued by the private sectors. Interest rate fluctuations are the main source of risk in fixed income securities.

> **Pause for thought:** The current value of a bond or debenture is the discounted value of its cash flows.

12.5.2 Bonds with Maturity

All bonds, whether issued by the government or PSUs or the corporate sectors, specify the interest rate and maturity period. The current value of a bond or debenture is the discounted value of its cash flows (coupon payments + maturity value of the bond). As mentioned above, bonds are

---

[6] There are 182 days in the semi-annual period.

314 SECURITY ANALYSIS AND PORTFOLIO MANAGEMENT

Scrip code	Scrip ID	Company name	Market lot	Issue price	Coupon rate (%)	Security type	Interest due Date1	Date2	Date3	Date4	Redemption date	Allotment date	Other details
112118	TISCO37	TISCO Discount	1	5100	-	Bonds	-	-	-	-	As on 01/11/2005, 2006, 2007 at Rs.	-	-
112116	TISCO35	TISCO Reg. Inc.	1	5000	17	Bonds	-	-	-	-	As on 01/11/2003, 2004, 2005, 2006 a	-	-
112188	ICICI87	ICICI - Deep Discount Bonds	1	2750	-	Bonds	-	-	-	-	As on 27/05/2022 at Rs. 100000/-.	5/28/97	Early redemption on 30/04
112189	ICICI88	ICICI - Deep Discount Bonds	1	5750	-	Bonds	-	-	-	-	As on 27/05/2017 at Rs. 100000/-.	5/28/97	Early redemption 30/04
112166	IDBDD66	IDBI Deep Discount Bonds	1	5500	-	Bonds	-	-	-	-	As on 31/01/2022 at Rs. 200000/-.	1/31/97	Early redemption on 30/04

(Source: www.bseindia.com)

discounted by appropriate discount rate; and it is the rate that investors might earn even on other instruments having similar characteristics. By comparing the present value of the bond with its current market value, it can be ascertained whether the bond is over-valued or under-valued. The following example is forwarded so as to enhance the understanding of the content being discussed.

Example: It is assumed that an investor is planning to purchase a five year maturity bond issued by ICICI, with face value of Rs. 5000 and coupon rate of 8% p.a. It is further assumed that the rate of return is 10%, looking at the fundamentals of ICICI (i.e., risk level), and investor's required rate[7] of return from similar type of investment. Now the question that arises is what should be the price of the bond if it matures at par?

In this case, investor will receive 8% p.a. of the face value, Rs. 5000, which is Rs. 400, as an interest rate (coupon rate) plus Rs. 5000, on maturity.

Thus, the present value of the bond is

$$P_0 = \frac{400}{(1.10)^1} + \frac{400}{(1.10)^2} + \frac{400}{(1.10)^3} + \frac{400}{(1.10)^4} + \frac{5400}{(1.10)^5}$$

$$= 4621.4$$

Thus, the current worth of the bond is Rs. 4621.4, if the required rate of return is 10%. Rs. 4621.4 consists of: interest payments of Rs. 1516.4 and maturity value of Rs. 3105 discounted at 10%. The price, Rs. 4621.4, indicates intrinsic value of the bond, implying that investors are ready to pay Rs. 4621.4 or less, to purchase this bond.

From this calculation we can derive the formula to find out value of the bond.

Bond value = Present value of interest + Present value of the maturity amount

$$\text{Bond value} = B_0 = \left[\frac{C_1}{(1+K_d)^1} + \frac{C_2}{(1+K_d)^2} + \ldots + \frac{C_n}{(1+K_d)^n}\right] + \frac{B_n}{(1+K_n)^n} \quad (1)$$

where,

$C_1, C_2, \ldots, C_n$ = interest of the bond.
K_d = cost of debt (here bond) capital, also known as discount rate or required rate of return.
B_n = amount payable, at maturity, of the bond.
n = number of years.
B_0 = price or value of the bond.

Equation (1) can also be written as

$$B_0 = \sum_{n=1}^{n} \frac{C}{(1+K_d)^n} + \frac{B_n}{(1+K_n)^n} \quad (2)$$

Or, $B_0 = C(\text{PVIFA}^8, K_d\%, n \text{ years}) + B_n(\text{PVIF}^9, K_d\%, n \text{ years})$ (3)

---

[7] The terms: required rate of return, discount rate, market interest rate, interest rate and required yield are used interchangeably in this chapter, as have been the terms bonds and debentures.
[8] Present value interest factor annuity.
[9] Present value interest factor

As the interest amount (coupon rate of face value) is known till the maturity of the bond and as also is the par value at maturity, the present value of annuity and present value of a single cash flow[10] concept can be applied to find out the value of the bond.

In the case of fixed coupon payment bonds coupon or interest payment is made at the end of each year for five years (as maturity of the bond is five years). Such a constant series of the coupon payment is named as annuity in finance parlance. And as all these coupon payments are discounted in terms of the present context they are referred to as present value of an annuity. The Table T4, given at the end of the book, be referred to in this context. In the first column years are mentioned. Looking horizontally, along the interest rate column of 10% and in the line of five years, PVIFA value is found to be 3.791. This is known as present value interest factor annuity. This is multiplied with coupon payment amount of Rs. 400 as in this example coupon payment is at the rate of 8%, of the face value Rs. 5000.

Here, face value of Rs. 5000 is received only once—at the end of the maturity. In this case it is at the end of the fifth year. So it is termed as a single cash flow. Since it is received at the end of the fifth year and as an investor we are interested in knowing the worth of 'this' Rs. 5000 in the present context, the present value of Rs. 5000 is to be found out. For this Table T3, given at the end of this book, be referred to. This table is named as PVIF (present value interest factor). In this table, from the row of 5 years and an interest rate of 10%, PVIF value, 0.621, is found out.

In the above equation, the left hand side represents the annuity factor and the right hand side, the present value of a single cash flow. From the above equation it can be observed that Rs. 400 is the annuity for five years and Rs. 5000 is received as a lump sum at the end of the fifth year. By using the present value at interest factor annuity (3.791) and present value of a single cash flow (0.621) from the present value Tables, T3 and T4 respectively, the present value of the bond is

$$= 400(PVIFA, 10\%, 5 \text{ years}) + 5000(PVIF, 10\%, 5 \text{ years})$$
$$= 400(3.791) + 5000(0.621)$$
$$= 1516.4 + 3105$$
$$= 4621.4$$

> **Pause for thought:** The bond value is the sum of the present values of the coupon and at par value, at maturity. At higher interest rates, the present value of the payments decreases and vice-versa.

12.5.3 Bond Values with Semi-Annual Interest

In the above example, coupon payment has been expressed as per annum. However, most of the bonds pay interests semi-annually. For the valuation of such bonds, and for that matter debenture, the coupon rate at the end of every six months has to be considered. Thus, the semi-annual value of the bond can be computed by modifying the above equation, which is for annual coupon payments. The following steps are involved in the calculation of bonds with semi-annual coupon payments:

— The annual interest and discount rate is divided by two to get the semi-annual coupon payment.
— The number of maturity years is doubled to get the number of half-yearly periods.

---

[10] Present value of annuity means series of coupon payment, so for that PVIFA is applied and maturity value is received at the end. Hence it is considered as a single cash flow and for that present value of a single cash flow PVIF is applied.

Thus, by applying these, the formula for semi-annual valuation of the bond is,

$$B_0 = \sum_{n=1}^{n} \frac{C/2}{[1+(K_d/2)]^n} + \frac{B_n}{[1+(K_n/2)]^{2n}} \quad (4)$$

Or, $B_0 = C/2(\text{PVIFA}, K_d/2\%, 2n \text{ years}) + B_n(\text{PVIF}, K_d/2\%, n \text{ years})$ (5)

where,

$K_d/2$ = discount rate for half-yearly coupon payments of the bond.

B_n = maturity amount of the bond.

$2n$ = number of years for half-yearly coupon payments.

B_0 = price or value of the bond.

$C/2$ = semi-annual coupon or interest payments.

The following illustration aids in the understanding of the concept of semi-annual payments.

A Rs. 1000 par value bond, with 10% coupon payment payable semi-annually, matures in five years. What should be the price of the bond, if the required rate of return is 12%?

By applying Equation (5), the value of the bond is,

B_0 = Rs. 5(PVIFA, 6%, 10 years) + Rs. 1000(PVIF, 6%, 10 years)

= Rs. 5(7.360) + Rs. 1000(0.558)

= Rs. 36.8 + Rs. 558

= Rs. 594.8

> **Pause for thought:** For the semi-annual bond values, the coupon rates and required rate of return are halved and the maturity period doubled, with respect to the annual value of the bond.

12.5.4 Value of the Bond with Principal Amortization

Many times a company issues the bond (or debenture) which is amortized every year. Under the circumstances, company does not pay the coupon payment on face value of the bond each year, but the principal declines every year and the interest is paid on the amount outstanding. It must be noted here that payment received on the bond decreases because outstanding balance decreases. However, one benefit investors receive is that compared to other (fixed and floating) types of bonds, every year investors receive comparatively larger amount of sum. As in the initial years large cash flow is received, the present value of such bonds is usually less and so its worth increases.

The following illustration should facilitate the understanding of the valuation of such bonds.

A value research company plans to issue a five year bond of Rs. 1000 at 10% of interest p.a. The required rate of return demanded by the investor is assumed to be 12%.

In such type of bonds the amount of interest decreases every year as the outstanding amount of the bond decreases, due to amortization. The principal amount is equally distributed over five years, i.e., Rs. 200 (Rs. 1000/5) per year. The balance outstanding for the first year is Rs. 1000, and interest is calculated on Rs. 1000. So, interest accrued at the rate of 10% is Rs. 100. The balance outstanding for the second year is Rs. 800 (Rs. 1000 - Rs. 200). Hence, the accrued interest is calculated on the outstanding balance of Rs. 800, which is Rs. 80. In a similar manner, it is calculated for the remaining years too.

∴ The value of the bond is,

$$B_0 = \frac{300}{(1.12)^1} + \frac{280}{(1.12)^2} + \frac{260}{(1.12)^3} + \frac{240}{(1.12)^4} + \frac{220}{(1.12)^5}$$

$= (300 \times 0.893) + (280 \times 0.797) + (260 \times 0.712) + (240 \times 0.636) + (220 \times 0.567)$

$= 267.90 + 223.16 + 185.12 + 152.64 + 124.74$

$= \text{Rs. } 953.56$

The formula for the amortized bond is, $B_0 = \sum_{t=1}^{n} \frac{CF_t}{(1+K_d)^t}$

where,

CF = cash flows of the bond—a sum of the interest and the amortized value of principal.

> **Pause for thought:** Amortization of principal is the situation whereby a company does not pay the coupon payment on face value of the bond each year. But the principal declines every year, and the interest is paid on the amount outstanding. Thus there is a decrease in the interest payable, with each progressing year.

12.5.5 Yield to Maturity (YTM)

It has been already stated that yield to maturity is the net yield obtained at maturity, of the bond.

In the earlier example of ICICI bond, coupon rate, maturity value of the bond and term to maturity, all were known. Thus with an assumed discount rate of 10% the price of the bond was found to be Rs. 4621.4. But, this does not provide any idea of the yearly earnings, by merely considering the present value of yearly coupon payment and maturity value. For that is needed the term, yield to maturity, which is, effectively the rate of return.

A given bond's yield can be calculated when its current price and cash flows (coupon + maturity value) are known. For the purpose of understanding, is considered the example of a bond whose price is Rs. 967.50, coupon rate is 7% p.a. for five years and it is also mentioned that after five year it will be redeemed at par (Rs. 1000).

There are different ways by which YTM can be calculated and here they are discussed one at a time, as follows.

YTM by trial-and-error method

$$947.50 = \frac{70}{(1+YTM)^1} + \frac{70}{(1+YTM)^2} + \frac{70}{(1+YTM)^3} + \frac{70}{(1+YTM)^4} + + \frac{70}{(1+YTM)^5}$$

YTM = 8.34% (as calculated)

Here we have obtained YTM = 8.34% by trial-and-error method by using Equations (2) and (3)

$$B_0 = \sum_{n=1}^{n} \frac{C}{(1+K_d)^n} + \frac{B_n}{(1+K_n)^n}$$

$B_0 = C(PVIFA, r\%, n \text{ years}) + B_n(PVIF, r\%, n \text{ years})$

The obvious query would be how the value of YTM, 8.34%, is arrived at. This is answered by the steps that follow.

It is being assumed that the said cash flows are discounted at the rate of 10%.

$$947.50 = \sum_{n=1}^{n} \frac{70}{(1+K_d)^n} + \frac{1000}{(1+K_n)^n}$$

$= 70(PVIFA 10\%, 5 \text{ years}) + 1000(PVIF 10\%, 5 \text{ years})$

$= 70 (3.791) + 1000 (0.621)$

$= Rs. 265.37 + Rs. 621$

$= Rs. 886.37$

The value on the right hand side, Rs. 886.37, is less than that on the left hand side, which is Rs. 947.50. This implies that the right hand side of the equation should be discounted by lower rate, till both values are equal or closer to each other.

Now by discounting at a rate of 9%, the right hand side comes out to be Rs. 922.3, as follows:

$947.50 = 70(PVIFA, 9\%, 5 \text{ years}) + 1000(PVIF, 9\%, 5 \text{ years})$

$= 70(3.890) + 1000(0.650)$

$= Rs. 272.3 + Rs. 650$

$= Rs. 922.3$

Thus even at the 9% discount rate, it is less than the left hand side value of Rs. 947.50. This means that the discount rate has to be lowered to, say, 8%,

∴ $947.50 = 70(PVIFA, 8\%, 5 \text{ years}) + 1000(PVIF, 8\%, 5 \text{ years})$

$= 70(3.993) + 1000(0.681)$

$= Rs. 279.51 + Rs. 681$

$= Rs. 960.51$

Hence, with the discount rate lowered to 8% the right hand side finally exceeds the left hand side, but not by much. Therefore, by considering two values of the bond, Rs. 922.3 (at 9% rate) and Rs. 960.51 (at 8% rate), it is apparent that price of the bond, Rs. 947.50, lies in between. This implies that the required rate of return, i.e., YTM must be somewhere between these two discount rates.

Here it has been discussed how the price of a bond changes when different discount rates: 8%, 9% and 10% are used. By observing the price of the bond it is thus concluded that higher the discount rate, lower the price of the bond. Using linear interpolation in the range of 8% and 9%, the value of YTM can be ascertained.

The procedure of interpolation entails the following steps:

— The difference between the present values of two rates has to be determined, which is here Rs. 38.21 (Rs. 960.51- Rs. 922.3).
— Next, the difference between the present value corresponding to the lower rate and bond price, i.e., between (in this case) Rs. 960.51 and Rs. 947.5 has to be ascertained. This is Rs. 13.01 in the example considered above.
— This value, obtained in the second step (Rs. 13.01), is divided by that obtained in the first step (Rs. 38.21) and it comes to 0.340 in the present example.
— The value in third step is multiplied by the interval width of 1% (9% - 8%) and it comes out to be 0.34% (0.340 × 1%) in the present context.
— The value obtained in step four is added to the interest rate of lower value, which is 8% in our case. Thus the value of YTM has turned out to be 8.34% (8 + 0.34).

$$\therefore \text{ YTM by trial-and-error method} = 8\% \times \frac{960.51 - 947.5}{960.51 - 922.3} \times (9\% - 8\%)$$

$$= 8.34\%$$

YTM by equation

We can also find out the YTM by the equation method. But this method actually leads to an approximate estimate of YTM. However, it is like a short-cut method to get a quick idea of the return generated by the bond.

$$\text{YTM} = \frac{C + (M - P)/n}{0.4M + 0.6P} \qquad (6)$$

where,

C = coupon rate.
M = maturity value.
P = price of the bond.
n = maturity period.

With the values available,

$$\text{YTM} = \frac{70 + (1000 - 947.5)/5}{(0.4 \times 1000) + (0.6 \times 947.5)}$$

$$= 8.31\%$$

It is thus apparent that the equation method has yielded an approximate value (8.31%), as compared to the trial-and-error method (8.34%), but is a close approximation.

> **Pause for thought:** YTM is the internal rate of return of the bond. There being an inverse relation between the bond prices and the yield, bond prices fall when the market rate increases and vice versa.

12.5.6 YTM and Realized Yield

The ongoing discussion on bonds has made us aware that the YTM of a bond is equal to the rate of return realized for the entire term of the bond, if all coupon payments are reinvested at an interest rate equal to the bond's YTM. The following illustration is presumed to enhance the understanding of the same.

The market price of Rs. 1000 par value bond, carrying a coupon rate of 11% and maturing after five years, is Rs. 1000. Calculate the realized yield to maturity if the reinvestment rate is 12%.

The YTM of this bond, by the equation method is,

$$YTM = \frac{C + (M - P)/n}{0.4 M + 0.6 P}$$

$$= \frac{110 + (1000 - 1000)/5}{(0.4 \times 1000) + (0.6 \times 1000)}$$

$$= \frac{110}{400 + 600}$$

$$= \frac{110}{1000}$$

$$= 11\%$$

If it is assumed that the received coupon payment is reinvested at the same rate of YTM in the market, the resultant value of the realized yield would be as shown below.

The realized yield

$= [110 \times (1.11)^4] + [110 \times (1.11)^3] + [110 \times (1.11)^2] + [110 \times (1.11)^1] + 110 + 1000$

$= Rs. 110 \times 6.228 + 1000$

$= Rs. 685.08 + 1000$

$= 1685.08$

In this calculation the value 6.228 can be obtained by calculation in the calculator only. The other way to find out this value is from Table T2 called future value interest factor annuity (FVIFA). The above is the example of future value annuity. Future value of an annuity is the constant series of the sum which an investor invests at the end of each year for 'n' years. Here, an investor invests constant sum of Rs. 1000 at the end of each year for five years. In this table the first column shows year and remaining row shows interest rate. From the table the value is found to be when interest rate is 11% and the year is fifth.

$$Rs.\ 1000(1 + r^*)^5 = Rs.\ 1685.08$$
$$(1 + r^*)^5 = 1.68508$$
$$(1 + r^*) = (1.68508)^{1/5} = 1.1100$$
$$r^* = 1.1100 - 1 = 0.11 = 11\%$$

where, r^* = realized yield.

This incidentally is equal to the YTM, calculated above by the equation method because reinvestment rate and YTM are the same. The following conclusions can be drawn thus:

— If the interest rate at which coupon payments are reinvested is higher than the YTM, the realized compound return would be more than the YTM.

— Other way round, with the reinvestment rate less than the YTM, realized compound yield will be less than the YTM.

Contradictions to these conclusions too exist, as follows:

— In reality it is difficult to predict the rate at which the coupon payments will be reinvested, since interest rates change over a period of time.

— Due to this reason YTM may not equal the realized compound yield.

— Neither the future interest rates are known nor can they be predicted.

— So, realized compound yield is computed only after the investment period is over.

— Because of this reason a distortion arises in the measurement of realized return.

Pause for thought: YTM of a bond is equal to the rate of return realized for the entire term of the bond, only if all coupon payments are reinvested at an interest rate equal to the bond's YTM.

12.5.7 Horizon Analysis

Forecasting the realized yield is thus not that simple and it forms the basis of horizon analysis.

Forecasting the realized compound yield over various holding periods is called horizon analysis. Thus it is actually the entire range of yields within the horizon of various holding periods. The projected, i.e., forecasted return depends upon two components:

— At what rate reinvestment of the coupon payments are possible.

— At what price the bond is sold in a market once the holding period is over.

Horizon analysis is further elaborated upon, using the following example.

Example: It is suppose that a 20 year bond is purchased, with coupon rate of 8%, compounded annually for Rs. 960. The YTM of this bond is 8.4%. It is assumed that an investor plans to hold this bond for 10 years only. Based upon economic and market data, the forecast for YTM of the bond is 9% when it is up for sale. Also forecasted is the coupon payment of Rs. 80 at the end of each year, to be reinvested at an interest rate of 7% p.a. As the investment horizon is 10 years, the remaining 10 years are left till the expiry of the bond. The sales price of this bond, at the forecasted YTM of 9%, will be Rs. 935.44. The coupon payment which would be received for 10 years and reinvested at a rate of 7% grows to: 80 × (FVIFA[11], 7%, 10 years) = 80 × (13.816) = Rs. 1105.28.

---

[11] Future value interest factor annuity.

Based upon these forecasted YTM and reinvestment rate, the invested Rs. 960 grows to Rs. 2040.72 (Rs. 935.44 + Rs. 1105.28) in 10 years.

In this forecasted rate, annualized compound return turns out to be:

$$P_0(1+r)^{10} = P^{10}$$
$$Rs.\ 960(1+r)^{10} = Rs.\ 2040.72$$
$$r = 1.078 - 1$$
$$r = 7.8\%$$

The above analysis thus leads to two types of risk that investors are exposed to:
— Interest rate risk.
— Reinvestment risk.

However, these risks offset one other. It is because, with a rise in the interest rates bond prices fall, and the value of the portfolio too falls, but coupon payments are reinvested at a higher rate.

> **Check yourself**
> For the above illustration of realized yield, find out the realized yield when reinvestment rate is: (i) 12% and (ii) 8%. Interpret your results.

> **Check yourself**
> Find out the YTM of the bond with coupon rate of 12% p.a., maturity of 5 years, with a selling price of Rs. 1050. Par value of the bond is Rs. 1000. What would be its realized yield if reinvestment rate is: (i) 14% and (ii) 9%.

The discussion on horizon analysis automatically leads us to the YTM for perpetual bonds, given the fact that these bonds do not have a fixed maturity value or period. These are purely open-ended, having continuity, and thus form a horizon of their own. So follows the YTM of perpetual bonds.

YTM of a perpetual bond

YTM of a perpetual bond is calculated as:

$$B_0 = \sum_{n=1}^{n} \frac{C}{(1+K_d)^n} \qquad (7)$$

For perpetual bond whose maturity is of infinite years, the above equation becomes:

$$B_0 = C/K_d \qquad (8)$$
$$\text{Or,}\quad K_d = C/B_0$$

where,

C = coupon rate.
K_d = cost of debt.

For example, if the rate of interest on Rs. 1000 par value bond is 7% and its price is Rs. 950, its YTM would be,

$$K_d = \frac{70}{950} = 7.36\%$$

> **Pause for thought:** Horizon analysis forecasts the entire range of yields within the horizon, comprised of various holding periods.

12.5.8 Bond Prices over Time

From the above discussion we know that bond price would be equal to its par value when coupon rate is equal to the market interest rate. In such cases the investor receives fair compensation, in terms of time-value of money in the form of recurring coupon payments. If the coupon rate is less than the market interest rate, such bonds would sell at less than par value to compensate the bond holder for the lesser coupon payment. Similarly, if the coupon rate is more than the market interest rate, investor's earnings are higher in the form of higher coupon payments. Such bonds are sold at premium, i.e., at a price higher than its par value.

In all three cases mentioned above, the bond holder receives a fair rate of return whether bonds are sold at discount, premium or at par values. In other words, in a perfect competitive market, the price of each bond gets so adjusted that investors end up with fair and competitive rate of return. However, investors may gain in the form of either capital gain or through the income from interest. If over a period of time, securities seem to be not faired priced, investors will immediately look to sell such low return securities. This brings down the price of such securities, till the return becomes at par with other competitive securities. In properly functioning efficient markets, prices continuously adjust till a fair market return is produced. This is shown in figure 12.1 below.

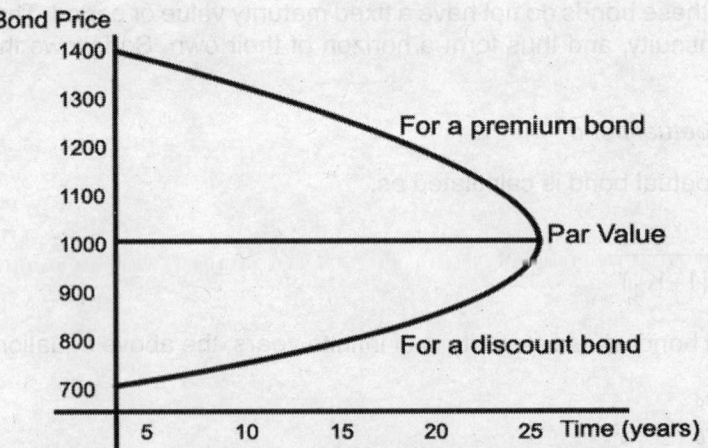

Figure 12.1: Bond prices over a time period

> **Pause for thought:** In a properly functioning efficient market, the prices of bonds continuously adjust till it produces fair market return for each investor.

12.6 YTM VERSUS HOLDING PERIOD RETURN (HPR)

In this section we discuss the YTM with respect to the holding period. It is matter of great interest as to how the YTM varies with the changes that occur during the holding period.

To understand bond prices with built-in capital gain and holding period of 10 years the following example is considered. A bond is assumed to have been issued few years ago when the market rate was 6%. The annual coupon payments for the bond was hence, also set at 6% p.a. With the assumptions that 4 years are left for maturity and the interest rates in a market has increased to 9% p.a., the price of the bond will be:

Rs. 60 (PVIFA, 9%, 4 years) + Rs. 1000 (PVIF, 9%, 4 years) = 60 (3.240) + 1000 (0.708)
= 194.4 + 708 = 902.4

It is apparent that the price of the bond is less than par value when 4 years are left for its maturity.

When three years are left (market rate is assumed to be same at. 9%), the price of the bond will be:

Rs. 60(PVIFA, 9%, 3 years) + Rs. 1000(PVIF, 9%, 3 years) = 60(2.531) + 1000(0.772)
= 151.86 + 772 = 923.86.

Thus, from the above calculation it can be said that the capital gain is Rs. 21.46 (923.86 – 902.4), when the time left to maturity is reduced from 4 years to 3 years. If we compute the return, provided by the bond (if investor purchases the bond at a price of Rs. 902.4 when 4 years are left till maturity and sells at Rs. 923.86 when 3 years are left) for 1 year, by considering coupon rate of 1 year and capital gain/loss of one year, it turns out to be

Rs. 60 + Rs. 21.46 = Rs. 81.46
Rs. 81.46/Rs. 902.4 = 9%

This indicates that the return earned by the investor is equivalent to the market rate prevailing in the market.

It is to be noted that in the above example, the holding period return (9%) and YTM (9%) are equal. The aspect discussed in the above example, is very commonly observed in the bond market. In other words, bonds must offer a rate of return that is equivalent to other comparable securities in a competitive market. Furthermore, when the bond's YTM changed from 6% to 9%, the rate of return on the bond also changed and it became equal to the revised yield (9%).

So when yields fluctuate, bond's rate of return also fluctuates. Since it is not certain as to when and to what extent market rates will change, it is difficult to say what will be the bond's return. As a consequence one cannot predict what will be the bond's holding period return. It has been already discussed above that as the bond's yield rises (falls), price of the bond falls (rises), and because of this holding period return of the bond can be less (more) than the initial yield. The relationship between YTM and holding period return can be better understood once the following example is studied.

The same bond, which was discussed above, having coupon rate of 6% p.a. and par value is Rs. 1000 is considered. The holding period, n = 5 years; and the initial YTM (the market rate) is 6%. Thus, the bond sells at the par value of Rs. 1000. And as YTM and coupon rates are 6%, bond's holding period return is also 6%. The yield is assumed to rise from 6% to 7%, with the price of the bond falling to Rs. 966.22[12] from Rs. 1000. In such a case, the holding period return will be:

$$HPR = \frac{Rs.\ 60 + (Rs.\ 966.22 - Rs.\ 1000)}{Rs.\ 1000} = 2.62\%$$

Thus is apparent the holding period return decreases, when yield rises and the bond prices fall. Converse too is true, as with a fall in the yield the market prices rise, and with it rises the holding period return.

For example, it is assumed that for a given bond, YTM falls from the initial 6% to 5% and hence the price rises to Rs. 1035.76[13].

$$\therefore \quad HPR = \frac{Rs.\ 60 + (Rs.\ 1035.76 - Rs.\ 1000)}{Rs.\ 1000} = 9.576\ \% = 9.58\%$$

Here the HPR is greater than the initial yield.

But then the question arises as to why does it happen so and what is the difference between yield to maturity and holding period return? These questions are adequately answered as follows.

YTM is considered as an average rate of return if the bond is held until it matures. In other words, YTM is the average return of the bond's coupon payment, current price and par value of the bond at maturity—all taken together. Compared to YTM, HPR is the rate of return of investment over a particular time period and depends upon: the coupon rate and difference of purchasing price and market price of the bond, at the end of the holding period. As the market price of the bond at the end of the holding period is not known, often it is forecasted and the HPR depends upon this forecasted value.

> **Pause for thought**: HPR varies inversely with the YTM but shows direct variation with the market rate of return on the bonds.

12.7 ZERO COUPON BONDS

Zero coupon bonds must sell for par values at the time of their maturity. Before maturity, they sell at discount value from par, because the time-value of money and price approaches par value at maturity. If the interest rates remain constant throughout the term of the bond, its price increases at a rate of interest till it reaches the maturity date. This aspect is clarified further through the following example and the calculations therein.

IDBI 2000 coupon bond, with 25 years of maturity, is assumed. The market rate is assumed to be 10%, and it remains constant throughout the period. The price of the bond today would be Rs. $1000/(1.10)^{25}$ = Rs. 1000 (PVIF 10%, 25 years) = Rs. 1000 (0.092) = Rs. 92. In a similar manner, when 24 years and 23 years are left till maturity, the prices are, Rs. 101.52, Rs. 111.68, and thus continue the calculation. Since the par value of the bond is discounted for 1 year hence, its price has increased by the 1-year discount factor.

> **Pause for thought:** Zero coupon bonds must sell for par values at the time of their maturity.

---

[12] 60 (PVIFA 7%, 4 years) + 1000 (PVIF 7%,4 years) = 60 (3.387) + 1000(0.763) = Rs. 966.22
[13] 60 (PVIFA 5%, 4 years) + 1000 (PVIF, 5%, 4 years) = 60 (3.546) + 1000 (0.823) = Rs. 1035.76

12.8 AFTER-TAX RETURNS

We know that the investor can earn return from zero-coupon bonds in the form of price appreciation only and it is considered as an implicit interest income of the bond holder. Even though the bond does not mature during that time period or is not sold, this is built-in price appreciation, considered as a taxable income by the tax authorities. The following example is meant to bring clarity to understanding of the concept.

For the given bond with a maturity of 25 years, it has been shown above that the price of the bond turns out to be Rs. 92. This means at present this bond should be issued at Rs. 92.

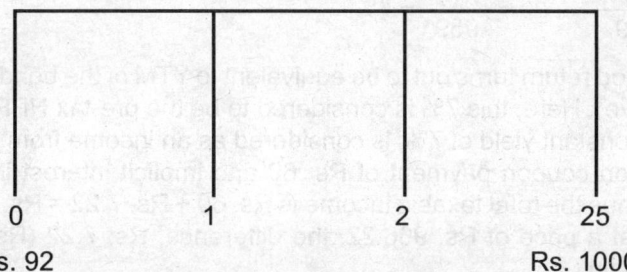

In the following year, if yield remains at 10%, the price of the bond turns out to be, Rs. 1000/$(1.10)^{24}$ = Rs. 101.53. So the implicit gain of this bond in 1 year is, Rs. 101.53 – Rs. 92.3 = Rs. 9.23. This amount, Rs. 9.23, is taxed. It is to be remembered that the implicit interest income, i.e., the built-in price appreciation is calculated on the basis of the assumption that yield of the bond remains constant.

The question that lurks is, what happens if yield of the bond changes? If it is assumed that in the following year (when 24 years are left for the maturity of the bond) yield falls from 10% to 9.5%, price of the bond will be, Rs. $1000/(1.095)^{24}$ = Rs. 113.56. In this case (when market rate falls from 10% to 9.5%), the bond is considered to have earned capital gain and hence is taxed at a rate allocated for capital gain. In case the bond is not sold, the price difference is an unrealized capital gain and is not subject to taxes for that year.

Conversely, if the yield rises from 10% to 10.5% after 1 year, the price of the bond will be Rs. $1000/(1.105)^{24}$ = Rs. 91.055. The difference between the prices at 10% and 10.5% yields, for n = 24 years, is Rs. -10.47 (Rs. 91.055 – Rs. 101.53), considered as a capital loss.

> **Pause for thought:** When the bond incurs a capital gain and it is sold the capital gain is taxed. But if the bond is not sold, the price difference is considered an unrealized capital gain and is not subject to taxes for that year.

12.8.1 Tax Treatment for Coupon Bearing Bonds

To understand how tax is computed for the coupon bearing bonds, the earlier example of bond with coupon rate of 6% p.a. and YTM of 7% is considered. As the YTM is more than coupon rate, this bond sells at a discounted price of:

60(PVIFA, 7%, 5 years) + 1000 (PVIF, 7%, 5 years) = 60(4.100) + 1000(0.713)
= 246 + 713
= Rs. 959.

Thus the bond sells at less than par value of Rs. 1000, because of low coupon rate compared to YTM. If the YTM is assumed to be 7% for remaining period of the bond, the bond would sell at Rs. 966.22 after 1 year.

$$60 \text{ (PVIFA, 7\%, 4 years)} + 1000 \text{ (PVIF, 7\%, 4 years)} = 60(3.387) + 1000(0.763)$$
$$= 203.22 + 763$$
$$= \text{Rs. } 966.22$$

In this case, the HPR for 1 year is,

$$\frac{60 + (966.22 - 959)}{959} = \frac{67.22}{959} = 7\%$$

The holding period return turns out to be equivalent to YTM of the bond (this theory has already been discussed above). Here, this 7% is considered to be the pre-tax HPR. The rise in bond price after 1 year, due to constant yield of 7%, is considered as an income from interest. As a result, the investors are taxed on coupon payment of Rs. 60 and implicit interest income of Rs. 7.22 (Rs. 966.22 – Rs. 959). Thus the total taxable income is Rs. 60 + Rs. 7.22 = Rs. 67.22. In case the bond is sold after 1 year at a price of Rs. 966.22, the difference, Rs. 7.22 (Rs. 966.22 – Rs. 959), is treated as a capital gain.

Conversely, if the YTM rises from 7 to 8% after 1 year (rather than staying constant at 7% as in the above example), the price of the bond turns out to be:

$$60 \text{ (PVIFA 8\%, 4 years)} + 1000 \text{ (PVIF 8\%, 4 years)} = 60(3.312) + 1000 (0.735)$$
$$= 198.72 + 735$$
$$= \text{Rs. } 933.72$$

In this case, the HPR for 1 year is,

$$\frac{\text{Rs. } 60 + (\text{Rs. } 933.72 - \text{Rs. } 959)}{\text{Rs. } 959} = 3.62\%$$

Thus, the HPR is evidenced to have decreased as yield has increased. Moreover, there is a capital loss of Rs. 25.28 (933.72 - 959). Tax would be hence charged on coupon payment of Rs. 60 plus implicit interest income of Rs. 7.22, while no tax will be charged—obviously—on capital loss of Rs. 25.28.

> **Pause for thought:** In case of capital gain, tax is charged while in case of loss it is not. Hence the returns generated correspond accordingly.

12.9 CURRENT YIELD

Current yield is the current rate of return. It is calculated by dividing the annual interest by current price of the bond. The calculation of current yield considers only the coupon rate, but not capital gain or loss. In the previous example, is considered the bond with coupon payment of Rs. 70, with the purchasing price (current investment) of the bond, Rs. 947.5. So, the current yield in this example is,

$$\text{Current yield} = \text{Coupon payment/ Price of the bond} \qquad (9)$$

$$= \frac{Rs.\ 70}{Rs.\ 947.5}$$

$$= 7.39\%$$

Usually bonds are redeemed at par and at the time of bond's maturity, due to capital gain, its overall rate of return is more than the current yield.

Certain variations of YTM that are significant are summarized as follows:

— For premium bonds, coupon rate is greater than the current yield, which in turn is greater than YTM and vice-versa. The reverse holds true for discount bonds too.

— If a bond's YTM is equal to the coupon rate, then the market price of such bonds is equal to its par value.

— If a bond's YTM is greater than its coupon rate, then the market price is less than its par value.

— If a bond's YTM is lower than its coupon rate, then its market price is more than its par value.

> **Pause for thought:** Current yield is the current rate of return. Its calculation involves dividing the annual interest by current price of the bond, with only the coupon rate being considered, and not capital gain or loss.

12.9.1 Yield to Call (YTC)

The callable bonds have been discussed in the segment on types of bonds. So we know that these are the bonds which can be called-in, before maturity. And now we strive to know what would be the yield when the bonds are called-in, that is redeemed prematurely. It so happens that sometimes such bonds, are issued by the companies. The call prices of these bonds are defined with respect to the corresponding call dates, which too are predetermined.

For understanding the yield of such bonds, an example is considered. It is assumed that a company issued bonds with maturity period of 20 years, when market interest rates were high. If interest rates fall after 6 years of issuance of the bonds, still the company cannot take the advantage of paying lower coupon rate (which prevails currently in the market). It is locked for 20 years for higher coupon payment. In such a circumstance, company may like to withdraw such high coupon bearing bonds and instead issue new bonds with lower coupon rates. This kind of situation can be effectively hedged by issuing callable bonds. It is advantageous for the company to issue callable bonds, which allows buying back of high coupon bearing bonds and reinvesting at the lower rate, as the market rate falls. This cost is levied on the bond holders as they have to forgo high coupon rate bonds. To ward off investors from foregoing such attractive coupon rates, issuers issue callable bonds with high coupon rates, with a higher YTM promised than non-callable bonds. The procedure applied for computing YTM is applied for computing YTC as well.

$$B_0 = \sum_{n=1}^{n} \frac{C}{(1+K_d)^n} + \frac{B_c^*}{(1+K_n)^{n^*}} \qquad (10)$$

where,

C = coupon rate of the bond.

K_d = cost of debt (here bond) capital, also known as discount rate or required rate of return.

B_c^* = call price of the bond.

n^* = number of years to the call date.

Suppose, a bond with 9% rate of return, 15 years maturity and face value of Rs. 1000, is callable in 5 years, at a price of Rs. 1060. The current price of the bond is Rs. 940. For this bond, YTC is,

$$940 = \sum_{n=1}^{n} \frac{90}{(1+YTC)^n} + \frac{1060}{(1+YTC)^{10}}$$

Solving the above equation by the trial-and-error method, YTC turns out to be 10.58%.

With the maturity period assumed to be 15 years, for the bond with face value of Rs. 1000, YTM, calculated by the trial-and-error method, is 9.75%.

The distinct features of the callable bonds are summarized as follows:

— Callable bonds are issued by corporate sector with call feature, which allows the company to call or buy back the bond before maturity.

— Refunding means the retirement or premature redemption of earlier high coupon bearing bonds by 'call' provision. This allows issuance of new bonds at a lower rate prevailing in the market.

— Callable bonds come with a provision of call protection, which means there is an initial time period during which these bonds are not callable. Bonds with such features are known as deferred callable bonds.

Pause for thought: Callable bonds are redeemable prematurely and are issued when non-callable bonds have to incur a loss during market fluctuations, bound by their lock-in period equal to the maturity period.

12.10 HOW COUPON RATE, REQUIRED YIELD AND PRICE MOVE TOGETHER?

From our prior discussion we know that there is an inverse relationship between price of the bond and yield. Hence, when the required yield (the required rate of return demanded by the investor) decreases the present value of the stream of cash flows increases and so the price increases too. Conversely, when required rate of return increases, the present value of the stream of cash flows decreases and so decreases price of the bond.

The price-yield relationship is understood with the following example. A 5-year maturity debenture issued by Excel Corporation, bearing a coupon rate of 11% and issued two years ago at Rs. 1000, is considered. The interest rate has decreased in last two years and now the investors are demanding 9% from this. As the maturity of the bond is 5 years, three years are left to maturity. In such a case the price of the bond is

$B_0 = C(PVIFA, K_d\%, n \text{ years}) + B_n(PVIF, K_d\%, n \text{ years})$

$= 110(PVIFA, 9\%, 3 \text{ years}) + 1000(PVIF, 9\%, 3 \text{ years})$

$= 110(2.531) + 1000(0.772)$

$= 278.41 + 772 = 1050.41$

Here, the rise of the bond price to Rs. 1050.41 is logical. Since the required rate of return demanded by the investor has decreased to 9% and if in such a time period the investor buys the bond of another company, the coupon payment on that company's bond would be Rs. 90 instead of Rs. 110, as paid by Excel Corporation. As the present coupon rate is Rs. 110, by holding the bond of Excel Corporation, Rs. 1050.41 (more than Rs. 1000 par value of bond), is being paid, while in case of another bond investor would have to pay a price of Rs. 1000 only as it pays coupon rate of 9% and investor's required rate of return is also 9%.. As all investors behave similarly (as per EMH), the price of the Excel Corporation's bond would be bid up to Rs. 1050.41. However, at this price the return provided by the bond is 9% (the same rate a new bond offers).

The ensuing discussion implies that as an investor we have two choices:

— Either we purchase the excel corporation's debenture, which is providing 11% coupon rate.
— Or we purchase another debenture issued by another company, which offers 9% coupon rate and selling at face value of Rs. 1000.

As interest rate has decreased in the market the required rate of return turns out to be 9% in the market. In this case, the yield or return from the second bond is also 9%, as it offers coupon rate of 9% and is available at face value of Rs. 1000.

$$\text{YTM of second bond} = \frac{C + (M - P)/n}{0.4M + 0.6P}$$

$$= \frac{90 + (1000 - 1000)/3}{(0.4 \times 1000) + (0.6 \times 1000)}$$

$$= 90/1000 = 9\%$$

The YTM of Excel Corporation

$$= \frac{110 + (1000 - 1050.41)/3}{(0.4 \times 1000) + (0.6 \times 1050.41)}$$

$$= \frac{110 - 16.80}{400 + 630.29}$$

$$= \frac{93.2}{1030.24}$$

$$= 9\%$$

In other words, the above calculation and this example indicate that the return or yield of both the investors remain same. In the case of Excel Corporation's debenture the investor has to pay a higher price of Rs. 1050.41 but is compensated by higher coupon rate of 11% p.a.; while in the case of second debenture investor has to pay only Rs. 1000 to acquire it but it offers only 9% coupon rate. The conclusion is that in both the cases investor ends up with same return or yield.

Another situation is considered, when two years from issuance of the bond by Excel Corporation's, interest rate rises in the market. Investors are assumed to demand 12% return from Excel Corporation. In such a case the price of the bond would be:

$$B_0 = 110(\text{PVIFA}, 12\%, 3 \text{ years}) + 1000(\text{PVIF}, 12\%, 3 \text{ years})$$
$$= 110(2.402) + 1000(0.712)$$
$$= 264.22 + 712$$
$$= 976.22$$

As other bonds are offering return of 12%, investors demand the same return from Excel Corporation (as it currently pays 11% of par value). Hence an investor discounts the bond by 12%, as a result of which the price of the bond turns out to be Rs. 976.22. At this price, the return or the yield provided by the bond is 12%.

$$\text{YTM} = \frac{110 + (1000 - 976.22)/3}{(0.4 \times 1000) + (0.6 \times 976.22)}$$
$$= 11.9\% \approx 12\%$$

Thus, it can be concluded that when investor's required rate of return increases (in this case 12%) more than the coupon rate, price of such bond falls. Similarly, when required rate of return is less than the coupon rate, price of such bond rises. In other words, market compensates the loss in terms of lower coupon rate by reducing price of the bond. Similarly, it increases cost by charging higher price when coupon rate is more than required rate of return.

12.10.1 Maturity of the Bond and Interest Rate Risk

As discussed in the segments on bond values and YTM, value of the bond depends upon the market interest rate; thaus changes with a change in the market rate of return. And the nature of the variation is inverse—value of the bond falls, when the required rate[14] rises and vice-versa.

The Table 12.2 below shows value of the perpetual bond to dip when the discount rate rises. For this perpetual bond of Rs. 1000 face value, coupon rate is assumed to be 10%. So, the value of the bond at the discount rate of 12% is,

$$B_0 = \frac{\text{INT}}{K_d} \qquad (11)$$

where,

INT = interest rate of the perpetual bond.

K_d = cost of the debt, i.e., discount rate (in other words, the market rate)

With the given values, the bond value turns out to be:

$$B_0 = \frac{100}{0.12} = \text{Rs. } 833.33$$

---

[14] The terms used in the chapter: required rate of return, market interest rate, discount rate, and interest rate convey the same meaning. It is the rate at which the promised cash flow of the bond is discounted.

The value falls to Rs. 1428.57 from Rs. 1666.67 when discount rate rises from 6% to 7%. Likewise, value of the bond, falls to Rs. 555.56, when the discount rate is 18%. It is apparent that at a discount rate of 10%, the value of the bond is equal to its par value, Rs. 1000.

Table 12.2: Values of the Perpetual Bond at Different Discount Rates

Discount rate (%)	Bond value (Rs.)
6.00	1666.67
7.00	1428.57
8.00	1250.00
9.00	1111.11
10.00	1000.00
11.00	909.09
12.00	833.33
13.00	769.23
14.00	714.29
15.00	666.67
16.00	625.00
17.00	588.24
18.00	555.56

From the figure below the inverse relationship between value of the bond and interest rate can be observed. The figure very clearly shows the value of a bond decreases when interest rate rises from 6 % to 18%.

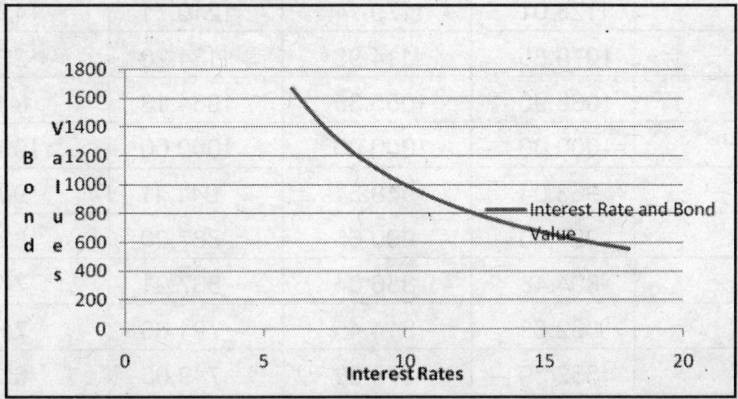

Figure 12.2: Interest rates and bond values

From the figure it can be further concluded that interest rates are always fluctuating. They have a tendency of rising or falling in the market, which exposes the bonds to the market interest rate risk.

> **Pause for thought:** Value of the bond depends upon the market interest rate; thus changes with a change in the market rate of return, with the nature of the change, inverse.

12.10.2 Interest Rate Sensitivity and Maturity of the Bonds

Sensitivity of the price of a bond towards the fluctuation in the interest rate, discussed above, is higher on bonds with longer maturities than bonds with shorter maturities. This is quite natural, given the fact that longer is the maturity period more liable is the bond to risk, as with the length of the duration probabilities of fluctuations too increase.

For the empirical analysis of this concept, the following table is to be referred. It represents the values of the bonds with maturity periods of: 5 years, 8 years, 10 years and that of a perpetual bond at the discount rate ranging from 7% to 18%. It is to be noted that at the discount rate of 10%, values of all four bonds with different maturities is Rs. 1000. It is evident, from the table below, when discount rate rises, the value of the bond with longer maturities falls more rapidly than does that of the bond with shorter maturity. When compared at different discount factors of 11%, 14%, 16%, and 18%, it can be observed that value of the bond falls more severely for bonds with longer maturity periods.

> **Pause for thought:** Assuming all other factors to be constant, the longer the maturity of the bond, greater the sensitivity of the price to fluctuations in interest rates.

Table 12.3: Bond Values at Different Interest Rates and with Different Maturity Periods

Discount rate (%)	Present value of the bonds			Perpetual bond
	Maturity period (in years)			
	5	8	10	
	Price of the bonds (Rs.)			
7	1123.01	1179.14	1210.71	1428.57
8	1079.85	1114.93	1134.20	1250.00
9	1038.90	1055.35	1064.18	1111.11
10	1000.00	1000.00	1000.00	1000.00
11	963.04	948.54	941.11	909.09
12	927.90	900.65	887.00	833.33
13	894.48	856.04	837.21	769.23
14	862.68	814.45	791.36	714.29
15	832.39	775.63	749.06	666.67
16	803.54	739.38	710.01	625.00
17	776.05	705.50	673.90	588.24
18	749.83	673.79	640.47	555.56

In a similar manner, the value of the long-term bond rises more rapidly when discount rate falls from 10% to 9%, 8%, and 7%. It can be noticed that at the discount rates of 7%, 8% and so on, the value of the perpetual bond is higher than the bond with 10 years maturity, which in turn is higher than a bond having a maturity period of 8 years, and thus the trend continues.

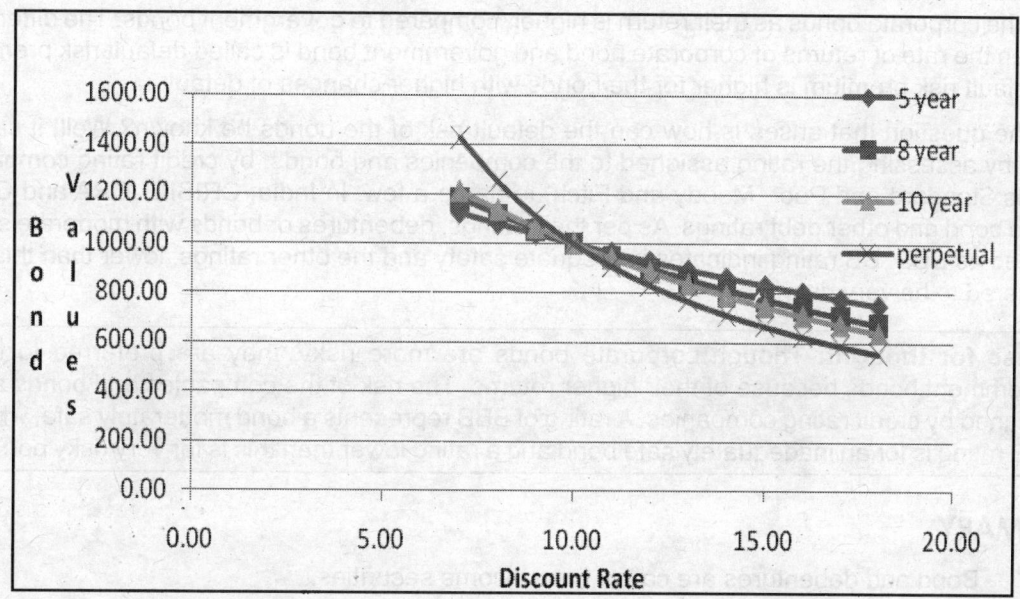

Figure 12.3: Value of the bond at different discount rates

The above Figure 12.3 is the pictorial representation of the table that precedes. From both, Table 12.3 and Figure 12.3, it can be interpreted that two bonds with the same ranking, in terms of default risk, have different sensitivity to interest rate risk, if their maturity period differs. The reason behind this different sensitivity is that in case of a bond with longer maturity, say 10 years or 8 years, investors are going to receive a specified coupon rate, even if the market interest rate changes. Contrary to this, in case of bonds with shorter maturity, investors can sell the bonds at the end of maturity and can reinvest the money at the prevailing (higher) interest rate in the market.

> **Pause for thought:** Susceptibility of the bond values, to the market interest risk, increases with increase in the length of the maturity period of the bond.

12.11 DEFAULT RISK AND CREDIT RATING

We know that bonds are issued by various agencies. Some of them are: central and state governments, government bodies, public and private sector companies and financial institutions. However, as already mentioned above, there is a difference in the bonds issued by public and private sector entities. Usually, investments are considered safe when in government or government–backed securities, as we presume that government will not default.

Contrary to this, investments in private sector are deemed extremely risky, as companies are not free from default risk. This makes them liable to incur financial crisis, even to the extent of bankruptcy. In such circumstances, bond holders may not get the promised payments from companies. This uncertainty is what is termed the default risk.

To avoid such risk, investors may prefer to park their funds only in government securities and not in corporate bonds. But if they do invest in corporate bonds, they should be made aware of the potential risk involved in the investment. Paradoxically, despite the greater element of risk, investors prefer the corporate bonds as their return is higher, compared to government bonds. The difference between the rate of returns of corporate bond and government bond is called default risk premium. The default risk premium is higher for the bonds with higher chances of default.

The question that arises is how can the default risk of the bonds be known? Well, it can be known by assessing the rating assigned to the companies and bonds, by credit rating companies such as Standard and Poor, Moody and Fitch, to name a few. In India, CRISIL, ICRA and CARE provide bond and other debt ratings. As per their ratings, debentures or bonds with moderate safety are rated as BBB. BB rating indicates inadequate safety and the other ratings, lower than this, are considered to be very risky.

> **Pause for thought:** Though corporate bonds are more risky, they are preferred to the government bonds because of their higher returns. The risk of the companies and bonds are assigned by credit rating companies. A rating of BBB represents a bond moderately safe, while a BB rating is for an inadequately safe bond and a rating lower than this is for very risky bonds.

SUMMARY

- ✓ Bond and debentures are called fixed income securities.
- ✓ In the case of bonds or debentures the stream of cash flows consists of annual interest payments and repayment of principal. As these cash flows are fixed and thus known in advance, the value of the bond or debenture is calculated by discounting at a rate of return.
- ✓ The present value of a bond is equal to the discounted value of stream of cash flows. The discount rate at which stream of the cash flows of the bond are discounted is the rate of return that investors expect from the securities of comparable risk.
- ✓ YTM is the internal rate of return of the bond.
- ✓ If the bond's price and series of the cash flows are given, its YTM is calculated by equating the present value of stream of cash flows with its price.
- ✓ Zero coupon bonds are issued at discounted price and so are also called deep discount bonds.
- ✓ Callable bonds promise higher YTM to compensate the investors for the loss from premature redemption.
- ✓ Puttable bonds provide the option to terminate prematurely, or extend the maturity, of the bond.
- ✓ Floating rate bonds pay a coupon rate at a fixed premium, over some reference rate.

BOND ANALYSIS

KEY CONCEPTS

Bonds	Zero Coupon Bonds	Yield To Maturity
Debenture	Floating Rate Bonds	Yield To Call
Par Value	Discount Rate	Current Yield
Face Value	Default Risk	Coupon Rate

REVIEW QUESTIONS

1. What are the characteristic features of a bond? What is the difference between bonds and debentures?
2. Explain the valuation of:
   (a) Bonds with fixed maturity.
   (b) Perpetual bonds.
3. How does the interest rate risk affect the value of the bond? Explain with example.
4. Why do bond prices go down when interest rates go up?

ILLUSTRATIONS

Q.1. Omega Company is planning to sell 12 year debentures of Rs. 10,000 each. The company is issuing this bond with the amortization of equal amount for each year. The interest rate is 8% p.a. If the investor's required rate of return is 9%, what is the bond's present value?

Ans: As the company is amortizing the debenture equally every year, the investor will receive a cash flow of Rs. 1000 in addition to coupon payments at the rate of 8% p.a., on the outstanding balance. The present value of the debenture is:

Year 1	Coupon payment 2	Amortized amount 3	Coupon + Amortized amount 4 (2 + 3)	PV factor, 9% 5	Present value 6 (4 × 5)
1	800.00	1000	1800.00	0.92	1651.38
2	736.00	1000	1736.00	0.84	1461.16
3	677.12	1000	1677.12	0.71	1188.11
4	622.95	1000	1622.95	0.65	1054.92
5	573.11	1000	1573.11	0.60	937.58
6	527.27	1000	1527.27	0.55	835.41
7	485.08	1000	1485.08	0.50	745.51
8	446.28	1000	1446.28	0.46	665.29
9	410.58	1000	1410.58	0.42	595.26
10	377.73	1000	1377.73	0.39	534.56
11	347.51	1000	1347.51	0.36	479.71
12	319.71	1000	1319.71	0.33	430.23
					10579.12

Rs. 10579.12 is the present value of the debenture.

Q.2. Consider two bonds of maturity periods 7 and 15 years. Each has a face value of Rs. 1000 and 9% coupon rates, with both selling at par. Assume that the yield of both the bonds falls to 7%. Find out the change in the bond prices due to the change in yield.

Ans: For the bond with maturity period of 7 years,

$$\text{Price} = (90/1.07) + [90/(1.07)^2] + [90/(1.07)^3] + [90/(1.07)^4]$$
$$+ [90/(1.07)^5] + [90/(1.07)^6] + [1090/(1.07)^7]$$
$$= 1107.7859$$

For the bond with maturity period of 15 years:

$$\text{Price} = (90/1.07) + [90/(1.07)^2] + [90/(1.07)^3] + [90/(1.07)^4] + [90/(1.07)^5] + [90/(1.07)^6]$$
$$+ [90/(1.07)^7] + [90/(1.07)^8] + [90/(1.07)^9] + [90/(1.07)^{10}] + [90/(1.07)^{11}]$$
$$+ [90/(1.07)^{12}] + [90/(1.07)^{13}] + [90/(1.07)^{14}] + [1090/(1.07)^{15}]$$
$$= 1182.1583$$

Q.3. There are three bonds, each with a face value of Rs. 1000. YTM is 9% and terms to maturity are 5, 12 and 18 years. Calculate the price of each bond. Plot a graph of the bond's discount versus their terms to maturity. Is the relationship linear?

Ans: For the bond with maturity period of 18 years:

$$\text{Price} = (100/1.09) + [100/(1.09)^2] + [100/(1.09)^3] + [100/(1.09)^4] + [100/(1.09)^5]$$
$$+ [100/(1.09)^6] \ldots \ldots [100/(1.09)^{17}] + [1100/(1.09)^{18}]$$
$$= 1087.556$$

For the bond with maturity period of 12 years:

$$\text{Price} = (100/1.09) + [100/(1.09)^2] + [100/(1.09)^3] + [100/(1.09)^4]$$
$$+ [100/(1.09)^5] \ldots \ldots + [100/(1.09)^{11}] + [1100/(1.09)^{12}]$$
$$= 1071.607$$

For the bond with maturity period of 5 years,

$$\text{Price} = (100/1.09) + [100/(1.09)^2] + [100/(1.09)^3] + [100/(1.09)^4] + [1100/1.09)^5]$$
$$= 1038.897$$

Q.4. Face values of both the bonds, A and B, are Rs. 10,000. They have 10% coupon rates and sell with YTM of 11%. Life of bond A is 15 years and that of B is 4 years. Calculate the price of the two bonds. Despite having same yields, why do their prices differ?

Ans: Price of bond A

$$= (1000/1.11) + [1000/(1.11)^2] + [1000/(1.11)^3] + [1000/(1.11)^4] + (1000/(1.11)^5]$$
$$+ [1000/(1.11)^6] + \ldots \ldots + [1000/(1.11)^{14}] + [1000/(1.11)^{15}]$$
$$= 9280.913$$

Price of bond B

$$= (1000/1.11) + [1000/(1.11)^2] + [1000/(1.11)^3] + ([1000/(1.11)^4]$$
$$= 9689.755$$

Q.5. Rs. 10,000 face value bond with a ten year term to maturity and 7% coupon rate currently sells so as to produce an 8% YTM. What is the bond's price? Calculate the bond's price, if its yield rises to 10% and 11% and falls to 6% and 7%?

Ans: When YTM is 8%:

Price = $(700/1.08) + [700/(1.08)^2] + [700/(1.08)^3] + [700/(1.08)^4]$
$+ \ldots\ldots\ldots + [700/(1.08)^9] + [10700/(1.08)^{10}]$

= 9328.992

When YTM is 10%:

Price = $(700/1.10) + [700/(1.10)^2] + [700/(1.10)^3 + [700/(1.10)^4]$
$+ \ldots\ldots + \ldots[700/(1.10)^9] + [10700/(1.10)^{10}]$

= 8156.63

When YTM is 11%:

Price = $(700/1.11) + [700/(1.11)^2] + [700/(1.11)^3] + [700/(1.11)^4]$
$+ \ldots\ldots + [700/(1.11)^9] + [10700/(1.11)^{10}]$

= 7644.307

When YTM is 6%:

Price = $(700/1.06) + [700/(1.06)^2] + [700/(1.06)^3] + [700/(1.06)^4]$
$+ \ldots\ldots + [700/(1.06)^9] + [10700/(1.06)^{10}]$

= 1 0736.01

When YTM is 7%:

Price = $(700/1.07) + [700/(1.07)^2] + [700/(1.07)^3] + [700/(1.07)^4]$
$+ \ldots\ldots + [700/(1.07)^9] + [10700/(1.07)^{10}]$

= 10000

Q.6. Rs. 1000 par value bond bears a coupon rate of 11% and matures after five years. Interest rate is payable annually and is available at the price of Rs. 975. What is the value of the bond if the required rate of return is 14%?

Ans: The YTM of this bond by the equation method is:

$$YTM = \frac{C + (M - P)/n}{0.4 M + 0.6 P}$$

$$= \frac{110 + (1000 - 975)/5}{(0.4 \times 1000) + (0.6 \times 975)}$$

$$= \frac{110 + 5}{400 + 585}$$

$$= \frac{115}{985}$$

= 11.67 % ≈ 12%

If it is assumed here that the received coupon payment is reinvested at the same rate of YTM in the market, the resultant value is the realized yield, calculated as:

The realized yield to maturity is

$= [110 \times (1.12)^4] + [110 \times (1.12)^3] + [110 \times (1.12)^2] + [110 \times (1.12)^1] + 110 + 1000$

= Rs. 1698.83

Rs. $1020(1 + r^*)^5$ = Rs. 1698.83

$(1 + r^*)^5 = 1.6655$

$r^* = (1.6655)^{1/5} - 1$

= 10.74%

PROBLEMS

Q.1. Rs. 1000 par value bond bears a coupon rate of 12% and matures after 5 years. Interest rate is payable semi-annually. What is the value of the bond, if the required rate of return is 14%?

Q.2. You have the following investment options, in the form of bonds with different parameters. Par value of all the bonds is Rs. 1000. Assume the income tax rate to be 20% and capital gain tax rate of 5%. Calculate pre-tax and post-tax yield to maturity of these bonds.

Bond	Coupon rate (%)	Maturity (in years)	Price (Rs.)
X	7	8	970
Y	8	6	990
Z	6	10	990

(**Hint:** Capital gain tax rate of 5% is paid at the time of maturity and it is paid on the difference between the purchase price and par value.)

Q.3. Ms Ramya Jagannathan holds 12% bonds of IDBI Ltd. The interest is payable quarterly. The current market price of the bond is Rs. 925 and its redemption value is Rs. 1000. What is the YTM of the bond?

Q.4. Find out the market value of the following bonds, which pay the interests annually.

Bond	Coupon rate (%)	Required rate of return (%)	Maturity period (in years)
P	7	12	12
Q	8	11	10
R	9	10	8
S	10	10	6
T	11	10	5

Q.5. A bond with 10 years maturity, 9% rate of return and face value of Rs. 1000 pays interest annually. It is callable in 8 years at a call price of Rs. 1100. What is the current YTM of this bond? Calculate YTC.

Q.6. There are four bonds: A, B, C and D. All have a face value of Rs. 1000. Bond A and B have coupon rates of 10% and 9% p.a., respectively; and maturity of both the bonds is 8 years. Bond C and D have coupon rates of 8% p.a. and 9% p.a., respectively and pay interests semi-annually. The maturity of bond C and D is 7 years. Calculate the price of all four bonds, if the required rate of return is 11%.

Q.7. A Rs. 1000 par value bond bears a coupon rate of 8%, payable semi-annually. Maturity of the bond is 5 years. What is the value of the bond, if the required rate of return is 10%, compounded semiannually?

Q.8. The market price of a Rs. 100 par value bond, carrying a coupon rate of 12% and maturing after 5 years, is Rs. 970. What is the YTM of this bond? What is the approximate YTM by the equation method? Calculate the realized YTM, if the reinvestment rate is 13%.

Q.9. A perpetual bond of Rs. 1000 is available at Rs. 970. The coupon rate of interest is 12% and relevant discount rate is 13%. Calculate the value of the bond. Should it be bought? What is its YTM?

Q.10. A Rs. 1000 par value bond, with the coupon rate of 9% p.a., will mature after 5 years. If the discount rate is 12%, what is the value of this bond?

Q.11. The market price of a Rs. 1000 par value bond, carrying a coupon rate of 12% and maturing after 5 years, is Rs. 1020. What is the YTM of this bond? What is the approximate YTM by the equation method? Calculate the realized YTM, if the reinvestment rate is 12%.

APPENDIX

Day count conventions used in calculating bond yield

Day count convention method is used to arrive at the holding period of a bond to calculate the accrued interest. For uniformity, all participants in the market should use the same method, as different day count convention method results in different amount of accrued interest and hence anomalous results. In Indian market, conventions used are as follows:

Bond market: The day count convention used in the bond market is 30/360. It means irrespective of actual number of days in a month, number of days in a month is taken as 30 and the number of days in a year, 360.

Money market: The day count convention method used in the money market is actual/365. That means actual number of days of the given month are taken as numerator while number of days in a year are taken as 365 days. As Treasury Bills is a money market instrument, it uses money market convention method.

Yield of T-bills

Yield of the treasury bills is calculated by the following formula:

Yield = (100 - P/P) × (365/D) × 100

where,

P = purchase price.

D = days to maturity.

ILLUSTRATION

Q.1. Assume the price of a 91 day T-bill, at issue, is Rs. 96.40. Find out the yield on this T-bill? If after 39 days T-bill is traded at a price of Rs. 98.10, what will be its yield?

Ans: Yield = (100 - 96.40/ 96.40) × (365/91) × 100 = 14.97 %

After 39 days, the price turns out to be Rs. 98.10.

∴ The remaining maturity = 91-39 = 52 days.

Yield = (100 - 98.10/98/10) × (365/52) × 100 = 13.59%

REFERENCES

1. http://www.waifem-cbp.org/v2/dloads/BOND%20YIELDS-DURATION.pdf
2. https://www.his.se/PageFiles/17648/riskmanagementwithduration.pdf
3. http://www.investopedia.com/university/advancedbond/advancedbond5.asp#axzz2E4qQ3tva
4. http://www.finpipe.com/duration.htm
5. http://www.scribd.com/doc/50978862/BOND-VALUATION-THEOREMS
6. http://www.investopedia.com/university/advancedbond/advancedbond2.asp#axzz2E4qQ3tva
7. http://www.investopedia.com/university/advancedbond/advancedbond3.asp#axzz2E4qQ3tva
8. http://www.investopedia.com/university/advancedbond/advancedbond6.asp#axzz2E4qQ3tva
9. http://www.investopedia.com/university/advancedbond/advancedbond1.asp#axzz2E4qQ3tva

13
THE TERM STRUCTURE OF INTEREST RATES

> **LEARNING OBJECTIVES**
> The purpose of this chapter is to enable you to understand:
> - Yield to maturity in detail.
> - What is spot rate?
> - The concepts of forward rates and future spot rates.
> - The intricacies of term structure theories.
> - Types of yield curves.

13.1 INTRODUCTION

In the previous chapter we dealt in detail with the various types of bonds and their characteristic utilities. We are concerned basically with the yield they provide at maturity. And also what happens if we have to, or we wish to under a given market condition, to redeem it before maturity. On these aspects too we have been discussing in the preceding chapters.

In this chapter we shall be devoting our attention especially to the fixed income securities and thus we will be concentrating on the yield obtainable at maturity. We will learn about the valuation of fixed income securities, which are risk-free, at least in terms of nominal payments. The only securities to fit in this category are those issued by the government or RBI on behalf of government. It is true that treasury bills are such securities where we assume default risk to be almost zero, as government can print money whenever it requires to. However, such securities may not protect the investor against the inevitable risk in the wake of inflation. During inflation the purchasing power of holders could deteriorate and thus the security cannot be considered fully secure, free from risk(s), in real terms. Yet, for the sake of simplifying, we assume that there are fixed income securities whose nominal and real rates are certain, and thus fixed.

13.2 YIELD TO MATURITY (YTM)

Yield to maturity is one of the methods for calculating interest rates. For the purpose of understanding we consider the example of three fixed income, risk-free securities, namely: X, Y,

Z and T. The following interest rates for one year zero coupon bonds have been quoted for them, at the end of each year, for four years in succession.

YTM is the measure of a bond's rate of return that considers both the income and capital gain or loss.

Table 13.1: Zero Coupon Bonds

Bond	Year	Interest rate
X	1	6%
Y	2	7%
Z	3	8%
T	4	8.8%

A face value of Rs. 1000 is assumed for all three bonds, mentioned above.

Similar is the case for coupon bearing bonds, U and V, as mentioned in the table below.

Table 13.2: Coupon Bearing Bonds

Bond	Year	Coupon	Interest rate
U	2	4%	6.7%
V	3	6%	7.12%

As we know that face value is Rs. 1000, the yield, from one year zero coupon bonds, is calculated as:

$$P = \frac{FV}{(1 + r_x)} \tag{1}$$

where,

P = price.

FV = face value.

$$P = \frac{Rs.\ 1000}{(1 + r_x)}$$

where r_x = annual compound rate of interest for bond X

As r_x is 6%.

$$P = \frac{Rs.\ 1000}{(1.06)^1}$$

= Rs. 943.39

Similarly, we can calculate the price of the bond, Y, to be quoted today, as we know the interest rates prevailing for the next two years are 6% and 7%.

For bond Y, the maturity period is two years.

$$\therefore P = \frac{Rs.\ 1000}{(1.07)^2}$$

$$= Rs.\ 873.43$$

From the above calculations we can say that the maturity and price of all three zero coupon bonds are as follows:

(i) X matures in one year and is now available at the price of Rs. 943.39.
(ii) Y will mature in two years and is now traded at the price of Rs. 873.43.
(iii) The current market price of bond Z is Rs. 793.83.

The coupon bearing bond, U, has 4% p.a. rate of interest. It will mature after two years and its current market price is Rs. 950. These bonds—all three of them—will be redeemed at par and investor will receive Rs. 1000 on maturity, on each of these three investments. Yield to maturity has a single interest rate. The interest rate compounds after a specific time period, taking into consideration income from both, interests as well as capital gain/loss. This is exemplified by the following calculation with bond X. As bond X is priced at Rs. 943.39, with maturity of one year and par value of Rs. 1000, YTM of this bond can be expressed and calculated as:

$$(1 + r_x) \times Rs.\ 943.39 = Rs.\ 1000$$

where, r_x = annual compound rate.

$$Rs.\ 943.39 = \frac{Rs.\ 1000}{(1 + r_x)}$$

r_x turns out to be 6%.

In a similar way, it turns out to be 7% and 8% for the bonds Y and Z.

Bond U is a two year coupon bond, with coupon rate of 4% p.a.

$$P_2 = \frac{C_1}{(1+r_z)^1} + \frac{M_2}{(1+r_z)^2} \qquad (2)$$

where,

C_1 = coupon payment for the first year.
M_2 = maturity value at the completion of the second year.
r_z = the annual compounded rate.

$$P_2 = \frac{40}{(1.067)^1} + \frac{1040}{(1.067)^2}$$

$$= Rs.\ 950$$

When the current value of a bond is known, we can find out the rate of interest. For coupon bearing bond U, we can apply the trial-and-error method. To do so, we can start at any hypothetical rate, 10%, then increase (decrease) the rate, if value on the left hand side is more (less) than value on the right hand side (here it is Rs. 950). Then by interpolation method or by using equation method (as discussed in earlier chapters), r_z is calculated and turns out to be 6.7%.

YTM is one of the simplest methods to calculate yield generated by the bond. It can also be used to compare yields of the different investment options; thus aids in subsequent investment decisions.

> **Pause for thought:** YTM is the net return received by the holder at the maturity of the security.

13.2.1 Spot Rates

We calculate the spot rate by measuring yield to maturity on one year zero coupon bonds and extend it to the coupon bearing bonds having a maturity period of more than one year. Spot rates also refer to interest rate associated with spot contract—it is the rate for an immediate transaction.

Referring to the earlier example of the zero coupon bonds, X and Y, their one year and two year spot rates were 6% and 7% respectively. In a similar manner, we can find out the spot rates for 3, 4 and thus for n years.

The equation used for the calculation is,

$$P_n = \frac{M_n}{(1 + S_n)^1} \tag{3}$$

where,

P_n = the present market price of zero coupon bond which matures in n years.
M_n = maturity value in the nth year.
S_n = the spot rate of nth year.
n = an integer, 1, 2, 3 ...

So, for bond X,

$$\text{Rs. } 943.39 = \frac{\text{Rs. } 1000}{(1 + r_x)}$$

Hence, spot rates can be determined for a zero coupon bond with maturity of 2 years, 3 years and so on, similarly. This can also be expanded for a coupon bearing bonds with maturity period of n years. In case of such a coupon bearing bond, spot rates can be calculated by,

$$P_2 = \frac{C_1}{(1 + S_1)^1} + \frac{M_2}{(1 + S_2)^2} \tag{4}$$

where,

C_1 = the coupon payment in the first year.
M_2 = the maturity value at the end of two years.
S_1 = the spot rate in the fist year.
S_2 = the spot rate in the second year.

The Term Structure of Interest Rates

To apply this concept to the coupon bearing bonds, we consider bond U by using the spot rate of bond X, which is 6%. As it is thus known that the one year spot rate is 6%, putting the values from Equation (2), in the above equation, we get,

$$\text{Rs. } 950 = \frac{40}{(1.06)^1} + \frac{1040}{(1+S_2)^2}$$

On calculation, S_2 is found to be 7%—same as earlier value of S_2, calculated for the zero coupon bond, Y. Thus, the spot rate for the second year is the same irrespective of its method (whether it is calculated directly from a two year zero coupon bond or two year coupon bearing bond). Sometimes there could be a marginal difference in spot rates calculated by these two methods.

> **Pause for thought:** Spot rates are 'on the spot' rates, applicable to the immediate, on the spot transactions.

13.2.2 Discount Factors

The reciprocal of spot rate,

$$d_n = \frac{1}{(1+S_n)^n} \tag{5}$$

where,

n = number of years, 1, 2, 3...n.

d_n = the discount factor.

S_n = the spot rate.

From Equation (5), the discount factor for the one year zero coupon bond, X, is 0.9433 ($1/1.06)^1$). Similarly, for a two year zero coupon bond, it turns to be $1/(1.07)^2$ = 0.873. Thus it can be applied to zero coupon bonds for 'n' years. These set of factors (reciprocal values) are sometimes referred to as the market discount function. In other words, market has determined the present value of Re. 1 as, $1/1.06 = 0.943$, to be paid in future, at the discount rate of 6% p.a. Or it could be interpreted as: today's Rs. 0.943 is tomorrow's Re.1! Similarly, as the two year spot rate is 7%, the present value of Re. 1, to be received (paid) after two years is, $1/(1.07)^2$ = 0.873. Once we have found out the discount function, the present value of any security can be determined by multiplying it with either C or M. Thus, by multiplying d_n with C_n we are converting the future value into its equivalent present value. So, $P_n = C_n d_n$.

This can be further extended to coupon bearing bonds as well. We assume that there is a two year coupon bearing bond with a coupon rate of 8% p.a. and maturity value of Rs. 1000. By applying the 1 year and 2 year discount factors, we can find out the price of the bonds to be:

$(80 \times 0.943) + (1080 \times 0.873) = 75.46 + 942.84 = 1018.3$.

This can be applied to any coupon bearing bonds with 'n' years of maturity.

Pause for thought: Discount function is the inverse of spot rate of a coupon. When the present value factor is multiplied with it, the future value of the bond is converted to its present equivalent.

13.2.3 Forward Rates

We have already seen how we arrived at the one year spot rate, of 6%, using the one year zero coupon bond, X, and 7%, with the two year zero coupon bond.

This can also be found out by a two step procedure. In this method, we have to discount Re. 1 two times, i.e., first time for the first year and second time for the second. This can be found out by applying equation, Re. $1/(1 + f_{12})$

$$\frac{\text{Re. } 1/(1 + f_{12})}{(1.06)} \tag{6}$$

Whichever route we opt for, the answer is

$$\frac{\text{Re. } 1/(1 + f_{12})}{1.06} = 0.8733$$

By solving the above equation,

Re. $1/(1 + f_{12}) = 0.8733 \times 1.06 = 0.9253$

$(1 + f_{12}) = 1/0.9253 = 1.0807$

$(1 + f_{12}) = f_{12} = 1.0807 - 1$

$f_{12} = 0.0807$

The term 'f' is known as the forward rate and f_{12} indicates forward rate from first to second year. This is the discount rate for calculating the equivalent value of a rupee one year from now. If we wish to have the discount rate we divide the discount factor 0.8573 into two parts. Part 1 we get 1 year hence and part 2 is that we would be getting 2 years hence.

In the example, the present value of Re. 1 which we will receive after 2 years is equivalent to Re. $1/1.0807 =$ Rs. 0.9253. By further discounting 0.9253 by spot rate, 6%, for 1 year.

0.9253/1.06 = 0.873

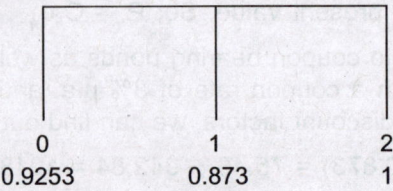

Thus to find out the 1-year forward rate, what we require is 1-year and 2-year spot rates and the equivalent terms as follows:

THE TERM STRUCTURE OF INTEREST RATES 349

$$\text{Re. } 1/(1 + S_2)^2 = \text{Re. } 1/(1 + f_{12})/(1 + S_1) \tag{7}$$

$$(1 + f_{12}) = \frac{(1 + S_2)^2}{(1 + S_1)}$$

$$(1 + S_1) \times (1 + f_{12}) = (1 + S_2)^2 \tag{8}$$

Generalizing the above equation for n spot rates (i.e., for $n - 1$ years)

$$(1 + f_{n-1}, n) = \frac{(1 + S_n)^n}{(1 + S_{n-1})^{n-1}} \tag{9}$$

$$(1 + f_{n-1, \underline{n}}) \times (1 + S_{n-1})^{n-1} = (1 + S_n)^n$$

Pause for thought: Forward rates are the compounded discount factors.

13.2.4 Forward Rates and Discount Factors

Equation (5), $d_n = 1/(1 + S_n)^n$, derives discount factor from the spot rate, as already discussed.

Similarly, using equation (8), $(1 + S_1) \times (1 + f_{12}) = (1 + S_2)^2$, leads to the discount factor for a forward rate

Using the same logic, we can find out the discount factor for 2 years. For that we need the discounted value of 1-year spot rate, multiplied with its forward rate. As we know that the discount factor for 2-year spot rate is,

$$d_2 = 1/(1 + S_2)^2$$

The discount factor for forward rate becomes,

$$d_2 = \frac{1}{(1 + S_1) \times (1 + f_{12})} \tag{10}$$

$$d_2 = \frac{1}{(1.06) \times (1.0807)}$$

$$d_2 = 0.8729 = 0.873$$

By generalizing the above equation for forward rate of $n - 1$ years, we get the discount factor for n years,

$$d_n = 1/(1 + S_{n-1})^{n-1} \times (1 + f_{n-1, n}) \tag{11}$$

It is to be noted that:

- Spot rate increases as time increases. Thus 1-year spot rate is less than 2-year spot rate, which in turn is less than the 3-year spot rate, and so is the trend.
- Spot rate also decreases as time increases. As an investor, we must watch the current trend and accordingly take a decision.

> **Pause for thought:** Thus again we are reminded that instead of going with generalizations it is better to weigh each case on its own merit.

13.3 YIELD CURVE

Yield curve relates the YTM and time to maturity. This can be understood by reverting to the earlier example of zero coupon bonds: X, Y, Z and T.

Table 13.3: Zero Coupon Bonds

Bond	Year	Interest rate
X	1	6%
Y	2	7%
Z	3	8%
T	4	8.8%

We calculate the quotes of the zero coupon bonds, to start with, and then the YTM, to get the yield curve.

We know that the price of the bond, X, is

$$\frac{Rs.\ 1000}{(1.06)^1} = Rs.\ 943.39$$

As the rates for next two years are 6% and 7%, the two year zero coupon bond Y will quote at

$$\frac{Rs.\ 1000}{(1.06) \times (1.07)} = Rs.\ 881.67$$

It can be expressed in a different manner as well. Thus, for bond Y,

$$\frac{Rs.\ 1000}{\left(1+r^2\right)} = Rs.\ 881.67 = 6.5\%$$

It implies that if we invest Rs. 881.67 today, it grows to Rs. 881.67 × 1.07 = Rs. 934.57; and this when reinvested at 7% will grow to Rs. 934.57 × 1.07 = Rs. 1000.

Likewise for bond, Z, it is,

$$\frac{Rs.\ 1000}{(1.06) \times (1.07) \times (1.08)} = Rs.\ 816.36$$

Or, by the different method, for bond Z (3 years),

$$\frac{Rs.\ 1000}{(1+r)^3} = Rs.\ 816.36 = 6.99\% = 7\%$$

Similarly for bond T (4 years), it is,

$$\frac{Rs.\ 1000}{(1.06) \times (1.07) \times (1.08) \times (1.088)} = Rs.\ 750.33$$

The yield of bond T is derived as,

$$\frac{Rs.\ 1000}{(1+r)^4} = Rs.\ 750.33 = 7.44\%$$

This can be generalized as,

$$P_v = \frac{1}{(1+r_1)(1+r_2)(1+r_3)\ldots(1+r_n)} \tag{12}$$

where,

P_v = present value of bond (or security).

r_i = one year interest rate that will prevail at the end of year, i.

The YTM as calculated above signifies that the interest rates may vary over time but there is one single rate at which bond's current value is equivalent to the discounted value of the future cash flows—and this equals the expected future cash flows, i.e., the YTM.

Table 13.4: YTM and Term

Term	1 year	2 years	3 years	4 years
YTM	6%	6.5%	7%	7.44%

Plotting time to maturity on X-axis and YTM on Y-axis, we get a graph, which is known as yield curve. Since in the example we have considered zero coupon bonds, it is called pure yield curve.

Now compare Table 13.1 and Table 13.4. For a 2 year bond Y, its YTM is 6.5% [(6 + 7)/2]. This is because yield is the measure of average return (determined from the market rates available for first and second year) over the maturity period of the bond. Looking at the bond, Z, whose maturity is 3 years, its YTM is found to be 7%. This is the arithmetic average over 3 years, i.e., (6 + 7 + 8) = (21/3) = 7%; again, same as three year yield we have derived in Table 13.3. Now for bond 4 (T), the arithmetic average turns out to be [(6 + 7 + 8 + 8.8)/4] = 7.45%. Hence, the arithmetic average and YTM differ slightly. This is the real situation in the market. This happens because of the compound interest rate of the bonds. To overcome this difference the geometric average has to be calculated rather than arithmetic average, as the latter is only an approximate assessment.

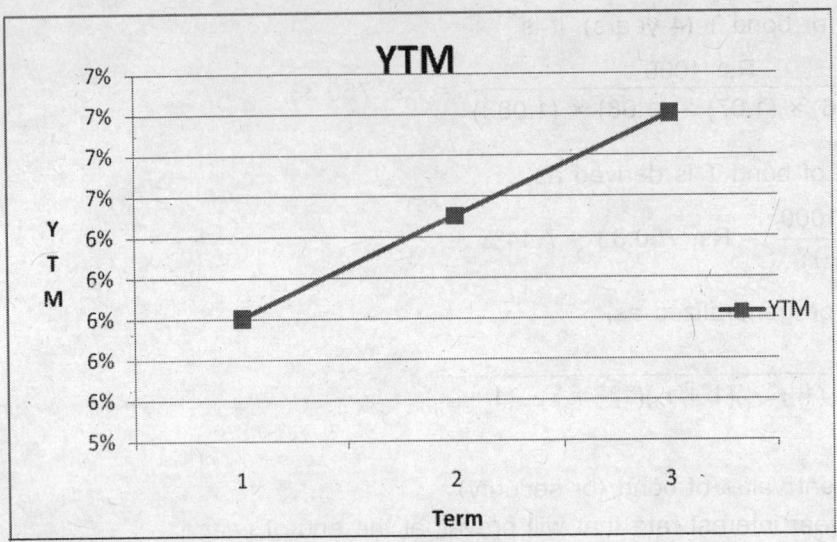

Figure 13.1: Yield curve

Only three bonds have been considered here for the purpose of our understanding. But in real life, larger number of bonds and their corresponding YTMs are plotted. The usual shape of the yield curve is as shown above.

Patterns of the yield curve

There are three main patterns created by the term structure of interest rates.

> **Pause for thought:** Yield curve gives the variation in the yield with the corresponding variation in the maturity periods.

13.3.1 Types of Yield Curves

1. *Normal yield curves*

This yield curve is obtained during normal market conditions, hence the name. By normal conditions is meant that long-term securities yield higher returns, than the short-term ones. The investors believe that economy will continue to grow at normal rate, with no substantial changes in the economy due to inflation and other factors. Thus, securities with long-term maturity will not be affected, is their belief. And in fact this has been the actual finding too, as securities with n-years of maturity ('n', the number of years, being quite appreciable), provides higher return in the future. Thus the normal expectation from the market materializes.

Yet the mechanism is not what the investors believe it to be. Inflation and other factors do exist. Uncertainty and risks are there aplenty in long-term securities, as compared to short-termed ones. We have been reiterating that higher is the risk, higher is the return. And that is why long-term securities give better return. But why do short-term securities have lower risk and return? This is so, because, short-term securities carry less risk than longer term securities because borrowers provide higher return to attract investors to invest in short-term securities, instead of long-term securities, which carry more risk.

The Term Structure of Interest Rates

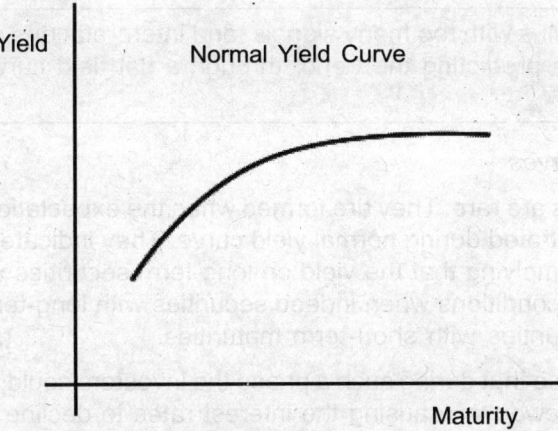

Figure 13.2: Normal yield curve

> **Pause for thought:** When the curve reflects a coherence between the expected (and considered normal) and obtained results, it is a normal yield curve.

2. *Flat yield curves*

There arise situations when market fails to give a signal that follow a steady pattern. Rather it gives mixed signals, combination of the expected and the unexpected. Furthermore, at times the group of investors interprets it in different ways. In presence of either of these conditions, and even more so when both are present, it becomes difficult for the market to determine in which directions the interest rate will move in the future. A flat curve is thus formed instead of one with a normal positive slope. During such a phase in the market, investors prefer to invest in fixed income securities, as they have high credit quality (discussed later).

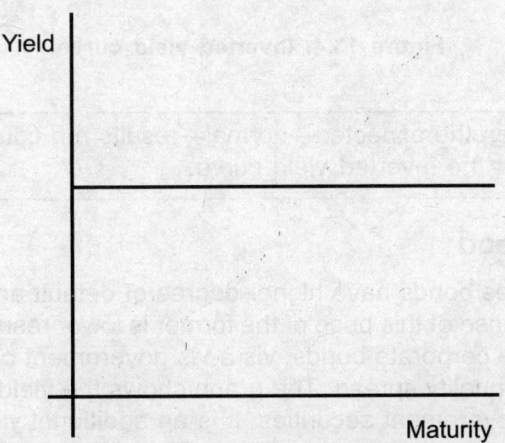

Figure 13.3: Flat yield curve

> **Pause for thought:** Thus with too many signals, and interpretations of the same, the market reflects the difficulty in predicting the trend, through a flat field curve—an averaged result of all.

3. Inverted yield curves

Inverted yield curves are rare. They are formed when the expectations of investors are almost reverse of those demonstrated during normal yield curve. They indicate that the interest rates will fall as time progresses, implying that the yield on long-term securities will be less. This happens during abnormal market conditions when indeed securities with long-term maturities provide less return, compared to securities with short-term maturities.

However, it is also true that during such a phase the investors could also believe that economy will experience further slowdown, causing the interest rates to decline further in the future. This would catalyze the belief that it is better to park the fund in long-term securities, at the current interest rates; because rates, and thus yields, in future may be even lower. Hence, despite the abnormal conditions, the investors might still land up with investing in long-term securities.

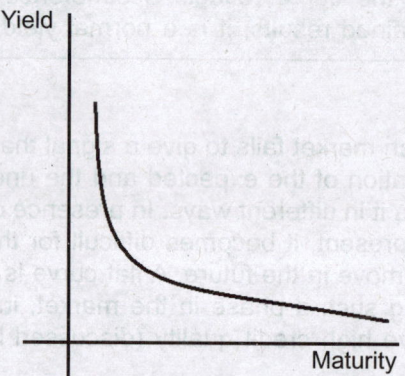

Figure 13.4: Inverted yield curve

> **Pause for thought:** When the expected—normal—results run counter to that obtained, the market reflects it through the inverted yield curve.

13.3.2 The Credit Spread

The corporate securities/bonds have higher degree of default and other risks, as compared to government bonds. Because of this price of the former is lower resulting in higher yields. These comparative yields from the corporate bonds, vis-à-vis government bonds, give rise to the credit spread; also known as the quality spread. The graph shows the yield curves of corporate bonds to be higher than that of government securities. It is an additional yield which investors receive for preferring corporate bonds to government bonds. The difference between the yield curves is known as credit spread or quality spread.

When the inflation rate rises, corporate bonds provide higher return to compensate for this rise in additional risk. Hence, the spread between these two securities increases as well. Contrary to this, with a fall in the inflation rate, and thus in the interest rates, the difference in yields from these two securities diminish. This is reflected by the shrinking of the quality spread. These yield curves, thus being an index of the quality spread, are used to price corporate bonds.

> **Pause for thought:** Credit (quality) spread is the difference in yields from the corporate and government securities. It is inversely related to the inflation rates.

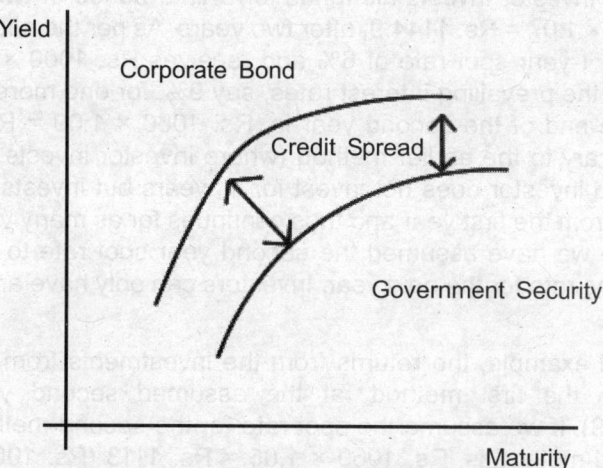

Figure 13.5: The credit spread

13.4 TERM STRUCTURE THEORIES

There are three basic theories which govern the term structure of interest rates. These theories analyze the rates, for the different maturity periods. An analysis is essential for proper evaluation of the risk-free securities.

1. *Pure expectations theory or unbiased expectations theory*

We already know what is meant by spot rates, courtesy our discussions on the same, in an earlier section. If the spot rate, on majority of the securities that are available in the market rises after a period of time, the investors are led to believe that the trend shall continue. Contrary to this, if there is a fall in the rates for majority of the risk-free securities, investors are convinced that spot rates will continue to fall in the future as well. Thus, according to this theory, the forward rate is a reflection of the average expectations of investors from their anticipated future spot rates.

To enhance the understanding of this theory, we again fall back on the earlier example of 1-year and 2-year spot rates. We assumed 1-year spot rate to be 6% and 2-year spot rate to be 7%. Thus, it reflects an increase in interest rates from the first to the second year. However, it could decrease as well. The former instance is called the upward sloping yield curve; while the latter is the example of a downward sloping yield curve.

As per the pure expectation theory, investors hold their funds for either:
— Maturity period of 'n' years.
— Or they can reinvest their fund from the proceeds of the previous year's earnings (principal and interest), for next year and so on.

With intent to simplify this discussion and enhance the understanding, let us assume that the investment horizon is of two years for investors. We stick with our assumption that the 1-year and 2-year spot rates are 6% and 7% respectively and the investment amount is Rs. 1000. As per the first method, as investor invests his funds for a time period of two year, he/she will end up with Rs. 1000 × 1.07 × 1.07 = Rs. 1144.9, after two years. As per the second method, investors invests Rs. 1000 at the 1-year spot rate of 6% and receives Rs. 1000 × 1.06 = Rs. 1060. The amount is reinvested at the prevailing interest rates, say 9%, for one more year. Hence, the total invested amount, at the end of the second year is, Rs. 1060 × 1.09 = Rs. 1155.4 (Rs. 1000 × 1.06 = Rs. 1060). Contrary to the earlier method (where investor invests for a fixed, 'n' number of years), in this method investor does not invest for 'n' years but invests for one year and then reinvests the proceeds from the first year and thus continues for as many years, as is the duration of the investment. Here we have assumed the second year spot rate to be 9%. But in real life it is difficult to assume the rate for the next year. Investors can only have an approximate estimate of it.

In this hypothetical example, the returns from the investments from the second method is more than those from the first method, at the assumed second year spot rate of 9% (Rs. 1155.4 > Rs. 1144.9). If we assume the spot rate for the second method to be 5%, then the returns from the second method is, Rs. 1060 × 1.05 = Rs. 1113 (Rs. 1000 × 1.06 = Rs. 1060). Thus in this case the first method is yielding more return than the second method (Rs. 1113 < Rs. 1144.9). If we assume the second year spot rate to be 8%, then the second method generates, Rs. 1060 × 1.08 = Rs. 1144.8 (Rs. 1000 × 1.06 = Rs. 1060). Hence, here both the methods give same return at the end of two years (Rs. 1144.9 ~ Rs. 1144.8). The summarized results of the above two methods are tabulated as follows.

Table 13.5: Comparison of 1-year and 2-year Spot Rates

1-year spot rate (%)	2-year spot rate (%)	Method 1	Method 2	Comparison
	7	Rs. 1144.9		
6	9		Rs. 1155.4	Rs. 1155.4 > Rs. 1144.9
6	5		Rs. 1113.0	Rs. 1113 < Rs. 1144.9
6	8		Rs. 1144.8	Rs. 1144.8 = Rs. 1144.9

Now we proceed to accord individual attention to each case.

If the expected future spot rate (spot rate for second year) is 9%, investors would prefer to invest in the second method—of reinvestment. If all, or majority of the investors, follow suit, soon supply for the second year spot rate increases, due to which the second year spot rate falls. At the same time, as majority of the investors prefer to invest in the reinvestment method, rather than the first method having a maturity period of 'n' years, supply of the fund falls short of demand.

This forces the 2-year spot rate to rise. Again, when the future spot rate is 5%, returns from the second method are comparatively less. Hence, more and more investors prefer to invest in the first method, involving of 'n' years' maturity. As a consequence, the 2-year spot rates decreases as supply of the fund increases compared to demand; and the second year future spot rate rises, as in reinvestment method supply falls short of demand.

We recall the forward rate, $f_{12} = 8.07\%$, as calculated above [vide Equation (6)]. If the expected future spot rate, one year hence, turns out to be 8.07%, instead of 9% or 5%, the second method generates Rs. 1060 × 1.0807 = Rs. 1145.54 (Rs. 1000 × 1.06 = Rs. 1060), which is equivalent to (Rs. 1000 invested at 2-year spot rate of Rs. 1000 × 1.07 × 1.07) Rs. 1144.9. This results in equilibrium, as both the investment methods turn out with the same return!

From the above analysis it can be concluded that the expected future spot rate is equal to the forward rate. The 1-year spot rate has been taken as 6%, and the second year rate rises to a level of 8.07% in one year resulting in the same return. Thus, here we have an upward sloping yield curve as two year spot rate is greater than the one year spot rate.

Till now our analysis, as per this theory, concludes that the expected future spot rate is equal to the forward rate:

$$(1 + S_1) \times (1 + f_{12}) = (1 + S_2)^2$$

But as $es_{12} = f_{12}$ the above equation becomes,

$$(1 + S_1) \times (1 + es_{12}) = (1 + S_2)^2$$

where, es_{12} = is the expected future spot rate.

Equation (12) reflects that the expected return, from both the methods is same. In our earlier discussion we had taken: 2-year spot rate, $S_2 = 7\%$; 1-year spot rate, $S_1 = 6\%$ and forward rate of 8.07%, which indicates towards upward sloping term structure. It can also be interpreted that longer the term, higher is the spot rate. In a similar manner, we can discuss the downward sloping yield term structure, where longer the term, lower the spot rate.

> **Pause for thought:** In a upward sloping term structure, investors expect the spot rate to rise in the future; while in downward sloping term structure, investors expect the spot rate to fall in the future.

Impact of inflation

What we have discussed in the pure expectation theory is that spot rates change from one year to the next. They either increase or decrease. Also, the spot rates that we have discussed are nominal rates, which is the result of real rate and inflation rate. If due to certain factors (or in absence of any concrete factors), real rate or inflation rates, or both, are expected to change in the future, the spot rate too is expected to change. To delve into this aspect we go back to our earlier example of 1-year spot rate, $S_1 = 6\%$ and also assume that the real rate is 4%, which will remain constant over a reasonable number of years. Nominal rate (spot rate) of 6% is the sum of real rate (4%) and inflation rate (2%). We have come to the forward rate of 8.07% for the second year, and at this rate resultant values are same from both methods of investment. Comparing the expected future spot rate 8.07% and 1-year spot rate 6%, we realize that as per this theory, there is a rise of 2.07%, from the 1-year spot rate of 6% to 8.07%. A question could arise as to why this increment of 2.07%? Well, it is because inflation rate is expected to rise by

2.07%. This indicates further that the current inflation rate is 2% and is expected to rise by 2.07%, resulting in 4.07% rise. Similarly when this mechanism is extended from the first year to the second (i.e., from 6% to 7%), inflation is expected to rise by 4.07%.

Economy has observed this phenomenon, whereby the term structure falls in the future when the current short-term spot rates are relatively high. Opposed to it, when the current spot rates are relatively low, the term structure is likely to rise in the future, as inflation too is expected to rise.

2. *The liquidity preference theory*

It is a common observation that investors value liquidity. Hence, they are interested in purchasing short-term securities. Following are the available options for investments:

— Investing for maturity period of 'n' years (i.e., with a lock-in period of certain years).
— Investing for a shorter period and/or with reinvestment options.

But investors would prefer to go for short-term securities. They wish to keep the options open for liquidation even before maturity. They also believe that they have to bear less 'price risk' if they invest in a short-term security. From the two methods discussed in the previous theory of term structure (unbiased expectation theory), investors would prefer the second method of investment, the liquidity preference theory. Because this method gives the option to reinvest the fund at the prevailing interest rates if investor does not need the cash. But if he/she needs the cash, the same can be withdrawn. Contrarily, if investors invest their funds as per method 1, the funds remain blocked for 'n' years. The investors lose the opportunity to reinvest if interest rates are favorable. And even if a need arises he/she cannot encash the investment before the maturity period.

Some investment options have the liquidation provisions before maturity. However, it is difficult to predict what price the investors will receive if they sell a security before its maturity period. Moreover, even if the return is same from both the methods, investors still prefer to invest via the second method. Thus considering all aspects, second method of reinvestment is superior to the first method. The n-year maturity method must provide higher return to attract the investors to invest in it. Thus to draw a large pool of investors for good subscription of securities, borrowers (i.e., issuers) must pay risk premium (i.e., higher expected return) to investors for securities with 'n' years of maturity. In practice, borrowers usually pay higher return on such securities; otherwise they have to go for frequent issuance of securities. This causes incurring of certain expenses like those for advertisements, registration and others, with every issuance. Also, the long-term securities reduce mental hassles for investors as they do not have to arrange for the funds frequently; at the same time they need not worry about the much desired higher expected rate. Thus, to motivate investors to invest for a longer period of time, borrowers have to provide higher return than the second method of reinvestment. For this the future spot rate must be less than the forward rate of 8.07%.

Let us assume that the spot rate is 7.5%. Then the value of Rs. 1000 in two years is, Rs. 1000 × 1.06 × 1.075 = Rs. 1139.5, as per second method of reinvestment. The value of the investment, as per the first method is, Rs. 1000 ×1.07 × 1.07 = Rs. 1144.9. Thus, n-year maturity method provides higher return, as it possesses higher degree of uncertainty, and thus risk.

Liquidity premium

The difference between 8.07% and 7.5% is known as liquidity premium. This is the extra return borrowers should provide to investors to invest in the long-term, n-year maturity, method (here it is for n = 2 years).

$$LP = f_{12} - es_{12}$$

where,

LP = liquidity premium.

f_{12} = the forward rate.

es_{12} = is the expected future spot rate.

In other words, we can say that

$[(1 + S_1) \times (1 + es_{12})] < (1 + S_2)^2$

$[(1.06)) \times (1 + es_{12})] < (1.07)^2$

Rs. 1.1395 < Rs. 1.1449

3. *The market segmentation theory*

This theory assumes that various investors and borrowers have certain preferences: tendency to invest in securities with certain maturity period; securities yielding certain interest rates—to name a few. Due to this, there is a separate market for each term-type securities: short-term, long-term and medium securities. The theory also deals with one crude assumption that usually investors and borrowers do not leave their market segmentation to invest in other segments, even though the other market is yielding higher return.

> **Pause for thought:** Market is divided into segments depending on the maturity period and each segment operates as a mutually exclusive separate market type.

SUMMARY

- ✓ The spot rate is the yield to maturity, on a pure discount security (i.e., zero coupon bonds).
- ✓ The yield to maturity of a security is the discount rate, at which the present value of all cash flows (interest payments and principals) are equal to the present value of the security.
- ✓ With the help of a spot rate of a zero coupon bond, spot rates for coupon bearing bonds can be determined.
- ✓ A forward rate is an interest rate, derived from spot rate. It is paid on the money borrowed at some specific time in future and it is repaid at even further distant time in future.
- ✓ Unbiased expectation theory, liquidity preference theory and market segmentation theory are the three theories used to discuss and derive term structure of interest rates. Majority of the evidences are in favor of the liquidity preference theory.
- ✓ A yield curve shows the relationship between yield to maturity and term to maturity, for risk-free securities. This relationship is known as the term structure of interest rates.

KEY CONCEPTS

Yield to Maturity	Spot Rate	Market Discount Function
Yield Curve	Forward Rate	Term Structure
Unbiased Expectation Theory	Liquidity Preference Theory	Market Segmentation Theory
Liquidity Premium	Quality Spread	Corporate Bonds
Inflation Rate	Real Rate	Market

REVIEW QUESTIONS

1. Distinguish between spot rates and forward rates.
2. You have learnt about the three theories of term structure. As per your analysis and judgment, which theory explains best the relationship between spot rates and yield to maturity?
3. Discuss how term structures have changed over a period of time and analyze the effect of such changes on T-bills, with different maturity periods, in India.
4. Collect the inflation rate of last ten to twenty years from www.rbi.org and analyze its impact on term structure of interest rates.
5. Calculate and compare the yield of corporate and government bonds and show your views for credit spread over a period of last ten years.

ILLUSTRATIONS

Q.1. The 1-year spot rate is 8% and 1-year forward rate, beginning today, is 9%. What is the 1-year forward rate, for two years, starting from today, if the 3-year spot rate is 10%?

Ans: Equivalent value of Re. 1, in three years

$$= (1.10) \times 3 = 1.331$$

Similarly, future value of Re. 1 in two years

$$= (1 + S_1) \times (1 + f_{12}) = 1.08 \times 1.09 = 1.1772$$

We know the equation

$$(1 + f_{n-1, n}) = \frac{(1 + S_n)^n}{(1 + S_{n-1})^{n-1}}$$

Similarly,

$$f_3 = \frac{(1 + S_3)^3}{(1 + S_2)^2} - 1$$

$$= \frac{1.331}{1.1772} - 1 = 0.1306 = 13.06\%$$

Q.2. If the 1-year spot rate is 6% and 1-year forward rate, starting one year from today, is 7%, what is the 2-year spot rate?

Ans: Equivalent value of Re. 1 in two years

$$= (1 + S_1) \times (1 + f_{12}) = 1.06 \times 1.07 = 1.1342$$

We know the equation

$$(1 + f_{n-1, n}) = \frac{(1 + S_n)^n}{(1 + S_{n-1})^{n-1}}$$

Similarly,

$$f_2 = \frac{(1 + S_2)^2}{(1 + S_1)^1} - 1$$

$$S_2 = \sqrt{(1.1342)} - 1$$

$$= 0.06498 = 6.49\%$$

PROBLEMS

Q.1. Given the following interest rates for various time periods, beginning from today, calculate forward rates for the years: one to two, two to three and so on.

Years from today	Spot rate (%)
1	6
2	6.5
3	7.5
4	8
5	8.5

Q.2. From the following forward rates, calculate: the 1, 2, 3 and 4-year spot rates.

Forward time period	Forward rate (%)
$f_{0,1}$	10.5
$f_{0,2}$	10
$f_{0,3}$	9.5
$f_{0,4}$	8.5
$f_{0,5}$	8

Q.3. Given below are two securities. Which one of them will have a lower yield to maturity if forward rates are upward sloping? What will be the answer, if they are downward sloping?

a. A 10 year zero coupon bond or a 12 year zero coupon bond?

b. A 10 year 8% coupon bond or a 10 year 9% coupon bond?

Q.4. Consider two bonds, each of Rs. 10000 face value, and each with five years remaining to maturity:

a. What is the yield to maturity of a zero coupon bond, which currently sells at Rs. 8020.50?

b. What is the yield to maturity of a bond, with 8% coupon rate p.a., currently selling at Rs. 9050? For this bond, the first interest payment is due one year from today.

Q.5. Find out the discount factors associated with three year, four year, five year and six year zero coupon bonds of Rs. 1000 face value, which sell for Rs. 900, Rs. 870, Rs. 830 and Rs. 750, respectively.

Q.6. The current spot rate of the market is 9%; and the forward rates for one year and two year are $f_{1,2}$ = 11% and $f_{2,3}$ = 12%, respectively. What should be the market price of a 10% p.a. coupon bond with face value of Rs. 1000, maturing three years from today? Assume that first interest payment is due one year from today.

SUGGESTED FURTHER READING FOR EMPIRICAL WORK

1. Miltersen, K.R. (1994), "An Arbitrage Theory of the Term Structure of Interest Rates", *The Annals of Applied Probability*, Vol. 4, No. 4.

2. Heath, D., Jarrow, R., and Morton, A. (1992), "Bond Pricing and the Term Structure of Interest Rates: A New Methodology for Contingent Claims Valuation", *Econometrica*, Vol. 60, No. 1.

3. Mishkin, S. (1995), "Nonstationarity of Regressors and Tests on Real-Interest-Rate Behavior", *Journal of Business & Economic Statistics*, Vol. 13, No. 1.

4. Rebonato, R. (2004), "Review Paper. Interest-Rate Term-Structure Pricing Models: A Review", *Proceedings: Mathematical, Physical and Engineering Sciences*, Vol. 460, No. 2043.

5. Ioffe, I.D., and Prisman, E.Z. (2003), "Term Structure of Interest Rates and Implied Market Frictions: The Min-Max Approach", *Management Science*, Vol. 49, No. 7.

6. Cuaresma, J.C., Gnan, E., and Ritzberger-Grünwald, D. (2005), "The Term Structure as a Predictor of Real Activity and Inflation in the Euro Area: A Reassessment work", *Review of World Economics / Weltwirtschaftliches Archiv*, Vol. 141, No. 2.

REFERENCES

1. http://www.investopedia.com/terms/t/termstructure.asp#axzz2E4qQ3tva

2. http://www.investopedia.com/university/advancedbond/advancedbond4.asp#axzz2E4qQ3tva

3. http://en.wikipedia.org/wiki/Yield_curve

4. https://www2.bc.edu/peter-ireland/ec261/chapter6.pdf

14
BOND PORTFOLIO MANAGEMENT

> **LEARNING OBJECTIVES**
>
> The purpose of this chapter is to enable you to understand:
> - Bond pricing theorems.
> - Variations related to duration of the bonds.
> - Distinction between the active and passive strategies for managing the bond portfolio.
> - What is meant by immunization, in this context?

14.1 INTRODUCTION

In this chapter we shall be discussing the ways to manage a portfolio, comprised of bonds. Which bonds are to be chosen and how an efficient portfolio can be created, through all these, we have already traversed. And in the previous chapter we dealt with the prices of bonds; yields generated by them and the relationship between them. But with this chapter, our approach takes a different route. Here we shall learn how to make the best of what we have. By that is meant, how we utilize to the maximum, the portfolio of bonds that we have chosen and entrusted with our funds. Various strategies for portfolio management are looked into which fall mainly under the two categories of:

— Active.
— Passive.

The strategy is considered passive, when portfolio managers try to attain and maintain the risk-return parameter, as per the market. While an active strategy is one in which systematic efforts are made to beat the market, by extracting superior performance through exploitation of the information available.

The active strategy, of bond portfolio management, is based on the assumption that bond market is not efficient. This gives investors an opportunity to earn above average returns. How? Well, if an investor can find out mis-priced (under-priced/over-priced) bonds and can identify the time to buy and sell, he/she can earn superior rate of return, irrespective of the market condition. It is all about intelligent use of the information and yes, it is about timing too! Passive strategy rests on the basic assumption that bond prices are in accordance with the semi-strong form of an efficient market. Hence, the current price of the bonds is presumed to reflect accurately all publicly available information. Thus this strategy acknowledges that bonds are fairly priced and return and risk are in perfect coherence. According to passive strategy it is almost impossible: to find under-priced bonds and identify the right time to buy and sell so as to earn superior, above average returns.

> **Pause for thought:** Passive strategy depends on the market trend. It prefers to be guided by the market. While active strategy looks to outsmart the market, by creating opportunities. Instead of going with the trend, or accepting the same as a rule of the book, it chooses to set a trend.

14.2 BOND PRICING THEOREMS

All theorems are representation of relationships. The first time we came across theorems is in geometry. If we recall, we would be led to the varied parameters of relationships therein.

Similarly, a bond pricing theorem too gives a relationship. It is a mathematical relationship between bond prices and bond yields at maturity. This takes us back to the relationship between bond price and yield to maturity; and its impact on market price of the bond, as discussed in the previous chapter. An understanding of these properties of bonds is important for envisaging the movement in bond prices as there is a change in interest rates. With this relationship as the reference, the five bonds pricing theorems have been derived.

1. Consider bond A, with maturity period of five years and a par value of Rs.1000. It pays coupon rate of 10% p.a., i.e., Rs.100 p.a. Its current yield is 10%, as it is selling at Rs.1000. How would the yield of the bond change, if the par value increases to Rs.1100 and then falls to Rs.900?

Ans.   P = 900, YTM = ?

$$YTM = \frac{C + (M - P/n)}{0.4 M + 0.6 P}$$

$$= \frac{100 + (1000 - 900/5)}{(0.4 \times 1000) + (0.6 \times 900)}$$

$$= 0.1276$$

$$= 12.76\%$$

P = 1100, YTM = ?

$$YTM = \frac{C + (M - P/n)}{0.4M + 0.6P}$$

$$= \frac{100 + (1000 - 1100/5)}{(0.4 \times 1000) + (0.6 \times 1100)}$$

$$= 0.0755$$

$$= 7.55\%$$

Interpretation: From the above calculation it stands proved that with an increase in market price of the bond, its yield decreases. Conversely, when the market price of the bond decreases, its yield increases.

> **Pause for thought: Theorem 1**: Market price and the yield of the bond show inverse variation.

2. Bond B matures in five years. It has a par value of Rs. 1000 and the annual coupon payment is Rs. 50. It generates 9% yield. Find out the price of the bond. After one year, if it still has the same yield, at what price it will be selling for? Show whether its discount has decreased or not.

Ans. When n = 5 years:

$$P_0 = (50/1.09) + (50/1.09^2) + (50/1.09^3) + (50/1.09^4) + (1050/1.09^5)$$

= Rs. 844.41

Difference = Par value − Price of the bond

= Rs. 1000 − Rs. 844.41

= Rs. 155.59

When n = 4 years:

$$P_0 = (50/1.09) + (50/1.09^2) + (50/1.09^3) + (1050/1.09^4)$$

= Rs. 870.41

Difference = Par value − Price of the bond

= Rs. 1000 − Rs. 870.41

= Rs. 129.59

When n = 3 years:

$$P_0 = (50/1.09) + (50/1.09^2) + (1050/1.09^3)$$

= Rs. 898.75

Difference = Par value − Price of the bond

= Rs. 1000 − Rs. 898.75 = Rs. 101.25

Similarly, when n = 2 years:

$$P_0 = (50/1.09) + (1050/1.09^2)$$

= Rs. 929.64

Difference = Rs. 1000 − Rs. 929.64

= Rs. 70.36

When n = 1 year:

$$P_0 = (1050/1.09)$$

= Rs. 963.30

Difference = Rs. 1000 − Rs. 963.30
= Rs. 36.7

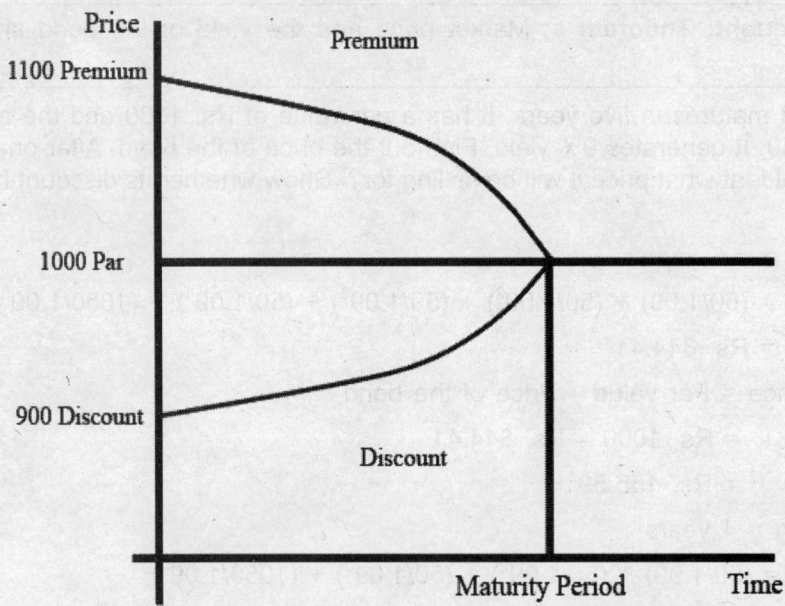

Figure 14.1: Relationship between bond price and maturity

The results obtained have been summarized in the table below.

Table 14.1: Maturity and Difference in the Price of the Bond

Years to maturity	5	4	3	2	1
Difference	155.59	129.59	101.25	70.36	36.70

Interpretation: The preceding calculation proves that when the yield of the bond remains unchanged over the entire maturity period, size of the discount or premium decreases as the maturity draws closer. It is evident from the table above that as the life of the bond shortens the difference between the par value and market price of the bond decreases. The Figure 14.1 above reflects that irrespective of whether the bond is selling at premium or discount, the prices of the bond will gradually converge at its par value as it approaches maturity. Ultimately, at the maturity value, premium or discount disappears.

Correspondingly, if there are two bonds with same coupon rate, par value and yield, one with shorter maturity period (n) will sell for smaller discount or premium. If we treat the bonds with five and four years maturity (from the above table), as two different bonds, we can affirm that the bond with five years maturity has discount of Rs. 155.59; while that with four years maturity has a discount of Rs. 129.59, for a change of Rs. 26.

> **Pause for thought: Theorem 2**: This applies when the yield remains constant for the entire term of maturity and proves that size of the discount (or premium) decreases as the maturity draws closer. And at the maturity value all discount and premium merge, preceded by gradual lessening of the difference between the par and market values of the bond.

3. We revert to the example of bond B to understand this theorem. If after two years, three years and subsequently as well, it still has a yield of 9%, what change takes place in its selling price?

Ans: For the purpose we will compare the difference or discount compared to Q.2.

Table 14.2: Maturity and Extent of Fall in the Price of the Bond

Years to maturity	5	4	3	2	1
P_0 (Rs.)	844.41	870.41	898.75	929.64	963.30
Difference	155.59	129.59	101.25	70.36	36.70
Change in price (Rs.)		26	28.34	30.89	33.66
Change from par value (%)		2.6	2.834	3.089	3.366

Interpretation: If the yield of the bond does not change during the maturity period, size of its discount (or premium) will decrease at an increasing rate as it approaches maturity.

> **Pause for thought: Theorem 3**: This is an extension of theorem 2. It states that with a constant yield during the term of the bond, the decrease in its premium or discount varies directly with the shortening of the time to maturity.

4. Bond C has a life span of five years and coupon rate of Rs. 80. Its yield is 8%, i.e., its price is equal to its par value, Rs. 1000. If its yield rises from 8 to 9%, then what will be the price? And if its yield falls from 8% to 7%, then what will be its price?

Ans: When YTM changes to 9%,

$$P_0 = (80/1.09) + (80/1.09^2) + (80/1.09^3) + (80/1.09^4) + (1080/1.09^5)$$

= Rs. 961.10

When YTM change to 7%,

$$P_0 = (80/1.07) + (80/1.07^2) + (80/1.07^3) + (80/1.07^4) + (1080/1.07^5)$$

= Rs. 1041

When YTM increases from 8% to 9%, then price falls by Rs. 38.9 (1000 − 961.10).

When YTM decreases from 8% to 7%, then price rises by Rs. 41 (1041 − 1000).

Interpretation: The calculation proves that decrease in yield of the bond from 8% to 7% raises the price of the bond by an amount of Rs. 41 (Rs. 1041 − Rs. 1000). It is greater in size than the subsequent fall of Rs. 38.9 (Rs. 1000 − Rs. 961.10) in the price of the bond, when the yield rises from 8% to 9%.

> **Pause for thought: Theorem 4**: The increase in the price of the bond with a decrease in the yield is greater than the fall in the price of the bond with an increase in the yield. But this applies when the decrease, and increase, in the yield is the same (1%).

5. We consider two bonds, C and D.

Table 14.3: Parameters of Bonds C and D

	Bond C	Bond D
Life	5	5
Coupon rate	8%	10%
Par value	1000	1000
Yield (YTM)	8%	8%
Price	1000	?
New YTM	9%	9%
Price	?	?

We calculate the unknown values and compare the percentage change in price of the two bonds, when yield rises from 8% to 9%.

Ans: For bond C:

YTM = 9%, P_0 = Rs. 961.10

Difference = 1000 − 961.10

= Rs. 38.90

Percentage = Rs. 38.90/Rs. 1000[1]

= 0.03890

= 3.89%

For bond D:

When YTM = 8%,

$P_0 = (100/1.08) + (100/1.08^2) + (100/1.08^3) + (100/1.08^4) + (1100/1.08^5)$

= Rs. 1079.85

When YTM = 9%,

$P_0 = (100/1.09) + (100/1.09^2) + (100/1.09^3) + (100/1.09^4) + (1100/1.09^5)$

= Rs. 1038.90

Difference = 1079.85 − 1038.90

= Rs. 40.95

Percentage = 40.95/1079.85 = 0.0379 = 3.79%

---

[1] Price when yield is 8%.

Interpretation: The above calculation shows that the percentage change in yield of bonds with higher coupon rate is comparatively smaller than that incurred by bonds with a lower coupon rate.

> **Pause for thought: Theorem 5**: The change in yield varies inversely with the coupon rates of bonds.

14.2.1 Convexity

The term convexity indicates a curve of a specific type—convex. But what implication(s) the term, 'convex', holds for the stock market, we proceed to discuss.

The previous section on 'bond theorems' elucidates the relation between the price of the bond and its yield (as it increases and decreases). The first and the fourth theorems lead to this new concept, called convexity. Theorem 1 states that there is an inverse relationship between bond price and yields. Yet theorem 4 leads to a non-linear relationship between yield and price of bonds. The non-linearity arises as the percentage rise in the price of the bond, with decrease in yield, is greater than the fall in the price with an increase in the yield. Even though the percentage change in the yield is same, in magnitude, the magnitude of change in the price of the bonds is not.

For a better understanding of this complexity of convexity we need to go back to theorem 4 and examine Figure 14.2. In the figure below yield to maturity are shown on X-axis and price of the bonds are shown on Y-axis.

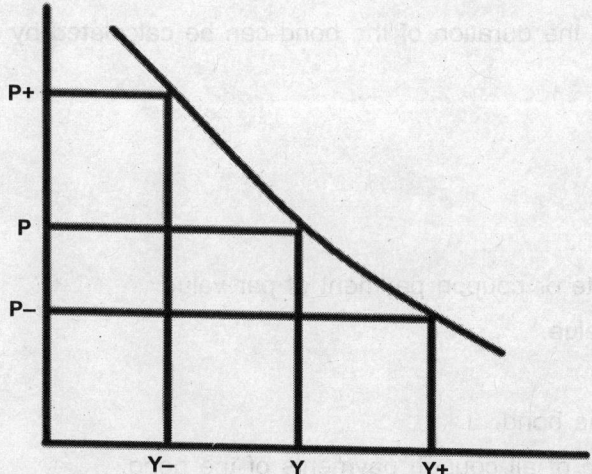

Figure 14.2: Convexity of the bond

By considering the example of bond theorem 4 we can draw two conclusions:

— We can see that when yield rises to Y^+ from Y, price falls from P to P^-. Similarly, when yield falls to Y^- from Y, price rises from P to P^+. This represents theorem 1 for bond pricing.

— From the figure above, it is also evident that when yield falls from Y to Y⁻, price rises to a greater extent, compared to an increase in the yield from Y to Y⁺ with the price falling from P to P⁻, validating theorem 4. The example for theorem 4 showed that, with 1% rise in yield, price fell from Rs. 1000 to Rs. 961.10 (Rs. 38.9); while for a 1% fall in the yield price rose from Rs. 1000 to Rs. 1041 (Rs. 41). Thus the relationship between the price and yield of the bond departs from linearity to convexity, even if to small extent. It happens so, because the percentage change in price of the bond is not same, even when the percentage yield is same (as has been iterated). This relationship between bond price and yield is represented by an upward curve. Thus it shows the convex relation between the price and the yield, which is referred to as convexity. This shape is most commonly observed for the bonds of the general type. However, one thing that should be kept in mind is that the shape is not a standard shape. It varies, with the degree of curvature depending upon coupon rate, life of the bond, its current market price, etc.

> **Pause for thought:** The relation between yield and price deviates from linearity, towards convexity, with the yield and price varying inversely (theorem 1); yet the magnitude of variation differs for the price, in spite of the magnitude of variation in the yield remaining the same (theorem 4).

14.2.2 Duration

Duration is a measure of the approximate maturity of a series of coupon payment bonds. For example, a bond, with a maturity period of 5 years, has an annual coupon payment of Rs. 70. Its par value is Rs. 1000 and yield to maturity, 11%. What is its current market price?

From the given data the duration of the bond can be calculated by two methods.

Method 1

$$D = \sum_{t=1}^{n} \frac{P_y(C_t)}{P_0} \times t \tag{1}$$

where,

C_t = coupon rate or coupon payment of par value.

P_v = present value.

t – time.

P_0 = price of the bond.

$\Sigma P_v(C_t)$ = summation of all coupon payments of the bond.

D = duration.

Table 14.4: Duration of the Bond

Time until receipt of the CF	Amount of CF	Present value @ 11%	Present value of CF	Present value of CF × Time
1	2	3	4	5 (4 ×1)
1	70	0.9009	63.0631	63.0631
2	70	0.8116	56.8136	113.6271
3	70	0.7312	51.1834	153.5502
4	70	0.6587	46.1112	184.4447
5	1000 + 70	0.5935	634.9929	3174.9646
			852.1641	3689.6497

Where, CF = cash flow.

$$\text{Duration} = \frac{3689.6497}{852.1641}$$

= 4.3297 years

Thus is validated the above definition of duration, as the approximate maturity (given maturity is 5 years) of a series of coupon payments bonds. It is so because the current price of the bond is equal to the sum of the present values of the cash flows.

$$P_0 = \sum_{t=1}^{n} P_y(C_t)$$

Rewriting Equation (1) in a slightly different way,

$$D = \sum_{t=1}^{n} \frac{P_y(C_t)}{P_0} \times t \times t \tag{2}$$

It can be thus stated, duration is a measure of the number of years, required for the price of a bond to be repaid by its internal cash flow. As zero coupon bonds do not involve coupon payments, the fund is available to the investor only on maturity. Duration of a zero coupon bond is equal to its maturity period. But coupon bearing bonds involve coupon payments. So price is realized much before the maturity period. Hence, duration of coupon bearing bonds is always less than its maturity period. The formula used above, to calculate duration, is also known as Macaulay duration. It is to be noted that duration differs from approximate maturity, as it takes into account various factors like intermediate coupon payment and principal repayment; while average maturity calculates only the average number of years a bond fund requires to repay its principal.

The steps to be followed, thus, for calculating duration are:

— The cash flow of the bond (coupon + principal) till maturity has to be determined.
— The present value for each year is to be calculated, by using YTM as the discount rate.
— The present value of the cash flows ascertained; coupon and principal payments are to be multiplied with P_v factor of step 2.

- The present values of all the cash flows are summed up, to determine the market price of the bond.
- Each present value is to be multiplied with that respective year.
- These values, obtained in the fifth step are to be summed up.
- The values obtained on summation in the sixth step is to be divided by market value of the bond.

Method 2: Semi-annual duration

We refer to the above example as we calculate the duration by this method. Duration of the bonds when coupon payments are semi-annual (Rs. 35), i.e., at the end of each six months, has to be calculated. For that calculation, the number of years is doubled and the YTM is halved.

Table 14.5: Duration of the Bond with Semi-annual Coupon Payments

Period	Time left till payment	Cash flows (CF)	P_v factor	P_v of cash flows	Weight	Duration
1	2	3	4	5 (3 × 4)	6	7 (2 × 6)
1.00	0.50	35.00	0.90	31.53	0.06	0.03
2.00	1.00	35.00	0.81	28.41	0.05	0.05
3.00	1.50	35.00	0.73	25.59	0.05	0.07
4.00	2.00	35.00	0.66	23.06	0.04	0.08
5.00	2.50	35.00	0.59	20.77	0.04	0.09
6.00	3.00	35.00	0.53	18.71	0.03	0.10
7.00	3.50	35.00	0.48	16.86	0.03	0.11
8.00	4.00	35.00	0.43	15.19	0.03	0.11
9.00	4.50	35.00	0.39	13.68	0.02	0.11
10.00	5.00	1035.00	0.35	364.51	0.65	3.26
				558.31		4.013

So, duration of the bond, at the time of semi-annual compounding, is 4.013.

For a bond portfolio, duration of the portfolio, as a whole, is nothing but the weighted average of the duration of the individual bonds; where the weights represent the proportion invested in each bond.

The duration of bond portfolio can be understood from the following example. If 70% of the entire fund is invested in a bond whose duration is 2.5 years and 30% of the amount is invested in a bond whose duration is 4.2 years, the duration of the portfolio is:

(0.70 × 2.5) + (0.30 × 4.2) = 3.01 years

> **Pause for thought:** Till now we have been evaluating the return of a bond, at maturity. But duration of a bond gives the approximate maturity period, calculated from the returns received. Furthermore, the duration of a portfolio of bonds is the weighted average of the individual bonds comprising the portfolio.

14.2.3 Features that Affect the Duration

Coupons and maturity

Duration of the bonds does not remain static over the entire term of the bond. Rather it changes as the coupons are gradually paid to the bond holder. When the bond holder receives coupon payment, the amount received is not counted as a future cash flow that has to be given to the bond holder (as they have already received it). Because of this, during the life span of the bond, the duration is continually decreasing as the time to maturity decreases. Thus, duration of the bond decreases as the maturity draws closer.

Coupon rates and yields

Bonds with high coupon rates and high yields have lower durations than bonds with lower coupon rates and yields. It so happens because with the holder of the bond receiving higher coupon rate, the holder receives repayment at a faster rate. The same holds true when the yield of the bond is high. Thus repayment made faster, the duration automatically decreases.

> **Pause for thought:** Coupons with high rates and yields reduce the duration of the bond. And during the term of the bond, with each payment made, duration shortens (thus is dynamic and not static) as the time to maturity shortens.

14.2.4 Application of Duration

Measuring interest rate risk

Interest rate risk is the unexpected variation in the interest rates. It consists of two components:

— Price or market risk
— Reinvestment risk.

Price risk is the significant variation from the unexpected change in markets prices of bonds and reinvestment risk is substantial variation from unexpected changes in the rate at which intermediate cash flows (i.e., coupon payments) are reinvested.

Price risk is the biggest risk faced by the investors. It is the risk, involving the decline of the price of a security or a portfolio. While reinvestment risk is the risk that future coupons cannot be reinvested at the prevailing interest rates when the initial purchase was made. Reinvestment risks are more likely when the price risk is high, with interest rates on the decline.

Duration measures the sensitivity of the value of a bond, with respect to the change in the interest rates. In other words, it measures the elasticity/flexibility of the bond.

14.2.5 Duration for Zero Coupon Bonds

Consider a zero coupon (also called, pure discount bond), where,

c = cash flow at maturity.

r = expected yield.

n = years to maturity.

The value of the bond at $t = 0$ (i.e., today), is given by,

$$P = c/(1 + r)^n \tag{3}$$

To analyze how the price changes with respect to the yield, Equation[2] (3) is differentiated,

$$dp/p = -n(dr/1 + r) \tag{4}$$

The equation thus derived, gives the percentage change in price as the yield changes. As discussed earlier, duration of a zero coupon bond is equal to the maturity period. From the above equation (4) it is apparent that 'n' represents duration of a zero coupon bond and change in the price of the bond is equal to the duration multiplied by the change in the yield.

Example: Consider a 3 years discount bond having a maturity period of 3 years and yield of 12%. Examine the price sensitivity of the discount bond, when rates rise to 13%.

$dp/p = -n(dr/1 + r)$

$dp/p = -3(0.01/1.12)$

$ = -2.7\%$

Thus, when the yield rises by 1% (from 12% to 13%), the value of the bond is found to decrease by 2.7%.

Example: Consider a zero coupon bond with 6 years maturity and a yield of 9%. Examine its price sensitivity, when rate falls to 8%.

$dp/p = -n(dr/1 + r)$

$dp/p = -6(0.01/1.09)$

$ = 5.50\%$

This shows that price of the bond rises to 5.50%, with a 1% fall in the yield (from 9% to 8%).

---

[2] $P = c/(1 + r)^n$ or $P = c(1 + r)^{-n}$

Or

$dp/dr = -nc(1 + r)^{-n-1}$

$dp = -n/(1 + r)^{n+1} dr$

$dp = -n \times c/(1 + r)^n [dr/(1 + r)]$

14.2.6 Duration for Coupon Bearing Bonds

The value of the coupon bearing bond is given by,

$$\text{Bond value} = B_0 = \left[\frac{C_1}{(1+k_d)^1} + \frac{C_2}{(1+k_d)^2} + \ldots \frac{C_n}{(1+k_d)^n}\right] + \frac{B_n}{(1+k_n)^n}$$

By analyzing the above equation,

$$dp/p = -D(dr/1 + r) \tag{5}$$

where, D = duration of the bond.

Example: We consider a coupon bond, with Rs. 1000 face value. Its maturity period is 8 years and coupon rate is 10%. Assuming the current yield to maturity to be 10%, find out the duration of the bond. What happens to the price of the bond if its yield rises to 11%?

Table 14.6: Duration of the Bond at 10%

Time until receipt of the CF	Amount of CF	Present value @ 10%	Present value of CF	Present value of CF × Time
1	2	3	4	5 (4 ×1)
1	100	0.909	90.9	90.9
2	100	0.826	82.6	165.2
3	100	0.751	75.1	225.3
4	100	0.683	68.3	273.2
5	100	0.621	62.1	310.5
6	100	0.564	56.4	338.4
7	100	0.513	51.3	359.1
8	1100	0.467	513.7	4109.6
			1000.4	5872.2

The duration of this bond is,

$$\text{Duration} = \frac{5872.2}{1000.4}$$

$$= 5.87$$

$dp/p = -D(dr/1 + r)$

$dp/p = -5.87(0.01/1.10)$

$\quad = -0.0533$

$\quad = -5.33\%$

It is apparent that when the yield of the bond rises from 10% to 11%, i.e., a 1% rise, price of the bond falls by –5.33%—from Rs. 1000 to Rs. 946.7.

From the above analysis we can infer that:
- Duration is a direct measure of the sensitivity of the yield of the bond.
- The sensitivity is measured with respect to the given percentage change in the market price.

Some key points to remember are as follows:
- By keeping the coupon rate and YTM constant, duration increases with time to maturity, but at a decreasing rate. Thus, there is a direct relationship between duration of the bond and its maturity.
- Duration is always less than its maturity for coupon bearing bonds.
- For a zero coupon bond duration is equal to its time to maturity.
- By keeping maturity and YTM constant, there is an inverse relationship between lower coupon bearing bonds and duration.
- Contrary to this, keeping the coupon and maturity constant, increases the duration with lower yield to maturity.
- It is always advisable to choose bonds with largest duration.
- Duration does not measure the complete risk of the bond. It measures volatility, which is only one of the components of risk.

14.2.7 Macaulay Duration

Macaulay duration was created by Frederick Macaulay in 1938[3] to calculate the bond's basic duration. Macaulay duration is calculated by adding the results, obtained by, multiplying the present value of each cash flow by the time it is received and divided by the total price of the security. The formula for Macaulay duration is

$$\text{Macaulay duration} = \frac{\sum_{t=1}^{n} \frac{t \times C}{(1+r)^t} + \frac{n \times M}{(1+r)^n}}{P} \qquad (6)$$

where,

n = number of cash flows.
t = time to maturity.
C = cash flow.
r = required rate of return.
M = maturity value.
P = bond price.

Now, the price of the bond is,

$$P = \frac{C\left[(1+r)^n - 1\right]}{r(1+r)^n} + \frac{M}{(1+r)^n} \qquad (7)$$

Or, P = C (PVIFA, r%, n years) + M (PVIF, r%, n years)

---

[3] However it was not used until 1970.

So, by putting the value of P in the equation for Macaulay duration,

$$\text{Macaulay Duration} = \frac{\sum \dfrac{t \times C}{(1+r)^t} + \dfrac{n \times M}{(1+r)^n}}{\dfrac{C\left[(1+r)^n - 1\right]}{r(1+r)^n} + \dfrac{M}{(1+r)^n}} \qquad (8)$$

Illustration

Find out the Macaulay duration of the bond whose maturity is 5 years; par value is Rs. 1000 and coupon rate is 5%. Coupon is paid annually and interest rate is 5%.

To find out the Macaulay duration of the bond, first of all price of the bond has to be ascertained as follows:

P = C(PVIFA, r%, n years) + M(PVIF, r%, n years)

= 50(PVIFA, 5%, 5 years) + 1000 (PVIF, 5%, 5 years)

= 50(4.329) + 1000(0.784)

= 216.45 + 784

= 1000.45 = 1000

Now, the Macaulay duration:

$$\text{Macaulay duration} = \frac{\sum \dfrac{t \times C}{(1+r)^t} + \dfrac{n \times M}{(1+r)^n}}{\dfrac{C\left[(1+r)^n - 1\right]}{r(1+r)^n} + \dfrac{M}{(1+r)^n}}$$

$$= \frac{\dfrac{(1 \times 50)}{(1.05)^1} + \dfrac{(2 \times 50)}{(1.05)^2} + \dfrac{(3 \times 50)}{(1.05)^3} + \dfrac{(4 \times 50)}{(1.05)^4} + \dfrac{(5 \times 50)}{(1.05)^5} + \dfrac{(5 \times 1000)}{(1.05)^5}}{1000}$$

= 4.55 years

Pause for thought: It came into being for calculating the bond's basic duration.

14.2.8 Modified Duration

Modified duration is a modified version of the Macaulay model that accounts for the changing interest rates. Modified duration shows how much the duration changes for every percentage change in yield. Bonds which are without any embedded features, bond price and interest rate move in opposite direction. Because of this reason, there is an inverse relationship between modified duration and an approximate 1% change in yield. The modified duration formula indicates how a bond's duration changes with fluctuations in interest rate. The modified duration formula is used to measure the volatility of a particular bond.

$$\text{Modified duration} = \frac{\text{Macaulay duration}}{[1+ (\text{YTM/No. of coupon period per year})]} \quad (9)$$

It can be also written as,

$$\text{Modified duration} = \frac{\text{Macaulay duration}}{(1 + \text{YTM}/n)}$$

The modified duration of the above illustration is,

$$\text{Modified duration} = \frac{4.55}{(1 + 0.05/5)}$$

$$= 4.33 \text{ years}$$

As has been already mentioned, duration measures the sensitivity (elasticity) of the bond price towards the variation in yields.

From Equation (5) we know that,

$dp/p = -D(dr/1 + r)$

Most portfolio managers rewrite the above equation as:

$$dp/p = -D/(1 + r) = -D^* \quad (10)$$

This substitution has been made, because in Equation (5) the scale factor $1/(1+r)$, is very cumbersome for portfolio managers. So, rather than taking it as a measure of elasticity, Equation (5) is simplified to Equation (10).

In equation (10), D^* is the modified duration. It is used in interest rate-risk management strategies. Hence it is also known as Macaulay's duration.

The following example should aid in the understanding of the ongoing discussion. A bond having 12% coupon rate; par value, Rs. 1000, 12% yield to maturity has a maturity period of 7 years. Duration of the bond is 5.11. What is the modified duration of the bond?

As the duration of the bond is 5.11, modified duration of the bond is,

$dp/p = -D/(1 + r) = -D^*$

$= -5.11/1.12 = -4.56\%$

The modified duration figure is interpreted as: with an increase of 1% in the interest rate, the bond price drops by -4.56%.

In other words, a decrease in yield of 100 basis points implies a 4.56% rise in the bond price.

Pause for thought: Modified duration is the variation in duration with the change in the yield

14.2.9 Relationship between Convexity and Duration

We have discussed at length the relationship between the yield, market price and maturity. Thus we know how convexity is an integral aspect of this relationship. Apart from these, duration, maturity and yield too are inter-linked. Thus by extrapolation we can state that convexity and duration are related. But we need to know the exact nature of the relation, and not an approximation. Hence it becomes imperative now to assess and analyze the relation between convexity and duration.

Convexity is the difference between the actual price change in a bond and that predicted by the duration statistics, for a given change in interest rate. As derived earlier, duration is the first derivative of the bond pricing equation with respect to its yield. On the other hand, convexity is the second derivative. Due to a downward sloping yield curve, the first derivative of price with respect to yield is negative, but the second derivative is positive. Figure 14.3 demonstrates this relationship graphically. Like Figure 14.2, Figure 14.3 too represents a bond that is currently selling for P and has a yield to maturity Y. The figure shows a straight line, which is tangent to the curve, at a point associated with current price (P) and yield.

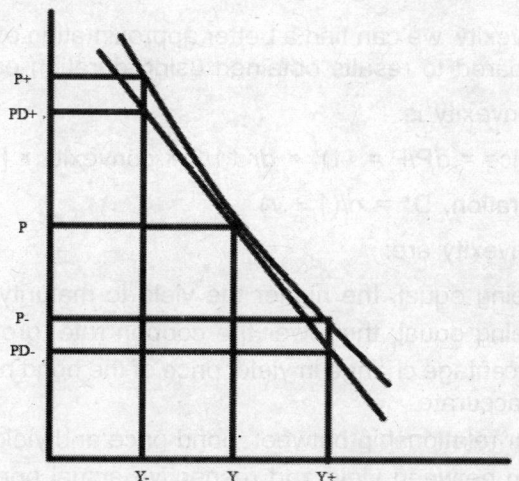

Figure 14.3: Relationship between convexity and duration

If yield of the bond increases from Y to Y^+, the corresponding prices of the bond decrease from P to P^-. Conversely, with a decrease in yield of the bond from Y to Y^-, the corresponding prices of the bond rise from P to P^+. One thing to be noted is that the fall in bond price decelerates when the yield increases. This is the reason why the shape of the curve is convex. The sharper is the curve the greater is the convexity.

There is another aspect that seeks attention and analyses. As per the equation, $dp/p = -D(dr/1 + r)$; the estimated prices of the bond when yield increases and falls will be PD^- and PD^+ respectively, and not, P^- and P^+. It is because the duration mentioned in the equation is not exact. The equation gives an approximate, and not an exact, price of a bond. Thus two things to be remembered, in this context are: it is an approximate equation and the percentage change in the price of a bond is linear function of its duration. Because of these, a new approximate price is represented by a straight line and the actual price by the curvature. The straight line which causes an error is a result of convexity. For example, in the case considered here, the errors are: $(P^- - PD^-)$ when yield rises; and $(P^+ - PD^+)$ when the yield falls. The equation underestimates the change in the price when yield changes. The actual relationship between yield change and bond price change is convex. The error becomes smaller for a lower percentage change in yield and is comparatively larger for a higher percentage change in yield. As the yield of the bond rises or falls, divergence occurs from the actual price changes and duration predicted price changes (tangent line). To get better (and thus improvised) approximation of the change in price for a given change in yield, the effect of duration on price, and the convexity on price, should be taken into account.

We can derive the convexity as second derivative of price change, with respect to yield, as follows:

Convexity = dp/dr^2

$$= \frac{1}{P}(1+r)^2 \sum_{t=1}^{} \frac{CF_t \times C_t(t+1)}{1(1+r)^t} \qquad (11)$$

With the help of convexity, we can find a better approximation of bond price change for every change in yield, as compared to results obtained using duration equation.

The equation for convexity is:

% change in price = $dP/P = -D^* \times dr + 1/2 \times$ convexity $\times [\Delta r]^2$ \qquad (12)

Where, modified duration, $D^* = d/(1 + r)$

Rules related to convexity are:

— Other things being equal, the higher the yield to maturity, lower is the convexity.
— Other things being equal, the lower the coupon rate, greater the convexity.
— For a larger percentage change in yield, price of the bond by using the duration equation becomes less accurate.
— There is a linear relationship between bond price and yield by using duration equation.
— The relationship between yield and respective actual bond price change is convex.
— Convexity increases for low coupon bearing, long maturity bonds and low YTM bonds.

> **Pause for thought:** As yield, price, maturity are all related to convexity—as well as to the duration—convexity and duration too are automatically related. Yet convexity gives a better approximation of the real market, with respect to the variation in price with every change in yield.

14.3 BOND PORTFOLIO MANAGEMENT

According to one of the bond pricing theorems, theorem 2, bond prices (discount and premium) converge at its par value as they approach maturity. Price and yield of bonds are reflections of change in interest rates. Hence bond portfolio management concerns itself mainly with altering the level of interest rate risk faced by the bonds, in the portfolio.

A preliminary, and quite detailed as well, discussion on the strategies adopted for managing portfolios—active and passive—we have already had in the introduction to this chapter. Now we proceed to accord them individual and more in-depth attention. On strategies depends the net output of the portfolios, whatever be the market conditions.

14.3.1 Passive Bond Management Strategies

Passive is the strategy, when the portfolio managers prefer to go by the book. They bank on the trend and projected return and yield, instead of trying out anything new. Passive strategy could be termed a safety-first approach. Passive strategy is of two types:

1. Buy and hold.
2. Indexing.

1. Buy and hold strategy

The portfolio managers examine certain factors related to the bond, such as: ratings given to the bond, coupon rate, maturity period, call/put feature, etc. Investors who opt for buy and hold strategy select bonds which match with their investment horizon, including maturities and duration. Such investors do not invest in bonds to earn profit by frequent trading. They prefer to invest and hold till maturity. However, investors may have to go for replacements of bonds as they mature. This is so because the individual bonds might have maturities shorter or longer than that desired by the investor. Thus, as per this strategy, bond portfolio manager would buy bonds with specific duration and as per pre-decided requirements would hold the same till maturity.

2. Indexing strategy

It is one of the most popular methods for bond portfolio managers. It works like index funds do for portfolio stocks. In an indexing strategy, bond portfolio manager replicates the investments characteristic of most popular bond market. The reason behind this investment strategy is that it is difficult to know and predict interest rate risk.

Pause for thought: Passive strategy is completely dependent on the precedence and projection of the market and is basically a safe approach.

14.3.2 Active Bond Management Strategies

Laddered and Barbell's strategies are the two well known active bond management strategies. Other active bond management strategies are: valuation analysis, credit analysis, etc.

As these strategies of active bond portfolio management depend upon uncertainty looming large over future interest rates, these are among the most risky strategies. The basic logic behind them is to hold capital when rise in interest rate is anticipated to end up with an attractive and significant capital gain, when interest rates are anticipated to fall. This attractive outcome is possible by altering the duration (i.e., maturity) structure of portfolio. The portfolio duration is decreased when the interest rates are expected to rise; and increased, when interest rates are expected to fall. Though yes, risk is indeed involved in these frequent restructuring of the portfolio, which is dependent on these duration alterations. Also, the restructuring of portfolios anticipating the fall of interest rates is very risky. Most important is the fact that, as an investment manager or a bond holder we assume that we are at peak of interest rates. Thus it is likely that the yield curve is downward sloping (resulting bond coupons will decline with maturity). Therefore, keeping such things in mind, the investor will shift his portfolio from short duration high coupon bonds to longer duration bonds, foregoing the current income. But if at this stage the interest rates rise, instead of our expectations for it to fall, our portfolio becomes susceptible to more price risk. Thus, the adjustment of the portfolio by predicting rise in interest rates involves comparatively less risk of an absolute capital loss. When maturity is reduced worst of worst that can happen is reduction in the income from interest and/or capital gain doesn't accrue.

Pause for thought: Active strategies prefer heightened activity—frequent trading—to safety. They are intent on generating better yields, defying the market logic. Risks are very high, but stakes are higher too—the returns that are delivered are high as well.

14.4 VALUATION ANALYSIS

Portfolio manager tries to select the bonds based only upon the evaluation of their intrinsic value. An intrinsic value of a bond depends upon various characteristics. Valuation analysis evaluates these characteristics with respect to the market. By evaluating the characteristics (all) of bonds, in terms of yield, required yield of the bond is derived from them. This gives the intrinsic value of the bond. Exercising this method on a number of bonds we can compare these derived bond values, with the prevailing market prices, to determine whether the bonds are under-priced or over-priced. Once the spectrum of prices is defined, investors buy under-priced bonds and over-priced bonds. For the valuation analysis it is important to understand and thus prioritize those characteristics which are important for evaluation of bonds. It is also extremely important to accurately estimate the yield cost of these characteristics over a period of time.

> **Pause for thought:** The intrinsic value of the bonds determines the composition of the portfolio. Thus evaluation of the same is done. Intrinsic value is decided by various characteristics. The individual evaluation of these characteristics, corresponding to the market, when summed, results in the intrinsic value. Yet some of the characteristics are more important than others in this evaluation.

14.4.1 Credit Analysis

To anticipate or determine the expected changes in the default risk, this strategy requires detailed analysis by the bond issuer. It is important to anticipate (based on performance) or project the likely changes in the ratings assigned to the bonds by rating agencies. We know that these ratings are subject to internal changes of the issuer (financial parameters, promoter, key resource person, etc.). Also the changes in the external environment (changes in industry and government policies for that particular industry) cause such changes in ratings. When economy is on the up and expanding, financially and fundamentally strong firms (issuers) thrive and excel. But during economic downturn, normal or even competent and good firms may find it difficult to maintain their financial health. Naturally companies go through these cyclic phases: ups and downs, in their ratings.

For the use of credit analysis as a bond portfolio management strategy, the prime requirement is to project rating changes before it is announced or rated by the rating agencies. Because when re-rating or rating is done by rating agencies, if it is a downgraded rating, market adjusts it swiftly. But the adjustment is not as swift, when the rating of a particular bond is upgraded. This manifests higher sensitivity of the market to adjustments for the downward rating, than for upward rating. So what is expected here is to acquire bond issues which are supposed to get upgrading and sell or avoid those bonds which are supposed to be downgraded.

> **Pause for thought:** Credit analysis analyzes the rating accredited, or likely to be, to the bonds.

14.4.2 Swaps

When a portfolio manager exchanges any existing bond or set of bonds with different bonds, it is a bond swap. Bond swapping has one or more of the following results:

- Increase in current income.
- Improved chances of price appreciation even when interest rates fall.
- Increase in yield to maturity.
- Leads to loss, to offset capital gain or taxable income.

> **Pause for thought:** Bond(s) in a portfolio are swapped with more profitable, as perceived, bonds.

Swaps are of 6 types and are discussed as follows:

1. *Substitution swaps*

This swap is used when portfolio manager wants to increase the current yield of the portfolio. For the purpose, the portfolio manager exchanges the bond with another bond, of similar risk characteristics and maturity. For example, a portfolio manager may replace a 10 year, 12% coupon bond, selling at a par value of Rs. 1000 with another 10 year, 12% coupon bond that sells for Rs. 960. The swap results in an increase in current yield. However, it is difficult to find desired replacements (as the one in this example) because bonds with same coupon and same risk would be selling at the same price.

Portfolio manager can adjust the portfolio's average duration by adjusting the holdings in the portfolio, if the scenario of interest rate is anticipated to change. Thus if the portfolio manager projects that interest rates are likely to rise he/she can decrease the portfolio's average duration to minimize the negative effect on prices. Reverse will happen when the managers expect the interest rates to fall. He/she can then lengthen the average duration of the portfolio to get the maximum benefit from such changes.

> **Pause for thought:** Substitution always means swapping with an entity of similar characteristics. Here too the same happens. To increase the current yield, bonds of almost similar risk features and maturity are swapped.

2. *Yield spread swaps*

The term yield spread means difference of yield in two markets. Thus in keeping with the difference, two such bonds are swapped to earn this spread. Obviously it involves bonds that trade in different markets, thus, pitting for example government bonds versus corporate bonds. Due to their different risk characteristics, they trade with different yields.

Example: We already know that government bonds have a lesser degree of risk as compared to private, corporate, bonds. However, sometimes a deviation from this perception is observed, with respect to the difference in yield. Such bonds can behave in unprecedented manner due to changing market conditions. Due to these deviations set in widening or narrowing of the spread between these markets. Portfolio managers exploit this difference in yield to gain from such trades. The deviation becomes extreme when during economic slowdowns investors discount corporate bonds and prefer government bonds. It is also known as inter-market spread swap.

> **Pause for thought:** The bonds are swapped on the basis of their performance in two different markets.

3. *Bond rating swaps*

Bonds with higher ratings have a comparatively lower yield to maturity, as they are considered to be less risky than the bonds with lower ratings. Two bonds with different ratings are swapped with each other, when one bond observes a change in the yield spread. If a portfolio manager predicts a change in the yield spread of a particular bond, he/she may swap such bonds with different ratings so as to produce capital gain, for slight increase in risk.

> **Pause for thought:** Bonds with different ratings are swapped, when one bond incurs a change in its yield spread. The swapping intends to increase the capital gain, despite the risk.

4. *Rate anticipation swaps*

This swap is put into effect by the bond portfolio manager when he/she wants to exploit the information on interest rate movements. Based upon the available information and believing in his/her anticipation about rise and fall in interest rates, he/she may replace the existing bonds to maximize gains. If the manager projects interest rates to go down, he/she would prefer to swap short-term bonds with long term-bonds. Conversely, if a rise in interest rates is anticipated, he/she might swap long-term bonds for short-term bonds. This swapping of long to short and vice-versa involves very high risk as investors have to rely upon uncertain predictions for future interest rates. But an expert bond portfolio manager designs the swap in such a way that one can end up with the least loss possible, when interest rates rises. One can also be led to a significant gain (by capital appreciation) when interest rates fall.

> **Pause for thought:** These swaps are purely based on the anticipation of what the rates would be, from the available information on the interest rate movements.

5. *Pure yield pick-up swaps*

Simply put, pure yield pick-up swaps is a transaction in which bonds with lower returns are swapped for bonds with higher returns. Sole purpose of this pure yield pick-up swap is to increase yield with new bonds having similar maturity and risk rating as the old bonds; only the coupon differs. For example, an investor who holds a treasury bond, with 5% yield, may sell it in the market and use the sale proceeds to purchase 6% yield bond.

This strategy is not put into effect with mis-priced (over or under-valued) bonds. But it becomes a tool for increasing returns by holding higher yield bonds. When the yield curve in the market is observed to be upward sloping, bond portfolio managers opt for the long-term bonds. This strategy is pursued to earn an expected term premium from higher yield bonds. However, investors are exposed to interest rate risk till the yield curve remains downward sloping during the holding period. Investors will earn a higher rate of return by swapping short-term bonds with long-term bonds. But if yield curve slides further downward, then the long-term bonds end up with substantial capital loss.

> **Pause for thought:** The bonds yielding low returns are replaced with those with higher returns. The yield becomes the sole determinant for the swapping.

6. *Tax swaps*

Tax swap means swapping in to similar bonds to receive tax benefit. Tax swap is used to exploit tax advantages. Tax swap can be realized in a situation when an investor sells a security which has declined in price since its purchase, to claim a capital loss for tax purpose and for simultaneous purchase of a similar or equivalent security (but not the same) of a company or industry. A tax swap allows the investor to reduce his/her tax liability. A bond incurring loss is swapped with another bond having similar characteristics (lower priced). This swap intends to realize the tax benefits accorded to the incurred capital loss. But this too comes with its share of risk, as the bonds that are swapped—sold and bought—are not exactly identical, thus differ in their individual responses to the different factors in the market that operate in tandem.

> **Pause for thought:** Bonds are swapped to gain tax benefits.

14.5 IMMUNIZATION

Immunization is the procedure of protecting the portfolio from interest rate risk(s). An immunized portfolio is insulated from any adverse effects related to future interest rates changes. This technique of bond portfolio management, very popular with portfolio managers, has evolved from the concept of duration. It ensures, and thus enables them to meet the promised stream of cash flow.

Immunization is achieved by calculating the duration of the promised cash flow, to subsequently invest the funds in a portfolio of bonds, whose duration of cash flow is identical to the weighted average duration of individual bonds in the portfolio. For example, we assume a bond portfolio, of two bonds. Out of these two bonds, X and Y, X has duration of 8 years and duration of Y is 4 years; one fourth of the total fund is invested in bond X and three fourths in bond Y.

Duration of the bond portfolio = [{(1/4) × 8} + {(3/4) × 4}]
$$= 2 + 3 = 5.$$

Now, we further assume a simple situation where a portfolio manager has one, and only one, cash outflow of Rs. 12,00,00,000, which he has to arrange from his portfolio and which has to be paid in two years. As there is only one cash outflow, its duration is thus two years. The bond portfolio manager considers investing in two different bonds. The first bond, XYZ, has the following characteristics: annual coupon payment of Rs. 65; maturity period is 3 years; par value of the bond is Rs. 1000 and yield to maturity is 8%. The price and duration of the bond are calculated as follows:

$$P_0 = \frac{65}{(1.08)^1} + \frac{65}{(1.08)^2} + \frac{1065}{(1.08)^3}$$

$$= Rs.\ 961.3$$

$$Duration = \frac{2707.933}{961.34}$$

$$= 2.82$$

Table 14.7: Duration of the Bond

Year	Cash flow	Discount factor @ 8%	P_v of Cash flow	Cash flow × Year
1	65	0.926	60.19	60.19
2	65	0.857	55.73	111.454
3	1065	0.794	845.93	2536.29
			961.34	2707.933

The second bond, PQR, has a maturity of 1 year and provides Rs. 1060 to its holder at the time of maturity. Rs. 1060 is generated from: Rs. 1000 (par value) and Rs. 60 (coupon payment). Bond PQR is currently selling at Rs. 981.48 and its yield to maturity is 8%.

There are three alternatives available to the portfolio manager:

(i) The entire fund of the portfolio can be invested in the 1 year bond (PQR bond). In this case, the maturity amount realized after one year has to be invested in another one year bond. Here lies the risk: if rate of interest falls at maturity, the amount generated would have to be reinvested at a lower rate than the current rate of 8%. Thus this option involves reinvestment risk.

(ii) The portfolio manager could choose to invest the entire fund in XYZ bond, whose maturity is 3 years. In this case, the bond has to be sold after two years as the portfolio manager has a cash outflow of Rs. 12,00,00,000, to be paid in two years. But, if at the end of 2 years, interest rate rises, bond prices would fall. This would make it difficult to generate cash flow of Rs. 12,00,00,000, for the payment. Thus, this alternative carries interest rate risk.

(iii) The third alternative is to partially invest in both the bonds, XYZ and PQR. The question herein pertains to the prospective ratio of the proportion of both, in the portfolio. Immunization strategy assesses this ratio by applying the following equation:

$$W_1 + W_2 = 1 \quad \ldots(I)$$
$$(W_1 \times 1) + (W_3 \times 2.82) = 2 \quad \ldots(II)$$

where,

W_1 = weight (proportion) of bond 1.

W_3 = weight (proportion) of bond 2.

1 = total weight (which should be equal to 1).

'1' in second equation = duration of bond 1 (PQR).

2.82 = duration of bond 2 (XYZ).

'2' in second equation = maturity (or number of years for cash flow).

Equation (II) also indicates that the weighted average of the duration of the bonds, in the portfolio, must be equal to the duration of the cash outflow.

We can re-write equation (I) as,

$W_1 = 1 - W_3$

By putting this value in to equation (II),

$[(1 - W_3) \times 1] + (W_3 \times 2.82) = 2$

$(1 - W_3) + 2.82 W_3 = 2$

$1.82 W_3 = 2 - 1$

$W_3 = 0.5494$

$W_1 = 0.4505$

The weights, $W_1 = 0.4505$ and $W = 0.5494$, indicate that the portfolio manager should invest 45.05% of the fund in PQR bond ($n = 1$ year) and 54.94% in XYZ bond ($n = 3$ year).

For that, the portfolio manager requires Rs. 10,28,40,000 [Rs. 12,00,00,000/$(1.08)^2$], to purchase bonds for complete immunization of the portfolio. Out of Rs. 102840000, Rs. 46329420 will be used to buy PQR bond ($n = 1$), and Rs. 56500296, to buy XYZ bond ($n = 3$). As the current market price of PQR bond is Rs. 981.48 (Rs. 46329420/Rs. 981.48), 47203.63 units of PQR bond and 58774.88 units (Rs. 56500296/Rs. 961.3) of XYZ bond, would be purchased.

We have discussed earlier that alternatives 1 and 2 entail reinvestment and interest rate risks, respectively. Thus, with a rise in interest rates, XYZ will give poor return; while with a decrease in interest rates, PQR will provide lower yield from reinvestment. This risk can be completely annulled (and the portfolio fully immunized) by the third alternative, which we have just analyzed.

But then how the process works?

In immunization strategy, both interest rate risk and reinvestment risk are set against each other. If the yield rises, the proceeds from selling XYZ, at the end of the two years, will be less (because price falls when interest rate rises). But an immunization will set in as PQR bond's proceeds will be reinvested at a higher rate. Thus the net effect sees the portfolio protected. Also coupon payment of XYZ bond will be reinvested at a higher rate. Conversely, if interest rate falls, then the proceeds from PQR bond and first year coupon payment of XYZ bond will be reinvested at lower rate. But the selling price of XYZ bond will rise, again compensating for the loss incurred by PQR bond. Thus, the third alternative, of putting the stakes in both the bonds, effectively immunizes (protects) the bond portfolio from interest rate movements.

The table below shows the proceeds from the portfolio, under different situations. It is apparent, irrespective of rise or fall in the interest rates, the value of the portfolio remains almost same, at Rs. 12,00,00,000—that is, the portfolio stays protected, courtesy the immunization.

Table 14.8: Immunized Portfolio at Different Discount Rates

YTM	Price of the bond			
	8%	9%	10%	11%
PQR bond at t = 2 [(Rs. 1060 × 47203.63 × (1 + y)]	54038715.62	54539074.1	55039432.58	55539791.05
XYZ bond at t = 1 [Rs. 65 × 58774.88 × (1 + y)]	4125996.58	4164200.25	4202403.92	4240607.59
XYZ bond at t = 2 [Rs. 65 × 58774.88]	3820367.2	3820367.2	3820367.2	3820367.2
XYZ bond at t = 2 [(Rs. 1065 × 58774.88/(1 + y)]	57958562.22	57426832.22	56904770.18	56392114.6
Portfolio value at the end of second year	119943642	119950474	119966974	119992880

Pause for thought: Rendering the portfolio immune to interest rate risks and reinvestment risks.

14.5.1 Issues with Immunization

Hypothetical examples, as seen above, may not work in real situation. Table 14.8 shows that many times value of the portfolio tends to be less than Rs. 12,00,00,000 at the end of two years. This happens because the interest rate risk of the bond, at times, cannot be measured accurately by the duration.

1. *Default and call risk*

Our calculation of duration and immunization is based on the assumption that the entire promised cash flows (coupon payments + par value), of all the bonds, will be paid in full and on time. Also it is assumed in the computation of duration and immunization that neither the bond will be called before maturity nor will it default. But if a particular bond is redeemed before its maturity, or if it defaults or delays in terms of coupon and par value payments, such bond portfolios are not immunized.

2. *Shift in the yield curve*

In our discussion we have assumed YTM of 8%, for both XYZ and PQR bonds. Also in the analysis of bond portfolio immunization, we assumed that it will rise or fall from 8% to 9%, 10%, 11% or 7%, and so on. Here, in this example, two assumptions are made: (i) shift in the yield curves are not parallel and (ii) change in yield does not occur from passing from one year to the other. In fact in real life, yield curves are not parallel; they may change frequently. It is not necessary that they will change at the end of the year only.

3. *Rebalancing*

Yield changes with time and so does duration of the bond. So, the duration computed earlier (at the time of designing of the portfolio) is no longer applicable. With the revised yield, a revised duration too becomes applicable. Therefore, immunization of new duration comes into effect. Thus the immunization strategy designed earlier does not immunize the portfolio actually. The portfolio needs to be rebalanced (restructured) every time the yield changes.

As yield changes during the period of the bond, existing bonds have to be replaced with others, whose duration match with the promised cash flow. This frequent selling and replacement (by purchasing) of bonds incurs the transaction cost. Sometimes it is difficult, even to get perfect replacement. Furthermore, frequent replacements may outweigh the benefit or gain from rebalancing. Thus, the decision for rebalancing has to be taken, taking into account, the gains from rebalancing and loss from transaction cost, necessitated by the rebalancing.

4. *Selection of the bond*

In the market there are 'n' numbers of portfolios whose duration may match with our promised cash outflow. In the above example, the promised cash outflow occurs at the end of two years. Hence, we can immunize the portfolio with a set of bonds whose maturity is two years. It depends on how the manager selects the portfolio of desired (or required) duration, from the available platter of portfolios. It is better, though, to select those bonds whose yield to maturity is highest among all the bonds that are available. The portfolio manager may choose the bond with lowest cost, as well. The other solution is that the portfolio manager selects the bonds whose maturity is closer to the promised cash outflow. In the example discussed here, the promised cash outflow of Rs. 12,00,00,000, occurs at the end of the two years. So, bond portfolio with bonds of 1 year and 3 year maturities are more preferred to the bonds with maturities of 1 and 4 years, respectively.

14.5.2 Contingent Immunization

Contingent immunization has the flavor of both active and passive bond portfolio management. As the yield rate is uncertain, so is the price of the bond. At times, immunization of a bond portfolio, by assuming fully favorable situation may not produce the desired result. In such circumstances, contingent immunization is applied.

In the example that has been repeatedly resorted to, by this ensuing discussion, the portfolio manager had to manage the promised cash outflow of Rs. 12,00,00,000 at the end of the two years, at the assumed yield of 8% and maturity of two years. We derived a strategy that portfolio can be completely immunized by investing Rs. 46329420 and Rs. 56500296 (as shown in Table 14.6) in bonds PQR and XYZ respectively.

However, there is another way to immunize this portfolio. It is done by investing the fund in only one bond, to match the cash outflow of Rs. 12,00,00,000 at the end of two years rather than investing in two bonds PQR and XYZ. We assume that the portfolio manager chooses to invest Rs. 104812647.3 in a two year maturity portfolio, C. That is, the portfolio manager will invest Rs. 104812647.3, at present, in bond C. It matures in two years, to give the maturity amount of Rs. 12,00,00,000, yielding 7% return. Here, the client (for whom the portfolio manager is immunizing) may accept the low yield of 7%, but expects a higher return.

> **Pause for thought:** A portfolio management immunization strategy that utilizes both the active and passive approaches is known as contingent immunization.

14.6 HORIZON ANALYSIS

The return of a bond depends on the purchasing and selling prices of the bond; as well as on the series of coupon payments. We know further that the price of a bond depends upon the YTM of the bond. Hence, price of the bond at the beginning of the holding period (purchasing price) and the selling price, both depend on the interest rates. It is extremely difficult to forecast the YTM when time horizon is too long. But at least in the initial phase the possible price changes must be analyzed by estimating: the yield change and the possible return from bond, in turn. This technique of actively managing bond portfolio by estimating the yield and analyzing its probable effect on bond is known as horizon analysis.

In horizon analysis, a single holding period return is selected for study, and a series of rates are tried for the holding period of the bond. In other words, we are dealing with a set of interest rates and their effects on price, over a given time horizon. But here we make a basic assumption: bonds will not default. Table 14.9, below, projects the hypothetical scenario, for bonds with 8% coupon.

The price change can be comprised of two parts.

Price change = Time effect + Yield change effect

We consider a bond with a maturity of 10 years, coupon rate of 7% p.a. and par value, Rs. 1000. The Table 14.9 shows the price of the bond per year (i.e., at the end of 1 year, 2 years, 3 years, extending to 10 years). For the purpose here, the spectrum of yield to maturity is assumed to be: 6.00, 6.50, 7.00, 7.50, 8.00, 8.50, 9.00, 9.50, 10.00, 10.50, 11.00, 11.50 and 12.00.

Table 14.9: Price of the Bond, with Different Yields to Maturity and Different Maturity Periods

YTM %	Maturity of the bond										
	10	9	8	7	6	5	4	3	2	1	0
6.0	1073.6	1068.0	1062.1	1055.8	1049.2	1042.1	1034.7	1026.7	1018.3	1009.4	1000.0
6.5	1035.9	1033.3	1030.4	1027.4	1024.2	1020.8	1017.1	1013.2	1009.1	1004.7	1000.0
7.0	1000.0	1000.0	1000.0	1000.0	1000.0	1000.0	1000.0	1000.0	1000.0	1000.0	1000.0
7.5	965.7	968.1	970.7	973.5	976.5	979.8	983.3	987.0	991.0	995.3	1000.0
8.0	932.9	937.5	942.5	947.9	953.8	960.1	966.9	974.2	982.2	990.7	1000.0
8.5	901.6	908.2	915.4	923.2	931.7	940.9	950.9	961.7	973.4	986.2	1000.0
9.0	871.6	880.1	889.3	899.3	910.3	922.2	935.2	949.4	964.8	981.7	1000.0
9.5	843.0	853.1	864.2	876.3	889.5	904.0	919.9	937.3	956.3	977.2	1000.0
10.0	815.7	827.2	840.0	853.9	869.3	886.3	904.9	925.4	947.9	972.7	1000.0
10.5	789.5	802.4	816.6	832.4	849.8	869.0	890.2	913.7	939.7	968.3	1000.0
11.0	764.4	778.5	794.2	811.5	830.8	852.2	875.9	902.3	931.5	964.0	1000.0
11.5	740.5	755.6	772.5	791.3	812.3	835.8	861.9	891.0	923.4	959.6	1000.0
12.0	717.5	733.6	751.6	771.8	794.4	819.8	848.1	879.9	915.5	955.4	1000.0

The above table shows the price matrix for a bond, with its yield varying in the market, at different maturity levels. The bond, in this example, has a coupon rate of 7% and par value of Rs. 1000. At the given YTM of 8% and term to maturity of 10 years, the bond is priced at Rs. 932.9. Thus it has a promised yield to maturity of 8%. For example, after 6 years, the time to maturity is 4 years. During this time, the yield also might have changed in the market. Suppose 6 years down the line, yield has changed and has reached 10% p.a. At the yield of 10% and term to maturity of 6 years, the price of the bond might be Rs. 904.9. We know that for any given time period, price of the bond is subject to the maturity period and change in the yield structure. From the table above we can say that bond price has reached to Rs. 904.9 from Rs. 932.9 due to two reasons: (i) change in yield (10% from 8%) and (ii) change in time (as 6 years have passed). It means, thus, the total price change, Rs. 28 (from Rs. 904.9 to Rs. 932.9) consists of two parts: (i) Rs. 34 (from Rs. 932.9 to Rs. 966.9, had the yield remained unchanged at 8%) and (ii) Rs. 62 (from Rs. 966.9 to Rs. 904.9 due to yield change effect for the maturity of 6 years). Thus,

Price change = Time effect + Yield change effect

Rs. 28 = Rs. 62 − Rs. 34

Let us take another example to emphasize how this works. In the given example, at a current yield of 8%, coupon rate of 7% p.a., the price of the bond is Rs. 932.9, for maturity period of 10 years. Suppose after 4 years, yield in the market shifts downward, to 6.5%. With 4 years already elapsed, 6 years are left to maturity for this bond. The price change, Rs. 91.3 (from Rs. 1024.2 to Rs. 932.9), consist of two parts: (i) Rs. 20.9 (from Rs. 953.8 to Rs. 932.9, due to time change and yield constant effect) and (ii) Rs. 70.4 (from Rs. 1024.2 to Rs. 953.8). In this case,

Price change = Time effect + Yield change effect

Rs. 91.3 = Rs. 20.9 + Rs. 70.4

From the above table we can also see that the coupon payment have not been considered for analysis of the change in price. But we must actually consider all cash flow and all possible yields to have a realistic picture.

> **Pause for thought:** In a portfolio with a wide time horizon, analyzing the probable effect on the bond, by estimating its yield first, forms the crux of horizon analysis.

SUMMARY

- ✓ There are five principles of bond pricing theorems: (i) If a bond's price increases (decreases), then its yield must decrease (increase). (ii) If the bond's yield remains same throughout the life of the bond, then the size of its discount (or premium) will decrease as maturity is approached. (iii) If the bond's yield remains same throughout the tenure of the bond, the size of its discount or premium will decrease at an increasing rate as maturity is attained. (iv) A decrease in the bond's yield will raise the price of the bond by an amount, which is greater in size than the corresponding fall in the bond's price, for a similar increase in the yield of the bond. (v) For a bond with a higher coupon rate, the percentage change in the bond's price will be smaller for a given change in yield.
- ✓ Duration of the bond is the average maturity of the bond, with a series of payments (coupon rate plus principal) associated with the bond. Duration is a weighted average

of time, till all the payments are made—where weights are equal to the present value of each cash flow in terms of price of the bond.

✓ The portfolio's duration is equal to the weighted average duration of the individual bonds in the portfolio.

✓ The construction of the bond portfolio, whose duration can match with liability in the future, is known as immunization technique.

KEY CONCEPTS

Coupon Payments	Bond Portfolio	Duration
Coupon Rate	Active Bond Management	Portfolio Duration
Yield to Maturity	Passive Bond Management	Convexity
Term to Maturity	Immunization	Duration and Convexity
Swaps	Horizon Analysis	

REVIEW QUESTIONS

1. The duration of the coupon bearing bond is always less than its time to maturity. Why?
2. Explain how immunization strategy helps a bond portfolio manager to mitigate interest rate and reinvestment risks.
3. What is the difference between the substitution swaps and inter-market swaps?
4. Prove the principle of bond convexity by using bond theorems 1 and 4. Support your answer with a figure.

ILLUSTRATIONS

Q.1. Calculate the duration of a bond with annual coupon payment of Rs. 75; maturity, 5 years; and par value, Rs. 1000. Its yield to maturity is 9%. Find out the price of the bond as well.

Ans:

Year	Discount factor	CF	P_v of CF	CF × Year
1	0.917431	75	68.80734	68.80734
2	0.84168	75	63.126	126.252
3	0.772183	75	57.91376	173.7413
4	0.708425	75	53.13189	212.5276
5	0.649931	1075	698.6762	3493.381
			941.6552	4074.709

Duration = 4.327

Q.2. For the bond in Q.1, find out by how much will the bond's price change if its yield increases to 10%.

Ans: $= dp/p = -D(dr/1 + r)$
$= -4.33[(0.10) - (0.09/1) + (0.09)]$
$= -0.0397$
$= -3.97\%$

Q.3. A bond has an annual coupon payment of Rs. 65; maturity, 3 years; and par value, Rs. 1000. Its yield to maturity is 8%. Find out the price of the bond and duration.

Ans: Bond price $= (65/1.08) + (65/1.08^2) + (1065/1.08^3)$
$= 961.34$

Duration:

Year	Discount factor	CF	P_v of CF	CF × Year
1	0.925926	65	60.18519	60.18519
2	0.857339	65	55.72702	111.454
3	0.793832	1065	845.4313	2536.294
			961.3435	2707.933
		Duration	2.816822	

Q.4. Consider a case in which a portfolio manager has to make only one cash outflow of Rs. 8,00,000, in two years. The bond portfolio manager considers investing in different bonds. The first bond is the one shown in Q.3, with a maturity of 3 years. The second bond issue involves a set of bonds that mature in 1 year, providing the holder of each bond with a single payment of Rs. 1060 (consisting of single coupon payment of Rs. 60 and a par value of Rs. 1000). These bonds (second bond) are currently selling for Rs. 972.47, and their yield to maturity is 8%. Calculate the immunization of the bond. Also construct the immunized portfolio (with discount rate of 8%, 9%, 10% and 11% respectively).

Ans: Weights of bonds:

W_1 = bond 1, its duration is 1 year.

W_2 = bond 2, its duration is 2.82 years.

Now, $W_1 + W_2 = 1$

$W_2 = 1 - W_1$

$(W_1 \times 1) + (W_2 \times 2.82) = 2$

$W_1 + 2.82 (1 - W_1) = 2$

$W_1 + 2.82 - 2.82W_1 = 2$

$1.82W_1 = 0.82$

$W_1 = 0.4505$

$W_2 = 1 - 0.4505$

$W_2 = 0.5495$

P_v of 8 lakhs,

$P_v = 8,00,000/(1.08)^2 = 6,85,871.0562$

$W_1 = (6,85,871.0562) \times (0.4505) = 3,08,985$

$W_2 = (6,85,871.0562) \times (0.5495) = 3,76,886$

Number of bonds:

$W_1 = 3,08,985/972.47 = 317.73$

$W_2 = 3,76,886/961.3435 = 392.04$

For bond 1 only:

$W_1 = 705.29$

$W_2 = 713.45$

	8%	9%	10%	11%
Bond 1 (1060 × 317.73 ×1.08)	3,63,737.304	3,67,105.242	3,70,473.18	3,73,841.118
Bond 2 (65 × 392.04 ×1.08)	27521.21	27776.03	28030.86	28285.69
(65 × 392.04)	25482.6	25482.6	25482.6	25482.6
(1065 × 392.04)/1.08	386595	383048.3	379566	376146.5
Total	803336.1	803412.2	803552.6	803755.9
Only bond 1	807416	814892.1	822368.1	829844.2
Only bond 2	799999.4	794008.7	788135.2	782376

Q.5. Mr. PQR owns a portfolio of four bonds with the following durations and weights:

Bond	Duration	Proportion
A	4.9	0.15
B	5.8	0.35
C	2.74	0.30
D	3.99	0.20

What is duration of Mr. PQR's portfolio?

Ans: Duration of Mr. PQR's portfolio

$= (4.9 \times 0.15) + (5.8 \times 0.35) + (2.74 \times 0.30) + (3.99 \times 0.20)$

$= 4.385$

Q.6. Consider a bond of 7.85 year duration. If its yield to maturity increases from 11% to 12%, what is the expected percentage change in the price of the bond?

Ans: $dp/p = -D (dr/1 + r)$
$= -7.85(0.12 - 0.11/1 + 0.11)$
$= -0.0708$
$= -7.08\%$

Q.7. A bond sells at its par value of Rs. 1000, with 8 years maturity and a 6.5% coupon rate p.a. Calculate the bond's duration.

Ans:

Year	Discount factor	CF	P_v	CF × Year
1	0.909091	65	59.09091	59.09091
2	0.826446	65	53.71901	107.438
3	0.751315	65	48.83546	146.5064
4	0.683013	65	44.39587	177.5835
5	0.620921	65	40.35989	201.7994
6	0.564474	65	36.69081	220.1448
7	0.513158	65	33.35528	233.4869
8	0.466507	1065	496.8304	3974.643
			813.2776	5120.693
		Duration	6.296365	

Q.8. Consider a 5 year term to maturity bond of Rs. 1000 face value and Rs. 100 annual coupon interest payments. The bond sells at par. What is the bond's percentage price change if the yield to maturity rises to 11% and 13% and falls to 8% and 9%.

Year	Discount factor	CF	P_v	CF × Year
1	0.909091	100	90.90909	90.90909
2	0.826446	100	82.64463	165.2893
3	0.751315	100	75.13148	225.3944
4	0.683013	100	68.30135	273.2054
5	0.620921	100	62.09213	310.4607
6	0.564474	100	56.44739	338.6844
7	0.513158	100	51.31581	359.2107
8	0.466507	1100	513.1581	4105.265
			1000	5868.419
		Duration	5.868419	

When the yield rises to 11%,

$$dp/p = -D(dr/1 + r)$$
$$= -5.87(0.11 - 0.10)/(1 + 0.10)$$
$$= -0.0534$$
$$= -5.34\%$$

When the yield rises to 13%,

$$dp/p = -D(dr/1 + r)$$
$$= -5.87(0.13 - 0.10)/(1 + 0.10)$$
$$= -0.1601$$
$$= -16.01\%$$

When the yield falls to 8%,

$$dp/p = -D(dr/1 + r)$$
$$= 5.87(0.10 - 0.08)/(1 + 0.10)$$
$$= 0.1067$$
$$= 10.67\%$$

When the yield falls to 9%,

$$dp/p = -D(dr/1 + r)$$
$$= 5.87(0.10 - 0.09)/(1 + 0.10)$$
$$= 0.0534$$
$$= 5.34\%$$

Q.9. Consider two bonds, A and B, whose face values are Rs. 10000; YTM is 7% and maturity period is 12 years. Both the bonds make annual interest payments. However, bond A has a 10% coupon rate while bond B sells at par. If the yield of both bonds decreases to 5%, calculate the percentage price changes of the two bonds.

Ans.: When YTM is 7%,

Price of bond A

$$= (1000/1.07^1) + (1000/1.07^2) + (1000/1.07^3) + (1000/1.07^4) + (1000/1.07^5)$$
$$+ (1000/1.07^6) + (1000/1.07^7) + (1000/1.07^8) + (1000/1.07^9) + (1000/1.07^{10})$$
$$+ (1000/1.07^{11}) + (11000/1.07^{12})$$

$$= 12382.8059$$

Price of bond B

$$= (700/1.07^1) + (700/1.07^2) + (700/1.07^3) + (700/1.07^4) + (700/1.07^5) + (700/1.07^6)$$
$$+ (700/1.07^7) + (700/1.07^8) + (700/1.07^9) + (700/1.07^{10})$$
$$+ (700/1.07^{11}) + (10700/1.07^{12})$$

$$= 10000$$

When YTM is 5%,
Price of bond A
= $(1000/1.05^1) + (1000/1.05^2) + (1000/1.05^3) + (1000/1.05^4) + (1000/1.05^5)$
$+ (1000/1.05^6) + (1000/1.05^7) + (1000/1.05^8) + (1000/1.05^9) + (1000/1.05^{10})$
$+ (1000/1.05^{11}) + (11000/1.05^{12})$
= 14431.6258

Price of bond B
= $(700/1.05^1) + (700/1.05^2) + (700/1.05^3) + (700/1.05^4) + (700/1.05^5) + (700/1.05^6)$
$+ (700/1.05^7) + (700/1.05^8) + (700/1.05^9) + (700/1.05^{10})$
$+ (700/1.05^{11}) + (10700/1.05^{12})$
= 11772.6503

% change in price:

Bond A = (14431.6258 − 12382.8059)/12382.8059
= 0.1655
= 16.55%

Bond B = (11772.6503 − 10000)/10000
= 0.1772
= 17.72%

PROBLEMS

1. A bond with 9% coupon payment p.a., sells at its par value of Rs. 1000. Its maturity period is 8 years. Calculate the bond's duration.

2. Mr. Sanjay owns a portfolio of six bonds with the following durations and proportions. Calculate the duration of Mr. Sanjay's bond portfolio.

Bond	Duration	Proportion
1	4.87	0.20
2	5.10	0.15
3	2	0.15
4	3.6	0.20
5	2.9	0.15
6	6.7	0.15

3. A bond has duration of 5.98 years and its yield rises from 9% to 9.6%. What is the expected percentage change in the price of the bond?

4. Consider a 10 year maturity bond, whose face value is Rs. 1000 and annual coupon payment rate is 10%. The bond sells at par value. What would be the percentage change in the price of the bond, if yield changes to 11% and 9%?

5. Consider a bond with annual coupon payment of Rs. 90; maturity, 3 years; and par value, Rs. 1000. Its yield to maturity is 8%. Find out the price of the bond and duration. Now, consider a case in which a portfolio manager has to make only one cash outflow of Rs. 10,00,000 in 2 years. The bond portfolio manager considers investing in different bond issues. The first bond issue is as shown in Q.4, which has a maturity of 3 years. The second bond issue involves a set of bonds that matures in one year, providing the holder of each bond with a single payment of Rs. 1080 (consisting of single coupon payment of Rs. 80 and a par value of Rs. 1000). These bonds (second bond) are currently selling for Rs. 990, and their yield to maturity is 9%. Calculate the immunization of the bond. Also construct the immunized portfolio (with discount rate of 8%, 9%, 10% and 11% respectively).

SUGGESTED FURTHER READING FOR EMPIRICAL WORK

1. Ronn, E.I. (1987), "A New Linear Programming Approach to Bond Portfolio Management", *The Journal of Financial and Quantitative Analysis*, Vol. 22, No. 4.
2. Fogler, H.R. (1984), "Bond Portfolio Immunization, Inflation, and the Fisher Equation", *The Journal of Risk and Insurance*, Vol. 51, No. 2.
3. Bierwag, G. O., Kaufman, G.G., and Toevs, A. (1983), "Duration: Its Development and Use in Bond Portfolio Management", *Financial Analysts Journal*, Vol. 39, No. 4.
4. Adler, M. (1983), "Global Fixed-Income Portfolio Management", *Financial Analysts Journal*, Vol. 39, No. 5.
5. Cremers, K.J.M., Nair, V.B., and Wei, C. (2007), "Governance Mechanisms and Bond Prices", *The Review of Financial Studies*, Vol. 20, No. 5.
6. Crack, T.F., and Nawalkha, S.K. (2000), "Interest Rate Sensitivities of Bond Risk Measures", *Financial Analysts Journal*, Vol. 56, No. 1.
7. Jeng H., and McLeod, R.W. (1995), "Intrayear Compounding and Fundamental Bond Valuation", *Quarterly Journal of Business and Economics*, Vol. 34, No. 3.
9. Cheng, P.L. (1962), "Optimum Bond Portfolio Selection", *Management Science*, Vol. 8, No. 4.
10. Maxwell, W.F. (1998), "The January Effect in the Corporate Bond Market: A Systematic Examination", *Financial Management*, Vol. 27, No. 2.
11. Zipkin, P. (1992), "The Structure of Structured Bond Portfolio Models", *Operations Research*, Vol. 40, Supplement 1: Optimization.
12. Ekeland, I., and Taflin, E. (2005), "A Theory of Bond Portfolios", *The Annals of Applied Probability*, Vol. 15, No. 2.
13. Resnick, B.G., and Shoesmith, G.L. (2002), "Using the Yield Curve to Time the Stock Market", *Financial Analysts Journal*, Vol. 58, No. 3.
14. Best, P., Byrne, A., and Ilmanen, A. (1998), "What Really Happened to U.S. Bond Yields" *Financial Analysts Journal*, Vol. 54, No. 3.

REFERENCES

1. http://www.cbe.wwu.edu/Hall/MBA542/bond_portfolio_management_strate.htm
2. http://www.investopedia.com/articles/bonds/08/bond-portfolio-strategies.asp#axzz2E4qQ3tva
3. http://seekingalpha.com/article/672131-strategies-to-position-your-bond-portfolio-for-interest-rate-moves
4. http://www.qfinance.com/asset-management-calculations/portfolio-analysis-duration-convexity-and-immunization
5. http://www.washingtoncrossingadvisors.com/LBP.pdf
6. http://www.investopedia.com/articles/bonds/08/bond-portfolio-strategies.asp#axzz2E4qQ3tva
7. http://www.thornburginvestments.com/research/articles/laddering_full.pdf

PART 5
FUNDAMENTAL ANALYSIS
(E-I-C FRAMEWORK)

15
ECONOMIC ANALYSIS

> **LEARNING OBJECTIVES**
> The purpose of this chapter is to enable you to understand:
> • The relationship between stock market and economy.
> • The factors that govern stock market.

15.1 INTRODUCTION

We come to this stage of the book with an understanding of the various aspects of stock market. The tools that operate to multiply our funds have been discussed in detail. The main purpose is to gain maximum returns and hence options are selected accordingly. Many generalizations are arrived at, which enable the arrival at a judicious decision. Yet these generalizations are made possible by exhaustive analysis of the market. Hence, in this chapter, we endeavor to analyze the functioning of market and thus of economy.

There are basically two types of analyses which guide us to our investment decisions:
— Fundamental analysis.
— Technical analysis.

Fundamental analysis is the analysis, wherein the investment decisions are taken on the basis of the financial strength of the company. There are two approaches to fundamental analysis, viz., E-I-C analysis or the 'top-down' approach and C-I-E analysis or the 'bottom-up' approach. In the following section, we shall be discussing the E-I-C approach. Fundamental analysis thus has obviously three components, and they are: economy-industry-company. This is usually done by the security analysts. The first step of this approach is to analyze the overall economy, in order to assess the general direction in which economy is heading. The key factor here is the relationship between economy and the stock price.

As per the efficient market hypothesis (discussed in Chapter 11), in a semi-strong and strong form of the efficient market, price of the stock does not depend upon past performances. Market discounts every hope and fear pertaining to economic and other factors. A rational investor intelligently adjudges the current economic situation and with a deep insight is able to forecast the status of the market. For an in-depth analysis of stock market and of particular stocks, it is imperative that one studies the economy and the economic factors involved, therein, to begin with. In this chapter we will discuss the factors which affect, and thus govern the stock market directly. But before that we take a look at the global economic environment.

15.1.1 The Global Economic Environment: an Overview

1980s to 1990s

During this period, the United States and Japan led the expansion with their highest GDP. They contributed their share of, 26.26% and 17.17% respectively, to the world GDP. However, 29.55% of the increment in world's GDP is attributed to the European Union alone.

1990s to 2000s

This phase was a phase of expansion, in economic output of 148 markets, by $16.9 trillion. It was dominated by the US alone, with its contribution being more than 41.37% of the world's incremental GDP, followed by Japan (16.04%), EU (14.48%) and China (8.05%).

2000 to 2010

2000-2006: The United States led the pack, but the period saw China catching up as well. Economic output of 176 markets expanded by $17.4 trillion. The five largest contributors to global output expansion were: The United States (20%), China (9%), Germany (6%), The United Kingdom (6%) and France (5%). While the economies to face the largest contraction in their output were: Japan (80%), Argentina (19%) and Uruguay (1%).

2007: China overtook the US and led the economic expansion, by contributing 12% to the world output. It was followed by the US (10%), Germany (6%) and the UK (6%). With nominal GDP, economic output of 183 markets expanded by $6.4 trillion during 2007.

2008: Genesis of credit crisis

It was the year of credit crisis for the US and other major countries of the world. During this year, economic output of 171 markets expanded by $5.8 trillion and 11 markets faced a contraction of $267 billion. Even though the crisis affected most of the countries of the world, it was not deep enough to forbid the reversal to growth.

2009: Credit crisis spreads

Economic output of 127 markets contracted by $4.1 trillion during 2009. The United Kingdom was the largest sufferer, accounting for 12% of the global output contraction, followed by Russia (11%) and Germany (8%). The remarkable thing during this period was almost all countries were affected by the credit crisis. China accounted for 61%—followed by Japan (20%) and Indonesia (4%)—of the global output expansion[1]. In terms of the purchasing power parity (PPP), India accounted for 17% of global output expansion.

2010: The recovery

At exchange rate, five largest contributors to global expansion were: China (17%), The United

---

[1] At current exchange rate basis.

States (10%), Brazil (9%), Japan (8%) and India (5%). Economic output of 35 markets contracted by $338.5 billion during 2010, while the economic output of 148 markets expanded by $5.3 trillion.

2011

This year largest economies in the world, with more than $2 trillion (€1.25 trillion), *by nominal GDP*, were: The United States, China, Japan, Germany, France, The United Kingdom, Brazil, and Italy. The largest economies in the world, with more than $2 trillion (€1.25 trillion) *by GDP (PPP)* were: The United States, China, Japan, India, Germany, Russia, The United Kingdom, Brazil and France.

2010 – 2016: The BRICs – engine for economic growth

The International Monetary Fund (IMF) predicted the contribution of BRIC (Brazil, Russia, India and China) nations' to the economic output, at exchange rate[2] and in terms of the PPP[3] theory. The IMF estimated the same for 40 countries of the world. The Table 15.1 below shows the list of predicted economy, for 10 countries, by the IMF.

Table 15.1: Predicted List of Economies by Incremental GDP (PPP), from 2010 to 2016

Rank	Country	Incremental GDP (billions of US$)	Share of global incremental GDP
—	World	29,103.681	100.00%
1	China	8,547.378	29.37%
2	United States	3,724.097	12.80%
—	European Union	3,080.774	10.59%
3	India	2,861.687	9.83%
4	Russia	809.035	2.78%
5	Brazil	787.335	2.71%
6	Japan	744.838	2.56%
7	Indonesia	609.759	2.10%
8	Germany	538.678	1.85%
9	South Korea	538.172	1.85%
10	Mexico	514.450	1.77%

---

[2] At exchange rate means at prevailing exchange rate between two countries.

[3] PPP means purchasing power parity. By using PPP, exchange rate between two countries are so adjusted that an identical good between two different countries has the same price when expressed in their respective currency.

Statistical Indicators

Economy

- GDP (GWP—gross world product): Purchasing power parity, PPP, exchange rates– $59.38 trillion (2005 est.), $51.48 trillion (2004), and $23 trillion (2002).
- GDP (GWP): Market exchange rates– $60.69 trillion (2008).
- GDP – real growth rate: 3.2% p.a. (2008), 3.1% p.a. (2000–07), 2.4% p.a. (1990–99) and 3.1% p.a. (1980–89).
- GDP – per capita: Purchasing power parity – $9,300, €7,500 (2005 est.), $8,200, €6,800 (92) (2003), $7,900 and €5,000 (2002).
- World median income: Purchasing power parity – $1,041, €950 (1993).
- GDP – composition by sector: Agriculture-4%; industry-32%; and services-64% (2004 est.).

Industry

- Industrial production growth rate: 3% (2002 est.)

Energy

- Yearly electricity – production: 15,850,000 GWh (2003 est.); and 14,850,000 GWh (2001 est.).
- Yearly electricity – consumption: 14,280,000 GWh (2003 est.); and 13,930,000 GWh (2001 est.).
- Oil – production: 79,650,000 bbl/d (12,663,000 m^3/d) (2003 est.); and 75,460,000 barrels per day (11,997,000 m^3/d) (2001).
- Oil – consumption: 80,100,000 bbl/d (12,730,000 m^3/d) (2003 est.); and 76,210,000 barrels per day (12,116,000 m^3/d) (2001).
- Oil – proved reserves: 1.025 trillion barrel (163 km^3) (2001 est.).
- Natural gas – production: 2,569 km^3 (2001 est.).
- Natural gas – consumption: 2,556 km^3 (2001 est.).
- Natural gas – proved reserves: 161,200 km^3 (1 January, 2002).

15.2 ASSESSING THE INDIAN ECONOMY

15.2.1 India's Economic Performance Post 1990-91

After 1990-91, the trajectory of India's economic growth has been high. The overall GDP grew at the rate of: 3.2% p.a., during 1971-81; 5.6% p.a. during 1981-1990; and accelerated further to an average of 6.4% p.a., during 1991-2001. Annual per capita GDP also increased correspondingly, during the mentioned phases. One of the most remarkable features of post reform period (1990-91) has been high growth rates, accompanied by an overall more stable growth pattern, with lesser deviations from trend.

But each coin has two faces. Thus this period has had its negative aspects too; one of them being the fact that though overall poverty levels have come down, disparities have widened[4]. It is not only the regional disparities that have widened, but interpersonal disparities too have increased[5]. And if that was not enough, one of the most alarming results has come out, in the survey by National Sample Survey Organization, on employment and unemployment. Their report—a decline in the rate of employment from 2.7%, in 1983, to 1.07%, in 2000!

15.2.2 Present Real Economy

The high growth phase of Indian economy—at 8.9%—during 2003-08, reduced to 6.7% in 2008-09 due to global crisis. It recovered marginally, as it rose to 7.4%, in 2009-10. However, the present growth rate leaves much scope for further enhancement. A resilient growth of service sector, accompanied by a remarkable recovery in the industrial sector has nullified, to an extent, the impact of a deficient south-western monsoon. This is significant, as the latter affected the output from the agriculture sector and would have impacted the net growth as well, otherwise. Figure 15.1, given below, shows an impressive contribution of service sector to the rise of Indian economy. Service sector, accounting for an average 53% of GDP, is the largest sector in the Indian economy. As opposed to this, share of agriculture sector has been on the decline persistently. The same applies to the industrial sector, as it too has recorded sluggish performance. The reason, behind performance of such magnitude by the service sector, while the others sectors have been lagging, is demographic. In light of this demographic factor, the structural change in the Indian economy stands explained, instead of appearing at odds. However, the abnormal feature of this structural change is a very low contribution of industry, to the GDP. In most of the Asian economies, the share of agriculture in GDP has declined as the incomes from other sources have increased. But, these countries have combated the fall in the share of agriculture, in GDP, with a substantial increase in the contribution from industry[6].

Implications of the above structural shift in GDP is that rise in the service sector must be accompanied by a corresponding rise in the industrial sector for a sustainable and balanced growth. Industrial growth holds the key, as it is the major source of employment, export and direct foreign investments. The service sector is continuing with its significant contribution. The performance of the service sector is driven by the major role played by the rise of domestic demands. Thus, if the demand for the service sector is driven internally, the sluggish growth of industry may itself put a break on the growth of service sector.

The fact of the matter, as of now, is, the growth of the service sector is mainly responsible for propelling the growth of the Indian GDP. Looking at the structure of the service sector, growth of the service sector and the overall growth may remain unsustainable, unless the two other sectors of the economy also register higher growth.

---

[4] As per the Economic Survey of 2000-01, 2006-06 and 2010-11, by The Ministry of Finance, Government of India, in 1983, some states like Orissa, Bihar, West Bengal and Tamil Nadu had more than 50% of their population below poverty line. By 1999-2000, while Tamil Nadu and West Bengal could reduce their poverty ratio by half, Orissa and Bihar continued to be the poorest states of India with poverty ratios of 47% and 43%, respectively.

[5] It means that while the income of the poor people has increased impressively in recent times, leading to a fall in the absolute poverty, the income of the non-poor on the other hand has increased faster leading to a rise in relative poverty. Thus, inequality in the distribution of income has magnified.

[6] The aggregate share of industry in GDP of: Indonesia is 46.5%; Korea is 41.4%; Malaysia is 49.6%; China is 51.1%; Philippines is 31.6%; and in Thailand it is 42.1%. From the above economies, only in Korea, Philippines and Thailand, the share of service sector was higher than industry. But in none of them, share of service sector exceeded 54% of GDP.

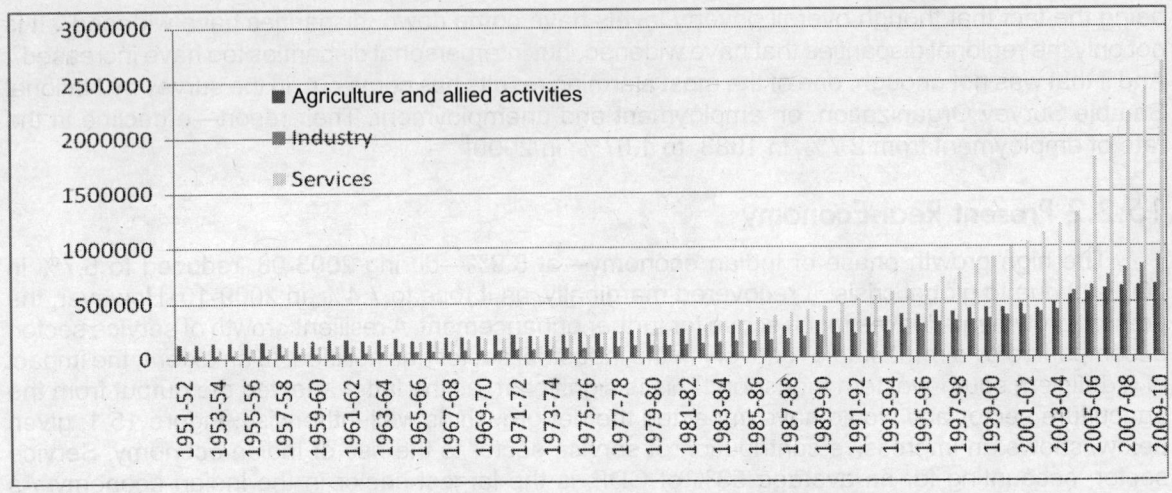

Figure 15.1: Components of GDP from 1951-52 to 2009-10

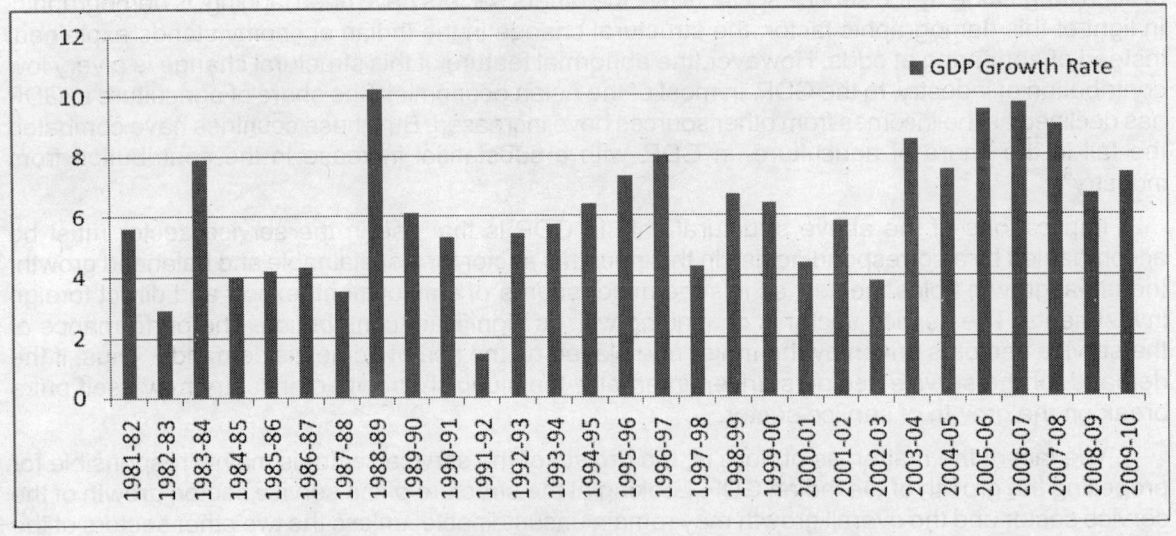

Figure 15.2: GDP growth rate from 1981-82 to 2009-10

(Source: Graph is plotted based on the data of India's GDP, from www.rbi.org.in/)

15.2.3 Agriculture

The agricultural GDP registered an increase of 0.2% in 2009-10, in spite of a deficient southwest monsoon. The overall impact of the deficient monsoon, on the recovery of growth rate was modest. This partly reflects the weak inter-sector linkage, especially in the case of agricultural sector. This admirable performance of the agriculture sector was due to its structural change. There is a decline in the proportion of food grains and commercial crops in total agriculture, with a corresponding rise in the share of horticulture, live-stock, forestry and logging. On an average, the growth of the agriculture sector has remained random, instead of being ordered, with its heavy dependence on monsoon. With a massive fall in the contribution of agricultural and allied services, to the GDP, it brings into focus the fact again the importance of these sectors. They seek attention and the lacunae have to be addressed, as around 52% of workforce relies on them. It is also required from the point of view of food security and stability of prices. The experiences, from the 1990s and continuing till date, indicate that marginal fall of 3-4% in food grain outputs can cause prices to escalate sharply.

The reasons behind the poor performance of the agricultural sector are: lack of public investments; operational inefficiencies; and improper delivery systems—to name a few. Another reason is the stagnated efforts of R&D towards: the development of new seeds; methods to reduce wastages; ways to increase yields; etc. It has been found that this sector has remained in isolation, ignored for far too long now, compared to the various reforms that have been taking place in other sectors.

15.2.4 Index of Industrial Production (IIP)

The very high index of industrial production would have sustained if the high growth period of 2005-06 had not been disturbed by global crisis. The IIP underwent a clock-wise growth from 2005-06 to 2010-11. The performance of the manufacturing sector was highest; followed by general mining; quarrying and the electricity sectors. The strong performance of the manufacturing sector, 2000 onwards, is attributed to the base effect[7]. The sector has been supported by increase in the demands of consumer durables and intermediate goods; accompanied by increase in the production of capital goods. Due to continued reduction in the outputs of crude oil and coal, the mining sector did not perform up to the mark, even with an appreciable increase in the production of natural gas, iron ore and other minerals.

Furthermore, due to low hydro-power generation (owing to deficient monsoon), performance of electricity sector lagged behind. One thing notable, about this performance of industry is that it is broad-based. The top five industries, with combined weight of 24.6%, have accounted for 63.5% of overall manufacturing output. In a similar manner, the remaining twelve industries have also contributed significantly to the overall output. The recovery in the growth rate of IIP suggests some stronger growth measures need to be looked at. Besides, concerns about the high industrial growth, with sustainability at the same pace, too needs to be addressed. Economists are of the view that weak external demands, combined with moderation in government expenditure on account of fiscal exit, may restrain the industrial growth. To sustain the current industrial growth, revival and continuation of internal demands are the prime requirements. Improvement in the agriculture sector and its allied activities, along with the implementation of sixth pay commission with changes in the income tax slab will further enhance the consumption demands.

On an average, manufacturing of industrial goods accounts for more than 71% of IIP; while non-consumer durables and consumer durables follow with 23% and 5%, respectively. One of the reasons for a comparatively sluggish growth of certain industry is that they do not have its own demands. It depends on the external demands—the derived demands. It implies that the biggest use of these products should stem from investment in infrastructure. This implies that demand of certain sector, viz., cement, steel, etc., relies on the infrastructural activity. So, when infrastructure

---

[7] Due to fiscal stimulus the sector received.

develops at good pace, industries like steel, cement, capital goods also perform very well. However, in case of utility and food sector they have their own demands as they do not rely on other sectors. The recent industrial revival is attributed to the stepping up of the investment in infrastructure. This has in turn generated fresh demand for industrial goods.

For a sustained growth in GDP, India needs to increase its investments.

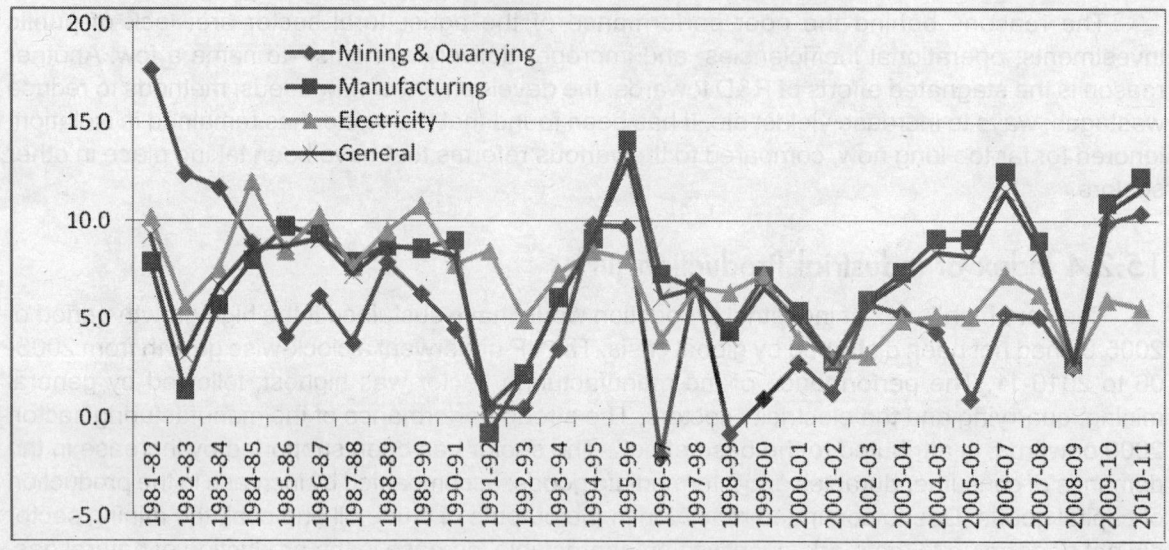

Figure 15.3: Components of IIP from 1981-82 to 2010-11.

(Source: Graph is plotted based on the data of IIP, from www.rbi.org.in/)

15.2.5 Infrastructure

Infrastructure has remained the major hindrance to the growth of Indian economy. In many cases time and cost overruns have acted as the primary hurdle in the actual realization of benefits of capacity addition (the infrastructural growth). Such capacity constraints are noteworthy in coal, ports, railways and power sectors, which thus inhibit high growth. However, the Indian infrastructure sector has performed relatively well since 2000. Growth had suffered a steep fall, in the year 1994-95, due to a change in weight and base value[8] of the index. Taking cognizance of this problem, central government has allocated 46% of the planned expenditure to infrastructure sector. Moreover, an initiative, led by the partnership of public and private sectors, will facilitate minimizing of many lacunae.

---

[8] Weight means proportion or composition of different industries in index of industrial production. Base value means value of the index in the base year.

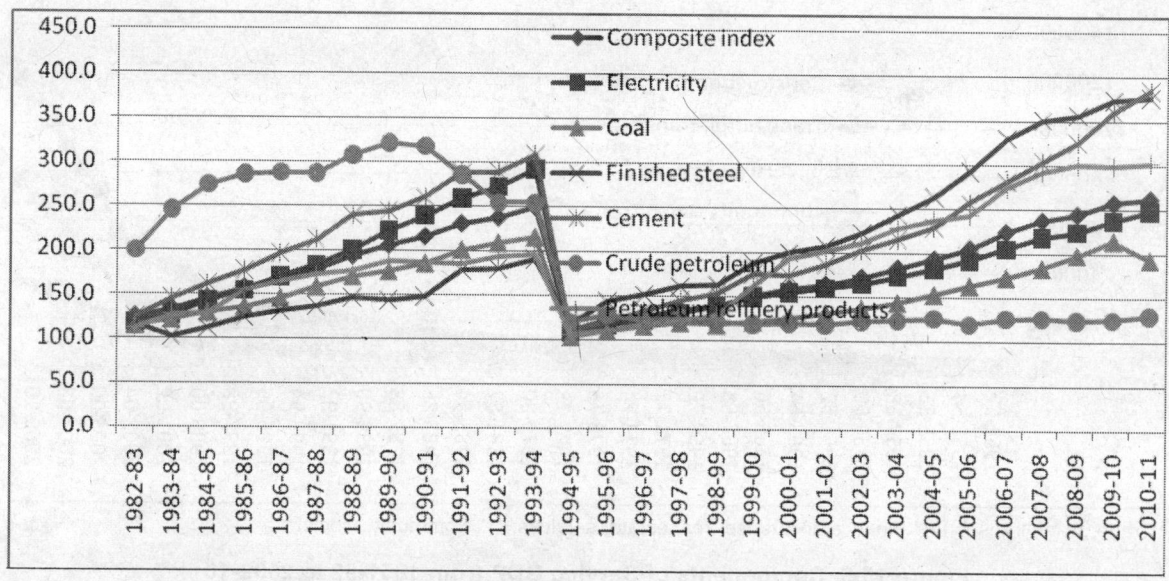

Figure 15.4: Components of Infrastructure IIP from 1982-83 to 2010-11.

(Source: Graph is plotted based on the data of index of infrastructure from www.rbi.org.in/)

15.2.6 Service Sector

Even though resilient, performance of the service sector is lower than what it was before the crisis period set in. But yes, services governed by domestic demands, such as, commercial vehicles, cell phone connections, construction activities, etc., have recorded high growth in the second half of 2009-10. Requirements for components of trade, hospitality sector and transportation have continuously surged, and thus contributed significantly to the GDP. They are followed by finance and insurance services; real estate and community, as well. Except community services and construction activities pertaining to real estate, the remaining three components have shown remarkable growth. Also, expansion of the national infrastructure has continued at a fast pace. The cellular phone sector, both the public as well as the private, has continuously registered a high growth rate. It was even immune to the 2008-09 global crises.

The service sector is likely to pick up further momentum, aided by the growth in the manufacturing sector. In addition to the existing business verticals (businesses and marketers[9], catering to the specific group of people within an industry), the emerging verticals like computing system, energy, infrastructure, industrial automation, education, financial and public services, viz., health care services will assume significance.

---

[9] One that sells goods or services in or to a market, especially one that markets a special commodity.

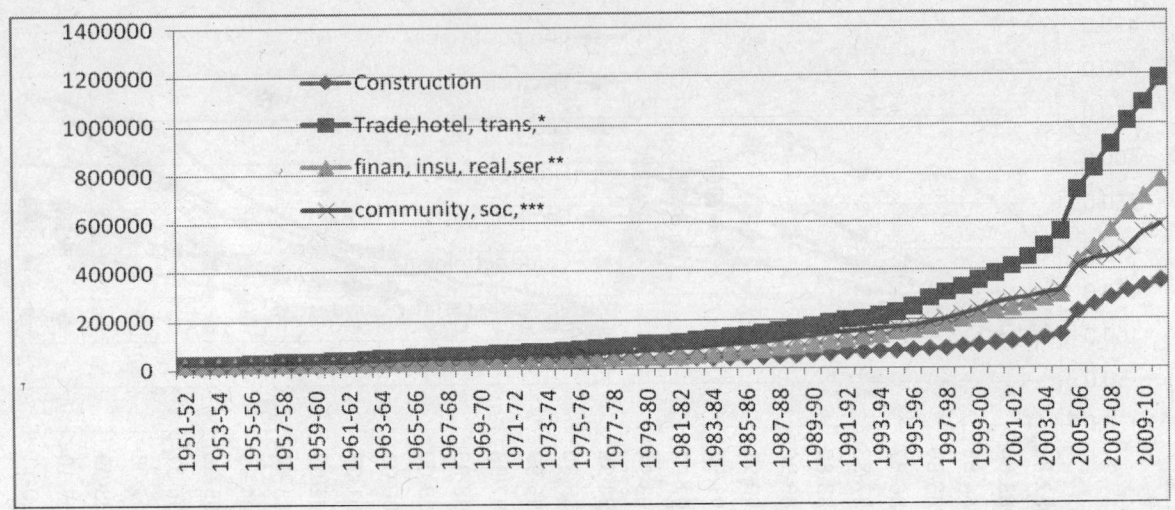

* Trade, hotel, transport; ** Finance, insurance, real estate, services; *** Community, social

Figure 15.5: Components of Service GDP from 1951-52 to 2009-10

15.2.7 Savings and Capital Formation

The aggregate savings rate changed slightly: from 36.4% in 2007-08, to 32.5% in the year 2008-09. This reflects a sharp fall in public sector savings, caused by fiscal stimulus measures. The investment rate reduced slightly in the year 2008-09 due to decline in investment in the private sector. The public sector savings remained subdued in the year 2009-10, owing to the revenue deficit of the government. It has recovered now due to improved profitability. The household savings, in: life insurance, public provident funds, small savings, mutual funds and senior citizen schemes too have recorded fast recovery.

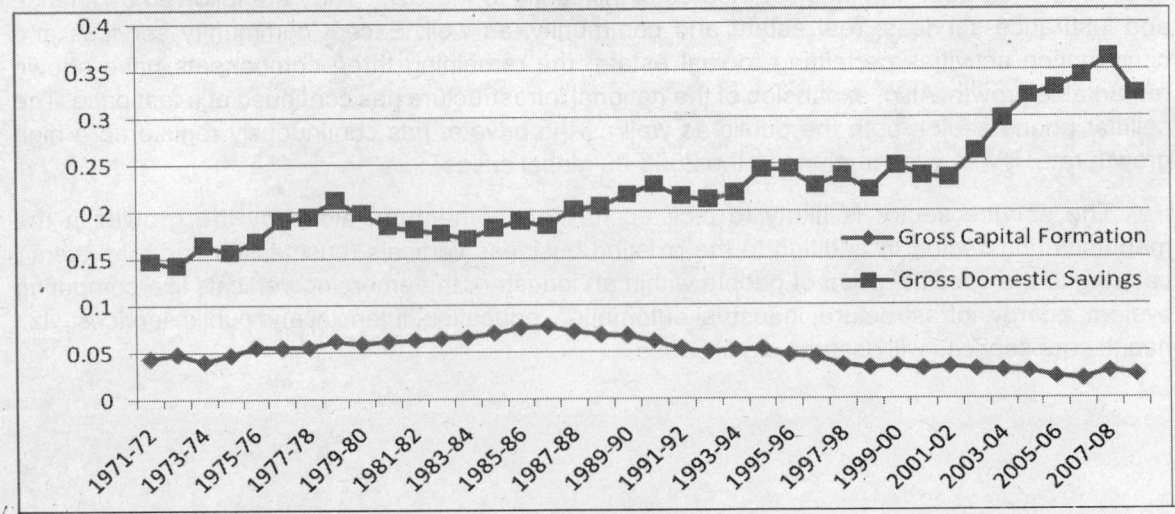

Figure 15.6: Gross Domestic Savings and Gross Capital Formation as a Percentage of GDP
(Source: Calculated as a percentage of GDP from National Income Statistics, CMIE, July, 2010)

15.2.8 Fiscal Policy

Fiscal policy is government's spending policies that influence macroeconomic conditions. These policies affect tax rates, interest rates and government spending, in an effort to control the economy.

Fiscal policy deals with the policies that govern government expenditures, its composition and financing[10]. The revenue component comes in the form of taxes. There exists a non-tax revenue component as well—the government revenue not generated from taxes. These include dividend and interest payments from various public sector undertakings. As per component of aggregate demand and supply (Y = C + I + G + X) fiscal policy can influence component of aggregate demand in several ways. Among these components, the government expenditure component can influence aggregate demand[11] by judicious combination of taxes and expenditures. But the question that arises is how government influences this aggregate demand? If the government expenditure is financed through borrowings, it augments government debt. It has also spillover effect for businesses, as it influences the current spending of private sector, and impacts the spending in the future as well. Similarly tax rates influence disposable income to individuals and companies. This effectively influences the total spending for consumption, and investment goods and services in the economy.

15.2.9 Business Cycles

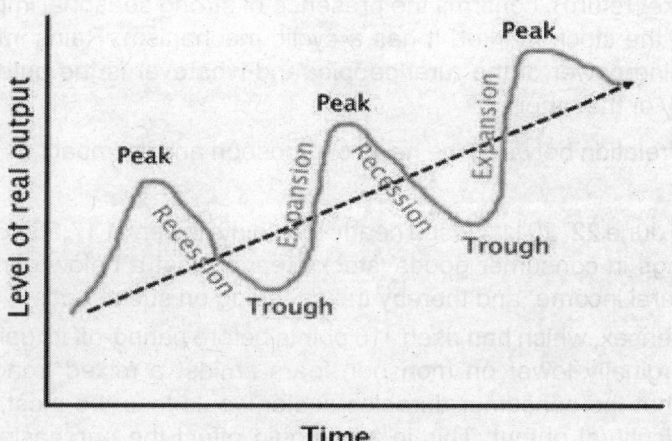

Figure 15.7: Phases of Business Cycles

The above graph represents the phases of business cycles. Peaks, manifesting expansion (growth), are followed by troughs—the valleys, depicting the reverse, that is, recession. The factor responsible for expansion is the aggregate demand, while aggregate output is the responsible for recession. In the graph above, Y-axis shows the level of real output, varying with time, which is

---

[10] Roy, Shyamal (2010), Fiscal Policy, "Macroeconomic Policy Environment: An Analytical guide for Managers", Tata McGraw Hill, New Delhi.

[11] It is obvious how it has increased during economic crises and influenced the aggregate demand. See graph 15.6.

plotted on the X-axis. The long-term investors prefer the long-term investments, as long-term growth remains intact, irrespective of the ups and down, which come and go.

15.2.10 Monsoon

A large number of people are affected by the monsoon in India. This is so because a high percentage (70) of the population is dependent on agriculture and allied activities. Hence the monsoons are looked forward to with great interest and anticipation. About 70% of the population depends on agriculture for their livelihood. This is significant further, as the rural economy contributes about 40% to GDP. Good rains boost the output of several commodities, and reduce the requirement for imports—a burden is thus lessened.

Most of the FMCG companies depend on the rural market, given the high percentage of population dependent on agriculture—the villagers, that is. Thus these companies have to depend upon the villagers, who account for two-thirds of the population. They have to bank on the agricultural commodities as raw material for their production purposes and thus are heavily reliant on them for the net output.

A good monsoon increases their purchasing power, whereas a drought usually leads to poor income. This causes additional burden on the government coffers as they have to increase the subsidies for the poor. Professor Ben Jacobsen, in his research paper (on the impact of seasonal factors on stock market return), confirms the presence of strong seasonal impacts; and especially that of monsoon, on the stock market. It has a cyclic mechanism. Rains impact the agricultural outputs and purchasing power of the rural people; and whatever is the outcome that affects the government, one way or the other.

Examples of correlation between the news of monsoon and its impact on the stock market are as follows:

— Sensex, on June 22, 2011, closed nearly ten points lower, at 17,550.63. Investors reduced their holdings in consumer goods' stocks fearing that a below normal monsoon would affect the rural income, and thereby the spending on such goods.

The BSE Sensex, which had risen 118 points before paring-off its gains in a choppy trade, settled marginally lower on monsoon fears amidst a mixed trend overseas. Brokers predicted that the consumer durables sector would lose the most, as less rains would impact agricultural output. This in turn would affect the purchasing power in the rural areas and thus slow down the overall economic growth.

"Less rains may reduce farm output and reduce the demand for household items such as fridge, two-wheelers and tractors for the people living in rural areas," said Delhi-based broker Mr. Manoj Choraria.

(Source: Business Line as on June 21, 2011)

— The monsoon has been 23% below the 10-year average during the four-month monsoon season that ended on September 30 2009. The benchmark, BSE Sensex, has risen by 15.5% to 17,127 during the same period.

This huge deviation of the index from the monsoon trend, according to some analysts, reflects the decreasing dependence of the Indian economy on rainfall. But there are some analysts who feel that at a time when the economy is still not out of the woods, the rainfall deficit can bring down the GDP growth rate, by as much as one percentage point. On top of that, despite the recent stability in agro-commodity prices globally, food price inflation is still a threat for the economy.

(Source: Times of India, September 31, 2009)

15.2.11 Budget Deficit

Budget deficit is the excess of the difference between government's expenditure and earning (revenue). To finance this gap, government has to borrow from the market, which ultimately results in crowding out of private investment. A shortfall in expenditure vis-à-vis revenue is offset by government borrowing. When interest rates on borrowing increase, the demand for the credit rises in the economy. It has been empirically proved by many researchers that borrowing of large amounts by the government crowds out private borrowing. When government borrows fund for its own and PSU's requirements, less proportion of fund remains available for private sector or they have to borrow the fund at the higher rate. Thus, private sector remains capital deficient—and this is known as crowding out.

15.2.12 Sentiment

The optimism or pessimism of the consumers, about the present economy and the projected economy in the future, is one of the major determinants of economic performance. Businesses too play their role. If businessmen (and manufacturers) have confidence in the present political system, their policy decisions will be taken in accordance. They will increase production by anticipating higher demand for their production. In a similar manner, if consumers trust that their income in the future will rise, they would be willing to spend more and entertain more demands. And their demand boosts the economy. Hence, trust has a huge role to play in the economic growth!

> **Pause for thought:** Thus for the overall growth of economy, growth has to encompass all the sectors, as they are the spokes on the wheel of growth. Apart from that, a highly favorable monsoon too is desired. Agriculture contributes significantly to economy with a major proportion of the population dependent on the same. In addition, there are certain sectors that are dependent on it as well. Last but not the least trust plays a huge role—in the government policies—for investments to be made for growth to be harvested, individually, nationally and globally.

SUMMARY

- ✓ It is the objective of the macroeconomic policy to maintain the full employment level, by balancing aggregate demand and supply.
- ✓ The present status of Indian economy is structured such that it relies more on the service sector rather than the industrial sector.
- ✓ The aggregate savings and capital formation rate has moderated in India, due to current level of deficit.
- ✓ It has been proved that large budget deficits crowds out private investment.
- ✓ Sentiment affects the stock market, and the entire economy pretty fast.

KEY CONCEPTS

Fiscal Deficit	Infrastructure	Business Cycles
GDP	Manufacturing Sector	Monsoon
IIPService Sector	Sentiments	

ASSIGNMENT QUESTIONS

1. Collect the various actions taken by the Indian government in terms of monetary policy and fiscal policy tools during recession. Prepare the list, by collecting the news clippings, of the various fiscal tools used by the government for the industry and how industry responded to it in the year 2008-09.

2. Analyze how industry performs and reacts when government changes monetary tools in the market.

3. Visit few units of the special economic zone. Interact with some of the businessmen and collect the list of different incentives offered to them. Analyze how it can affect the performance of the sector.

APPENDIX A

The analysis below shows the multiple regressions, by taking Sensex as the dependent variable and the other variables: GDP, inflation, interest rate, exchange rate and IIP as independent variables[12].

Table 1

Year	Sensex	GDP	Inflation	Interest rate	Exchange rate	IIP
1991	1908.85	2.136	13.87	11.5	22.74	8.2
1992	2615.37	4.385	11.788	11.84	25.92	0.6
1993	3346.06	4.938	6.362	13	30.49	2.3
1994	3926.9	6.199	10.212	13.5	31.37	6
1995	3110.49	7.352	10.225	12.5	32.43	9.1
1996	3085.2	7.56	8.949	14	35.43	13.1
1997	3658.98	4.128	7.399	13.82	36.31	6.1
1998	3055.41	6.02	13.24	12.82	41.26	6.6
1999	5005.82	7.238	4.658	12.35	43.06	4.1
2000	3972.12	5.83	3.906	11.89	44.94	6.6

---

[12] Sensex data has been taken from the BSE website. Those of GDP, IIP and inflation, have been taken from the IMF website. Data of interest rates are from the RBI website. The Forex data has www.x-rates.com as the source.

2001	3262.33	3.885	3.671	10.99	47.19	4.9
2002	3377.28	4.558	4.469	9.2	48.61	2.8
2003	5838.96	6.852	3.713	7.49	46.58	5.8
2004	6602.69	7.591	3.891	6.13	45.32	7
2005	9397.93	9.033	3.97	6.45	44.1	8.4
2006	13786.91	9.53	6.268	7.63	45.31	8
2007	20286.99	9.991	6.373	8.1	41.35	11.9
2008	9647.31	6.186	8.349	8.25	48.46	8.7
2009	17464.81	6.771	10.882	7.87	46.68	3.2
2010	20509.09	10.094	11.989	8.11	45.5	10.5
2011	15543.93	7.839	10.551	8.25	44.97	8.8

Table 2: Log Values of Data in Table 1

Year	Sensex	GDP	Inflation	Interest rate	Forex	IIP
1991	7.554256	0.758935	2.629728	2.442347035	3.124125	2.104134
1992	7.869161	1.47819	2.467082	2.471483629	3.255015	-0.51083
1993	8.115539	1.59696	1.850343	2.564949357	3.417399	0.832909
1994	8.275606	1.824388	2.323563	2.602689685	3.445852	1.791759
1995	8.042536	1.994972	2.324836	2.525728644	3.479084	2.208274
1996	8.034372	2.022871	2.191542	2.63905733	3.567559	2.572612
1997	8.20494	1.417793	2.001345	2.626116818	3.592093	1.808289
1998	8.024669	1.795087	2.583243	2.551006451	3.719894	1.88707
1999	8.518357	1.979345	1.538586	2.513656063	3.762594	1.410987
2000	8.287055	1.763017	1.362514	2.475697711	3.805328	1.88707
2001	8.090197	1.357123	1.300464	2.396985768	3.854182	1.589235
2002	8.124826	1.516884	1.497165	2.219203484	3.883829	1.029619
2003	8.672308	1.924541	1.31184	2.013568798	3.841171	1.757858
2004	8.795232	2.026963	1.358666	1.81319475	3.813748	1.94591
2005	9.148245	2.200885	1.378766	1.864080131	3.78646	2.128232
2006	9.531475	2.254445	1.835457	2.032087845	3.813528	2.079442
2007	9.917735	2.301685	1.85207	2.091864062	3.722072	2.476538
2008	9.174434	1.822289	2.122142	2.1102132	3.880739	2.163323
2009	9.767943	1.912649	2.38711	2.063058062	3.843316	1.163151
2010	9.928623	2.311941	2.48399	2.093097868	3.817712	2.351375
2011	9.651425	2.059111	2.356221	2.1102132	3.805996	2.174752

SPSS Output: 1 (Entered method)

Variables entered/removed

Model	Variables entered	Variables removed	Method
1	IIP, inflation, interest rate, GDP, Forex.		Enter

a. All requested variables entered

Model summary

Model	R	R square	Adjusted R square	Standard error of the estimate
1	0.901[a]	0.811	0.748	0.3742129

a. Predictors: (Constant), IIP, inflation, interest rate, GDP, Forex.
b. Dependent variable: Sensex

Model summary

Model	Change statistics				
	R square change	F change	Df1	Df2	Sig. F change
1	0.811	12.893	5	15	0.000

b. Dependent variable: Sensex

ANOVA

Model	Sum of squares	Df	Mean square	F	Sig.
1. Regression	9.027	5	1.805	12.893	0.000[a]
residual	2.101	15	0.140		
total	11.128	20			

a. Predictors: (Constant), IIP, inflation, interest rate, GDP, Forex.
b. Dependent variable: Sensex

Coefficients

Model		Un-standardized coefficients		Standardized coefficients	T	Sig.
		B	Std. error	Beta		
1	(Constant)	5.726	2.721		2.104	0.053
	GDP	0.780	0.297	0.391	2.627	0.019
	Inflation	0.563	0.219	0.354	2.572	0.021
	Interest rate	–1.367	0.400	–0.491	–3.422	0.004
	Forex	0.960	0.597	0.280	1.606	0.129
	IIP	0.007	0.134	0.006	0.048	0.962

a. **Dependent variable: Sensex**

Coefficients

Model		95.0% Confidence interval for B	
		Lower bound	Upper bound
1	(Constant)	–0.074	11.526
	GDP	0.147	1.413
	Inflation	0.096	1.030
	Interest rate	–2.219	–0.516
	Forex	–0.314	2.233
	IIP	–0.279	0.292

a. **Dependent variable: Sensex**

— R-squared value is 0.811, is fairly good and indicative of a strong positive relationship between dependent and independent variables.
— Equation:

$$Y = a + b_1 x_1 + b_2 x_2 + b_3 x_3 + b_4 x_4 + b_5 x_5$$

$$Y = 5.726 + 0.780\, GDP + 0.563\, Inflation - 1.367\, Interest\ Rate + 0.960\, Forex + 0.007\, IIP$$

— 1% increase in the GDP leads to 0.780% increase in Sensex.
— 1% increase in inflation leads to 0.563% increase in Sensex.
— 1% increase in the interest rates leads to 1.367% decrease in Sensex.
— 1% increase in the Forex leads to 0.960% increase in Sensex.
— 1% increase in the IIP leads to 0.007% increase in Sensex.

REFERENCES

1. Datt, Ruddar, Sundharam, K.P.M (2010), "Indian Economy", S.Chand, New Delhi, Pp. 891-931.
2. Handbook of Statistics on Indian Economy (2010), RBI, Government of India.
3. Agrawal A., (2002), "Indian Economy: Problems of Development and Planning", Vishwa Publication, New Delhi.
4. D'Souza, Errol (2008), "Macro Economics", Pearson Education, New Delhi.
5. Dornbusch, Rudiger (1993), "Policy Making in an open economy: concepts and case studies in economic performance", by World Bank, Washington D.C.
6. Roy, Shyamal (2010), "Macroeconomic Policy Environment: An Analytical Guide for Managers", Tata McGraw Hill, pp. 59.
7. Economic Survey (2001-02), Government of India.
8. Economic Survey (2002-03), Government of India.
9. Economic Survey (2003-04), Government of India.
10. Economic Survey (2004-05), Government of India.
11. Economic Survey (2005-06), Government of India.
12. Economic Survey (2006-07), Government of India.
13. Economic Survey (2007-08), Government of India.
14. Economic Survey (2008-09), Government of India.
15. Economic Survey (2009-10), Government of India.
16. Economic Survey (2010-11), Government of India.
17. www.rbi.org.in/database/currentstatistics/handbookofstatistics
18. www.mospi.gov.in

16
INDUSTRY ANALYSIS

> **LEARNING OBJECTIVES**
> The purpose of this chapter is to enable you to understand:
> - The life cycle of the industry.
> - The factors that affect performance of industry.
> - Michael Porter's five forces which affect the industry.

16.1 INTRODUCTION

Industry analysis is an investment research that begins by focusing on the status of an industry or an industrial sector. It is the second step of fundamental analysis, designed to assess the overall health of the industry. All analyses are basically of two types: qualitative and quantitative.

Industry analysis is a quantitative analysis, analyzing the characteristics of industry. Assessment of the current status is not the only purpose of the analysis. It is designed, so to assess the future prospects of an industry. When economy is not performing well, it is difficult for the industry to function and grow. This is not unusual as a troubled economy is not conducive to progress in any sector, for that matter.

There are different macroeconomic factors--referred to as variables--which, as they vary, affect the industries. Yet all factors do not affect all industries, either in an identical fashion or to an equal extent. This depends not only upon the sensitivity of the particular industry during that phase, but also on susceptibility of the industry towards specific factors.

16.1.1 The Industry Life Cycle

As the cycle of our life goes through various phases, the life cycle of an industry too goes through the same. It begins with the beginning of the industry, in the form of the entry of its first product in the market, to eventually end up in its decline.

The life cycle is a process of evolution and industries have been observed to evolve through at least four stages. They are:

- The pioneering stage.
- The expansion stage.
- The stabilization stage.
- The decline stage.

These phases are applicable to industries, as well as the product lines within the industry. The impact on the individual products, of the macroeconomic factors, determines the overall effect on the industry—and hence of the industry, on economy. Likewise are reflected the various phases.

> **Pause for thought:** Industry too undergoes various phases as does the human life cycle. Each phase has its own significance, individually as well as collectively. The nature of each phase impacts the net worth of the industry.

1. The pioneering stage: It is the initiation phase of the industry, wherein the first product is launched, that is, pioneered. This is a phase demanding rapid growth as the products are just being introduced and the technology is in transition from the innovative phase to the formative stage.

This being the initial phase, has the greatest of opportunities and the highest of risks. Companies have to wade through teething troubles and compete as well with other companies, in terms of technology, innovation, output, costs incurred, etc. Many companies fail in this stage itself as they aren't able to compete and thus cannot enjoy rapid growth—in production as well as and earnings. In the marketing parlance this stage is also referred to as a 'question mark' because the success of the product and life of the industry are yet to be proved and unknown. But the companies that do succeed attract other players also to enter this sector. A 'focus' strategy, is applied by the industry by emphasizing on the uniqueness of the product or service, to a small group of customers. It may happen that during this stage the profit of the firm may be negative as they have to pour funds to create new product, develop and test prototype, and market the product. Profit, if generated at this stage, is reinvested into the company to strengthen its position and to manage continued growth. So even if the competitive market sees the survival of the fittest, yet it is the fittest which encourage other companies to come forward, and enter the sector; and in the long run, help the sector as a whole, with their individual growths.

As is the norm of the market—high return for high risk—the same applies to investments made in companies still in their pioneering stage. While the company has high probability of failing, chances of succeeding too are high. Thus is high the expected return with an efficient performance of the industry. However, it is difficult to identify the likely survivor(s). Moreover, by the time such companies turn out to be winners, their prices rise to an extent to make investments in it difficult. In the late 1990s, IT companies, and at the beginning of the 1980s, companies in the capital goods sector, were in their pioneering stages.

As market demand grows from the introduction stage; and as life cycle experiences growth at an increasing pace, the industry enters phase of growth. It has also been found that during this early stage of the industry life cycle of firms may cluster together in close proximity to have access to key inputs such labor, technology, raw material, etc. US Silicon Valley is such a cluster for computer chip manufacturers. In India, such clusters have formed at Bangalore, Hyderabad, Pune and Gandhinagar, for the IT industry.

> **Pause for thought:** It is the phase when the industry takes birth, in the form of its first product. And this is the phase where it could survive or be decimated to non-existence, failing to keep up with competition and the requirements of growth.

2. The expansion stage: It is the second stage of an industry's life cycle and it is also known as growth stage. This is a phase for those companies which have survived the initial phase, and have in fact thrived and grown. Having proven their potential through their performance they pull the investors towards themselves. But then the problem crops, as cited above, that their prices by then are high enough to pose hindrance to the investments by general investors. Not all can invest, even if they wish to.

Like the introduction stage, growth stage requires a significant amount of capital. At the marketing front, goal of companies at this stage is to create differential advantage for their product over the competitor's in the industry. At this stage, the industry experiences product standardization which may encourage economies of scale and result in specific technology to achieve efficiency. Funds are spent for research and development—for the betterment of product and services to cater to the customer's needs and suggestions. If the firms become successful in this stage, growing demand for the product increases sales growth. Earnings and accompanying assets also grow, accruing profits for the firm.

At this stage, industry life cycle curve becomes steeper indicating very fast growth. In the marketing parlance, this stage is referred to as 'star' as they have high growth and market share. However, the concern at this stage is the introduction of intense rivalry as new entrants join the industry. Duration of this stage depends upon so many factors. For example, some firms may experience very short duration of growth and can immediately enter into maturity and decline. It happens for many electronic items as they achieve growth, maturity and decline very rapidly. Contrary to this, computer industry is such an example with long growth stage due to up gradation in hardware, product, services and other features. In this stage, firms tend to spread out geographically and continue to disperse during maturity and decline stage. To extend the growth stage and industry profit, companies may look for other countries and new markets.

The rate of growth is moderate as compared to the first phase. The survivors from the first phase now look to stabilize, opting for growth opportunities for steady and sustainable growth.

> **Pause for thought:** After establishing, through the first phase, this is a phase of expanding, through steady and sustained growth.

3. The stabilization stage: After the hectic pace of growth in the first phase, followed by the phase of expansion, with a moderation in growth, a steady stable phase is required.

The frenzy, though, cannot continue for long. Thus is entered the phase of stabilization. It is also referred to as maturity stage. The growth rate is found to be further moderated, as compared to that of the expansion phase. But given the acquired stability, it lasts usually for a longer period. At this stage, the companies compete mainly in terms of prices and innovation.

This stage is also known as maturity stage and during this period industry life cycle curve becomes noticeably flatter, which indicates slow growth. During such stage sales expand and earnings grow. However, their rate of growth falls compared to the growth stage. Also, at this stage the rate of expansion is equal to growth rate of economy. In the marketing parlance this stage is known as 'cash-cow'. In this stage, force or heat of the competition is experienced from the late entrants to the industry. These new entrants try to steal market share from existing customers. So, at this stage, company has to strength their marketing effort to showcase unique feature of their product from other low-cost offerings, or else, firms try to go for low-cost or low-price strategy to increase volume of their product and to beat the new entrant (s). Firms at this stage have excess cash to pay dividends to shareholders. There are very few firms which remain at this stage. However, those few who succeed to remain are the dominant firms.

Efficiency of the management helps to expand the stabilization phase by focusing on certain areas, such as: production improvement, just-in-time methods, automation, etc., which help to reduce cost and thus can enhance profit.

> *Check yourself*
>
> Find out the rate of dividends offered by ABB and ACC for the period 2007 to 2012. Also find out other firms which are regularly paying dividend. Check their industry life cycle stage by considering various factors, such as: market share, number of players in their sector, firm size, economies of scale, product offering, etc. What do you infer from your observation? Also check the industry life cycle stage for HUL and Nirma. What are your conclusions and the basis for the same?

> **Pause for thought:** The industry having survived and expanded now stabilizes and enjoys the proceeds with a steady growth.

4. The declining stage: It is difficult to enjoy the loyalty of the investors for too long. With the same trend applicable to the industry, a stage is arrived when it starts to stagnate and enters the phase of decline. Its growth rate dips. New companies come into the fray. And with the changing taste of the consumer, these companies capture their fancy and attract their investments. If companies cannot come out with some concrete measures for recovering their lost ground, with innovations or sops, they may even start incurring losses.

It happens when product innovation does not keep pace with other competing products/services/firms. Another possibility is that the innovation brought in by other industry in its product causes the existing industry to become obsolete. Its sales suffer and life cycle experiences decline. Its growth rate dips, with sales decreasing at an accelerating rate. Majority of the firms of the industry that tried to manage somehow in the maturity stage start leaving the industry. However, some firms try to remain and compete in the smaller market. Many times mergers and acquisitions are applied as remedy or firms try to apply other strategies to continue to stay in the market. This stage is also named as 'dog' in marketing parlance.

> **Pause for thought:** The inevitable happens, as in all life cycles. When the growth stops completely, the decline begins and if proper measures are not put in place this dip becomes irreversible.

16.1.2 An Assessment of the Industry Life Cycle

Study of life cycle is an important and internationally accepted concept which helps managers to better understand growth in sales of the firm—and other aspects—to introduce them to their investment purpose. Like industry, products also have life cycle. Furthermore, within an industry different individual companies may have different life cycle stages.

A proper assessment of the industry life cycle is essential to know its actual worth. This requires individual attention to each of the companies within an industry. Once the individual risks and returns are analyzed appropriate estimation can be made of its overall potential.

Industry analysis is general in nature. That is why assessment of the life cycle becomes all the more important. All the companies of an industrial sector may not necessarily belong to the same stage to which the industry as a whole belongs. Since individual companies retain their individuality thus, though they are a part of the sector, certain factors form major features of this assessment. They are:

- The risk and return of a particular company has to be found, rather than rigidly judging the industry from the stage to which it belongs as a whole.
- Investors who want to earn by capital gain should select that stock of the industry which is in the expansion phase.
- Companies in the maturity phase are selected if investors wish for higher income. As the companies undergo very moderate growth, and thus have fewer prospects for growth in maturity phase, they offer stable dividends.
- Companies in the decline stage are avoided by the investors. But to avoid such an investment it is essential that such a stage of company be identified primarily.
- The first stage, the pioneering phase, may attract the investors who are ready to bear high risk for a high return. However, it is a very risky stage as companies may not survive for long and have to exit from the market.

Pause for thought: An assessment of the industry life cycle lays emphasis on the assessment of the individual companies in the sector, as their status quite often varies from that of the industry as a whole. The approach is thus more individual, than general.

16.2 INDUSTRY STRUCTURE AND PERFORMANCE

Some industries may perform better, while others might not, over a length of time. Though it is a fact that current or future performances are not dependent on the past performance, experts and analysts derive useful trends from it to predict the future performances. Hence it should not be ignored. In practice, the past records of an industry's earning from sales are indeed analyzed.

The structure of an industry plays a major role in its performance. Apart from that there are various allied and interdependent factors, which too contribute to the same. Taking into account all of these, Michael Porter has presented the causes behind a performance and guidelines on how to deal with the prevailing conditions. It is actually a competitive strategy, comprising of five forces. These are called the five forces of Michael Porter's competitive strategy.

Pause for thought: There are factors which drive the performance of industry, an existing one as well as an entrant. These are explained as the five driving forces of Michael Porter.

16.2.1 Michael Porter's Five Forces

1. Threat from new entrants.
2. Bargaining power of buyers.
3. Bargaining power of suppliers.
4. Rivalry among the existing firms.
5. Threat from substitutes (products or services).

1. Threat from new entrants: New entrants to the industry put pressure on the prices and profit margin. Sometimes, even before it enters the market, it creates pressure on the prices and thus reduces the profit margin.

Entry of new players in the industry increases the capacity and size of the industry. It begins the competition for market share among firms and reduces cost of the goods or services. For example, compare the price of different telecommunication players such as Vodafone, Idea, Cellular, Bharti Airtel, Uninor, DOCOMO, *etc.*, in the early 2005-06 and in 2010-11. Similar is the case for aviation industry. It is a price-based competition amongst Jet Airways, Kingfisher, Indigo, Spice Jet and others. Thus, number of players increases industry size, capacity, innovations and benefits the consumers, as they can then avail product or services at a lower cost. Thus, the threat of entry by potential competitor more or less functions depending on to what extent entries are barred. The industry with high profit margin automatically attracts other players to enter.

These new entrants eventually decrease profitability of all firms in the industry. If it does not cost much for the new entrant—in terms of time and money, to enter the given industry and compete effectively; and existing firms are poor in terms of cost effectiveness, access and know-how of key technologies—the new firm can quickly enter the market and can rapidly excel and pierce profitability of the existing firms.

However, the new entrant faces challenges and resistance, as the existing firms might have created good brand loyalty, over a period, for their products/services in the market. Moreover, the existing firms might have the advantage of low cost production by backward and forward integration[1] and might have sound logistics for its business. Reliance Industries Ltd. and Tata Steel are the two good examples of vertical integration, which may not allow other companies to enter and share the profit margin.

For example, it is difficult to enter, as also exit from, certain industries like steel, petrochemicals, oil and gas, cement, etc. Such sectors require huge investment, technological and product know-how, license (or permission) from government, etc. Also, in such sectors break-even point is very high as their investment, in terms of fixed cost, is very high. It has been found that many times managers have to run such companies even though they incur losses (till the favorable time comes) as their fixed cost is very high. Compared to this, it is easy to enter, and exit from, certain sectors like: textiles, pharmaceuticals, IT, etc., as their investment, in terms of fixed cost and other factors, are manageable.

Also, some industries are characteristics of large economies. They can thus offer the product at a much cheaper rate than the new entrants. Further to this, brand loyalty, proprietary knowledge of patents, government regulation, absolute cost advantage, sound capital base, high fixed cost, scarcity of resources, high cost of switching for companies and some other factors, do not allow other players to enter and start the business.

> *Check yourself*
>
> Check the number of players in certain sectors like: IT, chemical, dyes, oil exploration, infrastructure, oil and gas, steel, etc. Why is there a huge difference, in terms of number of players of such industry? Try to study their financial statement from their websites.

> **Pause for thought:** New entrants threaten the existing companies, yet the latter pose resistance for the entrants with their earned brand loyalty, over the years.

2. Bargaining power of buyers: Buyers mean end-user of the product or the firms who distribute the industry's product to the final consumers. Bargaining power of buyers mean the potential of buyers to bargain down the prices charged by the firms. They (buyers) can also increase cost of the industry by demanding better quality of the goods or services. As they purchase in large quantities they can bargain in terms of quality, features of the product, terms and condition,

---

[1] For example, Tata Steel has its own captive iron ores and coal mines--to get the raw material at one end and network/subsidiaries for finished products like bearings, rod, bars, etc., on the other.

delivery place, after sale services and others. Sometimes they also pose threat for the backward integration of the product. In short, a customer as an individual or as a group has a large enough impact to affect company's margin and volume. Customers have such high bargaining power because switching to another product is easy. Products could be not that important for buyers; they might be price sensitive; there could be availability of good substitutes, etc.

If industry is characterized by small number of buyers, buyers have the upper hand. They put pressure on the price of the firm's product and enforce a reduction in the margin of profit. If the buyers buy the goods in large quantities, even that puts pressure on the price as they demand huge discounts.

> *Check yourself*
>
> Search on the internet and analyze the crisis or issues or problems faced by: 1. Jindal Steel; 2. The Kingfisher Group; 3. Essar Steel and 4. IPCL. What do you interpret?

> **Pause for thought:** The supply and demand theory gives buyers the edge, with their high bargaining powers, when they are lesser in number.

3. Bargaining power of suppliers: Suppliers mean firms which provide inputs to the industry. Bargaining power of suppliers mean, potential of the supplier to increase the price of the inputs, for example, labor, raw material, services, etc. They can pierce profit of the firm by increasing costs to firms in the industry. Also, they pose credible threat(s) for forward integration.

When supplier monopolizes the market, it puts pressure in terms of: price of the goods and on its other features, such as delivery agreements, etc. The problem compounds when the supplier possesses the right or license on some natural resources as well. But then if the market has substitute products, or there is a market for one, the supplier loses the monopoly of its product(s), and hence the bargaining power.

The suppliers have high bargaining power when:
- They have few or no substitutes at all.
- There are few suppliers of particular product.
- Their products are unique.
- The products have high switching cost.
- Their product is extremely important to the buyer.

Besides, suppliers might have high bargaining power also, when the supplying industry has a higher profitability than the buying industry.

> *Check yourself*
>
> Search on the internet about companies like Bharti Airtel, Idea Cellular, Vodafone, DOCOMO, Kingfisher, Spice Jet and other carriers. Who are the suppliers for such sectors? What is their bargaining power?

> **Pause for thought:** The monopoly of the supplier causes the supplier to be in demand, and the same is thus empowered with the bargaining power.

4. Rivalry among the existing firms : Rivalry, in market parlance, means the competitive struggle for market share among firms in an industry. Industries face intense competition between the existing companies, especially when the growth rate falls. Each one of them tries to maintain, or increase, its market share by alluring investors. This they do by cutting down on prices and/or providing some lucrative schemes. But a high fixed cost forces the industries to increase volume, as fixed costs put pressure on the industry to operate at full capacity.

The rivalry is reflected in the mature industry with very little growth. The extent of rivalry among established firms within an industry depends on certain factors, such as: extent of existing barriers; competitive structure of industry; presence of global players; amount of fixed costs; majority of the firms of same size (no dominant firm); little difference among competitor's product and services.

> **Pause for thought:** Market is always competitive, but in times of downturn the rivalry intensifies with all trying to survive, and thus making the most of that which is available.

5. Threat of substitute products or services : Substitute products or services refer to the products or services having the ability to satisfy customers' needs effectively. Substitute products or services pose a ceiling or upper return on the potential returns of an industry, by putting a price cap those firms can charge for their product. If there is lesser number of closer substitutes for a given industry, then such a firm has an opportunity to raise the price of their product(s). If the industry has large number of competitors, in the form of substitute products, and if these act as perfect substitutes, they reduce the profit margin of the industry by enforcing a reduction in its prices.

> *Check yourself*
>
> Search on the internet, substitutes that are available--in terms of electronic devices. Check the financial strength of such companies.

> **Pause for thought:** Substitutes eliminate monopoly and enforce reduction in prices, and thus in profits too.

16.3 INDUSTRY ANALYSIS

An industry is a group of companies, almost similar in terms of the nature of their products and the infrastructure for production. Companies are categorized into different industries on the basis of their manufacturing processes and products. On the other hand, industries are classified on the basis of their business cycles, into: growth, cyclical and defensive. There is another type, which is a mix of growth and cyclical.

Growth industries

The companies which have high rates of earnings and usually defy the business cycles are placed in this category. The growth and expansion of such industry depends upon the technological efficiency of the company, and not on the business cycles. For example, during the two phases of recession: 1997-98 and 2008-09, in Indian economy, growth was registered by the IT and telecommunication sectors respectively.

> **Pause for thought:** Growth industries are independent of business cycles.

Cyclical industries

These industries are dependent upon the business cycles. Hence their growth faces the ups and downs, as they move along, with the business cycles. During boom in the economy their profits rise and they enjoy growth. But during recession their growth slides.

Companies in cyclical industry deal with this kind of volatility by implementing cuts to compensations, and lay-offs during bad times. Conversely, it may pay bonuses and hire in masses during good time. Such industries may face serious trouble if they do not have cash or assets to weather a long recession. It includes those companies which produce durable goods, such as: raw materials and heavy equipments, automotive, construction, airlines, etc. It is advisable to buy the stock of such companies when they are at the bottom of the business cycle—and predict where the top of the cycle is—in order to sell at the optimal time. However, sometimes holding stock of such companies could be a wrong decision as their share price may take years to recover the loss which they have faced in economic downturn.

> **Pause for thought:** Cyclical industries experience growth and slide in cyclic fashion as they are dependent on business cycles.

Defensive industries

These industries also defy the business cycles as do the growth industries. Such industry remains stable during the various phases of the business cycle. During recession their performance is better than the market. However, during an expansion phase it performs below the market. Betas of defensive stock are less than one. An example will aid in the understanding and hence follows. Let us consider a stock whose beta is 0.4. If the expected fall in the market is 20%, then with the risk-free rate at 6%, the price of such stock would fall by 11.6% [6% + 0.4(20% − 6%)[2]]. Thus, such stock would feel less heat than the market at the time of downturn. Similarly, when market rises by 15%, at the time of boom, such price of such stock rises by 13.6% [6% + 0.4(15% − 6%)].

But the companies differ from the ones comprising the other, business-cycle-defying category of industries—the growth industry. Food industry forms a part of this class. They are independent of business cycles because irrespective of boom or recession the demand for basic needs does not go down. Rather they are always on the rise. However, like all defensive stocks, these industries too do not have very high growth. Instead, stocks of such companies, belonging to these industries, are held by investors who prefer steady earnings.

Also, like food industry, utility industry too is an example of defensive stocks because during all phases of the business cycles demand for gas, electricity, etc. is always there—and in fact is constantly on the rise.

> *Check yourself*
>
> Find the stock with negative beta from the market. Collect at least 10 such stocks and compare their share prices and returns, with that of the market, for the period: 2006 to 2012.

> **Pause for thought:** Defensive industries are those which are never short on demand, irrespective of the state of economy. Hence are independent of business cycles.

Cyclical Growth Industries

These types of industries intrinsically possess dual characteristics. They are growth, and at the same time cyclical industries.

---

[2] CAPM Model

> **Pause for thought:** An interesting mix of: dependence on, and at same time, independence from, business cycles, these industries reflect.

16.4 FACTORS AFFECTING INDUSTRY PERFORMANCE

There are various factors that affect the performance of an industry. They are enumerated and discussed at length, in this section as follows.

1. Nature of the product : The products of an industry are used by consumers and other industries. The performance and growth of various sectors, like steel and cement, depends upon the infrastructure for the consumption of the produces, from a sector. These sectors do not have their own demand. For the heavy engineering industry, its demand depends on the efficiency of manufacturing. The investor has to analyze the probable buyer(s) of such industry, to ascertain its demand and potential. For the consumer goods industry, the taste of the customers—thus the preferences—and fashion may change. And with them does the demand. Technological reasons and user friendliness are also the factors which affect the industry.

2. Government policy : Government policies on production capacities, tax rates, tax incentives, tax holidays, cash subsidies, interest rate subsidies, etc., are different for different industries. Government also regulates the pricing of certain products, during a certain period of time. Fertilizer and power sectors are given subsidies from time to time for the benefit of farmers. On the other hand, sugar and pharmaceuticals sectors face control/decontrol on the prices. Before the 1990's, there were government enforced restrictions on entering certain sectors, like airways and telecommunications. Private corporations were permitted to operate the domestic flights only.

3. Nature of the competition : The nature of competition a company faces in a particular industry determines the profitability and the price of the company's stock. After 1990-91 because of liberalization, privatization and globalization, nature of competition has changed significantly. For example, in the banking sector, entry of private and foreign banks has forced all the banks, including all public sector banks (PSBs) and co-operative banks, to do business at more competitive rates. Furthermore, they have had to equip themselves with the latest technologies and product portfolios. The banking industry has had to incorporate changes in its product, as well as services. Similar changes were faced by insurance, FMCG and elite goods industries. The competition becomes intense also in presence of too many firms within the industry. They mutually affect the profitability of the business and thus stock prices in the market. Thus, it is most important from the investor's point of view: to analyze the nature of competition and the market shares of a given company, before investing in the stock of that company.

> *Check yourself*
> Due to FDI route, allowed in retail sector, predict how the equation is likely to change for the Indian corporate sector.

4. Cost structure of the industry : The level of fixed and variable costs differ for industries and affect the company's cost of production and profitability. Certain sectors like steel, cement and petrochemicals cannot afford to remain small or medium-sized. They should be large or giant-sized. In such industries the breakeven point is also very high. They require greater sales volume to achieve their breakeven point. Once this breakeven point is achieved the profitability can increase significantly. Companies with a high level of fixed cost have a high degree of financial leverage.

When the economic conditions are good and the company's earnings before interest and taxes[3] (EBIT) also increases, then its earnings per share[4] (EPS) increases faster--with more debt in its capital structure. However, if economy is downward, its sales fall. With that, fall drastically both EBIT and EPS. Thus leverage is a double-edged sword. If the company decides not to employ debt in its capital structure, the financial risk is zero. But then, the company has to let go off the magical effect of debt on its EPS.

5. Operating risk : Operating risk means variability of EBIT in a company. The variability of EBIT is affected by both the internal and external environments. The EBIT varies mainly because of two reasons:

- Variability of sales.
- Variability of expenses.

Variability of sales is a key factor of operating risk. By assuming the sales variability to be constant, the variability in EBIT is further affected by the fixed and variable expenses. When sales are on the rise, higher operating leverage results in the rapid rise in EBIT. At the same time, during economic downturns, as the sales fall, EBIT falls at a significant rate.

> **Pause for thought:** There are various factors that affect the performance of industries. Yet one salient aspect that emerges is the fact that competition raises the bar of profits, and causes economic growth.

SUMMARY

✓ Industries differ in terms of fixed costs, sensitivity of business cycles, government policies, operating risks, etc.

✓ Industries are classified as growth industries, cyclical industries, defensive industries and cyclical growth industries.

✓ Life cycle of industry consists mainly of four stages: the pioneering stage, the expansion stage, the stabilization stage and the decline stage.

KEY CONCEPTS

Industry Life Cycle	Stabilization Stage	Cyclical Industries
Pioneering Stage	Decline Stage	Defensive Industries
Expansion Stage	Growth Industries	Defensive Cyclical industries

---

[3] EBIT is an indicator of a company's profitability. It is calculated by subtracting expenses, including interest and taxes, from revenues. In other words, EBIT is all profit before taking into account interest payment and taxes. The reason behind the widespread use of the EBIT is that it nullifies the effect of the different capital structure and tax rates. It is used for the purpose of cross-company comparisons. EBIT = Revenues – Operating expenses.

[4] EPS is considered to be the single most important variable in determining share prices. It shows a portion of a company's profit allocated to each outstanding share of common stock. It is a major component to calculate the price-to-earnings valuation ratio. EPS = (Net income - Dividends on preferred stock)/ Average outstanding shares.

ASSIGNMENT QUESTIONS

1. Study Michael Porter's five forces for the pharmaceutical industry. Also ascertain and analyze the stage at which the industry is performing. Study the cost structure and operating risk for the pharmaceutical sector.

2. Collect the news clippings for the steel industry and its major players like Jindal Steel, Tata Steel, SAIL, etc. Why do these companies differ in terms of profitability margin, even though they have similar cost structures and product portfolios? What are the problems that are being faced by this sector since 2008 and why? What role does the government or any other external factor play in the same?

3. Many companies of the pharmaceutical industry have shifted to Uttaranchal and other parts of the northern region. Why?

4. Analyze the factors responsible for the growth and expansion of IT industry.

5. Analyze the telecommunication sector. Have you noticed the problems they are facing because of the spectrum scam? What are they?

6. Make a study of the breakeven point and profitability margin for the automobile sector.

REFERENCES

1. www.investopedia.com

17
COMPANY ANALYSIS

> **LEARNING OBJECTIVES**
>
> The purpose of this chapter is to enable you to understand:
> - Analysis of company using the fundamental factors.
> - The financial strengths and weaknesses of a company by thoroughly analyzing P&L (profit and loss) and balance sheet of the company.
> - The prospects and risks of the company by analyzing its management, capital structure, terms and contracts with other companies and government, etc.
> - The competitive potential of the company.

17.1 INTRODUCTION

Company analysis is the third step of fundamental analysis, which follows the E-I-C framework. After the economy and industry analyses, we thus arrive at this chapter, which shows how company analysis is carried out by portfolio managers and security analysts. A good understanding of how the company related factors affect return on securities is essential for a student of finance, as well as for an investor.

Company analysis is conducted by assessing qualitative as well as quantitative factors of the company. Before analyzing company's financial statement it is required to look at some qualitative aspects of the company. Company analysis is carried out in the final stage of fundamental analysis after going through economic and industry analyses. Through this analysis it is tried to determine the intrinsic value of a company's stock. But, as we know from the definition, qualitative aspects represent those factors of a company's business that are difficult or impossible to quantify. This makes it difficult to incorporate such type of information to evaluate the price. However, it is also true that we cannot ignore this less tangible aspect of the company while analyzing it. This chapter, hence, considers both qualitative as well as quantitative factors for evaluating a company.

The purpose of this chapter is to convey the message that the stocks of well established companies may not necessarily be good investment options. It has been observed that the stock of a good company, with a high-quality management and strong performance (measured by sales and growth) can be priced so high that the intrinsic value of the stock is many times below its current market price. Hence, such a stock should not be acquired as it has the tendency to approach its intrinsic value sooner or later. Contrary to this, it has been also observed that the stock of companies with less success (based on its sales and growth) may have a current market price that is below its intrinsic value. Thus it becomes a wise decision to invest in such a company, even though the company apparently does not have a high profile.

An investment in a company requires integration of the observations. Analysis of a single aspect fails to lead us to good investment decisions. Only after comprehensively analyzing the company, we get to understand its potentials and risk. This has to be followed by the calculation of the intrinsic value of the company's stock. Then, this intrinsic value should be compared with the current market price to determine finally if the stock should be purchased. An investor should not confuse himself/herself with the notion that growth companies have growth stocks, because stock of growth companies may not necessarily be a growth stock.

17.1.1 Growth Companies and Growth Stocks

Generally, it is believed that growth companies are those which consistently register above average sales and earnings. But, this definition should not be followed blindly as many companies can yield the same through other means as well, such as: certain accounting procedures, mergers or other external events. According to Miller and Modigliani (1961), growth companies are those whose rates of return are greater than the required rate of return, WACC[1]. It means these are able to acquire capital at an average cost, of say 12%; and because of their prudent management and potential opportunities are able to earn much more return (say, 20% or above) than its WACC. Because of this, the earnings and the overall performance lead to a faster growth than the industry as a whole, or even faster than the growth of the entire economy. Usually, these companies retain large portion of their earnings in other profitable investment options such as in some projects or assets of the company which can further enhance growth in the subsequent years.

Hence, growth stocks are those stocks which earn higher return than other stocks in the market with similar risk characteristics. It is able to earn higher risk-adjusted rate of return because at some point of time the market had under-priced it, compared to the other stocks. The market is very prompt at reflecting the new information and adjusts the stock prices quickly. But the available information is not always accurate. As a consequence, many times the market fails to deliver as anticipated. The misinterpretation of information leads to this deviation, causing the stocks to be under or over-priced.

If the stock is under-valued, its price would eventually increase to reflect its intrinsic value, when the correct information is available (it is a law of nature, truth cannot be concealed!). An investor must observe that during this period of price adjustment, the actually realized return from the stock exceeds the required return for a stock with the given risk. Thus, during this period of adjustment, it will be considered a growth stock.

---

[1] WACC is the weighted average cost of capital. This shows the weighted average cost of capital of the firm depending upon their employment of fund from different sources and their respective proportion in the total fund. A company always strives to earn more than their WACC; as then only it can start earning. WACC can be also interpreted as the minimum required rate of return the company should earn on its investment. If the rate of return earned by the company is more (less) than its WACC or required rate of return, such company starts earning profit (loss).

Company Analysis

If the investor buys the stock of a growth company at its current market price, the return realized by him/her will be at par with the risk of the stock. In most of the cases it has been observed that the restless investors tend to overestimate the financial potentials of the growth company. Because of this the price of such a stock is inflated. The investors buying stocks at such inflated prices end up with a rate of return much less than the risk-adjusted required rate of return (even though the growth company experiences above average growth of sales and earnings).

Points to Remember

- As an analyst one should be more interested in finding out stocks outside the top tier of the companies (in the industry) that are scrutinized by numerous analysts. In other words, one should look for the neglected stocks.
- A future growth stock can be the stock of any (type of) company which is undervalued by the market.
- Several studies have confirmed that the stocks of many growth companies have underperformed.

> **Pause for thought:** A growth company is that which yields higher returns than that required.

17.1.2 Defensive Companies and Defensive Stocks

There are certain stocks that have relatively low business[2] and financial risks[3]. These are called defensive stocks and the companies, defensive companies. Hence the future earnings of defensive companies are likely to withstand an economic downturn. Companies that are in the business of public utility commodities, such as grocery chains, suffer less during economic slump. But that does not mean they are perfectly insulated from economic downturns. They too are affected. However, the decline in the return is less than the fall experienced by the overall market.

As per the CAPM theory, the stock with negative or slightly positive beta is considered a defensive stock because their returns are unlikely to be harmed significantly in a bear market.

> **Pause for thought:** Stocks of companies, affected to a lesser degree by economic downturns, are the defensive stocks of defensive companies.

---

[2] Business risk is a risk of the firm's assets when no debt is used. This risk is inherent in company's operation. Sales risk, input-cost risk, etc., are the factors which affect business risk. For example, when we compare an utility company with a textile company utility company always has a lesser business risk as it has stable earnings due to stable demand, compared to a textile company. So, business risk of the textile company is higher as its sales are affected by change in fashion, demographic factor, etc. Hence, the textile company would have lower optimal debt ratio making the investors feel risk regarding the company's ability to meet its responsibility in favorable and unfavorable times.

[3] Financial risk considers company's leverage. If a company has high amount of debt (i.e., leverage), the shareholders risk is high as company may turn bankrupt if unfavorable times persist. For example, for the airline industry the average leverage is very high—at times even more than 100%. So, it faces extreme financial risk and imminent bankruptcy.

17.1.3 Cyclical Companies and Cyclical Stocks

These are the companies whose earnings and other financial parameters are highly influenced by macroeconomic variables. Hence such companies perform very well during the growth phase of economy, while incur heavy losses during the recession. The steel, automobile and capital goods industries are some of the examples of cyclical companies. They have a very high level of business risk, which compounds their financial risk as well.

The earnings of cyclical companies are affected more than the overall market is. So, as per CAPM theory, these are the stocks with high positive betas.

> **Pause for thought:** The stocks dependent on the overall economy are cyclical stocks.

17.1.4 Speculative Companies and Speculative Stocks

Companies which follow the concepts of high risk and high return, such as companies in oil exploration, are the speculative companies. A speculative stock possesses a high probability of low or negative rates of return. At the same time it has a low probability of normal or high rates of return. This happens because speculative stocks are many times over-priced. So when the market adjusts their price corresponding to their intrinsic value that results into low or possibly negative rates of return. It means these are the over-valued stocks.

> **Pause for thought:** The speculative stocks abide by the high risk-return theory.

17.1.5 Value Stocks

Value stocks are those stocks which are undervalued, for reasons other than earnings and growth potentials. Usually, they have low price-earnings ratios.

> **Pause for thought:** Value stocks are the undervalued stocks with low price-earnings ratio.

17.2 COMPANY ANALYSIS AND FINANCIAL INFORMATION

The purpose of this discussion, on all types of stocks, is to affirm that it is absolutely necessary to examine the characteristics of a company (or its stock). Based on these characteristics and other information, the intrinsic value of the stock is estimated.

As has been already stated, this chapter explains how the security analysts carry out the fundamental analysis of companies, which requires an understanding of the factors that affect the returns earned from securities.

Security analysis is based on the financial information available. Financial data is needed to estimate, compare and analyze the earning potentials of the company. The financial information of an enterprise (company/firm/industry) is contained in the financial statements (the accounting reports).

Three basic financial statements are of great significance to investors and equity research firms: balance sheets; profit and loss accounts (P & L account), fund flow statement and cash flow statement. To illustrate the use of these financial statements for company analysis, financial statements of Reliance Industries Limited have been examined.

17.2.1 Company Analysis of Reliance Industries Limited

1. Profit and loss

Table 17.1: Profit and Loss Statements

	200903 (12)	200803 (12)	200703 (12)	200603 (12)	200503 (12)
Income					
Sales turnover	146328.07	139269.46	118353.71	89124.46	73164.10
Excise duty	4369.07	5463.68	6654.68	8246.67	7245.27
Net sales	**141959.00**	**133805.78**	**111699.03**	**80877.79**	**65918.83**
Other income	2148.40	6615.62	478.28	682.92	1603.38
Stock adjustments	427.56	−1867.16	654.60	2131.19	−524.35
Total income	**144534.96**	**138554.24**	**112831.91**	**83691.90**	**66997.86**
Expenditure					
Raw materials	107010.32	96311.56	78692.94	58342.31	45931.87
Power and fuel cost	3355.98	2052.84	2261.69	1146.26	907.94
Employee cost	2357.40	2049.95	2045.95	932.09	791.21
Other manufacturing expenses	3704.00	3951.40	3486.87	2217.72	1937.13
Selling and administration expenses	4619.24	4882.01	5342.31	5765.46	2826.38
Miscellaneous expenses	1379.92	547.30	588.85	461.19	352.09
Less: pre-operative expenses capitalized	3265.65	175.46	111.21	155.14	9.60
Total expenditure	**119161.21**	**109619.60**	**92307.40**	**68709.89**	**52737.02**
Operating profit	25373.75	28934.64	20524.51	14982.01	14260.84
Interest	1745.23	1077.36	1188.89	877.04	1468.66
Gross profit	**23628.52**	**27857.28**	**19335.62**	**14104.97**	**12792.18**
Depreciation	5195.29	4847.14	4815.15	3400.91	3723.50
Profit before tax	18433.23	23010.14	14520.47	10704.06	9068.68
Tax	1206.50	2604.96	1617.10	900.00	705.00
Fringe benefit tax	56.87	47.00	40.34	30.72	0.00
Deferred tax	1860.54	899.89	919.63	704.00	792.00
Reported net profit	15309.32	19458.29	11943.40	9069.34	7571.68
Extraordinary items	40.61	4111.75	−312.17	74.91	31.94
Adjusted net profit	**15268.71**	**15346.54**	**12255.57**	**8994.43**	**7539.74**

Adjusted below net profit	0.00	48.10	0.51	0.00	-4.17
P & L balance brought forward	4363.29	2765.37	3029.09	8967.86	5592.06
Statutory appropriations	0.00	0.00	0.00	0.00	0.00
Appropriations	14288.42	17908.47	12207.63	15008.11	4191.71
P & L balance carried down	5384.19	4363.29	2765.37	3029.09	8967.86
Dividend	1897.05	1631.24	1440.44	1393.51	1045.13
Preference dividend	0.00	0.00	0.00	0.00	0.00
Equity dividend (%)	130.00	130.00	110.00	100.00	75.00
Earnings per share	95.24	131.97	84.28	63.70	53.30
Book value	727.78	542.83	439.67	324.11	270.43

(*Sources:* Capitaline)

The profit and loss account reports the flow of funds from business operations that take place during a phase. The difference between income and expenditure represents profit or loss, accrued or incurred, during the period. At present, the creditors, bankers and financial analysts in India have started paying more attention to the firm's earning capacity, as a measure of its financial strength. Table 17.1 shows the profit and loss account of Reliance Industries Ltd from 2005 to 2009.

From this table, the net sales and income from other sources, added together under the term, total sales, amount to Rs.144107.4 crore (Rs.141959.00 crore and Rs.2148.40 crore). The proportion of income from other sources, in the year 2009, is 1.49% of the total sales. Thus, it can be stated that little information is lost by considering only the sales.

There are three major expense items which the analysts are usually interested in: cost of goods sold (COGS); selling and administrative expenses and interest expenses. Care should be taken while analyzing profit and loss statements of the company because when the CAGR of sales (excluding other income and stock adjustments) in the last five years is 16.58%, the growth in total expenditure is found to be 17.70%. This data is alarming for the investors. But, rationally, it should neither be the only criterion nor the major criterion for judging the financial health of an enterprise. Perhaps, this is the reason, for a significant fall of 12.30%, in the gross profit margin of the company, from 2008 to 2009. The reason behind this fall is also attributed to an increased investment and partial impact of recession. Analysis of the company's expenses shows a very steep rise, of 63.47%, in the expenses on power and fuel in just one year. From the details of the tax statement of the company it has been found that the company's tax management is very sound. Earnings from sales, deducting the cost of goods, are usually termed gross profit. While subtracting the selling and administrative expenses from the gross profit is termed as earnings before interest and taxes (EBIT). Many experts refer to EBIT as operating leverage or operating profit. Subtracting interest expenses from EBIT gives earning before tax (EBT), i.e., the pre-tax income. Deducting taxes from pre-tax incomes gives earnings after taxes. It is used to compute the earnings per share (EPS), unless the company has preference shares in their capital structure. Usually, EPS is calculated by dividing the earnings after tax by a weighted average of the number of common shares outstanding during the year.

> **Pause for thought:** The difference between the cost incurred and the income generated from sales, gives the profit and loss.

2. Balance sheet

Table 17.2: Balance Sheet Statements

	200903	200803	200703	200603	200503
Sources of funds					
Share capital	1642.78	1453.39	1453.35	1393.17	1393.09
Total reserves	124730.19	78312.81	62513.78	48411.09	39010.23
Total fund of shareholders	126372.97	79766.20	63967.13	49804.26	40403.32
Secured loans	10697.92	6600.17	9569.12	7664.90	7972.90
Unsecured loans	63206.56	29879.51	18256.61	14200.71	10811.69
Total debt	73904.48	36479.68	27825.73	21865.61	18784.59
Total liabilities	200277.45	116245.88	91792.86	71669.87	59187.91
Application of funds					
Gross block	149628.70	104229.10	99532.77	84970.13	55125.82
Less : accumulated depreciation	49285.64	42345.47	35872.31	29253.38	24872.83
Less: impairment of assets	0.00	0.00	0.00	0.00	0.00
Net block	100343.06	61883.63	63660.46	55716.75	30252.99
Lease adjustment	0.00	0.00	0.00	0.00	0.00
Capital work in progress	69043.83	23005.84	7528.13	6957.79	4829.29
Investments	21606.49	22063.60	16251.34	5846.18	17051.46
Current assets, loans advances					
Inventories	14836.72	14247.54	12136.51	10119.82	7412.88
Sundry debtors	4571.38	6227.58	3732.42	4163.62	3927.81
Cash and bank	22176.53	4280.05	1835.35	2146.16	3608.79
Loans and advances	13127.64	18130.67	12209.07	8144.85	13503.03
Total current assets	.54712.27	42885.84	29913.35	24574.45	28452.51
Less : current liabilities and provisions					
Current liabilities	32689.58	21045.47	16865.53	12563.50	13659.72
Provisions	3010.90	2992.62	1712.87	3890.98	3471.80

Total current liabilities	35700.48	24038.09	18578.40	16454.48	17131.52
Net current assets	19011.79	18847.75	11334.95	8119.97	11320.99
Miscellaneous expenses not written off	0.00	0.00	0.00	0.00	0.00
Deferred tax assets	247.51	310.53	297.64	121.70	366.64
Deferred tax liability	9973.81	8183.07	7279.66	5092.52	4633.46
Net deferred tax	−9726.30	−7872.54	−6982.02	−4970.82	−4266.82
Total assets	**200278.87**	**117928.28**	**91792.86**	**71669.87**	**59187.91**
Contingent liabilities	**19278.00**	**24308.69**	**28356.90**	**18339.06**	**9153.89**

(**Sources:** Capitaline)

The balance sheet shows the portfolio of assets of a corporation, as well as its portfolio of liabilities. Besides, it also represents the owner's equity, at a given point of time. It contains all information about the resources and obligations of a business entity. Furthermore, it reflects the business interests of the owner at a particular time. The balance sheet of RIL, shown in Table 17.2 is for the period 2005 to 2009.

Balance sheet helps in evaluating the capital structure of the company. Also, the net worth and outstanding debt is ascertained for the company, which enables one to infer its financial implications. From the table above, we can conclude that the company still has the scope to increase the fund by debt capital, as in the last five years the debt-equity ratio is less than 0.5. The debt capital has certain advantages in terms of low cost. And employment of debt component in the capital structure creates financial leverage. As revenues consistently grow, large amount of debt capital can increase the return, for the shareholder. On the other hand, if the sales fluctuate, employment of debt capital is risky as it brings with it fixed liabilities, in terms of interest payment. From the data of current assets and current liabilities, the liquidity position of the company is assessed. They help to figure out the overall ability of the company to pay its short-term obligations. The net current assets have reduced by 28.27% (from Rs.11320.99 crore to Rs.8119.97 crore) for during the year, 2005-06. Since then it has been an upward trend, till 2009. This reflects that the company is in a good position to repay its short-term debt obligation; yet at the same time have enough components of current assets for assets turnover. The contingent liability in the end is found to be unsteady. But contingent liabilities are not the actual liabilities; they are liabilities contingent upon the occurrence of some future event(s).

> **Pause for thought:** The balance sheet of a company reflects its portfolio of assets, portfolio of liabilities and equity—of the other owners—over a period of time.

As per the guidelines of SEBI, it is, compulsory for the companies to reveal cash flow statements in their annual report. For the purpose of analyses, cash flow statements can be divided in to three types:

- Cash flows from operational activities.
- Cash flows from investment activities.
- Cash flows from financing activities.

Table 17.3: Cash Flow Statements

	200903	200803	200703	200603	200503
Cash flow summary					
Cash and cash equivalents at beginning of the year	4280.05	1835.35	2146.16	3608.79	224.24
Net cash from operating activities	18245.86	17426.74	16870.55	10301.58	17288.58
Net cash used in investing activities	−24081.96	−23955.08	−17487.44	−12130.88	−8162.34
Net cash used in financing activities	23732.58	8973.04	306.08	366.67	−5741.69
Net (Inc)/Dec. in cash and cash equivalent	17896.48	2444.70	−310.81	−1462.63	3384.55
Cash and cash equivalents at end of the year	22176.53	4280.05	1835.35	2146.16	3608.79

Analyses from these perspectives give an account of the past performances and what can be expected from the company in the near future. For example, if the cash flow statement reveals that cash flows are more in operating activities, the investor can conclude that the present profit performance is short-lived, because: (i) major portion of the profit is sucked into the day-to-day operating activities and (ii) the cash consumed by operating activities doesn't enhance capital gain. On the other hand, cash flows from investment activities indicate that the company has acquired additional investments for the ongoing, or for future, projects. This raises the prospects of increased profitability of a company in the near future, if the project succeeds and earns a handsome return (or it increases risk if the investment in the project under-performs or fails).

On comparing the RIL's net cash flows from its operating, investment and financing activities over the period of last five years, it is found to be negative in the year 2006 and 2007. However, net cash flows in investment activities, is persistently negative over the entire period of assessment. It indicates the major cash outflow for purchase of fixed assets, investments, and movement in loans and advances. It comprises of good proportion of investment for RIL, further indicating better prospects for the company in future. This shows the company has good investment avenues. If it is compared for the last two years, net cash flows from operating activities reveals a major shift from Rs. 8973.04 crore in the year 2008 to Rs. 23,732.58 crore in the year 2009. Issuance of shares and warrants has raised the long term borrowings by more than 50%, causing this shift. Cash flows from operating activities is quite normal and as per expectation.

3. Fund flow statement : Fund flow statement gives an account of the sources, and application, of the funds. It also highlights the changes in the financial condition undergone by a firm between its two balance sheet dates. Thus the amount of funds generated or lost in operations can be evaluated from these statements.

The objectives of the fund flow statement analysis are:

- To find out the fund generating capacity of the company.
- To establish a relationship between inflow and outflow of the funds for the existing plans and for the expansion plans envisioned for the future.
- To find out the amount of funds: generated initially and injected from outside.

Table 17.4: Analysis of RIL's Fund Flow Statements

	200903	200803	200703	200603	200503
Sources of funds					
Cash profit	22249.49	25931.45	18562.33	13449.89	10730.77
Increase in equity	120.14	60.18	0.04	0.08	0.00
Increase in other net worth	20410.64	1435.09	5597.95	0.00	0.00
Increase in loan funds	37424.80	8653.95	5960.12	3081.02	0.00
Decrease in gross block	0.00	0.00	0.00	0.00	0.00
Decrease in investments	457.11	0.00	0.00	11205.28	0.00
Decrease in working capital	1689.72	0.00	0.00	3905.02	0.00
Others	69.25	0.00	60.14	0.00	0.00
Total inflow	**82421.15**	**36080.67**	**30180.58**	**31641.29**	**10730.77**
Application of funds					
Cash loss	0.00	0.00	0.00	0.00	0.00
Decrease in net worth	0.00	0.00	0.00	195.28	572.03
Decrease in loan funds	0.00	0.00	0.00	0.00	2160.07
Increase in gross block	80524.10	20174.04	15132.98	30052.50	3095.39
Increase in investments	0.00	5812.26	10405.16	0.00	3080.06
Increase in working capital	0.00	6622.28	1203.78	0.00	774.44
Dividend	1897.05	1631.24	1440.44	1393.51	1045.13
Others	0.00	1840.85	1998.22	0.00	3.65
Total outflow	**82421.15**	**36080.67**	**30180.58**	**31641.29**	**10730.77**

Analysis of the sources of funds

For the sake of a better understanding, we keep things simple and analyze the fund flow statement of only the previous year. It is observed that of the total inflow of funds, 27% has been generated internally; while approximately 46% has been collected from external sources, like issuance of equity shares and loan funds.

Analysis of applications of funds

In 2009, 97% of the fund was used for the purchase of fixed assets and 2.30% is used for paying dividends. There is no usage in terms of: working capital, repayment of loans and investment purposes.

From the sources of funds we can state that 27% is generated from cash profit, i.e., internally generated funds; and 46% is from issuance of the security. As opposed to this, 97% of the funds is used for the procurement of assets (the remaining, met out by decreasing the working capital and investments). So, in general large quantum of the fund is used for future expansion purposes.

This happened, with the company being in the expansion stage and its generating capacity likely to enhance further when the new investments in fixed assets are fully utilized. RIL has to rely more on the external sources of the funds and not on its internally generated funds. From the ratio analysis and other factors, it has been found that the internal rate of return is more than the cost of capital, for the firm. Hence it is expected to do very well in the future.

> **Pause for thought:** Fund flow statement states wherefrom the funds come (source) and where do they go (application).

17.3 DUPONT ANALYSIS

DuPont analysis is designed to measure the performance of a company. It is an evaluation of the firm's earning potential. With this method, assets are measured at their gross book-value, rather than at net book-value in order to produce a higher return on equity (ROE).

Table 17.5: DuPont Analysis of RIL

	200903	200803	200703	200603	200503
PBIDT/Sales (%)	17.34	20.78	17.34	16.81	19.49
Sales/Net assets	0.73	1.18	1.29	1.24	1.24
PBDIT/Net assets	0.13	0.25	0.22	0.21	0.24
PAT/PBIDT (%)	60.34	67.25	58.19	60.53	53.09
Net assets/Net worth	1.75	1.46	1.50	1.59	1.57
ROE (%)	15.69	21.64	22.45	21.90	21.82

According to DuPont analysis the ROE is affected by the following three factors:

- Operating efficiency, measured by profit margin.
- Asset efficiency, which is measured by assets turnover.
- Financial leverage, which is measured by the equity multiplier.

It helps the analyst to compare the performance of the firms across industries. Care should be taken though, with this analysis, as it is less useful for industries, like, investment banking because they do not use certain concepts of accountancy.

With DuPont analysis it becomes easier to understand that part of the business which is under-performing, as it divides ROE into three components. The assets are computed at gross value rather than net value, so as to produce a high return on equity. Thus is removed the incentives to avoid investing in new assets. Avoidance of new assets can occur, as financial accounting depreciation methods artificially produce lower ROEs in the initial years of an asset placed in service.

Asset turnovers measure the firm's efficiency at using its assets in generating sales or revenue. The higher the ratio better is considered the performance. It also sheds light on the pricing strategy. Companies with low profit margin tend to have high asset turnover; while those with high profit margin have low asset turnovers.

Financial leverage can be measured by equity multiplier. It is calculated as total assets/total shareholder equity. As it evaluates the way a company uses debt to finance its assets, financial leverage is also known as financial leverage ratio. A higher ratio indicates higher financial leverage, implying that the company relies more on debt for the purpose of financing its assets.

Profit margin is the quotient of net profit divided by sales. It measures the extent to which each rupee of sales a company actually earns. A high profit margin ratio indicates that the company has better control over costs, compared to its rival firms.

In the case of RIL, ROE has shown almost consistent performance except in the year 2009. Analysis of the data, of asset turnover and gross profit margin, helps us to conclude that an increase in the gross profit margin from 2007 to 2008 has reduced assets turnover ratio from 1.29 to 1.18. Equity multiplier has shown consistent performance for the period 2005 to 2007, but not in 2008 and 2009. It is surprising to note that the company started relying more on debt capital to finance its assets, in the year 2009, despite the fall in its gross profit margin. Moreover, the financial leverage data from year 2005 to 2007 indicates that the company has the scope to finance its assets by debt capital. Financial data of the company, for the last ten years, show an improvement in terms of its assets efficiency. And relying on the financial leverage will further improve its ROE.

In nutshell, ROE indicates how well the firm has used the resources of its owners. Since it reflects to what extent the objective of maximizing owner's return has been fulfilled, it serves as an indicator for the present as well as for the future, for both the management and the owners. It can also be compared with other companies of the industry and the industry as a whole.

> **Pause for thought:** DuPont analysis measures the performance of a company by evaluating its earnings.

17.3.1 Ratio Analyses

Ratio analysis is a tool, used to conduct the quantitative analysis of the information contained in the financial statement of a company. As it is a ratio, it correlates the various financial parameters. Ratio analysis is favored by the proponents of fundamental analysis.

There are many ratios, accounting for the company's performance, activity, financing and liquidity. Some of them have been discussed here.

> **Pause for thought:** Ratio analyses establish relation between the different financial parameters, contained in the financial statement.

17.3.2 Debt Equity Ratio

Debt equity ratio is given by,

$$\text{Debt equity ratio} = \frac{\text{Total debt}}{\text{Net worth}}$$

	200903	200803	200703	200603	200503
Debt equity ratio	0.57	0.45	0.47	0.49	0.57

It is clear from the table that the owners have contributed more than the lenders. It helps to analyze the long-term solvency of the firm. While the low debt-equity ratio indicates fewer burdens from the interest bearing liabilities, at the same time it indicates that the firm has under-utilized its capacity for financing its operations, by issuing debt capital. Ideally, the firm should increase its financial leverage by employing more debt capital in its capital structure to improve its earning of the shareholders.

> **Pause for thought:** Debt equity ratio is the extent to which debt has been employed for financing the operations.

17.3.3 Interest Coverage Ratio

Interest coverage ratio is calculated as,

$$\text{Interest coverage ratio} = \frac{\text{EBIT}}{\text{Interest}}$$

	200903	200803	200703	200603	200503
Interest coverage ratio	11.56	17.86	13.21	13.20	7.17

Debt equity ratio measures the extent to which debt has been employed by the firm to finance its operation; but it fails to reflect upon the debt repayment capacity of the firm. The interest coverage ratio is the debt serving capacity of the firm. It shows the number of times the interest charges are covered by funds that are ordinarily available for their payment. A high ratio indicates the extent to which even if the earnings fall, there will not be any embarrassment, as far as the payment of interest charges are concerned. Like current ratio, this ratio should not be followed blindly because a very high ratio indicates that the company is not using debt to its fullest capacity. In the case of RIL, interest coverage ratio has increased significantly from the year 2000 to 2009. Such a high ratio of RIL indicates that the company is not using debt to the best advantage of its owners.

> **Pause for thought:** Interest coverage ratio is the debt repayment capacity of the firm.

17.3.4 Inventory Turnover

Inventory turnover represented by,

$$\text{Inventory turnover} = \frac{\text{Cost of goods sold}}{\text{Average inventory}}$$

	200903	200803	200703	200603	200503
Inventory	10.06	10.56	10.64	10.17	9.99

Creditors, management and owners are always interested to know how different assets can generate sales and profit. In other words, turnover ratio gives an idea about the management of assets, like fixed assets, inventory, debtors, etc.

Inventory turnover ratio indicates the speed with which average inventory (average of the opening and closing balances of the inventory) are being converted (or turned over) into cost of the goods sold. RIL's inventory turnover ratio, for the last three years is approximately 10.42. It means RIL is turning its inventory of finished goods into sales 10.50 times per year, i.e., once in every 1.15 months (12 months/10.42) or once in every 34.54 days (360 days/10.42). This is the reciprocal of inventory turnover. Usually, higher inventory turnover ratio reveals better inventory management. In the data used here, RIL's inventory turnover ratio is observed to be consistently increasing since 2003. However, increase in this ratio should be interpreted carefully as it indicates very low level of inventory, which can lead to frequent stock-outs. Otherwise, higher turnover ratios may result when company replenishes its inventory with too many, small lot sizes (it can be costly for the firm in terms of per unit price of the inventory). Generally, this ratio should not be analyzed in a blanket way. Rather it must be compared with past ratios of the firm as well as with the industry average. RIL's efficiency in turning its inventories is continuously deteriorating in last two years, compared to what it was earlier.

> **Pause for thought:** It is the rate of conversion of average inventory into the cost of goods sold. The ratio can thus be taken as an interpretation of inventory management.

17.3.5 Debtors Turnover

Debtors turnover is given by the following relation,

$$\text{Debtors turnover} = \frac{\text{Credit sales}}{\text{Average debtors}}$$

	200903	200803	200703	200603	200503
Debtors	27.10	27.97	29.98	22.03	20.56

Like inventory turnover, debtor's turnover indicates the number of times debtors turnover each year. Usually, higher ratio reflects the efficiency of credit management. It is calculated by average, or year ending, balance of debtors. Credit sales are used as a marketing tool by companies to boost up their sales. When the company extends credit to its customers, it is converted into its account and from the account it is converted to cash over a short period of time (usually less than a year). As debtors account (quality and quantity both) for a significant portion of current assets, its management is very important. It affects the liquidity status of the firm.

Debtor's ratio of RIL has rapidly fluctuated over a period of time. But compared to the last five years (from 2000 to 2005), it has shown an upward trend; and an overall consistency from 2007 to 2009. By taking the average of last three years, the debtor's ratio turns out to be 28.35. Thus on an average, RIL is able to turnover its debtors 28.35 times in a year. In other words, debtors remain outstanding for, 12 months/28.35 = 0.4232 months (less than 15 days) or, 360 days/28.35 = 12.69 days. So, the average collection period is 12.69, which is approximately 13 days. Ideally, this average collection period should be compared with the firm's credit policy and credit period granted by the firm. The short collection period of RIL implies the good quality of debtors and also the prompt payment by the customers. However, too short a period may reflect a very restrictive credit policy of the firm.

> **Pause for thought:** It indicates the number of times debtors turnover each year and shows direct variation with the efficiency of credit management.

17.3.6 Fixed Assets Turnover

Fixed assets turnover is calculated as,

$$\text{Fixed assets turnover} = \frac{\text{Sales}}{\text{Net fixed assets}}$$

	200903	200803	200703	200603	200503
Fixed assets	1.21	1.39	1.34	1.34	1.42

The relationship between fixed assets and sales is known as fixed assets turnover. Like the inventory turnover, fixed assets turnover ratio of the firm has been fluctuating over a period of time (2005 to 2009). By taking the average of last three years it turns out to be 1.31 times. Its reciprocal is 0.7633, which implies that for generating a sale of one rupee, the company needs investment of Re.0.7633 in fixed assets.

> **Pause for thought:** Fixed asset turnover relates sales with the fixed assets.

17.3.7 Return on Assets (ROA)

It is the product of the ratios: net profit margin and total assets turnover.

$$ROA = \frac{Net\ profit}{Total\ income} \times \frac{Total\ income}{Total\ assets}$$

	200903	200803	200703	200603	200503
Return on assets (%)	6.22	12.96	10.15	9.73	9.35

It is computed to know the strategic success of the firm. Generally, companies have either cost leadership or differentiation strategy. How ROA performs, when compared to competitors, depends upon the company's strategy. If the company focuses on the cost leadership strategy, it should pay more attention to its total assets turnover ratio and try to maximize it. But if it follows differentiation strategy, ROA will rise, due to a rise in the net profit margin. This is so because under a differentiation strategy, company can charge a premium price and can control costs. On the other hand, with cost leadership strategy, it competes, penetrating through new markets, economies of scale[4] and increases the market share.

> **Pause for thought:** Net profit margin ratio multiplied by the ratio of the total asset turnover, is ROA.

17.3.8 Return on Capital Employed

It is denoted by,

$$ROCE = \frac{EBIT}{Total\ assets - Current\ liabilities}$$

	200903	200803	200703	200603	200503
ROCE (%)	13.21	18.66	20.12	18.76	19.31

It indicates the efficiency and profitability of the company's investments. It must be higher than the rate at which the company borrows. The significantly lower ratio indicates that further borrowings by a firm may reduce the investor's earnings markedly. In case of RIL, it was roughly consistent from 2005 to 2008, but fell substantially in the year 2009 (from an average 19.21%, over the period 2005-2008, to 13.21% in 2009). This is not a desirable result. It represents a hand-to-mouth existence for the company. Further reduction in ROCE can cause severe financial problems.

---

[4] Economies of scale give large companies access to a larger market by allowing them to operate with greater operational scale and geographical reach.

However, this ratio is not the sole criterion to judge the firm's financial strength, given the fact that the company's earning has substantially reduced in the year 2009, compared to 2008, due to recession (from Rs.24087.5 crore in the year 2008 to Rs.20178.46 in 2009).

> **Pause for thought:** It is the index of efficiency and profitability of the investments made by the company.

17.3.9 Return on Net Worth

Return on net worth (RONW) is given as,

$$\text{Return on net worth} = \frac{\text{Net income}}{\text{Shareholders' equity}}$$

	200903	200803	200703	200603	200503
RONW (%)	15.69	21.64	22.45	21.90	21.82

It is useful to compare the profitability of the company in the same industry. It measures company's profitability by revealing how much profit a company generates with the shareholders' money. Like ROCE, RONW has reduced drastically in the year 2009. It is also called return on equity (ROE).

> **Pause for thought:** It is the profit generated by the company, within the industry; with the investments of the shareholders in the company.

17.3.10 Enterprise Multiple

Enterprise multiple (EM) gives the value of the company. It is a more accurate representation of a firm's value than market capitalization. Its calculation involves market cap plus debt, minority interest and preferred shares, from which are deducted total cash and cash equivalents. The relation used for it is,

$$\text{Enterprise multiple} = \frac{\text{Enterprise value}}{\text{EBITDA}}$$

	200903	200803	200703	200603	200503
EV/EBIDTA	11.49	12.49	10.56	8.72	6.40

A low/high ratio indicates that the company may be under-valued/over-valued. It is different for different industries. So, it can be used for comparing the firms in the same industry. But inter-industry comparisons cannot be made. The good part of the EM is that it takes into account debt capital of the firm, which other conventional measures fail to (i.e., P/E). It is not directly useful for an investor. Generally, it is used by an acquirer. It is used by them for transnational comparison, as it ignores the distorting effects of a country's taxation policies. One positive sign for the RIL is that in spite of a reduction in profitability, its EM fell just marginally in the year 2009. Comparing with its performance in another year, EM has shown an impressive upward trend.

> **Pause for thought:** Enterprise multiple evaluates the company.

17.3.11 Current Ratio

Current ratio is calculated as,

$$\text{Current ratio} = \frac{\text{Current assets}}{\text{Current liabilities}}$$

	200903	200803	200703	200603	200503
Current ratio	1.06	0.98	0.90	1.03	1.10

Current ratio reflects short-term solvency of the firm. It indicates the margin of safety for creditors. Current ratio also shows the availability of current assets in rupees, for every one rupee of current liability. Ideally, ratio of 2:1 is considered satisfactory to evaluate the firm's short-term solvency. For RIL, the ratio is significantly lower than 2:1 each year. But it should not be interpreted as a short-term insolvency of RIL. Neither should it be followed blindly, because this ratio is a measure of quantity rather than quality. A firm with a current ratio more than 2:1, has struggled to meet its obligations. While firms with less than 2:1 ratio, but with good quality of current assets and tight collection policy, can manage their affairs smoothly. Contrarily, very tight current ratio of RIL represents: a good working capital management and fewer blockages of the funds in the form of current assets. Because everyone knows that returns from current assets, compared to fixed assets, is either nil or negative.

Pause for thought: Current ratio reflects the short-term solvency of the firm.

17.3.12 Price-Earnings Ratio

It is the reciprocal of earnings yield, i.e., earnings per share/market value per share. So,

$$\text{Price-earnings ratio} = \frac{\text{Market value per share}}{\text{Earnings per share}}$$

$$= \frac{MV}{EPS}$$

	200903	200803	200703	200603	200503
Price-earnings ratio (P/E)	15.99	17.16	16.24	12.50	10.24

In India, it is widely used by the security analysts to evaluate the firm's performance. It echoes investor's expectation with regards to the performance of a firm. P/E ratio should not be followed blindly and one should not compare P/E ratios across the industries, as industries differ in their growth prospects. It can be compared with the P/E ratio of other companies in a same industry, or with the past data, of the same company. The above table shows that P/E ratio has consistently increased from 2005 to 2008, except a marginal fall in the 2009. It is also known as price multiple or earning multiple—as RIL's P/E ratio of 15.99 in the year 2009 reflects the willingness of the investors to pay Rs.15.99 for every Re.1 of future earnings. Higher P/E ratio indicates that the investor is expecting higher growth for his earnings, compared to companies with lower P/E ratios. It is also linked with the other financial parameters like dividend payout, dividend growth rate and cost of the capital.

Usually, it is compared with industry and market. Investors can forecast the future P/E ratios and can compare with the present P/E ratio to assess the extent of under-pricing/over-pricing of the stock.

But the basic problem with this measure which should be taken in to account is that the denominator, *i.e.*, earning is based on the accounting measures for earnings and is thus susceptible to manipulation.

> **Pause for thought:** It is the ratio of the market value per share and the earnings per share.

17.3.13 Dividend Yield

Payout ratio measures the return to the shareholders, in the form of dividend, out of the company's profit.

$$\text{Percentage payout ratio} = \frac{\text{Dividend per share}}{\text{Earnings per share}} \times 100$$

The percentage of payout ratio is used to calculate the percentage of retained earnings.

Dividend yield is calculated by relating the dividend per share to the market price per share.

$$\text{Percentage dividend yield} = \frac{\text{Dividend per share}}{\text{Market price per share}} \times 100$$

The market price of the share, at which it is bought, is called cum-dividend share price. It is the actual cash flow received from the company. The market price is a measure of future discounted values, while the dividend per share is the present return from the investment. Hence, a high dividend yield means that the companies are undervalued in the market. But, it does not mean that the companies with low dividend yield are overvalued. Again, this cannot be generalized, as companies which do not pay dividend have no dividend yield at all.

	200903	200803	200703	200603	200503
Dividend (%)	130	130	110	100	75
Payout (%)	12.66	8.5	12.27	15.7	14.08
Dividend yield (%)	1.71	1.15	1.61	2.51	3.38

In case of RIL, divided yield reduced consistently during the period, 2005 to 2008, to recover marginally, in 2009, registering slight increase. For a better interpretation of dividend yield, it must be compared with the industry as a whole, and other rival firms.

> **Pause for thought:** Dividend yield is ratio of dividend per share to market price per share.

17.3.14 Earnings per Share (EPS)

It determines the earnings (that is, the profit) of the company, per share. EPS is calculated by dividing the earnings by the total number of shares.

$$\text{EPS} = \frac{\text{Net Profit}}{\text{Number of shares outstanding}}$$

Rather than absolute EPS, actual growth in EPS is a better measure of performance. It helps the investors to shortlist the companies.

	200903	200803	200703	200603	200503
EPS (Rs.)	95.24	131.97	84.28	63.7	53.3

RIL has again put up a good performance consistently, except in the year 2009.

> **Pause for thought:** EPS of a company is its profits accrued per share.

17.3.15 Tobin's q

Financial analysts use this ratio to determine whether the assets under the present management are under-performing or over-performing. It is calculated to get the idea as to how the market evaluated the performance of assets, under the particular company's ownership and control.

The ratio is given as,

$$\text{Price-to-book value ratio} = \frac{\text{Market price per share}}{\text{Book value per share}}$$

	200903	200803	200703	200603	200503
Price-to- book value (P/BV)	2.09	4.17	3.11	2.46	2.02

The firms would have an incentive to invest if q is greater than 1. But q value equal to 1 triggers reluctance towards an investment in the firm. A value greater than 1 indicates that the firm (management) is efficient and its assets have performed more than the expectation of the market. If q is less than 1, it paints the firm as a poor performer, pointing towards the necessity to utilize its assets in a more productive manner. This can be achieved by diversification or vertical integration of assets or by synergistic effects. The firm can become target for takeover by another firm if it has a q value less than 1.

It should be interpreted very cautiously as many times the book value is on historical costs rather than on replacement costs basis.

Analyzing RIL's price-to-book value ratio, for the last five years, it has been found to be much more than 2. This indicates a very efficient usage of the assets and a sound management of RIL.

> **Pause for thought:** It indicates whether an asset is under-performing or over-performing.

17.4 LEVERAGE ANALYSIS

Table 17.6: Financial leverage of companies in India

Name of the company	Debt/Equity ratio
SAIL	0.21
ONGC	0.19
Infosys	0.0
Bharti Airtel	0.30
ITC	0.02
Hindalco	0.40
Wipro	0.37
TCS	0.0
Tata Steel	0.78
Hindustan Zinc	0.0

Indian companies differ in terms of financial leverage as they depend upon number of factors, such as: size, nature of the product, technology, earning potential, economy, management attitude, credit worthiness, etc. The above table provides the financial leverage for some of the largest companies in India, as on 31st March, 2010.

17.4.1 Financial Leverage

The firm is able to magnify the return for shareholders, by increasing financial leverage, because usually debt capital is obtained at a lower rate than the firm's return on investment (ROI). Thus, the difference between the earnings generated by the assets, financed by the funds with fixed charges and costs of these funds, is distributed amongst the shareholders. This leads to an increase in the earnings per share or return on equity (ROE). But, the flip side is that the EPS or ROE will fall, if the rate of return on assets falls or is less than the cost of capital.

> **Pause for thought:** Financial leverage is the degree to which the borrowed money is utilized.

17.4.2 Estimating Earnings per Share

An estimation of EPS of a company is a function of the sales forecast and the estimated profit margin. The sales forecast is an analysis of the relationship of company's sales to various relevant economic series and to industry series. It reflects the performance of the company in terms of the overall economy and with respect to the rival firms.

For EPS estimation, an analysis of net profit margin includes the following three components:

- Identification of the company's strategy, viz., low cost or differentiation.
- Internal variables of the company, such as the current trend and probable future trend; and existence of any threat.
- How parallel the company is with the industry.

This analysis does not require the economy-company relationship because economic factors are reflected in the industry results itself (interpretation of the ROA ratio too provides it).

> **Pause for thought:** EPS estimation is a function of the sales forecast and the estimated profit margin.

17.5 Capital Structure of RIL

The assets of the company can be financed by increasing the claim of the owners or creditors. Owner's claim increases when the firm relies more upon equity shares or retains the earnings. On the other hand, the claim of creditors increases when the firm finances the assets by borrowings. Equity includes paid-up share capital, share premium, reserve and surplus (retained earnings). The debt capital is in the form of debentures and term loans from financial institutions. The proportion of debt and equity is known as capital structure of the company. The quantity and form of financing (both by debt and equity) is decided upon at the time of its promotion, expansion and modernization. It is a very significant decision on the part of the firm, as it affects the shareholders' return and risk. The mixture of debt and equity has direct impact on the shareholders' earnings and risk. And for the company as a whole, it influences the cost of capital and market value of the firm.

By analyzing RIL's balance sheet data of last five years, it can be concluded that the relative proportion of debt has reduced from the year 2005 to 2008 (from 0.57% to 0.45%) and has slightly increased in the year 2009 (0.57%). By looking at the period from 2000 to 2005, the company is found to have gradually redeemed its debt and reduced the proportion of debt in its capital structure. The company has enough provision to raise the capital by debt capital, as it is much below the prescribed level (2:1). In this way, the company can further increase the return of shareholders.

Furthermore, the return of shareholders can be increased manifold with the help of financial leverage (i.e., use of debt capital along with equity capital). Moreover, debt is a cheaper source of finance, with the interest being tax deductible. Firms can increase their earnings by increasing the leverage (procurement of funds by higher proportion of debt) during boom period. But, at the same time, leverage creates instability and increases fixed obligations. It may also lead to bankruptcy. Because of its debt capital being even lower than that prescribed, RIL could withstand the recession. As a consequence, its earnings per share did not fall drastically. So, judicious use of debt capital is advisable. It should be in accordance with the earning capacity and level of fixed assets.

The limit of the debt capital depends upon the firm's earning capacity and its fixed assets:

- Earnings limit of the debt: The use of the debt capital should be as per the earning potential of the firm. Interest coverage ratio is used to find out the limit of the debt. The ratio shows the firm's ability to pay the interest charges, the number of times the interest is covered by the earnings.
- Asset limit of the debt: Asset limit can be found out by calculating the fixed assets to debt ratio. For industrial units, the recommended level for this ratio is 0.5.

> **Pause for thought:** The proportion of debt and equity is known as capital structure of the company.

17.5.1 Management of RIL

In the year 1996-97, Reliance Industries Limited (RIL) became the first Asian company to issue bonds in the US. The company commissioned an 80,000 tonne bottle-grade PET chip plant at its Hazira manufacturing complex. Reliance's PET chips were accepted internationally due to their high quality. In the same year RIL proposed to invest around Rs.5000 crores (US $ 1,250 million) for building two world scale plants, at the site of the Jamnagar refinery in Gujarat. In 1998-99, RIL introduced packaged LPG in 15 kg cylinders under the brand name, Reliance Gas. In 1999-2000, RIL commissioned the world's largest (1.4 million tonnes per annum) Paraxylene (PX) plant at its newly integrated petrochemical complex at Jamnagar, which was planned in 1997-98. Reliance Petroleum Limited (RPL) merged with Reliance Industries Limited, in the year 2002-03. With this merger, Reliance came into the reckoning for a place in the Fortune Global 500, list of the world's largest corporations. The company has also amalgamated Indian Petrochemicals Corporations Limited (IPCL), and thus claims its place as a very strong competitor for a large base in the global market. Reliance discovered natural gas in its very first exploration. The well it drilled in the deep-water block of KG-D6, in the Krishna-Godavari basin, off Andhra Pradesh, hit the jackpot—natural gas, that is! In 2004-05, RIL acquired the polyester major, Trevira GmbH, headquartered in Frankfurt, Germany, having a capacity of 130,000 tonnes per annum of polyester staple fibers, polyester filament yarns and polyester chips.

In 2007, RIL was the largest producer of polyester fiber and yarn globally; 4th largest producer of Paraxylene (PX) and Purified Terephthalic Acid (PTA); 6th largest producer of Monoethylene Glycol (MEG) and 7th largest producer of Polypropylene (PP). Gujarat State Petronet Ltd. (GSPL) and

Reliance Industries Ltd. (RIL) have signed a gas transportation agreement. This permits them to transport 11 million standard cubic meters per day (MSCMD) of natural gas, from Bhadbhut in Bharuch to the RIL's refinery and petrochemical complex in Jamnagar. Similarly, Gujarat State Petroleum Corporation Ltd. (GSPC) has an agreement with Reliance Gas Transmission and Infrastructure Ltd. (RGTIL) for transportation of 3.5 MSCMD of natural gas, from its largest KG basin discovery at Kakinada, to Gujarat.

The Maharashtra state government has given the final nod to RIL to set up two captive power plants in Maharashtra--each of 1100 MW capacity--to meet the requirement of special economic zones, malls and other commercial setups. In return, RIL assured gas supply to the state's Mahgenco's Uran unit. RIL has invested an amount of Rs.25,000 crore to Rs.30,000 crore in a pipeline grid. This grid covers the main trunk lines for gas transport, supplemented by the spur lines; crisscrossing four major states initially, followed by a pan-India network, stretching 10,000 km across the country. RIL is entering the supply-deficient hospitality business and is in talks with big international names such as Walt Disney, Ritz Carlton and Four Seasons for managing some of their hotels. It is also keen to set up theme hotels, such as those run by Disney in the US. Having entered the consumer retail market and special economic zones in the last two years, Reliance considers hospitality business a natural addition to complement its existing businesses.

The company signed a letter of intent with NOVA Chemicals on May 2008, to enter into a joint venture (51:49), in the building and construction sector. This proposed joint venture between RIL and NOVA Chemicals is in a technological partnership for deploying eco-friendly building and construction technologies. It intends to design, engineer, fabricate and build a range of high-efficiency structures for the Indian sub-continent. RIL plans to invest Rs.17,000 crore in oil and gas exploration over the next few years. The company has already invested Rs. 9,000 crore for the same, so far. Surrender of the seven exploration blocks awarded to it by the Government, is also being strongly considered. (**Source:** Capitaline)

17.5.2 Shareholding Patterns of RIL

Table 17.7

Description as on	Number of shares 31/12/2009	% of holding 31/12/2009
Foreign (promoter and group)	0	0
Indian (promoter and group)	1522771300	46.5667
Total of promoter	1522771300	46.5667
Non- promoter (institution)	871519503	26.6513
Non-promoter (non-institution)	754798017	23.0819
Total non-promoter	1626317520	49.7332
Total promoter and non-promoter	3149088820	96.2999
Custodians (against depository receipts)	120997336	3.7001
Grand total	3270086156	100

17.5.3 Collaborations with Other Companies

The company has established 'Reliance Innovation Council' (RIC), under the chairmanship of Dr. R.A. Mashelkar (one of India's eminent scientist and a board member of the company). RIC's insights, suggestions and direction have changed the RIL's business paradigm and bolstered the innovation movement.

Table 17.8

Collaborator's name	Country	Purpose
Geon Co.	USA	Technical
Novacor	Canada	High density Polyethelene
Sinco Engineering	Italy	High density Polyethelene
DuPont Industry	Canada	Technical
Lummus Crest By	Holland	Technical
John Brown Engineers	UK	Technical
Imperial Chemical Industries	UK	Technical
U O P Process International Inc.	USA	Technical
E L DuPont	USA	Technical

17.5.4 The Competitive Edge of the Company

RIL's unique ability to increase its earnings, with a CAGR of more than 20%, over the period of last 30 years is because of several factors. These include its: flawless project execution, world class assets, time management (completion of the projects before due date; Patalganga is one such project), economies of scale, world class technology and financial discipline. With these characteristics, it thus stands tall, with the following distinctions to its credit:

- It has a unique distinction of operating plants at 90% of capacity utilization, which enables an earning of handsome margin.
- It has a strong on-the-ground capabilities and extensive distribution.
- Its superior product portfolio paves the way for profitable business integration.
- It has a rational production planning, with respect to the market demand.
- Despite the extreme volatility in the prices of chemical products, all over the world, RIL has maintained its market leadership in India.
- Till date, RIL has filed 120 patent applications, with 71 of them having been granted.
- At present it is operating two of the world's largest and most complex refineries. It accounts for 25% of the world's complex refining capacity.
- Its 1.24 million barrels per day (MBPD) of crude processing capacity is the largest for any single location in the world.
- It is emerging as the 4th largest producer of Polypropylene, globally.
- It is the world's largest producer of ultra-clean fuels at a single location.
- It has commenced production of hydrocarbons from its KG-D6 block in Krishna-Godavari

basin, with the production of sweet crude of 420 API. The production of oil in this block was commissioned within two years of its discovery, making it the world's fastest green-field deepwater oil development project. It was completed in less than six years from the time of its discovery, which is much faster than the time taken for similar production facilities elsewhere in the world.

- By commencing and increasing gas production from KG-D6 it has increased India's energy landscape. It accounts for 40% of the current hydrocarbon production in India. It will help in reducing our dependence on external sources for energy.
- Because of its overall competency, maintained for the fifth consecutive year, it featured in the Fortune Global 500, list of the world's largest corporations. Its current rankings are:
  - ❏ 264, based on sales.
  - ❏ 117, based on profits.

17.5.5 Overall Significance of RIL in Indian Economy

It plays a pivotal role in the growth of Indian economy and endeavors to contribute to the nation's progress. The following figures give a measure of its role:

- It accounts for 10.4% of India's total exports.
- 2.9% of the total market capitalization in India is attributed to RIL.
- It has a weightage of 13.6% in the BSE Sensex and 11.1% in the NSE S&P CNX Nifty.

17.5.6 Rating to RIL

Its long-term debt is rated AAA by CRISIL and AAA (Ind) by Fitch too.

17.5.7 Risk and RIL

RIL exports 61% of its total output. The major receivables are in US dollars. In addition to that, earnings in local currency are also based on import parity prices. So, it depends heavily on foreign exchange rates and thus is susceptible to the allied fluctuations and interest rate risks.

17.5.8 Future Scenario of RIL

In keeping with its current standing and vision, RIL envisions the future, as follows. Though yes, these are all projections, extrapolations and planning. How it actually unfolds, only time will tell.

- RIL intends to maximize the advantage of its high quality complex assets. It looks forward to realize the synergy between combined operations of both the refineries. This would aid in overcoming the ongoing challenges for the industry and sustaining superior margins.
- The entire global textile industry relies upon polyester; with this trend to rise further, according to the analysts. Moreover, they opine that the expected growth in India and in the world's GDP will raise, even further, the demand for polyester fiber and yarn by more than 3% over a period of five years.
- It is focusing on sustaining high operating rates, by improving efficiency and reducing operating costs.

- It aims to enhance its global reach by ensuring efficient product development (the continuing and sustainable growth of India will support this).
- In a developing economy of the world, the per capita consumption of plastics is in excess of 80 kg; while in India it is Rs.6 per kg, at present. With a growing per capita income and favorable demographic profile, demand for plastics in India is expected to grow, and thus RIL's demand too!
- It is playing an important role by significantly increasing investments in leno bag (used for vegetable and food packaging) and PPR piping (for hot and cold water applications).

SUMMARY

✓ It entails the basic financial variables of the company by studying its P&L, balance sheet, cash flows, fund flows, etc.

✓ Analysis of various financial ratios, like, leverage, assets turnover, working capital ratio, etc., of the last five years, help to ascertain financial condition of the firm. It aids in the identification of the strengths, weaknesses, future prospects and risk level of the firm.

✓ Analysis of the various ratios and their interpretation are very significant for the company.

✓ Study of the management of the company too sheds some light on prospects of the firm.

KEY CONCEPTS

Profit and Loss Account	Dividend Yield	EPS
Balance Sheet	Leverage Ratio	Tobin's Q
Cash Flow Statement	Assets Turnover Ratio	Leverage Analysis
Fund Flow Statement	Working Capital Ratio	DuPont Analysis

REVIEW QUESTIONS

1. How does the application of financial ratios help in judging the financial health, and that of the management, of the company? Explain.
2. Explain the importance and limitations of the leverage ratio in analyzing the financial strengths and weaknesses of the company.
3. What are the factors that have to be taken care of, while interpreting EPS of the company? Will you be able to compare it across industries and with different companies?

ASSIGNMENT QUESTIONS

1. Collect the financial statements of: (i) Profit and loss account; (ii) Balance sheet; (iii) Cash flow and (iv) Fund flow of the companies for the last five years. Collect these data for two companies in the power and IT sectors. Compare the performances of these two companies within the industry and outside the industry.
2. As in assignment question 1, collect the financial statements of at least five companies from the same sector, for the last five years. You can pick the healthcare sector for the purpose. Compute the ratios, as shown in the chapter, and interpret them. Compare these results from all the five companies.

3. Select ten companies from different sectors and study their ratios (as in ratio analyses) of the last five years. Show which company would withstand an economic downturn; which would be the worst affected and why?

4. Study and compare the capital structure of the IT companies and Cement companies. Interpret your results.

18
EQUITY VALUATION

> **LEARNING OBJECTIVES**
>
> The purpose of this chapter is to enable you to understand:
> - How the dividend discount model works to analyze value of an equity share.
> - The discussion on and real life examples of how free cash flow model works to derive fair or intrinsic value of the share.

18.1 INTRODUCTION

The discussion on company analysis, led us to the various other aspects of a company, which make an investment in it prudent or otherwise. By simply being a well-established company doesn't render it a good investment proposition, as has been repeatedly mentioned, supported by reasons. Now having come to this stage it is essential that we look into the methods which aid in the proper valuation of a company. This is more of a quantitative approach. Equity valuation is one such model used by market analysts to find out mis-priced (over-valued or under-valued) securities. This chapter thus presents the models which are used by the fundamental analysts to ascertain the intrinsic value of the company, using current as well as prospective factors.

For determining the total value of a company, reviewing the assets and revenue figures are not enough. It requires further parameters; thus is used equity valuation method. An equity valuation takes several financial indicators into account. These include both tangible and intangible assets, and provide prospective investors, creditors or shareholders with an accurate perspective of the true value of a company at any given time.

Equity valuations are conducted to measure the value of a company, given its current assets and position in the market.

18.1.1 Valuation of Ordinary Share

The fundamental purpose of this analysis is to identify those stocks which are mis-priced: undervalued or overvalued. The price of the stock is derived by projecting the available financial data. In India, as well as in foreign countries, there are various equity research firms which evaluate and furnish the data of the intrinsic value of a stock.

> **Pause for thought:** Comprehensive evaluation of the stocks is the main purpose, through the evaluation of its intrinsic value.

18.1.2 Intrinsic Value versus Market Price

It is difficult to evaluate an equity share, as compared to a bond. The reasons are as follows:

- The rate of the dividend is not fixed.
- It is not compulsory for the company to pay dividends.
- Equity shares do not generate the promised cash flow at the time of maturity (actually there is no maturity in the case of equity shares as per the norms[1]). So, the amount and timing of the cash flow are uncertain, compared to bond/debentures and preference shares (where rate of preference dividend is fixed).
- Moreover, the price of the share and amount of dividend are expected to rise and grow over a period of time. This uncertain and variable nature of dividend, on equity shares, makes the calculation difficult and many a time unreliable.

> **Pause for thought:** The variable nature of the dividend makes the evaluation of an equity share difficult as compared to that of a bond.

18.1.3 Single Period Valuation Model

As the name suggests, this evaluation method involves a single, definite period. We begin with a case where the investor wants to buy and hold the equity share for one year. We assume that the share will pay a dividend of Rs.5 next year (at the time of maturity) and the price of the share is expected to be Rs.125, at the same time. If we further assume that the investor's opportunity cost of capital (or required rate of return[2]) is 18% for the year, what should be the discounted price of the share in the present context?

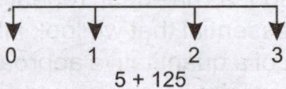

The current value of the equity share is determined by the current value of the expected dividend per share, Div1, at the end of the first year, plus the present value of the expected price of the share, one year hence.

---

[1] 'Going concern' concept of accounting principle.

[2] The required rate of return means the minimum expected yield by investors required in order to select a particular investment. In other words, it is a minimum acceptable rate of return at a given level of risk and it varies from investor to investor as their minimum expectation differs. Generally it is determined by a person's or institution's cost of capital. The required rate of return is also related to the amount of risk an investor is willing to accept. It is the minimum rate of return that an investment must provide or must be expected to provide in order to justify its acquisition. For example, an investor who can earn an annual rate of return of 8% in bank fixed deposits (FD), may set a required rate of return, say 18% on more risky stock investment, before considering to shift his investment from bank FD to stock.

Thus, required rate of return depends upon other available investment's return and of the risk level inherent in a particular investment. Terms like required rate of return, expected rate of return, return demanded by investor, opportunity cost of capital, capitalization rate or discount rate can be used interchangeably by analyst and practitioners.

Thus, the current price of the equity share is calculated as,

$$P_0 = \frac{Div_1 + P_1}{1+r} \quad (1)$$

$$= \frac{5+125}{1.18} = Rs.\ 110.17$$

Where,

P_0 = current price of the share.

Div_1 = dividend expected one year hence.

P_1 = expected price of the share, a year hence.

r = required rate of the return or opportunity cost of the capital.

From Equation (1) it can be concluded that the investor would buy this share, if the actual price of this share is Rs.110 or less. As per the efficient market hypotheses, in a well-functioning capital market, the investor has complete information and the exact value is reflected in the market price of the share. This is, in fact the case of a perfect financial market in efficient financial market[3]. There is no difference between the present value and market value of the share. However, the reality could differ as the market in which we operate may not be a strong form of efficient market. A share is considered under-valued, if its market price is less than the actual (present) value of the share. Similarly, a share is considered to be over-valued if its market price is higher than its actual value.

We can find out the expected growth rate (capital gain) from the present value and projected value of the share, one year hence.

$$g = \frac{125 - 110.17}{110.17}$$

$$= 0.1346\% = 13.46\%$$

Thus,
$$g = \frac{P_1 - P_0}{P_0} \quad (2)$$

Where, g = growth rate

Equation (2) implies that the investor expects a price appreciation of 13.46% for the given share, after one year. Therefore, if the share price is expected to grow at 'g'%, the price of the share one year hence is determined as:

$$P_1 = P_0(1 + g) \quad (3)$$

Substituting the value of P_1 from Equation (3) in Equation (1),

$$P_0 = \frac{Div_1 + P_0(1+g)}{1+r} \quad (4)$$

Simplification of Equation (4) leads to,

---

[3] This has been discussed, in depth, in Chapter 11--Market Efficiency

$$P_0 = \frac{Div_1}{r-g} \qquad (5)$$

Equation (5) indicates that the present value of a share is determined by discounting expected dividend by the difference of required rate of return and growth rate. From Equation (2), the growth rate is 13.46%. So, Equation (5) becomes,

$$P_0 = \frac{5}{0.18 - 0.1346}$$

$$= Rs.\,110.13$$

For calculating the expected rate of return, Equation (5) can also be written as,

$$r = \frac{D_1 + g}{P_0} \qquad (6)$$

Equation (6) can be used to calculate the required rate of return as noted in the following example. When the current market price of the share, predicted value of dividend and the expected growth rate, are given, what is rate of return that can be expected by investing in such a stock? In this case,

$$r = \frac{5}{110.17} + 0.1346$$

$$= 0.1768 = 17.68\%$$

> **Pause for thought:** Single period valuation model evaluates the expected rate of return for a stock—utilizing the present value of the stock—over a single fixed time period of one year.

18.1.4 Multi-Period Valuation Model

The preceding discussion on the single period valuation model involved the assumption that the investors were expected to hold the share for one year and sell it at the end of the same. The investor requires the dividend for one year (Div_1) and capital gain/loss $(P_1 - P_0)$ depending upon the price of the share when he sells the share at the end of the year. But when the holding period exceeds one year, investors expect the stream of cash flow in the form of dividends and liquidating price of the share at the end of his holding period. If it is assumed that the growth rate of a given equity share remains 13.46% p.a., and with the further assumption that share of the given firm is held for two years, dividend and selling price at the end of second year is further ascertained. The liquidating price of the share during his/her holding period becomes his selling price for the next year. This price depends upon the dividend at the end of the second year and is the accepted share price at the end of the second year. If we assume a constant growth rate of 13.46, then at this growth rate the dividend becomes,

$$Div_2 = Div_0\,(1+g)$$

$$Div_2 = 5(1.1346) = Rs.\,5.673$$

∴ And $\qquad P_2 = 125(1.1346) = Rs.\,141.83$

$$P_1 = \frac{Div_2 + P_2}{(1+r)}$$

∴ P_1 in this case is,

$$P_1 = \frac{5.673 + 141.83}{1.18}$$

$$= Rs.125$$

We have already calculated the present value (P_0) as the discounted value of the dividend over the next year and expected price of the share, one year hence (P_1). In a similar manner, the price, P_1, is estimated by discounting Div_2 and price at the end of the second year, P_2. Using the price P_2 and Div_2, the current price, P_0, can be calculated by discounting twice thus, as:

$$P_0 = \frac{Div_1}{1+r} + \frac{Div_2 + P_2}{(1+r)^2} \tag{7}$$

$$= \frac{5}{1.18} + \frac{5.673 + 141.83}{(1.18)^2}$$

$$= 4.28 + 105.93$$

$$= Rs.110.18$$

Likewise,
$$P_1 = \frac{Div_2 + P_2}{1+r}$$

As we have solved above, in equation (3), by further extending this formula

$$P_0 = \frac{Div_1}{1+r} + \frac{Div_2 + P_2}{(1+r)^2} \tag{8}$$

$$P_2 = \frac{Div_3 + P_3}{1+r}$$

$$P_0 = \frac{Div_1}{1+r} + \frac{Div_2}{(1+r)^2} + \ldots \frac{Div_n + P_n}{(1+r)^n} \tag{9}$$

$$P_0 = \sum_{t=1}^{n} \frac{Div_t}{(1+r)^t} + \frac{P_n}{(1+r)^n} \tag{10}$$

For a better understanding of how a multi-period relation gives the value of P_0 (the current price), examples below have to be considered.

Now, P_n is the expected price of the share at the end of 'n' years. By applying the dividend-discount method the value of P_n becomes the present value of the dividend stream, beyond the nth year as per the current evaluation.

So,
$$P_n = \frac{D_{n+1}}{(1+r)} + \frac{D_{n+2}}{(1+r)^2} + \ldots \frac{D_n}{(1+r)^n} \tag{11}$$

Substituting this value of P_n in the Equation (9) and simplifying it, leads to,

$$\sum_{t=1}^{n=\infty} \frac{Div_t}{(1+r)^t} \qquad (12)$$

Equation (12) is a generalized form of multi-period valuation. It is all-encompassing, as it stands for any and all dividend pattern(s): growth, downward, constant or randomly fluctuating.

The ongoing discussion can be understood only when an illustration is forwarded and thus the same follows.

Example: The current price of the share is assumed to be Rs.110.17 and is expected to grow at the rate of 13.46% p.a. It implies that, at this growth rate price at the end of one year will be Rs.110.17 × (1.1346) = Rs.125. Similarly, P_2 = Rs.141.83 and so on. It is also assumed that the expected dividend after a year (Div_1) is Rs.5. Thus, the expected dividend after two years will be 5 × (1.1346) = Rs.5.673 and thus it continues. If the required rate of return for the investor is 18%, and the holding period is 3 years, find out the current price of the share.

Calculation:

$$P_0 = \frac{Div_1}{(1+r)^1} + \frac{Div_2}{(1+r)^2} + \frac{Div_3}{(1+r)^3} + \frac{P_3}{(1+r)^3}$$

$$= \frac{5}{(1.18)^1} + \frac{5.673}{(1.18)^2} + \frac{6.44}{(1.18)^3} + \frac{160.92}{(1.18)^3}$$

$$= 4.24 + 4.074 + 3.9197 + 97.94$$

$$= Rs.110.18$$

Thus it is noted here that the current price, P_0, is equal to the present value, if present value of dividend for 3 years is added to the present value of the share at the end of the third year.

In real life, holding periods can be very long, varying between 10, 15, 20 years, or even more. In fact, according to the accounting principle[4], analysts assume the time period of infinity (∞). Within such a time horizon, the present value of the share becomes zero and current price of the share becomes equivalent to the present value of the infinite stream of dividend.

Referring to the Equations, (9) and (12),

$$P_0 = \frac{Div_1}{(1+r)^1} + \frac{Div_2}{(1+r)^2} + \ldots \frac{Div_{n=\infty}}{(1+r)^\infty} \qquad (13)$$

From Equation (12),

$$P_0 = \sum_{t=1}^{n=\infty} \frac{Div_t}{(1+r)^t}$$

Both, Equation (13) and Equation (12) ignore the liquidation value, that is, the terminal value of the share. The terminal value has not been incorporated, because when holding period becomes

---

[4] Going concern concept

too large, the gain is obtained only in the form of dividend stream. Thus the present value of terminal price approaches zero, hence, neglected.

> **Pause for thought:** Multi-period valuation model has no fixed, pre-determined maturity period and its dividend stream may be of infinite duration.

18.1.5 Zero Growth Model

The above analysis had assumed that the dividend per share grows at a constant growth rate of its original value; or may follow downward trend or random movement. In this section it is assumed that dividend per share remains constant--thus having zero growth rate and which we now refer to as D. Thus, with the dividend remaining constant, the present value of the share is given by,

$$P_0 = \frac{D}{(1+r)^1} + \frac{D}{(1+r)^2} + \ldots \frac{D_n}{(1+r)^n} + \ldots \infty \qquad (14)$$

On simplification, Equation (14) reduces to,

$$P_0 = \frac{D}{r} \qquad (15)$$

Equation (15) is nothing but the present value of perpetuity[5].

> **Pause for thought:** The zero growth model works with a constant dividend over the entire holding period, hence the name.

18.2 GROWTH IN DIVIDENDS

Dividends on equity shares do not remain constant over a period of time. The earnings and dividends of companies may grow, fall or fluctuate due to plenty of factors. Besides, the policy decisions and certain macroeconomic factors are major determinants of the fate of a company. As the analyses of financial reports indicate, majority of the companies retain substantial portion of their earnings for reinvestment purposes. This policy actually helps the company, as well as investors, to increase the earnings and price of the share in times to come.

> **Pause for thought:** With the dividends varying constantly, companies prefer to reinvest the major portion of their earnings. This causes increase in the price of the share, and growth of the company.

18.2.1 Constant Growth Model

This is one of the most popular dividend discount model and assumes that the dividend per share grows at a constant rate, 'g'. As per this model, value of the share in the present context is,

$$P_0 = \frac{D_1}{(1+r)^1} + \frac{D_1(1+g)}{(1+r)^2} + \ldots \frac{D_1(1+g)^n}{(1+r)^{n+1}} + \ldots \infty \qquad (16)$$

Simplification reduces the above equation to,

---
[5] Perpetuity means infinite series of dividend payment or interest payment, without realizing maturity value at the end of the holding period. It has been discussed in Chapter 12, in the context of bond prices and yields. It is similar to perpetual bonds.

$$P_0 = \frac{D}{r-g} \qquad (17)$$

The following example should enhance the understanding of this model.

Example: The dividend expected in one year is assumed to be Rs.5. Further, the constant rate at which the dividend grows is assumed to be 13.46% p.a. Find out the price of the share, if required rate of return (or opportunity cost of the capital) is 18%.

Putting these values in Equation (17),

$$P_0 = \frac{5}{0.18 - 0.1346}$$

$$= Rs.110.13$$

> **Pause for thought:** Constant growth and zero growth models differ, as the latter works with constant dividend, while the former is modeled on a dividend which has constant rate of growth, for the dividend.

18.2.2 Supernormal Growth and Normal Growth

In real life, the dividend of a company does not grow at a constant rate. The growth rate actually varies over a period of time. As per their observations the equity research analysts have concluded that majority of the firms experience growth in two stages. In the first stage the dividend grows at a supernormal rate. This is in the initial few years. Thereafter, the second stage sets in, with a normal growth rate for the dividend.

In the supernormal growth stage the company enjoys a very high growth rate because of the element of innovation. With its product, theme and concept being new for the market, there are no other firms to compete with. Thus, so long a competitor arrives in the market it can exploit its monopoly by charging premium prices and also enjoy a good share in the market. Subsequently with the entry of competitors this very scenario changes, and the second stage of growth is entered. The earnings and dividends grow at a normal rate. The value of the firm is hence determined in two parts:

- The supernormal growth rate is found out for a definite time period (till it enjoys monopoly).
- In the second part, present value of the dividend with constant growth rate is estimated for infinite time period.

The following example should lend clarity to the understanding of this concept.

Example: The EPS of a company was Rs.10 in the previous year. From it, it has paid dividend of Rs.4 as its dividend payout ratio is 40%. It is assumed that the earnings and dividends of a company grow at 18% p.a. for the first four years. It then will fall and finally stabilize at 10% p.a., over an infinite period of time. Find out the current price of the share, assuming the capitalization rate to be 21%.

Ans: From the above equation we can analyze the two-stage growth situation, with the supernormal growth rate being 18% p.a. and the normal growth rate, 10% p.a. The calculation is carried out in two parts:

Part 1

We determine the stream of dividends for the supernormal growth period, in the initial four years. The dividend per share (DPS) in the first year would be,

$$Div_0(1 + g) = Div_1$$

First year: $Div_1 = 4(1.18) = Rs.4.72$

Second year: $Div_2 = 4.72(1.18) = Rs.5.57$

$Div_3 = 5.57(1.18) = 6.57$

$Div_4 = 6.57(1.18) = 7.76$

Now, the current value of the dividend streams during the supernormal growth period is,

$$P_0 = (4.72/1.21) + (5.57/1.21^2) + (6.57/1.21^3) + (7.76/1.21^4)$$
$$= 3.900 + 3.8043 + 3.7087 + 3.6202$$
$$= Rs.15.033$$

This can also be calculated by using the present value of a growing annuity formula,

$$P_0 = Div_1 [(1/r - g) \times \{1 - (1 + g)/(1 + r)^n\}]$$
$$= 4.72[(1/(0.21 - 0.18) \times \{1 - (1.18)/(1.21)^4\}]$$
$$= Rs.15.033$$

Part 2

From the fifth year, growth rate falls from 18% to 10% and is assumed to be stable, subsequently.

For the second stage of normal growth rate, we can apply the constant dividend model, using Equation (17).

Hence, $P_4 = Div_5/(r - g_n)$

$$= 7.76(1.10)/(0.21 - 0.10)$$
$$= 8.536/0.11 = Rs.77.6$$

This is the value at the end of the fourth year. So, by discounting it to zero year, *i.e.*, in the present context, we get the value.

Therefore, $P_0 = P_4/(1 + r)^4$

$$= 77.6/(1.21)^4$$
$$= Rs.36.20$$

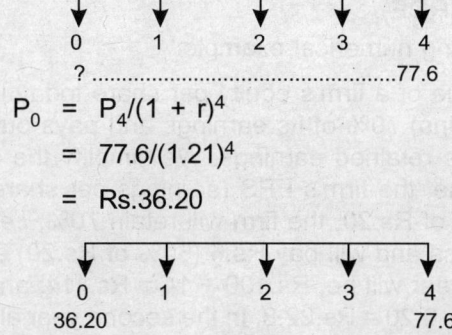

By adding the value of the two stages, we can get the current value of a share in the present context.

$$\text{Current value of the share} = \text{Rs.}15.033 + \text{Rs.}36.20 = \text{Rs.}51.23$$

The formula is now generalized for a two stage growth model as,

Current value (price) of the share = Present value of dividend during the finite supernormal growth period + present value of dividend during the infinite normal growth period.

$$P_0 = \sum_{t=1}^{n}[\text{Div}_0(1+g_s)^t/(1+r)^t] + \sum_{t=n+1}^{\infty}[\text{Div}_n(1+g_n)^{t-n}/(1+r)^3] \tag{18}$$

In the above equation, the first term gives the value of the dividend during supernormal growth rate, g_s. While the second term stands for the value of dividend, at normal growth rate, for infinite time period. It is to be noted that the latter gives the value of dividend growing at normal rate, perpetually. So, the second term can be written in a simplified manner, as,

$$P_n = \text{Div}_{n+1}/(r-g)$$

This reduces Equation (18) to,

$$P_0 = \sum_{t=1}^{n}[\text{Div}_0(1+g_s)/(1+r)] + P_n \tag{19}$$

> **Pause for thought:** The supernormal growth rate is the huge growth rate, above normal, of dividends; enjoyed by the company, in the initial years, courtesy, monopoly. Subsequently, this rate falls and stabilizes to a constant, normal growth of dividends, over an infinite period of time.

18.3 WHAT DETERMINES GROWTH?

The models on growth rate are based on the assumption that dividend grows, over time. But then it too is a fact that this growth rate is not identical or similar for all companies. Thus, inevitably we are led to the root question, and that is, what determines growth?

Well, there are two major factors which serve as the determinants. They are:

- Plough back ratio or retention ratio (b).
- Return on equity (ROE).

We consider the following numerical example.

Suppose, the book-value of a firm's equity per share today is Rs.100 and its ROE is 20%. The firm ploughs back (retains) 70% of its earnings and pays out 30% as dividend. The firm is expected to earn 20% on its retained earnings. We simplify the situation by assuming that the firm has no debt. In this case, the firm's EPS (earnings per share), after 1 year, will be, $EPS_1 =$ Rs.100 × 0.20 = Rs.20. Out of Rs.20, the firm will retain 70%, i.e., Rs.14 [so, b_1= Rs.14 (Rs.20 × 70%)], back in the business and will pay Rs.6 (30% of Rs.20) as dividend. The book-value of equity share in the second year will be, Rs.100 + 14 = Rs.114; and the firm's EPS in the second year will be, EPS_2 = Rs.114 × 0.20 = Rs.22.8. In the second year also it will retain 70% of earnings and distribute 30% as dividend. That is, b_2 = 15.96 (Rs.22.8 × 70%) and Div_2 = 6.84 (Rs.22.8 × 30%). By comparing the dividends of first and second year,

$$= (Div_2 - Div_1)/Div_1$$
$$= (6.84 - 6)/6$$
$$= 0.14 = 14\%$$

By comparing EPS_1 and EPS_2 we can say that EPS has grown by 14% [(22.8 − 20)/20]. The rise in the dividend from Rs.6 in the first year, to Rs.6.84 in the second year, *i.e.*, by Rs.0.84, is due to reinvestment of earnings. In this example, firm has been assumed to have retained 70% of earning of Rs.20, i.e., Rs.14. And on this Rs.14 the firm has earned additional earnings of Rs.2.8 (Rs.14 × 0.20) per share at the rate of 20%. 30% of the earning has been distributed amongst the shareholders. If the firm continues with the policy of reinvesting 70% of its earnings, dividend in subsequent year will continue to grow at 14% p.a. In this case, growth rate of 14% is calculated as,

$$g = b \times ROE[6]$$
$$= 0.70 \times 20\% = 14\%$$

From the above analysis it can be concluded that the growth rate will be higher if a greater percentage of earnings are retained for reinvestment purpose. A share valuation model should explicitly involve growth expectations.

If the first year dividend term is denoted as Div_1, dividend at the end of the first year will be,

$$Div_1 = Div_0 (1 + g)^1$$

At the end of the second year,

$$Div_2 = Div_1(1 + g) = Div_0(1 + g)^2, \text{ and so on, it continues.}$$

If we assume the growth rate of dividend to be constant, the above formula becomes

$$P_0 = Div_0(1 + g)/(1 + r) + Div_0(1 + g)^2/(1 + r)^2 + \ldots + Div_0(1 + g)^{n=\infty}/(1 + r)^{n=\infty} \quad (20)$$

$$P_0 = \sum_{t=1}^{n=\infty} Div_0(1+g)^1/(1+r)^1 \quad (21)$$

$$P_0 = Div_0(1 + g)/(r - g)$$

$$P_0 = Div_1/(r - g) \quad (22)$$

The above equation is also known as the perpetual growth model.

For this analysis the following are to be taken care of:

- The required rate of return (or the opportunity cost of capital) must be greater than the growth rate, *i.e.*, r>g. In the reverse case, results turn out to be absurd. For r = g, the resultant value will be a price that is infinite.

---

[6] The growth rate depends upon how much fund is reinvested back in the business and on it, return on equity earned by the firm. Reinvestment or retention ratio is the part of the firm's earning which the company is not spending or distributing as a dividend. This is the portion which when reinvested back in the business earns return equivalent to ROE and by the same extent the company's earnings per share increases. Proportion of retained earnings, and even dividend, magically grow in the future. So, growth rate of the company is equal to retention ratio and return on equity.

- The initial dividend per share, Div_1, must be greater than zero.

For the sake of simplicity, relationship between 'r' and 'g' is assumed to be constant.

Example 1: A company paid a dividend of Rs.5 in the previous year. The dividend in the future is expected to grow perpetually, at a rate of 7% p.a. Find out the current share price, if the required rate of return is 14%.

$$P_0 = Div_0(1 + g)/(r - g) = Div_1/(r - g) = 5.00(1.07)/(0.14 - 0.07) = Rs.76.43.$$

Example 2: A company has a book-value, per share, of Rs.140 and its return on equity is 18%. It retains 50% of its earnings. If the required rate of return is 22% find out the current price of the share.

Given: The company's book-value = Rs.140 and ROE = 18%. Its EPS one year hence is, EPS_1 = Rs.140 × 0.18 = Rs.25.2 and Div_1 = (1 − 0.50) × Rs.25.2 = Rs.12.6.

As dividend payout ratio is 50%, retention rate is also 50%.

Thus, the growth in dividend = g = 0.5 × 0.18 = 9% (∵ g = b × ROE)

If the dividend grows at a rate of 9% perpetually,

$$P_0 = 12.6/(0.22 - 0.09)$$
$$= Rs.96.92$$

> **Pause for thought:** Growth rate is directly proportional to the percentage of earnings reinvested.

18.3.1 Non-Payment of Dividends by Firms

The policies of a company, many a time, have been found to exclude payments of dividend; even though their returns are quite high every year. In fact, the companies which do not pay dividends in the current year enjoy a miraculous growth and premium share prices in the market. As discussed above, the current price is a discounted value of future expectations. Non-payment of dividend does not mean the company will not pay dividend ever. At some point of time company may start paying the dividend. Actually it is with this hope that the shareholders hold on to the shares of such company. So even in case of non-payment of dividend by the companies, the dividend discount model can be applied.

Example: It is assumed that a company is expected to pay dividend of Rs.6 per share on its share, from the eighth year to infinity. Furthermore, the original rate of return is assumed to be 16% and the perpetual sum, Rs.6, eighth year onwards.

Year	0	1	2	3	4	5	6	7	8	9	10	∞
Cash flows								?	6	6	6	∞

The present value, at the end of the seventh year is,

$$P_7 = 6/0.16 = Rs.37.5$$

Year	0	1	2	3	4	5	6	7	8	9	10
Cash flows ?								37.5	6	6	6 ...∞

Now by discounting Rs.37.5 by 7 years, at discount rate of 16%,

$$P_0 = 37.5/(1.16)^7 = 37.5 \times 0.354 = Rs.13.27$$

Year	0	1	2	3	4	5	6	7	8	9	10
Cash flows	13.27								6	6	∞

> **Pause for thought:** Even though companies do not pay dividend, and thus increment their net value, they sustain the loyalty of the investors. They hold the shares in the hope of dividend payouts by the company, in the near future.

18.4 EARNING CAPITALIZATION

Till now, in this chapter, only the dividend discount model has been discussed for the valuation of shares. Now, we shall study a new concept, called earning capitalization, for the same purpose. The earning capitalization method can be applied under the following circumstances:

- When the firm pays out 100% dividend, i.e., it does not plough any percentage of its earnings back in the business.
- When the firm's return on equity (ROE) is equal to its required rate of return.

In the first case, earnings of the firm will not grow over a period of time as the firm does not retain any earning, to reinvest it back in the business. Also, this model is applicable to those firms which do not use debt in their capital structure. In such firms, as all earnings are distributed as dividends, Div = EPS and growth rate $g = 0$ (because $b = 0$; hence, $g = b \times ROE = 0$). The value of a share is then determined by the formula,

$$P_0 = EPS_1(1-b)/(r-g) \qquad (23)$$

Since, $g = 0$, the above formula reduces to,

$$P_0 = EPS_1(1-b)/r \qquad (24)$$

Example 1: If EPS = Rs.4; b = 0.6; r = 14% and ROE = 20%, calculate the price of the share.

Ans: By applying Equation (23),

$$P_0 = EPS_1(1-b)/(r-g) = 4(1-0.6)/\{0.14 - (0.2 \times 0.6)\} = 1.6/(0.02) = Rs.80$$

The price of the share thus decreases when the earning is entirely (or a large portion) distributed as dividends. It happens because ROE (20%) is greater than the capitalization rate (14%).

Example 2: Calculate the price of the share, with all data remaining the same as in example 1; only the retention ratio is different: b = 0.

$$P_0 = EPS_1(1-b)/(r-g) = 4(1-0)/(0.14-0) = 4/(0.14) = Rs.28.57$$

The price of the share thus decreases when the earning is entirely (or a large portion) distributed as dividends. It happens because ROE (20%) is greater than the capitalization rate (14%).

As per the second criteria for the applicability of this model, return on equity has to be equal to the capitalization rate. This happens when the firms do not have growth opportunities in the market. They earn a return on equity equal to their cost of capital, thus contributing nothing to the firm. In such a case, $g = b \times ROE = b \times r$

Substituting the value of g in Equation (23),

$$P_0 = EPS_1(1 - b)/[r - (ROE \times b)] = EPS_1(1 - b)/[r - (r \times b)]$$
$$P_0 = EPS_1(1 - b)/r(1 - b) = EPS_1/r \qquad (25)$$

Example 3: Calculate the rate of return again, with all data of the above example remaining same, except the change in ROE to 14% from 20%.

When retention ratio is 60% and dividend payout ratio is 40%:

$$P_0 = 4(1 - 0.6)/[0.14 - (0.14 \times 0.6)] = 1.6/(0.14 - 0.084) = Rs.28.57$$

When retention ratio is 0% and dividend payout ratio is 100%:

$$P_0 = 4/0.14 = Rs.28.57$$

Thus, the above illustration indicates that irrespective of dividend payout ratio of the firm, the price of the share remains the same, when return on equity (ROE) is equal to the cost of equity capital or required rate of return for the firm. It happens because the company is able to employ the fund at the cost of 14% (here) and is earning the same return (14% ROE) on that fund. As ROE = r, such an instance will not help the firm to increase its share price.

> **Pause for thought:** The term 'capitalization' is used in quantitative aspect and refers to the amount at which a company's business can be valued. This model is used when either entire earning is given out as dividend or ROE is equal to the opportunity cost of capital or rate of capitalization.

18.4.1 Cost of Equity Capital

In this chapter, we have used the terms: cost of equity capital, equity capitalization rate and opportunity cost of the capital. All of these terms reveal the same meaning as it was assumed that all firms are equity financed firms, given that the proportion of debt capital is zero in such firms. In the discussion that follows now, we shall attend to the required rate of return (here, cost of equity capital).

The required rate of return = Risk-free rate + Risk premium

$$r = r_f + r_p$$

The risk premium is different for different shares; it is directly proportional to the risk.

We know from Equation (22),

$$P_0 = Div_1/(r - g).$$

Or,
$$r = (Div_1/P_0) + g$$

Thus, the required rate of return is equal to the ratio of dividend and current price of the share plus the growth rate.

> **Pause for thought:** Required rate of return is the sum, of the growth rate and ratio of the dividend and current price, of the share.

18.4.2 Stock Prices, Earnings and Dividends

There are basically two types of share:

- Growth share.
- Income share.

Growth share: Growth shares are those which offer greater opportunities for capital gain. Dividend yields of such shares are low as the company concerned ploughs back higher amount of earnings, instead of distributing dividends to its shareholders. But the share price rises, corresponding to the extent of its retention by the shareholders, hoping for dividends to follow in the future. The higher proportion of retained earnings and lesser dividends paid (if at all), in the initial years, enable the firm to increase the share prices substantially in later years. Such shares grow rapidly as growth rate increases because of high retention and good return on equity of such firms. The share price is also decided by the return on equity. The capital appreciation of such shares is very high.

> **Pause for thought:** Growth shares are those which do not yield dividends, but yield high capital gains.

Income share : In contrast to growth shares, income shares pay regular dividends. These have lesser scope of capital gains. When the payout ratio of companies is more than their earnings, the growth rate falls and share prices grow, but at a lower rate. For a regular flow of income, income shares are preferred, while for a substantial capital gain through price appreciation, growth shares are desirable.

> **Pause for thought:** From these shares one can have regular income in the form of dividends, yet the capital gain is not accrued.

Relation between share prices, earnings and dividends : A relation between share prices, earnings from them and dividends, does exist. And a study of the same does help in the evaluation of a company and hence with investment decisions. So now we look forward to establishing the above mentioned relationship. For the purpose we consider the following numerical example.

The expected earnings of a company, after a year, are assumed to be Rs.8 and its policy is to pay out 100% as dividend. The retention ratio (or plough back ratio) is zero. So in such a case, $EPS_1 = Div_1$. Also, the dividend and earnings of this firm will not grow in future, as $b = 0$ (since $g = b \times ROE$). If required rate of return is 15%, the current price of the share is,

$$P_0 = Div_1/(r - g) = EPS_1(1 - b)/(r - g) = 8(1 - 0)/(0.15 - 0) = Rs.53.33.$$

It is further assumed that out of an EPS of Rs.8, the company decides to pay dividend of Rs.6 (*i.e.*, 75% D/P ratio, and retention ratio is 25%); and reinvests Rs.2 back in the business at the ROE of 20%. In the light of this second additional assumption, find out the: payout ratio, retention ratio and growth rate of the company.

        Payout ratio = D/E = 6/8 = 75%
Where,   E = EPS.
                D = dividend.
    Retention ratio = 1 − D/E = 1 − 0.75 = 25%
        G = b × ROE = 0.25 × 0.20 = 5%

If for the sake of simplicity it is assumed that the company continues with this policy of having a dividend–payout ratio (D/P) of 75% and retention ratio of 25%, in future also, then the company will grow at a perpetual growth rate of 5% p.a.

In this case the current price of the share = $EPS_1(1 - b)/(r - g) = Div_1/(r - g) = 8(1 - 0.25)/[0.15 - (0.20 \times 0.25)] = 6/(0.15 - 0.05) = 60$.

The above calculation implies that at the given ROE and required rate of return, when company pays out 100% dividend and reinvestment is zero, in the business, price of the equity share will be Rs.53.33; but it will be Rs.60 when company's dividend payout is 75% and 25% is reinvested back in the business.

This difference of Rs.6.67 (Rs.60 – Rs.53.33) is the value of growth opportunities.

Now, the earlier price, P_0, of a share, when retention ratio b = 0, is compared with the P_0 when retention ratio, b = 25%. We can say that the price of the share increased from Rs.53.33 to Rs.60 when the company started reinvesting some portion of its earnings. Because, without retention, g = 0 and with a retention of 25%, g = 5%.

Subsequent assumptions are that the company mulls over plans of having 30% dividend payouts, with the remaining 70% retained for reinvesting it back in the business.

In this case,

$$\text{Dividend} = 0.30 \times 8 = 2.4$$
$$D/E = 2.4/8 = 30\%$$

Retention ratio, $b = 1 - D/P = 1 - 0.30 = 0.70 = 70\%$

Growth rate, $g = b \times ROE = 0.70 \times 0.20 = 14\%$

In this case the company will enjoy whopping growth rate of 14%, as 70% of its earnings are reinvested back in the business. If the company now decides to follow this policy forever, the company would grow at a perpetual growth rate of 14% p. a. In that case,

$$P_0 = EPS_1(1 - b)/(r - g)$$
$$= Div_1/(r - g)$$
$$= 8(1 - 0.70)/\{0.15 - (0.20 \times 0.7)\}$$
$$= 2.4/(0.15 - 0.14) = 2.4/0.01 = Rs.240$$

The price rise can be further shown to be increasing with further increase in the amount being reinvested. It is because in our hypothetical case, ROE>r. If by chance, ROE<K: then in such a case optimum policy for a company is to pay 100% dividend (or a huge percentage, even if 100% is not possible) out of their earnings.

> **Pause for thought:** The price rise is directly proportional to the amount of earning reinvested and inversely related to the dividend payout when ROE>r.

18.4.3 Value of Growth Opportunities

The previous section led us to the conclusion that retention of earnings raises the growth rate of the company and generates increased cash flows. But what is the mechanism behind this can be understood by the following example.

If, EPS = Rs.8, b= 25%, the retained earnings (RE) in the first year is RE_1 = Rs.8 × 0.25 = Rs.2. The ROE of this company is assumed to be 20%. The retained earnings would then be reinvested at a rate of 20% p.a. Hence the cash flow generated would be, 0.20 × 2 = Re. 0.4 in the first year. Here, the growth rate $g = b \times ROE = 0.25 \times 20\% = 5\%$.

So EPS in the second year will be increased by Re.0.4 and EPS_2 = 8 + 0.4 = Rs.8.4.

25% of Rs.8.4, company will be reinvested back in the business. So, RE_2 = Rs.8.4 × 0.25 = Rs.2.1. Thus the cash flow for the second year will be Rs.2.1 × 0.20 = Re. 0.42.

Therefore, in the third year EPS of the company will be, Rs.8 + Rs.0.4 + Rs.0.42 = Rs.8.82, of which 25% will be reinvested. So, RE_3 = 8.82 × 0.25 = Rs.2.205. When Rs.2.205 is reinvested at 20%, cash flow becomes Rs.2.205 × 0.20 = Re. 0.441. The similar procedure continues so long the retention ratio of the company remains 25% of its earnings.

The above procedure can be discussed in a slightly different manner, as follows.

When the company reinvested Rs.2 at the end of the first year, it expected to receive a perpetual cash flow of Re.0.4, second year onwards. So, by applying the NPV (net present value)[7] concept,

$$NPV_1 = (CF/r) - RE_1 \quad (26)$$
$$= (0.4/0.15) - 2$$
$$= Re.\ 0.67$$

The above equation states that the present value, at the end of the first year, is equal to difference between the present value of cash flow and retained earnings at the end of the first year. As the growth rate in this case is 5% (since, g = b × ROE = 0.25 × 0.2 = 5%), the cash flow at the end of the second year will be Rs.0.4 (1.05) = Rs.0.42

Hence, $$NPV_2 = \frac{Rs.\ 0.42}{0.15} - 2.1 = Rs.0.7$$

On comparing NPV_1 and NPV_2, we can say that NPV overall also grows at 5%.

$$NPV_2 = NPV_1 \times (1 + g)$$

Similarly,

$$NPV_n = NPV_{n-1} \times (1 + g)$$
$$NPV_2 = Rs.0.67 \times 1.05 = Rs.0.70.$$

Therefore, NPV_3 = Rs.0.7(1.05) = 0.735 and so on. Thus, calculating NPV values value of growth opportunities, Vg, is calculated as,

$$Vg = NPV_1/(1 + r) + NPV_2/(1 + r) + ... NPV_n/(1 + r) \quad (27)$$

Equation (27) is similar to the constant dividend growth model. Thus similarly, simplification reduces the above equation to,

$$Vg = NPV_1/(r - g) \quad (28)$$

Substituting the values of NPV_1, 'r', and 'g',

---

[7] NPV is the difference between present value of cash inflows and present value of cash outflows. In other words, it is the present value of money today to the present value of money in the future (projected), taking return in to account. It is one of the capital budgeting techniques to analyze the profitability of an investment or project. NPV analysis is sensitive to the reliability of future cash inflows that an investment or project will yield. NPV is the central tool in discounted cash flow (DCF) analysis and is a standard method for using a time value of money to appraise projects. It is widely used in economics, finance and accounting. It measures the excess or shortfall of cash flows, in present value terms, once financing charges are met.

$$Vg = 0.67/(0.15 - 0.05) = 0.67/0.10 = Rs.6.7$$

The price of the share, P_0, is now resolved into two components:

- Value of infinite stream of earnings, when growth is nil.
- Value of growth due to reinvestments.

$$P_0 = EPS/r + NPV_1/(r - g) \qquad (29)$$
$$= 8/0.15 + 0.67/(0.15 - 0.05)$$
$$= 53.33 + 6.7$$
$$= Rs.60.00$$

Rs.60 is the present value of growth opportunities. This is found to be equal to the price (Rs.60) when reinvestment rate is 25%. Rs.60 consists of Rs.53.33 from the zero retention rate component (the zero growth situation as mentioned above), and Rs.6.7 from the growth component (when retention rate is 25%).

Thus it can be stated that the current price, P_0, consists of: value of perpetual earnings, when $b = 0$ (and hence so is $g = 0$); and the value of growth resulting from the stream of cash flows, from the retained earnings.

By rewriting the Equation (26),

$$NPV_1 = (CF_1/r) - RE_1$$
$$= (b \times ROE \times EPS_1/r) - (b \times EPS_1)$$
$$= \{(b \times ROE \times EPS_1) - (b \times r \times EPS_1)\}/r$$
$$= [(b \times EPS_1)(ROE - r)]/r \qquad (30)$$

Substituting the value of NPV_1, from Equation (30) to Equation (29), the equation for growth opportunities is written as,

$$Vg = NPV_1/(r - g) = [b \times EPS_1(ROE - r)]/[r \times (r - g)] \qquad (31)$$
$$Vg = \{0.25 \times 8 (0.20 - 0.15)\}/0.15 \times (0.15 - 0.05)$$
$$= 6.7$$

Pause for thought: The NPV is composed of the values under zero investments, 100% dividend payouts and growth with some percentage of the earnings reinvested.

18.5 DISCOUNTED CASH FLOW VALUATION APPROACH

Now we come to another valuation approach, called the discounted cash flow valuation approach.

Discounted cash flow (DCF) is an attempt at current evaluation of the company, and in turn intrinsic value of the share, by making projections of the money to be generated in future. According to DCF (discounted cash flow), the present worth of the company is measured in terms of all the cash flows (projected) it will generate in future for the investor.

Basically two methods are used for DCF:

- Dividend discount model.
- Free cash flow to equity.

As an investment student, DCF analysis helps to estimate the real value of the share or the price at which that particular stock is traded in the market. For it, we need to analyze the factors which can affect the company's future growth and sales margins. This necessitates the analysis of the discount rate applicable to that particular company. The discount rate depends upon the risk-free rate, company's cost of capital and the risks faced by the company. All these factors will lead to the knowledge of what drives a company's share price and what should be the actual or fair or intrinsic value of the share of a given company.

The intrinsic value means the actual value of a security as opposed to its market price or book value[8]. In simple terms, intrinsic value gives the actual worth of the company or its share price (whichever may be the case). The market price of the share quoted in the market, *i.e.*, stock exchange, may be above or below the intrinsic value of the share. If market price is above the intrinsic value of the share, such shares are called over-valued and must be sold immediately; and can be bought in the near future when it reaches to its actual worth (because it is the tendency of any security to follow its actual value sooner or later). Similarly, when market price is below the intrinsic value, such stocks are called under-valued. Hence, must be bought without any delay—to be sold at a higher price in future.

The DCF analysis involves the following steps.

1. Forecasting period: The first step is to discount how far, into the future, an analyst should project the cash flows. The best way is to forecast the cash flows based upon the current status of the company and future prospects of the company, derived from company analysis. The table below gives an idea about the forecasting period for a company.

Table 18.1: Forecasting period

Company competitive position	Excess return Forecast period
Slow-growing company: operates in a highly competitive, low margin industry	1 years
Solid company: operates with advantages, such as strong marketing channels; recognizable brand name(s) or regulatory advantages.	5 years
Companies with outstanding growth: operates with very high barriers to entry for the new companies; dominant market position and/or prospects.	10 years

(**Source:** www.investopedia.com)

2. Forecasting revenue growth : After deciding the number of years to be considered as the forecasting period, the next step is to estimate the growth rate of revenue for that time period. To forecast the company's revenue growth rate, it is advisable to revert to the economy, industry and company analysis. These analyses help in forecasting the estimated revenue growth of the company. Moreover, it is better to forecast the revenue growth rate under different economic scenarios. In practice, like the multi-period dividend discount model, supernormal growth rate is

---

[8] Book value is based on the value of total assets, which is less than the value of the total liabilities. It attempts to measure the net assets a company has built up until the present time. In theory, it is the amount that the shareholders would receive if the company were to be completely liquidated.

estimated for the initial years and then normal growth rate is applied. The revenues and other components are forecasted by taking the respective CAGR values.

3. Forecasting free cash flows : Free cash flow is the net cash flow, of the expenses that flows through a company. In other words, free cash flow is the actual amount of residual cash the company is left with, from its operations. This can be used to maximize the wealth of shareholders by investing in growth opportunities.

Free cash flow = Revenues – All operating expenses

4. Discount rate: After projecting the company's cash flows for the coming years, in the next step the worth of the future cash flows, in terms of present context, has to be ascertained. This is done by applying appropriate discount rates to the projected cash flows for the future. Discount rate is determined by computing the cost of equity and the after-tax cost of debt. Cost of equity can be calculated by applying the CAPM formula, $R_e = R_f + \beta(R_m - R_f)$.

5. Fair value or intrinsic value of the share: In the final step, all the estimated free cash flows are discounted, at appropriate discount rates, as shown in step 4. Subsequently, debt is deducted from the summation of discounted cash flows and cash is added back. This, when divided by the number of shares, gives the intrinsic value of the share.

The calculation below shows the intrinsic value of the share derived as per the free cash flow-to-equity method.

Table 18.2: CAGR Calculation

(Rs. in cr.)

	Mar '09	Mar '08	Mar '07	Mar '06	Mar '05	CAGR
Net sales	141,959.00	133,805.78	111,699.03	80,877.79	65,918.83	46.58
Other income	1,264.03	6,595.66	236.89	546.96	1,573.70	–4.29
Stock adjustments	427.56	–1,867.16	654.6	2,131.19	–524.35	–196.00
Total income	143,650.59	138,534.28	112,590.52	83,555.94	66,968.18	16.49
Total expenses	118,234.17	109,506.10	91,947.72	68,550.24	52,684.32	17.55
						13.70
Operating profit	24,152.39	22,432.52	20,405.91	14,458.74	12,710.16	12.22
PBDIT	25,416.42	29,028.18	20,642.80	15,005.70	14,283.86	3.60
Interest	1,774.47	1,162.90	1,298.90	893.61	1,486.54	13.06
PBDT	23,641.95	27,865.28	19,343.90	14,112.09	12,797.32	6.54
Depreciation	5,195.29	4,847.14	4,815.15	3,400.91	3,784.57	
						15.40
Profit before tax	18,446.66	23,018.14	14,528.75	10,711.18	9,012.75	15.83
Tax	3,137.34	3,559.85	2,585.35	1,642.72	1,505.00	35.12
Net profit after tax	15,309.32	19,458.29	11,943.40	9,069.34	7,571.68	

Equity Valuation

Table 18.3: Projected Cash Flow

(Rs. in cr.)

	2010	2011	2012	2013	2014
Net sales	208086.03	305016.21	447098.2	655364.5	960644.97
Other income	1209.8303	1157.9547	1108.3033	1060.781	1015.2963
Stock adjustments	–410.46131	394.04642	–378.28798	363.1597	–348.63651
Total income	167338.24	194931.93	227075.75	264520	308138.76
Total expenses	138980.97	163368.25	192034.82	225731.6	265341.17
Operating profit	27461.353	31223.656	35501.407	40365.23	45895.405
PBDIT	28521.223	32005.3	35914.982	40302.26	45225.479
Interest	1838.4299	1904.6952	1973.349	2044.477	2118.1696
PBDT	26729.827	30221.012	34168.181	38630.89	43676.473
Depreciation	5535.1379	5897.2168	6282.981	6693.98	7131.8639
Profit before tax	21287.753	24566.422	28350.061	32716.44	37755.321
Tax	3633.8467	4208.9292	4875.0227	5646.53	6540.1344
Net profit after tax	20686.032	27951.074	37767.635	51031.82	68954.464
Depreciation	5535.1379	5897.217	6282.981	6693.98	7131.864
Cash flow	26221.17018	33848.29068	44050.61617	57725.804	76086.32791
PVIF	0.8797	0.7738	0.6807	0.5988	0.5267
Discounted cash flow	23066.7634	26191.80733	29985.25442	34566.211	40074.66891
Total DCF value	**153884.7054**				

The cost of equity as per CAPM model is 13.68%, as shown in the Table 18.4 below.

Table 18.4: Cost of Equity Capital

Risk-free rate	6.5
Market return	13.15
Risk premium	6.65
Beta	1.08
Cost of equity	13.68

Table 18.5: Intrinsic Value of the Share

Total discounted cash flows	15388470.54
Less debt	7,390,448.00
Add cash	1012500
Add investments	2,026,818.00
Equity value	11,037,340.54
Shares in issue	15,737.98
DCF per share (intrinsic value of share)	701.318755
Share price(March closing)	1223.2
Upside/Downside	– 42.67%

The intrinsic value is Rs.701.32. On comparing this with the closing market price in 2009 March (Rs.1223.3), it can be realized that the market price of RIL stock is more than its intrinsic value—which is found by the discounted cash flow technique. Thus, the stock is over-valued. However, market will soon intend to reach its intrinsic value. So, such stocks should be sold right away at the market price of Rs.1223.2 and can be bought later at a lower price (price will fall in the future as it will try to approach its intrinsic value).

> **Pause for thought:** DCF evaluates a company by projecting the amount of money it would generate in the future.

18.6 SENSITIVITY ANALYSIS

A technique used to determine how different values of an independent variable will impact a particular dependent variable under a given set of assumptions is referred to as sensitivity analysis. This technique is used within specific boundaries that will depend on one or more input variables, such as the effect that changes in interest rates will have on the price of a share.

Sensitivity analysis is a way to predict the outcome of a decision if a situation turns out to be different, compared to the key prediction(s).

The representations of sensitivity analyses are as follows:

1. When it is assumed that the return of the market changes from 13.15% to 15%, cost of equity is 15.68%. In that case the intrinsic value is even lesser, compared to what it was when the market return was 13.15%.

Risk-free rate	6.5
Market return	15
Risk premium	8.5
Beta	1.08
Cost of equity	15.68

Total discounted cash flows	14535715.71
Less debt	7,390,448.00
Add cash	1012500
Add investments	2,026,818.00
Equity value	10,184,585.71
Shares in issue	15,737.98
DCF per share (intrinsic value of share)	647.134239
Share price(March closing)	1223.2
Upside/Downside	−47.10%

2. If we assume that market return decreases from 13.15 to 11%, intrinsic value is Rs.769.89.

Risk-free rate	6.5
Market return	11
Risk premium	4.5
Beta	1.08
Cost of equity	11.36

Total discounted cash flows	16,467,716.72
Less debt	7,390,448.00
Add cash	1012500
Add investments	2,026,818.00
Equity value	12,116,586.72
Shares in issue	15,737.98
DCF per share (intrinsic value of share)	769.8946574
Share price(March closing)	1223.2
Upside/Downside	−37.06%

Pause for thought: It is an index of sensitivity (of a dependent variable), determined by assessing the impact of different values of an independent variable on a specific dependent variable.

SUMMARY

- ✓ Cash flows of an equity share consist of the stream of dividends and terminal price of the share.
- ✓ Unlike the valuation of bonds/debentures valuation of equity share is difficult, as the rate of dividend is not known. Furthermore, dividend payment is discretion, and not a compulsion, for the company.

- ✓ There are various approaches for the valuation of shares, viz., single period valuation model, multi-period valuation model, constant growth model, zero growth model, two stage growth model, etc.
- ✓ As per the dividend discount model, the current price of the share is equal to the discounted future dividend per share.
- ✓ The intrinsic value (fair value) of the share is determined by the discounted cash flow method. Basically two methods are used for DCF: (i) Free cash flow to equity and (ii) Dividend discount model.

KEY CONCEPTS

Equity Share	CAGR	Earning Capitalization
Income Shares	CAPM	Required Rate Of Return
Growth Shares	Beta	Risk-Free Rate
Dividend	Dividend Discount Model	Free Cash Flows To Equity
Single Period Valuation Model	Discounted Cash Flows	Projected Cash Flows
Multi-period Valuation Model	Intrinsic Value	Projected Revenue Growth Rate
Constant Growth Model	Present Value Of Growth Opportunities	

REVIEW QUESTIONS

1. Why is the valuation of equity shares difficult, compared to that of bonds and debentures?
2. Explain in detail the method of evaluating equity shares.
3. Explain present value growth opportunities.
4. Explain the steps for discounted cash flow method.

ASSIGNMENT QUESTIONS

1. Collect the financial statements (profit and loss and balance sheet) of BHEL for the last ten years. Apply the free cash flow to equity method, as shown in the chapter, by calculating company's CAGR for various components. Find the appropriate 'r' for discounting the cash flows. Carry out the scenario analysis (as shown in the text). Compare the current market price of BHEL and the intrinsic value derived by you. What does your comparison conclude?
2. For RIL, carry out the same exercise and find out the intrinsic value, for April 2012. For the purpose use the financial statements from 2007 to 2012. Compare it with the intrinsic value and current market price. What does your comparison indicate?

APPENDIX

Stock Market Indicators

P/E

For the valuation of the stocks, price-earnings ratio is one of the most widely used indicators in the market. It is a ratio of company's current share price to its earnings per share. But even as it is simple to calculate, its interpretation is difficult. While it is extremely informative in certain circumstances, it is almost meaningless at other times. Because of this unpredictability, P/E ratio often misguides.

$$P/E = \frac{\text{Market value per share}}{\text{Earnings per share (EPS)}}$$

For example, if current market price of the company is Rs.43 per share and earnings over the last twelve months, Rs.1.95 per share, the P/E ratio for the stock would be, (Rs.43/Rs.1.95) = 22.05

It is also known as price multiple or earnings multiple.

In practice, P/E ratio is calculated using EPS from the last four quarters, referred to as trailing P/E. However, EPS can also be calculated from the estimated earnings, expected over the next four quarters, referred to as leading (or projected or forward) P/E ratio. Sometimes EPS is also calculated by taking actual data of last two quarters and estimated data of the next two quarters.

A stock's P/E interprets the amount investors are willing to pay per rupee of earnings. For example, P/E of 20 means that investors are willing to pay Rs.20 for every Re.1 earned. As we are using the EPS of past four quarters to calculate P/E, it gives value of P/E in the present context. However, P/E is much more than merely the past performances of a company. It also takes in to account market expectations for a company's growth, because stock prices reflect what the company will be worth in the future. Future growth or expectations are discounted in current price of the company. Thus, a better way to interpret the P/E ratio is as a reflection of the market's optimism regarding growth prospects of the company.

If a company's P/E is higher than the market or industry average, it means the market is expecting much more over the next few months or years. A company with high P/E will have to eventually live up to the high expectations by increasing its earnings or the stock prices need to fall. Companies give reasonable attention to P/E, as a high ratio is the result of sustainable advantage that allows a company to grow over a period of time. The stock price can be increased by either of the ways: by increasing earnings or by an improved multiple, which the market assigns to those earnings.

A good example is Microsoft. Several years ago, when it was growing by leaps and bounds, its P/E ratio was over 100. Today, Microsoft is one of the largest companies in the world. However, its revenues and earnings can't maintain the same growth as before. As a result, its P/E had dropped to 43 by June 2002. This reduction in the P/E ratio is a common occurrence as high-growth startups solidify their reputations and turn into blue chips.

However, determining whether a particular P/E is high or low, without considering the following factors, is subject to error.

- Company growth rates: P/E of the company must be judged in terms of past growth rates, present growth rates and the expected rates of growth in the future. If the past growth rate is very poor, assuming it to be only 4-7%, yet still enjoying a very high P/E, then the stock could be over-priced.
- Industry: It is useful to compare the companies if they are from the same sector. For example, the utility industry is a stable industry, with a low growth and low P/E; while technology sector has a phenomenal growth rate and constant change in P/E. Thus, comparing P/E of these two sectors leads to a judgment that turns out meaningless. Ideally, high-growth companies should be compared with others in the same industry or with the industry average.

P/E ratio helps us to determine whether the company is overvalued or undervalued, but only under the right circumstances as discussed above. It cannot be generalized.

- Earnings: Earnings are used in the P/E, which is an accounting figure and includes non-cash items. Moreover, the guidelines to determine earnings are governed by GAAP[9] and are different in each country. As it is not enough, EPS can be explored, probed into various numbers depending upon the books. So, it may be possible that we end up comparing apples with oranges.

- Inflation: During high rates, inflation and depreciation costs[10] tend to be understated, because the replacement cost of goods and equipment increases with increase in the general price level. As earnings are unnaturally distorted upwards, the ratio is low during high inflation. So, to determine the trend, we must look at the P/E ratios over a period of time. It implies that as countries differ in their accounting standards, hence earnings of the company are calculated by different methods (due to GAAP) in different countries. In such a case, comparison of P/E of different companies across the world is meaningless. It can just mislead the investor or analyst without contributing anything in terms of a decision making tool, which it otherwise is. The term 'apples and oranges' refer to the situation when the P/E of such companies are being compared which should not be compared at all.

- Many interpretations: A low P/E does not always mean that the company is under-valued. But the market may interpret that the company is headed for trouble in the near future. It could also be interpreted otherwise, that the earnings may go down in the future than what is expected. Similarly, a high P/E could mean that the stock is overvalued, but there is no guarantee that it will fall in the near future.

As discussed above, various interpretations can be made from P/E. The table below provides a summary of the approximate indications P/E ratios give.

P/E	Interpretation
NA	A company with no earnings or losses has undefined P/E. However, mathematically negative P/E can be determined.
0-10	It means either the stock is undervalued or it is expected that the company's earnings are expected to fall. It further implies that the company has earned profit by selling assets; or current earnings are substantially above its earnings in the past.

---

[9] GAAP stands for generally accepted accounting principles. It is a widely accepted set of rules, conventions, standard and procedure for reporting financial information as established by the financial accounting and standard board. Indian GAAP is a set of accounting standards that every company, operating in India, has to follow when reporting its financial results. GAAP differs for each country as it incorporates policies and procedures that have to be followed for financial disclosure as per the standards set in each country.

[10] Depreciation costs are understated because at the time of high inflation, company's earning rises but depreciation cost remains as it is—calculated on the book-value of the assets. So, at the time of high inflation, depreciation cost remains understated. Similarly, when inflation is high, company's earning rises, while value of old equipment also rises if it is sold in the market.

10-17	For many companies, this range of P/E is considered as a desirable or fair range.
17-25	It may be a growth stock with further expectations of higher earnings in the near future. It can also be interpreted that the company's earnings has increased from the past published results.
25+	There is a further expectation of high growth in earnings in future or the stock may be just a speculative bubble.

The following are the important points to be remembered about P/E:
- Historically, the average P/E ratio in the market has been found to be around 15-25.
- P/E ratio must be judged by considering a firm's growth prospects and that of the industry.
- It is a better indicator as compared to the market price alone.
- At the time of high inflation, P/E ratios are usually low.
- It reflects the capital structure of the company.
- It has been found that when bonds yield high returns, investors pay less for a given EPS and P/E falls.
- To reduce the distortions in the P/E, and thus interpret it better, it is computed by using average earning of last 10 years.
- Current P/E should be compared with the current real interest rate, for better judgment.
- Also, the primary motivation for building conglomerates is to diversify earnings so that it can remain stable over time.

The market P/E: Ideally the market P/E should be calculated by taking weighted average of the constituents, not simple averages of the index constituents.

Price-to-Book value ratio : The legendary investor Benjamin Graham, Warren Buffet's mentor, was a big advocate of book-value and P/B in evaluating stocks. P/B ratio is the ratio of market price of the company's shares to its book-value of equity. The question that lingers is what price should we pay for the shares of a company? If our goal is to find out high-growth companies, which sell at low growth prices, price-to-book ratio offers a very handy, but a rather crude approach, to find undervalued companies. However, like P/E it may be an appropriate tool only under certain specific conditions.

$$\text{P/B ratio} = \frac{\text{Stock Price}}{\text{Total assets} - \text{Intangible assets and liabilities}}$$

The numerator is the current closing price of the stock while denominator is the last quarter's book-value. A low P/B ratio can mean that either the stock is undervalued or something is fundamentally wrong with the company. Like other ratios, it also varies with the industry. It also gives us some idea of whether we are paying too much for what would be left in case of an immediate bankruptcy for the company.

It is a tried and tested method to discover the low-priced stock that the market has somehow neglected. If a company's trading is less than its book-value, that is, its P/B is less than 1, it implies either the market believes the asset values are overstated or the company is earning a very poor return on its assets. If the first interpretation is true, the investor should try to liquidate the funds at the earliest, because the asset value of the company would soon face downward correction in the market. If the second assessment turns out to be true, there are chances that only a new management can turn around things and improve the return.

P/B greater than 1 indicates that the company has a very high share price, relative to its asset value, which generates very high return on the assets, and thus high earnings.

P/B and ROE

For a better judgment, and thus a better decision, P/B and ROE must be analyzed altogether.

- Many times overvalued growth stocks have a combination of low ROE and high P/B.
- If a company's ROE rises, then its P/B also rises.

P/B ratio is applicable only to capital intensive or financial businesses with ample assets on the book. The denominator of the formula completely ignores intangible assets like brand name, patent, intellectual property, good will etc. Because of this attribute, book-value does not carry much importance for service sectors where there are quite a few intangible assets. Stocks of Infosys, e-Bay, Google, Microsoft, etc., are examples of such stocks whose bulk value is determined by intellectual assets rather than physical assets. Due to this, P/B may be misleading for Infosys. Moreover, this ratio is not much of use for companies with high debt level or sustainable losses. A high level of debt may eat away substantial portion of its book-value, which may artificially raise P/B value. For companies with series of losses, book-value is negative and so P/B is meaningless. Because of inflation, book-value of assets becomes lesser than their current market value. Only for the start-up firms, book-value reflects original value. When firms get old, the book-value may increase or decrease and thus distorts the ratio. Over a period of time, companies may change their cash reserves, which in turn change the book-values, but without any change in operation. Share buy-back also distorts the book-value ratio. Like P/E, multiple P/B must be compared only within the industry. It is a rule of thumb that a P/B ratio greater than 3 would represent an overvalued and expensive stock than the stock actually is. On the other hand, a P/B ratio less than 1 indicates the stock to be an undervalued, cheap stock.

Doubling the P/B ratio in 8 months

The P/B ratio of BSE shares has doubled in eight months (April 2003 to December 2003); while it increased from being 1.41 times higher on April 25, 2003, to increasing 2.89 times on December 17, 2003. Also the P/B ratio of SENSEX constituents has moved from 1.99 times to 3.23 times (62%) during the same time period. This doubling of P/B indicates over-bought position in the stock market, indicating that the price per share has moved much faster than the book-value per share.

REFERENCES

1. Damodaran, Aswath (2009), *Damodaran on Valuation: Security Analysis for Investment and Corporate Finance*, 2nd edition, Wiley India, New Delhi.
2. Damodaran, Aswath (2008), *Corporate Finance: Theory and Practice*, 2nd edition, Wiley India, New Delhi.
3. Pastor Lubos and Veronesi Pietro (2003), "Stock Valuation and Learning about Profitability," *The Journal of Finance*, Vol.58, No.5, pp.1749-1789.
4. Molodovsky Nicholas (1968), "Stock Values and Stock Prices", *Financial Analyst Journal*, Vol.24, No.6, pp. 134-148.
5. www.investopedia.com

PART 6
TECHNICAL ANALYSIS

19
TECHNICAL ANALYSIS

> **LEARNING OBJECTIVES**
> The purpose of this chapter is to enable you to understand:
> - The price patterns.
> - The primary, secondary and daily fluctuations.
> - Dow Theory.
> - Types of charts involved in Dow Theory.
> - The market breadth theory.
> - Types of charts involved in the market breadth theory.
> - Moving averages.
> - Relative strength index (RSI).
> - Moving average convergence divergence.
> - Bollinger bands.

19.1 INTRODUCTION

As has been already mentioned, there are two approaches to analyze the movement of share prices: fundamental analysis (E-I-C Approach) and technical analysis. Chapters 15 to 17 have concentrated on fundamental analysis, which entails a thorough study of economic, industry and company variables. In this chapter attention is accorded to technical analysis.

Technical analysis reviews the past movements in prices to forecast their future dispositions. Thus, it runs completely contrary to the EMH. Technical analysis is applicable to stocks, indices, commodities, futures and to all such tradable instruments whose prices are influenced by the theory of demand and supply. In technical analysis, price refers to any combination of the opening, high, low and closing prices for a given security, over a specific time period. Time period can be intraday tick data (time intervals of 5 minutes, 15 minutes or hourly), daily, weekly, monthly or yearly. Some technical analysts also consider volume of data[1], open interest[2], etc., to study the price movement.

---
[1] Volume is the total number of transactions filled on each stock options contract for the day.
[2] Open interest is a calculation of the number of active trades for a particular market. It is calculated by using futures and options contracts—by adding all contracts that are associated with opening trades and subtracting all contracts that are associated with closing trades. It is used as an indication of the strength behind the market and thus serves as an indication of the strength of the price movement. But on its own it does not provide any indication of the direction of the price movement. Increasing open interest shows there is strength behind the current price movement and decreasing open interest shows that there is a weakening of the current price movement.

of shares. Technical analysis has become a very important tool for equity researchers, intraday traders and short-term investors. It is a powerful indicator of the volatility of the stocks, strengths and weaknesses of the momentum (of the market) and the anticipated interest of the investors to respond to the signals to buy or sell the stocks. A thoughtful application of this tool enables the investors to develop an expertise to beat the market. With the insights gathered, the investor then enters and exits at the right time to generate the maximum profit from the prevalent momentum in the market.

Technical analysis utilizes various types of charts and patterns to predict the movements of share prices. Thus, use of historical price charts lays the foundation of technical analysis. Over a period of time a number of indicators have been developed—with respect to the data provided by the charts—to ascertain these movements in the share prices. At the same time, each indicator has its own unique applicability, as well as, strengths and weaknesses.

As technical analysis is being discussed, it is imperative that we know what led to the inception of the same. There must have been some strong reasons, based on observations, behind it. Yes, indeed. Hence, follows the rationale behind technical analysis:

- Prices are influenced by the theory of demand and supply. Besides, various economic, industry, company and psychological factors too affect the prices.
- Prices follow trends and as new equilibrium is established in the market, periodically, they adjust to this new equilibrium.

With these as the reasons behind it, technical analysis is guided by the following principles to do the job for which it came into being: predicting the movements of share prices.

- Price discounts everything.
- Price movements are not totally random.
- 'What' is the change in price and 'what' is the extent of the same is more important than 'why' the change has occurred.

But then it is very seldom that any approach is completely free from weaknesses, just as returns are usually accompanied by inherent risks. Hence, similar is the case with technical analysis, which has its share of weaknesses, as follows:

- There is always a possibility of another trend in the market, completely different from that identified by the technical analyst.
- It is subject to the interpretation of charts and patterns. Two technical analysts may interpret the same chart differently and thus come up with different views and course of actions.
- Thus efficiency of technical analysis is dependent more on the efficiency of the analyst, than it is on the available data!
- Not all signals and patterns hence lead to the predicted outcomes.
- It has been criticized for being very slow with its interpretations. Because by the time a trend is identified, a significant move has already taken place.

19.1.1 History of Technical Analysis and Dow Theory

The history of technical analysis begins with Dow Theory, named after Charles Dow, the person who developed the theory. Charles Dow, journalist, founder and first editor of the *Wall Street Journal* presented this idea, of technical analysis, through his editorials in *Wall Street Journal*. He was co-founder of Dow Jones and Company. Though he is the father of this theory, he never got it published in the form of research papers. S.A. Nelson and William Hamilton, his colleagues and friends, subsequently formalized his idea into the theory for financial predictions of an economy, naming it the Dow Theory. Since then it has been worked on by Robert Rhea, who refined it and published a book on it.

Dow came up with this theory to explain the movement of the indices of Dow Jones Average. There are various assumptions of Dow Theory on which technical analyses of the stocks are based. They are as follows:

1. The manipulation of primary trend is not possible: It implies that though a large amount of money is at stake, it is impossible to manipulate the primary[3] trend. Intraday, day-to-day and even secondary[4] movements are prone to manipulation. Short movements, spanning from few hours to few weeks, can be subject to manipulation by large institutions, speculators, breaking news or rumors. Hamilton further stated that it is possible to manipulate one share, but not the entire market.

2. Price discounts everything: This means the market reflects all available information. Anything that is to know is already reflected in the market, in the form of prices. Prices discount the sum total of all hopes, fears, rumors and macroeconomic variables such as: interest rates, inflation rates, exchange rates, industrial policies, fiscal policies, revenue projections of the company, elections, war, monsoon, etc. If something unexpected happens, it affects the short-term trends, but the primary trend remains unaffected. At times market reacts negatively to good news, because before the news hits the market, it is already reflected contrarily in the price.

3. Technical analysis is a pseudo science: It is just a set of guidelines to assist the investors and traders with their own study of the market, but is not a guaranteed means of beating the market. As per Hamilton, while analyzing the market one should be objective and rational. This enables one to see what is there, and not what one wants to see! If an investor is long[5], he may want to see only bullish signs and may ignore any apparent bearish signals. On the other hand, when an investor is out of the market or short, he may be receptive to any negative aspects only, ignoring any bullish indicators. Dow Theory provides comparatively rational mechanism to render decisions less ambiguous.

4. History tends to repeat itself: It assumes that past patterns of price, of individual securities, tends to recur in the future. This happens because, people when confronted with similar set of circumstances, react in similar ways.

> **Pause for thought:** Technical analysis is purely based on the past data of stock prices and the philosophy of, "History repeats itself", as stock prices are predicted based on precedence.

19.2 TREND AND TREND LINES

Trend line shows direction of movement of security prices. The share prices can be either increasing or decreasing or could remain constant for a specific period of time. However, one notable aspect about the share prices is that they neither rise (or fall) constantly nor do they fluctuate in a

---

[3] In Dow Theory, primary trend is the major trend of the market, and is most important for the trader to determine it. It generally lasts between one to three years but can vary in some instances.

[4] Secondary movements or secondary trend moves in the opposite direction of the primary trend—or as a correction to the primary trend. In general, it lasts between three weeks to three months.

[5] Long means to buy and short means to sell. So, when an investor is long, i.e., he wants to buy, he always expects that the market will further go up. Similarly, when an investor is short means he is a seller—he sees bearish trend and concludes that market will fall.

straightforward manner. Each rise or fall is affected by a counter-move, causing their movement to follow a zigzag pattern. To properly identify the direction of price movements, straight lines are drawn, connecting either final prices that are attained or the initial price from which the trading begins, of the share. Such lines are straight lines, as can be evidenced from the Figure 19.1 below, depicting the three different types of trends and the corresponding trend lines.

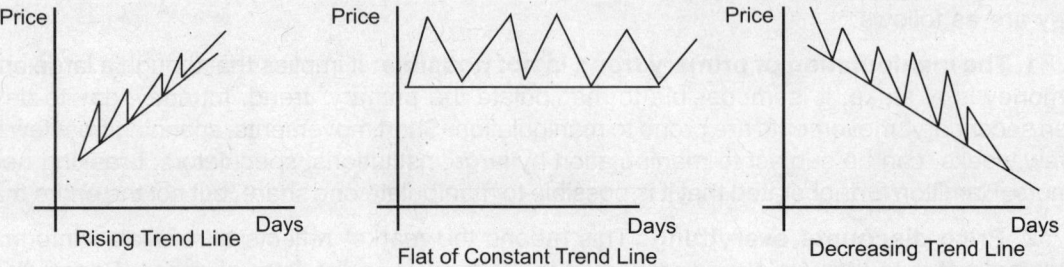

Figure 19.1: Trend and trend lines (rising, flat and falling trend)

> **Pause for thought:** The trend lines show the trend—upward or downward—of the movement of share prices. Though the movement is zigzag, the lines are straight as they result by connecting either the final prices of the share or their initial prices.

19.2.1 Market Movements

Dow and Hamilton identified three types of price movements for the Dow Jones Industrial and Rail averages. They are:

- Primary movements.
- Secondary movements.
- Daily fluctuations.

A primary movement could last from a few months to many years and signifies the underlying broad trend of the market. Secondary movements last from a few weeks to few months and move counter to the primary trend. Daily fluctuations can move with or against the primary trend and last from only a few hours to one week. Given the significant information that these trends provide, they demand a detailed discussion and thus being compiled as follows!

> **Pause for thought:** The price movements of the past, which forms the basis of technical analysis, have been identified to be of three types—primary, secondary and daily fluctuations—each providing characteristic information and thus having relevant significance.

19.2.2 Primary Movements

They represent the underlying broad trend of the price movements and can last from few months to many years. These movements are typically referred to as bull (upward trend) and bear (downward trend) markets. Once the primary trend has been identified, it will remain in effect, until proved otherwise. However, its length is mostly indeterminable. Moreover, it is difficult to know when and where the primary trend will stop. Hence, Hamilton opined that the objective should always be to utilize what we know, rather than haphazardly guessing about what we do not.

With a set of guidelines formed by the principles of Dow Theory, the identification of the trend and investment decisions are accordingly facilitated. Predicting the length and duration of the trend is a matter of expertise, gathered through practice. After all practice makes a person perfect! Hamilton and Dow were interested to tap the significance of the primary trend and according to them success is related to a timely identification of the trend and adhering to the same. A primary bear market is defined as a declining market, continuing over an appreciable length of time, because of deteriorating business conditions and subsequent decrease in demand for the stocks.

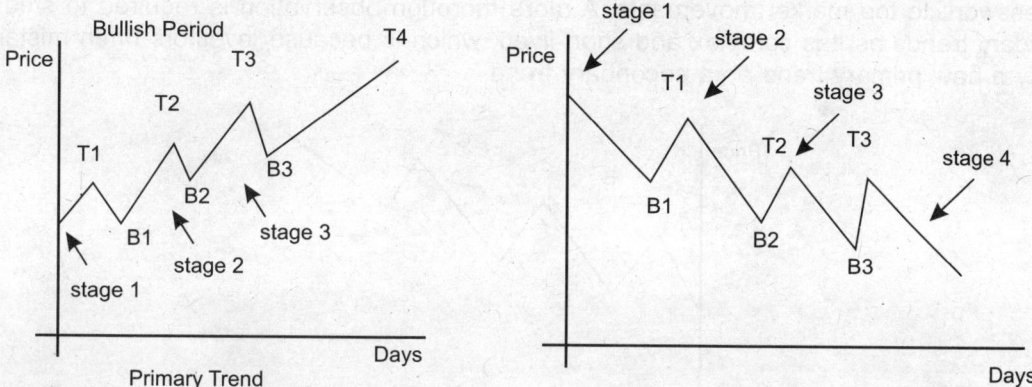

Figure 19.2: Primary trend-bullish market   Figure 19.3: Primary trend-bearish market

Pause for thought: Primary trends represent the underlying broad trend of the price movements and can stretch from few months to many years.

19.2.3 Secondary Movements

Secondary movements last from a few weeks to few months and run counter to the primary trend. Hence they can be referred to as reactionary in nature. In a bull market, secondary movements are considered as corrections[6]. Contrary to this, in a bear market, these movements are called reaction rallies[7]. Hamilton noted some characteristics of the secondary movements, common to both bull and bear markets. These characteristics should be considered as loose guidelines for investment decisions rather than accepting them as fixed rules. They are as follows:

- Based on the historical observations, Hamilton estimated that secondary movements retrace one-third to two-third of the primary moves, with 50% being the typical amount. Thus, according to this estimation, if the primary upward trend moved the Sensex from 10,000 to 12,500 (2500 points), the secondary trend would be expected to send the Sensex down at least 833 points (one-third of 2500).

---

[6] Market follows a trend, *i.e.*, it moves predominantly in a single direction over a given period of time. However, within that larger trend there will be periods when the market moves in a direction opposite to the prevailing trend. Such moves are called corrections.

[7] As discussed (foot note 4) secondary trend starts in an opposite direction to primary movement, and-or-as a correction to primary trend. When primary trend is bearish, *i.e.*, a falling trend, secondary movement will start opposite to it, which means the secondary movement will bring correction by going upward. This is known as reaction rallies.

- A secondary movement tends to be faster and sharper than the preceding primary movement.
- At the end of the secondary movement, there is a slack, just before the turnaround. Small movements in price, a decline in volume, or the combination of the two can mark this slack period.
- Lows are sometimes accompanied by a high volume washout day.

As per Dow and Hamilton, secondary movement is a necessary event to combat excessive speculation. Corrections and counter moves keep speculators in check and add a healthy dose of guesswork to the market movements. A more thorough observation is required to study the secondary trends as it is complex and short-lived, which is because investors often mistakenly identify a new primary trend as a secondary trend.

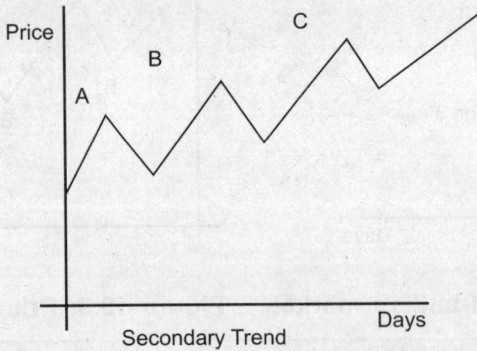

Figure 19.4: Secondary movement

> **Pause for thought:** Secondary movements last from a few weeks to few months and move counter to the primary trend.

19.2.4 Daily Fluctuations

Daily fluctuations become significant when considered as a group, as even when they are looked at individually, they can be dangerous and unreliable. Due to the extreme random nature of the prices, when considered on daily basis, forecasting the price from it is highly restricted. Moreover, excessive dependence on daily fluctuations may result in forecasting erroneous results, possibly even losses. On the other hand, careful analysis of daily price fluctuations can add valuable insight if viewed with a broader perspective. When a series of days is combined, a structure starts emerging, rendering the analysis better.

> **Pause for thought:** Daily fluctuations last from only a few hours to one week and can move with or against the primary trend.

19.3 TECHNICAL ANALYSIS VERSUS FUNDAMENTAL ANALYSIS

Fundamental analysis has been already discussed and technical analysis we have been discussing. And now their comparative study would forward the primary purpose here—to aid in the rational investment decisions.

Price of any security—be it stocks, bonds, currencies or commodities—are affected by two key factors: valuations and sentiments. Valuation means estimating the future cash flows from the assets and discounting them to the present value, using appropriate discount rates. Huge amount of time and money are invested for the research, which is essential to arrive at the intrinsic value of an asset. Technical analysts study the past trends; correlate it with the current scenario of the economy, industry and company; and based on the available information frame the future outlook. This approach of estimation leads to the valuation of the assets. Fundamental analysis is a tool used to arrive at these valuations. And it differs from technical analysis as is represented in the table below, which holds their contrasting characteristics.

Fundamental analysis	Technical analysis
"What to buy"	"When to buy"
It is a pure science; and includes pre-defined and tested parameters for investment.	It is a medley of science and art. It does not involve any formula.
Study of financial statements of the company.	Study of price charts and oscillators[8] derived theorem.
Studies price movements as random phenomena.	Does not subscribe to random walk theory.
Signals are generated by the corporate actions.	Signals are generated by market actions on the prices.
Chances of multiple interpretations are lower.	Chances of multiple interpretations are higher.
Gives signals in advance.	Generates delayed signals.

> **Pause for thought:** Each analysis has its unique contradicting features; merits and demerits; and a mutually inclusive approach, with respect to these analyses, enables the investor to generate the maximum benefits. Their differences, many, arise out of the elementary difference in their principles. While fundamental analysis concentrates on which assets are to be bought, technical analysis guides the investor to the right time for buying the asset. And once these two synergize, investor is a happy beneficiary!

19.3.1 Market Breadth Theory

The name implies that the theory takes cognizance of the volume of the change, synonymous with the breadth of the market. In simpler terms, it theorizes on the extent of changes in the market. But yes, the primal aspect is the direction, of the changes that occur in the market. The direction of the market can be identified by charting the volume, which implies charting of the new highs or lows (advances or declines data) of the market. Advances (declines) mean number of stocks whose prices have increased (decreased) from the previous day's trading. Breadth is the difference between the number of stocks that have advanced and declined during the same period (Table 19.1, column 5). The cumulative index of the net difference is a measure of the market breadth (Table 19.1, column 6). Breadth of the market indicates towards the number of stocks ticking up or down of a rally[9] or a retreat, representing the number of stocks included in a move, which an index or a simple price chart cannot.

---

[8] An oscillator is an indicator that is derived by applying a formula to the price data of a security.

[9] A rally is a term used to describe a sudden rise in stock prices, especially after a period of fall in the same. For example, if the stock market drops in the morning and investors rush in to buy stocks at cheaper prices, the stock market has rallied.

Market breadth theory is a theory of technical analysis, enabling the prediction of the strength of the market according to the number of stocks that advance or decline on a particular trading day. The utilities of the theory can be noted as follows:

- It is used as an indicator to gauge the number of stocks advancing or declining per day.
- If the breadth indicator is strong, it means the market will be rising; contrarily, it will fall.
- The advance/decline index, as a measure of market breadth, is used by the investors with long-term investments.
- When the advance/decline index rises, in spite of a downward trend in the market, bullish signal in a bear market is indicated. Contrary to this, when the advance/decline index falls, but in a rising market, it is a bearish signal in a bull market.
- Furthermore, when this index is more (less) than 1, it indicates advances are more (less) than decline.
- It was observed by H. A. Krow that if this ratio is more than 1.25, it is a signal to sell the stock. On the other hand, if this ratio is less than or close to 0.75, investors are urged to buy the stock. But then these observations by Krow are for short-term investments.

Advance/Decline index = (Advances - Declines) + Advance/Decline index value of the previous period

Table 19.1(a): Breadth of the Market

	Breadth of the market								
Date	Advances	Declines	Unchanged	Net	Breadth	Sensex		Nifty	
						Opening	Closing	Opening	Closing
1	2	3	4	5	6	7	8	9	10
18-01-2012	1028	422	67	606	606	16270.87	16466.05	4904.50	4967.30
19-01-2012	413	1054	40	−641	−35	16502.42	15451.47	4977.75	4980.65
20-01-2012	994	461	60	533	498	16573.87	16643.74	4995.00	5018.40
21-01-2012	623	813	72	−190	308	16745.01	16739.01	5044.85	5048.60
24-01-2012	707	737	65	−30	278	1667.02	16751.73	5025.35	5046.25
25-01-2012	888	557	75	331	609	16806.72	16995.77	5064.80	5127.35
26-01-2012	962	483	69	479	1088	17068.85	17077.18	5151.50	5158.30

Table 19.1(b): Breadth of the Market

Breadth of the market						
Index	Advances	Advances as % of total	Declines	Declines as % of total	Net	Breadth
Others	1138	46.34	1209	49.23	−71	−71
BSE 30	19	63.33	11	36.67	8	−63
BSE 500	225	45	272	54.4	−47	−110
BSE 200	95	47.5	105	52.5	−10	−120
BSE 100	56	56	44	44	12	−108

(www.bseindia.com, www. nseindia.com)

Advance-decline ratio: The advance-decline ratio (A/D ratio) shows the ratio of advancing issues to declining issues. It is calculated by dividing the number of advancing issues by the number of declining issues. The advantage of this ratio is that it remains constant regardless of the number of issues that are traded on the given exchange. A moving average of A/D ratio is used as an over-bought/over-sold indicator. Higher value indicates strong rally—and also chances of a correction. On the other hand, low value indicates over-sold condition and suggests that soon rally may come in the market.

A/D ratio = Advancing issues/Declining issues

Date	Advances	Declines	A/D ratio
1	2	3	4 (2/3)
18-01-2012	1028	422	2.436
19-01-2012	413	1054	0.392
20-01-2012	994	461	2.156
21-01-2012	623	813	0.766
24-01-2012	707	737	0.959
25-01-2012	888	557	1.594
26-01-2012	962	483	1.992

But then this index too is plagued by limitations, which are:

- The problem with this index is that it is not a time indicator. So, usually it is used along with other indicators, instead of being used individually. It has been mentioned above that if for a particular time period the market is attaining new highs, but at the same time the advance/decline index is falling, it is a bearish signal in a bull market. Now this signal arises because there are fewer securities which are causing the market to rise.
- Conversely, when the market is strongly moving in one direction the advance/decline index also follows this pattern.

Another parameter in the market breadth theory is the volume. Volume indicates the level of participation of traders. Volume data too serves as an indicator in a stock market and it is easy to read as well.

Volume

Volume means number of shares or contracts traded in a security, or on an entire market, during a given period of time. That is, it is the amount of shares that trade hands from sellers to buyers—as a measure of activity. Volume is an important indicator in technical analysis as it is used to measure the worth of a market move. According to Dow Theory, the main signals for buying and selling are based on the price movements of the indices. Volume is used as a secondary indicator to confirm what the price movement is suggesting. As per this definition, volume should increase when the price moves in the direction of the trend, and decrease when the price moves in the opposite direction of the trend. Thus, in case of an upward trend, volume should increase when the price rises—and fall when the price falls. The reason behind this is that uptrend shows strength when volume increases, because traders are more willing to buy an asset with the assumption that upward trend will continue.

Similarly, during correction, low volume gives the indication that most traders are not willing to close their positions because they believe the momentum for primary trend will continue.

Conversely, when volume runs counter to the trend, it is a sign of the weakness in the existing trend. For example, if the market is on the upward trend, but at the same time volume is weak or less on the upward trend it is a signal that buyers have started to dissipate. If buyers start leaving the market, or starts selling the shares, it indicates towards a very rare chance for the market to continue its upward journey. The same is applicable for increased volume on down days, which is an indication that more and more participants are becoming sellers in the market.

As per the Dow Theory, once a trend has been confirmed by volume, the majority of the money in the market should be moving with the trend, and not against it.

> **Pause for thought:** Market breadth theory enables the prediction of the strength of the market according to the number of stocks that advance or decline on a particular trading day. Breadth is the difference between the number of stocks to have advanced and declined during the same period. The cumulative index of net difference is a measure of the market breadth.

19.3.2 Types of Charts

We are aware that technical analysis utilizes charts for its purpose. The trend lines have already been discussed and now we are led to this very important tool of technical analysis—the charts. This section takes a detailed look into the various types of charts and their unique properties.

There are mainly four types of charts:

1. Line chart.
2. Bar chart.
3. Candlestick chart.
4. Point and figure chart.

1. Line chart: Line chart is developed by plotting the closing prices of the stock on daily basis, over a period of time, which, then are connected to form the chart. It is the simplest of the four types. The price is plotted on the Y-axis and the time period, on the X-axis. Its strength is its simplicity. The chart shown in Figure 19.5 below is the line chart of S&P CNX NIFTY for the period, January 2011 to November 2011.

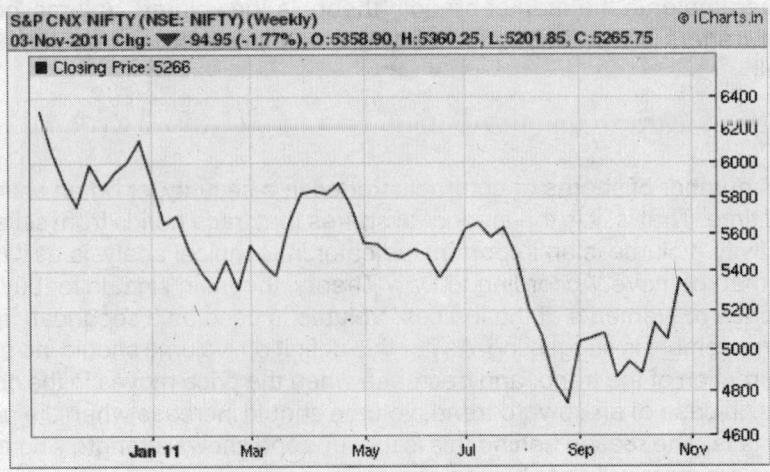

Figure 19.5: Line chart

Technical Analysis

> **Pause for thought:** It is the simplest chart of all, formed by connecting the closing prices of a stock, that are plotted on a daily basis over a period of time.

2. Bar chart : Bar chart is the most important charting method as it displays the high, low and closing prices of the security, for each day, during the specific time period. The highs and lows are represented by the top and bottom of the vertical bars respectively. The closing price is represented by the short horizontal line, present as an intercept on the vertical bar, jutting out to the right, from the bar. It can also be displayed by using all four prices for the day: opening, high, low and closing, of particular scrip. The addition of the opening price is displayed by the short horizontal line jutting out to the left, from the bar. It is an effective way to display a voluminous data. The figure below shows the bar chart of S&P CNX NIFTY for the time period: January 2011 to November 2011.

Figure 19.6: Bar chart

> **Pause for thought:** Bar chart is the most important charting method as it displays the high, low and closing prices of the security, for each day, during the specific time period. And the closing prices too can be incorporated, with each price-type having a specific pictorial representation.

3. Candlestick chart: These charts originated in Japan, over 300 years ago, and have become quite popular in recent times. For a candlestick chart, all four prices: opening, high, low and closing, for the day are required. A daily candlestick chart is based on the opening price, the intraday high and low prices, and the closing price. White (empty) or green candlesticks form when the closing is higher than the opening price, while black (solid) or red candlesticks are formed when the closing price is lower than the opening price. In other words, a white candle stick signifies profit, while a black candlestick stands for loss, during the day, for the stock.

In candlestick charting, body of the candlestick is the wide part of a candle that represents the range between the opening and the closing prices over a specific time period.

The white and black portion formed from the open and close is called the body (white body and black body). The lines above and below are called shadows and represent the high and low prices.

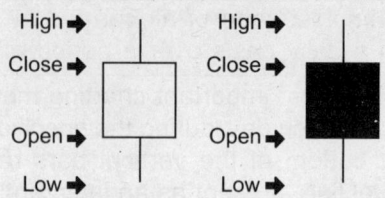

Figure 19.7: Candlestick chart

The Figure 19.8 below represents the candlestick chart of S&P CNX NIFTY from January 2011 to November 2011.

Figure 19.8: Candlestick chart of S&P CNX Nifty

Pause for thought: A candlestick chart is created out of the opening price, the intraday high and low prices and closing price for the day, of a stock. A white (empty) or a green candlestick represents profitable trading, while a black or red candlestick stands for loss incurred by the stock. The width of the candlestick, called its body, is a measure of the difference between opening and closing prices of the stock—thus an indication of the extent of profit and loss as well.

4. Point and figure chart: In the charting methods discussed above, all plot one data point for each period of time, irrespective of whether there is a price movement or not. The plotting of the data for each day, over the given length of the time period, is a routine matter. Thus there is a dot, a bar and a candlestick plotted to mark the price, even if it is constant.

The point and figure chart is a complete departure from this norm. It only takes the significant price movements into cognizance, while time is not considered as a factor at all. There is an X-axis but it does not extend evenly across the chart. It shows only the significant price changes and omits volume (the data spread, over a period of time) completely. Even though the X-axis represents time, specific calendar time is unimportant.

TECHNICAL ANALYSIS 501

As shown in the Figure 19.9 below, the flat crosses are used to show upward movement, while the ellipses show downward movement. The cross or ellipse is plotted only for a significant price movement. When prices do not move at all or move very little, over a period of time, they are not depicted on the chart. This focus, on only the significant price movements, makes it easier to identify the support and resistant levels, bullish breakouts and bearish breakdowns.

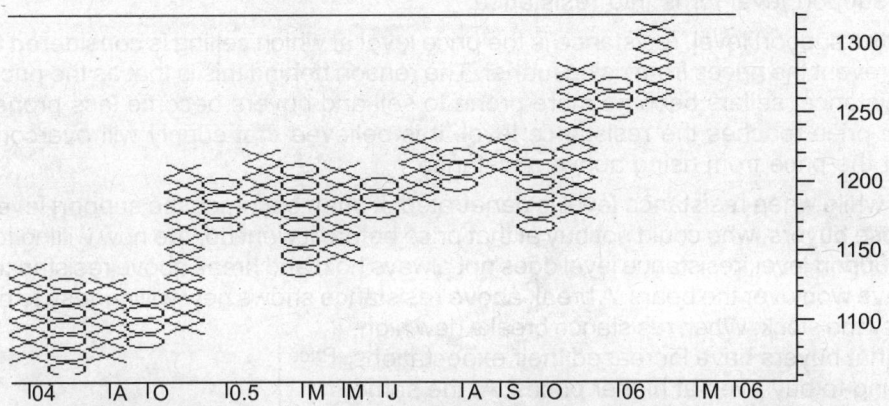

Figure 19.9: Point and figure chart

> **Pause for thought:** In point and figure chart only the significant price changes appear as points in the figure, with time being not a factor in its construction.

19.3.3 Support and Resistance

Support and resistance are two major indicators of technical analysis. They define natural boundaries for advancing and declining prices, just like a ball bounces when it hits the floor or drops after being thrown to the ceiling.

We know that prices are driven by supply and demand, with an excessive supply pushing down the prices while an excess demand for the stock raising its price. Thus, demand, synonymous with buying, leads to a bullish trend. Contrarily, supply is synonymous with selling (which increases the supply) leading to a bearish trend in the market. When supply and demand are equal, prices move sideways as bulls and bears strike it out of control. In other words, the price at which trade takes place is the price at which a bull and a bear agree to do business, representing the consensus of both the parties.

Support is the price level at which demand is considered to be strong enough to prevent the price from declining further. The logic behind this is that as the price declines towards support and gets cheaper, buyers become more inclined to buy and sellers become less inclined to sell. By the time the price reaches the support level, it is believed that demand will overcome supply and prevent the price from falling further. In other words, support level indicates the price at which majority of the investors believe that prices will no longer go down, rather they move higher. Resistance level indicates the rise in prices, at which the majority of investors feel prices will go down.

When the support level is penetrated, it becomes resistance level. It is because investors want to limit their losses and will sell later, when prices approach the former level. It means, as nothing is permanent same applies to the support level! Support does not always hold and a break below, signals, bears have won over bulls. A decline of the price, below support level, indicates a new willingness to sell (with a fear that prices may fall further) or a lack of incentive to buy. When support breaks a new low, it indicates that sellers have reduced their expectations and buyers cannot be persuaded to buy till the price decreases below support level. Once support is broken, another support level is established at the lower level. Thus, once the price breaks below a support level, the broken support level turns into resistance.

Unlike the support level, resistance is the price level at which selling is considered to be strong enough to prevent the prices from rising further. The reason behind this is that as the prices advance towards resistance, sellers become more prone to sell and buyers become less prone to buy. By the time the price reaches the resistance level, it is believed that supply will overcome demand and prevent the price from rising above resistance.

After a while when resistance level is penetrated, it often becomes the support level. This is so because those buyers, who could not buy at that price before it went up, are now willing to buy at that price. Like support level, resistance level does not always hold and break above resistance, indicates, that bulls have won over the bears. A break above resistance shows new willingness to buy and less interest to sell the stock. When resistance breaks new high, it indicates that buyers have increased their expectations and are willing to buy even at higher prices. At the same time sellers cannot be persuaded to sell (in an expectation that price may rise even further). Once resistance is broken, a new resistance level is established at the higher level. Thus, as the price advances and crosses the resistance level, it signals changes in supply and demand. The breakout above resistance indicates that the forces of demand have overwhelmed the forces of supply. If the price returns to this level, the demand increases and support level is found.

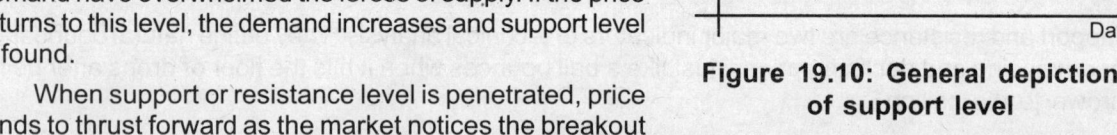

Figure 19.10: General depiction of support level

When support or resistance level is penetrated, price tends to thrust forward as the market notices the breakout and tries to tap this opportunity by buying or selling. This happens because price has a memory. Those prices, at which a significant number of buyers and sellers entered the market in the past, will tend to generate a similar mix of players when prices again touch that level.

Buyers and sellers are constantly in competition with each other. Support defines that level where buyers are strong enough to keep the prices from falling further, while resistance is that level where sellers are strong enough to push the prices further up. Support and resistance play different roles in upward and downward trends. In an upward trend, support is where a pull-back[10] from rally should end; and in a downward journey, resistance is where a pull-back from a decline should end. Below is the chart (Figure 19.12) of BHEL with the support and resistance indications. The interchanging (penetration) of support and resistance too can be seen in the chart.

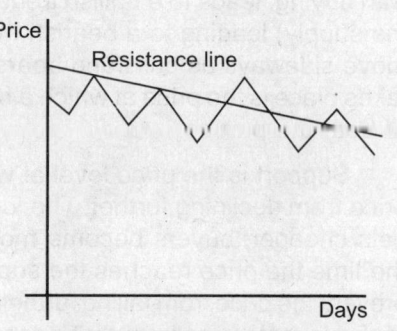

Figure 19.11: General depiction of resistance level

---

[10] Pull-back means buying weakness and selling strength. Stocks that are in up-trends will pull back, offering a low-risk buying opportunity and stocks that are in down-trend will show rally (that is, rise or upward movement) and thus will offer low-risk selling opportunity.

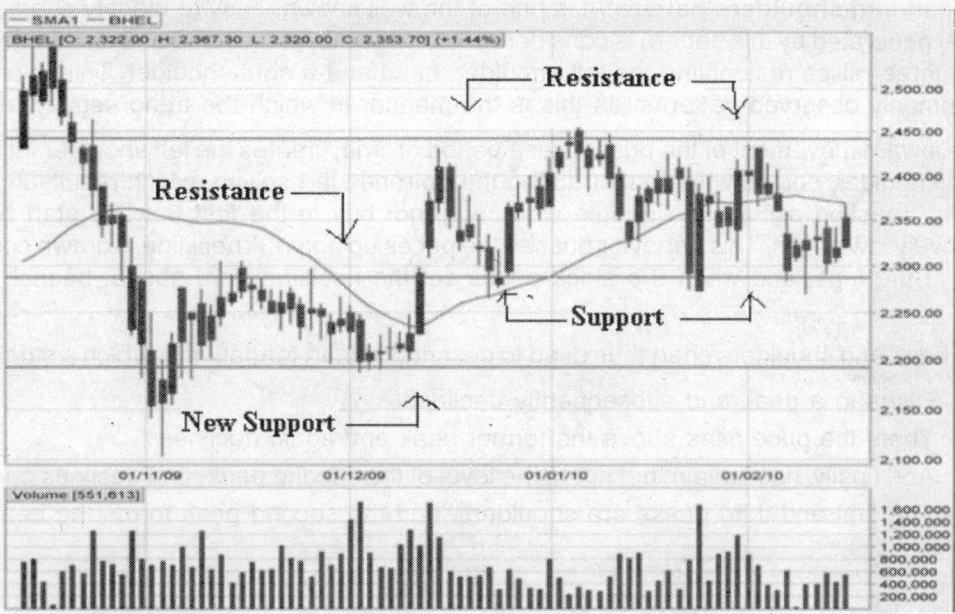

Figure 19.12: Support and resistance chart of the stock of BHEL

> **Pause for thought:** Support and resistance are two major indicators of technical analysis. They define natural boundaries for advancing and declining prices. Support defines that level where buyers are strong enough to keep the prices from falling further, while resistance is that level at which sellers are strong enough to push the prices further up.

19.3.4 Chart Patterns

A fundamental belief of technical analysis is that security prices move in trends, and these trends do not last forever. Prices rise and fall. But these changes in the direction of the movement of prices rarely occur in an identical manner. Instead, prices typically decelerate, pause and then reverse. These different phases occur as investors form new expectations. As a consequence, the demand and supply line changes. These changes in expectations cause different pattern of prices to emerge. It is to be recalled that no two markets are identical, but their price patterns are often found to be similar. And a predictable price behavior often follows this pattern. These patterns can last from days to months, extending to even few years, at times. Usually, it has been found that the more striking is the movement in price, longer a pattern takes to emerge.

It is evident that there are quite a few chart patterns, given the varied manner in which the stock prices move. These patterns, mentioned below, are subsequently discussed for an in-depth idea of the same.

1. Head and shoulders pattern.
2. Head and shoulders reverse pattern.
3. Triangle pattern.
4. Flag pattern.
5. Cup and handle.
6. Rounding bottom.

1. Head and shoulders pattern: It is one of the well known, easy to identify chart patterns. The signal generated by this pattern is considered to be reliable. In the head and shoulders pattern, there are three rallies resembling the left shoulder, head and a right shoulder. This is one of the most commonly observed patterns, as this is the manner in which the trend usually reverses.

The upward movement of the price, over a period of time, creates the left shoulder. At the peak of the left shoulder, people who bought during the uptrend start selling, which results in a dip. At the bottom, reaction occurs and people who could not buy in the first uptrend start buying at comparatively low prices. This behavior pushes the prices up again. A neckline is drawn connecting the lows of the tops, and when the stock prices cut the neckline from above, bearish trend is signaled.

The head and shoulders chart thus used to describe a chart formation in which a stock's price:

- Rises to a peak and subsequently declines.
- Then, the price rises above the former peak and again declines.
- And finally, rises again, but not to the level of the second peak, and declines once more.
- The first and third peaks are shoulders, and the second peak forms the head.

Figure 19.13: Head and shoulders chart of Wipro Ltd.

From the above head and shoulders chart of Wipro Ltd. we can say that neckline (shoulder) is at a price of Rs.450 and the price Rs.535 corresponds to the head. The difference between height of the head and neckline is Rs.85. So target is the fall in price to the extent of Rs.85 from the neckline, *i.e.*, Rs.450 – Rs.85 = Rs.365.

Here, the left shoulder is formed at the price of Rs.450 and head is at the price of Rs.535. Once we can identify this, we can affirm that on the right hand side approximately similar fall will take place to form the right shoulder. So, it is anticipated that the price will fall approximately by Rs.85. It gives the signal for the investor to buy the stock later on, when the price approximately falls by Rs.85.

Pause for thought: It is one of the most reliable chart patterns. It consist of two shoulders and a head, marking three peaks, with the first and third being referred to as shoulders and the maxima, the second peak, is hailed as head.

2. Head and shoulders reverse pattern : Head and shoulder reverse pattern shows the characteristics as implied by the name—the reverse of the head and shoulders pattern. The fall of stock's price, followed by its rise creates a reversed right shoulder; and the continuous fall, followed by rise in price, forms the head and the left shoulder. The neckline is drawn by connecting the tops of the inverted head and shoulders. When the price pierces the neckline from below, it marks the end of the bearish trend and beginning of the bullish. This pattern must be confirmed with the volume and trend of the market. The head and shoulder reverse pattern indicates change in trend and sentiment. This is formed when prices move up from first low, with an increase in volume up to a certain level and then decreases to a new low. This forms the left shoulder. After that the price recovers and is supported by more volume than seen before, which forms the head. Subsequently, a corrective reaction on low volume occurs by forming the right shoulder.

As have been noted, the characteristics of the head and shoulders pattern, how the same be not followed for the reverse pattern? Hence, the reverse pattern is described as a chart pattern used in technical analysis to predict the reversal of a current downtrend. This pattern is identified when the price action of a security meets the following characteristics:

- The price falls to a trough and then rises.
- The price falls below the former trough and then rises again.
- Finally, the price falls again, but not as far as the second trough.
- Once the final trough is generated, the price heads upward toward the resistance-- found near the top of the previous troughs. The first and third troughs are considered shoulders and the second one forms the head.

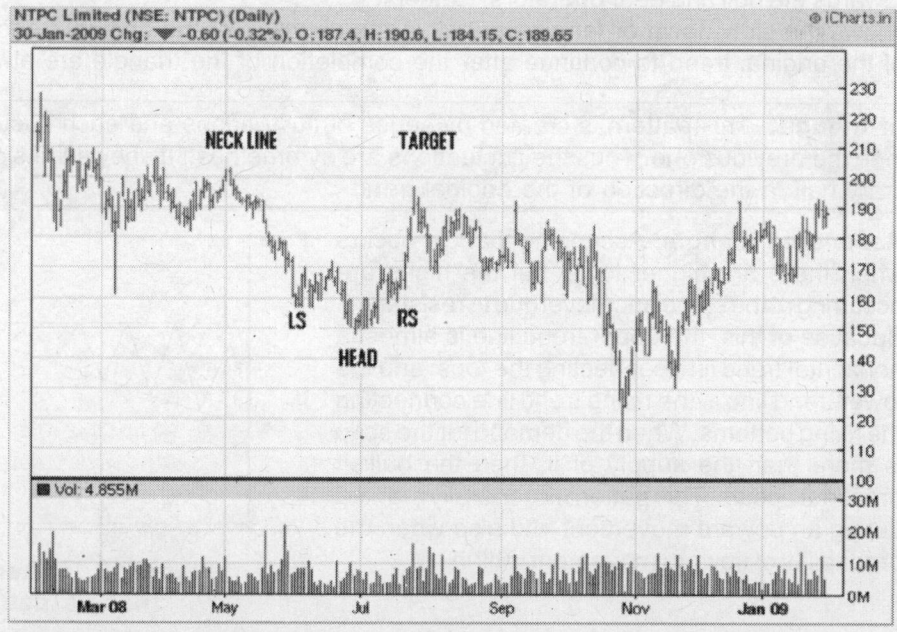

Figure 19.14: Head and shoulders reverse chart of NTPC Limited

For NTPC Limited, the neckline is at Rs. 170 and depth of the head is, Rs.170 – Rs.150 = Rs.20. So, target after the completion of the pattern is Rs. 170 + Rs. 20 = Rs. 190.

Here, the price at the left shoulder is Rs.170, while the head is at Rs.150. Thus, it indicates that it has fallen by Rs.20. So, approximately it is estimated that the right shoulder will be created by rise of almost Rs.20 from head. Hence, the price can rise from Rs.150 to Rs.170 [Rs.150 (head) + 20 (difference)]; and the maximum it rises to is Rs.190 [Rs.170 (price at left shoulder) + Rs.20 (difference)].

> **Pause for thought:** This too consists of three peaks, but inverted! In other words, it is comprised of three troughs, with the first and third forming the shoulders (reversed) and the second one, the minima in this case, the inverted head.

3. Triangle pattern : Triangle pattern is very common, easy to identify and popular in technical analysis. Triangle patterns are of three types of: symmetrical, ascending and descending

- **Symmetrical triangle:** This pattern is created by series of fluctuations and each fluctuation is smaller than the previous one. In a symmetrical triangle, peaks do not attain the height of the previous peaks; while troughs are higher than the previous ones. By connecting the diminishing peaks, which are thus slanted downward, symmetrical triangle results. In a similar manner, connecting the rising troughs, which are slanted upward, the lower trend line is formed. This pattern does not have any bias towards the bull and bear operators. Rather it shows the slow down or temporary halt in the direction of the original trend. Chances of the original trend to continue after the completion of the triangle are always there.

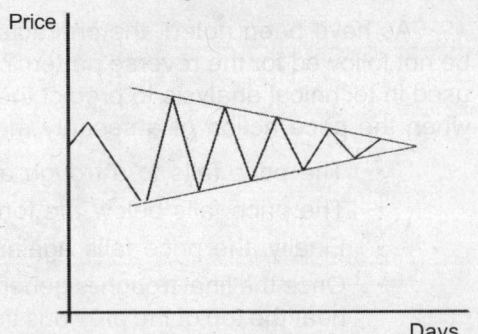

Figure 19.15: Symmetrical triangle

> **Pause for thought:** This pattern is created by series of fluctuations and each fluctuation is smaller than the previous one. Thus the fluctuations are symmetrical! It shows the slow down or temporary halt in the direction of the original trend.

- **Ascending triangle:** Ascending triangle occurs when there are higher lows, but the highs are occurring at the same price level due to resistance. Because of this, the upper trend line is almost a horizontal trend line connecting the tops; and the lower trend line is the rising trend line connecting the rising bottoms. When the demand for the scrip is more than the supply of it, then the bullish breakout occurs. This pattern is generally marked during an upward movement and also when the probability of upward movement is high.

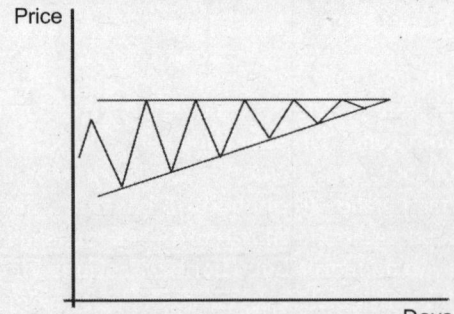

Figure 19.16: Ascending triangle pattern

Findings and interpretations: In contrast to the symmetrical triangle pattern, an ascending triangle has a certain bullish trend, or bias, before the actual breakout. It is clear from the above discussion that symmetrical triangle is a neutral formation that relies on the impending breakout to indicate the direction of the next move. The upper line on the ascending triangle shows the overhead supply that prevents security from falling to such levels. It is analogous to having large selling orders at this level, but which takes number of weeks or months to execute—thus preventing the price from rising further. The higher low indicates increased buying pressure and gives the ascending triangle its bullish bias.

> **Pause for thought:** Ascending triangle occurs when there are higher lows, but the highs are occurring at the same price level due to resistance.

- *Descending triangle*: Like the earlier triangle patterns, this one too is made up of similar fluctuations and each top is lower than the previous tops. The upper trend line is falling and by connecting the lower tops, becomes the upper trend line. The lower trend line is almost horizontal connecting the bottoms, indicating the support level. There are chances of downward bearish breakdown, as the overall movement reflects that the bearish players are more powerful than the bullish players. Usually this pattern is observed during the downward trend.

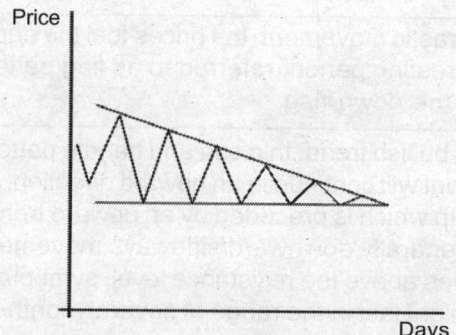

Figure 19.17: Descending triangle pattern

Findings and interpretations: It has a bearish bias compared to symmetrical triangle. In the descending triangle the lower line indicates demand that prevents the security from declining below a certain level. It is analogous to having large number of buy orders which are placed at this level, but it takes more time to execute—preventing thus further decline in price. Even if price does not decline below this level, reaction makes it to decline. The lower high on the upper line shows increased selling pressure and gives the descending triangle a bearish bias.

> **Pause for thought:** All its attributes are reverse of those for the ascending triangle pattern.

4. Flag pattern: It is easiest to identify and commonly seen on the price charts. After a strong movement, prices usually need to take rest. Pattern emerging during this resting period is known as 'flag'. The flags are two types:

- Up flag.
- Down flag.

These patterns show the market corrections of the over-bought or over-sold scrips. This pattern emerges within a very short time. Each rally and set back lasts only for two-three days. If the pattern is wider, it may take relatively more time.

When prices have moved higher (lower) and have consolidated, channel of support and resistance is created. When prices penetrate, to close above the rising resistance line, time is deemed right to buy the scrip. Similarly, when prices penetrate, to close below the support line, it marks the signal to sell the scrip.

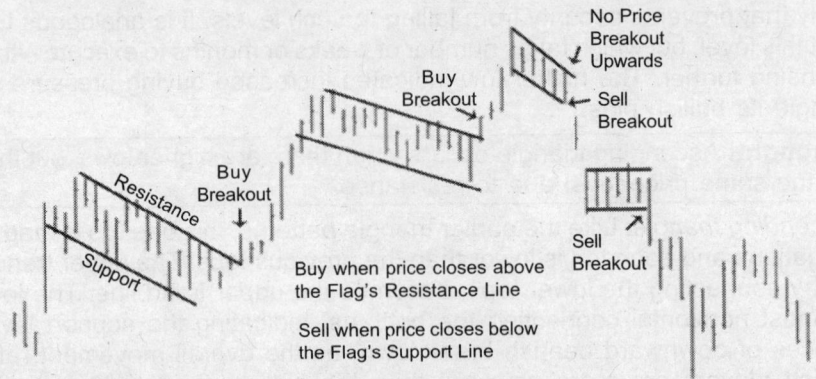

Figure 19.18: Flag patterns—up flag and down flag

> **Pause for thought:** After a drastic movement, the prices feel the need to rest and characteristic patterns emerge during this resting period, referred to as flag patterns and observed to be of two types—the up flag and the down flag.

5. Cup and handle : It is a bullish trend. In a cup and handle pattern upward trend continues, in which upward trend might halt, but will continue in an upward direction, once the pattern is confirmed. The price pattern looks like a cup which is preceded by an upward trend. The handle follows the cup formation and is formed by a generally downward/sideways movement in the price of the security. Once the price movement pushes above the resistance level, symbolized by the handle, the upward trend continues. This pattern might last in the range of several months to several years.

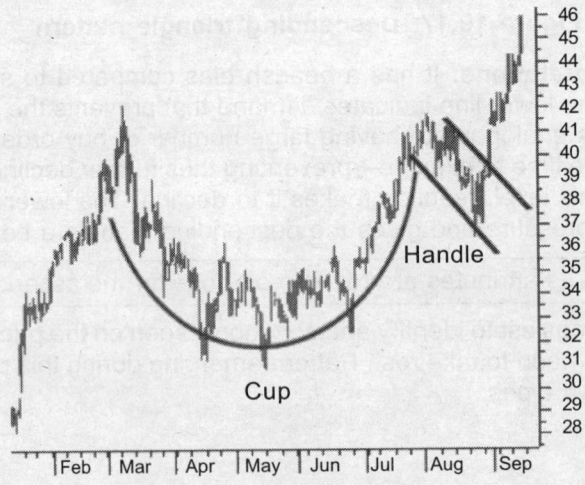

Figure 19.19: Cup and handle

> **Pause for thought:** It represents a bullish trend, with the price pattern resembling a cup which is preceded by an upward trend. The handle follows the cup formation facilitated by a downward/sideways movement in the security's price.

6. Rounding bottom: A rounding bottom is a long-term reversal pattern, indicating a shift from downward to an upward trend. This pattern is traditionally thought to last anywhere from several months to several years. It looks similar to cup and handle pattern, but without the handle! As per the chartist view, it is difficult to identify and interpret.

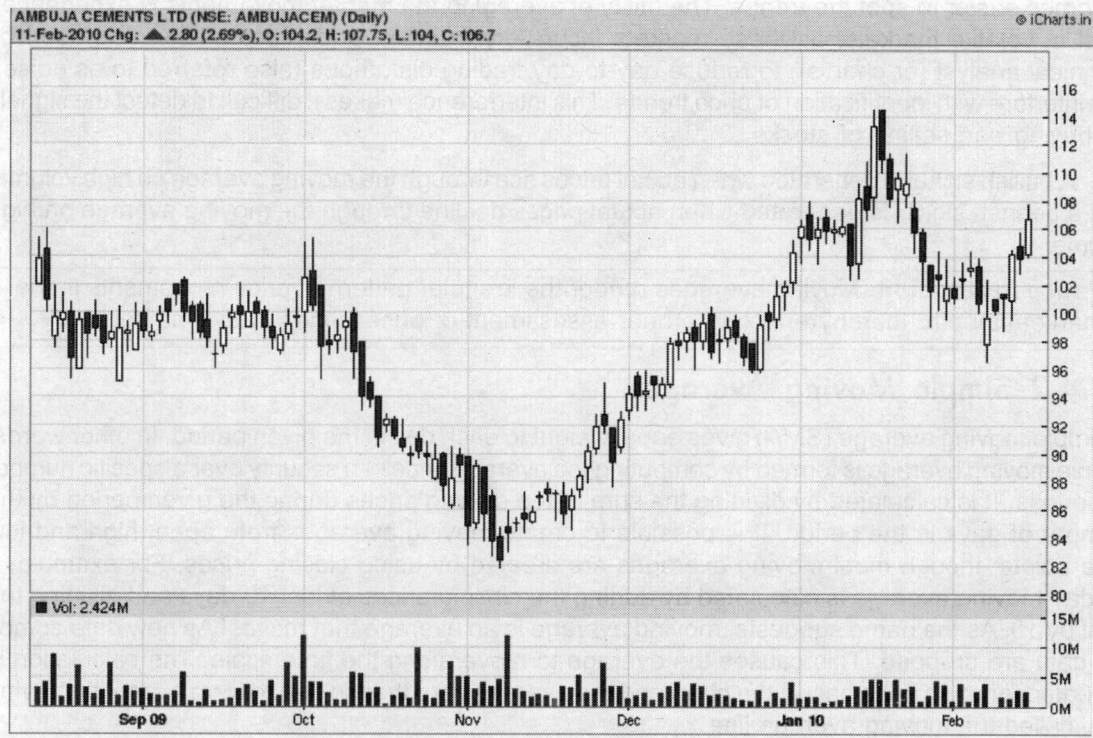

Figure 19.20: Rounding bottom

> **Pause for thought:** A rounding bottom is a long-term reversal pattern, marking a shift from a downward to an upward trend. Thus, signals the reversal of a bearish trend to a bullish trend.

19.4 TECHNICAL ANALYSIS INDICATORS

The different charts and varied patterns of charts, discussed in the preceding sections, all have significant information quotient. Over and above these, technical analysts make use of further indicators to enhance the efficiency of their analysis. The indicators used are moving averages of different types: simple, weighted, exponential, triangular variable and long-term. As to what are they, and how they aid in the said purpose, forms the subject matter of the following section. But before that, what are moving averages needs to be known, and thus begins the discussion with the same.

19.4.1 Moving Averages

Moving averages are one of the most popular and easy to use tools, available to the technical analyst. The security prices, and hence market indices, do not rise or fall in a straight line. The upward and downward movements are interrupted by counter moves. These counter moves, causing an irregular pattern, makes it difficult to envisage the trend of the market movement. The underlying trend can be studied only by smoothening of the data and it is for that very purpose the moving average technique is used. It provides an averaged view of the market movement—a smoothened interpretation of the price trends. Thus with the moving averages smoothening a data series, it becomes easier to spot the trends. The utility of averaging the market movements is experienced most in volatile markets, as these markets incur very frequent price fluctuations. It is used by technical analyst (or chartist) to reduce day-to-day trading distortions (also referred to as noise), that interfere with identification of price trends. This interference makes it difficult to detect the signals for buying and selling of stocks.

A bullish signal is generated when actual prices rise through the moving average on high volume; and a bearish signal is generated when actual prices decline through the moving average on high volume.

> **Pause for thought:** Moving averages render the irregular pattern of price movements in the market smooth, thereby enabling proper assessment of price trends in the market.

19.4.2 Simple Moving Averages

A simple moving average (SMA) gives equal weight to each day in the given period. In other words, simple moving average is formed by computing the average price of a security over a specific number of periods. It is calculated by dividing the sum of the closing prices during the given period by the number of days in the period. It is possible to create moving averages from open, high and low data points, though most moving averages are created by using closing prices. For example, a 10 day-moving average is calculated by adding the closing prices of last 10 days and dividing the total by 10. As the name suggests, moving average is an average that moves! As new data comes old data are dropped. This causes the average to move along the time scale. The calculation is repeated for each price bar on the chart and the averages are then joined to form a smooth curving line, called the moving average line.

The example below shows the 5-day moving average that evolved over three days.

Daily closing prices: 100, 110, 120, 130, 140, 150, 160, 170.

First day of 5-day SMA: (100 + 110 + 120 + 130 + 140)/5 = 120

Second day of 5-day SMA: (110 + 120 + 130 + 140 + 150)/5 = 130

Third day of 5-day SMA: (120 + 130 + 140 + 150 + 160)/5 = 140

Thus, from the above calculation it is noted that the moving average rises from 120 to 140 over a 3-day calculation period. It is also inferred that each moving average value is just below the last price. For example, the moving average for day 1 equals 120 and the last price is 140. It shows that prices of previous day are lower and this causes the moving average to lag.

Thus is noted:

Indicator *Simple moving average.*

Formula *Sum of 'x' period of closing price divided by 'x'.*

The table below shows the 5-day, 10-day, 20-day and 50-day simple moving averages for the stock of HDFC from the given price data.

Table 19.2: Simple Moving Average of HDFC

Date	Opening price	High price	Low price	Closing price	SMA-5	SMA-10	SMA-20	SMA-50
20-10-03	317.5	323	312.15	315.45				
21-10-03	314	314.6	308.1	310.15				
22-10-03	312	313.7	298	301.15				
23-10-03	301	303.45	298	299.5				
24-10-03	300.3	308.9	296.15	307.85	306.82			
25-10-03	310.7	312	305.05	305.9	304.91			
27-10-03	305.5	314	299.5	300.75	303.03			
28-10-03	302.6	314	302.05	312.05	305.21			
29-10-03	313	319	312.3	315.3	308.37			
30-10-03	313	320	313	317.5	310.3	308.56		
31-10-03	320.05	321.5	312	316.35	312.39	308.65		
3-11-03	320	322	316	318.4	315.92	309.475		
4-11-03	320	322	308	309.45	315.4	310.305		
5-11-03	311.4	312.9	307.25	308.8	314.1	311.235		
6-11-03	303.25	309.95	303	307.8	312.16	311.23		
7-11-03	307.5	309.45	302	305.4	309.97	311.18		
10-11-03	310.45	312	303	309.95	308.28	312.1		
11-11-03	312	312	304.95	308.05	308	311.7		
12-11-03	309	309	298	299.5	306.14	310.12		
13-11-03	303.75	304.4	298	299.45	304.47	308.315	308.4375	
14-11-03	300.65	303.75	295.25	296.65	302.72	306.345	307.4975	
15-11-03	298.9	300.45	297.1	299.95	300.72	304.5	306.9875	
17-11-03	299.95	304.9	298.5	304	299.91	303.955	307.13	
18-11-03	305.75	306	300.35	301.85	300.38	303.26	307.2475	
19-11-03	300	304.45	293.8	301.75	300.84	302.655	306.9425	
20-11-03	300	302	296	297	300.91	301.815	306.4975	
21-11-03	290.25	305	290.25	302.95	301.51	301.115	306.6075	
24-11-03	305	306	301.05	302.1	301.13	300.52	306.11	
25-11-03	303	306	301.1	302.8	301.32	300.85	305.485	
27-11-03	303.5	309	300.1	301.45	301.26	301.05	304.6825	
28-11-03	305	307.75	299	302.45	302.35	301.63	303.9875	

1-12-03	304.9	314.9	304.5	309.65	303.69	302.6	303.55	
2-12-03	314.5	320	311	318.25	306.92	304.025	303.99	
3-12-03	318.5	330.6	318.5	328.7	312.1	306.71	304.985	
4-12-03	330	335.1	327	334.4	318.69	309.975	306.315	
5-12-03	337.2	337.2	325	328	323.8	313.075	307.445	
8-12-03	326	333.95	321	329.4	327.75	315.72	308.4175	
9-12-03	334	336.75	330.05	331.1	330.32	318.62	309.57	
10-12-03	320.25	343	320.25	340.1	332.6	322.35	311.6	
11-12-03	339.8	352	337	350.6	335.84	327.265	314.1575	
12-12-03	351.2	366	346.05	360.45	342.33	333.065	317.3475	
15-12-03	363	366	350	353.4	347.13	337.44	320.02	
16-12-03	357.7	360.4	352.05	355.75	352.06	341.19	322.6075	
17-12-03	357	360.1	356	358	355.64	344.12	325.415	
18-12-03	360	360	351.55	354.1	356.34	346.09	328.0325	
19-12-03	358	360	351.05	355.8	355.41	348.87	330.9725	
22-12-03	357	360	355.15	358.8	356.49	351.81	333.765	
23-12-03	360	364	350.55	351.9	355.72	353.89	336.255	
24-12-03	354.5	360.45	351.5	359.7	356.06	355.85	339.1	
26-12-03	358.25	363	353.5	358.3	356.9	356.62	341.9425	320.362

> **Pause for thought:** It is the average closing price of stocks for a given period of time, giving equal weight to the price data of each day.

19.4.3 Weighted Moving Averages

A weighted moving average (WMA) is calculated by multiplying each data of the previous day by a weight. Since the recent prices are considered to be more relevant, and hence more important than the not so recent ones, the calculation of WMA assigns more weight to recent data and less weight to the past data.. For example, in the computation of simple moving average of 200 days, data of each day is given equal weight. Thus a data which is more than 6 months old, and could be considered slightly out of date, too is given the same importance as is accorded to the data 1 month old. The table below shows the 5-day, 10-day and 15-day weighted moving averages.

The calculation of a 5-day weighted moving average can be understood with reference to the table below. For the share prices shown in the table (column 5), the value of weight for the tenth day is 10; weight on the ninth day is 9 and so it continues with the value of weight for the first day is 1.0. All the values are the summed up and divided by 55 (weighted average of 10 days and the sum of 10 days = 1 + 2 + 3 + 4 + 5 + 6 + 7 + 8 + 9 + 10 = 55).

Thus the formula for the WMA is:

Formula $WMA = [(n \times P_n) + \{(n-1) \times (P_n - 1)\} + \{(n-2) \times (P_n - 2)\} + \ldots \{(n) - (n-1)\} \times \{P_n - (n-1)\}]/[\{n + (n-1) + \ldots + \{(n) - (n-1)\}]$

n = running number associated with the period calculated.

Pn = previous day's closing price for the n number of days.

Table 19.3: Weighted moving averages of HDFC

Date	Opening price	High price	Low price	Closing price	WMA-5	WMA-10	WMA-20
20-10-03	317.5	323	312.15	315.45			
21-10-03	314	314.6	308.1	310.15			
22-10-03	312	313.7	298	301.15			
23-10-03	301	303.45	298	299.5			
24-10-03	300.3	308.9	296.15	307.85	305.0967		
25-10-03	310.7	312	305.05	305.9	304.79		
27-10-03	305.5	314	299.5	300.75	303.4033		
28-10-03	302.6	314	302.05	312.05	306.41		
29-10-03	313	319	312.3	315.3	309.7733		
30-10-03	313	320	313	317.5	312.8167	309.5673	
31-10-03	320.05	321.5	312	316.35	314.8333	310.9836	
3-11-03	320	322	316	318.4	316.8367	312.7564	
4-11-03	320	322	308	309.45	314.68	312.7518	
5-11-03	311.4	312.9	307.25	308.8	312.48	312.4782	
6-11-03	303.25	309.95	303	307.8	310.38	311.8536	
7-11-03	307.5	309.45	302	305.4	308.1267	310.7936	
10-11-03	310.45	312	303	309.95	308.12	310.57	
11-11-03	312	312	304.95	308.05	308.0433	309.8336	
12-11-03	309	309	298	299.5	305.21	307.6155	
13-11-03	303.75	304.4	298	299.45	302.98	305.6755	307.9517
14-11-03	300.65	303.75	295.25	296.65	300.3733	303.5545	306.829
15-11-03	298.9	300.45	297.1	299.95	299.45	302.3918	306.1102
17-11-03	299.95	304.9	298.5	304	300.5433	302.3009	305.8257
18-11-03	305.75	306	300.35	301.85	301.19	301.9182	305.3229
19-11-03	300	304.45	293.8	301.75	301.6467	301.6436	304.7993
20-11-03	300	302	296	297	300.3667	300.6155	303.8524
21-11-03	290.25	305	290.25	302.95	301.0467	300.8218	303.5145
24-11-03	305	306	301.05	302.1	301.2433	301.0009	303.0852
25-11-03	303	306	301.1	302.8	301.8	301.4155	302.77

27-11-03	303.5	309	300.1	301.45	301.8433	301.5245	302.3857
28-11-03	305	307.75	299	302.45	302.24	301.7791	302.1731
1-12-03	304.9	314.9	304.5	309.65	304.6733	303.2373	302.7124
2-12-03	314.5	320	311	318.25	309.5267	306.0827	304.1124
3-12-03	318.5	330.6	318.5	328.7	316.7867	310.5691	306.4657
4-12-03	330	335.1	327	334.4	324.22	315.6036	309.2671
5-12-03	337.2	337.2	325	328	327.3233	318.8809	311.3324
8-12-03	326	333.95	321	329.4	329.19	321.8491	313.4233
9-12-03	334	336.75	330.05	331.1	330.3067	324.6455	315.5836
10-12-03	320.25	343	320.25	340.1	333.5667	328.5509	318.4912
11-12-03	339.8	352	337	350.6	339.5667	333.6873	322.2055
12-12-03	351.2	366	346.05	360.45	347.77	339.7209	326.6143
15-12-03	363	366	350	353.4	351.46	343.4182	330.0479
16-12-03	357.7	360.4	352.05	355.75	354.3333	346.7473	333.4507
17-12-03	357	360.1	356	358	356.3133	349.8036	336.8214
18-12-03	360	360	351.55	354.1	355.8	351.6182	339.5533
19-12-03	358	360	351.05	355.8	355.62	353.3836	342.1979
22-12-03	357	360	355.15	358.8	356.75	355.1891	344.8481
23-12-03	360	364	350.55	351.9	355.22	355.2055	346.5752
24-12-03	354.5	360.45	351.5	359.7	356.5467	356.2618	348.8081
26-12-03	358.25	363	353.5	358.3	357.2933	356.7073	350.6367

> **Pause for thought:** WMA too is a moving average, but unlike the simple moving average, which gives equal weight to the data of each day, it assigns more weight to the recent data, after weighing out the comparative significance of the recent and not so recent data. It is calculated by multiplying each data of the previous day by the said weights.

19.4.4 Exponential Moving Averages

The exponential moving average (EMA) is used to identify and study the trend reversals. Calculation of EMA is complex than that of simple moving average, but has an advantage over the calculation of SMA. A voluminous data, covering each and every closing price, over the last 200 days (or more) is not required. EMA only requires the closing prices of two days—the day on which it is being calculated and the day previous to it.

The exponent has to be calculated for EMA, as the name suggests. For the purpose one should take the number of days' EMA that one wants to calculate, adding one to the number of days that one is considering. Exponential moving average reduces lag by providing more weight to recent prices. The weight applied to most recent period depends on the number of periods in the moving average. To begin with, the simple moving average is calculated. So, a simple moving average is used as the previous day's EMA in the initial calculation. After that weighting multiplier is calculated.

Then the final step gives the exponential moving average. That is, for a 10-day EMA, 1 has to be added to get to 11 for the purpose of calculation. This is called (days + 1) method. The exponent can be calculated by taking number 2 and dividing this by number of (days + 1).

So, the exponent for a 10-day moving average = 2/11 = 0.1818. Likewise the exponent for a 30-day moving average = 2/31 = 0.0645 and for a 200-day moving average the exponent = 2/201 = 0.0099.

After the exponent is ascertained, previous day's EMA is required. The previous day's moving average is nothing but the simple moving average of that many number of days. Thus, to calculate a 10-day EMA, the first EMA is needed, which is actually a 10 day-SMA. This value, with the closing price for the day, finally leads to the EMA.

∴ EMA = [Current day's closing price × exponent] + [Previous day's EMA × (1–exponent)]

The Figure 19.21 below is an example of a 10-day EMA.

- 10-day period sum/10.
- Multiplier: (2/(Time period + 1)) = (2/(10 + 1)) = 0.1818.
- EMA: [Close – EMA (previous day)] × multiplier + EMA (previous day).

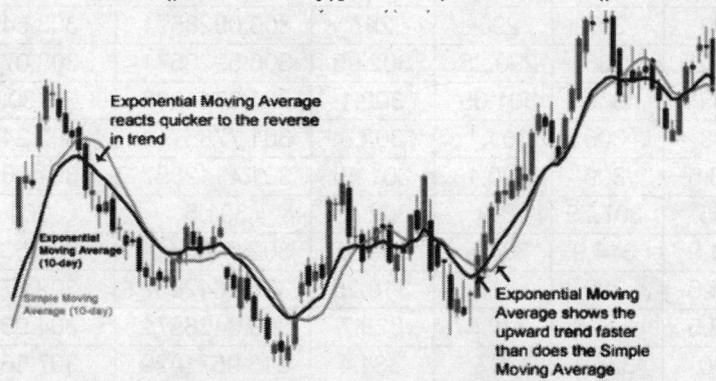

Figure 19.21: Exponential moving average

Table 19.4: Exponential moving averages of HDFC

Date	Opening price	High price	Low price	Closing price	Average of 7 days	Average of 7 days	Decision
20-10-03	317.5	323	312.15	315.45			
21-10-03	314	314.6	308.1	310.15			
22-10-03	312	313.7	298	301.15			
23-10-03	301	303.45	298	299.5			
24-10-03	300.3	308.9	296.15	307.85			
25-10-03	310.7	312	305.05	305.9			
27-10-03	305.5	314	299.5	300.75	305.8214286		
28-10-03	302.6	314	302.05	312.05	305.3357143		
29-10-03	313	319	312.3	315.3	306.0714286		
30-10-03	313	320	313	317.5	308.4071429		

31-10-03	320.05	321.5	312	316.35	310.8142857		
3-11-03	320	322	316	318.4	312.3214286		
4-11-03	320	322	308	309.45	312.8285714		
5-11-03	311.4	312.9	307.25	308.8	313.9785714	309.9	Buy
6-11-03	303.25	309.95	303	307.8	313.3714286	309.3535714	Buy
7-11-03	307.5	309.45	302	305.4	311.9571429	309.0142857	Buy
10-11-03	310.45	312	303	309.95	310.8785714	309.6428571	Buy
11-11-03	312	312	304.95	308.05	309.6928571	310.2535714	Sell
12-11-03	309	309	298	299.5	306.9928571	309.6571429	Sell
13-11-03	303.75	304.4	298	299.45	305.5642857	309.1964286	Sell
14-11-03	300.65	303.75	295.25	296.65	303.8285714	308.9035714	Sell
15-11-03	298.9	300.45	297.1	299.95	302.7071429	308.0392857	Sell
17-11-03	299.95	304.9	298.5	304	302.5071429	307.2321429	Sell
18-11-03	305.75	306	300.35	301.85	301.35	306.1142857	Sell
19-11-03	300	304.45	293.8	301.75	300.45	305.0714286	Sell
20-11-03	300	302	296	297	300.0928571	303.5428571	Sell
21-11-03	290.25	305	290.25	302.95	300.5928571	303.0785714	Sell
24-11-03	305	306	301.05	302.1	301.3714286	302.6	Sell
25-11-03	303	306	301.1	302.8	301.7785714	302.2428571	Sell
27-11-03	303.5	309	300.1	301.45	301.4142857	301.9607143	Sell
28-11-03	305	307.75	299	302.45	301.5	301.425	Buy
1-12-03	304.9	314.9	304.5	309.65	302.6285714	301.5392857	Buy
2-12-03	314.5	320	311	318.25	305.6642857	302.8785714	Buy
3-12-03	318.5	330.6	318.5	328.7	309.3428571	304.9678571	Buy
4-12-03	330	335.1	327	334.4	313.9571429	307.6642857	Buy
5-1203	337.2	337.2	325	328	317.5571429	309.6678571	Buy
8-1203	326	333.95	321	329.4	321.55	311.4821429	Buy
9-12-03	334	336.75	330.05	331.1	325.6428571	313.5714286	Buy
10-12-03	320.25	343	320.25	340.1	329.9928571	316.3107143	Buy
11-12-03	339.8	352	337	350.6	334.6142857	320.1392857	Buy
12-12-03	351.2	366	346.05	360.45	339.15	324.2464286	Buy
15-12-03	363	366	350	353.4	341.8642857	327.9107143	Buy
16-12-03	357.7	360.4	352.05	355.75	345.8285714	331.6928571	Buy
17-12-03	357	360.1	356	358	349.9142857	335.7321429	Buy
18-12-03	360	360	351.55	354.1	353.2	339.4214286	Buy
19-12-03	358	360	351.05	355.8	355.4428571	342.7178571	Buy
22-12-03	357	360	355.15	358.8	356.6142857	345.6142857	Buy
23-12-03	360	364	350.55	351.9	355.3928571	347.2714286	Buy
24-12-03	354.5	360.45	351.5	359.7	356.2928571	349.0785714	Buy
26-12-03	358.25	363	353.5	358.3	356.6571429	351.2428571	Buy

> **Pause for thought:** Though the calculation is far more complex than that of SMA, EMA requires only the closing prices of two days—the day on which it is being calculated and the day previous to it; as compared to the voluminous data that SMA requires, as it takes equal cognizance of the entire data spanning the entire period.

19.4.5 Triangular Moving Averages

In this method, more weight is given to the middle part of a price series. It involves taking the simple moving average of a simple moving average. This double smoothening process reduces distortions even further and generates a smooth curved line.

> **Pause for thought:** It is the simple moving average of a simple moving average!

19.4.6 Variable Moving Averages

It is an exponential moving average and it factors in the volatility of security prices. For comparatively more volatile prices, the averages are smoothed more and relatively higher weight is assigned to current data.

Most of the moving average calculation methods are not able to compensate for the trading range (when price moves sideways in a narrow range) versus trending market (when prices move up or down over an extended period). In the trading ranges moving averages with shorter term can produce numerous false signals. In trending markets, longer term moving averages slowly react to reversals in trend. In such circumstances, variable moving average smoothes out sensitivity and performs better in both the markets.

> **Pause for thought:** It is an exponential moving average, with the volatility of the security prices factored in.

19.4.7 Long-Term Moving Averages

A 200-day simple moving average is the most often used moving average in the Indian stock market to study and interpret the long-term trend. Some chartists use the equivalent moving average, which in weekly terms is the 40-week moving average.

> **Pause for thought:** It is the moving average which aids in the interpretation of long-term trend in the Indian stock market.

Guidelines for the application of moving averages: The ensuing discussion has been on the various moving averages, wherein the significance of the same have has been entailed. Given the extent of their utility, summarizing the ways to apply the moving averages, renders the study more systematic and allows one to maximize its use.

- It is a useful technical indicator tool which indicates when to buy and sell stocks.
- To effectively apply the moving averages for investment decisions, the most suitable moving average has to be identified.
- The next step is to select the appropriate time period (10 days, 30 days, 100 days and the like), depending on one's objective and volatility of the stock market.
- Longer is the time period, greater is the significance of the trend once a signal emerges. A relatively long-term trend provides fewer, more reliable signals, but can miss parts of the trend.

- A short-term moving average reveals lost signals, but many of them are generally false. When the security prices pierce the moving averages from below, it is an indicator of the onset of an uptrend. Conversely, when it penetrates from above, it marks the beginning of a downtrend.
- It is always advisable to use short-term moving averages with long-term moving averages, to get clear trading signals because this leads to fewer, more definitive crossings of the two lines.

Main uses of the moving averages

The two main uses of moving averages are:

- Trend identification.
- Identification of the support and resistance levels.

Figure 19.22: 50-day and 200-day moving averages of SBI

Moving averages are used with the prices of the scrip. In the figure, both the moving averages show upward penetration. This shows that the price of SBI stock will rise, which thus is a signal for buying the stock. Similarly, downward penetration indicates that the stock prices will fall and hence selling of the stock is signaled.

19.5 RELATIVE STRENGTH INDEX (RSI)

The relative strength index, most popularly known as RSI, was introduced by W. Wilder in an article, in commodities magazine, way back in June 1978. The name of the oscillator, 'relative strength index', is actually a misnomer, as it does not measure the relative strength of two securities. RSI instead is a measure of the internal strength of a single security. Relative strength chart compares the two market indices, which is often referred to as comparative relative strength.

It is defined as a technical momentum indicator that compares the magnitude of recent gains to recent losses, in an attempt to determine over-bought and over-sold conditions of an asset.

RSI analysis is based on the assumption that prices of some securities rise rapidly during the bullish trend, but fall slowly during the bearish trend, with respect to the market as a whole. In other words, such securities possess greater internal strength relative to the market, and hence outperform the market.

When Wilder introduced RSI, he suggested using 14-day RSI. But then 9-day and 25-day RSI have also gained popularity. It is always better to select the period of RSI analysis which goes best with the investment criteria of investors.

RSI is based on the ratio of the average up-close to the average down-close over a period of time. In other words, when the security closes higher than on the previous day, RSI measures the strength of this upward move.

The formula for calculation of RSI is as given below:

$$RSI = 100 - \frac{100}{1+RS}$$

Average gain = (Total gains/n)

Average loss = (Total losses[11]/n)

RS = (Average gain/Average loss)

Certain conclusions are drawn, which envisage the characteristics of RSI with respect to the above mentioned average gain and loss. These provide important insights for the investment decision, which, after all is the reason for this entire text! These inferences are as follows:

- When the average gain is greater than the average loss, the RSI rises and it will be greater than 1.
- But when the average loss is greater than the average gain, the RSI decreases and becomes less than 1.
- Thus the RSI oscillates between 0 and 1.
- By looking at the movements over a period of time, RSI can serve as an overall momentum behind price swings.
- If RSI>70, it shows an over-bought condition and indicates that the security has moved too high too quickly. When RSI<30, it shows an over-sold condition and indicates that the security has moved too low too quickly.
- In other words, if the RSI rises above 30, it is considered bullish trend for the stock, and when the RSI falls below 70, it is considered bearish trend for the stock.
- To get the idea of long-term trade, one can look for divergences between price and the RSI. Divergence occurs when the price makes a new high that is not confirmed by a new high in the RSI.
- Bullish divergence sets in when prices are slanting down and the RSI is slanting up. Conversely, a bearish divergence occurs when prices are slanting up and the RSI is slanting down.

Chart formation of the RSI

The RSI forms chart patterns, such as head and shoulders and triangles, which may or may not be visible on the price chart. Levels of support and resistance, on number of occasions, have been found to be reflected by the RSI with much more clarity, compared to what the actual prices convey.

---

[11] Losses should be taken as positive values and not as negative values. Thus, the minus sign should be ignored.

Table 19.5: Relative Strength Index for ACC Cement

Date	Closing price	Gain	Loss
10/20/2003	209.65		
10/21/2003	198.75		10.9
10/22/2003	198.9	0.15	
10/23/2003	196.9		2
10/24/2003	199.35	2.45	
10/25/2003	206.1	6.75	
10/27/2003	205.4		0.7
10/28/2003	202.1		3.3
10/29/2003	203.45	1.35	
10/30/2003	204.6	1.15	
10/31/2003	214.2	9.6	
11/3/2003	228.8	14.6	
11/4/2003	233.85	5.05	
11/5/2003	233.5		0.35
11/6/2003	233.55	0.05	
11/7/2003	229.2		4.35
11/10/2003	229.75	0.55	
11/11/2003	242.2	12.45	
11/12/2003	234.95		7.25
11/13/2003	228.15		6.8
11/14/2003	222.9		5.25
11/15/2003	229.1	6.2	
11/17/2003	229.65	0.55	
11/18/2003	225		4.65
11/19/2003	219.4		5.6
11/20/2003	219.35		0.05
11/21/2003	221.3	1.95	
11/24/2003	219.75		1.55
11/25/2003	219.65		0.1
11/27/2003	218.75		0.9
11/28/2003	227.05	8.3	
12/1/2003	230.6	3.55	
12/2/2003	234.5	3.9	
12/3/2003	233.7		0.8
12/4/2003	231.75		1.95
12/5/2003	226.1		5.65
12/8/2003	218.6		7.5
12/9/2003	223.3	4.7	
12/10/2003	223.25		0.05
12/11/2003	221.55		1.7
12/12/2003	227	5.45	

12/15/2003	228.05	1.05	
12/16/2003	226.15		1.9
12/17/2003	224.8		1.35
12/18/2003	228.05	3.25	
12/19/2003	230.65	2.6	
12/22/2003	231.45	0.8	
12/23/2003	232.25	0.8	
12/24/2003	232		0.25
12/26/2003	249.35	17.35	

Total Gain = 114.6

Total Loss = 74.9

Average Gain = 114.6/25[12] = 4.584

Average Loss = 74.9/24[13] = 3.121

RS = Average Gain/Average Loss = 4.584/ 3.121 = 1.469

RSI = 100 – 100/(1+RS)

RSI = 59.49

> **Pause for thought:** The name, relative strength index (RSI), is a misnomer as RSI doesn't measure the relative strength of two securities. Rather it is a measure of the innate strength of a single security. It assumes that price of some securities rises sharply during the bullish trend, but falls slowly during the bearish trend, with respect to the overall market, thereby proving their greater internal strength with respect to the market.

19.6 GAP

A gap refers to an area on the price chart which reflects zero trading. A gap is defined as the difference between the opening price of a stock for the day and its closing price, the day before.

For example, it is assumed that XYZ scrip closed at Rs.450.83 on December 12, 2011 and opened at Rs.451.27 on December 13, 2011. The gap = Rs.451.27 – Rs.450.83 = 0.44. All gaps are ultimately filled. It could take an hour or week or sometimes even a year, to fill the gap. The exact time required for the gap to fill cannot be predicted with any certainty. However, if the gap is small, chances of its getting filled faster are higher. There are many scrips in the market for whom gap occurred on October 10, 2008 (during the stock market crash), which were filled up on November 11, 2009, indicating that it took more than a year to fill the gap.

One needs to be careful about one thing while studying the gap with respect to the securities. Gap analysis does not apply to stocks with low volumes. The correct gap analysis for price movements can produce huge profits. Occurrence of gap indicates that something important has happened to fundamentals or psychology of the investors, which marks this market movement.

But then how does a gap occur?

- Gap occurs as an outcome of underlying fundamental or technical aspects. For example, the company's financial performance could be much higher than expected; its stock may gap-up the next day, i.e., the stock price could open higher than it closed the day before, thus resulting in a gap.

---

[12] Total number of gains

[13] Total number of losses

- Gaps occur frequently in Forex market and widen the bid-ask spread[14].
- Gaps usually occur more frequently on daily charts, while gaps on weekly and monthly charts are rare. Weekly gap occurs between Friday's closing and Monday's opening; while monthly gaps occur between the last trading day of the month and the first trading day of the next month.

> **Pause for thought:** Gap is that area in the price chart of a stock which marks zero trading. It arises as a result of the difference between the opening price of the stock for the day and its closing price, the day before.

19.6.1 Types of Gaps

There are four types of gaps:
1. Common.
2. Breakaway.
3. Runaway.
4. Exhaustion.

1. Common gaps: These gaps are known as common gaps because they get filled up easily and occur without any event. It is also known as trading gap or area gap. This type of gaps rarely produces trading opportunities.

> **Pause for thought:** These occur without any event, get filled up easily and rarely produce any trading opportunities.

2. Breakaway gaps: This gap occurs when price action breaks out of their trading range or congestion area[15]. During breakaway gaps volume also rises considerably because many are holding positions on the wrong side of the breakout and need to cover it. Same holds true for increased volume and downward breakaway gap.

> **Pause for thought:** It occurs when price action break out of their trading range (also known as congestion area).

3. Runaway gaps : These types of gaps arise because of increased interest in the stocks. The upside runaway gaps represent the traders who missed the earlier opportunity to enter into the market during uptrend and waited for the correction in the price, yet concluded that it is not going to happen. Because of this, there is a sudden increase in interest towards buying and the price gaps are evidenced above the previous day's close. This gap represents panic situation in the market.

> **Pause for thought:** This arises because of a sudden increase in interest for a stock, marked by its random purchase by investors.

4. Exhaustion gaps: These occur near the end of a good up or downtrend. At times it is difficult to differentiate between runaway and exhaustion gaps. It too reflects a state of panic. If the gaps occur during downtrends, pessimism sets in. Usually, during these times investors liquidate their entire holdings. These gaps are filled up when price trend starts reversing. An exact reversal is

---

[14] The difference between the buying and selling prices.

[15] Congestion area is a kind of price range over which market has traded for some period of time. The area near the top (bottom) of the congestion is resistance (support), when it is approached from below (above). To break away from this area, market requires enthusiasm and for that it requires either more buyers than sellers for upside breakouts; or more sellers than buyers for downside breakouts.

observed with bullish trend of the market. During bullish excitement, buyers may not get enough of the stocks. At the same time prices gap up with huge volume and high profit opportunity arises, which ultimately leads to fall in the demand of the stocks. Hereon, price drops and reversal occurs, marking the onset of a bearish trend.

> **Pause for thought:** Exhaustion gaps open up at the end of a good up or downtrend.

SUMMARY

- ✓ The rationale of the technical analysis is that prices are moved by demand, supply and many EIC factors. Also, they move in trends and adjust to new equilibrium from time to time.
- ✓ The basics of technical analysis were developed by Charles Dow, developed later on by S.A. Nelson and William Hamilton, into a theory.
- ✓ The pillars of technical analysis are the three price trends: primary, secondary and daily fluctuations (tertiary).
- ✓ Fundamental analysis is the answer for 'what to buy' while technical analysis suggests 'when to buy'.
- ✓ Market breadth theory predicts the strength of the market according to the number of stocks that advance or decline on a particular trading day. Market breadth index is an advance/decline index, depicting total number of advancing and declining security prices in the stock market.
- ✓ There are mainly four types of charts: line, bar, candlestick and point and figure.
- ✓ Support and resistance define natural boundaries for advancing and declining prices, just like a ball bounces when it hits the floor or drops after being thrown to the ceiling.
- ✓ The major chart patterns are: head and shoulders; reverse head and shoulders; triangle; flag; cup and handle; and rounding bottom.
- ✓ Moving averages are one of the most popular and easy to use tools available to the technical analysts. There are five types of moving averages: simple, weighted average, exponential, triangular, variable and long-term.
- ✓ Relative strength chart compares the two market indices, and this comparison leads to an index which is often referred to as relative strength index (RSI).
- ✓ A gap refers to an area on the price chart in which there are no trades. Gaps are of four types: common, breakaway, runaway and exhaustion.

KEY CONCEPTS

Technical Analysis	Moving Averages	Pennants
Price Patterns	Primary Movement	Wages
Charts	Secondary Movement	Wedges
Volume	Daily Fluctuations	Convergence
Market Breadth	Trend Lines	Divergence
Price Breakouts	Triangles	Moving Average Convergence and Divergence
Gap Analysis	Relative Strength Index	

REVIEW QUESTIONS

1. Explain the difference between the fundamental and technical approaches to investment.
2. It is a technical analyst's view that one can predict the future price changes by using the past price changes data. Do you agree? Give reasons for your answer.
3. Compute the RSI by taking 14 days price of ICICI stock.
4. Compute the moving averages and exponential moving averages of RIL by taking 50, 100 and 200 days price data.

Websites for Further Reference and Chart Patterns

1. www.icharts.in
2. www.nseindia.com
3. www.stockcharts.com
4. www.investopedia.com
5. www.gstock.com
6. www.etradezone.com
7. www.onlinetradingconcepts.com

APPENDIX

This section contains the concepts that have already been dealt with in the chapter. Herein, they are being extended and elaborated to enhance the understanding further.

Price Patterns

An uptrend is formed when higher highs (HH) are 'up' than higher lows (HL). In other words, it is defined by higher lows and higher highs in price. A downtrend is formed when lower highs (LH) are more than lower lows (LL). And hence it is defined by lower lows and lower highs in the price.

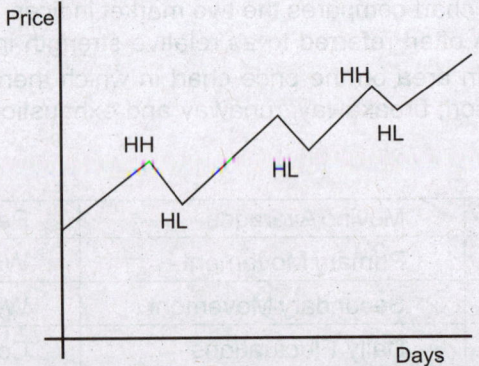

Markets tend to follow a trend about 20-30% of the time. When no trend is observed in a market, it is said that prices are consolidating with time, i.e., prices are being consolidated by range and not by direction. It is difficult to identify a trend because sometimes markets might be trending up on a 5 minute chart and trending down on a 30 minute chart.

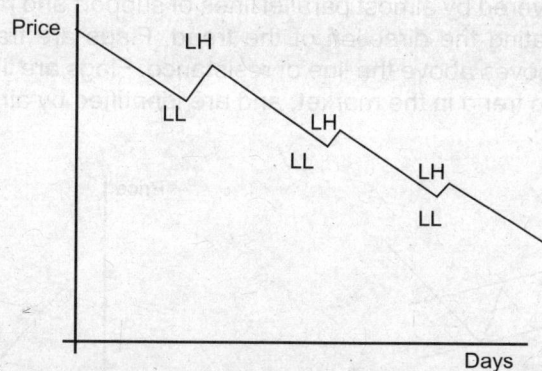

Research has shown that the more significant trends form 45 degree angles. A sharper angle could mean unpredictability and tentative rally, while an acute angle may indicate that a reversal in trend is just round the corner.

Generally, a trend line can be drawn from as few as two top/bottom levels. However, the more top/bottom levels touch the trend line, the more stable the trend is, as a higher number of points reflect a stable base for the trend.

Consolidation and Continuation Patterns

Consolidation patterns occur after rapid rise or fall in the stock prices. After moving rapidly in a particular direction (rise or fall), price needs to rest. This could mean it may remain almost flat, *i.e.*, constant for the time being, before continuing with the original trend or opting for a reversal. It is also known as the trading range.

Continuation pattern indicates that there are chances of temporary diversion in the movement of stock prices, but eventually it will continue with its existing trend. If such price pattern lasts for 2 to 3 months, accuracy of its signals is quite high. Triangles, wedges and flags are the common types of continuation patterns.

Triangles: Triangle patterns suggest that a trend is going to face a temporary change and will eventually follow its original trend. It is characterized by consolidation over a few weeks or months, followed by an accelerated breakout of the pattern in the direction of the original trend.

Triangles are of three types: symmetrical, ascending and descending.

A symmetrical triangle shows consolidation, stretching from few weeks to few months, during its existing upward and downward trends. The symmetrical triangle has: a line of support that slopes upward and a line of resistance with downward sloping.

An ascending triangle shows period of consolidation during its rising trend. It occurs when price moves between a line of resistance, which is relatively flat or constant, and a line of support which is sloping upward. When such trend continues these lines converge, and breakout occurs. This pattern ends when price moves strongly above the line of resistance.

A descending triangle represents a period of consolidation during its downward trend. It arises when price action moves between a line of resistance which is downward, and a line of support that is relatively flat or constant. Breakout occurs when these two lines converge. When price moves forcefully, below the line of support, the descending triangle formation closes and the downtrend continues.

Flag : Flags are covered by almost parallel lines of support and resistance. They usually have a little bit of slant indicating the direction of the trend. Flags are transient. Significant breakout occurs when the price moves above the line of resistance. Flags are like a temporary pause during the upward or downward trend in the market, and are identified by almost horizontal entry into the pattern.

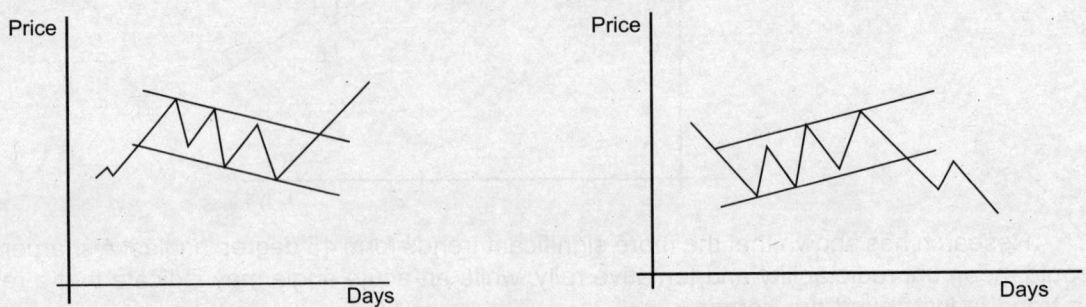

Wedges : Wedges resemble flags as well as symmetrical triangle patterns. They are treated in an almost similar manner like triangles are, and indicate sharp breakout in the direction of the prevailing trend.

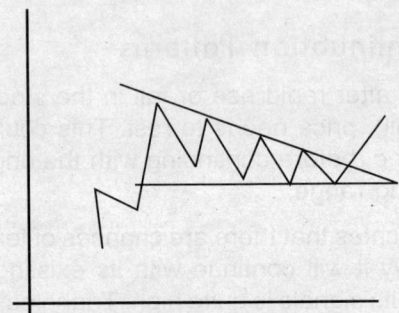

Pennants : Like flags, pennant is a continuation pattern and shows period of 'rest' or 'halt' before continuing with the prior trend. It consolidates, before breaking out to continue with prevailing trend. It is formed either in falling or rising trends. The given chart is for a rising trend.

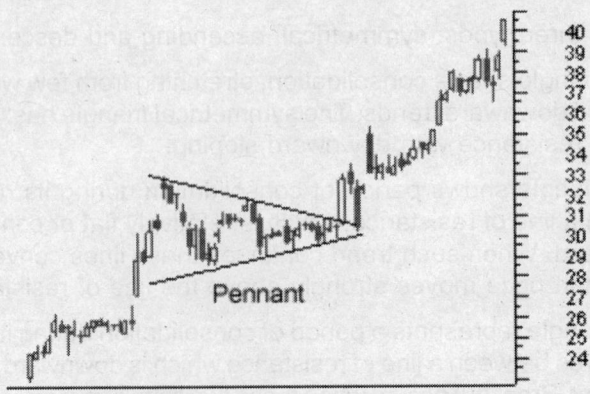

Double Top and Double Bottom : As the name suggests, the double top pattern is made up of two consecutive peaks that are almost equal with a modest trough in between. It is a very commonly observed pattern and its shape resembles the alphabet 'M'. A peak is reached before a small decline, followed by another peak. Thus a valley is created between the first and second peaks. The second peak is roughly equal to the first. After the second peak the price falls, marking the onset of a new downtrend. But actually it is difficult to identify and predict double top. It is because, a simple uptrend with each new wave of buying, interspersed with minor reactions and profits, would appear as a double top formation. Moreover, we know from our earlier discussion that price can move in either direction.

Double bottom resembles the alphabet 'W' and indicates bullish trend, with a major reversal at the bottom of a downtrend. It happens during a downward trend in the stock market. Usually in a double bottom trend, it has been found that stock prices may possibly bounce off the level of support and rise approximately to around 10-20% of the previous downtrend. This will form peak of the double bottom, W. At this level any hesitation in buying the stock indicates buying pressure which is not enough for it to breakout. Subsequently, the price gets back to the previous low on the line of support. This is usually done on lower volume than before. For the formation of the double bottom, the previous level of support is important. In the final stage of formation, of the double bottom, volume increases to support it.

Moving Average Convergence Divergence (MACD): It was created by Gerald Apple and shows the characteristics of both a trending indicator and an oscillator. The MACD line represents the difference between the 12-day and 26-day EMA. A single line represents a 9-day EMA of the MACD line. An EMA applies a percentage of today's value to yesterday's moving average value. A 'buy signal' can be identified when the MACD line 'crosses-up' through the signal line. Similarly, it is a 'sell signal' when the MACD line 'crosses-down' through the signal line. This signal is strongest at the higher end of the MACD range. Signals can also be identified when both lines cross above or below the baseline. Of the two EMAs that make up MACD, the 12-day EMA is the faster than the 26-day EMA. Closing prices are used to form the moving averages. Usually, a 9-day EMA of MACD is plotted to act as a signal line.

A 'bullish crossover' occurs when MACD moves above its 9-day EMA, while a 'bearish crossover' occurs when MACD moves below its 9-day EMA. The histogram is positive when MACD is above its 9-day EMA, and negative when below. If MACD is positive and rises, then the gap between the 12-day EMA and the 26-day EMA is widens. This indicates that the rate of change of the faster moving average is higher than the rate of change of the slower moving average. If MACD is negative and declining further, then the negative value between the faster moving average and the slower moving average is expanding. This indicates an increase in the downward momentum is increasing, representing a bearish period for the security.

MACD 'centerline crossovers' occur when the faster moving average crosses the slower moving average.

Moving average convergence divergence of HDFC

Date	Closing price	12-EMA	26-EMA	MACD	Single line	MACD-single line
20-10-03	315.45					
21-10-03	310.15					
22-10-03	301.15					
23-10-03	299.5					
24-10-03	307.85					
25-10-03	305.9					
27-10-03	300.75					
28-10-03	312.05					
29-10-03	315.3					
30-10-03	317.5					
31-10-03	316.35					
3-11-03	318.4	310.0292				
4-11-03	309.45	309.5292				
5-11-03	308.8	309.4167				
6-11-03	307.8	309.9708				
7-11-03	305.4	310.4625				
10-11-03	309.95	310.6375				
11-11-03	308.05	310.8167				
12-11-03	299.5	310.7125				
13-11-03	299.45	309.6625				
14-11-03	296.65	308.1083				
15-11-03	299.95	306.6458				
17-11-03	304	305.6167				
18-11-03	301.85	304.2375				
19-11-03	301.75	303.5958				
20-11-03	297	302.6125	306.5365	–3.92404		
21-11-03	302.95	302.2083	306.0558	–3.84744		
24-11-03	302.1	301.9333	305.7462	–3.81282		
25-11-03	302.8	301.3375	305.8096	–4.47212		
27-11-03	301.45	300.7875	305.8846	–5.09712		
28-11-03	302.45	301.0333	305.6769	–4.64359		
1-12-03	309.65	301.8833	305.8212	–3.93782		

2-12-03	318.25	303.6833	306.4942	−2.8109		
3-12-03	328.7	306.0792	307.1346	−1.05545	−3.733475783	2.678027066
4-12-03	334.4	308.6125	307.8692	0.743269	−3.21488604	3.958155271
5-12-03	328	310.7917	308.2731	2.51859	−2.507549858	5.026139601
8-12-03	329.4	313.0958	308.775	4.320833	−1.603810541	5.924643875
9-12-03	331.1	315.9375	309.2635	6.674038	−0.365349003	7.039387464
10-12-03	340.1	319.0333	310.4423	8.591026	1.155555556	7.435470085
11-12-03	350.6	323.075	312.05	11.025	2.896509972	8.128490028
12-12-03	360.45	327.8792	314.075	13.80417	4.86784188	8.936324786
15-12-03	353.4	332.2083	315.9212	16.28718	6.989850427	9.29732906
16-12-03	355.75	336.65	317.6827	18.96731	9.21460114	9.752706553
17-12-03	358	340.6792	319.6038	21.07532	11.47371795	9.601602564
18-12-03	354.1	343.6667	321.7038	21.96282	13.63418803	8.328632479
19-12-03	355.8	345.925	323.8712	22.05385	15.60452279	6.449323362
22-12-03	358.8	347.9583	326.2615	21.69679	17.27371795	4.423076923
23-12-03	351.9	349.95	328.2596	21.69038	18.72920228	2.961182336
24-12-03	359.7	352.475	330.4019	22.07308	19.95676638	2.116310541
26-12-03	358.3	354.7417	332.5731	22.16859	20.88614672	1.28244302

Bollinger Bands: Bollinger bands are tools of technical analysis, developed by John Bollinger in the 1980s. They came into being from the observation that volatility is inherently a dynamic condition and not static, varying widely with time. As per the Bollinger band theory, prices are considered high at the upper band and low at the lower band. This simple definition of high and low helps to find out the highs and lows even in a complicated pattern. It is useful in comparing price action for the systematic trading decisions.

Certain stocks may continue with a trend for long period of time and during this time some volatility might be observed. It has been discussed earlier in the chapter that traders use moving averages for smoothening of the trend and to filter price action. Bollinger bands add price channels for the better monitoring of the price behavior. These price channels are designed to encompass the trading activity around the trend.

In a Bollinger band, a set of three curves are drawn in relation to the price of securities. The graph below shows a middle curve, which is a SMA and it serves as a base for the upper and lower bands. The graph in this case is of middle Bollinger bands, for a 20-day SMA.

The space between the upper bands and the middle line, and the lower bands and the middle line, is known as volatility. In other words, it is the standard deviation of stock prices obtained from the moving average.

Certain formulations, established in this context, are as follows:

Upper Bollinger band = Middle Bollinger band + (2 × 20-day period standard deviation)
Lower Bollinger band = Middle Bollinger band − (2 × 20-day period standard deviation)

Band width = (Upper Bollinger band – Lower Bollinger band)/Middle Bollinger bands

% of b = (Last – Lower Bollinger band)/(Upper Bollinger band – Lower Bollinger band)

As Bollinger bands use standard deviation as one of the measures, they adjust themselves to the market conditions. When the market becomes more volatile, the bands expand (i.e., move away from the average in both the direction) and when market is less volatile, the bands contract (*i.e.*, they move closer to the average).

It is often viewed by the technical analysts that if the bands are tightened for a reasonable period of time some volatility is bound to arise. It has also been observed that when prices move closer to the lower band, the more over-sold the market is; and when prices move closer to the upper band, the more over-bought the market is.

Bollinger bands comprise of a centerline and two price channels: one price channel above the centerline and one below it. The centerline is calculated by the EMA method and the price channels are the standard deviation of the stocks. In Bollinger bands the upper and lower bands are set as price targets.

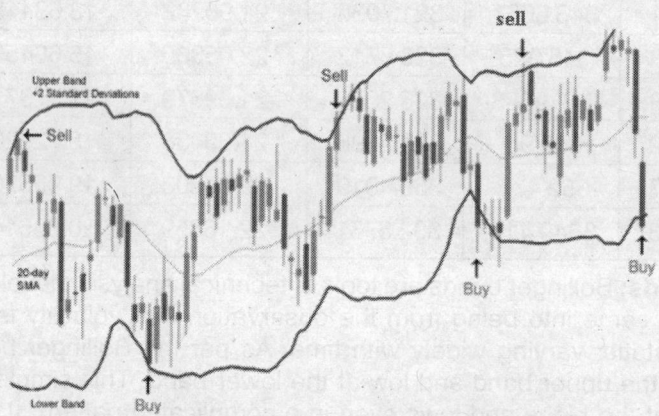

REFERENCES

1. www.icharts.in
2. www.nseindia.com
3. www.stockcharts.com
4. www.etradezone.com
5. www.onlinetradingconcepts.com

PART 7
PORTFOLIO MANAGEMENT

20
MARKOWITZ PORTFOLIO THEORY

> **LEARNING OBJECTIVES**
>
> The purpose of this chapter is to enable you to understand:
> - How an optimal portfolio of risky assets is constructed by applying the efficient frontier theory.
> - The construction of a portfolio of risky securities on the basis of high return, low return, high beta, etc.
> - How the optimal portfolio is selected, from the portfolios lying on the north-western region.

20.1 INTRODUCTION

In Chapter 5, Introduction to Portfolio Theory, we have already discussed the profitability of investing the funds in more securities, instead of one. Thus, investing in different assets, like stocks of IT, steel, FMCG, energy, etc., and in gold, as well as real estate is better than entrusting the entire wealth to only one security. Because in such cases the wealth is not at all secure. If the security faces a slump, then the entire fund faces the adverse effects. While holding diverse assets, and thus a well-diversified portfolio, sees a diversion in the risk too! The Markowitz model guides the selection of an optimal portfolio by establishing the risk-return relationship of securities. It utilizes the concept of efficient portfolio. This chapter concentrates on the selection of an optimal portfolio.

20.1.1 Modern Portfolio Theory

The modern portfolio theory (MPT) was developed by Harry Markowitz. Till it was, it is only the returns that concerned the investors. And thus investment decisions were based on the same, with no thoughts spared for risk. Market volatility, which represents the risk involved, as it affects the risk quotient of a security, didn't feature as a criterion for investment decisions. Hence portfolios used to be constructed randomly.

Markowitz model is a mathematical formulation, designed to produce the best of portfolios, at least theoretically. It is based on the logic that when the investors are given set of portfolios with same return, but different risks, they simply opt for the one with the least risk for a given return. Likewise, for a given level of risk, the portfolio with highest return is chosen. Theoretically, constructing the best portfolio becomes thus a balancing act. While one with the least risk for a given (expected) return is selected, so is chosen the one with the highest (expected) return for a given level of risk. This balancing is the optimization of a portfolio so as to generate the maximum earning, through the optimal use of the financial parameters, mainly risk and return. The MPT seeks thus to optimize a portfolio by establishing a framework within which return, risk, covariance or correlation with other assets function. The framework of MPT establishes relationship between return and risk, whose effects can be optimized through diversification.

> **Pause for thought:** MPT is a mathematical formulation to create an optimal portfolio by diversification and thus optimizing the effects of the risk-return relationships.

20.1.2 Theoretical Framework for Portfolio Selection Model

It has been already stated above, how the advent of Markowitz changed the concept of, and thus precepts for, investment decisions. With his mathematical formulation, to enable the selection of an optimal portfolio, he actually revolutionized the whole selection procedure. This model considers the evaluation of a security based on its mean and standard deviations; besides its correlation with other securities in the portfolio, to be the best mode of evaluation. By providing the detailed mathematics of diversification, and proving its efficacy, he proposed that investors should select the portfolios based on their overall risk-return characteristics, instead of merely compiling portfolios with securities which individually have attractive risk-return characteristics. In other words, investors should select portfolios, based on their cumulative proficiency, and not on the productivity of individual securities. It is a single period model where an investor forms a portfolio at the beginning of the period with an objective to maximize the expected return from the portfolio, for a given level of risk. Or the other way round, minimize the risk for a given level of expected return. These assumptions of: single time period[1] and the risk-averse nature of investors, allows risk to be measured by the variance (standard deviation) of the portfolio's return.

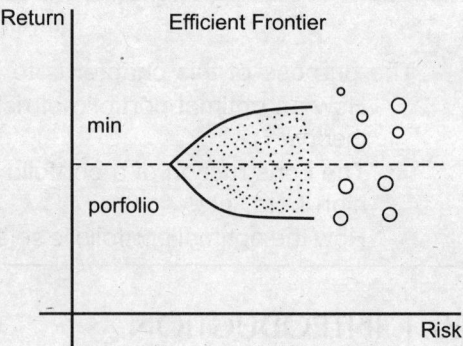

Figure 20.1: Efficient frontier of portfolios compared to individual securities

When securities are added to a portfolio, the expected return and standard deviation changes in a very specific manner. The variance depends on how these securities correlate with, and vary with respect to the other securities, which are already present in the portfolio. From the available data on expected returns, variances and covariance, minimum variance portfolio can be computed and thus constructed, for any targeted return. In Figure 20.1, above, X-axis represents standard deviation (risk) of the individual security (or portfolio); while Y-axis represents expected return of the individual security (or portfolio). It is to be noted that the bigger dots show the risk and return of individual assets and are lying more towards the north-east. The comparatively smaller dots show the risk and return of portfolios. It is evident from these graphs that small dots are relatively on the north-western region, compared to the large dots of individual securities. It implies that the individual securities are inefficient, because of higher risk that has to be borne for a given level of return. Contrary to this, the diversified portfolios of more than one security lead to higher expected returns, with lower risks. All the portfolios that lie on the upper left side (north-western region), and

---

[1] This trait has been discussed in detail in Chapter 7—Risk-Free Lending and Borrowing.

not on the lower right side (south-eastern region), are optimal portfolios. The north-western regions, where the optimal portfolios reside are called the efficient frontier. Optimal portfolios are effectively the efficient portfolios. Hence, the name, efficient frontier, is accorded to the region where these portfolios reside. The investors choose the portfolios from these efficient portfolios and this is the essence of modern portfolio theory.

The portfolios or securities lying on the lower side are with higher standard deviation and lower return; hence this region is inefficient. The portfolios (or securities) lying on the right hand side have higher risk for a given level of return. Hence, this frontier is inefficient as well. The theory assumes that investors act rationally through decisions aimed at maximizing the return, for the accepted level of risk.

The Figures, 20.2 and 20.3, below, have been incorporated to enable the identification of efficient frontier and the efficient portfolio(s) on it.

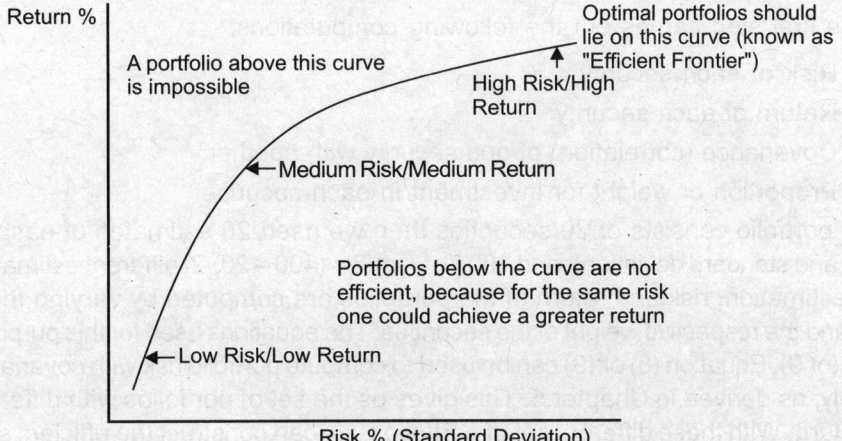

Figure 20.2: Efficient frontier of portfolios with the concept of risk and return

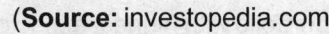

(**Source:** investopedia.com)

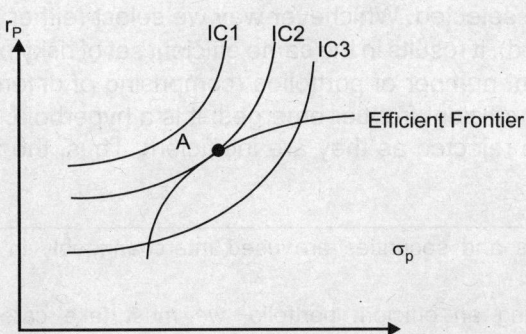

Figure 20.3: Efficient frontier with indifference curves

In a portfolio the risk of a security, individually, is not actually considered in isolation. It is the mass effect that is of interest. Thus the risk quotient of a portfolio is a cumulative measure, with the contribution of each security aggregating to the risk of the portfolio. Nevertheless, the inclusion of a large number of scrips[2] in a portfolio is not wholly applicable to the diversification of risks in portfolio as the returns of different securities are correlated.

If we keep on adding securities blindly and by chance majority of such securities have positive correlation with each other, then such diversification—even with 'n' number of securities—will not help us to reduce risk of the portfolio. Thus, mere diversification does not reduce the risk of the portfolio. Securities selected judiciously with low risk—and negative or poor correlation with other—help to reduce risk. When there is positive correlation amongst securities in a portfolio diversification benefits are non-existent.

Hence, it can be stated that that risk cannot be eliminated completely, irrespective of the number of securities included in the portfolio. We shall now discuss the steps involved in the construction of a portfolio.

1. The first step carries out the following computations:

- Risk of each security.
- Return of each security.
- Covariance (correlation) of one security with another.
- Proportion or weight for investment in each security.

If our portfolio consists of 20 securities then we need 20 estimates of each: return and risk (variances and standard deviation); and 190 $[(n^2 - n)/2 = (400 - 20)/2]$ different estimates of covariance. After this estimation, risk and return of the portfolios are computed by varying the combination of securities and the respective weight of the securities. The equations used for this purpose are Equations (1) and (8) (or 9). Equation (8) or (9) can be used to compute portfolio risk with covariance or correlation respectively, as derived in Chapter 5. This gives us the set of portfolios with different values of net risk and return. With these different set of portfolios, we can construct the efficient set of risky assets by taking risk (standard deviation) on the X-axis and return on Y-axis.

The fundamental idea behind this frontier set is that for any level of risk, we can select the portfolio with highest expected return. In other words, the portfolio with minimum risk for any targeted expected return should be selected. Whichever way we select (either based on highest expected return or lowest risk involved), it results in the same efficient set of risky portfolios. When this process is carried out with sufficient number of portfolios (comprising of different securities with different weights), the shape of the efficient frontier emerges; it is a hyperbola. The portfolios, lying lowest on the right hand side are rejected as they are inefficient. Thus, the first step generated the list of efficient portfolios[3].

---

[2] The terms: scrips, stocks and securities are used interchangeably in this chapter and throughout the book.

[3] When we are constructing an efficient portfolio, we must take care of the following points: (i) Sometimes, investors restrict the inclusion of securities to only those with a regular dividend payment record. In such a case, the task of the portfolio manager is to identify such securities. (ii) At times some institutions do not take short positions with respect to any assets. Under such reservations, a portfolio manager must construct the portfolio without short sales. (iii) Investors may also limit the investment by choosing not to invest in particular scrip or industry due to ethical or other reasons. This leads to lower reward-to-volatility ratio than the efficient set of the portfolios with no restrictions.

2. In step two, risky securities are identified and the optimal portfolio of risky securities is constructed in such a way that it results in a sharp vertical CAL, on the extreme (as much as possible) left hand side[4].

3. In step three, risk-free assets are added to the portfolio of risky securities. Different combinations are tried with different set of risky portfolios (as well as individual securities) and risk-free assets. The one which is tangent to the capital allocation line (CAL) is selected. We select the portfolios on the CAL which is tangent to the efficient frontier and has the highest reward-to-volatility ratio. The portfolio manager would offer the same risky portfolio to all clients, irrespective of their preference (or aversion) for risks, and extent of the same. Investors will thus choose the appropriate point on the CAL depending upon their aversion to risk. But optimal portfolio of risky assets is kept as the reference point. Thus, greater is the risk aversion, higher will be the investment in the risk-free assets and less in the optimal portfolio. On the other hand, higher affinity for risk would lead the investor to invest more in optimal portfolio of risky securities and less in risk-free assets. This preference of the investors, based upon their risk tolerance capacity, is known as the separation property.

In real life, different portfolio managers or mutual fund companies may have different input list (data of: number of scrips from industry, their weight, expected return, risk, etc.). So, different efficient frontiers are derived, leading thus to different optimal portfolios. However, if the quality of the selected scrips and their composition is poor, it will result in a low quality efficient frontier and a sub-standard optimal portfolio. Under the circumstances, a passive portfolio such as the market index[5] is a better alternative. Furthermore, the efficient frontier depends upon various other factors, viz., the input list and restrictions levied by the clients, to name a couple. However, the framework of this analysis is such that even a limited number of portfolios are capable of providing sufficient choices for the efficient set. It can also cater to the needs of wide a range of investors. This is the fundamental principle on which the mutual fund industry works.

> **Pause for thought:** Mutual fund industry works on the principle of catering to the financial needs of as large a cross-section of investors as possible.

Portfolio risk: The n-asset case--the miraculous effect of diversification

We have constructed the portfolio with two risky securities and three risky securities in Chapter 5, Introduction to Portfolio Theory. Similarly, portfolios can be constructed with 8, 10, 12, 15 and even more number of securities. As the number of securities rise, the calculation of risk becomes increasingly difficult. It has been already mentioned above that a portfolio of 20 securities requires 230 (20 return, 20 variances and 190 covariance) estimates. Now that is a huge number! The number of return and variances (standard deviation) equals the number of securities, but the number of

---

[4] Step 2 and step 3 have been discussed in chapters 7 and 8.

[5] Active portfolio is such a portfolio in which securities are selected by portfolio manager, by thorough analysis as per the E-I-C framework and tries to achieve maximum return for a given level of risk-that is, tries to reduce the risk for a given level of return. In nut shell, such portfolios are derived by active involvement and active management by portfolio managers. Also, portfolio manager reshuffles the securities--their weights etc., to gain the best result.

On the other hand, when portfolio manager or investor do not want to follow the lengthy analysis of the E-I-C framework, he may follow any index and would invest in those securities which are included in the index-and will try to remain at par with the market. So, such portfolio construction strategy does not require active involvement or management-but is just a replica of the market.

538 SECURITY ANALYSIS AND PORTFOLIO MANAGEMENT

covariance (and also correlation) is much higher. Their number increases in direct variation with the number of securities in a portfolio. When 'n' is too large, portfolio risk depends upon the covariance between the securities.

Let us derive the relation for portfolio risk, with 'n' securities and with equal weights of each.

Portfolio variance = σ_p^2 = n[1/n^2] × average variance + n(n – 1) [1/n^2] × average covariance (1)

$\qquad\qquad\qquad\quad$ = [1/n] × average variance + [1 – 1/n] × average covariance $\qquad$ (2)

From the above equation, we can observe that portfolio variance is the weighted sum of the average variance and average covariance of the securities. If the number of securities in a portfolio is too large, the first term of the above equation becomes negligible (almost equal to zero). Then the average covariance term becomes the measure of portfolio variance.

Thus, for a large value of 'n', Equation (2) reduces to,

The variance of the portfolio = average covariance $\qquad\qquad\qquad\qquad\qquad\qquad\qquad$ (3)

Furthermore, Equation (2) indicates that when number of securities in a portfolio increases variance of portfolio decreases. This is the effect of diversification, *i.e.*, an increase in the number of securities in a portfolio.

> **Pause for thought:** The basic paradigm of selection for an optimal portfolio is the ratio of risk and return. Either it is comprised of securities to generate highest expected return for the given level of risk. Or otherwise, it comprises of securities which lead to lowest risk, for the given value of expected return

20.1.3 Construction of Efficient Portfolio as per the Markowitz Model[6]

Preceded by the theoretical interpretation of Markowitz model, we now proceed to the empirical application of the theories. For the purpose, the efficient frontier is constructed from all 50 scrips of Nifty by taking the data[7] of last 10 years. They are tabulated in Table 20.1.

A passive portfolio is thus created as scrips from indices have been taken, instead of selecting them on the basis of our own judgment of risk, return and other characteristics. But we intend to compare both sets of portfolios: active and passive. For that, an active portfolio is constructed with effort towards selecting the right scrips from the market, going first through detailed economic, industry and company analyses. The proportion of each security is determined based upon risk, return and correlation data. Also, a number of scrips are replaced with other potential scrips from time to time, maintaining the proportion. In contrast to this, passive portfolio selects only those securities which are on indices like Nifty, Sensex or others. It is believed that such securities represent the market and they are the best investment alternatives compared to others. So, the construction of passive portfolio spares the efforts of E-I-C analysis. Such passive portfolios give results that reflect the market, provided the proportions of securities selected in the portfolio are identical to that in the index.

---

[6] Here we have not included risk-free assets in the construction of Markowitz's optimal portfolio. The portfolio has been constructed with risky securities only.

[7] Risk and return of all the 50 securities of Nifty is calculated by taking data from 2001 to 2010, except for those scrips which are new to the market. For such scrip, risk and return is calculated based on their prices available for the given year.

20.1.4 Passive Portfolio

As mentioned above it is constructed with the securities of Nifty 50

Table 20.1: List of the Securities of Nifty 50

ABB	GAIL	INFOSYSTCH	PNB	SIEMENS
ACC	HCLTECH	ITC	POWERGRID	STER
AMBUJACEM	HDFC	JSWSTEEL	RANBAXY	SUNPHARMA
AXISBANK	HDFCBANK	JPASSOCIAT	RCOM	SUZLON
BHARTIARTL	HEROHONDA	KOTAKBANK	RELCAPITAL	TATASTEEL
BHEL	HINDALCO	LT	RELIANCE	TATAMOTORS
BPCL	HINDUUNILVR	M&M	RELINFRA	TATAPOWER
CAIRN	ICICIBANK	MARUTI	RPOWER	TCS
CIPLA	IDEA	NTPC	SAIL	UNITECH
DLF	IDFC	ONGC	SBIN	WIPRO

Table 20.2: Return and Risk of the Securities of Nifty 50

Scrip	Return (%)	Risk (%)	Scrip	Return (%)	Risk (%)
ABB	30.88	60.77	LT	31.14	57.44
ACC	29.73	34.62	M&M	35.64	52.71
AMBUJACEM	5.48	36.75	MARUTI	29.62	26.69
AXISBANK	57.7	52.37	NTPC	18.68	23.86
BHARTIARTL	46.6	67.03	ONGC	33.12	44.24
BHEL	43.61	44.88	PNB	53.98	61.09
BPCL	21.24	20.43	POWERGRID	−4.23	8.97
CAIRN	17.3	17.45	RANBAXY	2.6	30.34
CIPLA	−5.9	31.42	RCOM	−8.85	51.7
DLF	−21.35	28.43	RELCAPITAL	50.53	83.54

GAIL	36.21	47.12	RELIANCE	20.64	43.51
HCLTECH	9.95	40.99	RELINFRA	28.24	54.72
HDFC	16.19	30.37	RPOWER	−21.6	46.27
HDFCBANK	30.73	24.84	SAIL	67.1	101.14
HEROHONDA	24.26	36.65	SBIN	35.3	24.17
HINDALCO	2.45	51.71	SIEMENS	34.36	78.14
HINDUUNILVR	6.95	14.14	STER	118.01	184.99
ICICIBANK	33.44	39.33	SUNPHARMA	10.23	16.56
IDEA	−16.76	19.68	SUZLON	−10.08	57.17
IDFC	31.82	57.39	TATASTEEL	29.36	52.76
INFOSYSTCH	−0.3037	29.63	TATAMOTORS	41.1	54.9
ITC	−0.7059	34.57	TATAPOWER	35.17	37.64
JSWSTEEL	46.24	90.43	TCS	0.5138	34.47
JPASSOCIAT	23.08	74.85	UNITECH	37	92.57
KOTAKBANK	44.17	72.23	WIPRO	−9.22	25.58

9 portfolios have been constructed on the basis of the following parameters:

1. 21 scrips selected from Nifty 50, on the basis of high return.
2. 14 scrips selected from Nifty 50, on the basis of high return.
3. 10 scrips selected from Nifty 50, on the basis of high return.
4. 5 scrips selected from Nifty 50, on the basis of high return.
5. 20 scrips selected from Nifty 50, on the basis of low risk.
6. 15 scrips selected from Nifty 50, on the basis of low risk.
7. 10 scrips selected from Nifty 50, on the basis of low risk.
8. 8 scrips selected from Nifty 50, on the basis of low risk.
9. 12 scrips selected from Nifty 50.

The following tables (1 to 9) have the inputs: name of the scrip, weight, return-risk (variance and standard deviation) and covariance of securities with respect to each other in a given portfolio. We can also construct an efficient portfolio by selecting an active portfolio[8] (considering macroeconomic, industry and company factors).

---

[8] The later part of this chapter shows the efficient portfolio derived from the active portfolio.

Table 1

RISK AND RETURN BY MARKOWITZ MODEL

Sr. No.	SCRIP	RETURN	RISK	VARIANCE	WEIGHTS	(WEIGHTS)^2	W²*Ri	VARIANCE*W^2	2*Wi*Wj*Cov ij	ABB	AXIS	BHARTI	BHEL	GAIL	HDFC	ICICI	IDFC	JSW	KOTAK	LT	M&M	ONGC	PNB	RELCA	SAIL	SBIN	SIEMENS	TATAM	TATAP	UNITECH
1.00	ABB	30.88	60.77	3692.99	0.05	0.00	1.47	8.37		8.37																				
2.00	AXISBANK	57.70	52.37	2742.62	0.05	0.00	2.75	6.22		8.60	8.61																			
3.00	BHARTIARTL	46.60	67.03	4493.02	0.05	0.00	2.22	10.19		10.87	6.48																			
4.00	BHEL	43.61	44.88	2014.21	0.05	0.00	2.08	4.57		10.57	6.95	8.61																		
5.00	GAIL	36.21	47.12	2220.29	0.05	0.00	1.72	5.03		5.82	8.98	4.34	4.96																	
6.00	HDFCBANK	30.73	24.84	617.03	0.05	0.00	1.46	1.40		4.11	3.55	2.72	2.64	1.76																
7.00	ICICIBANK	33.44	39.33	1546.85	0.05	0.00	1.59	3.51		8.11	7.61	5.30	5.85	5.44	3.44															
8.00	IDFC	31.82	57.39	3293.61	0.05	0.00	1.52	7.47		2.63	2.63	4.72	1.01	6.23	4.83	6.23														
9.00	JSWSTEEL	46.24	90.43	8177.58	0.05	0.00	2.20	18.54		1.36	11.48	6.15	0.01	9.46	6.79	8.49	18.65													
10.00	KOTAKBANK	44.17	72.23	5217.17	0.05	0.00	2.10	11.83		1.46	8.74	6.55	1.57	9.69	1.70	4.49	16.12	25.50												
11.00	LT	31.14	57.44	3299.35	0.05	0.00	1.48	7.48		10.08	6.38	6.81	6.08	3.70	4.94	7.43	8.04	11.41	5.78											
12.00	M&M	35.64	52.71	2778.34	0.05	0.00	1.70	6.30		8.99	9.26	7.42	7.74	8.13	2.20	6.07	2.05	2.72	4.56	1.95										
13.00	ONGC	33.12	44.24	1957.18	0.05	0.00	1.58	4.44		5.15	4.86	3.49	4.12	6.58	-0.12	2.88	0.90	1.07	5.91	2.60	5.93									
14.00	PNB	53.98	61.09	3731.99	0.05	0.00	2.57	8.46		8.78	10.20	6.55	7.73	10.89	1.22	6.06	2.04	3.24	7.36	2.20	12.55	10.00								
15.00	RELCAPITAL	50.53	83.54	6978.93	0.05	0.00	2.41	15.83		7.17	10.11	11.65	5.43	5.29	6.13	8.35	19.10	28.94	14.20	15.55	3.33	-1.58	0.17							
16.00	SAIL	67.10	101.14	10229.30	0.05	0.00	3.20	23.20		9.84	18.89	10.09	9.65	18.21	3.34	10.58	13.76	21.55	22.89	5.66	16.43	11.54	20.28	16.02						
17.00	SBIN	35.30	24.17	584.19	0.05	0.00	1.68	1.32		4.32	4.75	3.04	3.06	3.78	1.93	3.65	4.80	6.77	4.43	4.23	3.47	2.11	3.73	5.37	7.59					
18.00	SIEMENS	34.36	78.14	6105.86	0.05	0.00	1.64	13.85		15.20	11.47	7.80	11.56	9.83	3.46	9.37	1.42	0.60	2.17	12.38	11.74	9.72	15.66	4.47	16.24	4.86				
19.00	TATAMOTORS	41.10	54.90	3014.01	0.05	0.00	1.96	6.03		8.71	7.73	1.30	5.86	7.83	2.32	5.99	3.52	4.17	4.02	4.71	8.25	7.36	11.14	-0.84	11.98	3.74	12.69			
20.00	TATAPOWER	35.17	37.64	1416.77	0.05	0.00	1.67	3.21		3.62	6.87	5.73	3.28	5.29	2.43	4.37	7.84	12.24	7.70	3.54	5.25	1.53	5.23	9.30	12.53	2.90	3.91	2.59		
21.00	UNITECH	37.00	92.57	8569.20	0.05	0.00	1.76	19.43		16.55	7.08	17.23	12.43	4.34	4.01	8.10	1.43	0.60	-2.53	17.36	8.79	6.47	11.28	8.06	4.65	3.34	22.69	6.80	2.71	

RETURN	40.75	
SUM		187.4841531	1493.198804
VARIANCE	1681	
STD DEV	41	

Table 2

AVERAGE RETURN

YEAR	2001	2002	2003	2004	2005	2006	2007	2008	2009	2010
AXISBANK		4.63	161.37	73.92	51.45	58.53	92.54	9.76	-7.66	74.85
BHARTIARTL			29.34	111.27	21.75	26.57	27.17	-52.51	-73.11	-90.48
BHEL		-34.05	67.64	38.60	34.12	37.61	-24.03	-60.52	-42.12	-17.24
GAIL		-4.15	108.29	4.03	-24.12	-24.71	19.81	-42.97	-49.06	12.88
JSWSTEEL						-57.14	142.64	-56.66	-66.75	37.91
KOTAKBANK		53.36	85.48	-28.42	-48.10	-41.45	132.64	-46.89	-78.46	-28.15
M&M		-44.89	110.79	52.54	-14.40	-6.11	-13.50	-67.57	-13.24	-3.62
PNB			129.00	51.56	-18.56	-48.47	-33.15	-55.17	-32.10	6.89
RELAPITAL		-73.94	18.55	-5.75	71.14	16.80	170.18	-50.33	-107.94	-38.71
SAIL		-35.90	234.73	-15.35	-49.53	-44.04	92.20	-72.63	-77.66	-31.82
SBIN		-12.59	35.02	2.71	0.37	9.42	21.56	-32.23	-38.32	14.45
TATAMOTORS		7.72	86.42	8.97	-19.19	0.87	-39.69	-83.37	-39.49	77.76
TATAPOWER		-40.84	49.73	26.47	-14.67	-13.68	62.72	-25.09	-38.60	-6.05
UNITECH		-15.80	42.12	123.31	160.23	-16.94	-78.53	-76.11	-112.97	-25.30

COVARIANCE MATRIX

	AXISBANK	BHARTIARTL	BHEL	GAIL	JSWSTEEL	KOTAKBANK	M&M	PNB	RELAPITAL	SAIL	SBIN	TATAMOTOR	TATAPO	UNITECH
AXISBANK	1427.96													
BHARTIARTL	1531.54	1898.08												
BHEL	1980.04	957.69	1093.14											
GAIL	2530.34	1356.69	2.07	2087.00										
JSWSTEEL	1927.80	1443.47	345.35	2137.15	5622.87									
KOTAKBANK	2041.85	1637.16	1706.89	1792.64	599.68	1005.21								
M&M	2248.95	1443.82	1703.48	2400.15	714.09	1622.30	2767.54							
PNB	2228.51	2569.91	1197.75	1165.80	6380.83	3130.67	735.20							
RELAPITAL	4165.31	2225.91	2128.83	4015.28	4752.05	5046.36	3622.21	36.86						
SAIL	1046.49	670.04	675.56	832.71	1493.79	976.28	764.99	4470.99	3532.54					
SBIN	1704.87	286.28	1292.03	1726.59	919.09	887.21	1820.08	823.47	1183.03	1673.10				
TATAMOTOR	1515.53	1264.17	2128.33	1165.56	2699.44	1698.58	1156.63	2455.39	-186.21	2641.24	824.45			
TATAPOWER	1561.42	3800.13	722.44	832.71	132.15	-558.15	1937.82	1152.24	2094.93	2761.95	640.26	571.65		
UNITECH	1561.42	3800.13	2740.41	956.65				2486.78	1777.28	1026.37	737.56	1499.09	598.10	

MARKOWITZ PORTFOLIO THEORY

Table 2 (Contd.)

RISK AND RETURN BY MARKOWITZ MODEL

Sr. No.	SCRIP	RETURN	RISK	VARIANCE	WEIGHTS	Wi*Ri	VARIANCE*Wi^2	2*Wi*Wj Cov ij	AXIS	B/BHARTI	BHEL	GAIL	JSW	ST KOTAK	M&M	PNB	RELCA	SAIL	SBIN	TATAM	TATAP	UNITECH
1	AXISBANK	57.70	52.37	2742.62	0.07	4.12	13.99															
2	BHARTIARTL	46.60	67.03	4493.02	0.07	3.33	22.92	14.57														
3	BHEL	43.61	44.88	2014.21	0.07	3.12	10.28	15.63	19.37													
4	GAIL	36.21	47.12	2220.29	0.07	2.59	11.33	20.20	9.77	11.15												
5	JSWSTEEL	46.24	90.43	8177.58	0.07	3.30	41.72	25.82	13.84	0.02	21.30											
6	KOTAKBANK	44.17	72.23	5217.17	0.07	3.16	26.62	19.67	14.73	3.52	21.81	57.38										
7	M&M	35.64	52.71	2778.34	0.07	2.55	14.18	20.84	16.71	17.42	18.29	6.12	10.26									
8	PNB	53.98	61.09	3731.99	0.07	3.86	19.04	22.95	14.73	17.38	24.49	7.29	16.55	28.24								
9	RELCAPITAL	50.53	83.54	6978.93	0.07	3.61	35.61	22.74	26.22	12.22	11.90	65.11	31.95	7.50	0.38							
10	SAIL	67.10	101.14	10229.30	0.07	4.79	52.19	42.50	22.71	21.72	40.97	48.49	51.49	36.96	45.62	36.05						
11	SBIN	35.30	24.17	584.19	0.07	2.52	2.98	10.68	6.84	6.89	8.50	15.24	9.96	7.81	8.40	12.07	17.07					
12	TATAMOTOR	41.10	54.90	3014.01	0.07	2.94	15.38	17.40	2.92	13.18	17.62	9.38	9.05	18.57	25.05	-1.90	26.95	8.41				
13	TATAPOWER	35.17	37.64	1416.77	0.07	2.51	7.23	15.46	12.90	7.37	11.89	27.55	17.33	11.80	11.76	21.38	28.18	6.53	5.83			
14	UNITECH	37.00	92.57	8569.20	0.07	2.64	43.72	15.93	38.78	27.96	9.76	1.35	-5.70	19.77	25.38	18.14	10.47	7.53	15.30	6.10		

RETURN	45.025
SUM	317.1818429 1633.5
VARIANCE	1950.646
STD DEV	44.16611

Table 3

AVERAGE RETURN

SCRIP/YEAR	2001	2002	2003	2004	2005	2006	2007	2008	2009	2010
AXISBANK		4.63215	161.367	73.920646	51.44922	58.52967414	92.5428	9.760782259	-7.664315486	74.85
BHARTIARTL			29.3412	111.26837	21.74774	26.56500505	27.1732	-52.51108725	-73.10713044	-90.48
BHEL		-34.05	67.6358	38.599153	34.1179	37.60688492	-24.029	-60.51778936	-42.1191246	-17.24
JSWSTEEL						-57.1370633	142.638	-56.65741623	-66.74893102	37.905
KOTAKBANK		53.3558	85.4798	-28.41788	-48.1028	-41.4549352	132.637	-46.89107529	-78.4569495	-28.15
PNB			129.003	51.562596	-18.5602	-48.4733469	-33.153	-55.16635751	-32.10390879	6.8909
RELCAPITAL		-73.941	18.5471	-5.746452	71.14456	16.7950309	170.184	-50.33334696	-107.9379798	-38.71
SAIL		-35.897	234.732	-15.35227	-49.5313	-44.0420191	92.1984	-72.63462979	-77.6569201	-31.82
TATAMOTORS		7.71845	86.419	8.9664685	-19.1855	0.874995579	-39.692	-83.36934054	-39.49173646	77.76
UNITECH		-15.801	42.1226	123.30529	160.2306	-16.9444129	-78.532	-76.11028639	-112.9742	-25.3

Table 3 (Contd.)

COVARIANCE MATRIX

	AXISBANK	BHARTIARTL	BHEL	JSWSTEEL	KOTAKBAI	PNB	RELAPIT,SAIL	TATAMOTORS	UNITECH
AXISBANK									
BHARTIARTL	1427.96322								
BHEL	1531.54192	1898.08							
JSWSTEEL	2530.3388	1356.69	2.06986						
KOTAKBANK	1927.79681	1443.47	345.354	5622.8687					
PNB	2248.95497	1443.82	1703.48	714.09076	1622.305				
RELAPITAL	2228.51286	2569.91	1197.75	6380.8287	3130.674	36.85917901			
SAIL	4165.31039	2225.91	2128.83	4752.0488	5046.365	4470.992438	3532.54		
TATAMOTOF	1704.87459	286.28	1292.03	919.09227	887.2122	2455.385965	-186.21	2641.235181	
UNITECH	1561.41639	3800.13	2740.41	132.15016	-558.146	2486.777256	1777.28	1026.36885	1499.086384

RISK AND RETURN BY MARKOWITZ MODEL

Sr. No.	SCRIP	RETURN	RISK	VARIANCE	WEIGHTS	(WEIGHTS)^2	Wi*Ri	VARIANCE*Wi^2	2*Wi Wj Cov ij		AXISBANK	BHARTI	BHEL	JSWSTI	KOTAK	PNB	RELCA	SAIL	TATAM	UNITECH
1	AXISBANK	57.70	52.37	2742.62	0.10	0.01	5.77	27.43			27.43									
2	BHARTIARTL	46.60	67.03	4493.02	0.10	0.01	4.66	44.93			28.56	44.93								
3	BHEL	43.61	44.88	2014.21	0.10	0.01	4.36	20.14			30.63	37.96	20.14							
4	JSWSTEEL	46.24	90.43	8177.58	0.10	0.01	4.62	81.78			50.61	27.13	0.04	81.78						
5	KOTAKBANK	44.17	72.23	5217.17	0.10	0.01	4.42	52.17			38.56	28.87	6.91	112.46	52.17					
6	PNB	53.98	61.09	3731.99	0.10	0.01	5.40	37.32			44.98	28.88	34.07	14.28	32.45	37.32				
7	RELAPITAL	50.53	83.54	6978.93	0.10	0.01	5.05	69.79			44.57	51.40	23.95	127.62	62.61	0.74	69.79			
8	SAIL	67.10	101.14	10229.30	0.10	0.01	6.71	102.29			83.31	44.52	42.58	95.04	100.93	89.42	70.65	102.29		
9	TATAMOTOF	41.10	54.90	3014.01	0.10	0.01	4.11	30.14			34.10	5.73	25.84	18.38	17.74	49.11	-3.72	52.82	30.14	
10	UNITECH	37.00	92.57	8569.20	0.10	0.01	3.70	85.69			31.23	76.00	54.81	2.64	-11.16	49.74	35.55	20.53	29.98	85.69
						RETURN	48.80													
						SUM		551.68	1843.01											
						VARIANCE	2394.70													
						STD DEV	48.94													

Table 4

AVERAGE RETURN

SCRIP/YEAR	2001	2002	2003	2004	2005	2006	2007	2008	2009	2010
AXISBANK		4.632153	161.3668	73.920646	51.44922	58.52967414	92.5428	9.760782259	-7.6643	74.85
BHARTIARTL			29.34122	111.26837	21.74774	26.56500505	27.1732	-52.51108725	-73.107	-90.48
PNB				129.0032	51.562596	-18.5602	-48.47334685	-33.153	-55.16635751	-32.104	6.8909
RELAPITAL				-73.9407	18.54709	-5.746452	-18.5602	16.7950309	170.184	-50.33334696	-107.94	-38.71
SAIL				-35.8973	234.7319	-15.35227	-49.5313	-44.04201911	92.1984	-72.63462979	-77.657	-31.82

COVARIANCE MATRIX

	AXISBANK	BHARTIAR	PNB	RELAPITAL	SAIL
AXISBANK	1427.963				
BHARTIARTL	2248.955	1443.824			
PNB	2228.513	2569.907	36.85918		
RELAPITAL	4165.31	2225.908	4470.992	3532.5437	

RISK AND RETURN BY MARKOWITZ MODEL

Sr. No.	SCRIP	RETURN	RISK	VARIANCE	WEIGHTS	(WEIGHTS)^2	W i*Ri	VARIANCE*Wi^2	2*Wi Wj Cov ij	AXISBAN	BHARTI	PNB	RELCAPI	SAIL
1	AXISBANK	57.70	52.37	2742.62	0.20	0.04	11.54	109.70						
2	BHARTIAR	46.60	67.03	4493.02	0.20	0.04	9.32	179.72		114.24				
3	PNB	53.98	61.09	3731.99	0.20	0.04	10.80	149.28		179.92	115.51			
4	RELCAPITA	50.53	83.54	6978.93	0.20	0.04	10.11	279.16		178.28	205.59	2.95		
5	SAIL	67.10	101.14	10229.30	0.20	0.04	13.42	409.17		333.22	178.07	357.68	282.60	
					RETURN		55.18							
					SUM			1127.03	1948.06					
					VARIANCE		3075.10							
					STD DEV		55.45							

Table 5

COVARIANCE MATRIX

	ACC	BPCL	CAIRN	CIPLA	DLF	HDFCBANK	HEROHON	HINDUNIL	IDEA	INFOSYS	ITC	MARUTI	NTPC	POWER	RANBA	SBIN	SUNPH	TATAP	TCS	WIPRO
ACC	-115.91																			
BPCL	376.01	138.92																		
CAIRN	-76.14	133.64	80.83																	
CIPLA	334.57	59.54	279.66	-128.36																
DLF	615.56	-45.70	361.05	-205.52	426.09															
HDFCBANK	232.27	-39.99	7.40	316.54	-351.32	197.40														
HEROHONDA	115.91	-159.51	-36.41	223.92	-75.15	-29.95	86.90													
HINDUNILVR	382.86	128.81	226.38	42.79	342.02	388.31	-63.06	-45.51												
IDEA	94.03	205.82	335.00	712.76	149.98	59.49	416.94	117.62	311.89											
INFOSYSTCH	-550.32	377.42	-11.30	-80.78	-61.49	-74.90	269.63	-312.94	-21.65	65.29										
ITC	570.11	164.05	70.05	178.86	-257.92	247.99	361.91	31.27	8.16	228.95	-26.82									
MARUTI	265.09	-81.94	21.16	-479.71	57.99	321.36	-450.94	-97.13	29.27	-334.97	-87.26	-36.88								
NTPC	214.21	88.71	100.97	75.98	115.93	190.02	57.70	-14.36	107.96	212.98	1.25	87.77	6.20							
POWERGRID	-237.36	437.93	346.72	201.29	416.35	44.88	143.18	-211.81	374.30	374.27	749.25	86.91	-156.79	181.40						
RANBAXY	467.24	132.44	334.86	-142.13	437.00	426.55	-76.04	-103.55	368.38	77.63	-3.84	181.24	339.58	169.98	152.21					
SBIN	172.86	-204.95	-107.93	-44.13	-133.17	48.40	-162.34	124.82	-117.22	-130.97	-325.71	58.77	222.93	-55.94	-309.41					
SUNPHARMA	309.03	150.73	184.91	-406.06	293.72	536.19	-49.36	-244.70	213.76	-124.31	448.31	137.36	655.25	86.03	315.06	640.26	-20.39			
TATAPOWER	682.80	236.71	553.90	203.71	605.84	490.37	401.80	-28.64	586.27	581.39	-90.67	282.53	-157.06	298.66	415.11	386.54	-259.32	2.20		
TCS	149.80	157.65	494.71	-101.22	72.11	240.43	69.08	112.89	559.67	168.71	229.30	-18.37	125.90	297.76	81.12	-2.46	136.14	-52.87		
WIPRO	-1.17																		173.52	

RISK AND RETURN BY MARKOWITZ MODEL

SR. NO.	SCRIP	RETURN	RISK	VARIAN	WEIGHTS (WEIGHTS)	W²*Ri	VARIANC	2*Wi*Wj Cov ij	ACC	BPCL	CAIRN	CIPLA	DLF	HDFCBA	HEROHK	HINDUN	IDEA	INFOSY	ITC	MAR	NTPC	POWER	RANBA	SBIN	SUNPI	TATAP	TCS	WIPRO
1	ACC	29.73	34.62	1198.54	0.05	1.49	3.00	-0.58																			
2	BPCL	21.24	20.43	417.38	0.05	1.06	1.04	1.88	0.69																		
3	CAIRN	17.3	17.45	304.50	0.05	0.87	0.76	-0.38	0.67	0.40																	
4	CIPLA	-5.9	31.42	987.22	0.05	-0.30	2.47	1.67	0.30	1.40	-0.64																
5	DLF	-21.35	28.43	808.26	0.05	-1.07	2.02	3.08	-0.23	1.81	-1.03	2.13															
6	HDFCBAN	30.73	24.84	617.03	0.05	1.54	1.54	1.16	-0.20	0.04	1.58	-1.76	0.99														
7	HEROHON	24.26	36.65	1343.22	0.05	1.21	3.36	0.58	-0.80	-0.18	1.12	-0.38	-0.15	-0.32													
8	HINDUUN	6.95	14.14	199.94	0.05	0.35	0.50	1.91	0.64	1.13	0.21	1.71	1.94	0.43	-0.23												
9	IDEA	-16.76	19.68	387.30	0.05	-0.84	0.97	0.47	1.03	1.68	3.56	0.75	0.30	-0.15	0.59	1.56											
10	INFOSYSTI	-0.3037	29.63	877.94	0.05	-0.02	2.19	-2.75	1.89	-0.06	-0.40	-0.31	-0.37	2.08	-1.56	-0.11	0.33										
11	ITC	-0.7059	34.57	1195.08	0.05	-0.04	2.99	2.85	0.82	0.35	0.89	-1.29	1.24	1.35	0.16	0.04	1.14	-0.13									
12	MARUTI	29.62	26.69	712.36	0.05	1.48	1.78	1.33	-0.41	0.11	-2.40	0.29	1.61	1.81	-0.49	0.15	-1.67	-0.44	0.18								
13	NTPC	18.68	23.86	569.30	0.05	0.93	1.42	1.07	0.44	0.50	0.38	0.58	0.95	-2.25	-1.06	0.54	1.06	-0.44	0.03								
14	POWERGR	-4.23	8.97	80.46	0.05	-0.21	0.20	-1.19	2.19	1.73	1.01	2.08	0.22	0.29	0.72	1.87	0.01	0.44	0.18								
15	RANBAXY	2.6	30.34	920.52	0.05	0.13	2.30	2.34	0.66	1.67	0.22	1.01	2.13	-0.38	-0.52	1.84	3.75	0.43	0.91								
16	SBIN	35.3	24.17	584.19	0.05	1.77	1.46	0.86	-1.02	-0.54	-0.71	-0.67	0.24	-0.81	0.62	0.39	-0.02	0.91	0.85	0.76							
17	SUNPHAR	10.23	16.56	274.23	0.05	0.51	0.69	1.55	0.75	0.92	-0.22	-2.03	2.68	-0.25	-1.22	-0.59	-0.65	-1.63	0.29	1.11	-0.28	-1.55					
18	TATAPOW	35.17	37.64	1416.77	0.05	1.76	3.54	3.41	1.18	2.77	1.47	1.02	2.45	2.01	-0.14	1.07	-0.62	2.24	1.70	0.43	1.58	3.20	0.01				
19	TCS	0.5138	34.47	1188.18	0.05	0.03	2.97	3.41	1.18	2.77	1.02	3.03	2.45	2.01	-0.14	2.93	2.91	-0.45	0.69	2.08	1.93	-1.30	-0.26				
20	WIPRO	-9.22	25.58	654.34	0.05	-0.46	1.64	-0.01	0.75	0.79	2.47	-0.51	0.36	1.20	0.35	0.56	2.80	0.84	1.15	-0.09	0.63	1.49	0.41	-0.01	0.68	0.87

RETURN 10.19271
SUM 36.84192 119.5387709
VARIANCE 156.3807
STD DEV 12.50523

Table 6

COVARIANCE MATRIX

	BPCL	CAIRN	CIPLA	DLF	HDFCBA	HINDUNILVR	IDEA	INFOSYSTCH	MARUTI	NTPC	POWERGR	RANBAXY	SBIN	SUNPH	WIPRO
BPCL	138.92														
CAIRN	133.64	80.83													
CIPLA	59.54	279.66	-128.36												
DLF	-45.70	361.05	-205.52	426.09											
HDFCBANK	-159.51	-36.41	223.92	-75.15	-29.95										
HINDUNILVR	128.81	226.38	42.79	342.02	388.31	-45.51									
IDEA	205.82	335.00	712.76	149.98	59.49	117.62	311.89								
INFOSYSTCH	164.05	70.05	178.86	-257.92	247.99	31.27	8.16	228.95							
MARUTI	-81.94	21.16	-479.77	57.99	321.36	-97.13	29.27	-334.97	36.88						
NTPC	88.71	100.97	75.98	115.93	190.02	-14.36	107.96	212.98	87.77	6.20					
POWERGRID	437.93	346.72	201.29	416.35	44.88	-211.81	374.30	374.27	86.91	-156.79	181.40				
RANBAXY	132.44	334.86	-142.13	437.00	426.55	-103.55	368.38	339.58	181.24	339.58	169.98	152.21			
SBIN	-204.95	-107.93	-44.13	-133.17	48.40	124.82	-117.22	77.63	58.77	222.93	-55.34	-309.41			
SUNPHARMA	149.80	157.65	494.71	-101.22	72.11	69.08	112.89	-130.97	229.30	-18.37	125.90	297.76	81.12	-2.46	
WIPRO								559.67							

SR. NO.	SCRIP	RETURN	RISK	VARIANCE	WEIGHT	(WEIGHT)Y2	W i*Ri	VARIANCE*Wi2	Wi Wj Covij											
									BPCL	CAIRN	CIPLA	DLF	HDFCBA	HINDU	IDEA	INFOSY	MARU	POWER	RANBA	SBIN	SUNPH	WIPRO
1	BPCL	21.24	20.43	417.38	0.07	0.00	1.42	1.86														
2	CAIRN	17.3	17.45	304.50	0.07	0.00	1.15	1.35	1.23													
3	CIPLA	-5.9	31.42	987.22	0.07	0.00	-0.39	4.39	1.19	0.72												
4	DLF	-21.35	28.43	808.26	0.07	0.00	-1.42	3.59	0.53	2.49	-1.14											
5	HDFCBANK	30.73	24.84	617.03	0.07	0.00	2.05	2.74	-0.41	3.21	-1.83	3.79										
6	HINDUUNI	6.95	14.14	199.94	0.07	0.00	0.46	0.89	-1.42	-0.32	1.99	-0.67	-0.27									
7	IDEA	-16.76	19.68	387.30	0.07	0.00	-1.12	1.72	1.14	2.01	0.38	3.04	3.45	-0.40								
8	INFOSYSTC	-0.3037	29.63	877.94	0.07	0.00	-0.02	3.90	1.83	2.98	6.34	1.33	0.53	1.05	2.77							
9	MARUTI	29.62	26.69	712.36	0.07	0.00	1.97	3.17	1.46	0.62	1.59	-2.29	2.20	0.28	0.07	2.04						
10	NTPC	18.68	23.86	569.30	0.07	0.00	1.25	2.53	-0.73	0.19	-4.26	0.52	2.86	-0.86	0.26	-2.98	0.33					
11	POWERGRI	-4.23	8.97	80.46	0.07	0.00	-0.28	0.36	0.79	0.90	0.68	1.03	1.69	-0.13	1.89	0.78	0.06					
12	RANBAXY	2.6	30.34	920.52	0.07	0.00	0.17	4.09	3.89	3.08	1.79	3.70	0.40	-1.88	3.33	0.77	-1.39	1.61				
13	SBIN	35.3	24.17	584.19	0.07	0.00	2.35	2.60	1.18	2.98	-1.26	3.88	3.79	-0.92	3.27	1.61	3.02	1.51	1.35			
14	SUNPHARM	10.23	16.56	274.23	0.07	0.00	0.68	1.22	-1.82	-0.96	-0.39	-1.18	-1.04	1.11	-1.16	0.69	1.98	-0.50	-2.75			
15	WIPRO	-9.22	25.58	654.34	0.07	0.00	-0.61	2.91	1.33	1.40	4.40	-0.90	0.43	0.64	1.00	0.61	4.97	-0.16	1.12	2.65	0.72	-0.02
					RETURN		7.66															
					SUM			37.31	99.05													
					VARIANCE				136.36													
					STD DEV				11.68													

Table 7

COVARIANCE MATRIX

	BPCL	CAIRN	HDFCBANK	HINDUNILVR	IDEA	NTPC	POWERGRID	SBIN	SUNPHARMA	WIPRO
BPCL										
CAIRN	138.92									
HDFCBANK	-45.70	361.05								
HINDUNILVR	-159.51	-36.41	-29.95							
IDEA	128.81	226.38	388.31	-45.51						
NTPC	-81.94	21.16	321.36	-97.13	29.27					
POWERGRID	88.71	100.97	190.02	-14.36	107.96	6.20				
SBIN	132.44	334.86	426.55	-103.55	368.38	339.58	169.98			
SUNPHARMA	-204.95	-107.93	48.40	124.82	-117.22	222.93	-55.94	-20.39		
WIPRO	149.80	157.65	72.11	69.08	112.89	-18.37	125.90	81.12	-2.46	

SR. NO.	SCRIP	RETURN	RISK	VARIANCE	WEIGHT	(WEIGHTS)^2	Wi*Ri	VARIANCE*Wi^2	2*Wi Wj Cov ij									
									BPCL	CAIRN	HDFCBANK	HINDUNILVR	IDEA	NTPC	POWERGRID	SBIN	SUNPHARMA	WIPRO
1	BPCL	21.24	20.43	417.38	0.10	0.01	2.12	4.17										
2	CAIRN	17.3	17.45	304.50	0.10	0.01	1.73	3.05	2.78									
3	HDFCBAN	30.73	24.84	617.03	0.10	0.01	3.07	6.17	-0.91	7.22								
4	HINDUUN	6.95	14.14	199.94	0.10	0.01	0.70	2.00	-3.19	-0.73	-0.60							
5	IDEA	-16.76	19.68	387.30	0.10	0.01	-1.68	3.87	2.58	4.53	7.77	-0.91						
6	NTPC	18.68	23.86	569.30	0.10	0.01	1.87	5.69	-1.64	0.42	6.43	-1.94	0.59					
7	POWERGR	-4.23	8.97	80.46	0.10	0.01	-0.42	0.80	1.77	2.02	3.80	-0.29	2.16	0.12				
8	SBIN	35.3	24.17	584.19	0.10	0.01	3.53	5.84	2.65	6.70	8.53	-2.07	7.37	6.79	3.40			
9	SUNPHAR	10.23	16.56	274.23	0.10	0.01	1.02	2.74	-4.10	-2.16	0.97	2.50	-2.34	4.46	-1.12	-0.41		
10	WIPRO	-9.22	25.58	654.34	0.10	0.01	-0.92	6.54	3.00	3.15	1.44	1.38	2.26	-0.37	2.52	1.62	-0.05	
					RETURN		11.02											
					SUM			40.89	78.09									
					VARIANCE			118.97										
					STD DEV			10.91										

Table 8

Covariance Matrix

	BPCL	CAIRN	HDFCBANK	HINDUNILVR	IDEA	POWERGRID	SBIN	SUNPHARMA
BPCL								
CAIRN	138.92							
HDFCBANK	-45.70	361.05						
HINDUNILVR	-159.51	-36.41	-29.95					
IDEA	128.81	226.38	388.31	-45.51				
POWERGRID	88.71	100.97	190.02	-14.36	107.96			
SBIN	132.44	334.86	426.55	-103.55	368.38	169.98		
SUNPHARMA	-204.95	-107.93	48.40	124.82	-117.22	-55.94	-20.39	

Sl. NO.	SCRIP	RETURN	RISK	VARIANCE	WEIGHT	(WEIGHTS)^2	W i*Ri	VARIANCE*W i^2	2*Wi Wj Cov ij	BPCL	CAIRN	HDFC	HINDU	IDEA	POWER	SBIN	SUNPH
1	BPCL	21.24	20.43	417.38	0.13	0.02	2.66	6.52			4.34	-1.43	-4.98	4.03	2.77	4.14	-6.40
2	CAIRN	17.3	17.45	304.50	0.13	0.02	2.16	4.76				11.28	-1.14	7.07	3.16	10.46	-3.37
3	HDFCBANK	30.73	24.84	617.03	0.13	0.02	3.84	9.64					-0.94	12.13	5.94	13.33	1.51
4	HINDUUNI	6.95	14.14	199.94	0.13	0.02	0.87	3.12						-1.42	-0.45	-3.24	3.90
5	IDEA	-16.76	19.68	387.30	0.13	0.02	-2.10	6.05							3.37	###	-3.66
6	POWERGR	-4.23	8.97	80.46	0.13	0.02	-0.53	1.26								5.31	-1.75
7	SBIN	35.3	24.17	584.19	0.13	0.02	4.41	9.13									-0.64
8	SUNPHARI	10.23	16.56	274.23	0.13	0.02	1.28	4.28									
						RETURN	12.60										
						SUM		44.77	74.85								
						VARIANCE	119.61										
						STD DEV	10.94										

Table 9

COVARIANCE MATRIX

	ACC	AXISBANK	BHEL	BPCL	CAIRN	HDFCBANK	ICICIBANK	MARUTI	NTPC	PNB	SUNPH	TATAPOWER
ACC	719.49											
AXISBANK	1005.96	1531.54										
BHEL	-115.91	342.77	148.44									
BPCL	376.01	506.12	205.03	131.92								
CAIRN	615.56	783.65	581.84	-43.70	361.05							
HDFCBANK	885.45	1677.19	1289.13	143.52	534.30	757.47						
ICICIBANK	570.11	275.49	628.38	164.05	70.05	247.99	363.85					
MARUTI	265.09	551.21	187.10	-8.94	21.16	321.36	405.64					
NTPC	219.32	2248.95	1703.48	962.55	308.59	268.79	1335.56	36.88				
PNB	172.86	-167.69	-58.26	-204.95	-107.93	48.40	-70.98	511.28	-74.37			
SUNPHARMA	309.03	1515.53	722.44	150.73	184.91	536.19	964.36	58.77	222.93	-593.75		
TATAPOWER								137.36	655.25	1152.24	2.20	

RISK AND RETURN BY MARKOWITZ MODEL

SR NO	SCRIP	RETURN	RISK	VARIANCE	WEIGHT	(WEIGHTS)^2	W I*Ri	VARIANCE*Wi^2	2*Wi Wj Cov ij
								ACC	AXISBAN BHEL BPCL CAIRN HDFC ICICIB MARUTI NTPC PNB SUNPH TATAPOWER
1	ACC	29.73	34.62	1198.54	0.08	0.01	2.48	8.32	0.00 0.00 0.00 0.00 0.00 0.00 0.00 0.00 0.00 0.00 0.00
2	AXISBANK	57.7	52.37	2742.62	0.08	0.01	4.81	19.05	9.99 0.00 0.00 0.00 0.00 0.00 0.00 0.00 0.00 0.00 0.00
3	BHEL	43.61	44.88	2013.21	0.08	0.01	3.63	13.99	13.97 21.27 0.00 0.00 0.00 0.00 0.00 0.00 0.00 0.00 0.00
4	BPCL	21.24	20.43	417.38	0.08	0.01	1.77	2.90	-1.61 4.76 2.06 0.00 0.00 0.00 0.00 0.00 0.00 0.00 0.00
5	CAIRN	17.3	17.45	304.50	0.08	0.01	1.44	2.11	5.22 7.03 2.85 1.93 0.00 0.00 0.00 0.00 0.00 0.00 0.00
6	HDFCBAN	30.73	24.84	617.03	0.08	0.01	2.56	4.28	8.55 10.88 8.08 -0.63 5.01 0.00 0.00 0.00 0.00 0.00 0.00
7	ICICIBANK	33.44	39.33	1546.85	0.08	0.01	2.79	10.74	12.30 23.29 17.90 2.02 7.42 10.52 0.00 0.00 0.00 0.00 0.00
8	MARUTI	29.62	26.69	712.36	0.08	0.01	2.47	4.95	7.92 3.83 8.73 2.28 2.02 7.42 3.44 5.05 0.00 0.00 0.00 0.00
9	NTPC	18.68	23.86	569.30	0.08	0.01	1.56	3.95	3.68 7.66 2.60 -1.14 0.29 4.46 5.63 0.51 0.00 0.00 0.00
10	PNB	53.98	61.09	3731.99	0.08	0.01	4.50	25.92	3.05 31.24 23.66 13.37 4.29 3.73 18.55 7.10 -1.03 0.00 0.00
11	SUNPHAR	10.23	16.56	274.23	0.08	0.01	0.85	1.90	2.40 -2.33 -0.81 -2.85 -1.50 0.67 -0.99 0.82 3.10 -8.25 0.00
12	TATAPOW	35.17	37.64	1415.77	0.08	0.01	2.93	9.84	4.29 21.05 10.03 2.09 2.57 7.45 13.39 1.91 9.10 16.00 0.03

RETURN	31.79	
SUM		107.96	410.89
VARIANCE	518.85	
STD DEV	22.78	

Markowitz Portfolio Theory

Table 20.3: Summary of Risk and Return Profile of all Portfolios

	Selection of portfolio on the basis of high return		
	No. of scrip	Return (%)	Risk (%)
Portfolio 1	21	40.75	41.00
Portfolio 2	14	45.03	44.17
Portfolio 3	10	48.80	48.94
Portfolio 4	5	55.18	55.45

	Selection of portfolio on the basis of low risk		
	No. of scrip	Return (%)	Risk (%)
Portfolio 1	21	10.19	12.51
Portfolio 2	15	7.65	11.68
Portfolio 3	10	11.02	10.91
Portfolio 4	8	12.60	10.94

	Return (%)	Risk (%)
Portfolio 1	40.75	41.00
Portfolio 2	45.03	44.17
Portfolio 3	48.80	48.94
Portfolio 4	55.18	55.45
Portfolio 5	10.19	12.51
Portfolio 6	7.65	11.68
Portfolio 7	11.02	10.91
Portfolio 8	12.60	10.94
Portfolio 9	31.78	22.78

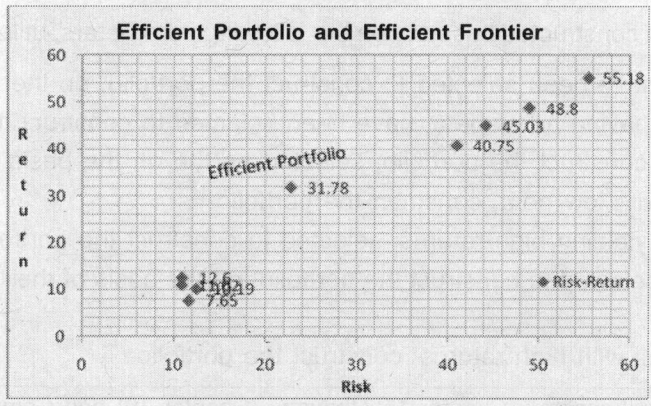

Figure 20.4: Efficient frontier and efficient portfolio

From the risk and return profile of the 9 portfolios, it is evident that portfolio 9 is the most efficient portfolio, compared to the rest, with better reward-to-volatility ratio. The graph below shows the efficient frontier of all 9 portfolios. Portfolio 9 is deemed to be the most efficient portfolio, lying on the north-western region, compared to the rest. Shape of the efficient set is concave and the portfolio lying to its left is portfolio 9. Hence, it is an efficient portfolio.

> **Pause for thought:** A passive portfolio is created taking scrips from indices, instead of selecting them on the basis of our own judgment of risk, return and other characteristics.

20.1.5 Active Portfolio

Since we wish (already stated above) to compare the active and passive portfolios in the paradigm of Markowitz model, an active portfolio is constructed. The E-I-C framework[9] forms the basis of this construction. In all, 34 companies are selected from 10 sectors and the data of their share prices have been collected from Bombay Stock Exchange. The prices are on yearly basis, from 2004-05 to 2008-09. Out of these 34 securities, top 25 securities (with comparatively higher return) have been finalized for the construction of the efficient set.

Table 20.4: Top 25 companies selected on the basis of E-I-C analysis

JINDAL STEEL	RELIANCE POWER	TATA COMM.	ICICI BANK	HUL
SAIL	SBI	GSFC	MARUTI SUZUKI	TATA STEEL
BHARTI AIRTEL	HDFC	ULTRATECH	GRASIM	ONGC
SPICE JET	ACC	HERO HONDA	DABUR INDIA	CADILA HEALTH
BHEL	NTPC	MAHINDRA & MAHINDRA	GAIL	TATA MOTORS

> **Pause for thought:** Quite contrary to the passive portfolio active portfolio selects the securities taking into cognizance the human judgment.

20.2 MARKOWITZ OPTIMIZATION MODEL

7 portfolios have been constructed based upon the following parameters, utilizing Markowitz model.

1. 15 scrips have been selected to construct the portfolio, on the basis of low beta.
2. 12 scrips, having a low beta, have been selected to construct the portfolio.
3. 10 scrips, construct the portfolio, selected on the on the basis of low beta.
4. 8 scrips, with low beta, construct the portfolio.
5. 12 scrips, yielding high returns, selected to construct the portfolio.
6. 10 scrips selected to construct the portfolio, on the basis of their comparatively higher returns.
7. 8 scrips, all with high returns, construct the portfolio.

---

[9] Refer to chapters on Economy (Chapter 15), Industry (Chapter 16) and Company Analysis (Chapter 17) under Fundamental Analysis (E-I-C framework).

Assumption 1: Selecting the low beta scrips

Table 20.5: Top 15 scrips, with low beta

No.	Scrips	Average rate of return (%)	Standard deviation, S.D. (%)	W_i
1	JINDAL STEEL	94.03	176.42	0.0667
2	SAIL	37.12	70.79	0.0667
3	BHARTI AIRTEL	36.51	50.86	0.0667
4	SPICE JET	33.26	95.29	0.0667
5	BHEL	31.14	41.51	0.0667
6	RELIANCE POWER	29.33	42.75	0.0667
7	SBI	28.88	28.70	0.0667
8	HDFC	28.56	28.67	0.0667
9	ACC	27.70	45.07	0.0667
10	NTPC	25.28	22.21	0.0667
11	TATA COMM.	24.20	38.63	0.0667
12	GSFC	23.87	46.78	0.0667
13	ULTRATECH	23.63	50.22	0.0667
14	HERO HONDA	22.43	25.41	0.0667
15	MAHINDRA & MAHINDRA	22.40	69.95	0.0667
	Return	32.56%	Standard[10] deviation	33.56%

Table 20.6: 12 scrips with low beta

No.	Scrips	Average rate of return (%)	Standard deviation, S.D. (%)	W_i
2	SAIL	37.12	70.79	0.083333
3	BHARTI AIRTEL	36.51	50.86	0.083333
4	SPICE JET	33.26	95.29	0.083333
5	BHEL	31.14	41.51	0.083333
6	RELIANCE POWER	29.33	42.75	0.083333
7	SBI	28.88	28.70	0.083333
8	HDFC	28.56	28.67	0.083333
10	NTPC	25.28	22.21	0.083333
11	TATA COMM.	24.20	38.63	0.083333
12	GSFC	23.87	46.78	0.083333
14	HERO HONDA	22.43	25.41	0.083333
15	MAHINDRA & MAHINDRA	22.40	69.95	0.083333
	Return	28.58%	Standard deviation	24.36%

[10] Risk of all the portfolios are calculated by the long formula with covariance/correlation of portfolio risk. Appendix at the end of the chapter shows the covariance values for all mentioned securities.

Table 20.7: 10 scrips with low beta

No.	Scrips	Average rate of return (%)	Standard deviation, S.D. (%)	W_i
2	SAIL	37.12	70.79	0.1
3	BHARTI AIRTEL	36.51	50.86	0.1
6	RELIANCE POWER	29.33	42.75	0.1
7	SBI	28.88	28.70	0.1
8	HDFC	28.56	28.67	0.1
10	NTPC	25.28	22.21	0.1
11	TATA COMM.	24.20	38.63	0.1
12	GSFC	23.87	46.78	0.1
14	HERO HONDA	22.43	25.41	0.1
15	MAHINDRA & MAHINDRA	22.40	69.95	0.1
	Return	27.86%	Standard deviation	21.76%

Table 20.8: 8 scrips with low beta

No.	Scrips	Average rate of return (%)	Standard deviation, S.D. (%)	W_i
3	BHARTI AIRTEL	36.51	50.86	0.125
6	RELIANCE POWER	29.33	42.75	0.125
7	SBI	28.88	28.70	0.125
8	HDFC	28.56	28.67	0.125
10	NTPC	25.28	22.21	0.125
11	TATA COMM.	24.20	38.63	0.125
12	GSFC	23.87	46.78	0.125
15	MAHINDRA & MAHINDRA	22.40	69.95	0.125
	Return	27.38%	Standard deviation	23.09%

Assumption 2: Selection of the scrips on the basis of their comparatively higher average rate of returns

Table 20.9: Top 12 Scrips with Higher Returns

No.	Scrips	Average rate of return (%)	Standard deviation, S.D. (%)	W_i
1	JINDAL STEEL	94.03	176.42	0.083333
2	SAIL	37.12	70.79	0.083333
3	BHARTI AIRTEL	36.51	50.86	0.083333
4	SPICE JET	33.26	95.29	0.083333
5	BHEL	31.14	41.51	0.083333
6	RELIANCE POWER	29.33	42.75	0.083333
7	SBI	28.88	28.70	0.083333
8	HDFC	28.56	28.67	0.083333
9	ACC	27.70	45.07	0.083333
10	NTPC	25.28	22.21	0.083333
11	TATA COMM.	24.20	38.63	0.083333
12	GSFC	23.87	46.78	0.083333
	Return	34.99%	Standard deviation	41.73%

Table 20.10: Top 10 Scrips with Higher Returns

No.	Scrips	Average rate of return (%)	Standard deviation, S.D. (%)	W_i
1	JINDAL STEEL	94.03	176.42	0.1
2	SAIL	37.12	70.79	0.1
3	BHARTI AIRTEL	36.51	50.86	0.1
4	SPICE JET	33.26	95.29	0.1
5	BHEL	31.14	41.51	0.1
6	RELIANCE POWER	29.33	42.75	0.1
7	SBI	28.88	28.70	0.1
8	HDFC	28.56	28.67	0.1
9	ACC	27.70	45.07	0.1
10	NTPC	25.28	22.21	0.1
	Return	37.18%	Standard deviation	43.34%

Table 20.11: Top 8 Scrips with Higher Returns

No.	Scrips	Average rate of return (%)	Standard deviation, S.D. (%)	W_i
1	JINDAL STEEL	94.03	176.42	0.125
2	SAIL	37.12	70.79	0.125
3	BHARTI AIRTEL	36.51	50.86	0.125
4	SPICE JET	33.26	95.29	0.125
5	BHEL	31.14	41.51	0.125
6	RELIANCE POWER	29.33	42.75	0.125
7	SBI	28.88	28.70	0.125
8	HDFC	28.56	28.67	0.125
	Return	39.85%	Standard deviation	48.54%

20.2.1 Evaluation of Portfolio

Having constructed the sets of portfolios now we come to their evaluation, and thus to their efficiencies.

Table 20.12: Markowitz optimization model[11] as per the E-I-C analysis

Basis of portfolio construction	Higher average rate of return		Lower beta of the securities	
No. of scrips	Expected rate of return (%)	Standard deviation (%)	Expected rate of return (%)	Standard deviation (%)
15 scrips	32.55	33.55	32.55	33.55
12 scrips	34.99	41.73	28.58	24.35
10 scrips	37.18	43.36	**27.86**	**21.76**
8 scrips	39.85	48.54	27.38	23.09

Considering the risk and return of these eight portfolios, the portfolio constructed by taking lower beta from 10 scrips is the portfolio which lies on the north-western region, compared to the other portfolios. This has been shown in bold, in Table 20.12.

From the above figure it can be concluded the portfolios containing scrips with lower beta are more efficient, compared to the ones constructed on the basis of average returns of the scrips. From Table 20.12 above, it can be concluded that the portfolio of 10 scrips, with low beta is the

---

[11] In the construction of Markowitz Optimal Portfolio, we have not included the third step, introduction of risk-free assets, in the portfolio.

optimal portfolio, with comparatively higher return for a relatively lesser risk. From the Figure 20.5 it is to be noted that it stays more toward north-western region of the efficient set.

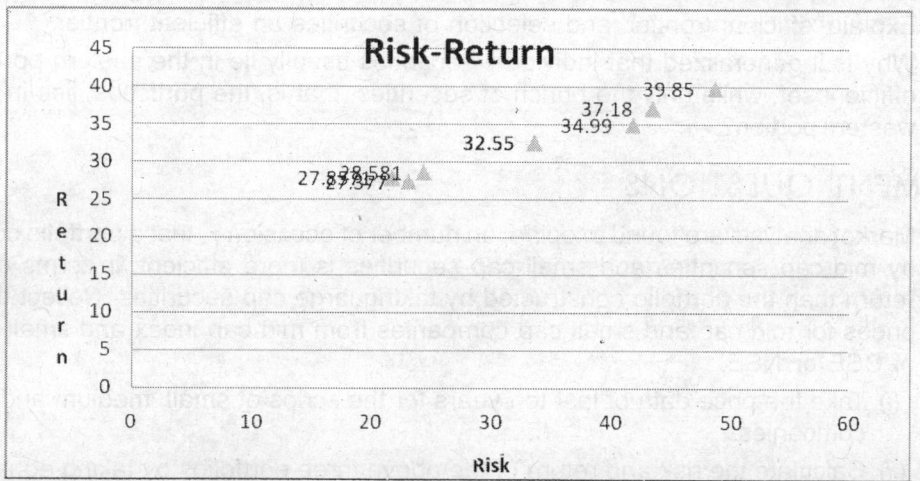

Figure 20.5: Risk and return of Markowitz portfolio as per the E-I-C analysis

> **Pause for thought:** Portfolios comprised of scrips with low beta are more efficient and form optimal portfolios with higher returns, with lesser risk.

SUMMARY

- Markowitz was the first to recognize that diversification reduces unsystematic risk of the portfolio.
- Investors can construct the portfolios with the various securities that are available. However, all of them do not result in a comparatively low risk and high return portfolio. The return-risk relationship depends on the correlation amongst the securities and on their proportion invested in a portfolio.
- Of the constructed portfolios, very few are attractive and efficient portfolios.
- Efficient portfolios are those which give highest returns for a given level of risk or they involve lesser risk for the given return.
- Efficient portfolios form the efficient frontier.
- The portfolios lying on the 'north-western' region of efficient frontier are preferred to the portfolios lying on 'south-eastern' region. These are called the optimal portfolios.

KEY CONCEPTS

Modern Portfolio Theory	North-Western Region	Average Covariance
Markowitz Optimization Model	South-Eastern Region	Beta
Efficient Portfolio	Active Portfolio Set	Scrip
Efficient Frontier	Passive Portfolio Set	CAL
Diversification	Portfolio Variance	

REVIEW QUESTIONS

1. Explain Markowitz diversification with the help of the algorithm developed by him.
2. Explain 'efficient frontier' and selection of securities on efficient frontier.
3. Why is it generalized that individual securities usually lie in the eastern portion of the efficient set, while only the bunch of securities, that is, the portfolios, lies in the north-western portion?

ASSIGNMENT QUESTIONS

1. Market analysts are found to opine, on number of occasions, that a portfolio constructed by mid cap securities and small cap securities is more efficient, in terms of risk and return than the portfolio constructed by taking large cap securities. Collect the data of prices for mid cap and small cap companies from mid cap index and small cap index of BSE or NSE.
   (i) Take the price data of last ten years for the scrips of small, medium and large cap companies.
   (ii) Calculate the risk and return of the above three portfolios by taking equal weights.
   (iii) Construct the two separate portfolios consisting of mid cap and small cap companies and compare this with the portfolio constructed of large scale company.
2. Construct the portfolio of small, medium and large cap companies separately as discussed in assignment question 1. Calculate the portfolio beta of all three portfolios.
3. Plot on the graph the results of these three portfolios, of assignment question 1, by taking risk on the x-axis and return on the y-axis. Show where the optimal portfolio lies.

PROBLEMS

Q.1 The Shah Brothers has come to you for evaluation of their current investment portfolio and for suggestions on the changes required. The Shahs have invested 100% in portfolio D. The Shahs are comfortable to bear more risks in lieu of higher returns. But, still, they have targeted an expected return of 15% and prefer to minimize the risk associated with that level of return. Statistics of return and risk for the Shahs' portfolio are shown below. (Only one among them is a risk-free security, while the others are all risky stocks).

Portfolio	Expected return (%)	Standard deviation (%)
A	28	23
B	18	16
C	27	22
D	13	17
E	17	16
F	8	0
G	7	12
I	19	10
J	14	8

K	4	4
L	24	19
M	16	18
N	11	12
O	12	16
P	15	19
Q	23	22
R	25	29
S	14	14

(i) Plot the portfolio on a graph in excel sheet with return on the vertical (y) axis and standard deviation on the horizontal (x) axis. Draw the efficient frontier. Which of these are not efficient?

(ii) Calculate the extra return that the Shahs can earn without altering their risk level? Plot this portfolio as new portfolio (NP) on the graph.

(iii) How low could the Shahs reduce their risk without reducing their current level of expected return? Plot this portfolio as NP1 on the graph.

(iv) Construct a mixed portfolio with risk-free securities and risky securities which can produce the desired level of expected return sought by the Shahs.

(v) Draw the capital market line

(vi) Identify the market portfolio.

Q.2 Complete the table, filling up the missing values, by taking the data of last five years.

Security	Expected return	Standard deviation	Correlation with market portfolio	Beta
ACC				
Ambuja Cement				
Axis Bank				
Bharti Airtel				
BHEL				
Market portfolio				
Risk-free asset				

CASE STUDY

Mr. Vidish Malhotra recently completed his MBA. He and his classmate, Mr. Nishit Reddy, both were employed in the FMCG sector. Both were earning handsomely and were single, with no other responsibilities. At the end of the first year, as they planned their finances they realized that it was high time for them to choose the right stock(s). But as both of them were not aware of how the stock market functions they felt that they might have missed the opportunity. They were 22 years of age and thought they could take risks. They had enough fund and wished to invest it judiciously rather than keeping it idle in a bank. Moreover, they were not happy with the performance of the instrument they had selected last year, as a tax saving investment. They approached an agent, who dealt with mutual funds. He advised them to go for either MIP or SIP, as a mode of regular investment. However, both of them were not happy with the fact sheet of different schemes. They found charges to be too high and felt it would be better to invest on their own, instead of investing in any of these schemes. They had read a lot about Warren Buffet. Inspired by him they were eager to invest in the market and opted for long-term investments. They approached one of their alumni, Mr. Devershi Gupta, on this matter. Mr. Gupta worked with the investment sector and had a very good knowledge of the market. Mr.Gupta explained to them the two ways to investing: (i) active and (ii) passive. He told that the former method requires the investor to thoroughly analyze the market fundamentals (industry structure and company analysis). Subsequent to that the scrips were to be selected on the basis of their past performance and expected returns. In this way the portfolio could be constructed and be re-structured when fundamentals of the market underwent change(s). The second method, the passive method, does not require the investors to carry out any analysis of market, industry and company. Only those scrips, which were in the popular indices like Nifty, Sensex, Dollex, Nifty 500, BSE 200, etc., had to be selected. As experienced and thus believed, best scrips selected from the indices is always a better method to construct the portfolio. Mr. Malhotra and Mr. Reddy decided to opt for both modes, having mutually agreed that Mr. Malhotra would go for with the passive strategy while Mr. Reddy went with the active strategy. Initially, both of them wanted to invest a fund of Rs.1,00,000 individually. As an investment student, suppose they have approached you. Help them to construct the portfolio vide both the strategies. For that you are required to following these instructions:

For passive portfolio management

Select the index (either Sensex or Nifty) first. Then find out from their websites www.bseindia.com and www.nseindia.com, proportion of each security in the given indices, i.e., the weight of each security in Nifty 50 and 30 scrips in BSE Sensex. Invest in either Nifty or Sensex in the same proportion and watch their performance. Calculate the holding period returns of each security and weekly, monthly, quarterly, half-yearly and yearly returns of the portfolio.. Show your results to Mr. Malhotra and Mr. Reddy.

For active portfolio management

As a finance student, you are aware of the market. Study carefully the E-I-C factors for Mr. Malhotra and Reddy and pick up the right securities. You need to select the securities not only from indices, but even those which you find to have performed well in last five-ten years. Before including such securities watch their performance over the last five to ten years, by analyzing the individual security returns, financial performance, management of the company, their competence, number of projects they are currently dealing in, etc. You can pick up the stocks from mid cap and small cap segments of Nifty or BSE as well. After the elementary study, invest the given fund in selected securities and watch their performance. If you find any of them to be not performing well or the price of some securities fall, reconstruct your portfolio. Decide the weight of each security on the basis of the fundamentals of market security. Calculate the holding period return of each security and weekly, monthly, quarterly, half-yearly and yearly returns of the portfolio. Show your results to Mr. Malhotra and Mr. Reddy.

APPENDIX
Correlation of top 25 scrips of active portfolio set

Correl(Jindal, SAIL)	0.952366517	Correl(SAIL, Bharti Airtel)	0.478693
Correl(Jindal, Bharti Airtel)	0.702128882	Correl(SAIL, Spice Jet)	−0.11285
Correl(Jindal, Spice Jet)	0.166104747	Correl(SAIL, BHEL)	0.196071
Correl(Jindal, BHEL)	0.409999062	Correl(SAIL, Reliance Power)	0.995408
Correl(Jindal, Reliance Power)	0.971855688	Correl(SAIL, SBI)	0.87949
Correl(Jindal, SBI)	0.953589861	Correl(SAIL, HDFC)	0.725651
Correl(Jindal, HDFC)	0.863694053	Correl(SAIL, ACC)	0.227471
Correl(Jindal, ACC)	0.394184992	Correl(SAIL, NTPC)	0.898691
Correl(Jindal, NTPC)	0.987691043	Correl(SAIL, Tata Comm)	0.474514
Correl(Jindal, Tata Comm)	0.719912835	Correl(SAIL, SFC)	0.476353
Correl(Jindal, GSFC)	0.709330938	Correl(SAIL, ULTRATECH)	0.476353
Correl(Jindal, ULTRATECH)	0.407371716	Correl(SAIL, HERO HONDA)	−0.69219
Correl(Jindal, HERO HONDA)	−0.66706266	Correl(SAIL, Mahindra & Mahindra)	−0.607
Correl(Jindal, Mahindra & Mahindra)	−0.525469531		
Correl(Bharti Airtel, Spice Jet)	0.603917969	Correl(Spice Jet, BHEL)	0.698601009
Correl(Bharti Airtel, BHEL)	0.85710942	Correl(Spice Jet, Reliance Power)	−0.047321171
Correl(Bharti Airtel, Reliance Power)	0.525017302	Correl(Spice Jet, SBI)	0.249263905
Correl(Bharti Airtel, SBI)	0.813332497	Correl(Spice Jet, HDFC)	0.443111478
Correl(Bharti Airtel, HDFC)	0.91785832	Correl(Spice Jet, ACC)	0.489855615
Correl(Bharti Airtel, ACC)	0.821598132	Correl(Spice Jet, NTPC)	0.255862865
Correl(Bharti Airtel, NTPC)	0.796834857	Correl(Spice Jet, Tata Comm)	0.722330814
Correl(Bharti Airtel, Tata Comm)	0.953810771	Correl(Spice Jet, GSFC)	0.778578879
Correl(Bharti Airtel, GSFC)	0.933286565	Correl(Spice Jet, ULTRATECH)	0.167747044
Correl(Bharti Airtel, ULTRATECH)	0.697655599	Correl(Spice Jet, HERO HONDA)	0.322137125
Correl(Bharti Airtel, HERO HONDA)	−0.338777827	Correl(Spice Jet, Mahindra & Mahindra)	−0.045877976
Correl(Bharti Airtel, Mahindra & Mahindra)	−0.192452553		
Correl(BHEL, Reliance Power)	0.216495	Correl(Reliance Power, SBI)	0.889651206
Correl(BHEL, SBI)	0.634768	Correl(Reliance Power, HDFC)	0.745190686
Correl(BHEL, HDFC)	0.809792	Correl(Reliance Power, ACC)	0.230206811
Correl(BHEL, ACC)	0.963987	Correl(Reliance Power, NTPC)	0.928106849
Correl(BHEL, NTPC)	0.495479	Correl(Reliance Power, Tata Comm)	0.539272911
Correl(BHEL, Tata Comm)	0.757848	Correl(Reliance Power, GSFC)	0.527434154

Correl(BHEL, GSFC)	0.853995	Correl(Reliance Power, ULTRATECH)	0.307575764
Correl(BHEL, ULTRATECH)	0.822055	Correl(Reliance Power, HERO HONDA)	−0.717947221
Correl(BHEL, HERO HONDA)	0.167255	Correl(Reliance Power, Mahindra & Mahindra)	−0.558728252
Correl(BHEL, Mahindra & Mahindra)	−0.37427		

Correl(SBI, HDFC)	0.965295	Correl(HDFC, ACC)	0.797656
Correl(SBI, ACC)	0.644073	Correl(HDFC, NTPC)	0.902178
Correl(SBI, NTPC)	0.959645	Correl(HDFC, Tata Comm)	0.856375
Correl(SBI, Tata Comm)	0.762693	Correl(HDFC, GSFC)	0.900514
Correl(SBI, GSFC)	0.794413	Correl(HDFC, ULTRATECH)	0.747632
Correl(SBI, ULTRATECH)	0.654778	Correl(HDFC, HERO HONDA)	−0.35175
Correl(SBI, HERO HONDA)	−0.50525	Correl(HDFC, Mahindra & Mahindra)	−0.54429
Correl(SBI, Mahindra & Mahindra)	−0.60817		

Correl(ACC, NTPC)	0.473804	Correl(NTPC, Tata Comm)	0.80924
Correl(ACC, Tata Comm)	0.651758	Correl(NTPC, GSFC)	0.781038
Correl(ACC, GSFC)	0.73937	Correl(NTPC, ULTRATECH)	0.457906
Correl(ACC, ULTRATECH)	0.940841	Correl(NTPC, HEROHONDA)	−0.67014
Correl(ACC, HERO HONDA)	0.09815	Correl(NTPC, Mahindra & Mahindra)	−0.43561
Correl(ACC, Mahindra & Mahindra)	−0.3807		

Correl(TATA Comm, GSFC)	0.964906724	Correl(GSFC, ULTRATECH)	0.546638657
Correl(TATA Comm, ULTRATECH)	0.463156889	Correl(GSFC, HERO HONDA)	−0.166669798
Correl(TATA Comm, HERO HONDA)	−0.354793118	Correl(GSFC, Mahindra & Mahindra)	−0.347409001
Correl(TATA Comm, Mahindra & Mahindra)	−0.136301138		

Correl(Ultratech, HERO HONDA)	−0.017449824	Correl(HERO HONDA, Mahindra & Mahindra)	−0.140940423
Correl(Ultratech, Mahindra & Mahindra)	−0.449132827		

Suggested Further Reading for Empirical Work

1. Sharpe, W.F. (1963), "A Simplified Model for Portfolio Analysis", *Management Science*, Vol. 9, No. 2.
2. Cheng, P.L. (1971), "Efficient Portfolio Selections Beyond the Markowitz Frontier", *The Journal of Financial and Quantitative Analysis*, Vol. 6, No. 5.
4. Jobson, J. D., and Korkie, B. (1980), "Estimation for Markowitz Efficient Portfolios", *Journal of the American Statistical Association*, Vol. 75, No. 371.
5. Rubinstein, M. (2002), "Markowitz's "Portfolio Selection": A Fifty-Year Retrospective", *The Journal of Finance*, Vol. 57, No. 3.

6. Markowitz, H.M. (1976), "Markowitz Revisited", *Financial Analysts Journal*, Vol. 32, No. 5.
7. Steinbach, M.C. (2001), "Markowitz Revisited: Mean-Variance Models in Financial Portfolio Analysis", *SIAM Review*, Vol. 43, No. 1.
8. Konno, H., and Yamazaki, H. (1991), "Mean-Absolute Deviation Portfolio Optimization Model and Its Applications to Tokyo Stock Market", *Management Science*, Vol. 37, No. 5.
9. Blog, B., Hoek, G., Kan, R., and Timmer, G. T. (1983), "The Optimal Selection of Small Portfolios", *Management Science*, Vol. 29, No. 7.
10. Draviam, T., and Chellathurai, T. (2002), "Generalized Markowitz Mean-Variance Principles for Multi-Period Portfolio-Selection Problems", *Proceedings: Mathematical, Physical and Engineering Sciences*, Vol. 458, No. 2027.
11. Michaud, R.O. (1989), "The Markowitz Optimization Enigma: Is 'Optimized' Optimal?", *Financial Analysts Journal*, Vol. 45, No. 1.

21
SHARPE'S SINGLE INDEX MODEL

LEARNING OBJECTIVES

The purpose of this chapter is to enable you to understand:

- How is the return of a security related to the index return.
- How beta measures the systematic risk.
- The calculation of systematic and unsystematic risks using Sharpe's model. The flexibility of Sharpe's model, in terms of the input data, compared to the Markowitz model.
- The flexibility of Sharpe's model, in terms of the input data, compared to the Markowitz model.

21.1 INTRODUCTION

In the preceding chapters various tools and techniques have been introduced and discussed to identify an optimal portfolio. But the optimal portfolios have been shown to be constructed of securities, when a large number of these were available to choose from. The foundation of modern portfolio theory was laid by Markowitz in 1951. In 1964, William F. Sharpe extended upon the work of Markowitz. Sharpe worked with Linter (1965) and Mossin (1966); and shared the Nobel Prize with Markowitz and Miller in 1990, for his contribution to the capital asset pricing model (CAPM). While Markowitz was awarded the Nobel Prize for proving that diversification leads to reduction in the portfolio risk.

We have already seen how on applying Markowitz portfolio theory led to a curved efficient set. To it when was added lending or borrowing at the risk-free rate, the tangency portfolio on the linear efficient set too was identified. But then it is seldom that a theory is free from any limitations. The same applies to Markowitz model, which has two major limitations:

— It involves huge number of estimates, for: return, variance and covariance.
— It does not provide any guideline for predicting the risk-premium of a security, which is essential for constructing the efficient frontier of risky assets.

As per the Markowitz model, in order to construct the portfolio of 20 stocks (already discussed in the previous chapter, it is being reiterated for easy recollection) we need to calculate:

$n = 20$ estimates of expected return.

$n = 20$ estimates of variances.

$(n^2 - n)/2 = 190$ estimates of covariance.

Thus a total of 230 estimates are required for the purpose. This in itself is a huge number, for the purpose of estimation. And to think of the fact that a portfolio of 20 securities is quite small! For a portfolio of 50 securities we need a total 1325 estimates; and for portfolio of 100 securities it is 5150 estimates that are needed. These calculations, given their girth are enough to cause repulsion.

In this chapter we shall be moving further from the curved efficient set of Markowitz model, towards processes of portfolio construction by using Sharpe's Model.

21.2 SHARPE'S SINGLE INDEX MODEL

The basic intention of investors is to earn more, at the cost of least risk. But we have already seen how the earlier investment decisions used to be based merely on return and how the paradigm of decision was changed by Markowitz. At the same time the limitations inherent in Markowitz model too have been mentioned above. The excessive data required for estimates, leading to a huge number of estimates, $n(n + 3)/2$, required a remedy. And it this remedy that William Sharpe has provided.

Sharpe's model simplifies the construct of Markowitz model by considering only a single index for analyzing the performance of a portfolio. The model assumes that the return on a security is linearly related to a single index. As the Sharpe's model links the return to a single index it also breaks up the risk of each security into two parts:

— The market related risk (also called systematic risk), which cannot be diversified away. That is, diversification cannot reduce systematic risk. Systematic risk is measured by the beta coefficient.

— The unsystematic risk which can be eliminated via diversification, and thus is also termed diversifiable risk.

The single index model provides an alternative expression for portfolio variance, which is easier to calculate than that provided by the Markowitz analysis.[1] As per the definition of market index, it should consist of all securities that are financially traded in the market. It is practically difficult to construct a portfolio containing all such securities. So, a broad based market index, like Nifty 50, BSE 100, BSE 500, BSE Sensex, Bankex, etc., is used as a proxy for this purpose. A portfolio of 250 securities would require: 250 estimates of beta, 250 estimates of residual variance and one estimate of the variance of the market portfolio. Sharpe's model thus needs $(3n + 2)$ estimates (bits of information), as compared to the $[n(n + 3)/2]$ estimates required by Markowitz model.

The single index model can be expressed by the following equation:

$$R_i = \alpha_i + \beta_i R_m + e_i$$

---

[1] W. Sharpe, "A Simplified model for portfolio analysis", Management Science (January 1963): 277-293.

where,

R_i = expected return on security i.

α_i = that part of the return on a security, i, which is independent of market performance (intercept of the straight line or alpha coefficient).

β_i = a constant, measures the expected change in the dependent variable, R_i, for a given change in the independent variable, R_m (slope of the straight line or beta coefficient).

R_m = return on the market index.

e_i = random residual error.

The single index model resolves the return of a security into two components:

— Market independent component, α_i, a unique feature.
— Market dependent component, $\beta_i R_m$.

The unique feature that α_i is, is actually a microeconomic factor. It affects a single company and not all companies or the market in general. This effect is explained by the factors that are company specific, like R&D, invention of new design(s), drug or product, labor and management problems, etc.

The market dependent part is a macroeconomic factor and is represented by $\beta_i R_m$. It affects all the companies as it affects the entire economy. Some of the examples of such factors are: changes in monetary policies, industrial policies, fiscal policies; country specific recession or global recession, etc. β_i measures the sensitivity of the return with respect to the market. If beta of the security is greater than 1, the return on the security is expected to increase by more than 1% when market return increases by 1% and vice versa. Similarly, beta less than 1, leads to a less than 1% change in the return, when market return changes by 1%. Beta equal to 1 indicates that return on the security and market return move in tandem. Given these values, the error term (e_i) is the difference between the return on security 'i' and the sum of the two components of the return. Because by definition, the single index model, equality, the two sides must be the same.

> **Pause for thought:** The model assumes that the return of a security is linearly related to a single index.

The basic constructs on which Sharpe's model functions and the limitations experienced by this model are summarized as follows.

Assumptions

Sharpe's single index model is based on the simplified (with respect to Markowitz) assumptions, as follows:

— The key assumption of the single index model is that the stocks show covariance only because of their common relationship to the market index.
— No fundamental effect can cause the simultaneous movements of stocks.
— The expected return, standard deviation and covariance of the single index model represent the joint movement of securities.

Limitations

— It is difficult to accept that the model depends only on such simple assumptions.
— It has been criticized for assuming that stock prices move together because of common relationship to market index. Many researchers have observed that there are other influences, beyond the market; such as industry related factors, sensitivity of the company to some particular macroeconomic factor, etc.

Leaving aside the criticisms, that are faced by all theories, and from which something better always develops, we proceed to take note of the calculations and derivations involved in the single index model. At least this much is a fact that it has taken care of the limitations of Markowitz model. Isn't it?

Derivations

The mean return is, $R_i = \alpha_i + \beta_i R_m + e_i$

The variance of the return, $\sigma^2 = \beta_i^2 \sigma_m^2 + \sigma^2 e_i$

The variance, σ^2, represents two types of risks: systematic (or market risk) and unsystematic risk (or unique risk).

The variance, when multiplied by the beta of the security, represents the systematic risk.

Systematic risk = $\beta_i^2 \sigma_m^2$

The other unexplained part of the risk is called the unsystematic risk.

Unsystematic Risk = Total risk − Systematic risk

$\sigma^2 e_i$ = Total risk − Systematic risk

$= \sigma_i^2 - \beta_i^2 \sigma_m^2$

So, Total risk = Systematic risk + Unsystematic risk

$= \beta_i^2 \sigma_m^2 + \sigma^2 e_i$

The market risk accounts for that part of the variance that cannot be diversified away. This is evidenced when the security responds to the fluctuations in the market. The second term is the security's unsystematic risk (also called the residual variance). It accounts for that part of the variability occurring due to deviations from the fitted relationship between security return and market return.

The covariance of return, between securities, 'i' and 'j', is given by

$\sigma_{ij} = \beta_i \beta_j \sigma_m^2$

Similarly, the variance of the portfolio is calculated as:

Total portfolio variance = Portfolio market risk
                        + Portfolio unsystematic risk (residual variance)

$\sigma_p^2 = \beta_p^2 \sigma_m^2 + \sigma^2 e_p$

where, β_p = beta of a portfolio and it can be calculated as,

$$\beta_p = \sum_{i=1}^{n} x_i \times \beta_i$$

$\sigma^2 e_p$ is called unsystematic risk of the portfolio and it can be calculated as,

$$\sigma^2 e_p = \sum_{i=1}^{n} x_i^2 \times \sigma^2 e_i$$

σ_p^2 = variance of the portfolio.

σ_m^2 = variance of market.

$\sigma^2 e_i$ = variation in return of the security, which is not related to the market.

x_i = proportion (weight) of the security, 'i', in the portfolio.

Beta of a portfolio is a measure of the volatility or systematic risk of portfolio, as compared to the market as a whole. It is the weighted average of the beta values of its component securities, determined by using their respective weights in the portfolio.

> **Pause for thought:** Beta of a portfolio (β_p) measures the systematic risk of the portfolio, with respect to the market as a whole.

The expected return of a portfolio can be estimated by calculating α_i and β_i.

Hence, $$R_p = \sum_{i=1}^{n} x_i(\alpha_i + \beta_i R_m)$$

It is the weighted average return of the portfolio determined by estimating the return of each security in the portfolio and multiplying with the weights equivalent to the proportion of the respective security in the portfolio.

Alpha of a portfolio (α_p)

$$\alpha_p = \sum_{i=1}^{n} x_i \times \alpha_i$$

where,

n = number of securities in the portfolio.

α_i = value of alpha for security, i.

x_i = proportion of investment in security, i.

α_p = value of the alpha for the portfolio.

Alpha is a measure of performance on a risk-adjusted basis. Alpha considers the volatility (price risk) of the portfolio or a mutual fund and compares its risk-adjusted performance with a benchmark index. The excess return of the fund, relative to the return of the benchmark index, is the alpha[2] of the fund.

---

[2] Investopedia dictionary

> **Pause for thought:** Alpha measures the performance of a portfolio on a risk-adjusted basis.

21.2.1 Components of Risk: Systematic Risk and Unsystematic Risk

We have already discussed at length on these two variants of risk, in Chapter 6, Beta and Risk Estimation. So, instead of getting into those details again, we head straightway to the application of the same, represented by an example. That will enhance our understanding of the risk components of a security.

Table 21.1: Risk-return and Beta of Market Index, SBI and Maruti

	Average return	Standard deviation	Beta
SBI	37.39	24.84	0.2521
Maruti	30.15	26.71	0.4252
Market index (Nifty)	28.63	39.52	1
Correlation coefficient between SBI and Maruti	0.334		
r^2	0.11		

Systematic risk of SBI,

$$\beta_i^2 \sigma_m^2 = (0.2521)^2 \times (39.52)^2$$
$$= 99.311$$

Unsystematic risk of SBI,

$$\sigma^2 e_i = \sigma_i^2 - \beta_i^2 \sigma_m^2$$
$$= (24.84)^2 - 99.311$$
$$= 617.02 - 99.311$$
$$= 517.70$$

Therefore, total risk = 99.311 + 517.70 = 617.01

The contributions of the respective components of risk, to the total risk of the security, are very much evident, thus.

Similarly,

Systematic risk of Maruti, $\beta_i^2 \sigma_m^2 = (0.4251)^2 \times (39.52)^2$
$$= 282.38$$

Unsystematic risk of Maruti, $\sigma^2 e_i = \sigma_i^2 - \beta_i^2 \sigma_m^2$
$$= (26.71)^2 - 282.38$$
$$= 713.42 - 282.38$$
$$= 431.04$$

Hence, total risk = 282.38 + 431.04 = 713.42

The composition of the total risk is made clear thus, for the stock of Maruti.

> **Pause for thought:** The ratio of systematic to unsystematic risk varies for different securities.

21.2.2 Sharpe's Optimal Portfolio

In contrast to the Markowitz optimal portfolio, Sharpe's optimal portfolio is based on a ratio called Sharpe's ratio, which measures risk-adjusted performance. The Sharpe ratio is calculated by subtracting the risk-free rate (such as that of the 10-year U.S. Treasury bond) from the rate of return for a portfolio and dividing the result by the standard deviation of the portfolio returns.

The formula for Sharpe's ratio

$$= \frac{\bar{r}_p - r_f}{\sigma_p}$$

where

$\bar{r}_p$ = Expected portfolio return

r_f = Risk free rate

σ_p = Portfolio standard deviation

Sharpe's ratio tells us whether a portfolio's returns are due to smart investment decisions or a result of excess risk. This measurement is very useful because although higher returns are always preferred, but it is to be considered a good investment only if it does not involve too much additional risk. The greater a portfolio's Sharpe's ratio, the better its risk-adjusted performance is. A negative Sharpe's ratio indicates that a risk-less asset would perform better than the security being analyzed.

> **Pause for thought:** Sharpe's optimal portfolio is decided by Sharpe's ratio, which measures risk-adjusted performance. The ratio and the performance share direct variation, while a negative value indicates that a risk-less security would perform better than the one being analyzed.

21.2.3 Construction of Sharpe's Optimal Portfolio

Now that we know what is meant by Sharpe's optimal portfolio and Sharpe's ratio, we need to know how to construct the portfolio. The construction of the portfolio involves the following steps.

1. Ratio of excess return to systematic risk (β)

The first step in selecting any security in a portfolio depends upon the ratio of excess return to beta (β). The excess return on the security is the difference between the expected return and the return at risk-free rate (risk-free rate of return is provided by government on securities like RBI bonds, T-Bills, etc.). The ratio measures the excess return earned by the security over the risk-free rate, per unit of the systematic risk. It is also known as return-to-risk ratio. Portfolio managers prefer to include such securities which record higher ratio of excess return to beta.

This ratio is expressed as: $\dfrac{R_i - R_f}{\beta}$

where,

R_i = expected return of stock, i.

R_f = risk-free rate of return.

β = beta (systematic risk) of stock, i.

2. After calculating the excess return-to-beta (risk) ratio, securities are ranked in descending order of their excess return-to-risk ratio.

3. After the securities have been ranked, the different components of C_i are calculated. C_i is formulated as:

$$C_i = \frac{\sigma_m^2 \frac{\Sigma(R_i - R_f)\beta_i}{\sigma^2 e_i}}{1 + \sigma_m^2 \sum_{i=1}^{N} \frac{\beta_1^2}{\sigma^2 e_i}}$$

where,

σ_m^2 = variance in the market.

$\sigma^2 e_i$ = variance of a security's movement that is not associated with the movement of the market index (the unsystematic risk of the security).

The components of C_i have to be calculated as:

(a) The first component of C_i is calculated. It is the difference of required rate of return and the risk-free rate, multiplied by the beta of the respective security and divided by unsystematic risk:

$$\frac{(R_i - R_f)\beta_i}{\sigma^2 e_i}$$

(b) The cumulative value of step 3(a) is determined.

(c) The ratio of systematic risk to unsystematic risk, for each security, is calculated, using the term:

$$\frac{\beta_i^2}{\sigma^2 e_i}$$

(d) The cumulative value of the ratio, calculated in step 3(c), is ascertained.

4. All these calculated values are substituted in the formula of C_i. The initial values of C_i are found to fluctuate and subsequent to that it starts decreasing. The stage from where the fall begins is taken as the cut-off rate (C*). The securities above the cut-off point are selected. Once the cut-off rate is ascertained the investor knows how many securities are qualified for the optimum portfolio. Thus, Sharpe's optimum portfolio is constructed using these qualified securities.

5. Having determined the securities that qualify for the portfolio, the next task is to find out their respective proportion required. The formula used for the purpose is,

$$X_i = \frac{Z_i}{\Sigma Z_i}$$

where,

$$Z_i = \frac{\beta_i(R_i - R_f)}{\sigma^2 e_i \beta_i} - C^*$$

C^* = cut-off rate.

R_i = expected return of stock, *i*.

R_f = risk-free rate of return.

β_i = beta of stock, *i*.

$\sigma^2 e_i$ = unsystematic risk of stock, *i*.

Thus, the above expression determines the relative investment in each security.

6. As already stated, only those securities whose C_i value is greater than the C^* (cut-off rate) qualify for the optimal portfolio. The C_i values, which are greater than C^*, are effectively the values of the ratio of excess return-to-beta. The values lower than this are ignored. And it is these unique C_i values, higher than the cut-off, C^*, which are the values of the Sharpe's ratio— essential for securities to qualify for Sharpe's optimal portfolio.

Sharpe's ratio is also formulated as:

$$\text{Sharpe's ratio} = \frac{(R_i - R_f)}{\sigma_p}$$

where,

R_i = expected return of stock, *i*.

R_f = risk-free rate of return.

σ_p = standard deviation of the portfolio return.

This ratio provides a relationship between the potential risk and its reward. It measures the excess return on a security, per unit of a systematic risk.

> **Pause for thought:** Optimal portfolio is thus comprised of those securities whose excess return-to-risk ratio is above the cut-off rate. And this ratio is the Sharpe's ratio, prerequisite thus for the securities to qualify for Sharpe's optimal portfolio.

21.2.4 Sharpe's Optimal Portfolio: Illustration

An illustration, of the theoretical discussion that precedes, would be beneficial for the purpose of understanding. Hence, follows.

The return, unsystematic risk and beta of the securities, shown in the table below, is computed by taking the prices of the securities from 2001 to 2010. The risk-free rate, R_f, is assumed to be 8%. Standard deviation of the market, as calculated, is 39.53%, for the same time period.

Table 21.2

1	2 Name of the scrip	3 Return (R_i)	4 Beta (β)	5 Unsystematic risk ($\sigma^2 e_i$)	6 $R_i - R_f$	7 $(R_i - R_f)/\beta_i$
1	PNB	56.89	0.21	5883.98	48.89	231.65
2	JSWSTEEL	48.59	0.45	7969.77	40.59	90.63
3	AXIS BANK	57.71	0.56	2252.40	49.71	88.71
4	KOTAKBANK	45.34	0.46	5002.39	37.34	80.53
5	RELCAPITAL	52.51	0.60	6416.04	44.51	74.28
6	TATAMOTORS	43.66	0.49	2698.02	35.66	72.93
7	BHEL	43.61	0.50	1624.90	35.61	71.34
8	STER	118.02	2.13	27135.53	110.02	51.65
9	SAIL	69.28	1.24	7724.62	61.28	49.35
10	BHARTIARTL	46.60	1.34	1456.89	38.60	28.84

Column 6 shows the excess return the particular scrip has provided over risk-free rate, while column 7 shows the excess return-to-beta ratio. The risk-free rate of return, R_f, is 8%.

Table 21.3

$[(R_i - R_f) \times \beta]/\sigma^2 e_i$	$\beta_i^2/\sigma^2 e_i$	$\Sigma[(R_i - R_f) \times \beta]/\sigma^2 e_i$	$\Sigma \beta_i^2/\sigma^2 e_i$	$[(\sigma_m^2) \times \Sigma\{(R_i - R_f) \times \beta]/\sigma^2 e_i\}]$	$1+(\sigma_m^2) \times (\Sigma\beta_i^2/\sigma^2 e_i)$
8 [(6 × 4)/5]	9 [(4 × 4)/5]	10 (cumulative of column 8)	11 (cumulative of column 9)	12 (market variance × column 9)	13 (1+market variance × coulmn 11)
0.0017538	0.00000757	0.0017538	0.00000757	2.74	1.012
0.002281001	0.00002517	0.004034801	0.00003274	6.30	1.051
0.012367267	0.00013942	0.016402068	0.00017216	25.63	1.269
0.003460019	0.00004296	0.019862087	0.00021512	31.04	1.336
0.004156944	0.00005596	0.02401903	0.00027108	37.53	1.424
0.006463566	0.00008863	0.030482596	0.00035971	47.63	1.562
0.010938296	0.00015332	0.041420893	0.00051303	64.72	1.802
0.008636044	0.00016720	0.050056937	0.00068023	78.22	2.063
0.009850703	0.00019962	0.059907639	0.00087985	93.61	2.375
0.035470155	0.00123007	0.095377794	0.00210992	149.03	4.297

Column 8 shows the excess return multiplied by beta and the product divided by unsystematic risk; while column 9 shows the ratio of the beta squared, to unsystematic risk. Columns 12 and 13 show the values of the numerator and denominator respectively, for the calculation of C_i. Column 14, in the Table 21.4 below, shows the calculation of C_i, obtained by substituting the values of column 12 in the numerator and 13 in the denominator.

The value of C_i, in column 14, is calculated using the formula,

$$C_i = \frac{\sigma_m^2 \dfrac{\Sigma(R_i - R_f)\beta_i}{\sigma^2 e_i}}{1 + \sigma_m^2 \sum_{i=1}^{N} \dfrac{\beta_1^2}{\sigma^2 e_i}}$$

$$\therefore \; C_i = \frac{2.74}{1.012}$$

$$= 2.708$$

Likewise, it is calculated for other securities as well. Column 14 of the table below shows that the value of C_i is increasing; but after attaining a peak value of 39.418, the fall begins. The peak value is known as the cut-off rate, C^*. The table below shows, $C^* = 39.418$. Thus securities with Ci value higher than 39.418 are included in the portfolio; while those below, are excluded. The stocks ranked above C^* have high excess return-to-beta ratio, C_i, than the cut-off and all stocks ranked below C^* have low excess return-to-beta.

Table 21.4: Cut-off rate

C_i		Z_i	X_i	Return
14 (12/13)		15	16	17 (16 × 3)
2.708		0.001455	0.057693033	3.28
5.998		0.001289	0.051093214	2.48
20.196		0.006872	0.272410146	15.72
23.228		0.001767	0.070026967	3.17
26.364		0.001951	0.07733827	4.06
30.492		0.00297	0.117734195	5.14
35.924		0.004895	0.194043208	8.46
37.916		0.002045	0.081085503	9.57
39.418	C^*	0.001982	0.078575464	5.44
34.684				
		$\Sigma Z_i = 0.025226$	$\Sigma X_i = 1$	Return = 57.34%

Calculation of X_i has to be preceded by the evaluation of Z_i. Hence, column 15, in the above Table 21.4, records the proportion, Z_i, of each qualified security (those having scores above the cut-off rate).

$$Z_i = \frac{\beta_1(R_i - R_f)}{\sigma^2 e_i \beta_i} - C^*$$

After the value of Z_i has been derived X_i is computed, as shown in column 16.

$$X_i = \frac{Z_i}{\Sigma Z_i}$$

X_i for the first scrip $= \dfrac{0.001455}{0.025226} = 0.05767$

Column 16 shows the ratio of Z_i value for the respective security to summation of Z_i values. Column 15 shows the respective proportion (weight) of each security required for the construction of the portfolio. By multiplying the return (column 3) of the security with the respective weights (X_i: column 16), security's portfolio return is found out, and then summing up the return of all securities it turns out to be 57.34%.

21.2.5 Constructing an Optimal Portfolio by Sharpe's Index Model of Nifty 50

Now we proceed to put to test our understanding of the construction of Sharpe's optimal portfolio, by extending it to all the fifty scrips of Nifty 50. For the purpose, the average returns of all the scrips[3] are being considered here. Betas too, of all fifty scrips have been calculated (column 6). The first column shows the serial number of scrips, while columns 2 and 3 enlist the names and average returns of the securities respectively. Column 4 holds the risk-free rate, which is assumed to be 8%. Excess return of the security is the difference of the average return of respective securities and their risk-free rate of return (see column 5). Unsystematic risk, shown in column 7, is calculated by subtracting systematic risk from total risk (as shown on page 569, for SBI). Column 8 represents the ratio of column 5 to column 6, i.e., excess return-to-beta ratios.

Table 21.5: Average Return, Beta and Excess Return-to-Beta Ratios of all 50 Securities of Nifty 50

Sr. no.	Name of scrip	Average return (R_i)	Risk-free return (R_f)	Excess return ($R_i - R_f$)	Beta	Unsystematic risk	Excess return-to-beta ratio [($R_i - R_f$)/β_i]
1	2	3	4	5	6	7	8
1	STERLITE	118.02	8	110.02	2.13	27135.53	51.65
2	SAIL	69.28	8	61.28	1.24	7724.62	49.34
3	AXIS BANK	57.71	8	49.71	0.56	2252.41	88.77

[3] Here average return has been calculated by taking the data from 2002 to 2010. For new scrips, average returns have been calculated from the data available for the given year.

4	PNB	56.89	8	48.89	0.21	5883.98	231.71
5	REL CAPITAL	52.51	8	44.51	0.60	6416.04	74.31
6	JINDAL STEEL	48.59	8	40.59	0.45	7969.77	90.60
7	BHARTI AIRTEL	46.60	8	38.60	1.34	1456.89	28.81
8	KOTAK BANK	45.34	8	37.34	0.46	5002.39	81.17
9	TATA MOTORS	43.66	8	35.66	0.49	2698.02	72.92
10	BHEL	43.61	8	35.61	0.50	1624.90	71.36
11	UNITECH	38.70	8	30.70	0.01	8775.02	3449.33
12	SBIN	38.39	8	30.39	0.25	500.05	121.56
13	TATA POWER	37.64	8	29.64	0.36	1264.38	82.78
14	GAIL	36.22	8	28.22	0.46	1886.50	61.35
15	ONGC	35.78	8	27.78	0.25	1996.79	112.45
16	M&M	35.64	8	27.64	0.75	1912.71	37.10
17	SIEMENS	35.53	8	27.53	0.37	6006.72	75.01
18	ICICI BANK	33.44	8	25.44	0.41	1289.57	62.05
19	TATA STEEL	32.73	8	24.73	0.57	2384.28	43.39
20	L&T	32.54	8	24.54	0.08	3411.85	306.76
21	IDFC	31.82	8	23.82	0.27	3113.74	88.22
22	ABB	30.89	8	22.89	0.56	3207.82	40.88
23	HDFC BANK	30.74	8	22.74	0.21	547.29	108.29
24	MARUTI	30.16	8	22.16	0.43	412.70	52.13
25	ACC	29.73	8	21.73	0.31	1047.24	70.10
26	REL INFRA	29.33	8	21.33	0.24	2921.06	87.42
27	HERO HONDA	24.62	8	16.62	0.34	1166.76	49.46
28	JPASSOCIATE	23.85	8	15.85	0.75	4581.71	21.10
29	RELIANCE	21.74	8	13.74	0.35	1721.03	39.25
30	BPCL	21.24	8	13.24	0.11	398.83	120.36
31	NTPC	20.94	8	12.94	0.17	532.94	77.46
32	HDFC	18.32	8	10.32	0.17	872.56	60.00
33	CAIRN	17.30	8	9.30	−0.03	299.41	−269.45
34	SUN PHARMA	11.18	8	3.18	0.02	273.74	186.76
35	HCL TECH	9.96	8	1.96	0.37	1471.11	5.34
36	HINDUUNIVER	6.96	8	−1.04	−0.02	199.64	61.66

37	AMBUJA CEMENT	5.48	8	−2.52	0.07	1341.91	−34.52
38	RANBAXY	4.01	8	−3.99	−0.07	916.30	56.97
39	HINDALCO	2.45	8	−5.55	0.10	2657.27	−55.52
40	TCS	2.01	8	−5.99	0.07	1225.19	−86.87
41	INFOSYSTEM	−0.30	8	−8.30	0.22	802.94	−37.75
42	ITC	−0.71	8	−8.71	0.00	1195.31	33484.62
43	POWERGRID	−3.04	8	−11.04	0.02	84.15	−690.00
44	CIPLA	−5.90	8	−13.90	0.10	972.26	−141.98
45	WIPRO	−8.31	8	−16.31	0.30	520.24	−53.82
46	RCOM	−8.66	8	−16.66	0.08	2648.79	−208.19
47	SUZLON	−9.86	8	−17.86	−0.01	3297.64	1930.27
48	IDEA	−16.77	8	−24.77	−0.08	357.80	302.15
49	DLF	−21.35	8	−29.35	−0.27	−312.03	110.33
50	R POWER	−21.61	8	−29.61	−0.82	579.35	36.14

Once the excess return-to-beta ratio has been determined, the calculation of the cut-off rate is the next step. The formula for the cut-off rate is,

$$C_i = \frac{\sigma_m^2 \frac{\Sigma(R_i - R_f)\beta_i}{\sigma^2 e_i}}{1 + \sigma_m^2 \sum_{i=1}^{N} \frac{\beta_1^2}{\sigma^2 e_i}}$$

Securities with negative returns are now removed from the 50 securities enlisted in the table above and the following calculation is performed on the remaining 35 securities. In the Table 21.6 below, the cut-off rates are recorded by utilizing the different components as per the above equation. Calculation of the excess return-to-beta ratio enables the ranking of the securities in the descending order: from the highest to the lowest. In the following Table, 21.6, column 2 has UNITECH with highest excess return-to-beta ratio, followed by L&T and the others. Column 3 represents the ratio of, excess return multiplied by beta, to unsystematic risk. Column 4 records the cumulative values of column 3. Column 5 has squared beta values and column 6 is for the ratio of squared beta to unsystematic risk.

Table 21.6 has been generated by eliminating the negative return securities from Table 21.5 and subsequently finding out the cut-off point for all 35 positive return securities.

Table 21.6: Data of 35 Securities with Positive Returns, Ignoring the 15 Securities, With Negative Returns, of the Total of 50 Securities (Table 21.5) of Nifty 50

Sr. no.	Name of the scrip	$[(R_i - R_f) \times \beta_i]/\sigma^2 e_i$	Cumulative of column (3)	σ_i^2	$\beta_i^2/\sigma^2 e_i$
1	2	3	4	5	6
1	UNITECH	0.0000311	0.0000311	0.0001	0.00000001
2	L&T	0.0005754	0.0006066	0.0064	0.00000188
3	PNB	0.0017532	0.0023598	0.0445	0.00000757
4	SUN PHARMA	0.0001972	0.0025569	0.0003	0.00000106
5	SBIN	0.0151935	0.0177505	0.0625	0.00012499
6	BPCL	0.0036517	0.0214022	0.0121	0.00003034
7	ONGC	0.0034357	0.0248379	0.0610	0.00003055
8	HDFC BANK	0.0087255	0.0335634	0.0441	0.00008058
9	JINDAL STEEL	0.0022817	0.0358450	0.2007	0.00002518
10	AXIS BANK	0.0123591	0.0482041	0.3136	0.00013923
11	IDFC	0.0020655	0.0502696	0.0729	0.00002341
12	REL INFRA	0.0017817	0.0520513	0.0595	0.00002038
13	TATA POWER	0.0083912	0.0604425	0.1282	0.00010136
14	KOTAK BANK	0.0034336	0.0638761	0.2116	0.00004230
15	NTPC	0.0040536	0.0679297	0.0279	0.00005233
16	SIEMENS	0.0016820	0.0696117	0.1347	0.00002242
17	REL CAPITAL	0.0041554	0.0737671	0.3588	0.00005592
18	TATA MOTORS	0.0064632	0.0802303	0.2391	0.00008863
19	BHEL	0.0109357	0.0911660	0.2490	0.00015324
20	ACC	0.0064324	0.0975984	0.0961	0.00009176
21	ICICI BANK	0.0080883	0.1056867	0.1001	0.00013035
22	GAIL	0.0068811	0.1125678	0.2116	0.00011217
23	HDFC	0.0020343	0.1146021	0.0296	0.00003390
24	MARUTI	0.0228162	0.1374183	0.1806	0.00043766
25	STERLITE	0.0086359	0.1460542	4.5369	0.00016719
26	HERO HONDA	0.0047862	0.1508404	0.1129	0.00009676
27	SAIL	0.0098526	0.1606929	1.5426	0.00019969
28	TATA STEEL	0.0059121	0.1666050	0.3249	0.00013627

29	ABB	0.0039960	0.1706010	0.3136	0.00009776
30	RELIANCE	0.0027941	0.1733951	0.1225	0.00007118
31	M&M	0.0107658	0.1841609	0.5550	0.00029018
32	BHARTI AIRTEL	0.0355030	0.2196639	1.7956	0.00123249
33	JPASSOCIATE	0.0025974	0.2222613	0.5640	0.00012310
34	HCL TECH	0.0004864	0.2227476	0.1340	0.00009106
35	CAIRN	−0.0010711	0.2216765	0.0012	0.00000398

In the Table 21.7 below, column 9 shows the cumulative value of column 6, which is in fact the cumulative of the ratio of squared beta to unsystematic risk. Column 10 is for the variance of the market; here variance has been calculated by considering all the 50 scrips of Nifty. The product of column 4 and Nifty variance are shown in column 11. Column 12 is the sum of 1 and product of Nifty variance and column 9. The last column, 13, shows the cut-off point. The highest C_i value is the cut-off point, which is 57.029 in this case, and thus the C*. From column 13 it is evident that cut-off point, C_i, for respective securities, starting from UNITECH increases till the 23rd security, HDFC. After that the cut-off rate, C_i, slides. So, a total of 23 securities are selected, marked in red. Actually there is no need to calculate C_i value once C* has been found out. The stocks ranked above C* have high, excess return-to-beta ratio, than the cut-off, C_i, and all those ranked below C* have low, excess return-to-beta ratio.

Table 21.7: Continuation of Table 21.6

Sr. no.	Name of the scrip	Cumulative of column (6)	Nifty variance × column (4)	Nifty variance	1+ [(Nifty variance] × column (9)	Cut-off point
7	8	9	10	11	12	13
1	UNITECH	0.00000001	1562.57	0.05	1.000	0.049
2	L&T	0.00000188	1562.57	0.95	1.003	0.945
3	PNB	0.00000945	1562.57	3.69	1.015	3.634
4	SUN PHARMA	0.00001051	1562.57	4.00	1.016	3.931
5	SBIN	0.00013549	1562.57	27.74	1.212	22.890
6	BPCL	0.00016583	1562.57	33.44	1.259	26.560
7	ONGC	0.00019639	1562.57	38.81	1.307	29.698
8	HDFC BANK	0.00027697	1562.57	52.45	1.433	36.604
9	JINDAL STEEL	0.00030215	1562.57	56.01	1.472	38.047
10	AXIS BANK	0.00044138	1562.57	75.32	1.690	44.578
11	IDFC	0.00046479	1562.57	78.55	1.726	45.503
12	REL INFRA	0.00048517	1562.57	81.33	1.758	46.262

13	TATA POWER	0.00058654	1562.57	94.45	1.917	49.280
14	KOTAK BANK	0.00062884	1562.57	99.81	1.983	50.343
15	NTPC	0.00068117	1562.57	106.15	2.064	51.418
16	SIEMENS	0.00070359	1562.57	108.77	2.099	51.811
17	REL CAPITAL	0.00075951	1562.57	115.27	2.187	52.710
18	TATA MOTORS	0.00084814	1562.57	125.37	2.325	53.914
19	BHEL	0.00100138	1562.57	142.45	2.565	55.543
20	ACC	0.00109315	1562.57	152.50	2.708	56.314
21	ICICI BANK	0.00122350	1562.57	165.14	2.912	56.715
22	GAIL	0.00133567	1562.57	175.90	3.087	56.978
23	HDFC	0.00136957	1562.57	179.07	3.140	57.029
24	MARUTI	0.00180723	1562.57	214.73	3.824	56.153
25	STERLITE	0.00197443	1562.57	228.22	4.085	55.865
26	HERO HONDA	0.00207119	1562.57	235.70	4.236	55.637
27	SAIL	0.00227088	1562.57	251.09	4.548	55.205
28	TATA STEEL	0.00240715	1562.57	260.33	4.761	54.676
29	ABB	0.00250491	1562.57	266.58	4.914	54.247
30	RELIANCE	0.00257609	1562.57	270.94	5.025	53.915
31	M&M	0.00286627	1562.57	287.76	5.479	52.524
32	BHARTI AIRTEL	0.00409876	1562.57	343.24	7.405	46.355
33	JPASSOCIATE	0.00422186	1562.57	347.30	7.597	45.716
34	HCL TECH	0.00431291	1562.57	348.06	7.739	44.973
35	CAIRN	0.00431689	1562.57	346.39	7.745	44.721

Having determined the 23 securities that qualify for the optimum portfolio, the next task is to find out the corresponding weight of each security, for construction of the optimum portfolio. The proportion of funds to be invested in each security is estimated by the following equation:

$$X_i = \frac{Z_i}{\Sigma Z_i}$$

where,

$$Z_i = \frac{\beta_1 (R_i - R_f)}{\sigma^2 e_i \beta_i} - C^*$$

The Z_i value for UNITECH:

Z_i = 0.0000010 × (3449.33 − 57.029)
    = 0.003393 = 0.0035

The ratio of beta to unsystematic risk is taken from column 3 (the third row, Table 21.8), excess return-to-beta ratio is taken from column 4 (the same third row, Table 21.8) and cut-off point, C* = 57.029, has been derived from Table 21.6.

Once the Z_i value is calculated, X_i, the proportion to be invested in each security, is determined. For that, summation of Z_i values, for each security, is found out and in this case it is 0.2038. The value of X_i for UNITECH:

$$X_i = \frac{Z_i}{\Sigma Z_i}$$

$$= \frac{0.0035}{0.2038}$$

$$= 0.01717 = 0.0172$$

Similarly, the Z_i and X_i values are calculated for other securities as well. As per the results of these calculations, maximum is invested in the security of State Bank of India and the minimum in that of HDFC.

Table 21.8: Calculation of Z_i and X_i Values of the Top 23 Securities

Sr. no.	Name of the scrip	Beta-to-unsystematic ratio	Excess return-to-beta ratio	Z	X	Individual return	Proportion return
1	2	3	4	5	6	7	8
1	UNITECH	0.0000010	3449.33	0.0035	0.0172	38.699	0.6641
2	L&T	0.0000234	306.76	0.0072	0.0352	32.541	1.1445
3	PNB	0.0000359	231.71	0.0082	0.0401	56.89	2.2822
4	SUN PHARMA	0.0000621	186.76	0.0114	0.0557	11.175	0.6224
5	SBIN	0.0005000	121.56	0.0493	0.2420	38.39	9.2890
6	BPCL	0.0002758	120.36	0.0259	0.1269	21.24	2.6954
7	ONGC	0.0001237	112.45	0.0102	0.0502	35.775	1.7962
8	HDFC BANK	0.0003837	108.29	0.0275	0.1349	30.74	4.1472
9	JINDAL STEEL	0.0000562	90.60	0.0030	0.0145	48.59	0.7041
10	AXIS BANK	0.0002486	88.77	0.0110	0.0539	57.71	3.1100
11	IDFC	0.0000867	88.22	0.0037	0.0182	31.82	0.5782
12	REL INFRA	0.0000835	87.42	0.0034	0.0169	29.33	0.4946
13	TATA POWER	0.0002831	82.78	0.0095	0.0465	37.636	1.7511

14	KOTAK BANK	0.0000920	81.17	0.0028	0.0139	45.34	0.6305
15	NTPC	0.0003134	77.46	0.0082	0.0400	20.936	0.8380
16	SIEMENS	0.0000611	75.01	0.0014	0.0070	35.529	0.2470
17	REL CAPITAL	0.0000934	74.31	0.0020	0.0099	52.51	0.5193
18	TATA MOTORS	0.0001812	72.92	0.0034	0.0169	43.66	0.7379
19	BHEL	0.0003071	71.36	0.0049	0.0238	43.61	1.0392
20	ACC	0.0002960	70.10	0.0041	0.0200	29.73	0.5950
21	ICICI BANK	0.0003179	62.05	0.0017	0.0083	33.44	0.2782
22	GAIL	0.0002438	61.35	0.0011	0.0052	36.22	0.1893
23	HDFC	0.0001971	60.00	0.0006	0.0029	18.32	0.0526
	Sum			0.2038	1		34.4057

The return of this optimum portfolio, comprising of 23 securities turns out to be 34.40%.

Table 21.9: Calculation (same as table 21.6) of the proportion return of only those securities, of the selected 23, whose returns are more than 35

Sr. no.	Name of the scrip	Z = G × H	X	Individual return	Proportion return
1	2	3	4	5	6
1	UNITECH	0.0039	0.0354	38.699	1.369258
2	PNB	0.0081	0.0733	56.89	4.168336
3	SBIN	0.0493	0.4440	38.39	17.04654
4	ONGC	0.0104	0.0933	35.775	3.336332
5	JINDAL STEEL	0.0030	0.0267	48.59	1.297888
6	AXIS BANK	0.0110	0.0989	57.71	5.707201
7	TATA POWER	0.0095	0.0859	37.636	3.231488
8	KOTAK BANK	0.0028	0.0255	45.34	1.157038
9	SIEMENS	0.0014	0.0129	35.529	0.457018
10	REL CAPITAL	0.0020	0.0182	52.51	0.954604
11	TATA MOTORS	0.0035	0.0311	43.66	1.356833
12	BHEL	0.0049	0.0438	43.61	1.910859
13	GAIL	0.0012	0.0111	36.22	0.403116
Sum		0.1111	1		42.3965

Table 21.10: Covariance Matrix of the Top 13 Securities Included in the Optimal Portfolio

COVARIANCE MATRIX	UNITECH	PNB	SBIN	ONGC	JINDAL	AXIS	TATA	KOTAK	NTPC	SIEMEN	TATA	BHEL	GAIL
UNITECH	589.93	128.7873	75.32189	−73.0064	573.1505	167.3893	131.7838	180.9527	−25.4749	−488.866	451.7439	−216.506	202.4886
PNB.	128.7873	3401.907	862.2152	2270.012	698.5067	2248.955	1228.005	1652.05	−75.4291	3499.06	2476.548	1703.485	2400.147
SBIN	75.32189	862.2152	532.8033	507.9488	1524.533	1062.263	662.9246	990.2618	345.1973	1118.928	855.9317	695.2479	854.2791
ONGC	−73.0064	2270.012	507.9488	1860.337	216.8629	1099.098	401.0815	1406.829	−63.2583	2241.591	1693.568	935.2128	1495.046
JINDAL STEEL	573.1505	698.5067	1524.533	216.8629	6761.059	2588.136	2777.778	5760.342	1564.841	104.5059	914.732	44.48571	2117.926
AXIS BANK	167.3893	2248.955	1062.263	1099.098	2588.136	2438.296	1556.865	1909.682	561.5012	2549.133	1710.087	1531.542	1980.042
TATA POWER	131.7838	1228.005	662.9246	401.0815	2777.778	1556.865	1302.336	1737.579	669.0245	934.8035	612.0619	760.7731	1216.187
KOTAK BANK	180.9527	1652.05	990.2618	1406.829	5760.342	1909.682	1737.579	4745.078	1401.419	506.8601	928.0118	337.2093	2153.569
NTPC	−25.4749	−75.4291	345.1973	−63.2583	1564.841	561.5012	669.0245	1401.419	488.9959	−238.645	−150.332	203.1494	362.5581
SIEMENS	−488.866	3499.06	1118.928	2241.591	104.5059	2549.133	934.8035	506.8601	−238.645	5525.945	2861.242	2571.171	2195.04
TATA MOTORS	451.7439	2476.548	855.9317	1693.568	914.732	1710.087	612.0619	928.0118	−150.332	2861.242	2730.375	1299.134	1740.517
BHEL	−216.506	1703.485	695.2479	935.2128	44.48571	1531.542	760.7731	337.2093	203.1494	2571.171	1299.134	1790.374	1093.144
GAIL	202.4886	2400.147	854.2791	1495.046	2117.926	1980.042	1216.187	2153.569	362.5581	2195.04	1740.517	1093.144	1973.893
Sum	1697.695	22494.25	10087.86	13991.32	25646.86	21402.99	13991.2	23709.84	5043.547	23380.77	18123.62	12748.42	19784.84

Risk of the portfolio = 40.267562

Sharpe's ratio = (42.3965 − 8)/(40.267562)

= 0.8541

21.2.6 Optimum Portfolio with Short Sales

A market transaction in which an investor sells borrowed securities in anticipation of a price decline and is required to return an equal number of shares at some point in the future is known as short sale.

Hence, short sales mean selling the shares which the investor doesn't own actually. Investors usually short sale securities in the anticipation that they will buy such securities at a lower price in the future. The procedure that has been discussed is without short sales. But the procedure to calculate the optimum portfolio, with short sales, is almost similar to the one discussed above. The stocks are ranked first as per their excess return-to-beta ratio and all stocks are considered for the portfolio construction. Here the final cut-off point to be considered is 44.721, as per table 21.7 column 13. Z_i values are calculated next, for each security. The stocks with a positive Z_i value will be held long, and if negative, it will be sold short. By taking $C^* = 44.721$, the calculation of Z_i value for a stock of UNITECH is carried out.

$$Z_i = \frac{\beta_1(R_i - R_f)}{\sigma^2 e_i \beta_i} - C^*$$

$$= (0.00000101) \times (3449.326 - 44.721)$$

$$= 0.003438$$

Similarly, it is calculated for other stocks as well. The 35 stocks enlisted here, starting from UNITECH to CAIRN, are held long and the remaining securities such as Tata Steel, ABB, Reliance, Mahindra and Mahindra, Bharti Airtel, JP Assocoiate and HCL Tech., are sold short as their Z values are negative.

Table 21.11: Portfolio with Short Sales

Sr.	Name of Scrip	$R_i - R_f/\beta_i$	Beta (β)	Unsystematic Risk ($\sigma^2 e_i$)	$\beta_i/\sigma^2 e_i$	Z
1.	UNITECH	3449.326	0.0089	8775.021	0.00000101	0.003453
2.	L&T	306.7625	0.08	3411.854	0.00002345	0.006144
3.	PNB	231.7062	0.211	5883.977	0.00003586	0.006705
4.	SUN PHARMA	186.7647	0.017	273.7354	0.00006210	0.008821
5.	SBIN	121.56	0.25	500.0484	0.00049995	0.038416
6.	BPCL	120.3636	0.11	398.83	0.00027581	0.020863
7.	ONGC	112.4494	0.247	1996.793	0.00012370	0.008378
8.	HDFC BANK	108.2857	0.21	547.2928	0.00038371	0.02439
9.	JINDAL STEEL	90.60268	0.448	7969.766	0.00005621	0.002579
10.	AXIS BANK	88.76786	0.56	2252.405	0.00024862	0.010951
11.	IDFC	88.22222	0.27	3113.737	0.00008671	0.003772
12.	REL INFRA	87.41803	0.244	2921.057	0.00008353	0.003567
13.	TATA POWER	82.78212	0.358	1264.384	0.00028314	0.010777

14.	KOTAK BANK	81.17391	0.46	5002.387	0.00009196	0.003352
15.	NTPC	77.46108	0.167	532.94	0.00031336	0.010259
16.	SIEMENS	75.0109	0.367	6006.715	0.00006110	0.001851
17.	REL CAPITAL	74.30718	0.599	6416.043	0.00009336	0.002762
18.	TATA MOTORS	72.92434	0.489	2698.02	0.00018124	0.005112
19.	BHEL	71.36273	0.499	1624.899	0.00030710	0.008182
20.	ACC	70.09677	0.31	1047.244	0.00029602	0.007512
21.	ICICI BANK	62.04878	0.41	1289.567	0.00031794	0.005509
22.	GAIL	61.34783	0.46	1886.504	0.00024384	0.004054
23.	HDFC	60	0.172	872.5609	0.00019712	0.003012
24.	MARUTI	52.13176	0.425	412.702	0.00102980	0.007632
25.	STERLITE	51.65211	2.13	27135.53	0.00007849	0.000544
26.	HERO HONDA	49.46429	0.336	1166.764	0.00028798	0.001366
27.	SAIL	49.33816	1.242	7724.619	0.00016078	0.000742
28.	TATA STEEL	43.38596	0.57	2384.277	0.00023907	–0.00032
29.	ABB	40.875	0.56	3207.82	0.00017457	–0.00067
30.	RELIANCE	39.25429	0.35	1721.027	0.00020337	–0.00111
31.	M&M	37.10067	0.745	1912.706	0.00038950	–0.00297
32.	BHARTI AIRTEL	28.80597	1.34	1456.89	0.00091977	–0.01464
33.	JPASSOCIAT	21.09987	0.751	4581.709	0.00016391	–0.00387
34.	HCL TECH	5.34153	0.366	1471.109	0.00024879	–0.0098
35.	CAIRN	–269.449	–0.0345	299.41	–0.00011523	0.036201

The proportion (X_i) of each stock in the portfolio is calculated as above, utilizing the formula,

$$X_i = \frac{Z_i}{\Sigma Z_i}$$

Table 21.12: Return of the Optimum Portfolio with Short Sales

Sr. no.	Name of the scrip	Z	X	Individual return	Proportion return
1	UNITECH	0.003453	0.016172	38.699	0.625827
2	L&T	0.006144	0.028775	32.541	0.936368
3	PNB	0.006705	0.031403	56.89	1.78649

4	SUN PHARMA	0.008821	0.041313	11.175	0.461672
5	SBIN	0.038416	0.17991	38.39	6.906751
6	BPCL	0.020863	0.097705	21.24	2.075258
7	ONGC	0.008378	0.039236	35.775	1.403655
8	HDFC BANK	0.02439	0.114225	30.74	3.51128
9	JINDAL STEEL	0.002579	0.012079	48.59	0.586901
10	AXIS BANK	0.010951	0.051286	57.71	2.95974
11	IDFC	0.003772	0.017666	31.82	0.562121
12	REL INFRA	0.003567	0.016703	29.33	0.489898
13	TATA POWER	0.010777	0.05047	37.636	1.899482
14	KOTAK BANK	0.003352	0.015699	45.34	0.711771
15	NTPC	0.010259	0.048047	20.936	1.005906
16	SIEMENS	0.001851	0.008667	35.529	0.307933
17	REL CAPITAL	0.002762	0.012936	52.51	0.679261
18	TATA MOTORS	0.005112	0.023939	43.66	1.045187
19	BHEL	0.008182	0.038316	43.61	1.67097
20	ACC	0.007512	0.035179	29.73	1.045861
21	ICICI BANK	0.005509	0.025801	33.44	0.86277
22	GAIL	0.004054	0.018987	36.22	0.687708
23	HDFC	0.003012	0.014105	18.32	0.258404
24	MARUTI	0.007632	0.035741	30.156	1.077792
25	STERLITE	0.000544	0.002548	118.019	0.300706
26	HERO HONDA	0.001366	0.006397	24.62	0.157496
27	SAIL	0.000742	0.003477	69.278	0.240858
28	TATA STEEL	−0.00032	−0.00149	32.73	−0.04892
29	ABB	−0.00067	−0.00314	30.89	−0.09713
30	RELIANCE	−0.00111	−0.00521	21.739	−0.11319
31	M&M	−0.00297	−0.0139	35.64	−0.49541
32	BHARTI AIRTEL	−0.01464	−0.06855	46.6	−3.19461
33	JPASSOCIATE	−0.00387	−0.01813	23.846	−0.43239
34	HCL TECH	−0.0098	−0.04588	9.955	−0.45677
35	CAIRN	0.036201	0.169537	17.296	2.932308
Sum		**0.2135**	**1**		**32.3519**

The above Table 21.12 shows the proportion to be invested in each security of the portfolio whose return turns out to be 32.35%.

> **Pause for thought:** Short sale is selling of the borrowed securities with hopes of buying them at a lower price later.

SUMMARY

- In Markowitz model, portfolio return and risk is computed easily with $(n^2 - n)/2$ parameters, for portfolio of 'n' securities. While Sharpe's single index model is solved by $n(n + 3)/2$ parameters and is simpler than Markowitz model.
- Sharpe's single index model also gives the ideal proportion to be invested in each security and it discards the securities with lower return.
- Sharpe's model also indicates the number of securities to be sold short. Markowitz model does not say anything about either the proportion or short selling.
- Sharpe's model is based on the relationship between the index return and rate of return on the security. It takes into account both systematic and unsystematic risks.

KEY CONCEPTS

Beta	Markowitz Portfolio Theory	Short Sales
Systematic Risk	Sharpe's Single Index model	Risk-Free Rate
Unsystematic Risk	Optimal Portfolio	
Market Risk	Cut-Off Point	

REVIEW QUESTION

1. Explain how Sharpe's single index model differs from the Markowitz model.

ASSIGNMENT QUESTIONS

1. Collect the prices of five scrips for the last five years. The scrips should be from different sectors, viz., FMCG, power, oil and gas, IT, healthcare, small cap and mid cap.
   (i) Calculate for each: return, risk, correlation coefficient and coefficient of determination.
   (ii) Interpret your results.
   (iii) Are the systematic and unsystematic risks different for the different sectors? Is there any specific trend? Or is it random? Show your results.
2. (i) Construct the Sharpe's single index model by collecting all 30 scrips of BSE Sensex.
   (ii) Find out their risk, return, beta, correlation coefficient, and coefficient of determination, systematic and unsystematic risks, from the data of last 10 years.
   (iii) Calculate the return and risk of the portfolio, on the basis of the weight assigned by the model to each security.

ILLUSTRATION

Calculate the systematic and unsystematic risks for the given securities from the following data.

	Average return (%)	Standard deviation	Beta
Tata Power	33.90	126.34	0.36
Mahindra & Mahindra	25.09	106.70	0.74
Market index (Nifty)	28.63	39.52	1
Correlation coefficient between SBI and Maruti	0.90		
r^2	0.81		

Ans: The systematic risk of Tata Power

$= \beta_i^2 \sigma_m^2$

$= (0.36)^2 \times (39.52)^2$

$= 202.41$

The unsystematic risk of Tata Power,

$\sigma^2 e_i = \sigma_i^2 - \beta_i^2 \sigma_m^2$

$= (126.34)^2 - 202.41$

$= 15961.8 - 202.41$

$= 15759.38$

Thus, out of total risk (variance), 15961.8, of the security of Tata Power, 202.41 is due to the systematic risk and 15759.38 is due to the unsystematic risk.

Similarly, the systematic risk of the stock of Mahindra & Mahindra

$= \beta_i^2 \sigma_m^2$

$= (0.74)^2 \times (39.52)^2$

$= 855.26$

And the unsystematic risk of the stock of Mahindra & Mahindra,

$\sigma^2 e_i = \sigma_i^2 - \beta_i^2 \sigma_m^2$

$= (106.70)^2 - 855.26$

$= 11384.9 - 855.26$

$= 10529.63$

Thus, the total risk, 11384.9, of Mahindra & Mahindra is made up of 855.26 and 10529.63 as systematic risk and unsystematic risk respectively.

PROBLEMS

1. Calculate the systematic and unsystematic risk from the following data of ABB and ACC.

	Average return (%)	Standard deviation (%)	Beta
ABB	30.89	60.77	0.56
ACC	29.73	34.62	0.31
Market index (Nifty)	28.63	39.52	1
Correlation coefficient between SBI and Maruti	0.86		
r^2	0.74		

2. Consider the following data. Calculate return and risk of the portfolio applying Sharpe's model. The risk-free rate is assumed to be 8%. Return of the Sensex for the period 2004-2009 is 32.95% and risk of the market, 50.21%.

Name of the company	Avg. rate of return	Variance	S.D.	Beta	Systematic risk	Unsystematic risk ($\sigma^2 e$)
JINDAL STEEL	94.03	31123.90	176.42	0.97	2366.92	28756.98
SAIL	37.12	5010.84	70.79	1.24	3846.63	1164.20
BHARTI AIRTEL	36.51	2586.42	50.86	0.79	1554.56	1031.86
SPICE JET	33.26	9079.96	95.29	0.87	1887.42	7192.54
BHEL	31.14	1723.43	41.51	0.99	2463.64	−740.21
RELIANCE POWER	29.33	1827.90	42.75	1.04	2720.72	−892.82
SBI	28.88	823.44	28.70	1.20	3614.82	−2791.38
HDFC	28.56	821.84	28.67	1.19	3568.49	−2746.64
ACC	27.70	2030.99	45.07	0.72	1314.05	716.95
NTPC	25.28	493.27	22.21	0.59	892.12	−398.86
TATA COMM.	24.20	1492.63	38.63	0.71	1271.80	220.83
GSFC	23.87	2188.62	46.78	0.76	1466.75	721.86
ULTRATECH	23.63	2521.87	50.22	0.58	851.51	1670.36
HERO HONDA	22.43	645.52	25.41	0.60	919.32	−273.80
MAHINDRA & MAHINDRA	22.40	4893.07	69.95	1.03	2668.59	2224.48
ICICI BANK	21.72	1361.02	36.89	1.48	5494.70	−4133.68
MARUTI SUZUKI	18.72	463.30	21.52	0.69	1184.89	−721.59
GRASIM	16.54	1511.13	38.87	0.69	1210.26	300.87

DABUR INDIA	14.00	1641.47	40.52	0.29	211.56	1429.91
GAIL	11.59	777.92	27.89	0.67	1133.95	−356.02
HUL	10.90	77.60	8.81	0.35	309.15	−231.55
TATA STEEL	8.54	1290.22	35.92	1.42	5097.96	−3807.74
ONGC	7.72	181.63	13.48	0.79	1565.27	−1383.64
CADILA HEALTH	4.83	1176.85	34.31	0.22	121.23	1055.62
TATA MOTORS	1.98	943.69	30.72	1.22	3739.03	−2795.34

CASE STUDY

Mr. Aarav Mishra is actively involved in the stock market. In the past he has served as an investment advisor to his family, friends and relatives. He used to be a strong believer in playing safe and always advocated investing in safe options, like FDs in bank; savings schemes offered by the post office and life insurance. Recently he attended a workshop on the workings of financial market and learnt few techniques to invest in the market. Initially he hesitated to invest according to these new techniques. But he was eager as well to invest in the market, seeing how his friends had built their wealth through rational investments in the stock market. He decided to apply both methods of portfolio construction: (i) Markowitz model and (ii) Sharpe's index model, which he had learnt at the workshop. He thought both the models were empirically tested. He came to know of the advantages of the Sharpe's model. Sharpe's model facilitates selection of securities, from the given set of securities. Moreover, Sharpe's model indicates which securities should be held long and which should be sold short. Furthermore, the number of parameters for estimating risk and return are less if the portfolio is constructed as per the Sharpe's model, compared to those required by Markowitz's model. In spite of that, his friend Mr. Sudhir Kulkarni advised him to construct the portfolio as per Markowitz theory. Mr. Kulkarni told that all mutual fund companies and wealth management companies construct the portfolios on the basis of Markowitz model. But Vijay, his neighbor's son, advised him to go with Sharpe's model as it is less cumbersome. Vijay is a final year finance student and offered his help to Mr. Mishra with the construction of the portfolio, by both the methods. Now Vijay is seeking your help and advice on the same. Mr. Mishra has Rs. 2,00,000 for investing in the market, to begin with. Assist Vijay by keeping in mind the following suggestions for constructing the portfolio:

Pick up the right securities from the market, based upon the fundamental analysis of the security. Also, analyze and assess the future prospects of the company, before investing in it. Collect around 20 potential scrips from the market and construct the Markowitz model by taking: (i) Equal weights of securities; weights are based upon the potential of the security (i.e., by consulting risk-return profile of each security); (ii) Compute the risk and return of the portfolio by taking the weights as per method (i); (iii) Construct a portfolio using the Sharpe's model with the same 20 scrips and calculate risk and return of the thus constructed Sharpe's portfolio.

Compare these risks and returns and guide Mr. Mishra to invest in the market. What does your analysis lead to?

SUGGESTED FURTHER READING FOR EMPIRICAL WORK

1. Varian, H. (1993), "A Portfolio of Nobel Laureates: Markowitz, Miller and Sharpe", *The Journal of Economic Perspectives*, Vol. 7, No. 1.
2. Sharpe, W.F. (1963), "A Simplified Model for Portfolio Analysis", *Management Science*, Vol. 9, No. 2.
3. Bilbao, A., Arenas, M., Jiménez, M., Gladishl, B. P., and Rodríguez, M.V. (2006), "An Extension of Sharpe's Single-Index Model: Portfolio Selection with Expert Betas", *The Journal of the Operational Research Society*, Vol. 57, No. 12.
4. Hodgson, D.J., and Vorkink, K.P. (2003), "Efficient Estimation of Conditional Asset-Pricing Models", *Journal of Business & Economic Statistics*, Vol. 21, No. 2.
5. Konno, H., and Yamazaki, H. (1991), "Mean-Absolute Deviation Portfolio Optimization Model and Its Applications to Tokyo Stock Market", *Management Science*, Vol. 37, No. 5.
6. Jobson, J.D., and Korkie, B.M. (1981), "Performance Hypothesis Testing with the Sharpe and Treynor Measures", *The Journal of Finance*, Vol. 36, No. 4.
7. Kwan, C.C.Y. (1984), "Portfolio Analysis Using Single Index, Multi-Index, and Constant Correlation Models: A Unified Treatment", *The Journal of Finance*, Vol. 39, No. 5 .
8. Vasicek, O.A., and McQuown, J.A. (1972), "The Efficient Market Model", *Financial Analysts Journal*, Vol. 28, No. 5.
9. Lo, A.W. (2002), "The Statistics of Sharpe Ratios", *Financial Analysts Journal*, Vol. 58, No. 4.

REFERENCES

1. Sharpe F William (1963), "A Simplified Model for Portfolio Analysis", *Management Science*, Vol.9, No.2, pp.277-293.
2. Frankfurter M. George; Phillips E. Herbert and Seagle P. John (1976), "Performance of the Sharpe Portfolio Selection Model: A Comparison", *The Journal of Financial and Quantitative Analysis*, Vol.11, No.2, pp. 195-204.

22
PORTFOLIO SELECTION

LEARNING OBJECTIVES

The purpose of this chapter is to enable you to understand:

- Indifference curves and feasible set to identify the location of the portfolio, in terms of risk and return.
- The importance of efficient frontier to determine the optimal portfolio of risky assets.
- The application of the Markowitz optimization technique, called corner portfolio and adjacent portfolio.
- The derivation of an optimal portfolio from the efficient set.

22.1 INTRODUCTION

The basics of portfolio theory have been discussed in Chapter 5; and in Chapters 20 and 21 we discussed two specific models of portfolio theory. While Chapter 20 led us through the revolutionary work of Markowitz, it also made us aware of some limitations of the same. These very limitations are countered very well by William Sharpe, through his single index model, as we found in Chapter 21. With these as the proper foundation, this chapter journeys through the modalities and essentials of portfolio selection. All that we have learnt are being revisited by studying their applications. And through it all, we hope to achieve what we wish to, for our funds—a judicious selection of portfolio.

When options are few, one has no choice but to select from only those. But when options are infinite—and potential too—the selection too passes through infinite choices, before a decision is reached. It is so with the portfolios, there being innumerable options to choose from. Hence, this chapter. The theories are discussed for constructing efficient portfolios—as are the derivations of optimal portfolios—along with the funds, to be allocated to them.

22.2 THE THEORY OF INDIFFERENCE CURVES

Indifference curves have been discussed in Chapter 7. So we are aware that just as the individual securities get ranked by these curves, graphically, the same holds true for the portfolios.

Indifference curves aid in the selection of the most desirable portfolio, from the available combinations, depending upon the investor's risk-return preferences. The graph is plotted with the X-axis as the measure of risk, while the Y-axis, that of the return. And graphical representation of each portfolio leads us to the most suitable portfolio for an investor with specific risk-return preferences.

Prior to the application of indifference curves, a discussion on the basic information these curves provide, is required. Thus the same is the subject of attention as follows. In the figure below, each curved line represents one indifference curve. These curves represent the combination of portfolios that provide the investor with the desired level of returns. These curves have various characteristics and their study would enhance the understanding of the implications of these curves.

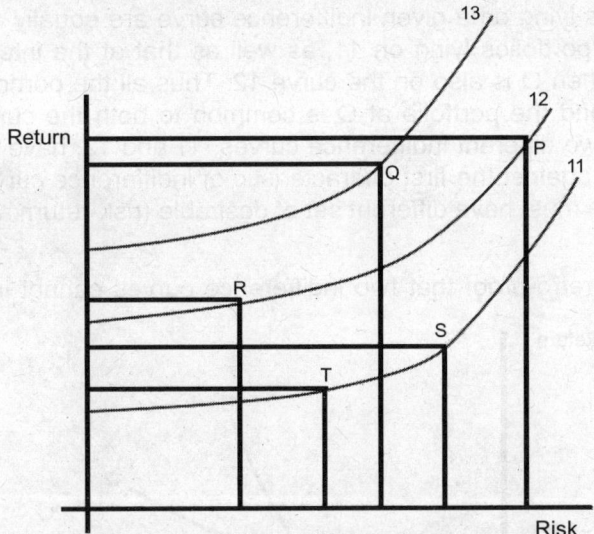

Figure 22.1: Set of indifference curves

1. *All portfolios that lie on a given indifference curve are equally desirable to investors.*

A set of indifference curves is shown graphically in the Figure 22.1 above. These curves represent portfolios with different risk-return characteristics. From these we consider two portfolios, T and S, on the curve 11. It is evident that portfolio, T, has a lower return compared to the portfolio, S. So, from the perspective of returns, portfolio S appears to be more desirable than T. But a higher return is always accompanied by a corresponding high risk. Hence, S is the preferred portfolio for an investor ready to bear high risk for the sake of high return. Otherwise, portfolio T (with lower risk and lower return) would be the choice. Thus, portfolios lying on the same indifference curves are equally desirable, subject to the preferences of the investors, with respect to the risk-return ratio of the portfolios.

Thus, here, it can be said approximately (without exact calculation) that both the portfolios, T and S, have the same risk-return trade-off. Choice of the portfolio depends upon the preference of the investor. Similar is the case for the portfolios, R and P, as they both lie on the same indifference curve, 12. The investor can choose any portfolio depending upon his preferred risk-return trade-off. Only two portfolios have been shown here on indifference curves, 11 and 12. In real life, investor can choose any portfolio or any point lying on it. Herein, it can be further inferred that the indifference curve, 11, is chosen by comparatively more risk-averse investors as it carries less risk, even though it provides less return. Indifference curves, 12 and 13, are chosen by risk-neutral and risk-lover investors respectively.

But these desirable portfolios that have been discussed are with respect to the chosen indifference curve. So how this curve is chosen from the available lot one needs to know. That forms the context of the discussion later.

2. *Indifference curves cannot intersect.*

To prove the truth of this statement we assume two indifference curves to be intersecting at the point O (in the Figure 22.2, below). As per the first characteristic of indifference curves, just discussed, all portfolios lying on a given indifference curve are equally desirable. It signifies equal suitability for all the portfolios lying on 11, as well as that at the intersection point O, as O too is on curve 11. But then O is also on the curve 12. Thus all the portfolios lying on 12 and 11 are equally desirable; and the portfolio at O is common to both the curves. This means all the portfolios lying on the two different indifference curves, 11 and 12, have the same risk-return characteristics. And that is against the first characteristic of indifference curve, which states that different indifference curves must have different set of desirable (risk-return ratio is the parameter of desirability) portfolios.

Hence, we reach the retro-proof that two indifference curves cannot intersect each other.

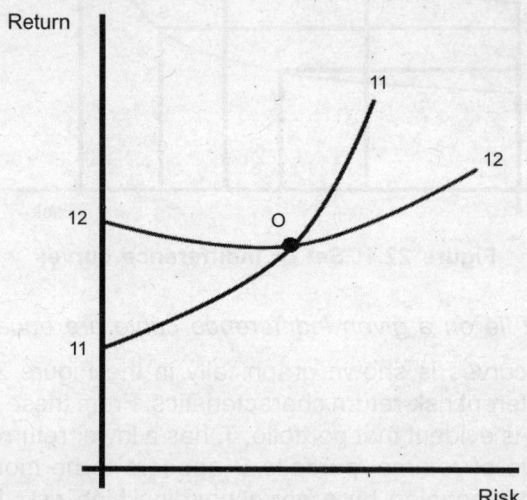

Figure 22.2: Indifference curves with intersection

3. *The portfolio(s) lying on the north-western region of indifference curves is (are) more desirable than the rest, lying elsewhere.*

To understand the region-specificity for the selectivity of portfolios we resort to Figure 22.1 and carry out a comparative study. For the purpose, the portfolios Q (on curve 13), P (on curve 12) and S (on curve 11) are compared, in terms of their risk-return characteristics. Portfolio Q is more desirable compared to portfolio S since it has a lower risk and higher return. Again, portfolio

Q has a marginally lower return, compared to P. But this marginal gap is over-compensated by the substantial lesser risk. Thus in this case it is a lower return, but much lower risk, than P, which makes Q a better choice than even P. Hence, Q is found to be the most desirable of the three portfolios compared: P, Q and S. And this is so because of the north-western region where the portfolio Q lies.

Similarly, if as an investor we can find out another portfolio, which lies further to the north-west than Q, it becomes more desirable than Q.

4. *There are innumerable indifference curves.*

Given the innumerable options for portfolio selection, the various permutations and combinations thus render the number of indifference curves infinite. Simply put, it means, an investor can have 'n' number of indifference curves. That is why, in Figure 22.1, indifference curves can be plotted above 13, below 11; and in between 11–12 and 12–13 respectively.

> **Pause for thought:** These represent the preference of investor for a portfolio, and at the same time indifference to all other available options.

22.2.1 Selection of Indifference Curves

How does an investor choose his/her indifference curves?

This is a question which seeks answer, as we have to select the portfolios from the chosen indifference curve. Furthermore, to reach a rational decision, options have to be narrowed down to a select few, from the innumerable that are available.

We already know that investors are divided into categories, with risk-return ratio as the parameter. So, Figure 22.1 is not a universal or standard representation of all investors in a market. As a consequence the correct representation would be, different indifference curves for the three main type of investors: the aggressive (those who love to take risks), those who are averse to risks and the ones who are neutral towards risk.

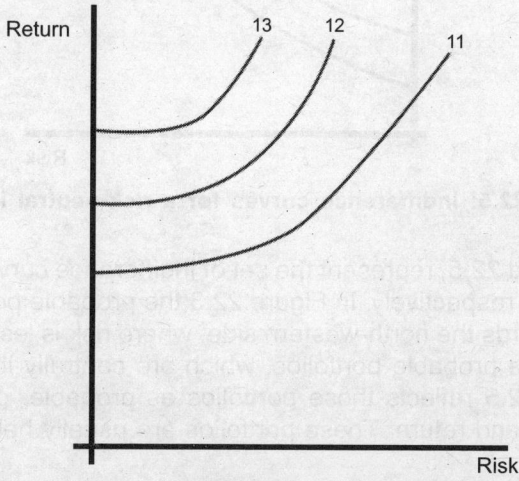

Figure 22.3: Indifference curves for an investor averse to risk

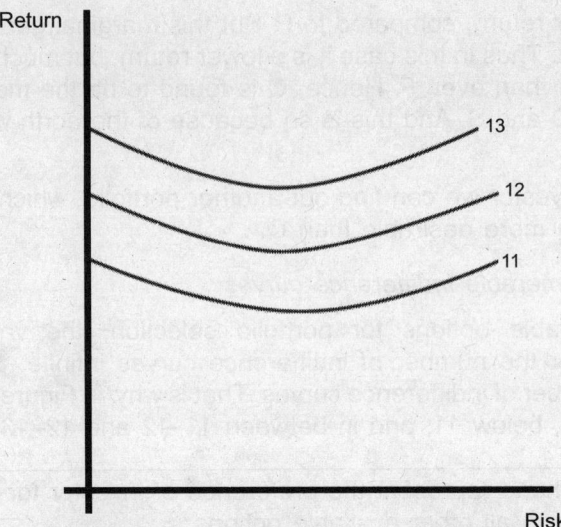

Figure 22.4: Indifference curves for an investor who takes risk

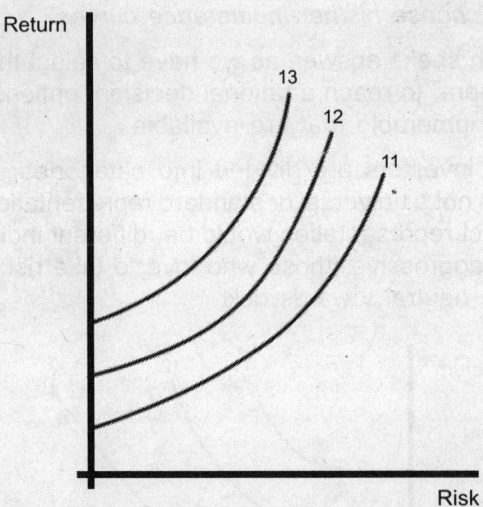

Figure 22.5: Indifference curves for a risk-neutral investor

Figures 22.3, 22.4, and 22.5, represent the set of indifference curves for the risk-averse, risk-taker and neutral investors respectively. In Figure 22.3 the probable portfolios on the indifference curves are lying more towards the north-western side, where risk is less and thus return too could be less. In Figure 22.4, the probable portfolios, which are centrally located, have high risk, but moderate return. Figure 22.5 reflects those portfolios as probable, on the indifference curves, which have moderate risk and return. These portfolios are usually held by the neutral investors.

> **Pause for thought:** Out of the innumerable, the most preferred indifference curve is chosen, in accordance with the type of investor. And the portfolios lying on the north-western region of this curve are selected as the suitable portfolio.

22.3 THE EFFICIENT SET

The earlier section on indifference curves has been an important learning on how the indifference curves serve the purpose of selecting portfolios. Thus we know how a specific region of these curves is considered the zone of eligibility, and thus desirable to the investors. These regions represent a particular risk-return ratio. 'n' number of portfolios can be constructed from the available securities. This can be achieved by combining the available securities in different proportions. Thus an investor and a student of investment must evaluate the risk-return ratio of all possible portfolios to finally select the one as per preference.

But constructing innumerable portfolios is practically not possible. Generating 'n' number of portfolios, via various permutations and combinations, is not at all feasible. Hence, only a small part, of the entire range of available portfolios, has to be considered and evaluated. Thus we are saved from the tedious task of constructing 'n' number of portfolios and calculating their risk and return. This small subset of portfolios that are considered, preferentially chosen from the entire set, is known as the efficient set.

In other words, efficient set is such a region within the feasible set which represents a set of portfolios that maximize the expected return, at each level of portfolio risk. By applying efficient set theorem to the feasible set, the efficient set can be located. As per efficient set theorem all the portfolios in the efficient set are located on the 'north-west' boundary of the feasible set (this north-western region is also called the efficient frontier). Plotting an indifference curve on the same figure (of efficient frontier) and then choosing the portfolio, which is 'farthest northwest', gives the optimal portfolio.

For choosing the efficient set there is a theorem, which provides the guidelines. According to it, there are two parameters, on which this choice of portfolios is to be based:

— Return: highest expected return for different levels of risk.
— Risk: lowest risk for different levels of expected return.

The group of portfolios which satisfies these two criteria is known as efficient set and forms the efficient frontier. Thus the efficient frontier actually is so called, as the portfolios therein perform efficiently, with respect to risk and return.

> **Pause for thought:** The small subset of portfolios, selected from the entire set of portfolios, is the efficient set.

22.3.1 The Feasible Set

Figure 22.6, below, represents the feasible set (also known as the opportunity set). The feasible set means collection of all feasible portfolios. And feasible portfolio means a portfolio that an investor can construct, with the assets available. Given the feasible set or portfolio, opportunity set (as discussed in Chapter 5)—which is a collection of assets—allows the potential investors to choose from them a portfolio configuration that matches their level of risk tolerance.

From the feasible set the efficient set can be found. The feasible set is the set of all portfolios that can be formed from the combinations of the available 'n' securities. These possible portfolios lie either on the boundary or within the boundary of the feasible set. The points: A, B, C, D and E, have been identified as portfolios on this feasible set to enhance the understanding. The feasible set is usually umbrella-shaped, as shown in Figure 22.6. This shape may flatten (i.e., become thinner) and there might be a change in its position: it may move vertically or laterally. The movement depends upon the number of securities and their correlation with each other—and in turn on their risk and return, as that decides the volume of the feasible set.

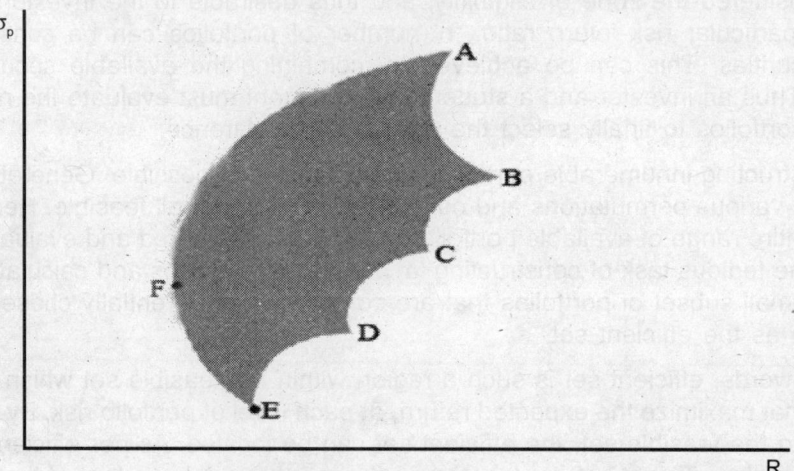

Figure 22.6: The feasible set

Pause for thought: The efficient set is the subset of the feasible set.

22.3.2 The Efficient Set and the Feasible Set

The above segment has mentioned that we can identify the efficient set from the feasible set. But to do so we need to study the above figure carefully. The horizontal axis records the risk while the vertical axis represents the return. The points: A, B, C, D, E and F, have been marked as selected portfolios, as on the given feasible set. However, the portfolios are not limited to only five. With 'n' number of securities, we can have 'n' number of combinations on the feasible set. From the above figure, it is evident that portfolio A provides the highest return, while portfolio E has the least return. As far as risk is concerned—the second parameter (for selection of the subset)—the figure shows portfolio A involves maximum risk. Thus, for a given level of return portfolio A possesses highest risk. Portfolio F is seen to be offering least risk. The other two portfolios, C and D, are not preferred by investors. Even though portfolios C and F provide almost the same return, the level of risk is much higher for C. Similarly, portfolio D provides a marginally higher return than portfolio E, but its risk is much higher. Hence, portfolios, C and D, find no takers.

These conclusions are indicated in the following Figure 22.7, with the region-specificities marked.

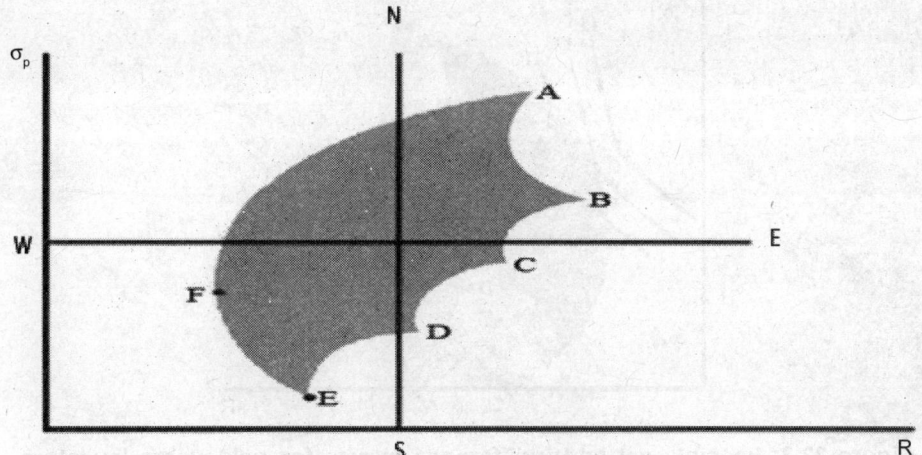

Figure 22.7: Feasible set with direction

The analysis of Figure 22.7 too leads to the same conclusions: the portfolios in the feasible set that lie on the north-western region possess minimum risk for varying levels of expected return, hence preferred. At the same time, those lying on the north-eastern offer maximum expected return, but for a varying level of risk. Hence is the corroboration: the efficient portfolio is one which is lying on the northwest region of the feasible set. From this efficient set, investor can find his/her optimum portfolio, depending upon the individual preferences. Portfolios lying on the south–eastern region are graphically shown to possess high degree of risk for a given expected return, thus to be discarded.

> **Pause for thought:** The subset that efficient portfolio is, of the feasible set, is comprised of the portfolios lying on the north-western region of the feasible set.

22.3.3 Feasible Set and Indifference Curves

Once the efficient set is determined, one question that still remains unanswered is how an investor selects optimal portfolio from the given feasible set. As we know that investors differ in their risk bearing capacities, affinity or otherwise for risks and the returns that they expect. Hence, their selection of an optimal portfolio is not distinct from that of the efficient set, from the feasible set as discussed above. As a consequence, irrespective of the category to which the investors belong, the selection of optimal portfolios takes them too to the north-western region only.

As shown in Figure 22.8, investors would plot his/her indifference curve on the efficient set as per the risk-return preferences. Thus are plotted three different indifference curves, as shown in the Figures 22.8, 22.9 and 22.10, below. In Figure 22.8, out of the three indifference curves, 12, intersects the feasible set at point O. And there is a chance that an investor may prefer to select the portfolio on 13, as of all three it lies maximum to the north-west. However, it is the depiction of an ideal situation. In reality it is not possible as no such feasible set of portfolio exists. Several portfolios are lying on the indifference curve 11, but they are inferior in terms of the risk and return parameters, compared to those on O (which is on 12). Hence none of the portfolios on 11 is selected. Figures, 22.9 and 22.10, show how the optimum portfolios are selected for a neutral and a risk-loving investor, respectively, by using indifference curves.

600 SECURITY ANALYSIS AND PORTFOLIO MANAGEMENT

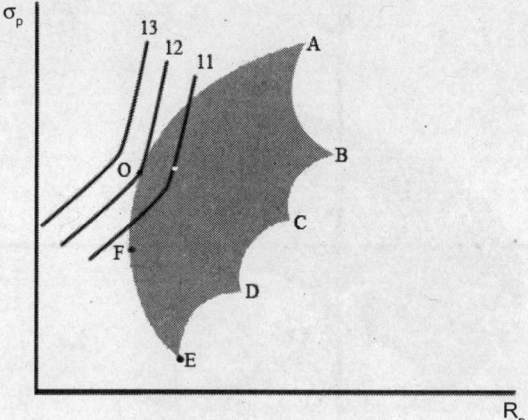

Figure 22.8: Feasible set and indifference curves for risk-averse investors

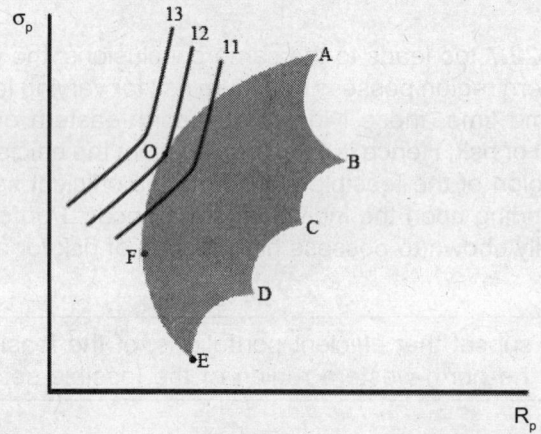

Figure 22.9: Feasible set and indifference curves for neutral investors

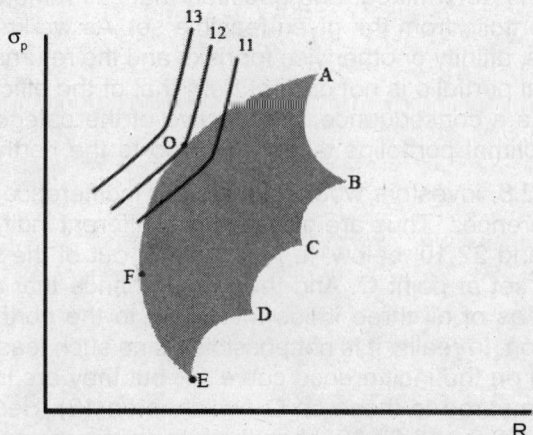

Figure 22.10: Feasible set and indifference curves for risk-loving investors

22.4 DERIVING THE LOCATION OF THE EFFICIENT SET

Till now we have been continuously discussing about the efficient set, the optimal portfolio and how they are selected from the feasible set. The indifference curves, serving as the tool for the purpose, too we have discussed at length. Thus we know that the portfolios lying on the north-western region of the feasible set qualify as the efficient portfolios and form the efficient frontier. But primary selection, essential, is that of the indifference curve on which these efficient portfolios reside.

This derivation leads us to a link between the feasible set, the efficient set and the corner portfolio. And as the segment progresses the following relation too will unfold:

$$\text{Feasible set} \Rightarrow \text{Efficient set} \Rightarrow \text{Corner portfolio}$$

We know that it is possible to construct 'n' number of portfolios by taking different proportions of given securities in a portfolio. But our aim is to select the optimal portfolio, out of the possible 'n' number of portfolios. And even if the selection of optimal portfolio is the aim, a rational investor should concern himself/herself with the selection of only those portfolios which lie on the efficient set. Yet again the number of portfolios causes a problem, as 'n' number of portfolios lie on the efficient set as well. It thus is a very cumbersome task to select the portfolios from the infinite portfolios lying on the efficient set.

However, as we have already discussed, Markowitz has simplified this task. He developed an algorithm to solve it (the solution though doesn't form a part of the discussion here, which is restricted only to highlighting its function.[1]). And with that he derived the location of the efficient set.

Here, the location of the efficient set is derived by taking the three securities of: HDFC, HDFC Bank and BPCL. The return and risk of these securities are calculated from the data of prices over the period 2001 to 2010.

Security = [HDFC, HDFC Bank, BPCL]
Return = [18.32, 30.74, 21.24]
Risk (variance) = [918.70, 617.22, 417.47]

Covariance:

Stock	Covariance
HDFC and HDFC Bank	497.79
HDFC Bank and BPCL	–51.41
BPCL and HDFC	–326.70

Return on the risk-free asset is 8%.

Markowitz identified and constructed the corner portfolios[2] by taking the algorithm of the

---

[1] Markowitz, Harry (1956), "The Optimization of a quadratic function subject to Linear Constraints", Naval Research Logistics Quarterly, 3, Nos. 1-2.

[2] From out of the many efficient portfolios, there is a need to identify the efficient portfolios which are on the boundary extreme north-west. This can be found out by selecting limited number of portfolios on this boundary. The series of the efficient portfolios lying on the north-east boundary of the efficient set are known as corner portfolios.

security with highest return. In this sample, of the three securities, that of HDFC Bank has the highest return of 30.74%. The only way to earn the highest return for the portfolio of these three securities is to invest 100% of the available fund in HDFC Bank. If the portfolios are constructed by taking different combinations of: either two or three securities, out of the above mentioned three, the returns of the portfolios will be less than 30.74%. The notation W1 = (0, 1, 0) means 0% of the funds is invested in HDFC and BPCL, while 100% of the fund has been invested in HDFC Bank. Thus, as follows, three corner portfolios are constructed: C1, C2 and C3, with varying proportions of the three securities: HDFC, HDFC Bank and BPCL.

Corner portfolio, C1

W1 = (0, 1, 0). The return and standard deviation are 30.74% and 24.84% respectively. It can be denoted as C1.

Corner portfolio, C2

Now the algorithm identifies second portfolio as (0, 0.95, 0.05) which consists of 95% of investment in HDFC Bank and 5% in BPCL. Its expected return and risk are 30.26% and 23.52% respectively. Its symbolic representation is C2.

The first and second corner portfolios are adjacent efficient[3] portfolios and the derivation of the efficient portfolio in-between, is as follows:

$$(0.5 \times C1) + (0.5 \times C2) = [0.5 \times (0, 1, 0)] + [0.5 \times (0, 0.95, 0.05)]$$
$$= (0, 0.975, 0.015)$$

When the proportion of investments is: 0% in HDFC, 97.5% in HDFC Bank and 1.5% in BPCL, the expected return and risk turns out to be 30.50% and 24.18% respectively.

Corner portfolio, C3

Similarly, the third corner portfolio is identified, with the composition of (0.1, 0.8, 0.1) and return and risk: 28.55% and 21.75% respectively. It is denoted by C3.

If hypothetically, the investment ratio is 50:50 or any other combination, in the second and third corner portfolios, the resulting portfolio is found to have the following composition:

$$(0.5 \times C2) + (0.5 \times C3) = [0.5 \times (0, 0.95, 0.05)] + [0.5 \times (0.1, 0.8, 0.1)]$$
$$= (0.05, 0.875, 0.075)$$

The return and risk, of this hypothetical resultant portfolio, are 29.41% and 22.61% respectively.

As mentioned above, only the adjacent corner portfolios are efficient. That is, the portfolios constructed by taking weights of two neighboring (adjacent) corner portfolios C1 and C2; C2 and C3; C3 and C4—and so on—are deemed efficient. But the portfolios constructed by taking non-adjacent corner portfolios are not considered to be efficient. Thus, the portfolios constructed by taking weight of corner portfolios C1 and C3; C2 and C4; C1 and C4; C2 and C5; etc., are inefficient portfolios.

---

[3] Adjacent portfolios mean neighboring portfolios of corner portfolios. Here in an attempt to find out the optimal portfolio from the given corner portfolio—by trial and error—two neighboring portfolios are tried out in order to maximize return for a given level of risk and vice-versa.

Having calculated the composition of adjacent portfolios, now we carry out the calculations for the non-adjacent corner portfolios: C1 and C3

$$(0.5 \times C1) + (0.5 \times C3) = [0.5 \times (0, 1, 0)] + [0.5 \times (0.1, 0.8, 0.1)]$$
$$= (0.05, 0.9, 0.05)$$

The return and risk of this portfolio turns out to be 29.64% and 23.28% respectively. But, this is an inefficient portfolio, because its expected return, 29.64%, lies between the expected returns of the second (30.26%) and third (28.55%) corner portfolios. At the same time, the risk of this non-adjacent portfolio is more than that of portfolio created out of the adjacent corner portfolios, C2 and C3—it is 22.61% and that of the corner portfolio C3 is 21.75%.

The efficient portfolio with the targeted return of 29.64% (i.e., equal to that of the non-adjacent portfolio), can be constructed with the help of the following equation.

$$29.64\% = (C2 \times Y) + [C3 \times (1 - Y)]$$
$$29.64\% = 30.26\%Y + 28.55\% (1 - Y)$$
$$29.64\% = 28.55\% + 1.71\%Y$$
$$1.09Y = 1.71\%Y$$
$$Y = 0.63$$

That is, $1 - Y = 0.37$

This implies that with an investment of 63% in C2 and the remaining 37% fund in C3, the composition of the resultant portfolio is:

$$[0.63 \times (0, 0.95, 0.05)] + [0.37 \times (0.1, 0.8, 0.1)] = (0.037, 0.8945, 0.0685)$$

The resultant portfolio with the composition of (0.037, 0.8945, 0.0685) provides 29.63% return and 22.85% risk. The standard deviation of this portfolio is lower than the standard deviation of non-adjacent portfolio composed of C1 and C3. This is the reason why portfolios constructed with two non-adjacent corner portfolios is called an inefficient portfolio.

Corner portfolio, C4

The fourth corner portfolio, C4, has the three securities in the proportion (0, 0.7, 0.3), i.e., (0%, 70%, 30%). The return and risk of the portfolio are 27.89% and 17.84% respectively.

The adjacent portfolio constructed by investing in the corner portfolios, C3 and C4, in a 50:50 ratio, is

$$(0.5 \times C3) + (0.5 \times C4) = [0.5 \times (0.1, 0.8, 0.1)] + [0.5 \times (0, 0.7, 0.3)]$$
$$= (0.05, 0.75, 0.2)$$

The return and risk of this portfolio are 28.22% and 19.53% respectively.

As above, when a resultant portfolio is constructed with two non-adjacent corner portfolios, C2 and C4, in 50:50 hypothetical ratio, the composition of the portfolio is,

$$(0.5 \times C2) + (0.5 \times C4) = [0.5 \times (0, 0.95, 0.05)] + [0.5 \times (0, 0.7, 0.3)]$$
$$= (0, 0.825, 0.175)$$

The return and risk of this resultant portfolio are 29.08% and 20.44% respectively. Its return lies in-between that of C2 and C3. But the risk, 20.44%, is higher than the resultant portfolios of C2 and C3 (risk of the resultant portfolio of the adjacent portfolios, C3 and C4, is 19.53%; while risk of the corner portfolio C4 is 17.84%).

So this resultant portfolio is a non-efficient portfolio.

Corner portfolio, C5

The next corner portfolio, C5, is constructed with the composition of 10%, 60% and 30% in HDFC, HDFC Bank and BPCL respectively. Thus, C5 = (0.1, 0.6, 0.3). The return and risk of the corner portfolio, C5, is 26.65% and 17.05% respectively.

The resultant portfolio of the adjacent portfolios, C4 and C5, with C4 and C5 in 50:50 ratio, has the composition,

$$(0.5 \times C4) + (0.5 \times C5) = [0.5 \times (0, 0.7, 0.3)] + [0.5 \times (0.1, 0.6, 0.3)]$$
$$= (0.05, 0.65, 0.3)$$

The return and risk of this portfolio is 27.27% and 17.41% respectively.

Similarly, the compositions of the other corner portfolios are identified. Table 22.1, below, shows the return and risk of corner portfolios, C6 and C7. The next corner portfolio, from the given exhibit, is C8 with the composition of (0.4, 0, 0.6). The return and risk of this portfolio are 20.07% and 11.85% respectively. From the given exhibit[4], it is evident that the portfolio composed of investments in the proportion of 40% in HDFC, 0% in HDFC Bank and 60% in BPCL securities respectively has the least risk. It means it is the final point for the construction of the portfolio.

Table 22.1: Proportion, Risk and Return of Corner Portfolios

Corner portfolio for a three security case					
	Weight			Corner portfolio	
Corner portfolio	HDFC	HDFC Bank	BPCL	Expected return (%)	Standard deviation (%)
C1	0	1	0	30.74	24.84
C2	0	0.95	0.05	30.26	23.52
C3	0.1	0.8	0.1	28.55	21.75
C4	0	0.7	0.3	27.89	17.84
C5	0.1	0.6	0.3	26.65	17.05
C6	0.2	0	0.8	20.66	14.12
C7	0.3	0	0.7	20.36	12.25
C8	0.4	0	0.6	20.07	11.85

---

[4] The given exhibit shows the sample of portfolios, constructed by taking different weights of the above three securities. It is not the complete set of portfolios. The construction of the algorithm is beyond the scope of this book. Here an effort has been made to make readers aware of how efficient portfolios are derived, as simply as possible.

Table 22.2: Proportion, Risk and Return of Adjacent Portfolios

Adjacent portfolio	Corresponding corner portfolio	Weight			Expected return (%)	Standard deviation (%)
		HDFC	HDFC Bank	BPCL		
1	C1 and C2	0	0.975	0.015	30.50	24.18
2	C2 and C3	0.05	0.875	0.075	29.41	22.61
3 (non-adjacent)	C1 and C3	0.05	0.9	0.05	29.64	23.28
4	C3 and C4	0.05	0.75	0.2	28.22	19.53
4 (non-adjacent)	C2 and C4	0	0.825	0.175	29.08	20.44
5	C4 and C5	0.05	0.65	0.3	27.27	17.41

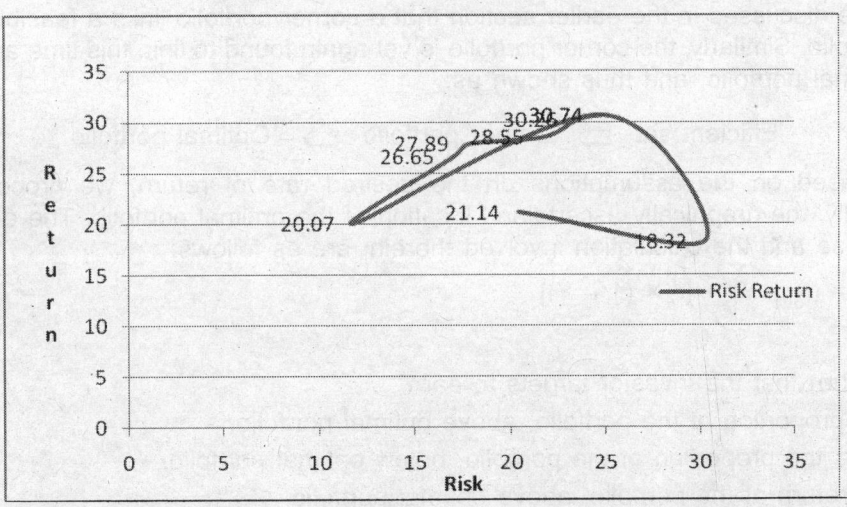

Figure 22.11: Location of the corner portfolios

> **Pause for thought:** From the feasible set is selected the efficient set. Yet there is another entity, corner portfolio, which serves as the link in-between. Corner portfolios are those which have predominant investment in one of the securities. And two adjacent corner portfolios combined together give an efficient portfolio—with the return-risk falling in the desirable zone. While the resultant portfolio, of the combination of two non-adjacent corner portfolios, lead to an inefficient portfolio, obviously because of its unfavorable risk-return characteristics. All these assessments lead to the derivation of the location of the efficient portfolio, derived from the position of the corner portfolios.

22.4.1 Optimal Portfolio

After deriving the location for Markowitz's efficient set, the task left is the identification of an optimal portfolio from a given efficient set. The optimal portfolio should correspond to the tangency point of efficient set and investor's indifference curve. The identification and selection of the portfolio is done from the graph of the corner portfolio itself. We have already discussed that the selection of the optimal portfolio depends upon risk bearing capacity of the investor and on his/her risk-return trade-off. So, the optimal portfolio is not the same for all types of investors. From the above figure it can be concluded that a risk-averse investor will try to identify his/her optimal portfolio between C6 and C7 or between C7 and C8. Any portfolio lying between C6 and C7 or between C7 and C8 has a comparatively lesser risk, with the return in the range of around 20%. Conversely, for a risk-loving investor, the optimal portfolio might be between C1 and C2 or between C2 and C3. In this region comparatively higher return can be generated, in lieu of high risk. If a region between these two extremes are chosen, by assuming that the investor wants to earn a return somewhere around 25%, the investor will be led to select two corner portfolios, C5 and C6, as 25% lies in between. Furthermore, from the Figure 22.11 it is apparent that out of all the corner portfolios, the returns of C5 and C6 are lying more towards the north-west. Thus two parameters support C5 and C6: the desired range of return, 25%, lies in-between and these two are situated on the north-western region.

We have discussed in the earlier section that a corner portfolio links a feasible set and an efficient portfolio. Similarly, the corner portfolio is yet again found to link, this time an efficient set and the optimal portfolio, and thus shown as:

$$\text{Efficient set} \Rightarrow \text{Corner portfolio} \Rightarrow \text{Optimal portfolio}$$

Now, based on the assumptions on the desired rate of return, we proceed to prove mathematically, the graphically ascertained location of the optimal portfolio. The equation used for the purpose and the calculation involved therein, are as follows:

$$R^* = (r_a \times Y) + [r_b \times (1 - Y)]$$

where,

R^* = return that the investor targets to earn.
Y = the proportion of the portfolio, above optimal portfolio.
$(1 - Y)$ = the proportion of the portfolio, below optimal portfolio.
r_a = the return of the portfolio, above optimal portfolio.
r_b = return of the portfolio, below optimal portfolio.

$$25\% = (26.65\% \times Y) + [20.66\% \times (1-Y)]$$
$$4.34 = 5.99Y$$
$$Y = 4.34/5.99 = 0.7245$$
$$Y = 0.7245 = \text{proportion invested in the corner portfolio, C5.}$$
$$1 - Y = 0.2755 = \text{proportion invested in the corner portfolio, C6.}$$

Substituting these values of proportion in corner portfolios C5 and C6, we get the resultant portfolio

= (0.7245 × C5) + (0.2755 × C6)
= [0.7245 × (0.1, 0.6, 0.3)] + [0.2755 × (0.2, 0, 0.8)]
= 0.1275 + 0.4347 + 0.4377 = 0.9999 ≃ 1

The return and risk of this portfolio are 25% and 14.51% respectively. The risk-return characteristics of the resultant portfolio indicate that the target portfolio, in this case the optimal portfolio, will lie more towards the north-west region, than C5 and C6 corner portfolios.

> **Pause for thought:** An investor's optimal portfolio is defined by the tangency point between the efficient set and the investor's indifference curve.

SUMMARY

- ✓ 'n' number of portfolios can be constructed by applying Markowitz model. From these 'n' portfolios, investors can select only those portfolios which are on the given indifference curves corresponding to their risk-return preferences.

- ✓ An indifference curve shows different combinations of risk and return that an investor can derive and are equally desirable by using different proportions of given securities.

- ✓ Portfolios lying on the north-west region are more desirable than the portfolios lying on the south-eastern region. Deeper the portfolio in north-west region, more preferred it is than the portfolio lying just on the north-western boundary.

- ✓ By efficient set is meant the set of those portfolios which provide maximum return for varying level of risk, and minimum risk for varying levels of expected return.

- ✓ Investors prefer to select the optimal portfolio from the given set of portfolios lying on the efficient set.

- ✓ From the 'n' number of portfolios lying on the efficient set, investors can construct the corner portfolios, which in turn lead to the identification of the optimal portfolio.

- ✓ An optimal portfolio is identified with the help of corner portfolios and is tangent to the indifference curve and efficient set.

KEY CONCEPTS

Optimal Portfolio	Risk-Loving Investors	Feasible Set
Efficient Set	Risk-Averse Investors	Adjacent Portfolio
Corner Portfolio	Neutral Investors	Efficient Portfolio
Tangency Point	Indifference Curves	Inefficient Portfolio

REVIEW QUESTIONS

1. Why do the indifference curves move upwards, to the right?
2. Why is it not possible for two indifference curves to intersect each other?
3. It is always preferable to select the portfolios lying on the north-west region of the indifference curve. Why? Explain with reasons.
4. Why do the indifference curves of risk-loving investors lie towards north-east region?
5. "Generally the individual securities lie on the northern region of the feasible set, while the portfolios lie on the north-western region of the feasible set." Is this statement it true? Give reasons for your answer.
6. Explain why is it important to identify the corner portfolios for ascertaining the composition of the efficient set.

CASE STUDY

Mr. C. R. Dhola, aged 60, has recently retired from the Surat Municipal Corporation. He had joined SMC at the age of 22. Mr. Dhola was the only earning member of his family when he began working for SMC. At that time responsibility of two younger sisters, mother and wife rested on him. His mother had few gold ornaments. Those helped them to marry off the two daughters in the family, as at that time Mr. Dhola had negligible savings. But now at the age of 60, having fulfilled all his social obligations, he wants to leave a peaceful life. He has savings of approximately 20 lakhs in a bank—in the form of fixed deposits in bank and the amount he received from his provident fund, to name a couple of them. Mr. Sanjay Dhola, one of the three sons Mr. Dhola has, is on a trip to India from the US, for 20 days. His other two sons stay in India and have small businesses of their own, but these are not stable. From these two sons he has two grandsons and one granddaughter. Mr. Dhola wishes to set aside few lakhs now for financing the higher education of these grandchildren of his. Grandsons are aged 8 and 6 while the granddaughter is just 3 years of age. Mr. Dhola is confused and is unable to decide on his own on how he should invest his funds so that he would be able to meet the financial demands for their education in the future. He has come across several insurance and mutual fund agents and has gone through the different policies, modes of investment and probable benefits, the risk factor, etc. Mr. Dhola strongly believes in investing in safer options like buying land and investing in gold. He believes that stock market will not give desired return 10, 20 and 25 years down the line. On the other hand, he also feels that returns from fixed deposits in the bank are not enough to fulfill his objective. His NRI son is insisting that his father invests in the stock market. And for that he is specifically emphasizing on IT and pharmaceutical sectors, which he believes will give good returns. As per his suggestion, Mr. Dhola has collected the prices of the following scrips from the internet. He has also calculated their annual return to have a detailed idea of their performance. He has also collected gold prices from 2002 to 2011, to compare with these scrips.

Year	Zydus (Return %)	Infosys (Return %)	IBM (Return %)	Gold (Price in Rs.)
2002	−60.78	17.08	−12.53	4200
2003	207.38	16.84	1.96	5400
2004	357.27	−62.73	4.32	6522
2005	126.89	42.77	−7.80	7553
2006	−36.34	−25.32	5.71	9356
2007	79.48	−21.12	2.42	10134
2008	−45.91	−36.41	3.97	12571
2009	268.88	131.58	2.84	17973
2010	113.68	32.19	2.19	20553
2011	−10.26	−19.52	3.21	26364

Exhibit A

Portfolio	HDFC	HDFC Bank	BPCL	Return	Risk
1.00	0.10	0.20	0.70	22.85	14.08
2.00	0.20	0.30	0.50	23.51	13.25
3.00	0.30	0.40	0.30	24.16	16.35
4.00	0.40	0.50	0.10	24.82	21.76
5.00	0.50	0.40	0.10	23.58	22.25
6.00	0.60	0.40	0.00	23.29	25.85
7.00	0.50	0.50	0.00	24.53	25.16
8.00	0.40	0.60	0.00	25.77	24.66
9.00	0.30	0.50	0.20	25.11	18.80
10.00	0.10	0.60	0.30	26.65	17.05
11.00	0.00	0.70	0.30	27.89	17.84
12.00	0.00	0.80	0.20	28.84	19.88
13.00	0.00	0.90	0.10	29.79	22.25
14.00	0.00	0.10	0.90	22.19	18.30
15.00	0.90	0.10	0.00	19.56	28.98
16.00	0.90	0.00	0.10	18.61	26.26
17.00	0.80	0.10	0.10	19.85	24.99
18.00	0.70	0.20	0.10	21.10	23.89

19.00	0.60	0.20	0.20	21.39	20.23
20.00	0.50	0.30	0.20	22.63	19.49
21.00	0.10	0.10	0.80	21.90	15.23
22.00	0.20	0.10	0.70	21.61	12.99
23.00	0.20	0.20	0.60	22.56	12.68
24.00	0.30	0.20	0.50	22.26	12.77
25.00	0.30	0.30	0.40	23.21	14.28
26.00	0.90	0.00	0.10	18.61	26.26
27.00	0.10	0.00	0.90	20.95	16.99
28.00	0.20	0.00	0.80	20.66	14.12
29.00	0.00	0.00	1.00	21.24	20.43
30.00	1.00	0.00	0.00	18.32	30.31
31.00	0.00	1.00	0.00	30.74	24.84
32.00	0.00	0.50	0.50	25.99	15.26
33.00	0.50	0.00	0.50	19.78	13.06
34.00	0.60	0.20	0.20	21.39	20.23
35.00	0.20	0.60	0.20	26.36	18.88
36.00	0.20	0.20	0.60	22.56	12.68
37.00	0.30	0.30	0.40	23.21	14.28
38.00	0.30	0.40	0.30	24.16	16.35
39.00	0.40	0.30	0.30	22.92	16.49
40.00	0.10	0.80	0.10	28.55	21.75
41.00	0.00	0.95	0.05	30.27	23.52
42.00	0.45	0.45	0.10	24.20	21.97
43.00	0.45	0.50	0.05	24.68	23.41
44.00	0.00	0.20	0.80	23.14	16.60
45.00	0.20	0.00	0.80	20.66	14.12
46.00	0.90	0.00	0.10	18.61	26.26
47.00	0.10	0.00	0.90	20.95	16.99
48.00	0.30	0.00	0.70	20.36	12.25
49.00	0.00	0.60	0.40	26.94	16.26
50.00	0.10	0.10	0.80	21.90	15.23
51.00	0.10	0.50	0.40	25.70	15.28

52.00	0.70	0.00	0.30	19.20	18.72
53.00	0.15	0.50	0.35	25.55	15.76
54.00	0.00	0.30	0.70	24.09	15.44
55.00	0.00	0.70	0.30	27.89	17.84
56.00	0.00	0.85	0.15	29.32	21.03
57.00	0.10	0.35	0.55	24.27	13.79
58.00	0.10	0.50	0.40	25.70	15.28
59.00	0.40	0.00	0.60	20.07	11.85

SUGGESTED FURTHER READING FOR EMPIRICAL WORK

1. Feinstein, C.D., and Mukund, N. (1993), "Reformulation of a Mean-Absolute Deviation Portfolio Optimization Model", *Management Science*, Vol. 39, No.12.
2. Parkhe, A. (1991), "International Portfolio Analysis: A New Model", *MIR: Management International Review*, Vol. 31, No.4.
3. Perold, A.F. (1984), "Large-Scale Portfolio Optimization", *Management Science*, Vol. 30, No.10.
4. Lee, S., and Chang, K. (1995),"Mean-Variance-Instability Portfolio Analysis: A Case of Taiwan's Stock Market", *Management Science*, Vol. 41, No.7
5. Lim, A.E.B.,and Zhou, X.Y.(2002),"Mean-Variance Portfolio Selection with Random Parameters in a Complete Market", *Mathematics of Operations Research*, Vol. 27, No. 1.
6. Bird, R., and Tippett, M. (1986), "Naive Diversification and Portfolio Risk-A Note", *Management Science*, Vol. 32, No.2.
7. Hui, T., Kwan, E.K., and Lee, C. (1993), "Optimal Portfolio Diversification: Empirical Bayes versus Classical Approach", *The Journal of the Operational Research Society*, Vol. 44, No.11.
8. Jorion, P. (2003), "Portfolio Optimization with Tracking-Error Constraints", *Financial Analysts Journal*, Vol. 59, No.5.
9. Finkelshtain, I., and Chalfant, J.A. (1993), "Portfolio Choices in the Presence of Other Risks", *Management Science*, Vol. 39, No.8.
10. Scherer, B. (2002), "Portfolio Resampling: Review and Critique", *Financial Analysts Journal*, Vol. 58, No.6.
11. Simaan, Y. (1993), "Portfolio Selection and Asset Pricing-Three-Parameter Framework", *Management Science*, Vol. 39, No.5.
12. Devinney, T.M., and Stewart, D.W. (1988), "Rethinking the Product Portfolio: A Generalized Investment Model", *Management Science*, Vol. 34, No. 9.

13. Goldfarb, D., and Iyengar, G. (2003), "Robust Portfolio Selection Problems", *Mathematics of Operations Research*, Vol. 28, No.1.
14. Best, M.J., and Grauer, R.R. (1991), "Sensitivity Analysis for Mean-Variance Portfolio Problems", *Management Science*, Vol. 37, No.8.

REFERENCES

1. http://www.scribd.com/doc/72384268/50/The-Feasible-Set
2. http://www.norstad.org/finance/port.pdf
3. http://en.wikipedia.org/wiki/Efficient_frontier
4. http://www.orsj.or.jp/~archive/pdf/e_mag/Vol.39_1_099.pdf
5. http://www.risklatte.com/Articles_new/Portfolioanalysis/PT_22.php
6. http://www.slideshare.net/akashbakshi/4corner-portfolio

23
PORTFOLIO PERFORMANCE EVALUATION

> ### LEARNING OBJECTIVES
> The purpose of this chapter is to enable you to understand:
> - The evaluation of the performance of a portfolio, using risk-adjusted measures.
> - Analysis of the security market line for the portfolio.
> - The application of Jenson, Sharpe and Treynor's method for evaluating the performance of a portfolio.

23.1 INTRODUCTION

The selection of portfolios—efficient as well as optimal—depending upon the risk preferences of the investors doesn't mean that they would continue to be effective with changing times. The performance of the portfolios requires evaluation, periodically, as the macroeconomic and microeconomic factors are seldom static. So under this dynamic state, the portfolios too reflect changes in their behaviour.

Hence this chapter is dedicated to the principles, and their applications, for evaluating the performance of a portfolio. These evaluations serve as a feedback to the portfolio managers. So as is the need, they can change strategies to enhance the performance of the portfolio; or if need be, shift the investment(s) to another portfolio. For the purpose of evaluating and managing a portfolio, this chapter begins with 'return' of the portfolio as the parameter. Subsequent to it, the measure of an adjusted-risk too is incorporated in this process. And these principles are all explained by applying them to real portfolios, using the different tools available for the evaluation.

23.1.1 Measuring Portfolio Performance: the Conventional Way

There are certain conventional methods to evaluate the performance of a portfolio. And these include some over-simplifications too. So before proceeding to the complex methods we take another look at the conventional ones.

Based on dividend, opening price and closing price of a stock

The current price of the stock of a hypothetical company, PQR, is assumed to be Rs. 100. It is further assumed that the stock pays a dividend of Rs. 5 and its closing price is Rs. 110, at which the stock is sold off. The return expected by the investor is calculated in the conventional manner as:

$$\frac{\text{Dividend income} + \text{Capital gain/loss}}{\text{Buying price of the stock}} = \frac{5+10}{100} = 15\%$$

The rate of return, calculated above, is also ascertained by discounting the cash flow (as has been discussed in the equity valuation model in Chapter 18). Taking the same data as above, the expected return, vide this method too, comes out to be the same:

$$100 = \frac{(5+110)}{(1+r)} = 15\%$$

> **Pause for thought:** These calculations primarily utilize the concept of capital gain/loss, i.e., the difference between the prices at which the stocks are bought and sold.

Time-weighted return versus rupees-weighted return

Time-weighted rate of return is the measure of the compound rate of growth in a portfolio. It is also known as the geometric mean return. This method eliminates the distortion created by inflow of fund in investment. The method assumes that all cash distributions of the investment are reinvested in the portfolio and exactly same periods are used for comparisons. By using this method, the effect of varying cash inflows is eliminated by assuming a single investment at the beginning of a period, and measuring the growth or loss of the market value, at the end of the period. It is used to measure and compare the return earned by investment managers. Rupees-weighted return measures rate of return for a single asset or portfolio of assets. As this method incorporates size and timing of the cash flow, it is an effective method to measure the return of the portfolio. It is equivalent to internal rate of return (IRR).

Time-weighted concepts are usually cumulative approaches, and hence applied to multi-period investments. How this functions, should be clear from the following discussion for which the same example, as above, is chosen.

It is supposed that the investor wants to purchase another share of the PQR Co. at the end of the first year. But the price at the end of the first year is Rs. 110, compared to the purchasing price, Rs. 100, at the beginning of the first year. It is assumed that both shares are held till the end of the second year. At the end of the second year, the price is taken as Rs. 115.

In this case, the total investment is,

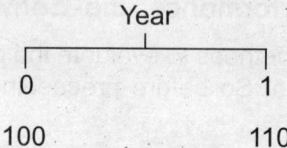

Cash inflow from dividend,

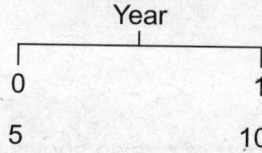

Cash flow from investment proceeds

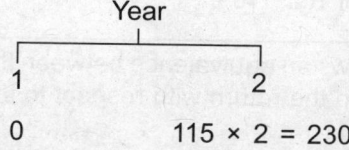

By using the DCF technique the average return over 2 years is determined by equating the present values of cash inflow and outflow. Total outflow is Rs. 100 in the first year to buy the share, and it is Rs. 110 in the second year for buying another stock of PQR.

Similarly, total inflow is comprised of: Rs. 5 (dividend in the first year); Rs. 5 (as dividend in the second year on the share purchased in the first year) and again Rs. 5 (dividend on the other share purchased in the second year). Thus it amounts to: Rs. 10 + Rs. 5 (in form of dividend) and Rs. 230[1], the proceeds from the sale two shares at the end of the second year[2].

$$-100 - \frac{110}{1+r} = \frac{5}{1+r} + \frac{240}{(1+r)^2}$$

$$r = 10\%$$

'r' (10%) is the internal rate of return. The return, in the second year, when stocks are purchased at a comparatively higher price (Rs. 110), has a greater influence on the overall return on the investment, than that for the first year. Hence, it is also called the rupees-weighted return on the investment.

Per year return is,

$$r_1 = \frac{110 + 5 - 100}{100} = 15\%$$

$$r_2 = \frac{115 + 5 - 110}{110} = 9.09\%$$

As stated above, is demonstrated through the calculations of geometric change. The return from the first year is 15%; and as the stock is purchased at comparatively higher price, the return in the second year is less than that obtained in the first year.

---

[1] Sales proceeds from two shares, Rs. 115 × 2 = Rs. 230.

[2] Here Rs. 240 consists of Rs. 230 (sales proceeds from two shares plus Rs. 10, dividends of the first and second years).

Geometric return is,

$$r_G = (r_1 \times r_2)^{1/2} - 1$$
$$= (1.15 \times 1.0909)^{1/2} - 1$$
$$= 1.12 - 1 = 0.12 = 12\%$$

A lower value of r_2, compared to that of r_1, also shows that rupees-weighted average is less than time-weighted average. The return in the second year is less, as the stock is purchased at a comparatively higher price of Rs. 110.

> **Pause for thought:** This draws an equivalence between the return with respect to the holding period (time) of the stock and the return with respect to the income generated (cash) during the same time.

23.1.2 Performance Measurement by Adjusting Risk

It has been mentioned at the outset that the evaluation process would take into cognizance the risk element and the return generated. In keeping with that, calculation of return by conventional methods has been discussed above. And now we proceed to the element of risk and how the performance is measured by adjusting the same. This leads us to a measure of the risk-adjusted performance of the portfolio.

We know that the risk involved in the portfolio (and for securities in general) is measured by the standard deviation (positive square root of the variance) and risk is comprised of two components: market risk (measured by beta, the systematic risk) and unique risk (unsystematic risk). So once the returns of a portfolio are estimated, we move towards evaluating its performance. But for that, we need to calculate the risk, as comparing the risk with the return enables the evaluation of the performance. Thus, the calculation and analysis of risk becomes very crucial, to be used judiciously for arriving at a rational decision. For example, a client, Mr. X, is assumed to have many assets[3]. Under the circumstances, market risk[4] of the portfolio provides the appropriate measure of the portfolio's impact on Mr. X's overall level of risk. But if this portfolio is the only one portfolio or investment possessed by Mr. X, and if it is not well-diversified portfolio, then the total risk of the portfolio is a better measure of risk. In such a case, it is not advisable to rely on market risk for a given portfolio (as the given portfolio is not well-diversified). So, when performance is measured with respect to risk, it is a practice to take into account either market risk or total risk. It is because of this the unsystematic risk and its impact on portfolio performance[5] will not be addressed here.

Suppose we want to measure the performance of a particular portfolio by considering its market price data of the last 10 years. In such a case, the average return of the portfolio is denoted by r_p simply,

---

[3] Here 'many assets' means the portfolio of Mr. X is very much diversified. So, for such a portfolio the relevant measure of performance is the market risk.

[4] Because it is believed that by efficient diversification, unique risk is eliminated. Hence, the risk that remains is only the market risk.

[5] It is assumed that portfolio consists of enough number of securities to eliminate unique risk completely.

$$r_p = \sum_{t=1}^{t} r_{pt} \qquad (1)$$

where,

r_p = average return of the portfolio.

r_{pt} = return of the portfolio at time, t (which is ex-post or historical).

t = total time interval or period (in this case it is 10).

For the same portfolio, the variance and then standard deviation of the portfolio are calculated by the equations:

$$\sigma_p^2 = \sum_{t=1}^{t} \frac{(r_{pt} - r_p)^2}{t-1} \qquad (2)$$

$$\sigma_p = (\sigma_p^2)^{1/2} \qquad (3)$$

It gives the amount of total risk that the portfolio carried during the selected time period of 10 years. Thus, by using ex-post average return (r_p) and standard deviation (σ_p), as measures to evaluate the performance of the portfolios, the portfolios can be compared.

In the Table 23.1 below, example of ICICI Equity Fund (Growth) has been used to show the portfolio performance evaluation.

Table 23.1: Return and Risk of the Portfolio

\multicolumn{5}{c}{ICICI Equity Fund (Growth)}				
Year 1	NAV 2	$[P_1 - P_0]/P_0 \times 100$ 3	$[r - E(r)]$ 4	$[r - E(r)]^2$ 5
2001	10.19			
2002	8.85	–13.15	–61.80	3819.20
2003	38.09	330.40	281.75	79380.78
2004	13.09	–65.63	–114.28	13060.73
2005	16.91	29.18	–19.47	378.96
2006	32.83	94.15	45.50	2069.88
2007	40.58	23.61	–25.04	627.16
2008	58.26	43.57	–5.08	25.82
2009	32.08	–44.94	–93.59	8758.34
2010	52.64	64.09	15.44	238.40
2011	65.92	25.23	–23.42	548.57
		Return = 48.65%	108907.84	**Variance = 12100.87** **S.D. = 110.00%**

The average return of the portfolio is 48.65% and the standard deviation is 110%.

> *Check yourself*
> Collect the NAV of different mutual fund (sector wise and general) schemes from www.bajajcapital.com for a period of 10 years. Calculate their average return and risk and compare then with the appropriate market index. Find out how many mutual funds have outperformed the market? These mutual funds are sector specific or general?

> **Pause for thought:** The risk-adjusted measure of performance utilizes the average return of the portfolio and return of the portfolio over a specified time interval. The risk-adjusted return is the difference between the average return of the portfolio and the return of the benchmark portfolio. This difference is commonly referred to as alpha of the portfolio.

23.1.3 Measuring Performance of Portfolios

It is to be noted that the discussions in this chapter are on the portfolios that have been constructed and are managed by the active strategy of portfolio management. The comparison of the performance of such portfolios is desired to be on a relevant basis—by comparing with the performance of others—and not on an absolute basis. So, different mutual funds will be analyzed, using different evaluation criteria, to judge their relative performances.

Thus, staying with our Mr. X, it is further assumed that according to his portfolio manager, the return earned by his portfolio (constructed by investing in diversified assets), last year, is 28%. This is a huge return. And if it is a fact that last year the BSE Sensex went up by 12%, then Mr. X's portfolio has performed very well. But had the Sensex gone up by 35%, then the same 28% return, that Mr. X's portfolio earns, will not be considered a great performance. In fact it would be received as a bad news. Hence, it is realized that to know whether the return of a given portfolio is superior or inferior it must be compared with either an actively or passively managed portfolio (i.e., some benchmark portfolio).

Ideally such benchmark portfolio(s) should be: comprised of enough diversified assets, practical and known in advance. To be a benchmark portfolio, it has to be acknowledged as an ideal portfolio, as compared to the one which is being evaluated. It is all relative. The characteristics are all with respect to the other. Thus the benchmark portfolio too is not a standard portfolio. It consists of only particular types of assets. The purpose of the benchmark portfolio is to reflect the objective of the client. Hence it differs for each client, and also varies with time. For example, if the objective of Mr. X is to earn superior return by investing in a portfolio (which consist of only medium scale companies' stock), then BSE Sensex is not the appropriate benchmark for him. In such a case BSE mid cap or Nifty mid cap is a better indicator of performance.

Furthermore, return too has to be compared along with the risk. So, return of the portfolio under evaluation must be compared with that of the benchmark portfolio. Figure 23.1, as shown below, represents such a comparison for hypothetical portfolio of equities. The performance of this equity portfolio, for each year, is measured by diamond. The performance of other hypothetical portfolios (of equity stocks only) is represented by the box surrounding the diamond. This box is most commonly referred to as a box plot or a floating bar chart. The figure summarises the rankings for the performance over five periods: 1 year, 2 years, 3 years, 4 years and 5 years.

The top and bottom line of the box indicates the return of the fifth and ninety fifth percentile comparison portfolio respectively. The dashed line (top and bottom) shows the rate of return of the twenty fifth and seventy fifth percentiles. The solid line, in the middle, shows the average rate of return of the portfolio. The diamond is drawn at the average rate of return of the given portfolio. Also, the diamond in the given box represents the performance of a given portfolio, relative to other comparable portfolios from the entire population of portfolios, in the given context. In this comparison, risk of the other comparable portfolios is assumed to be similar to that of the benchmark equity fund. When such criteria (portfolios of same type, similar risk-return levels during given time period) are not maintained, the evaluation of the performance of the portfolio might be invalidated. Finally, the return of the portfolio being evaluated must be compared with performance of the related index.

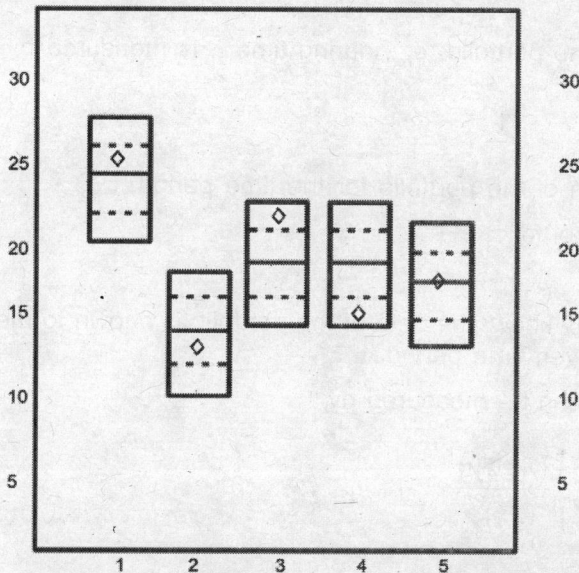

Figure 23.1: Comparison of portfolio return

> **Pause for thought:** The measure of the performance of a portfolio is had, with respect to the risk-return levels of the benchmark portfolio. It is a portfolio of equities and though is not an ideal portfolio, but is considered so, compared to the one which is evaluated.

23.2 BETA OF THE PORTFOLIO

The beta of the portfolio is calculated by calculating the covariance of the portfolio with that of the index. This is then divided by variance of the related index. The covariance is estimated by comparing the excess return of the portfolio is compared with that of the related market index, during the time period, t.

$$\beta_p = \frac{\left(t \sum_{t=1}^{t} Er_{mt} \, Er_{pt}\right) - \left(\sum_{t=1}^{t} Er_{pt} \sum_{t=1}^{t} Er_{mt}\right)}{\left(t \sum_{t=1}^{t} Er_{mt}\right)^2 - \left(\sum_{t=1}^{t} Er_{pt}\right)^2} \tag{4}$$

where,

Er_{mt} = excess return of the market portfolio for the time period, t.

The excess return of the market portfolio is measured by the relation,

$Er_{mt} = r_{mt} - r_{ft}$

Excess return on the portfolio, e_{rpt}, during time t, is measured by

$Er_{pt} = r_{pt} - r_{ft}$

where,

Er_{pt} = excess return of the portfolio for the time period, t.

r_{pt} = return of the portfolio.

r_{ft} = risk-free rate.

Thus, as we already know, the beta of the portfolio is shown to measure the market risk of the portfolio over the given time period, t.

Alternatively, beta can be measured by,

$$\beta_p = \frac{(n * \Sigma xy) - (\Sigma x \, \Sigma y)}{(n * \Sigma x^2) - (\Sigma x)^2} \tag{5}$$

where,

x and y = return of the market and portfolio respectively.

n = time period.

Beta of the ICCI Equity Fund (Growth) has been shown below, in Table 23.2.

Table 23.2: Beta of the Portfolio

No.	Year	Market Return (X) (%)	Portfolio Return (Y) (%)	$[R_x - E(R_x)]$	$[R_x - E(R_x)] \times [R_x - E(R_x)]$	$[R_y - E(R_y)]$	$[R_x - E(R_x)] \times [R_y - E(R_y)]$
1	2001						
2	2002	−11.43	−13.15	−29.18	851.52	−61.80	1803.36
3	2003	35.38	330.40	17.63	310.65	281.75	4965.87
4	2004	−4.94	−65.63	−22.70	515.17	−114.28	2593.94
5	2005	55.59	29.18	37.84	1431.72	−19.47	−736.59

6	2006	17.23	94.15	−0.52	0.27	45.50	−23.82
7	2007	19.18	23.61	1.43	2.04	−25.04	−35.76
8	2008	−14.46	43.57	−32.21	1037.42	−5.08	163.66
9	2009	40.49	−44.94	22.74	516.93	−93.59	−2127.79
10	2010	31.47	64.09	13.72	188.28	15.44	211.86
11	2011	9.01	25.23	−8.74	76.36	−23.42	204.67
		E(x) =17.75%	E(y) = 48.65		4930.36		7019.40
					547.82		Cov = 779.93
					S.D.=23.41		

$$\beta_p = \frac{Cov_{(R_{Portfolio}, R_{market})}}{\text{Variance of market}}$$

$$\beta_p = \frac{\sigma_{pm}}{\sigma_m^2} = \frac{779.93}{547.82} = 1.42$$

> **Check yourself**
> Calculate beta of the portfolio of at least ten randomly selected mutual fund schemes, by using historical data of at least 10 years. Now compare them with the current year's return and risk of those mutual funds. Do all the mutual funds, whose beta is higher/lower, perform better/poor than the market? Is beta, found out with the help of historical data, good measure to check whether a given mutual fund is superior or inferior compared to the market?

> **Pause for thought:** Beta of the portfolio is the systematic risk of the portfolio, hence market dependent and undiversifiable.

23.2.1 Security Market Line (SML) of a Portfolio (Ex-Post)

For the given time period (assumed to be 10 years, in this case), ex-post SML is estimated by finding out the average risk-free return and market return.

$$r_f = \sum_{t=1}^{t} \frac{r_{ft}}{t} \tag{6}$$

where,

r_f = average risk-free return.

r_{ft} = risk-free return at time, t.

t = number of periods in a given time period.

In a similar manner, the average market return is computed by,

$$r_m = \sum_{t=1}^{t} \frac{r_{mt}}{t} \qquad (7)$$

where,

r_m = average market return.

r_{mt} = return of market at time, t.

t = number of periods, in a given time period.

From the values of r_f and r_m, we can solve the equation of SML (security market line).

We know that SML (from Chapter 9) for an individual security is given by,

$$r_i = r_f + \beta(r_m - r_f)$$

Similarly, SML for a given portfolio is,

$$r_p = r_f + \beta_p(r_m - r_f) \qquad (8)$$

The ex-post characteristics line for a portfolio of ICICI Fund Co. can be calculated on the basis of the above formulations.

We consider the average return of T-bills of last 10 years, 6.09%[6], and the average market return, 17.75 % (table 23.2).

$$r_p = 6.09\% + 1.42(17.75\% - 6.09\%)$$
$$= 6.09\% + 1.42(11.66\%)$$
$$= 6.09\% + 16.55\%$$
$$= 22.65\%$$

This shows that the given equity portfolio of ICICI equity fund is supposed to give return of 22.65%, as its beta is 1.42 and market return (which is benchmark portfolio in the given case) is 17.75%. However, from Table 23.2 it can be inferred that the given portfolio has performed far better than its anticipated return of 22.65%.

> **Pause for thought:** SML gives the return of the portfolio by considering benchmark return of the portfolio, as a reference, for a given value of beta.

23.2.2 Alpha

The risk-adjusted performance of a portfolio is measured by the difference between its average return and return of the relevant benchmark portfolio. This difference is commonly termed as alpha (α) of the portfolio.

Thus, alpha of the portfolio is denoted by,

$$\alpha_p = r_p - r_m \qquad (9)$$

---

[6] www.rbi.org.

where,

α_p = alpha of the portfolio (ex-post).

r_p = average return of the portfolio.

r_m = average return of the relevant market index (or benchmark portfolio).

Here, alpha (α_p) for the assumed portfolio, is calculated by the approximate method, and value is thus found to be,

$$\alpha_p = 48.65\% - 17.75\% = 30.9\%$$

Where, the portfolio return is the return of the mutual fund being considered, ICICI Equity Fund (Growth) and return of the benchmark portfolio is the market return (in this case, Sensex).

> *Check yourself*
> Collect at least ten mutual fund schemes whose alpha is positive (found out with help of historical data). We know that positive value of alpha indicates such mutual funds are under-priced and so have chances to perform better in near future. What does it indicate? What is your observation when you compare those mutual funds having positive alpha, with their returns in the current year?

> **Pause for thought:** The risk-adjusted return is the difference between the average return of the portfolio and the return of the benchmark portfolio. This difference is commonly referred to as alpha of the portfolio.

23.2.3 Interpretation of Alpha

The positive value of alpha indicates that the average return of the portfolio is greater than the average return of the benchmark portfolio (generally some relevant market index; for example, for a portfolio of medium sized companies, benchmark portfolio is usually the mid cap index of BSE or NSE). Hence, a positive alpha value indicates superior performance of the portfolio, being evaluated, as compared to the benchmark portfolio. Conversely, a negative value of alpha indicates that the portfolio has an average return less than that of the benchmark portfolio. Obviously then, a negative alpha indicates inferior performance.

In the example considered here, the positive value of alpha for the portfolio of the concerned mutual fund of ICICI thus represents superior performance, compared to the market return.

By substituting the value of α_p in Equation (9), we get the portfolio's alpha (ex-post) based on the SML (ex-post).

$$\alpha_p = r_p - [r_f + (r_m - r_f)\beta_p] \qquad (10)$$

Thus, the ex-post characteristics line for the portfolio return can be calculated as,

$$r_p - r_f = \alpha_p + \beta_p(r_m - r_f) \qquad (11)$$

Therefore, the characteristics line for the given fund is,

$$r_p - r_f = 30.9 + 1.42\,(r_m - r_f)$$

For the given portfolio of ICICI, the average return, over the last 10 years is 48.65% and the beta, 1.42. The beta value (greater than 1) indicates that the fund is comparatively aggressive. From the values of beta and average return, the exact vertical distance of the portfolio of ICICI to the ex-post SML is calculated as:

$$\alpha_p = r_p - [r_f + (r_m - r_f)\beta_p] \quad (12)$$

Figure 23.2, below, shows the SML. From the figure it can be seen that its ex-post alpha is positive, which indicates superior performance (intercept of 30.9% on Y-axis, in the graph). By taking the values of alpha and beta the characteristics line can be drawn as in Figure 23.2:

$$r_p - r_f = -\alpha + \beta(r_m - r_f) \quad (13)$$

As the ICICI fund is below the SML (see the characteristics line, Figure 23.2), its ex-post alpha is positive (more than 1) and indicates superior performance. By using the values of alpha and beta, the characteristics line (ex-post) becomes,

$$r_p - r_f = 30.9 + 1.42\,(r_m - r_f)$$

The following steps are involved in the calculation of alpha and beta (ex-post) of the portfolio:

— The average rate of return of the portfolio, market index (i.e., Sensex) and risk-free security (e.g.: T-bills) are calculated.
— Beta (ex-post) of the portfolio is to be calculated.
— This is followed by the calculation of alpha (ex-post) of the portfolio.
— Using the average return of the portfolio, the relevant market index, risk-free rate, alpha and beta, the characteristics line (ex-post) is determined.

Alpha and beta of the portfolio are also calculated by using simple linear regression method.

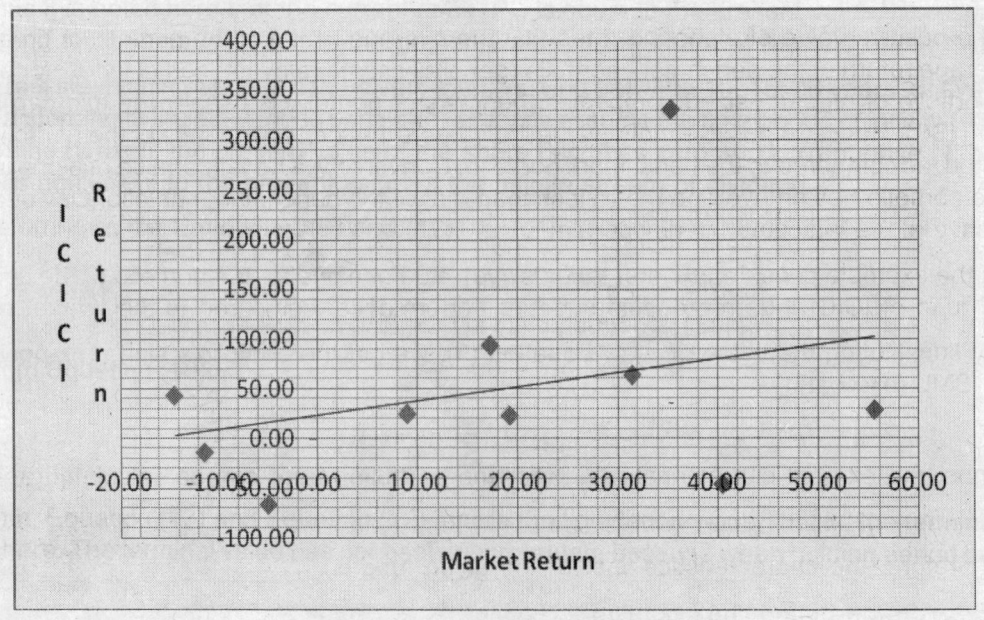

Figure 23.2: Characteristics line

The regression line in the above figure shows the best fit for the scatter diagram.

> **Pause for thought:** A positive value of alpha indicates that the performance of the portfolio being evaluated is superior to that of the benchmark portfolio, while the reverse is true for a negative alpha.

23.2.4 Standard Deviation of Random Error Term

Error is the general term for any departure, of the outcome from its true or expected outcome. Analytical errors can be random or unpredictable deviations between replicates, quantified with standard deviations.

The standard deviation of random error term is formulated as:

$$[\Sigma Y^2 - (\text{Alpha} \times \Sigma Y) - \{\text{Beta} \times (\Sigma X \times Y)\}]/(T-2)\}^{1/2} \qquad (14)$$

Table 23.3: Standard Deviation of Random Error Term

Year	Return: X (%)	Return: Y (%)	Y^2	X^2	XY
2001	-	-			
2002	−11.43	−13.15	172.93	150.28	130.61
2003	35.38	330.40	109161.17	11688.66	1251.59
2004	−4.94	−65.63	4307.83	324.56	24.45
2005	55.59	29.18	851.62	1622.27	3090.30
2006	17.23	94.15	8863.37	1622.02	296.83
2007	19.18	23.61	557.26	452.78	367.89
2008	−14.46	43.57	1898.19	−629.85	208.99
2009	40.49	−44.94	2019.29	−1819.41	1639.32
2010	31.47	64.09	4107.50	2017.15	990.60
2011	9.01	25.23	636.45	227.41	81.25
	$\Sigma X = 177.52$	$\Sigma Y = 486.50$	$\Sigma Y^2 = 132575.61$	$\Sigma X^2 = 15655.87$	$\Sigma XY = 8081.85$

The standard deviation of random error term, for the portfolio of ICICI being considered, thus turns out to be 111.22, when the corresponding values are substituted in Equation (14).

Alpha

Alpha of the portfolio = $(\Sigma Y/T) - \{\text{Beta} \times (\Sigma X/T)\}$ (15)

Thus, alpha for the ICICI stock = 23.38

Standard error of beta

The beta calculated for a given portfolio, XYZ, would remain static for that time period. It will only change if the time period is changed and one or other components (i.e., assets) of the portfolio are changed. Hence, as the duration of the portfolio changes, beta too does. Also, a change in even one of the components of the portfolio causes the beta to change. The standard error of beta tries to indicate the extent of such estimation errors.

Standard error of beta
= Standard deviation of random error term$/\Sigma X^2 - \{(\Sigma X)^2/T\}^{1/2}$ (16)

Standard error of beta for the ICICI fund = 1.58

Standard error of alpha

In the same manner the standard error of alpha measures the magnitude of the possible sampling error that might have occurred during the estimation of the portfolio.

Standard Error of alpha
= Standard deviation of random error term$/[T - \{(\Sigma X)^2/\Sigma X^2\}]^{1/2}$ (17)

Standard Error of alpha for the given ICICI stock = 45.01

> **Pause for thought:** The error terms are actually a measure of the magnitude of estimation errors that creeps in during the construction of a portfolio.

Correlation coefficient

$$\text{Correlation coefficient} = \frac{(\Sigma X \times Y) - (\Sigma X)(\Sigma Y)}{[\{(N\Sigma Y^2) - (\Sigma Y)^2\}\{(N\Sigma X^2) - (\Sigma X)^2\}]^{1/2}}$$

Putting the corresponding values in the above equation, it is found that,

Correlation coefficient for the considered ICICI fund = 0.3029

> **Pause for thought:** Correlation coefficient is a measure of the how well the portfolio correlates to the market index.

Coefficient of determination

Coefficient of determination = (correlation coefficient)^2

∴ Coefficient of determination for the ICICI fund = $(0.3029)^2$ = 0.091

> **Pause for thought:** Coefficient of determination explains the extent of variation, in the excess return of the portfolio, as a function of the market index.

Coefficient of non-determination

Coefficient of non-determination = 1 − Coefficient of determination

Coefficient of non-determination for the ICICI fund = 1 − 0.091 = 0.909

> **Pause for thought:** When market index is not the determinant of the variation in the excess return of a portfolio, the variation is given by the coefficient of non-determination.

We know that the correlation coefficient ranges from –1 to +1. In this case, the correlation coefficient for the portfolio of ICICI is 0.3029, which indicates a very poor relationship between the ICICI portfolio and the market index. The value of r^2—the coefficient of determination—explains the percentage of variation in the excess return of the portfolio, in relation to the variation in the excess return of the market. In the example under consideration, a value of 0.091 indicates that a movement of 9.1%, in the excess return of ICICI portfolio, is because of the movement in excess return of the market index. Coefficient of non-determination explains the movement of the excess return of the ICICI fund, which is not related to the excess return of the market. It can be cited here that 90.9% return of the given fund of ICICI is not related to the market index.

In Table 23.4, the evaluated performances of five mutual funds: (i) Birla Sun Life Dividend Yield Plus–Growth; (ii) Escorts Income Fund; (iii) ICICI Prudential FMCG Fund–Growth; (iv) Reliance Banking Fund–Growth; and (v) Reliance Pharma Fund–Growth, have been recorded. All of these five mutual funds are compared with the relevant market index.

Table 23.4: The ex-post Performance Measures of Selected Funds

Performance evaluation measures	I	II	III	IV	V
Beta	–0.20	–0.05	–0.17	–0.34	–0.11
Alpha	50.76	17.82	41.98	56.00	25.43
Standard deviation of random error term	55.53	11.28	42.12	64.06	26.10
Standard error of beta	0.50	0.10	0.38	0.58	0.24
Standard error of alpha	23.66	4.80	17.94	27.29	11.12
Correlation coefficient	–0.47	–0.46	–0.65	–0.53	–0.35
Coefficient of determination	0.22	0.21	0.42	0.28	0.12
Coefficient of non–determination	0.78	0.79	0.58	0.72	0.88

23.3 TREYNOR'S PERFORMANCE INDEX: REWARD-TO-VOLATILITY RATIO

The reward-to-volatility ratio is equal to the difference of average portfolio return and average risk-free return, divided by the portfolio beta.

$$\text{Treynor's measure} = \frac{r_p - r_f}{\beta_p} \qquad (18)$$

where,

r_p = average return of the portfolio.

r_f = average risk-free return of the portfolio.

For the ICICI portfolio, under consideration here, the average return is 48.65% and the average return of the risk-free security is 6.09%.

So, the average excess return for the portfolio = 48.65% - 6.09 = 42.56%.

The beta of the portfolio is 1.42. Substituting these values in Equation (18), Treynor's measure turns out to be 29.97.

Treynor's performance index = $\dfrac{(48.65\% - 6.09\%)}{1.42}$ = 29.97%

This value is quite close to the alpha (ex-post) value, 23.38, as a measure of portfolio performance and the SML (ex-post) is used as a benchmark portfolio for the purpose of evaluation.

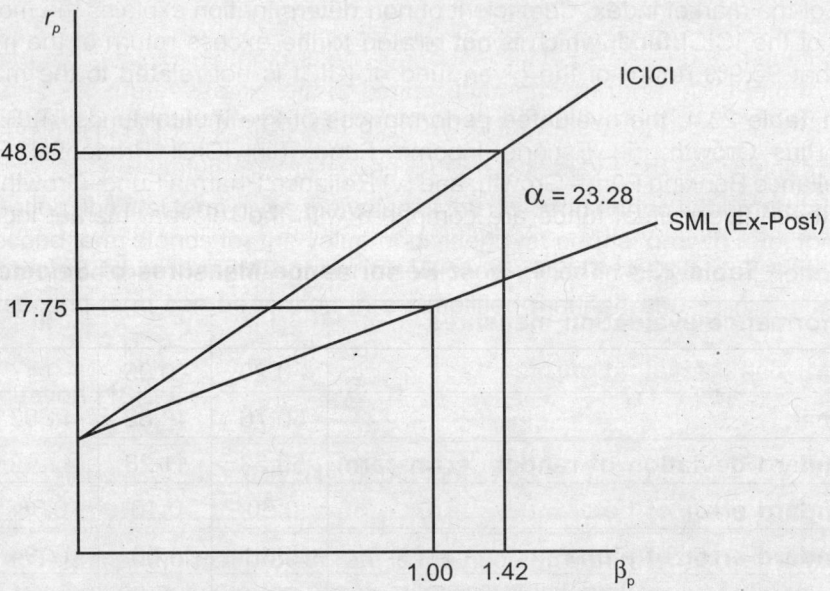

Figure 23.3: Treynor's Portfolio Measure and SML

In the Figure 23.3 above, origin of the slope of the line, at the risk-free rate, is to be noted. The vertical distance between two points, divided by horizontal distance between the two points, gives the slope. In this figure, the vertical distance between two points is ($r_p - r_f$) and the horizontal distance is ($\beta_p - 0$). So, here the slope becomes equal to the formula for Treynor's measure.

Treynor's measure = $\dfrac{r_p - r_f}{\beta_p}$

For the ICICI portfolio, the SML (ex-post) for the period of 10 years is shown by the solid line. A value of 1.42, on X-axis shows the beta of the ICICI, while 48.65% on Y-axis shows the return offered by ICICI fund. From the graph it can be seen that a line passes from risk-free interest rate r_f = 6.09% on Y-axis. Comparing this with the SML (as a benchmark measure for performance), it is clear that if the value of Treynor's measure is higher than the SML it means that the given portfolio performed better than the market. The reverse is true, if Treynor's measure for the portfolio is less than the SML. It can be seen that the particular portfolio has not performed as well as the market has, thus reflecting an inferior performance.

There are certain aspects that have to be kept in mind while measuring the performance of the portfolio by the SML and Treynor's method. They are:

PORTFOLIO PERFORMANCE EVALUATION **629**

- Both tools provide with the same assessment of a portfolio in comparison to the market portfolio (here, index).
- Also, any portfolio whose alpha is positive would lie above the SML, with a slope greater than that of SML.
- Similarly, a portfolio with negative alpha lies below the SML, with the slope lesser than that of SML and thus represents inferior performance, as compared to the market index. Since the portfolio of ICICI is shown to be having positive alpha value, it lies above SML and thus reflects a superior performance.

However care should be taken if the tools for the measurement are the SML and Treynor's ratio. When used for two or more mutual funds, or portfolios, their results are not necessarily consistent. It is because of the fact that though a mutual fund might be ranked first as per the Treynor's measure, and second vide SML; another mutual fund could be ranked first as per SML and second by Treynor's performance index.

> **Pause for thought:** Treynor's evaluation index is the reward-to-volatility (in this case, systematic risk) ratio, which is the difference between average return and the average risk-free return, divided by the beta of the portfolio. And it uses SML as the benchmark.

23.3.1 Sharpe's Measure: Reward-to-Variability Ratio

Unlike the reward-to-systematic risk ratio (i.e., Treynor's performance index, which uses the SML as a benchmark), reward-to-variability ratio measures the risk-adjusted performance, using capital market line (CML) as the benchmark. Thus, while Treynor's ratio measures risk-adjusted performance in terms of systematic risk, Sharpe's ratio measures risk-adjusted performance in terms of total risk (i.e., standard deviation of the portfolio).

$$\text{Sharpe's measure} = \frac{r_p - r_f}{\sigma_p} \tag{19}$$

where,

r_p = average return of the portfolio.

r_f = average risk-free rate.

σ_p = standard deviation (the total risk) of the portfolio.

Thus as per Equation (19),

$$\text{Sharpe's measure for the ICICI fund is} = \frac{48.65\% - 6.09\%}{23.41\%}$$

$$= 1.82$$

In Figure 23.4 below, the standard deviation of the portfolio is plotted on the X-axis and the average return of the portfolio on Y-axis. The CML passes from these two points. In the graph, the first point is the vertical intercept and is equal to the risk-free rate (in this case it is an average of 10 years). The second point above the vertical intercept, r_f, marks the location of the market portfolio. The slope is the vertical distance between two points divided by the horizontal distance.

Hence it is formulated as, slope = $r_m - r_f/(\sigma_m - 0)$.

Substituting the corresponding values, slope = $(48.65\% - 6.09\%)/(23.41 - 0) = 1.82$

Graph of Sharpe's measure

By using vertical intercept r_f, the equation for the CML is,

$$r_m = r_f + \frac{(r_m - r_f)}{\sigma_m}\sigma_p \qquad (20)$$

By putting the respective values in Equation (20),

$$r_m = 6.09\% + \frac{(17.75\% - 6.09\%)\sigma_p}{23.41\%}$$

$$= 6.09\% + (0.498 \times \sigma_p)$$

For the portfolio of ICICI, the average return and standard deviation are 48.65% and 23.41% respectively.

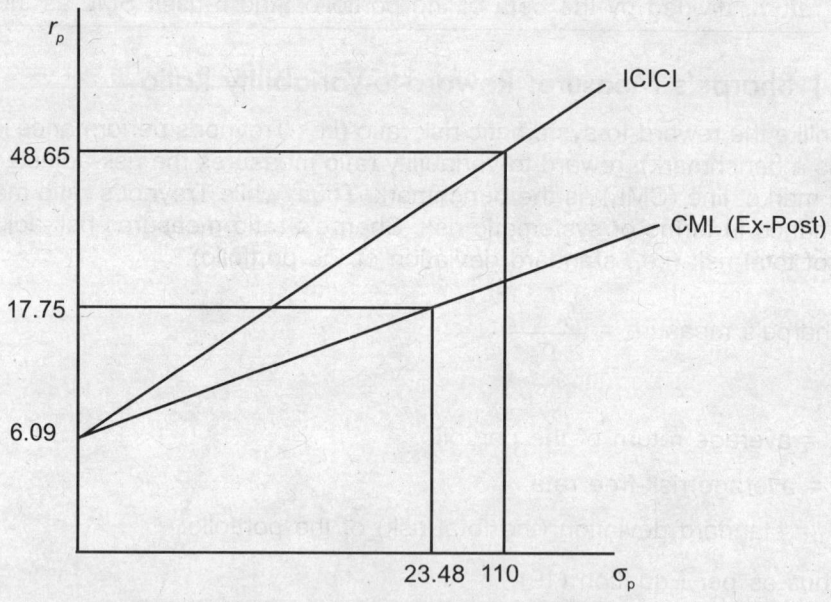

Figure 23.4: Sharpe's performance measure and CML

As with the reward-to-systematic risk ratio, the slope of the line (CML) of reward-to-variability ratio too is the vertical distance between the two points $(r_p - r_f)$, divided by the horizontal distance between these two points $(\sigma_p - 0)$.

In the above Figure 23.4, first line starting from r_f represents portfolio of ICICI while second line shows CML.. We already know from our discussions on CML (in Chapter 9) that it is the product of a combination of risk-free lending (or borrowing) with risky security and risky portfolio. And as discussed above, CML acts as a benchmark portfolio for evaluating the performance of the given portfolio. The performance of the portfolio of ICICI is superior to the market index as it is above the CML.

If the given portfolio is above the CML (or if the slope of given portfolio is greater than the slope of CML), the given portfolio has given superior performance than the market. Conversely, a lower value of Sharpe's ratio than the CML represents a portfolio that lies below the CML (ex-post) and thus has a performance inferior to the market.

> *Check yourself*
> Calculate Treynor's measure and Sharpe's measure of top 10 mutual fund schemes. Rank them as per both the measures. Do both the measures arrive at the same ranking? Give reasons for your observation.

> **Pause for thought:** Sharpe's measure of the performance of a portfolio is based on reward-to-variability ratio. It measures the risk-adjusted performance in terms of total risk (i.e., standard deviation, as compared to beta in Treynor's method). CML is used as the benchmark while Treynor used SML. A portfolio above CML indicates a better performing portfolio, while the one below CML represents an inferior performance, compared to the market.

23.3.2 Comparison of Treynor's Method and Sharpe's Method

Having discussed both, the Treynor's performance index and SML (ex-post) and Sharpe's ratio and use of CML, we would benefit from comparisons of these two methods. The purpose being the evaluation of the performances of portfolios, this comparison would enable us to choose the better option under a given condition, and thus reach the best conclusion. In practice, it has been observed that for a given portfolio, Treynor's and Sharpe's measures can lead to different assessments compared to market portfolio, even when the evaluation is carried out at the same time. Thus for a given time period, a portfolio may be assessed to outperform the market as per Treynor's method, while conclusions form Sharpe's method might be in contradiction. These two methods are found to oppose each other when the given portfolio has a large amount of unsystematic risk. We know that Treynor's measure takes into account only the market risk of the portfolio, while Sharpe's ratio takes into account the total risk of the portfolio (the denominator of both the formulae be noted). Also we know that total risk is equal to the market risk and unique (unsystematic) risk. Because of this difference in measurement parameters in both the ratios, variation occurs in their assessment of portfolios.

> **Pause for thought:** Since Treynor's method uses only the market (systematic) risk, while Sharpe utilizes the total risk (systematic and unsystematic) of the portfolios, the evaluation by these two methods contradict when the unsystematic risk of the portfolio is large.

23.3.3 Issues in Using Risk-Adjusted Performance Measures

Use of market Indices

Appropriate market indices have been used for both the measures: reward-to-systematic risk ratio (Treynor's method) and reward-to-variability (Sharpe's method). Usually NSE 50 or BSE Sensex is used as the market portfolio. From both the methods it is evident that the performance (and hence ranking) of the portfolio depends upon the use and selection of market indices. If the market index is changed for a given portfolio, for the same time period, the performance, and more specifically rank of the portfolio, changes. However, it has been also proved that for most commonly used indices results do not vary much.

> **Pause for thought:** Given that both methods use market index as the reference portfolio, changes in the market index brings about changes in the performance of the portfolios, to some extent.

23.4 JENSON'S DIFFERENTIAL RETURN MEASURE

Like Treynor's method, Jenson's evaluation of portfolios too is based on the capital asset pricing model (CAPM). The expected return for any security, and more specifically for a portfolio (p), is given by

$$r_p = \alpha_p + \beta_p(r_m - r_f) \tag{21}$$

where,

r_p = average return of portfolio.

r_f = risk-free rate of interest.

α = the intercept.

β = measure of systematic risk.

r_m = average market return.

Jenson's method is a measure of absolute risk-adjusted return because it measures the performance against a definite standard. This standard (benchmark) is based upon the portfolio manager's predicting abilities. The chances of earning higher return depend upon manager's aptitude in anticipating and estimating the returns as efficiently as possible.

We know that beta is the measure of systematic risk. And we also know that ideally beta of this portfolio should be 1, if the portfolio manager uses all securities available in the market to construct the portfolio. But beta of the portfolio constructed by the manager can be more, or less, than 1 (as practically, it is not possible to invest in all securities of the market to construct the portfolio). If beta of the portfolio is greater than 1, it reflects the presence of riskier securities in the portfolio, than a portfolio of all market securities.

$$r_p = \alpha_p + \beta_p(r_m - r_f) \tag{22}$$

It is to be remembered that the above equation is ante-period. This equation can be applied to the ex-post period if the investor's expectations are realized on an average. Empirically, Equation (22) can be approximated as,

$$r_p = r_f + \beta_p(r_m - r_f) + \varepsilon_p \tag{23}$$

where,

r_p = return of the portfolio.

r_f = risk-free rate of return.

r_m = market return.

ϵ_p = random error term of the portfolio.

β_p = systematic risk of the portfolio.

Equation (23) implies the summation of the risk-free rate, portfolio's risk-premium and an error term gives the return on portfolio at any given time. The risk-premium of a portfolio is a function of the market risk-premium and systematic risk. When the systematic risk is high, the risk-premium too is large.

Equation (23), can be rewritten as

$$r_p - r_f = \beta_p(r_m - r_f) + \epsilon_p \tag{24}$$

where,

$r_p - r_f$ = risk-premium of the portfolio.

Equation (24) indicates that the portfolio's risk premium is equal to the sum of the error term, and the product of the beta of the portfolio and the market risk premium. Thus, it can be said that the risk-premium of the given portfolio is in proportion to the risk-premium of the market portfolio.

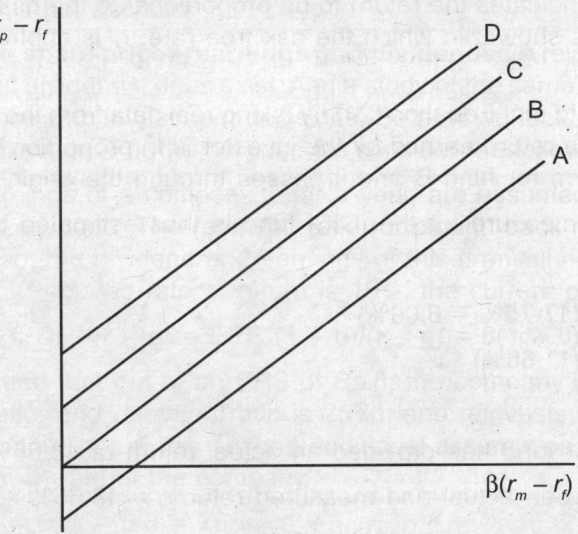

Figure 23.5: Jenson's measure for different portfolios

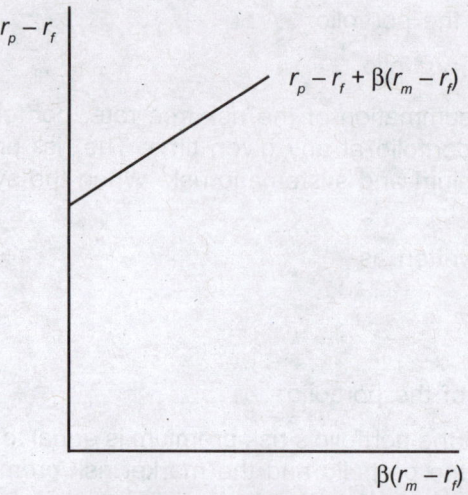

Figure 23.6: Portfolio's beta and return

Fund B in Figure 23.5 indicates the return to be proportional to the risk. The characteristics line in excess return form is shown, in which the risk free rate, r_f, is subtracted from portfolio's return and the market return.

It is practically possible to test Equation (24) by taking real data from the market. In the above figure, fund B shows that the return earned by the investor is in proportion to the risk assumed. So, there is no intercept term for fund B and it passes through the origin.

Jenson's performance measure for the ICICI fund is thus estimated to be,

$r_p = r_f + \beta_p(r_m - r_f)$

$= 6.09\% + 1.42(17.75\% - 6.09\%)$

$= 6.09\% + 1.42(11.66\%)$

$= 22.65\%$

We know that the ICICI fund has provided an actual return of 48.65%.

So, the difference between actual and measured returns = 48.65% – 22.65% = 26%.

To find out whether the performance of the portfolio is superior or inferior, to the market index, Jenson added an intercept term, α, in Equation (24).

$$r_p - r_f = \alpha_p + \beta_p(r_m - r_f) + \epsilon_p \qquad (25)$$

where ϵ_p is assumed to be zero.

As per the CAPM model, the equilibrium condition should result in a zero intercept term. As alpha (α) denotes the average incremental rate of return, per period, beyond the return attributed to the level of risk, alpha measures the contribution from the portfolio manager.

We can infer the following relation between the portfolios, A, B, C and D, based upon their values of alpha:

- Portfolio D indicates a performance superior to that of the other portfolios as its alpha is significantly positive (compared to A, B and C). It can be noted in Figure 23.5 that portfolio D has a positive intercept.
- Portfolio A performs the worst among all the portfolios as its alpha is negative. Figure 23.5 reflects a negative intercept for portfolio A.
- For portfolio B, alpha passes through the origin indicating its value to be zero. This proves that the portfolio manager's prediction on the market return, for a given risk, came out to be true.
- Portfolio C also indicates superior performance, but is less than that of D as its alpha value is slightly less than that of portfolio D. This fact is evident from the figure.

By rearranging Equation (25) we get,

$$\alpha_p = (r_p - r_f) - [\beta_p(r_m - r_p)] \qquad (26)$$

Thus, α_p is the difference between actual excess return of the portfolio and excess return of the market, multiplied by systematic risk of the portfolio. This difference can be positive, negative or zero, depending upon the portfolios, as well as time.

The superiority of Jenson's measure, over the other two, is that it estimates both alpha and beta simultaneously for the given portfolio. However, it should be kept in mind that while measuring performance of the given portfolio, the return from each period needs to be compared, along with the average return for the entire period.

> **Pause for thought:** Jenson's method is based on CAPM and it measures the absolute risk-adjusted return, given that the reference used for evaluation is a definite standard. It estimates both the alpha and beta of the portfolio, during the same time period. Thus, is more comprehensive and superior, to both Treynor's and Sharpe's methods.

23.5 MARKET TIME AND SELECTION OF PORTFOLIO

We have been discussing the selection of portfolios based on varied parameters. And having come to this stage we proceed to take a look how time becomes a factor in this selection procedure. It has been stated innumerable times that beta is a measure of systematic (market) risk. Thus, we are very much aware that an aggressive portfolio, compared to the market, has a high value of beta. Conversely, a portfolio with a low beta indicates relatively conservative nature (and thus performance) of the portfolio, compared to the market. We have also discussed that the expected return of a portfolio is a linear function of its beta, given as:

$$r_p = \alpha_p + r_f + (r_m - r_f)\beta_p$$

where,

r_p = return of the portfolio.

α_p = alpha of the portfolio.

r_f = risk-free rate of return.

r_m = return of the market (related index).

β_p = beta of the portfolio.

In practice it has been found that it is preferable to hold a portfolio with high positive beta when the market is expected to perform better (i.e., relatively higher returns are expected). During the high expectation phase, return of a portfolio with high beta is more than that of a low beta portfolio. Conversely, when the market is expected to slump (and thus provide relatively lower returns), portfolios with negative beta are preferred, as return from a negative beta portfolio is more than that of positive beta portfolio in these situations.

Thus, it can be summarised, when:

$r_m > r_f$, buy and hold portfolios with high positive beta.

$r_m < r_f$, buy and hold portfolios with negative beta.

Portfolios constructed on this framework outperform the market portfolio, which has a constant beta of 1.

> *Check yourself*
> Collect randomly 25 mutual fund schemes from the market and find out their beta from their historical NAV. Out of these 25 mutual fund schemes how many mutual funds have negative beta? Check such mutual funds' performance in the year 2008 when market performed poorly. Compare the performances of mutual funds with negative and positive betas during that phase, providing explanations for the same.

> **Pause for thought:** The portfolios are evaluated, held and constructed on the basis of the expected market return and beta values of the portfolios. Thus the selection of the portfolio is related to time, with beta and expected market return as the intermediaries.

23.6 A COMPARATIVE STUDY OF ALL THREE MEASURES

Sharpe measures the performance of a portfolio using the standard deviation, return and diversification. On the other hand, Treynor's method evaluates the portfolio on the basis of systematic risk only. We can construct and rank the portfolios on the basis of Sharpe and Treynor's methods. But either of the measures is incapable of estimating the extent to which a particular portfolio outperforms or underperforms, compared to some benchmark (or standard) fund. Until some modifications are made Jenson's measure cannot be ideally used to rank the portfolio's performance. The agreement between these methods is absolute when a well-diversified portfolio is evaluated. They come up with unanimous rankings for these portfolios, because for a fully diversified portfolio, total variance becomes equal to the systematic variance. However, one thing should be taken care of while evaluating the portfolios. When the portfolio is not completely diversified, Treynor and Jenson's measures may give relatively higher ranking than the Sharpe's method. Sharpe measures the performance taking into cognizance both systematic and unsystematic risk as it considers the total risk. Also, Sharpe and Treynor's measures use average return for the performance period, while Jenson uses the periodic returns.

The table below shows the performance of select mutual funds for the time period 2001-2011. The risk-free rate is assumed to be 8%.

Table 23.5: Comparison of Portfolios on the Basis of the Three Methods

Scheme name	S.D.	Sharpe's ratio	Beta	Alpha	Treynor's ratio	Jenson's ratio
SBI MagnumEquity Fund–Growth	43.79	0.38	–0.5	35.12	16.49	–0.21
ICICI PrudentialFMCG–Growth	114.72	0.09	1.42	23.38	9.75	21.88
LIC Nomura MutualFund (Tax Plan Dividend)	49.17	0.34	–0.39	17.59	16.49	1.61
Canara RebecoBalance–Growth	30.62	0.54	–0.29	31.41	16.49	3.28
Kotak Gilt SavingPlan–Growth	36.52	0.45	–0.34	25.92	16.49	2.33
UTI Pharma andHealthcare Fund–Dividend	30.71	0.45	–0.17	18.83	13.74	5.69
TATA Life Science and Technology Fund–Dividend	47.96	0.28	–0.15	26.77	13.64	5.97
Sahara Income Fund–Growth	19.53	0.84	0.06	5.5	16.49	8.99

Check yourself

Collect sector specific mutual fund schemes and relate their performance with the related indices. For example UTI Pharma and Healthcare Fund must be analyzed with Healthcare Index only. Interpret your answers.

Problems in portfolio measurement: the limitations

The three measures discussed above have certain limitations and they should be taken care of while judging the performance of a portfolio on the basis of either of them.

— Risk-free rate: Risk-free rate, considered for these measures, is the T-bill rate. But the T-bill rate is not an appropriate proxy for the risk-free rate, for an individual investor.

— Market portfolio: In all three methods, market portfolio means portfolio of all available securities of the market. But construction of the market portfolio, by considering all assets, is practically impossible. In practice, indices like Sensex or Nifty are used as a proxy for the market portfolio. However, it creates potential measurement errors.

For better evaluation: the solution

For a better evaluation of the portfolio, following things should be considered:

— A long time period should be selected.

— For a short-term portfolio, the ability of the portfolio manager to predict correctly the expected market returns may overshadow the actual performance. But it might have also happened due to the portfolio manager's luck or due to some other reason(s). However, it is very unlikely that the trend—of outperforming the market—will continue for long. So, for a better judgement, it is better to rely on the performance of the mutual funds over a longer period.

— Global investment trends may change the efficient frontier when foreign securities are added to the portfolio. It also changes the beta of the portfolio.

> **Pause for thought:** Sharpe measures the performance of portfolios taking into cognizance both systematic and unsystematic risk, given that it considers the total risk. But Treynor considers only the market risk. Also, Sharpe and Treynor's measures use average return for the performance period, while Jenson uses the periodic returns. Jenson's method is a measure of absolute risk-adjusted return because it measures the performance against a definite standard. These three methods are in absolute agreement only when a well-diversified portfolio is being evaluated.

SUMMARY

- ✓ Portfolios are evaluated to assess their return and risk, compared to the benchmark portfolio.
- ✓ The performance of the portfolio is adjudged as superior or inferior, on the basis of its return with respect to the market return. It is also analyzed whether the performance is due to skill or luck.
- ✓ Treynor's measure indicates the fund's performance in terms of market risk.
- ✓ Sharpe's ratio measures the risk-premium related to total risk.
- ✓ Jenson's ratio measures the actual return of the portfolio with the calculated ex-post data or the expected return.
- ✓ Jenson's method is a measure of absolute risk-adjusted return because it measures the performance against a definite standard.

KEY CONCEPTS

Rupees-Weighted Return	Alpha	Benchmark Or Standard Portfolio
Time-Weighted Return	Beta	Treynor's Measure
Coefficient Of Correlation	Random Error Term Of Alpha	Sharpe's Measure
Coefficient Of Determination	Random Error Term Of Beta	Jenson's Measure
Coefficient Of Non-Determination	Random Error Term Of Standard Deviation	Characteristics Line

REVIEW QUESTION

1. Why do we need to compare the performance of a particular portfolio with that of a related market index or benchmark portfolio? How would you define the term related here?

ASSIGNMENT QUESTIONS

1. Take any top performing mutual fund from the market. Refer to www.bajajcapital.com and from that collect the NAVs of last ten years. Calculate: return, risk, alpha and beta of the portfolio.

2. Repeat the assignment question 1 for 10 other mutual funds. Compare their return, risk, alpha, beta, correlation coefficient and coefficient of determination. Interpret them.
3. As in questions 1 and 2, carry out the similar exercise for the sectoral funds. Take the NAVs of the sector-wise mutual funds and compare them with the appropriate index. For example, compare the Reliance Pharma mutual fund with the Healthcare index for the same time period. Do it for at least 5-8 sectors and interpret your results.
4. Calculate all the components of the portfolio evaluation as shown in Table 23.4 for five mutual funds.
5. Calculate Sharpe, Jenson and Treynor's measures respectively, by using the data of last 10 years and 5 years. Interpret your results. Repeat these calculations for 15 mutual funds.
6. Read the recent updates and news on mutual funds from the following websites and interpret your results: www.bajajcapital.com, www.amfi.com, www.moneycontrol.com, www.bseindia.com and www.nseindia.com.

ILLUSTRATIONS

Q.1. Following are the NAVs of the portfolio of Principal Balanced Fund, from 2005 to 2011. For the same time period the closing prices of the market are also given. By using these data, calculate: alpha, beta, random error term of standard deviation, standard error of alpha, standard error of beta, coefficient of correlation, coefficient of determination and coefficient of non-determination, of the portfolio.

Year	Market prices (Rs.)	NAV of Principal Balanced Fund (Rs.)
2005	9397.93	14.32
2006	13786.91	21.61
2007	20286.99	20.48
2008	9647.31	24.81
2009	17464.81	18.53
2010	20509.09	30.04
2011	15873.95	30.77

Ans:

Principal Balanced Fund	
Beta	1.004338
Alpha	1.008359
Standard deviation of random error term	37.98958
Standard error of beta	0.020833
Standard error of alpha	15.68261
Correlation coefficient	0.999141
Coefficient of determination	0.998283
Coefficient of non-determination	0.001717

Q.2. From the following data of SBI Magnum Equity Fund-Growth, calculate: return, risk, alpha and beta. Draw the characteristics line.

Year	Market (Rs.)	NAV (Rs.)
2001	-	12.39
2002	3377.28	8.01
2003	5838.96	8.51
2004	6602.69	13.16
2005	9397.93	15.65
2006	13786.91	21.98
2007	20286.99	27.87
2008	9647.31	47.27
2009	17464.81	21.08
2010	20509.09	39.04
2011	15873.95	46.12

Ans:

Return and risk of SBI Magnum Equity Fund

SBI Magnum Equity Fund-Growth				
Year	NAV	$(p_1 - p_0)/p_0 \times 100$	$[r - E(r)]$	$[r - E(r)] \times [r - E(r)]$
1	2	3	4	5
2001	12.39			
2002	8.01	-35.35	-58.27	3395.94
2003	8.51	6.24	-16.68	278.27
2004	13.16	54.64	31.72	1006.03
2005	15.65	18.92	-4.00	16.02
2006	21.98	40.45	17.52	307.08
2007	27.87	26.80	3.87	15.00
2008	47.27	69.61	46.69	2179.51
2009	21.08	-55.41	-78.33	6135.39
2010	39.04	85.20	62.28	3878.25
2011	46.12	18.14	-4.79	22.93
				17234.43
	Average return = 22.92			Variance = 1914.94 S.D.= 43.76

Beta and alpha of the portfolio

No.	Year	Market Return (X) (%)	Portfolio Return (Y) (%)	$[R_x - E(R_x)]$	$[R_x - E(R_x)] \times [R_x - E(R_x)]$	$[R_y - E(R_y)]$	$[R_x - E(R_x)] \times [R_y - E(R_y)]$
1	2001						
2	2002	3.53	−35.35	−20.95	439.00	−58.27	1220.99
3	2003	72.55	6.24	48.07	2310.50	−16.68	−801.84
4	2004	12.43	54.64	−12.05	145.24	31.72	−382.25
5	2005	41.82	18.92	17.34	300.59	−4.00	−69.40
6	2006	46.32	40.45	21.83	476.69	17.52	382.60
7	2007	46.71	26.80	22.23	493.99	3.87	86.09
8	2008	−52.54	69.61	−77.02	5932.30	46.69	−3595.77
9	2009	79.67	−55.41	55.18	3045.15	−78.33	−4322.41
10	2010	17.37	85.20	−7.11	50.60	62.28	−442.98
11	2011	−23.02	18.14	−47.51	2257.08	−4.79	227.49
		Average return = 24.49	Average return = 22.92		15451.15		−7697.47
							−855.27
					Variance = 1716.79 S.D. = 41.43		

Beta = $-\dfrac{855.27}{1716.79} = -0.498$

Alpha = 35.12

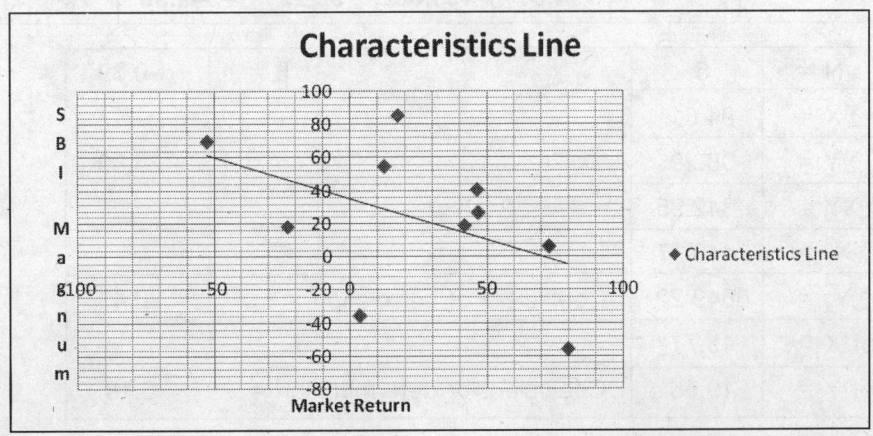

As the beta of this portfolio is negative, the characteristics line of this fund is sloping downward.

642 SECURITY ANALYSIS AND PORTFOLIO MANAGEMENT

Q.3. Calculate the alpha, beta, r and r^2 for the UTI Pharma fund. Use the healthcare index given below as an appropriate measure of performance.

	Healthcare Index		UTI Pharma Fund NAV
Year	Opening NAV	Closing NAV	NAV
2006	3103.76	3792.05	20.58
2007	3794.69	4418.65	22.44
2008	4425.12	2966.19	25.02
2009	2968.04	5018.33	18.52
2010	5043	6734.19	30.68
2011	6755.39	5833.07	42.36

Ans:

Year	Mid cap market			NAV		XY	X^2	Y^2
	Opening NAV	Closing NAV	Return (X)	NAV	Return (Y)			
2006	3103.76	3792.05	22.18	20.58	–	–	–	–
2007	3794.69	4418.65	16.44	22.44	9.04	148.61	270.37	81.68
2008	4425.12	2966.19	–32.97	25.02	11.50	–379.06	1086.97	132.19
2009	2968.04	5018.33	69.08	18.52	–25.98	–1794.62	4771.90	674.92
2010	5043	6734.19	33.54	30.68	65.66	2201.89	1124.62	4311.07
2011	6755.39	5833.07	–13.65	42.36	38.07	–519.78	186.41	1449.36
Total	–	–	94.61	159.60	98.29	–342.95	7440.27	6649.22

	N =	5		β =	–0.39
	ΣX =	94.61			
	ΣY =	98.29		α =	25.80
	ΣXY =	–342.95			
	ΣX² =	7440.27			
	ΣY² =	6649.22	Coefficient of correlation =		–0.43
Avg. of X =		15.77			
Avg. of Y =		19.66	Coefficient of determination =		0.18

Q.4. Following are the details of the DSP Black Rock Tech Fund and IT Index. Calculate alpha, beta, r and r^2 for the given fund.

No.	Year	Tech. Index		DSP Rock Tech. Fund
		Opening NAV	Closing NAV	NAV
1	2006	3540.52	3660.8	15.90
2	2007	3662.85	4015.03	23.75
3	2008	4015072	1947.04	37.22
4	2009	1963.15	3277.04	15.09
5	2010	3288.23	4046.74	31.04
6	2011	4051.41	3380.25	35.52

Ans:

No.	Year	Opening	Closing	Return	NAV	Return	XY	X^2	Y^2
1	2006	3540.52	3660.8	3.40	15.90	–	–	–	–
2	2007	3662.85	4015.03	9.61	23.75	49.37	474.70	92.45	2437.50
3	2008	4015072	1947.04	–99.95	37.22	56.72	–5668.83	9990.30	3216.68
4	2009	1963.15	3277.04	66.93	15.09	–59.46	–3979.34	4479.31	3535.17
5	2010	3288.23	4046.74	23.07	31.04	105.70	2438.21	532.11	11172.31
6	2011	4051.41	3380.25	–16.57	35.52	14.43	–239.10	274.44	208.31
	Total	–	–	–13.51	158.52	166.76	–6974.36	15368.60	20569.97

N =	5		β =	–0.43
ΣX =	–13.51			
ΣY =	166.76		α =	32.20
ΣXY =	–6974.36			
ΣX² =	15368.60			
ΣY² =	20569.97	Coefficient of correlation =		–0.43
Avg. of X =	–2.70			
Avg. of Y =	33.35	Coefficient of determination =		0.18

PROBLEMS

Q.1. Following are the NAVs of ING Balanced Fund from 2005 to 2011. For the same time period, the market closing prices are also given. By using these data, calculate: alpha, beta, random error term of standard deviation, standard error of alpha, standard error of beta, coefficient of correlation, coefficient of determination and coefficient of non-determination, of the portfolio.

Year	Market prices (Rs.)	NAV of ING Balanced Fund (Rs.)
2005	9397.93	11.72
2006	13786.91	17.35
2007	20286.99	17.78
2008	9647.31	20.81
2009	17464.81	15.5
2010	20509.09	23.73
2011	15873.95	25.89

Q.2. Following are the details of the Canara Rebeco Balance Fund and IT Index. Calculate: alpha, beta, r and r^2 for the given fund.

Year	Market return	Canara Rebeco Balance Fund
2002	3.53	−9.53
2003	72.55	13.00
2004	12.43	58.93
2005	41.82	21.35
2006	46.32	41.67
2007	46.71	36.89
2008	−52.54	43.34
2009	79.67	−37.79
2010	17.37	59.28
2011	−23.02	16.77

Q.3. Calculate Jenson, Treynor and Sharpe's ratio for the following mutual funds.

Year	Market prices (Rs.)	Tata Balanced Fund	Kodak Growth Fund	ING Nomura Balanced Fund
2005	9397.93	24.4	32.48	11.29
2006	13786.91	37.56	61.09	14.43
2007	20286.99	35.48	63.25	9.73
2008	9647.31	39.6	82.77	10.56
2009	17464.81	30.47	57.32	8.36
2010	20509.09	48.36	95.33	11.4
2011	15873.95	52.66	105.23	11.67

Q.4. Following are the NAVs of ING Balanced Fund from 2005 to 2011. For the same time period, the market closing prices are also given. By using these data, calculate: alpha, beta, random error term of standard deviation, standard error of alpha, standard error of beta, coefficient of correlation, coefficient of determination and coefficient of non-determination, of the fund.

Year	Tata Balanced Fund (NAV) (Rs.)	Market prices (Rs.)
2005	24.4	9397.93
2006	37.56	13786.91
2007	35.48	20286.99
2008	39.6	9647.31
2009	30.47	17464.81
2010	48.36	20509.09
2011	52.66	15873.95

CASE STUDY

Mr. Jay Patel attended a seminar organized by the Kotak Fund. In the context of the changing and an uncertain financial environment, Kotak made presentations on investments and retirement planning in general; and went on to give the details of their Kotak 50 Growth Fund. Their presentation covered the following points:

— Deterioration in the purchasing power due to high inflation rates.
— The abolition of the pension option for government employees since 2002.
— Investment in savings a/c of bank or FDs in bank, actually provide negative or very less return, compared to the inflation rate.
— Due to better medical facilities and other supporting tools, life expectancy rate has increased.

Mr. Jay is employed in a private sector pharmaceutical company and is working in the QC department since 2004. He holds Bachelor degree in Pharmacy and has very little knowledge of the stock market and aspects of the same, such as equity, inflation, mutual funds, return, etc. However, he follows a daily routine of minutely reading all information related to the stock market and economy. He is very keen to learn about all these financial aspects so that he can make better financial decisions.

The presentations made by the Kotak Fund emphasized that one should start investing early, to take advantage of the low NAVs. Most of the participants in this seminar were in the age group of 30-35, considered the peak time to start investing.

Mr. Saurabh Chandra has recently joined Kotak Securities as a management trainee. He recently passed out from one of the renowned B-schools of India and holds a Masters degree in business administration. The participants were science and/or pharma graduates in the seminar. Mr. Arun Shroff, Area Head, therefore requested to Mr. Chandra to seek the answers to the following and present in front of the audience to make them better versed with the same:

1. If at present the minimal requirement for a family of 4 persons is Rs. 400,000 p.a., what will be the requirement for the same standard of living, when they are 20, 30, 40 and 50 years of age? Most of the participants in this seminar are in the age group of 30-35.
2. If the present targeted audience retires at the age of 60 and starts saving (from the current year) with Rs. 1,00,000, p.a., what will be the amount he/she can accumulate as savings at the age of 60?
3. Is the present Kotak 50 Growth Fund's return sufficient, if a person decides to invest in it from the current year and holds the investment till he/she turns 60?
4. What other information is required to effectively hedge an investor's future uncertainty of the income?
5. Also if the present portfolio of Kotak 50 Growth is not sufficiently rewarding, construct the portfolio of securities and advise Mr. Jay Patel.

Mr. Saurabh has collected the following data from internet to present his views.

Year	Gold price	Sensex	Inflation rate	Interest rate	Kotak 50 Growth Fund
2004	6522	6602.69	3.891	6.13	
2005	7553	9397.93	3.97	6.45	32.48
2006	9356	13786.91	6.268	7.63	61.09
2007	10134	20286.99	6.373	8.1	63.25
2008	12571	9647.31	8.349	8.25	82.77
2009	17973	17464.81	10.882	7.87	57.32
2010	20553	20509.09	11.989	8.11	95.33
2011	26364	15543.93	10.551	8.25	105.23

APPENDIX

1. IT Mutual Funds

Name of the MF scheme	2007	2008	2009	2010	2011
Birla Sunlife New Millenium Fund	20.26	24.25	10.55	19.27	22.41
DSP Black Rock Tech. Fund	23.75	37.22	15.09	31.04	35.52
Franklin Infotech Fund	55.93	45.79	23.85	54.91	72.25
ICICI Prudential Tech. Fund	15.46	17.54	6.41	14.21	20.4
SBI Magnum Umbrella IT Fund	27.63	24.95	9.08	20.27	25.26
Total	143	149.8	64.98	139.7	175.8
Average(Y)	**28.606**	**29.95**	**13**	**27.94**	**35.17**

BSE Tech. Index

Year	Return (X)
2007	9.61
2008	−51.51
2009	66.92
2010	23.07
2011	−16.57
Total	31.52
Average	6.304

Beta = −0.15

2. **Pharma Funds**

Name of the MF scheme	2007	2008	2009	2010	2011
Franklin Pharma	24.52	26.16	31.05	30.88	32.58
JM Healthcare Fund	20.2	21.69	23.65	24.86	26.23
Reliance Pharma Fund	20.61	30.91	20.28	43.91	58.32
SBI Magnum Pharma Fund	36.32	39.12	19.81	35.78	46.38
UTI Pharma & Healthcare	22.44	25.02	18.52	30.68	42.36
Total	124.09	142.9	113.31	166.11	205.87
Average (Y)	24.82	28.58	22.66	33.22	41.17

BSE Healthcare Index

Year	Return (X)
2007	16.44
2008	−32.97
2009	69.08
2010	33.54
2011	−13.1
Total	72.99
Average	14.598

Beta = −0.09

REFERENCES

1. Dichev D. Illia (2007), "What are Stock Investors' Actual Historical Returns? Evidence from Dollar-Weighted Returns?", *The American Economic Review*, Vol.97, No.1, pp.386-401.

2. Jobson J.D. and Korkie M. Bob (1981), "Performance Hypothesis Testing with Sharpe and Treynor Measures", *The Journal of Finance*, Vol. 36, No.4, pp.889- 908.

3. Kothari S.P. and Warner B. Jerold (2001), "Evaluating Mutual Fund Performance", *The Journal of Finance*, Vol.56, No.5, pp. 1985-2010.

4. Ippolito A. Richard (1989), "Efficiency with Costly Information: A Study of Mutual Fund Performance, 1965-1984", *The Quarterly Journal of Economics*, Vol. 104, No.1, pp.1-23.

5. Greenblat Mark and Titman Sheridan (1993), "Performance Measurement Without Benchmarks: An Examination of Mutual Fund Returns", *The Journal of Business*, Vol. 66, No.1, pp.47-68.

6. Lee-Few Cheng and Rehman Shafigur (1990), "Market Timing Selectivity and Mutual Fund Performance: An Empirical Investigation", *The Journal of Business*, Vol. 63, No.2, pp. 261-278.

7. http://www.mutualfundsindia.com/

8. http://www.moneycontrol.com/mutualfundindia/

9. http://www.indiainfoline.com/MutualFunds/

10. http://www.amfiindia.com/

FACTOR TABLES

Table T1
Future Value of a Single Cash Flow (FVIF)
Interest Rate (%)

Year	1	2	3	4	5	6	7	8	9	10	11	12	13	14	15
1	1.010	1.020	1.030	1.040	1.050	1.060	1.070	1.080	1.090	1.100	1.110	1.120	1.130	1.140	1.150
2	1.020	1.040	1.061	1.082	1.103	1.124	1.145	1.166	1.188	1.210	1.232	1.254	1.277	1.300	1.323
3	1.030	1.061	1.093	1.125	1.158	1.191	1.225	1.260	1.295	1.331	1.368	1.405	1.443	1.482	1.521
4	1.041	1.082	1.126	1.170	1.216	1.262	1.311	1.360	1.412	1.464	1.518	1.574	1.630	1.689	1.749
5	1.051	1.104	1.159	1.217	1.276	1.338	1.403	1.469	1.539	1.611	1.685	1.762	1.842	1.925	2.011
6	1.062	1.126	1.194	1.265	1.340	1.419	1.501	1.587	1.677	1.772	1.870	1.974	2.082	2.195	2.313
7	1.072	1.149	1.230	1.316	1.407	1.504	1.606	1.714	1.828	1.949	2.076	2.211	2.353	2.502	2.660
8	1.083	1.172	1.267	1.369	1.477	1.594	1.718	1.851	1.993	2.144	2.305	2.476	2.658	2.853	3.059
9	1.094	1.195	1.305	1.423	1.551	1.689	1.838	1.999	2.172	2.358	2.558	2.773	3.004	3.252	3.518
10	1.105	1.219	1.344	1.480	1.629	1.791	1.967	2.159	2.367	2.594	2.839	3.106	3.395	3.707	4.046
11	1.116	1.243	1.384	1.539	1.710	1.898	2.105	2.332	2.580	2.853	3.152	3.479	3.836	4.226	4.652
12	1.127	1.268	1.426	1.601	1.796	2.012	2.252	2.518	2.813	3.138	3.498	3.896	4.335	4.818	5.350
13	1.138	1.294	1.469	1.665	1.886	2.133	2.410	2.720	3.066	3.452	3.883	4.363	4.898	5.492	6.153
14	1.149	1.319	1.513	1.732	1.980	2.261	2.579	2.937	3.342	3.797	4.310	4.887	5.535	6.261	7.076
15	1.161	1.346	1.558	1.801	2.079	2.397	2.759	3.172	3.642	4.177	4.785	5.474	6.254	7.138	8.137
16	1.173	1.373	1.605	1.873	2.183	2.540	2.952	3.426	3.970	4.595	5.311	6.130	7.067	8.137	9.358
17	1.184	1.400	1.653	1.948	2.292	2.693	3.159	3.700	4.328	5.054	5.895	6.866	7.986	9.276	10.761
18	1.196	1.428	1.702	2.026	2.407	2.854	3.380	3.996	4.717	5.560	6.544	7.690	9.024	10.575	12.375
19	1.208	1.457	1.754	2.107	2.527	3.026	3.617	4.316	5.142	6.116	7.263	8.613	10.197	12.056	14.232
20	1.220	1.486	1.806	2.191	2.653	3.207	3.870	4.661	5.604	6.727	8.062	9.646	11.523	13.743	16.367
21	1.232	1.516	1.860	2.279	2.786	3.400	4.141	5.034	6.109	7.400	8.949	10.804	13.021	15.668	18.822
22	1.245	1.546	1.916	2.370	2.925	3.604	4.430	5.437	6.659	8.140	9.934	12.100	14.714	17.861	21.645
23	1.257	1.577	1.974	2.465	3.072	3.820	4.741	5.871	7.258	8.954	11.026	13.552	16.627	20.362	24.891

650 SECURITY ANALYSIS AND PORTFOLIO MANAGEMENT

24	1.270	1.608	2.033	2.563	3.225	4.049	5.072	6.341	7.911	9.850	12.239	15.179	18.788	23.212	28.625
25	1.282	1.641	2.094	2.666	3.386	4.292	5.427	6.848	8.623	10.835	13.585	17.000	21.231	26.462	32.919
26	1.295	1.673	2.157	2.772	3.556	4.549	5.807	7.396	9.399	11.918	15.080	19.040	23.991	30.167	37.857
27	1.308	1.707	2.221	2.883	3.733	4.822	6.214	7.988	10.245	13.110	16.739	21.325	27.109	34.390	43.535
28	1.321	1.741	2.288	2.999	3.920	5.112	6.649	8.627	11.167	14.421	18.580	23.884	30.633	39.204	50.066
29	1.335	1.776	2.357	3.119	4.116	5.418	7.114	9.317	12.172	15.863	20.624	26.750	34.616	44.693	57.575
30	1.348	1.811	2.427	3.243	4.322	5.743	7.612	10.063	13.268	17.449	22.892	29.960	39.116	50.950	66.212
31	1.361	1.848	2.500	3.373	4.538	6.088	8.145	10.868	14.462	19.194	25.410	33.555	44.201	58.083	76.144
32	1.375	1.885	2.575	3.508	4.765	6.453	8.715	11.737	15.763	21.114	28.206	37.582	49.947	66.215	87.565
33	1.389	1.922	2.652	3.648	5.003	6.841	9.325	12.676	17.182	23.225	31.308	42.092	56.440	75.485	100.700
34	1.403	1.961	2.732	3.794	5.253	7.251	9.978	13.690	18.728	25.548	34.752	47.143	63.777	86.053	115.805
35	1.417	2.000	2.814	3.946	5.516	7.686	10.677	14.785	20.414	28.102	38.575	52.800	72.069	98.100	133.176
36	1.431	2.040	2.898	4.104	5.792	8.147	11.424	15.968	22.251	30.913	42.818	59.136	81.437	111.834	153.152
37	1.445	2.081	2.985	4.268	6.081	8.636	12.224	17.246	24.254	34.004	47.528	66.232	92.024	127.491	176.125
38	1.460	2.122	3.075	4.439	6.385	9.154	13.079	18.625	26.437	37.404	52.756	74.180	103.987	145.340	202.543
39	1.474	2.165	3.167	4.616	6.705	9.704	13.995	20.115	28.816	41.145	58.559	83.081	117.506	165.687	232.925
40	1.489	2.208	3.262	4.801	7.040	10.286	14.974	21.725	31.409	45.259	65.001	93.051	132.782	188.884	267.864
41	1.504	2.252	3.360	4.993	7.392	10.903	16.023	23.462	34.236	49.785	72.151	104.217	150.043	215.327	308.043
42	1.519	2.297	3.461	5.193	7.762	11.557	17.144	25.339	37.318	54.764	80.088	116.723	169.549	245.473	354.250
43	1.534	2.343	3.565	5.400	8.150	12.250	18.344	27.367	40.676	60.240	88.897	130.730	191.590	279.839	407.387
44	1.549	2.390	3.671	5.617	8.557	12.985	19.628	29.556	44.337	66.264	98.676	146.418	216.497	319.017	468.495
45	1.565	2.438	3.782	5.841	8.985	13.765	21.002	31.920	48.327	72.890	109.530	163.988	244.641	363.679	538.769
46	1.580	2.487	3.895	6.075	9.434	14.590	22.473	34.474	52.677	80.180	121.579	183.666	276.445	414.594	619.585
47	1.596	2.536	4.012	6.318	9.906	15.466	24.046	37.232	57.418	88.197	134.952	205.706	312.383	472.637	712.522
48	1.612	2.587	4.132	6.571	10.401	16.394	25.729	40.211	62.585	97.017	149.797	230.391	352.992	538.807	819.401
49	1.628	2.639	4.256	6.833	10.921	17.378	27.530	43.427	68.218	106.719	166.275	258.038	398.881	614.239	942.311
50	1.645	2.692	4.384	7.107	11.467	18.420	29.457	46.902	74.358	117.391	184.565	289.002	450.736	700.233	1083.657

Table T1 (Contd.)
Future Value of a Single Cash Flow (FVIF)
Interest Rate (%)

Year	16	17	18	19	20	21	22	23	24	25	26	27	28	29	30
1	1.160	1.170	1.180	1.190	1.200	1.210	1.220	1.230	1.240	1.250	1.260	1.270	1.280	1.290	1.300
2	1.346	1.369	1.392	1.416	1.440	1.464	1.488	1.513	1.538	1.563	1.588	1.613	1.638	1.664	1.690
3	1.561	1.602	1.643	1.685	1.728	1.772	1.816	1.861	1.907	1.953	2.000	2.048	2.097	2.147	2.197
4	1.811	1.874	1.939	2.005	2.074	2.144	2.215	2.289	2.364	2.441	2.520	2.601	2.684	2.769	2.856
5	2.100	2.192	2.288	2.386	2.488	2.594	2.703	2.815	2.932	3.052	3.176	3.304	3.436	3.572	3.713
6	2.436	2.565	2.700	2.840	2.986	3.138	3.297	3.463	3.635	3.815	4.002	4.196	4.398	4.608	4.827
7	2.826	3.001	3.185	3.379	3.583	3.797	4.023	4.259	4.508	4.768	5.042	5.329	5.629	5.945	6.275
8	3.278	3.511	3.759	4.021	4.300	4.595	4.908	5.239	5.590	5.960	6.353	6.768	7.206	7.669	8.157
9	3.803	4.108	4.435	4.785	5.160	5.560	5.987	6.444	6.931	7.451	8.005	8.595	9.223	9.893	10.604
10	4.411	4.807	5.234	5.695	6.192	6.727	7.305	7.926	8.594	9.313	10.086	10.915	11.806	12.761	13.786
11	5.117	5.624	6.176	6.777	7.430	8.140	8.912	9.749	10.657	11.642	12.708	13.862	15.112	16.462	17.922
12	5.936	6.580	7.288	8.064	8.916	9.850	10.872	11.991	13.215	14.552	16.012	17.605	19.343	21.236	23.298
13	6.886	7.699	8.599	9.596	10.699	11.918	13.264	14.749	16.386	18.190	20.175	22.359	24.759	27.395	30.288
14	7.988	9.007	10.147	11.420	12.839	14.421	16.182	18.141	20.319	22.737	25.421	28.396	31.691	35.339	39.374
15	9.266	10.539	11.974	13.590	15.407	17.449	19.742	22.314	25.196	28.422	32.030	36.062	40.565	45.587	51.186
16	10.748	12.330	14.129	16.172	18.488	21.114	24.086	27.446	31.243	35.527	40.358	45.799	51.923	58.808	66.542
17	12.468	14.426	16.672	19.244	22.186	25.548	29.384	33.759	38.741	44.409	50.851	58.165	66.461	75.862	86.504
18	14.463	16.879	19.673	22.901	26.623	30.913	35.849	41.523	48.039	55.511	64.072	73.870	85.071	97.862	112.455
19	16.777	19.748	23.214	27.252	31.948	37.404	43.736	51.074	59.568	69.389	80.731	93.815	108.890	126.242	146.192
20	19.461	23.106	27.393	32.429	38.338	45.259	53.358	62.821	73.864	86.736	101.721	119.145	139.380	162.852	190.050
21	22.574	27.034	32.324	38.591	46.005	54.764	65.096	77.269	91.592	108.420	128.169	151.314	178.406	210.080	247.065
22	26.186	31.629	38.142	45.923	55.206	66.264	79.418	95.041	113.574	135.525	161.492	192.168	228.360	271.003	321.184
23	30.376	37.006	45.008	54.649	66.247	80.180	96.889	116.901	140.831	169.407	203.480	244.054	292.300	349.593	417.539
24	35.236	43.297	53.109	65.032	79.497	97.017	118.205	143.788	174.631	211.758	256.385	309.948	374.144	450.976	542.801
25	40.874	50.658	62.669	77.388	95.396	117.391	144.210	176.859	216.542	264.698	323.045	393.634	478.905	581.759	705.641
26	47.414	59.270	73.949	92.092	114.475	142.043	175.936	217.537	268.512	330.872	407.037	499.916	612.998	750.468	917.333
27	55.000	69.345	87.260	109.589	137.371	171.872	214.642	267.570	332.955	413.590	512.867	634.893	784.638	968.104	1192.533
28	63.800	81.134	102.967	130.411	164.845	207.965	261.864	329.112	412.864	516.988	646.212	806.314	1004.336	1248.855	1550.293
29	74.009	94.927	121.501	155.189	197.814	251.638	319.474	404.807	511.952	646.235	814.228	1024.019	1285.550	1611.022	2015.381
30	85.850	111.065	143.371	184.675	237.376	304.482	389.758	497.913	634.820	807.794	1025.927	1300.504	1645.505	2078.219	2619.996
31	99.586	129.946	169.177	219.764	284.852	368.423	475.505	612.433	787.177	1009.742	1292.668	1651.640	2106.246	2680.902	3405.994

32	115.520	152.036	199.629	261.519	341.822	445.792	580.116	753.292	976.099	1262.177	1628.761	2097.583	2695.995	3458.364	4427.793
33	134.003	177.883	235.563	311.207	410.186	539.408	707.741	926.550	1210.363	1577.722	2052.239	2663.930	3450.873	4461.290	5756.130
34	155.443	208.123	277.964	370.337	492.224	652.683	863.444	1139.656	1500.850	1972.152	2585.821	3383.191	4417.118	5755.064	7482.970
35	180.314	243.503	327.997	440.701	590.668	789.747	1053.402	1401.777	1861.054	2465.190	3258.135	4296.653	5653.911	7424.032	9727.860
36	209.164	284.899	387.037	524.434	708.802	955.594	1285.150	1724.186	2307.707	3081.488	4105.250	5456.749	7237.006	9577.002	12646.219
37	242.631	333.332	456.703	624.076	850.562	1156.269	1567.883	2120.748	2861.557	3851.860	5172.615	6930.071	9263.367	12354.332	16440.084
38	281.452	389.998	538.910	742.651	1020.675	1399.085	1912.818	2608.520	3548.330	4814.825	6517.495	8801.190	11857.110	15937.089	21372.109
39	326.484	456.298	635.914	883.754	1224.810	1692.893	2333.638	3208.480	4399.930	6018.531	8212.044	11177.511	15177.101	20558.844	27783.742
40	378.721	533.869	750.378	1051.668	1469.772	2048.400	2847.038	3946.430	5455.913	7523.164	10347.175	14195.439	19426.689	26520.909	36118.865
41	439.317	624.626	885.446	1251.484	1763.726	2478.564	3473.386	4854.110	6765.332	9403.955	13037.441	18028.208	24866.162	34211.973	46954.524
42	509.607	730.813	1044.827	1489.266	2116.471	2999.063	4237.531	5970.555	8389.011	11754.944	16427.175	22895.824	31828.687	44133.445	61040.882
43	591.144	855.051	1232.896	1772.227	2539.765	3628.866	5169.788	7343.782	10402.374	14693.679	20698.241	29077.697	40740.720	56932.144	79353.146
44	685.727	1000.410	1454.817	2108.950	3047.718	4390.928	6307.141	9032.852	12898.944	18367.099	26079.784	36928.675	52148.121	73442.466	103159.090
45	795.444	1170.479	1716.684	2509.651	3657.262	5313.023	7694.712	11110.408	15994.690	22958.874	32860.527	46899.417	66749.595	94740.782	134106.817
46	922.715	1369.461	2025.687	2986.484	4388.714	6428.757	9387.549	13665.802	19833.416	28698.593	41404.265	59562.259	85439.481	122215.608	174338.862
47	1070.349	1602.269	2390.311	3553.916	5266.457	7778.796	11452.810	16808.937	24593.436	35873.241	52169.373	75644.069	109362.536	157658.135	226640.520
48	1241.605	1874.655	2820.567	4229.160	6319.749	9412.344	13972.428	20674.992	30495.860	44841.551	65733.410	96067.968	139984.046	203378.994	294632.676
49	1440.262	2193.346	3328.269	5032.701	7583.698	11388.936	17046.362	25430.240	37814.867	56051.939	82824.097	122006.320	179179.579	262358.902	383022.479
50	1670.704	2566.215	3927.357	5988.914	9100.438	13780.612	20796.561	31279.195	46890.435	70064.923	104358.362	154948.026	229349.862	338442.984	497929.223

Table T2
Future Value of Interest Factor Annuity (FVIFA)
Interest Rate (%)

Year	1	2	3	4	5	6	7	8	9	10	11	12	13	14	15
1	1.000	1.000	1.000	1.000	1.000	1.000	1.000	1.000	1.000	1.000	1.000	1.000	1.000	1.000	1.000
2	2.010	2.020	2.030	2.040	2.050	2.060	2.070	2.080	2.090	2.100	2.110	2.120	2.130	2.140	2.150
3	3.030	3.060	3.091	3.122	3.153	3.184	3.215	3.246	3.278	3.310	3.342	3.374	3.407	3.440	3.473
4	4.060	4.122	4.184	4.246	4.310	4.375	4.440	4.506	4.573	4.641	4.710	4.779	4.850	4.921	4.993
5	5.101	5.204	5.309	5.416	5.526	5.637	5.751	5.867	5.985	6.105	6.228	6.353	6.480	6.610	6.742
6	6.152	6.308	6.468	6.633	6.802	6.975	7.153	7.336	7.523	7.716	7.913	8.115	8.323	8.536	8.754
7	7.214	7.434	7.662	7.898	8.142	8.394	8.654	8.923	9.200	9.487	9.783	10.089	10.405	10.730	11.067
8	8.286	8.583	8.892	9.214	9.549	9.897	10.260	10.637	11.028	11.436	11.859	12.300	12.757	13.233	13.727
9	9.369	9.755	10.159	10.583	11.027	11.491	11.978	12.488	13.021	13.579	14.164	14.776	15.416	16.085	16.786
10	10.462	10.950	11.464	12.006	12.578	13.181	13.816	14.487	15.193	15.937	16.722	17.549	18.420	19.337	20.304
11	11.567	12.169	12.808	13.486	14.207	14.972	15.784	16.645	17.560	18.531	19.561	20.655	21.814	23.045	24.349
12	12.683	13.412	14.192	15.026	15.917	16.870	17.888	18.977	20.141	21.384	22.713	24.133	25.650	27.271	29.002
13	13.809	14.680	15.618	16.627	17.713	18.882	20.141	21.495	22.953	24.523	26.212	28.029	29.985	32.089	34.352
14	14.947	15.974	17.086	18.292	19.599	21.015	22.550	24.215	26.019	27.975	30.095	32.393	34.883	37.581	40.505
15	16.097	17.293	18.599	20.024	21.579	23.276	25.129	27.152	29.361	31.772	34.405	37.280	40.417	43.842	47.580
16	17.258	18.639	20.157	21.825	23.657	25.673	27.888	30.324	33.003	35.950	39.190	42.753	46.672	50.980	55.717
17	18.430	20.012	21.762	23.698	25.840	28.213	30.840	33.750	36.974	40.545	44.501	48.884	53.739	59.118	65.075
18	19.615	21.412	23.414	25.645	28.132	30.906	33.999	37.450	41.301	45.599	50.396	55.750	61.725	68.394	75.836
19	20.811	22.841	25.117	27.671	30.539	33.760	37.379	41.446	46.018	51.159	56.939	63.440	70.749	78.969	88.212
20	22.019	24.297	26.870	29.778	33.066	36.786	40.995	45.762	51.160	57.275	64.203	72.052	80.947	91.025	102.444
21	23.239	25.783	28.676	31.969	35.719	39.993	44.865	50.423	56.765	64.002	72.265	81.699	92.470	104.768	118.810
22	24.472	27.299	30.537	34.248	38.505	43.392	49.006	55.45676	62.87334	71.40275	81.21431	92.50258	105.491	120.436	137.6316
23	25.716	28.845	32.453	36.618	41.430	46.996	53.436	60.893	69.532	79.543	91.148	104.603	120.205	138.297	159.276
24	26.973	30.422	34.426	39.083	44.502	50.816	58.177	66.765	76.790	88.497	102.174	118.155	136.831	158.659	184.168
25	28.243	32.030	36.459	41.646	47.727	54.865	63.249	73.106	84.701	98.347	114.413	133.334	155.620	181.871	212.793

26	29.526	33.671	38.553	44.312	51.113	59.156	68.676	79.954	93.324	109.182	127.999	150.334	176.850	208.333	245.712
27	30.821	35.344	40.710	47.084	54.669	63.706	74.484	87.351	102.723	121.100	143.079	169.374	200.841	238.499	283.569
28	32.129	37.051	42.931	49.968	58.403	68.528	80.698	95.339	112.968	134.210	159.817	190.699	227.950	272.889	327.104
29	33.450	38.792	45.219	52.966	62.323	73.640	87.347	103.966	124.135	148.631	178.397	214.583	258.583	312.094	377.170
30	34.785	40.568	47.575	56.085	66.439	79.058	94.461	113.283	136.308	164.494	199.021	241.333	293.199	356.787	434.745
31	36.133	42.379	50.003	59.328	70.761	84.802	102.073	123.346	149.575	181.943	221.913	271.293	332.315	407.737	500.957
32	37.494	44.227	52.503	62.701	75.299	90.890	110.218	134.214	164.037	201.138	247.324	304.848	376.516	465.820	577.100
33	38.869	46.112	55.078	65.210	80.064	97.343	118.933	145.951	179.800	222.252	275.529	342.429	426.463	532.035	664.666
34	40.258	48.034	57.730	69.858	85.067	104.184	128.259	158.627	196.982	245.477	306.837	384.521	482.903	607.520	765.365
35	41.660	49.994	60.462	73.652	90.320	111.435	138.237	172.317	215.711	271.024	341.590	431.663	546.681	693.573	881.170
36	43.077	51.994	63.276	77.598	95.836	119.121	148.913	187.102	236.125	299.127	380.164	484.463	618.749	791.673	1014.346
37	44.508	54.034	66.174	81.702	101.628	127.268	160.337	203.070	258.376	330.039	422.982	543.599	700.187	903.507	1167.498
38	45.953	56.115	69.159	85.970	107.710	135.904	172.561	220.316	282.630	364.043	470.511	609.831	792.211	1030.998	1343.622
39	47.412	58.237	72.234	90.409	114.095	145.058	185.640	238.941	309.066	401.448	523.267	684.010	896.198	1176.338	1546.165
40	48.886	60.402	75.401	95.026	120.800	154.762	199.635	259.057	337.882	442.593	581.826	767.091	1013.704	1342.025	1779.090
41	50.375	62.610	78.663	99.827	127.840	165.048	214.610	280.781	369.292	487.852	646.827	860.142	1146.486	1530.909	2046.954
42	51.879	64.862	82.023	104.820	135.232	175.951	230.632	304.244	403.528	537.637	718.978	964.359	1296.529	1746.236	2354.997
43	53.398	67.159	85.484	110.012	142.993	187.508	247.776	329.583	440.846	592.401	799.065	1081.083	1466.078	1991.709	2709.246
44	54.932	69.503	89.048	115.413	151.143	199.758	266.121	356.950	481.522	652.641	887.963	1211.813	1657.668	2271.548	3116.633
45	56.481	71.893	92.720	121.029	159.700	212.744	285.749	386.506	525.859	718.905	986.639	1358.230	1874.165	2590.565	3585.128
46	58.046	74.331	96.501	126.871	168.685	226.508	306.752	418.426	574.186	791.795	1096.169	1522.218	2118.806	2954.244	4123.898
47	59.626	76.817	100.397	132.945	178.119	241.099	329.224	452.900	626.863	871.975	1217.747	1705.884	2395.251	3368.838	4743.482
48	61.223	79.354	104.408	139.263	188.025	256.565	353.270	490.132	684.280	960.172	1352.700	1911.590	2707.633	3841.475	5456.005
49	62.835	81.941	108.541	145.834	198.427	272.958	378.999	530.343	746.866	1057.190	1502.497	2141.981	3060.626	4380.282	6275.405
50	64.463	84.579	112.797	152.667	209.348	290.336	406.529	573.770	815.084	1163.909	1668.771	2400.018	3459.507	4994.521	7217.716

Table T2 (Contd.)
Future Value of Interest Factor Annuity (FVIFA)
Interest Rate (%)

Year	16	17	18	19	20	21	22	23	24	25	26	27	28	29	30
1	1.000	1.000	1.000	1.000	1.000	1.000	1.000	1.000	1.000	1.000	1.000	1.000	1.000	1.000	1.000
2	2.160	2.170	2.180	2.190	2.200	2.210	2.220	2.230	2.240	2.250	2.260	2.270	2.280	2.290	2.300
3	3.506	3.539	3.572	3.606	3.640	3.674	3.708	3.743	3.778	3.813	3.848	3.883	3.918	3.954	3.990
4	5.066	5.141	5.215	5.291	5.368	5.446	5.524	5.604	5.684	5.766	5.848	5.931	6.016	6.101	6.187
5	6.877	7.014	7.154	7.297	7.442	7.589	7.740	7.893	8.048	8.207	8.368	8.533	8.700	8.870	9.043
6	8.977	9.207	9.442	9.683	9.930	10.183	10.442	10.708	10.980	11.259	11.544	11.837	12.136	12.442	12.756
7	11.414	11.772	12.142	12.523	12.916	13.321	13.740	14.171	14.615	15.073	15.546	16.032	16.534	17.051	17.583
8	14.240	14.773	15.327	15.902	16.499	17.119	17.762	18.430	19.123	19.842	20.588	21.361	22.163	22.995	23.858
9	17.519	18.285	19.086	19.923	20.799	21.714	22.670	23.669	24.712	25.802	26.940	28.129	29.369	30.664	32.015
10	21.321	22.393	23.521	24.709	25.959	27.274	28.657	30.113	31.643	33.253	34.945	36.723	38.593	40.556	42.619
11	25.733	27.200	28.755	30.404	32.150	34.001	35.962	38.039	40.238	42.566	45.031	47.639	50.398	53.318	56.405
12	30.850	32.824	34.931	37.180	39.581	42.142	44.874	47.788	50.895	54.208	57.739	61.501	65.510	69.780	74.327
13	36.786	39.404	42.219	45.244	48.497	51.991	55.746	59.779	64.110	68.760	73.751	79.107	84.853	91.016	97.625
14	43.672	47.103	50.818	54.841	59.196	63.909	69.010	74.528	80.496	86.949	93.926	101.465	109.612	118.411	127.913
15	51.660	56.110	60.965	66.261	72.035	78.330	85.192	92.669	100.815	109.687	119.347	129.861	141.303	153.750	167.286
16	60.925	66.649	72.939	79.850	87.442	95.780	104.935	114.983	126.011	138.109	151.377	165.924	181.868	199.337	218.472
17	71.673	76.979	87.068	96.022	105.931	116.894	129.020	142.430	157.253	173.636	191.735	211.723	233.791	258.145	285.014
18	84.141	93.406	103.740	115.266	128.117	142.441	158.405	176.188	195.994	218.045	242.585	269.888	300.252	334.007	371.518
19	98.603	110.285	123.414	138.166	154.740	173.354	194.254	217.712	244.033	273.556	306.658	343.758	385.323	431.870	483.973
20	115.380	130.033	146.628	165.418	186.688	210.758	237.989	268.785	303.601	342.945	387.389	437.573	494.213	558.112	630.165
21	134.841	153.139	174.021	197.847	225.026	256.018	291.347	331.606	377.465	429.681	489.110	556.717	633.593	720.964	820.215
22	157.415	180.1721	206.3448	236.4385	271.0307	310.7813	356.4432	408.8753	469.0563	538.1011	617.2783	708.0309	811.9987	931.0438	1067.28
23	183.601	211.801	244.487	282.362	326.237	377.045	435.861	503.917	582.630	673.626	778.771	900.199	1040.358	1202.047	1388.464
24	213.978	248.808	289.494	337.010	392.484	457.225	532.750	620.817	723.461	843.033	982.251	1144.253	1332.659	1551.640	1806.003
25	249.214	292.105	342.603	402.042	471.981	554.242	650.955	764.605	898.092	1054.791	1238.636	1454.201	1706.803	2002.616	2348.803
26	290.088	342.763	405.272	479.431	567.377	671.633	795.165	941.465	1114.634	1319.489	1561.682	1847.836	2185.708	2584.374	3054.444
27	337.502	402.032	479.221	571.522	681.853	813.676	971.102	1159.002	1383.146	1650.361	1968.719	2347.751	2798.706	3334.843	3971.778
28	392.503	471.378	566.481	681.112	819.223	985.548	1185.744	1426.572	1716.101	2063.952	2481.586	2982.644	3583.344	4302.947	5164.311
29	456.303	552.512	669.447	811.523	984.068	1193.513	1447.608	1755.683	2128.965	2580.939	3127.798	3788.958	4587.680	5551.802	6714.604
30	530.312	647.439	790.948	966.712	1181.882	1445.151	1767.081	2160.491	2640.916	3227.174	3942.026	4812.977	5873.231	7162.824	8729.985
31	616.162	758.504	934.319	1151.387	1419.258	1749.632	2156.839	2658.404	3275.736	4034.968	4967.953	6113.481	7518.735	9241.043	11349.981

32	715.747	888.449	1103.496	1371.151	1704.109	2118.055	2632.344	3270.836	4062.913	5044.710	6260.620	7765.121	9624.981	11921.946	14755.975
33	831.267	1040.486	1303.125	1632.670	2045.931	2563.847	3212.460	4024.129	5039.012	6306.887	7889.382	9862.703	12320.976	15380.310	19183.768
34	965.270	1218.368	1538.688	1943.877	2456.118	3103.254	3920.201	4950.678	6249.375	7884.609	9941.621	12526.633	15771.849	19841.600	24939.899
35	1120.713	1426.491	1816.652	2314.214	2948.341	3755.938	4783.645	6090.334	7750.225	9856.761	12527.442	15909.824	20188.966	25596.664	32422.868
36	1301.027	1669.994	2144.649	2754.914	3539.009	4545.685	5837.047	7492.111	9611.279	12321.952	15785.577	20206.477	25842.877	33020.696	42150.729
37	1510.191	1954.894	2531.686	3279.348	4247.811	5501.279	7122.197	9216.297	11918.986	15403.440	19890.828	25663.225	33079.883	42597.698	54796.947
38	1752.822	2288.225	2988.389	3903.424	5098.373	6657.547	8690.080	11337.045	14780.543	19255.299	25063.443	32593.296	42343.250	54952.030	71237.031
39	2034.273	2678.224	3527.299	4646.075	6119.048	8056.632	10602.898	13945.566	18328.873	24070.124	31580.938	41394.486	54200.360	70889.119	92609.141
40	2360.757	3134.522	4163.213	5529.829	7343.858	9749.525	12936.535	17154.046	22728.803	30088.655	39792.982	52571.998	69377.460	91447.963	120392.883
41	2739.478	3668.391	4913.591	6581.496	8813.629	11797.925	15783.573	21100.476	28184.715	37611.819	50140.157	66767.437	88804.149	117968.873	156511.748
42	3178.795	4293.017	5799.038	7832.981	10577.355	14276.489	19256.959	25954.586	34950.047	47015.774	63177.598	84795.645	113670.311	152180.846	203466.272
43	3688.402	5023.830	6843.865	9322.247	12693.826	17275.552	23494.490	31925.140	43339.058	58770.718	79604.773	107691.469	145498.998	196314.291	264507.153
44	4279.546	5878.881	8076.760	11094.474	15233.592	20904.418	28664.278	39268.923	53741.432	73464.397	100303.014	136769.166	186239.718	253246.436	343860.299
45	4965.274	6879.291	9531.577	13203.424	18281.310	25295.346	34971.419	48301.775	66640.376	91831.496	126382.798	173697.840	238387.839	326688.902	447019.389
46	5760.718	8049.770	11248.261	15713.075	21938.572	30608.368	42666.131	59412.183	82635.066	114790.370	159243.325	220597.257	305137.434	421429.684	581126.206
47	6683.433	9419.231	13273.948	18699.559	26327.286	37037.126	52053.680	73077.985	102468.482	143488.963	200647.590	280159.517	390576.915	543645.292	755465.067
48	7753.782	11021.500	15664.259	22253.475	31593.744	44815.922	63506.490	89886.922	127061.917	179362.203	252816.963	355803.586	499939.451	701303.427	982105.588
49	8995.387	12896.155	18484.825	26482.636	37913.492	54228.266	77478.917	110561.913	157557.778	224203.754	318550.374	451871.554	639923.498	904682.421	1276738.264
50	10435.649	15089.502	21813.094	31515.336	45497.191	65617.202	94525.279	135992.154	195372.644	280255.693	401374.471	573877.874	819103.077	1167041.323	1659760.743

Table T3
Present Value of a Single Cash Flow (PVIF)
Interest Rate (%)

Year	1	2	3	4	5	6	7	8	9	10	11	12	13	14	15
1	0.990	0.980	0.971	0.962	0.952	0.943	0.935	0.926	0.917	0.909	0.901	0.893	0.885	0.887	0.870
2	0.980	0.961	0.943	0.925	0.907	0.890	0.873	0.857	0.842	0.826	0.812	0.797	0.783	0.769	0.756
3	0.971	0.942	0.915	0.889	0.864	0.840	0.816	0.794	0.772	0.751	0.731	0.712	0.693	0.675	0.658
4	0.961	0.924	0.888	0.855	0.823	0.792	0.763	0.735	0.708	0.683	0.659	0.636	0.613	0.592	0.572
5	0.951	0.906	0.863	0.822	0.784	0.747	0.713	0.681	0.650	0.621	0.593	0.567	0.543	0.519	0.497
6	0.942	0.888	0.837	0.790	0.746	0.705	0.666	0.630	0.596	0.564	0.535	0.507	0.480	0.456	0.432
7	0.933	0.871	0.813	0.760	0.711	0.665	0.623	0.583	0.547	0.513	0.482	0.452	0.425	0.400	0.376
8	0.923	0.853	0.789	0.731	0.677	0.627	0.582	0.540	0.502	0.467	0.434	0.404	0.376	0.351	0.327
9	0.914	0.837	0.766	0.703	0.645	0.592	0.544	0.500	0.460	0.424	0.391	0.361	0.333	0.308	0.284
10	0.905	0.820	0.744	0.676	0.614	0.558	0.508	0.463	0.422	0.386	0.352	0.322	0.295	0.270	0.247
11	0.896	0.804	0.722	0.650	0.585	0.527	0.475	0.429	0.388	0.350	0.317	0.287	0.261	0.237	0.215
12	0.887	0.788	0.701	0.625	0.557	0.497	0.444	0.397	0.356	0.319	0.286	0.257	0.231	0.208	0.187
13	0.879	0.773	0.681	0.601	0.530	0.469	0.415	0.368	0.326	0.290	0.258	0.229	0.204	0.182	0.163
14	0.870	0.758	0.661	0.577	0.505	0.442	0.388	0.340	0.299	0.263	0.232	0.205	0.181	0.160	0.141
15	0.861	0.743	0.642	0.555	0.481	0.417	0.362	0.315	0.275	0.239	0.209	0.183	0.160	0.140	0.123
16	0.853	0.728	0.623	0.534	0.458	0.394	0.339	0.292	0.252	0.218	0.188	0.163	0.141	0.123	0.107
17	0.844	0.714	0.605	0.513	0.436	0.371	0.317	0.270	0.231	0.198	0.170	0.146	0.125	0.108	0.093
18	0.836	0.700	0.587	0.494	0.416	0.350	0.296	0.250	0.212	0.180	0.153	0.130	0.111	0.095	0.081
19	0.828	0.686	0.570	0.475	0.396	0.331	0.277	0.232	0.194	0.164	0.138	0.116	0.098	0.083	0.070
20	0.820	0.673	0.554	0.456	0.377	0.312	0.258	0.215	0.178	0.149	0.124	0.104	0.087	0.073	0.061
21	0.811	0.660	0.538	0.439	0.359	0.294	0.242	0.199	0.164	0.135	0.112	0.093	0.077	0.064	0.053
22	0.803	0.647	0.522	0.422	0.342	0.278	0.226	0.184	0.150	0.123	0.101	0.083	0.068	0.056	0.046
23	0.795	0.634	0.507	0.406	0.326	0.262	0.211	0.170	0.138	0.112	0.091	0.074	0.060	0.049	0.040
24	0.788	0.622	0.492	0.390	0.310	0.247	0.197	0.158	0.126	0.102	0.082	0.066	0.053	0.043	0.035
25	0.780	0.610	0.478	0.375	0.295	0.233	0.184	0.146	0.116	0.092	0.074	0.059	0.047	0.038	0.030

26	0.772	0.598	0.464	0.361	0.281	0.220	0.172	0.135	0.106	0.084	0.066	0.053	0.042	0.033	0.026
27	0.764	0.586	0.450	0.347	0.268	0.207	0.161	0.125	0.098	0.076	0.060	0.047	0.037	0.029	0.023
28	0.757	0.574	0.437	0.333	0.255	0.196	0.150	0.116	0.090	0.069	0.054	0.042	0.033	0.026	0.020
29	0.749	0.563	0.424	0.321	0.243	0.185	0.141	0.107	0.082	0.063	0.048	0.037	0.029	0.022	0.017
30	0.742	0.552	0.412	0.308	0.231	0.174	0.131	0.099	0.075	0.057	0.044	0.033	0.026	0.020	0.015
31	0.735	0.541	0.400	0.296	0.220	0.164	0.123	0.092	0.069	0.052	0.039	0.030	0.023	0.017	0.013
32	0.727	0.531	0.388	0.285	0.210	0.155	0.115	0.085	0.063	0.047	0.035	0.027	0.020	0.015	0.011
33	0.720	0.520	0.377	0.274	0.200	0.146	0.107	0.079	0.058	0.043	0.032	0.024	0.018	0.013	0.010
34	0.713	0.510	0.366	0.264	0.190	0.138	0.100	0.073	0.053	0.039	0.029	0.021	0.016	0.012	0.009
35	0.706	0.500	0.355	0.253	0.181	0.130	0.094	0.068	0.049	0.036	0.026	0.019	0.014	0.010	0.008
36	0.699	0.490	0.345	0.244	0.173	0.123	0.088	0.063	0.045	0.032	0.023	0.017	0.012	0.009	0.007
37	0.692	0.481	0.335	0.234	0.164	0.116	0.082	0.058	0.041	0.029	0.021	0.015	0.011	0.008	0.006
38	0.685	0.471	0.325	0.225	0.157	0.109	0.076	0.054	0.038	0.027	0.019	0.013	0.010	0.007	0.005
39	0.678	0.462	0.316	0.217	0.149	0.103	0.071	0.050	0.035	0.024	0.017	0.012	0.009	0.006	0.004
40	0.672	0.453	0.307	0.208	0.142	0.097	0.067	0.046	0.032	0.022	0.015	0.011	0.008	0.005	0.004
41	0.665	0.444	0.298	0.200	0.135	0.092	0.062	0.043	0.029	0.020	0.014	0.010	0.007	0.005	0.003
42	0.658	0.435	0.289	0.193	0.129	0.087	0.058	0.039	0.027	0.018	0.012	0.009	0.006	0.004	0.003
43	0.652	0.427	0.281	0.185	0.123	0.082	0.055	0.037	0.025	0.017	0.011	0.008	0.005	0.004	0.002
44	0.645	0.418	0.272	0.178	0.117	0.077	0.051	0.034	0.023	0.015	0.010	0.007	0.005	0.003	0.002
45	0.639	0.410	0.264	0.171	0.111	0.073	0.048	0.031	0.021	0.014	0.009	0.006	0.004	0.003	0.002
46	0.633	0.402	0.257	0.165	0.106	0.069	0.044	0.029	0.019	0.012	0.008	0.005	0.004	0.002	0.002
47	0.626	0.394	0.249	0.158	0.101	0.065	0.042	0.027	0.017	0.011	0.007	0.005	0.003	0.002	0.001
48	0.620	0.387	0.242	0.152	0.096	0.061	0.039	0.025	0.016	0.010	0.007	0.004	0.003	0.002	0.001
49	0.614	0.379	0.235	0.146	0.092	0.058	0.036	0.023	0.015	0.009	0.006	0.004	0.003	0.002	0.001
50	0.608	0.372	0.228	0.141	0.087	0.054	0.034	0.021	0.013	0.009	0.005	0.003	0.002	0.001	0.001

Table T3 (Contd.)
Present Value of a Single Cash Flow (PVIF)
Interest Rate (%)

Year	16	17	18	19	20	21	22	23	24	25	26	27	28	29	30
1	0.862	0.855	0.847	0.855	0.833	0.826	0.820	0.813	0.806	0.800	0.794	0.787	0.781	0.775	0.769
2	0.743	0.731	0.718	0.706	0.694	0.683	0.672	0.661	0.650	0.640	0.630	0.620	0.610	0.601	0.592
3	0.641	0.624	0.609	0.593	0.579	0.564	0.551	0.537	0.524	0.512	0.500	0.488	0.477	0.466	0.455
4	0.552	0.534	0.516	0.499	0.482	0.467	0.451	0.437	0.423	0.410	0.397	0.384	0.373	0.361	0.350
5	0.476	0.456	0.437	0.419	0.402	0.386	0.370	0.355	0.341	0.328	0.315	0.303	0.291	0.280	0.269
6	0.410	0.390	0.370	0.352	0.335	0.319	0.303	0.289	0.275	0.262	0.250	0.238	0.227	0.217	0.207
7	0.354	0.333	0.314	0.296	0.279	0.263	0.249	0.235	0.222	0.210	0.198	0.188	0.178	0.168	0.159
8	0.305	0.285	0.266	0.249	0.233	0.218	0.204	0.191	0.179	0.168	0.157	0.148	0.139	0.130	0.123
9	0.263	0.243	0.225	0.209	0.194	0.180	0.167	0.155	0.144	0.134	0.125	0.116	0.108	0.101	0.094
10	0.227	0.208	0.191	0.176	0.162	0.149	0.137	0.126	0.116	0.107	0.099	0.092	0.085	0.078	0.073
11	0.195	0.178	0.162	0.148	0.135	0.123	0.112	0.103	0.094	0.086	0.079	0.072	0.066	0.061	0.056
12	0.168	0.152	0.137	0.124	0.112	0.102	0.092	0.083	0.076	0.069	0.062	0.057	0.052	0.047	0.043
13	0.145	0.130	0.116	0.104	0.093	0.084	0.075	0.068	0.061	0.055	0.050	0.045	0.040	0.037	0.033
14	0.125	0.111	0.099	0.088	0.078	0.069	0.062	0.055	0.049	0.044	0.039	0.035	0.032	0.028	0.025
15	0.108	0.095	0.084	0.074	0.065	0.057	0.051	0.045	0.040	0.035	0.031	0.028	0.025	0.022	0.020
16	0.093	0.081	0.071	0.062	0.054	0.047	0.042	0.036	0.032	0.028	0.025	0.022	0.019	0.017	0.015
17	0.080	0.069	0.060	0.052	0.045	0.039	0.034	0.030	0.026	0.023	0.020	0.017	0.015	0.013	0.012
18	0.069	0.059	0.051	0.044	0.038	0.032	0.028	0.024	0.021	0.018	0.016	0.014	0.012	0.010	0.009
19	0.060	0.051	0.043	0.037	0.031	0.027	0.023	0.020	0.017	0.014	0.012	0.011	0.009	0.008	0.007
20	0.051	0.043	0.037	0.031	0.026	0.022	0.019	0.016	0.014	0.012	0.010	0.008	0.007	0.006	0.005
21	0.044	0.037	0.031	0.026	0.022	0.018	0.015	0.013	0.011	0.009	0.008	0.007	0.006	0.005	0.004
22	0.038	0.032	0.026	0.022	0.018	0.015	0.013	0.011	0.009	0.007	0.006	0.005	0.004	0.004	0.003
23	0.033	0.027	0.022	0.018	0.015	0.012	0.010	0.009	0.007	0.006	0.005	0.004	0.003	0.003	0.002
24	0.028	0.023	0.019	0.015	0.013	0.010	0.008	0.007	0.006	0.005	0.004	0.003	0.003	0.002	0.002
25	0.024	0.020	0.016	0.013	0.010	0.009	0.007	0.006	0.005	0.004	0.003	0.003	0.002	0.002	0.001
26	0.021	0.017	0.014	0.011	0.009	0.007	0.006	0.005	0.004	0.003	0.002	0.002	0.002	0.001	0.001
27	0.018	0.014	0.011	0.009	0.007	0.006	0.005	0.004	0.003	0.002	0.002	0.002	0.001	0.001	0.001
28	0.016	0.012	0.010	0.008	0.006	0.005	0.004	0.003	0.002	0.002	0.001	0.001	0.001	0.001	0.001
29	0.014	0.011	0.008	0.006	0.005	0.004	0.003	0.002	0.002	0.002	0.001	0.001	0.001	0.001	0.001
30	0.012	0.009	0.007	0.005	0.004	0.003	0.003	0.002	0.002	0.001	0.001	0.001	0.000	0.000	0.000
31	0.010	0.008	0.006	0.005	0.004	0.003	0.002	0.002	0.001	0.001	0.001	0.001	0.000	0.000	0.000

660 Security Analysis and Portfolio Management

32	33	34	35	36	37	38	39	40	41	42	43	44	45	46	47	48	49	50
0.000	0.000	0.000	0.000	0.000	0.000	0.000	0.000	0.000	0.000	0.000	0.000	0.000	0.000	0.000	0.000	0.000	0.000	0.000
0.000	0.000	0.000	0.000	0.000	0.000	0.000	0.000	0.000	0.000	0.000	0.000	0.000	0.000	0.000	0.000	0.000	0.000	0.000
0.000	0.000	0.000	0.000	0.000	0.000	0.000	0.000	0.000	0.000	0.000	0.000	0.000	0.000	0.000	0.000	0.000	0.000	
0.000	0.000	0.000	0.000	0.000	0.000	0.000	0.000	0.000	0.000	0.000	0.000	0.000	0.000	0.000	0.000	0.000	0.000	0.000
0.001	0.000	0.000	0.000	0.000	0.000	0.000	0.000	0.000	0.000	0.000	0.000	0.000	0.000	0.000	0.000	0.000	0.000	0.000
0.001	0.001	0.001	0.000	0.000	0.000	0.000	0.000	0.000	0.000	0.000	0.000	0.000	0.000	0.000	0.000	0.000	0.000	0.000
0.001	0.001	0.001	0.001	0.000	0.000	0.000	0.000	0.000	0.000	0.000	0.000	0.000	0.000	0.000	0.000	0.000	0.000	0.000
0.001	0.001	0.001	0.001	0.001	0.000	0.000	0.000	0.000	0.000	0.000	0.000	0.000	0.000	0.000	0.000	0.000	0.000	0.000
0.002	0.001	0.001	0.001	0.001	0.001	0.001	0.000	0.000	0.000	0.000	0.000	0.000	0.000	0.000	0.000	0.000	0.000	0.000
0.002	0.002	0.002	0.001	0.001	0.001	0.001	0.001	0.000	0.000	0.000	0.000	0.000	0.000	0.000	0.000	0.000	0.000	0.000
0.003	0.002	0.002	0.002	0.001	0.001	0.001	0.001	0.001	0.001	0.000	0.000	0.000	0.000	0.000	0.000	0.000	0.000	0.000
0.004	0.003	0.003	0.002	0.002	0.002	0.001	0.001	0.001	0.001	0.001	0.001	0.000	0.000	0.000	0.000	0.000	0.000	0.000
0.005	0.004	0.004	0.003	0.003	0.002	0.002	0.002	0.001	0.001	0.001	0.001	0.001	0.001	0.000	0.000	0.000	0.000	0.000
0.007	0.006	0.005	0.004	0.004	0.003	0.003	0.002	0.002	0.002	0.001	0.001	0.001	0.001	0.001	0.001	0.001	0.000	0.000
0.009	0.007	0.006	0.006	0.005	0.004	0.004	0.003	0.003	0.002	0.002	0.002	0.001	0.001	0.001	0.001	0.001	0.001	0.001

Table T4
Present Value of Interest Factor Annuity (PVIFA)
Interest Rate (%)

Year	1	2	3	4	5	6	7	8	9	10	11	12	13	14	15
1	0.990	0.980	0.971	0.962	0.952	0.943	0.935	0.926	0.917	0.909	0.901	0.893	0.885	0.877	0.870
2	1.970	1.942	1.913	1.886	1.859	1.833	1.808	1.783	1.759	1.736	1.713	1.690	1.668	1.647	1.626
3	2.941	2.884	2.829	2.775	2.723	2.673	2.624	2.577	2.531	2.487	2.444	2.402	2.361	2.322	2.283
4	3.902	3.808	3.717	3.630	3.546	3.465	3.387	3.312	3.240	3.170	3.102	3.037	2.974	2.914	2.855
5	4.853	4.713	4.580	4.452	4.329	4.212	4.100	3.993	3.890	3.791	3.696	3.605	3.517	3.433	3.352
6	5.795	5.601	5.417	5.242	5.076	4.917	4.767	4.623	4.486	4.355	4.231	4.111	3.998	3.889	3.784
7	6.728	6.472	6.230	6.002	5.786	5.582	5.389	5.206	5.033	4.868	4.712	4.564	4.423	4.288	4.160
8	7.652	7.325	7.020	6.733	6.463	6.210	5.971	5.747	5.535	5.335	5.146	4.968	4.799	4.639	4.487
9	8.566	8.162	7.786	7.435	7.108	6.802	6.515	6.247	5.995	5.759	5.537	5.328	5.132	4.946	4.772
10	9.471	8.983	8.530	8.111	7.722	7.360	7.024	6.710	6.418	6.145	5.889	5.650	5.426	5.216	5.019
11	10.368	9.787	9.253	8.760	8.306	7.887	7.499	7.139	6.805	6.495	6.207	5.938	5.687	5.453	5.234
12	11.255	10.575	9.954	9.385	8.863	8.384	7.943	7.536	7.161	6.814	6.492	6.194	5.918	5.660	5.421
13	12.134	11.348	10.635	9.986	9.394	8.853	8.358	7.904	7.487	7.103	6.750	6.424	6.122	5.842	5.583
14	13.004	12.106	11.296	10.563	9.899	9.295	8.745	8.244	7.786	7.367	6.982	6.628	6.302	6.002	5.724
15	13.865	12.849	11.938	11.118	10.380	9.712	9.108	8.559	8.061	7.606	7.191	6.811	6.462	6.142	5.847
16	14.718	13.578	12.561	11.652	10.838	10.106	9.447	8.851	8.313	7.824	7.379	6.974	6.604	6.265	5.954
17	15.562	14.292	13.166	12.166	11.274	10.477	9.763	9.122	8.544	8.022	7.549	7.120	6.729	6.373	6.047
18	16.398	14.992	13.754	12.659	11.690	10.828	10.059	9.372	8.756	8.201	7.702	7.250	6.840	6.467	6.128
19	17.226	15.678	14.324	13.134	12.085	11.158	10.336	9.604	8.950	8.365	7.839	7.366	6.938	6.550	6.198
20	18.046	16.351	14.877	13.590	12.462	11.470	10.594	9.818	9.129	8.514	7.963	7.469	7.025	6.623	6.259
21	18.857	17.011	15.415	14.029	12.821	11.764	10.836	10.017	9.292	8.649	8.075	7.562	7.102	6.687	6.312
22	19.660	17.658	15.937	14.451	13.163	12.042	11.061	10.201	9.442	8.772	8.176	7.645	7.170	6.743	6.359
23	20.456	18.292	16.444	14.857	13.489	12.303	11.272	10.371	9.580	8.883	8.266	7.718	7.230	6.792	6.399
24	21.243	18.914	16.936	15.247	13.799	12.550	11.469	10.529	9.707	8.985	8.348	7.784	7.283	6.835	6.434
25	22.023	19.523	17.413	15.622	14.094	12.783	11.654	10.675	9.823	9.077	8.422	7.843	7.330	6.873	6.464

26	22.795	20.121	17.877	15.983	14.375	13.003	11.826	10.810	9.929	9.161	8.488	7.896	7.372	6.906	6.491
27	23.560	20.707	18.327	16.330	14.643	13.211	11.987	10.935	10.027	9.237	8.548	7.943	7.409	6.935	6.514
28	24.316	21.281	18.764	16.663	14.898	13.406	12.137	11.051	10.116	9.307	8.602	7.984	7.441	6.961	6.534
29	25.066	21.844	19.188	16.984	15.141	13.591	12.278	11.158	10.198	9.370	8.650	8.022	7.470	6.983	6.551
30	25.808	22.396	19.600	17.292	15.372	13.765	12.409	11.258	10.274	9.427	8.694	8.055	7.496	7.003	6.566
31	26.542	22.938	20.000	17.588	15.593	13.929	12.532	11.350	10.343	9.479	8.733	8.085	7.518	7.020	6.579
32	27.270	23.468	20.389	17.874	15.803	14.084	12.647	11.435	10.406	9.526	8.769	8.112	7.538	7.035	6.591
33	27.990	23.989	20.766	18.148	16.003	14.230	12.754	11.514	10.464	9.569	8.801	8.135	7.556	7.048	6.600
34	28.703	24.499	21.132	18.411	16.193	14.368	12.854	11.587	10.518	9.609	8.829	8.157	7.572	7.060	6.609
35	29.409	24.999	21.487	18.665	16.374	14.498	12.948	11.655	10.567	9.644	8.855	8.176	7.586	7.070	6.617
36	30.108	25.489	21.832	18.908	16.547	14.621	13.035	11.717	10.612	9.677	8.879	8.192	7.598	7.079	6.623
37	30.800	25.969	22.167	19.143	16.711	14.737	13.117	11.775	10.653	9.706	8.900	8.208	7.609	7.087	6.629
38	31.485	26.441	22.492	19.368	16.868	14.846	13.193	11.829	10.691	9.733	8.919	8.221	7.618	7.094	6.634
39	32.163	26.903	22.808	19.584	17.017	14.949	13.265	11.879	10.726	9.757	8.936	8.233	7.627	7.100	6.638
40	32.835	27.355	23.115	19.793	17.159	15.046	13.332	11.925	10.757	9.779	8.951	8.244	7.634	7.105	6.642
41	33.500	27.799	23.412	19.993	17.294	15.138	13.394	11.967	10.787	9.799	8.965	8.253	7.641	7.110	6.645
42	34.158	28.235	23.701	20.186	17.423	15.225	13.452	12.007	10.813	9.817	8.977	8.262	7.647	7.114	6.648
43	34.810	28.662	23.982	20.371	17.546	15.306	13.507	12.043	10.838	9.834	8.989	8.270	7.652	7.117	6.650
44	35.455	29.080	24.254	20.549	17.663	15.383	13.558	12.077	10.861	9.849	8.999	8.276	7.657	7.120	6.652
45	36.095	29.490	24.519	20.720	17.774	15.456	13.606	12.108	10.881	9.863	9.008	8.283	7.661	7.123	6.654
46	36.727	29.892	24.775	20.885	17.880	15.524	13.650	12.137	10.900	9.875	9.016	8.288	7.664	7.126	6.656
47	37.354	30.287	25.025	21.043	17.981	15.589	13.692	12.164	10.918	9.887	9.024	8.293	7.668	7.128	6.657
48	37.974	30.673	25.267	21.195	18.077	15.650	13.730	12.189	10.934	9.897	9.030	8.297	7.671	7.130	6.659
49	38.588	31.052	25.502	21.341	18.169	15.708	13.767	12.212	10.948	9.906	9.036	8.301	7.673	7.131	6.660
50	39.196	31.424	25.730	21.482	18.256	15.762	13.801	12.233	10.962	9.915	9.042	8.304	7.675	7.133	6.661

Table T4 (Contd.)
Present Value of Interest Factor Annuity (PVIFA)
Interest Rate (%)

Year	16	17	18	19	20	21	22	23	24	25	26	27	28	29	30
1	0.862	0.855	0.847	0.840	0.833	0.826	0.820	0.813	0.806	0.800	0.794	0.787	0.781	0.775	0.769
2	1.605	1.585	1.566	1.547	1.528	1.509	1.492	1.474	1.457	1.440	1.424	1.407	1.392	1.376	1.361
3	2.246	2.210	2.174	2.140	2.106	2.074	2.042	2.011	1.981	1.952	1.923	1.896	1.868	1.842	1.816
4	2.798	2.743	2.690	2.639	2.589	2.540	2.494	2.448	2.404	2.362	2.320	2.280	2.241	2.203	2.166
5	3.274	3.199	3.127	3.058	2.991	2.926	2.864	2.803	2.745	2.689	2.635	2.583	2.532	2.483	2.436
6	3.685	3.589	3.498	3.410	3.326	3.245	3.167	3.092	3.020	2.951	2.885	2.821	2.759	2.700	2.643
7	4.039	3.922	3.812	3.706	3.605	3.508	3.416	3.327	3.242	3.161	3.083	3.009	2.937	2.868	2.802
8	4.344	4.207	4.078	3.954	3.837	3.726	3.619	3.518	3.421	3.329	3.241	3.156	3.076	2.999	2.925
9	4.607	4.451	4.303	4.163	4.031	3.905	3.786	3.673	3.566	3.463	3.366	3.273	3.184	3.100	3.019
10	4.833	4.659	4.494	4.339	4.192	4.054	3.923	3.799	3.682	3.571	3.465	3.364	3.269	3.178	3.092
11	5.029	4.836	4.656	4.486	4.327	4.177	4.035	3.902	3.776	3.656	3.543	3.437	3.335	3.239	3.147
12	5.197	4.988	4.793	4.611	4.439	4.278	4.127	3.985	3.851	3.725	3.606	3.493	3.387	3.286	3.190
13	5.342	5.118	4.910	4.715	4.533	4.362	4.203	4.053	3.912	3.780	3.656	3.538	3.427	3.322	3.223
14	5.468	5.229	5.008	4.802	4.611	4.432	4.265	4.108	3.962	3.824	3.695	3.573	3.459	3.351	3.249
15	5.575	5.324	5.092	4.876	4.675	4.489	4.315	4.153	4.001	3.859	3.726	3.601	3.483	3.373	3.268
16	5.668	5.405	5.162	4.938	4.730	4.536	4.357	4.189	4.033	3.887	3.751	3.623	3.503	3.390	3.283
17	5.749	5.475	5.222	4.990	4.775	4.576	4.391	4.219	4.059	3.910	3.771	3.640	3.518	3.403	3.295
18	5.818	5.534	5.273	5.033	4.812	4.608	4.419	4.243	4.080	3.928	3.786	3.654	3.529	3.413	3.304
19	5.877	5.584	5.316	5.070	4.843	4.635	4.442	4.263	4.097	3.942	3.799	3.664	3.539	3.421	3.311
20	5.929	5.628	5.353	5.101	4.870	4.657	4.460	4.279	4.110	3.954	3.808	3.673	3.546	3.427	3.316
21	5.973	5.665	5.384	5.127	4.891	4.675	4.476	4.292	4.121	3.963	3.816	3.679	3.551	3.432	3.320
22	6.011	5.696	5.410	5.149	4.909	4.690	4.488	4.302	4.130	3.970	3.822	3.684	3.556	3.436	3.323
23	6.044	5.723	5.432	5.167	4.925	4.703	4.499	4.311	4.137	3.976	3.827	3.689	3.559	3.438	3.325
24	6.073	5.746	5.451	5.182	4.937	4.713	4.507	4.318	4.143	3.981	3.831	3.692	3.562	3.441	3.327
25	6.097	5.766	5.467	5.195	4.948	4.721	4.514	4.323	4.147	3.985	3.834	3.694	3.564	3.442	3.329
26	6.118	5.783	5.480	5.206	4.956	4.728	4.520	4.328	4.151	3.988	3.837	3.696	3.566	3.444	3.330
27	6.136	5.798	5.492	5.215	4.964	4.734	4.524	4.332	4.154	3.990	3.839	3.698	3.567	3.445	3.331
28	6.152	5.810	5.502	5.223	4.970	4.739	4.528	4.335	4.157	3.992	3.840	3.699	3.568	3.446	3.331
29	6.166	5.820	5.510	5.229	4.975	4.743	4.531	4.337	4.159	3.994	3.841	3.700	3.569	3.446	3.332
30	6.177	5.829	5.517	5.235	4.979	4.746	4.534	4.339	4.160	3.995	3.842	3.701	3.569	3.447	3.332
31	6.187	5.837	5.523	5.239	4.982	4.749	4.536	4.341	4.161	3.996	3.843	3.701	3.570	3.447	3.332

32	6.196	5.844	5.528	5.243	4.985	4.751	4.538	4.342	4.162	3.997	3.844	3.702	3.570	3.447	3.333
33	6.203	5.849	5.532	5.246	4.988	4.753	4.539	4.343	4.163	3.997	3.844	3.702	3.570	3.448	3.333
34	6.210	5.854	5.536	5.249	4.990	4.755	4.540	4.344	4.164	3.998	3.845	3.703	3.571	3.448	3.333
35	6.215	5.858	5.539	5.251	4.992	4.756	4.541	4.345	4.164	3.998	3.845	3.703	3.571	3.448	3.333
36	6.220	5.862	5.541	5.253	4.993	4.757	4.542	4.345	4.165	3.999	3.845	3.703	3.571	3.448	3.333
37	6.224	5.865	5.543	5.255	4.994	4.758	4.543	4.346	4.165	3.999	3.846	3.703	3.571	3.448	3.333
38	6.228	5.867	5.545	5.256	4.995	4.759	4.543	4.346	4.166	3.999	3.846	3.703	3.571	3.448	3.333
39	6.231	5.869	5.547	5.257	4.996	4.759	4.544	4.346	4.166	3.999	3.846	3.703	3.571	3.448	3.333
40	6.233	5.871	5.548	5.258	4.997	4.760	4.544	4.347	4.166	3.999	3.846	3.703	3.571	3.448	3.333
41	6.236	5.873	5.549	5.259	4.997	4.760	4.544	4.347	4.166	4.000	3.846	3.703	3.571	3.448	3.333
42	6.238	5.874	5.550	5.260	4.998	4.760	4.544	4.347	4.166	4.000	3.846	3.704	3.571	3.448	3.333
43	6.239	5.875	5.551	5.260	4.998	4.761	4.545	4.347	4.166	4.000	3.846	3.704	3.571	3.448	3.333
44	6.241	5.876	5.552	5.261	4.998	4.761	4.545	4.347	4.166	4.000	3.846	3.704	3.571	3.448	3.333
45	6.242	5.877	5.552	5.261	4.999	4.761	4.545	4.347	4.166	4.000	3.846	3.704	3.571	3.448	3.333
46	6.243	5.878	5.553	5.261	4.999	4.761	4.545	4.348	4.166	4.000	3.846	3.704	3.571	3.448	3.333
47	6.244	5.879	5.553	5.262	4.999	4.761	4.545	4.348	4.166	4.000	3.846	3.704	3.571	3.448	3.333
48	6.245	5.879	5.554	5.262	4.999	4.761	4.545	4.348	4.167	4.000	3.846	3.704	3.571	3.448	3.333
49	6.246	5.880	5.554	5.262	4.999	4.761	4.545	4.348	4.167	4.000	3.846	3.704	3.571	3.448	3.333
50	6.246	5.880	5.554	5.262	4.999	4.762	4.545	4.348	4.167	4.000	3.846	3.704	3.571	3.448	3.333

Z-SCORE TABLES

Values of the Cumulative Distribution Function for a Standard Normal Random Variable:

z	0.00	0.01	0.02	0.03	0.04	0.05	0.06	0.07	0.08	0.09
0.00	0.5000	0.5040	0.5080	0.5120	0.5160	0.5199	0.5239	0.5279	0.5319	0.5359
0.10	0.5398	0.5438	0.5478	0.5517	0.5557	0.5596	0.5636	0.5675	0.5714	0.5753
0.20	0.5793	0.5832	0.5871	0.5910	0.5948	0.5987	0.6026	0.6064	0.6103	0.6141
0.30	0.6179	0.6217	0.6255	0.6293	0.6331	0.6368	0.6406	0.6443	0.6480	0.6517
0.40	0.6554	0.6591	0.6628	0.6664	0.6700	0.6736	0.6772	0.6808	0.6844	0.6879
0.50	0.6915	0.6950	0.6985	0.7019	0.7054	0.7088	0.7123	0.7157	0.7190	0.7224
0.60	0.7257	0.7291	0.7324	0.7357	0.7389	0.7422	0.7454	0.7486	0.7517	0.7549
0.70	0.7580	0.7611	0.7642	0.7673	0.7704	0.7734	0.7764	0.7794	0.7823	0.7852
0.80	0.7881	0.7910	0.7939	0.7967	0.7995	0.8023	0.8051	0.8078	0.8106	0.8133
0.90	0.8159	0.8186	0.8212	0.8238	0.8264	0.8289	0.8315	0.8340	0.8365	0.8389
1.00	0.8413	0.8438	0.8461	0.8485	0.8508	0.8531	0.8554	0.8577	0.8599	0.8621
1.10	0.8643	0.8665	0.8686	0.8708	0.8729	0.8749	0.8770	0.8790	0.8810	0.8830
1.20	0.8849	0.8869	0.8888	0.8907	0.8925	0.8944	0.8962	0.8980	0.8997	0.9015
1.30	0.9032	0.9049	0.9066	0.9082	0.9099	0.9115	0.9131	0.9147	0.9162	0.9177
1.40	0.9192	0.9207	0.9222	0.9236	0.9251	0.9265	0.9279	0.9292	0.9306	0.9319
1.50	0.9332	0.9345	0.9357	0.9370	0.9382	0.9394	0.9406	0.9418	0.9429	0.9441
1.60	0.9452	0.9463	0.9474	0.9484	0.9495	0.9505	0.9515	0.9525	0.9535	0.9545
1.70	0.9554	0.9564	0.9573	0.9582	0.9591	0.9599	0.9608	0.9616	0.9625	0.9633
1.80	0.9641	0.9649	0.9656	0.9664	0.9671	0.9678	0.9686	0.9693	0.9699	0.9706
1.90	0.9713	0.9719	0.9726	0.9732	0.9738	0.9744	0.9750	0.9756	0.9761	0.9767
2.00	0.9772	0.9778	0.9783	0.9788	0.9793	0.9798	0.9803	0.9808	0.9812	0.9817
2.10	0.9821	0.9826	0.9830	0.9834	0.9838	0.9842	0.9846	0.9850	0.9854	0.9857
2.20	0.9861	0.9864	0.9868	0.9871	0.9875	0.9878	0.9881	0.9884	0.9887	0.9890
2.30	0.9893	0.9896	0.9898	0.9901	0.9904	0.9906	0.9909	0.9911	0.9913	0.9916
2.40	0.9918	0.9920	0.9922	0.9925	0.9927	0.9929	0.9931	0.9932	0.9934	0.9936
2.50	0.9938	0.9940	0.9941	0.9943	0.9945	0.9946	0.9948	0.9949	0.9951	0.9952
2.60	0.9953	0.9955	0.9956	0.9957	0.9959	0.9960	0.9961	0.9962	0.9963	0.9964
2.70	0.9965	0.9966	0.9967	0.9968	0.9969	0.9970	0.9971	0.9972	0.9973	0.9974
2.80	0.9974	0.9975	0.9976	0.9977	0.9977	0.9978	0.9979	0.9979	0.9980	0.9981
2.90	0.99813	0.99819	0.99825	0.99831	0.99836	0.99841	0.99846	0.99851	0.99856	0.99861
3.00	0.99865	0.99869	0.99874	0.99878	0.99882	0.99886	0.99889	0.99893	0.99896	0.99900

Values of the Cumulative Distribution Function for a Standard Normal Random Variable (Cont.)

z	0.00	0.01	0.02	0.03	0.04	0.05	0.06	0.07	0.08	0.09
-0.1	0.4602	0.4562	0.4522	0.4483	0.4443	0.4404	0.4364	0.4325	0.4286	0.4247
-0.2	0.4207	0.4168	0.4129	0.4090	0.4052	0.4013	0.3974	0.3936	0.3897	0.3859
-0.3	0.3821	0.3783	0.3745	0.3707	0.3669	0.3632	0.3594	0.3557	0.3520	0.3483
-0.4	0.3446	0.3409	0.3372	0.3336	0.3300	0.3264	0.3228	0.3192	0.3156	0.3121
-0.5	0.3085	0.3050	0.3015	0.2981	0.2946	0.2912	0.2877	0.2843	0.2810	0.2776
-0.6	0.2743	0.2709	0.2676	0.2643	0.2611	0.2578	0.2546	0.2514	0.2483	0.2451
-0.7	0.2420	0.2389	0.2358	0.2327	0.2296	0.2266	0.2236	0.2206	0.2177	0.2148
-0.8	0.2119	0.2090	0.2061	0.2033	0.2005	0.1977	0.1949	0.1922	0.1894	0.1867
-0.9	0.1841	0.1814	0.1788	0.1762	0.1736	0.1711	0.1685	0.1660	0.1635	0.1611
-1.0	0.1587	0.1562	0.1539	0.1515	0.1492	0.1469	0.1446	0.1423	0.1401	0.1379
-1.1	0.1357	0.1335	0.1314	0.1292	0.1271	0.1251	0.1230	0.1210	0.1190	0.1170
-1.2	0.1151	0.1131	0.1112	0.1093	0.1075	0.1056	0.1038	0.1020	0.1003	0.0985
-1.3	0.0968	0.0951	0.0934	0.0918	0.0901	0.0885	0.0869	0.0853	0.0838	0.0823
-1.4	0.0808	0.0793	0.0778	0.0764	0.0749	0.0735	0.0721	0.0708	0.0694	0.0681
-1.5	0.0668	0.0655	0.0643	0.0630	0.0618	0.0606	0.0594	0.0582	0.0571	0.0559
-1.6	0.0548	0.0537	0.0526	0.0516	0.0505	0.0495	0.0485	0.0475	0.0465	0.0455
-1.7	0.0446	0.0436	0.0427	0.0418	0.0409	0.0401	0.0392	0.0384	0.0375	0.0367
-1.8	0.0359	0.0351	0.0344	0.0336	0.0329	0.0322	0.0314	0.0307	0.0301	0.0294
-1.9	0.0287	0.0281	0.0274	0.0268	0.0262	0.0256	0.0250	0.0244	0.0239	0.0233
-2.0	0.0228	0.0222	0.0217	0.0212	0.0207	0.0202	0.0197	0.0192	0.0188	0.0183
-2.1	0.0179	0.0174	0.0170	0.0166	0.0162	0.0158	0.0154	0.0150	0.0146	0.0143
-2.2	0.0139	0.0136	0.0132	0.0129	0.0125	0.0122	0.0119	0.0116	0.0113	0.0110
-2.3	0.0107	0.0104	0.0102	0.0099	0.0096	0.0094	0.0091	0.0089	0.0087	0.0084
-2.4	0.0082	0.0080	0.0078	0.0075	0.0073	0.0071	0.0069	0.0068	0.0066	0.0064
-2.5	0.0062	0.0060	0.0059	0.0057	0.0055	0.0054	0.0052	0.0051	0.0049	0.0048
-2.6	0.0047	0.0045	0.0044	0.0043	0.0041	0.0040	0.0039	0.0038	0.0037	0.0036
-2.7	0.0035	0.0034	0.0033	0.0032	0.0031	0.0030	0.0029	0.0028	0.0027	0.0026
-2.8	0.0026	0.0025	0.0024	0.0023	0.0023	0.0022	0.0021	0.0021	0.0020	0.0019
-2.9	0.00187	0.00181	0.00175	0.00169	0.00164	0.00159	0.00154	0.00149	0.00144	0.00139
-3.0	0.00135	0.00131	0.00126	0.00122	0.00118	0.00114	0.00111	0.00107	0.00104	0.00100

INDEX

abnormal profit 273, 277
abnormal returns 169
absolute cost advantage 426
absolute risk-adjusted return 632
absolute solution 126
absolute value 126
account holder 231
accountancy 443
accounting beta 175
accounting report 436
accrued interest 312
acquirer 51
active bond management strategies
    barbell 381
    credit analysis 381
    laddered 381
    valuation analysis 381
active portfolio 538, 540, 552
active return 169, 182
actively managed portfolio 618
activity 444
actual cash flow 450
actual data 255
actual liabilities 440
actual price change 379
actual return 634
actual return 77, 84, 180, 182
actual standard deviation 116
actual values 119
ADR 30, 43
ADR route 30
advance decline index 496
advance-decline ratio (A/D ratio) 497
advances 495
after-tax returns 327
aggregate demand 413
aggregate market capitalization 57
aggregate market risk 253
aggregate savings rate 412
aggressive investor 224
aggressive stock 247

agricultural GDP 408
agriculture 406, 414
algorithm 601
allocation
    of capital 221, 224
    of funds 62, 224, 225
alpha 158, 168, 169, 622
    calculation of 624
    fundamental indicators 168
    inferior performance 623
    intercept 169
    interpretation of 623
    measure of diversifiable risk 184
    measure of performance 568
    negative value 247, 523
    of the portfolio 184
    positive value 247
    positive value 623
    risk-adjusted measure 169
    standard error of 626
    superior performance 623
    value of 568
    zero value of 168
alpha coefficient 566
alpha value 168, 635
    greater than zero 168
American depository receipts 30
AMEX 30
amortization 317
amortized bond 318
amount of cash flow 460
analyses 8
analysis 278
analyst 78, 415, 443
analyst's report 43
analytical framework 244
annual compound rate
    of interest 344
    of return 76
annual compounded rate 345
annual coupon rate 308

annual per capita GDP 406
annual rate of return 74
annual return 78
annualized compound return 323
annualized standard deviation 62
annuity factor 316
ante-period 632
application of funds
    analysis of 442
appreciation 29
approval route 34
approximate maturity 371
APT 169, 269
    fundamental principle 263
    law of one price 263
APT and CAPM
    comparative study 264
    linear relationship 264
APT model 264
arbitrage 59, 263
    meaning 262
arbitrage opportunity 268
arbitrage pricing theory (APT) 262
arbitrageur 263
area gap 522
arithmetic average 351
arithmetic mean 75, 78
ascending triangle 506
asset 115, 222, 229, 243, 262, 289
    reallocation 226
    allocation 231
asset backed bonds 311
asset beta 178
asset class 249
asset efficiency 443
asset limit 453
asset management companies (AMC) 24, 42
asset turnover 443, 444
asset under management (AUM) 24
assets 442, 445, 495
    efficiency 444
    in a portfolio 158
    turnover 440, 443
assets
    financial 249
        bonds 249
        futures 249
        options 249
        stocks 249
    real 5, 249
        antique collection 249
        gold 249
        real estate 249
        silver 249

assumption 256, 462
auto-correlation 280
auto-correlation test 279
automatic route 34
average covariance 159, 160, 162, 538
    of scrips 163
    of securities 164
average excess return
    for portfolio 627
average gain 519
average growth 435
average incremental rate of return 634
average inventory 445
average loss 519
average maturity 371
average portfolio return 627
average profits 83
average rate of return 75, 79, 326
average rate of returns 554
average return 78, 108, 181, 196, 351, 615
    of portfolio 629
    of risk-free security 627
average returns 109, 111, 136
average risk-free return 627
average variance 160, 538

backward integration 426
balance sheet 289, 436, 439-440, 452
balanced scheme 25
bank account 18
bank deposits 17, 18
bank notes 11
bank, fixed deposit (FD) 7, 18
banker 438
banker's draft 12
Bankex 42, 565
banking institution 18
bankrupt 289
bankruptcy 14, 336, 453
banks 8
bar 500
bar chart 498, 499
bargaining power 427
base market capitalization 57
base period 60
base price 278
base year 48, 59
bear market 492
bearer bonds 11
bearer debentures 12
bearer instruments 16

bearish breakdown 501
bearish divergence 519
bearish signals 491
bearish trend 9, 505
bears 9
bell-shaped curve 84
benchmark 42, 55, 632
benchmark equity fund 619
benchmark index 59, 169, 568
benchmark measure
    for performance 628
benchmark portfolio 618, 623
    portfolio 630
benchmarked index 62
benchmarking fund portfolios 60
benefit 63
benefits 5
benefits of diversification 136
beta (systematic risk) 245
beta 158, 164, 170, 182, 569
    determinants 175
    market value 164
    measure of risk and return 170
    measure of undiversifiable risk 184
    value 247
beta coefficient 565, 566
beta
    calculation of 624
    of portfolio 184, 619, 620
    of security 179, 183, 247
    standard error of 625
bid-ask spread 59, 62, 522
bills of exchange 12
blockage period 22
Bollinger bands 529
Bombay Stock Exchange (BSE) 43
bond 225
    elasticity 373
    flexibility 373
    maturity value 366
    over-priced 363
    par value of 385
    properties 364
    under-priced 363
    yield 366
bond holder 305, 324
bond indenture 306
bond issuer 382
bond management
    active strategy 382
    passive strategy 380-381
bond portfolio immunization 388

bond portfolio management 363, 380-381
bond price 324, 364
bond pricing equation 379
bond pricing theorem 363, 364
bond rating swap 384
bond swap 382
bond theorem 369
bond value 313, 382
bond yield, at maturity 364
bonds 7, 12, 13, 103
    characteristics 306
    evaluation 382
    periodic payment 306
    types of 307-312
bonus issues 56
bonus share 56, 273, 285
book value per share 289
book value
    of equity share 468
boom period 453
boon of diversification 111
borrow 4, 208, 244
borrowed fund 229
borrowers 34
borrowing 15, 206, 564
    of fund 206
borrowings 413, 452
bottom-up approach 403
brand loyalty 426
breadth 43
    indicator 496
breakaway gaps 522
break-even point 426
BRIC nations 405
broker 231
broker's commission 62
brokerage 274
brokerage charges 8, 58, 274
brokerage costs 244
BSE *100* 23, 565
BSE *200* 42
BSE *30* 42
BSE 49
BSE *500* 565
BSE index cell 55
BSE index committee 45
BSE indices 51
BSE PSU index 51
BSE reality index 42
BSE Sensex 41, 50, 175, 414, 456, 565
BSE tech 42
built-in capital gain 325

built-in price appreciation 327
bull market 492
bullish breakout 501, 506
bullish divergence 519
bullish indicators 491
bullish signal 508
bullish signs 491
bullish trend 9
bulls 9
bunch of securities 106
business conditions 175
business cycle risk 262
business cycles 175, 413
    cyclical 428
    defensive 428
    growth 428
    peaks 414
    troughs 414
business entity 440
business interest 440
Business Line 44
business risk 435, 436
business-cycle-defying industry 429
buy and hold 381, 460
buy-back of shares 57
buyer 502
buying 59

CAGR 7, 77, 438, 478
CAL 201, 208, 228, 231
    slope 201
call date 329
call option 306
call price 306, 329
call risk 388
callable bond 306, 329
candlestick chart 498-500
capacity addition 410
capacity constraints 410
capacity utilization 455
capital 221, 228, 423, 434, 472
    opportunity cost of 472
    optimal distribution 221
capital allocation 225
capital allocation decision 224
capital allocation line (CAL) 201, 221, 228, 537
    derivation 220
capital appreciation 6, 8, 9, 473
capital appreciation/losses 24
capital asset pricing model (CAPM) 243, 247, 564, 632
capital deficient 415
capital gain (loss) 73

capital gain 9, 25, 30, 72-74, 381-383, 441, 461, 473
capital gain or loss 175
capital gain, realization 70
capital gain/loss 81, 105, 345
capital gains 244
capital goods 409, 410, 436
capital indexed bond 309
capital loss 327, 381
capital market 24, 30, 81, 244, 262
capital market instruments 24
capital market line (CML) 243, 247, 629
capital market theory (CMT) 243
capital reallocation 226
capital stock 9
capital structure 178, 431, 438, 440, 444, 452, 471
capitalization issue 56
capitalization rate 466, 471
CAPM 169, 243-256, 262
    assumptions 244, 248
    expected return 255
    formula 478
    implications 254
    limitations 255
    linear efficient set 250
    market portfolio 256
    rate of return 255
    separation principle 248
    theory 435
CAPM model 634
CARE 336
cash cow 423
cash equivalent 13, 448
cash flow 13, 72, 385, 475, 476, 615
cash flow statement 436, 440
cash flows 273, 306
    from financing activities 440
    from investment activities 440
    from operational activities 440
cash inflow 72, 615
cash outflow 385, 615
cash profit 442
cash subsidies 430
catastrophe bonds 312
certainty equivalent rate of return 223
certificate of deposits 11, 12, 16
certificates, KVP 17
challenges 456
characteristics line (ex-post) 624
characteristics line 170, 245
characteristics line equation 247
chart patterns 503
    cup and handle 503, 508
    flag pattern 503, 507
    head and shoulders 503, 504
    head and shoulders reverse pattern 503, 505

triangle pattern 503, 506
        rounding bottom 503, 509
chartist 42, 275, 278, 292
charts 490
charts, types of 498
cheques 11, 12
C-I-E analysis 403
circuit filters 62
circular notes 12
close-ended schemes 24
closing price 6, 489, 498
closing share price 70, 72
clusters 422
CML
        intercept 249
        slope 250
        straight line equation 250
        vertical intercept 250
CMT 263
CNX *100* 23, 44
CNX Mid Cap Index 61
CNX Nifty *50* 256
CNX Small Cap Index 60
coefficient of variation (cv) 118, 291
coefficient
        of determination 158, 173, 626-627
        of non-determination 626-627
COGS 438
collection period 446
collection policy 449
commercial banks 15
commercial loans 31
commercial paper 12, 15
committee 55
commodities 28, 414, 489
commodity 79
common factors 265
common gaps 522
common shares 438
common stocks 13
co-movement 108
companies 42, 43, 50, 104
Companies Act 14
company 26, 42, 49, 104, 473
        evaluation 473
company analysis 433-457, 459
company fundamentals 81
company strategy 447
company, share capital 13
comparative relative strength 518
compensation 29, 169, 324
competency 456

competition 427
competitive market 422
competitive rate of return 324
competitive strategy 425
complete elimination 161
complete portfolio 226, 228
component of risk 161, 376
components of risk
        systematic 158, 160, 245
        unsystematic 158, 160, 245
compound annual growth rate 7, 77
compound interest 351
compound rate of growth 614
compounded annual growth rate (CAGR) 7
compounded annually 21
compounded half-yearly 17, 21
computation, risk-return ratio 135
concave 197
congestion area 522
conservative securities 253
consoles 307
consolidation pattern 524
constant dividend growth model 475
constant dividend model 467
constant growth model 465
constant growth rate 462, 465
constitution
        of minimum variance portfolio 125
        of portfolio 158, 243
consumer durables 409
consumer goods industry 430
consumer retail market 454
consumption demands 409
contingent immunization 389
contingent liabilities 440
continuation pattern 524
contractual terms 29
convertible bond 309
convertible debentures 14
convertible preference shares 15
convex relation 370
convexity 369, 378, 380
co-operative bank 430
co-operative society 21
corner portfolio 601, 606
        adjacent portfolio 603
        composition of 604
        hypothetical ratio 603
        inefficient portfolio 603
        non-adjacent portfolio 603
        resultant portfolio 603
        return and standard deviation 602

corporate action 55, 62, 495
corporate bodies 51
corporate insiders 277, 292
corporate restructuring 57
corporate securities/bonds 354
corporation 21
corrections 493, 494
correlation 83, 116, 117, 158, 160, 167, 227, 279, 536
    of securities 117
correlation coefficient 103, 109-111, 116, 121, 158, 279, 626, 627
        negative 110
        positive 110
        zero 110
cost leadership 447
cost leadership strategy 447
cost of capital 443, 449, 452
cost of debt capital 330
cost of equity 478
cost of goods sold (COGS) 438, 445
cost structure, of industry 430
costs of capital measurement 255
counter moves 494, 507
counter-cyclical 104
countries, market efficiency 274
country specific recession 566
coupon 373
coupon bearing bond 344, 345
        duration 375
coupon payment 13, 306, 308, 345, 346, 371, 390
coupon rate 306, 331, 373
covariance 103, 106, 108, 111, 117, 139, 162, 196, 198, 227, 534, 536
    of individual securities 162
    of portfolio 121
    of returns 108, 121
    of risk-free security 200
    of securities 540
    of security 251
covariance matrix 244, 583
covariance terms 159
covariance, estimates of 565
covariance-expected return relationship 252
credit 273
credit analysis 381, 382
credit crisis 404
credit management 446
credit period 446
credit policy 446
credit rating 335
credit rating agencies 14
credit rating companies 336

credit reserve ratio 161
credit sales 446
credit spread 354
credit worthiness 452
creditor 438, 445, 452
CRISIL 44, 60, 336
cross holding 51
crowding out 415
CRR 161
cumulative value 579
cup and handle 507
currency devaluation 275
current account 18
current assets 440, 446, 449, 459
current closing price 289
current income 6, 383
current liabilities 440
current liability 449
current market price 345
current price 275, 284, 476
current ratio 445, 449
current share price 286, 289
current spot rates 358
current stock price 276
current trend 452
current yield 328
curvature, degree of 370
curved efficient set 564, 565
cut-off point 571, 577, 579, 581
cut-off rate 571, 574
cut-off spread 308
CV 288
cyclical companies 436
cyclical industries 428
cyclical stocks 436

daily fluctuation 492, 494
data point 500
data, volume of 489
day-to-day movement 491
DCF technique 615
debentures 7, 12-14, 305, 452
debt 178, 431, 448, 452, 456, 471
debt capital 440, 444, 448, 452, 453
debt market 14
debt repayment capacity 445
debt securities 7, 57
debt trap 308
debt, after-tax cost 478
debt-equity ratio 440, 444
debtors turnover 446
decline 423

decline stage 425
declines 495
deep discount bond 307
default 196
default risk 5, 7, 22, 196, 198, 305, 335, 343, 382, 388
default risk premium 336
defensive companies 435
defensive industries 429
defensive stock 429, 435
defensive strategy 104
deferred callable bonds 330
deficits 15
degree of
    curvature 370
    diversification 160
    freedom 79, 107
    operating leverage 175-176
    risk 5
    risk aversion 209, 223, 234
    variation 118
delivery agreement 427
delivery system 409
demand 501
demand and supply principle 249
demat 28
demographic profile 457
denominations 17
Department of Post, Government of India 21
deposit receipt 17, 30
depository charges 58
depository participants (DPs) 28
deposits 7
derivative
    negative 379
    positive 379
derivatives 12, 23
descending triangle 507
determinants of beta
    financial leverage 175
    nature of business 175
    operating leverage 175
developed countries 274
developing economy 457
development financial institutions (DFIs) 16
development project 456
deviation 79, 85, 108
    from average return 79
DFI 16
differentiation 452
differentiation strategy 447
direct method 105
directors of the company 50

discount 6, 14, 16, 24
discount bond 329, 374
discount factor 347
discount rate 254, 306, 348, 478
discounted cash flow 319
    valuation approach 476
discounted price 460
discounted value 306, 450
dispersion 119
distribution 229
distribution value 85
divergence 519
diverse securities 104, 111
diversifiable risk 162, 565
diversification 104, 115-116, 160-163, 245, 451, 565
    of a portfolio 117
    of funds 112
    of investment 104
diversification benefit 131
    possibility of 134
diversified assets 618
diversified portfolio 60
dividend 6, 14, 30, 61-63, 72, 273, 442, 472, 615
dividend amount 460
dividend discount model 465, 470, 476
dividend growth rate 449
dividend option 25
dividend payout 449
dividend payout ratio 470, 472, 473
dividend per share (dps) 73, 74, 81, 450, 465, 467
    downward trend 465
    random movement 465
    zero growth 465
dividend rate 460
dividend warrants 12
dividend yield 73, 74, 81, 105, 175, 450, 473
dividend
    constant rate 466
    non-payment 470
    variable nature 460
dividends 104, 244
dock warrant 17
Dollex 42
domestic capital market 23
domestic market 265
dominate 117
dominated stock 117
dot 500
double bottom **527**
double top **527**
Dow Jones **Average** 491
Dow Jones Industrial and Rail averages 492

Dow Jones Industrial Average (DJIA) 44, 46, 279
Dow theory 490
    assumptions 491
down flag 507
downgraded rating 382
downside risk 86
downturn 429
downward movement 501
downward sloping yield curve 379
downward sloping yield term structure 357
downward trend 492
drafts 11
DuPont analysis 443
duration 370, 378
    zero coupon bond 374
    coupon bearing bond 375

earning 444, 472
earning capacity 438, 453
earning capitalization 471
earning multiple 449
earning potential 443, 452, 453
earnings 436
earnings after tax 438
earnings before interest and taxes (EBIT) 430, 438
earnings before tax (EBT) 438
earnings limit 453
earnings per share (EPS) 430, 438, 450, 452, 453
EBIT 438
EBT 438
ECB 34
    automatic route 34
    approval route 34
economic analyses 433
economic condition 81, 430
economic downturn 429, 431, 435
economic factors 452
economic growth 406, 414
economic index 48
economic output 404
economic performance, determinant 415
economic revival 79
economic scenario 105
economic slump 435
economic stages 82
economics 6
Economics Times Index 48
economies of scale 447, 455
economy 13, 26, 42, 112, 175, 431, 452
economy-company relationship 452
efficiency 158, 447
    of management 424

efficiency structure 454
efficient financial market 461
efficient frontier 198, 247, 535, 537, 538
efficient frontier set 244
efficient frontier theory 533
efficient market 262, 272-274
efficient market hypothesis (EMH) 272-274, 292, 403, 461
efficient market theory, validity 292
efficient performance 422
efficient portfolio 122, 124, 197, 243, 249, 252, 552
    construction of 538
    rates of return 247
efficient portfolio manager 42
efficient product development 457
efficient set 103, 136, 197, 212, 537, 597-599, 606
    concave shape 552
    construction of 552
    deriving location of 601
    empirical property 197
    theory 197
efficient set theorem 197
efficient market 168
    semi-strong form 276, 292, 284
    strong form 277, 292
    weak form 276, 278
E-I-C analysis 403
E-I-C approach 489
E-I-C framework 433, 552
elasticity 373
electricity sector 409
electronic limit order book (ELOB) 58
elimination of risk 162
ellipses 501
EMH 272, 276, 292
    validation 280
    weak form of 292
empirical evidence 292
empirical studies 277
empirical test 255
empirical work 275
employee welfare trust 51
employment of debt 440
end-user 426
energy landscape 456
energy
    consumption 406
    production 406
enterprise multiple (EM) 448
EPS 438
    estimation 452
equal probabilities 119

INDEX 675

equation method 345
equilibrium condition 634
equilibrium price 263, 275
equities 48
equity 225, 440, 452
equity beta 178
equity capital 178, 472
    cost of 472
equity capitalization rate 472
equity fund 178
equity market 73
equity market fluctuation 73
equity multiplier 443
equity research 175
equity research firm 254, 436
equity researcher 490
equity securities 57, 459
equity share 7, 8, 12, 15, 254, 442, 452, 460
    current value 460
equity stock 198
equity valuation 459
equity valuation model 614
equivalent value 348
error term 566
e-silver 28
ESOP 43
estimated profit margin 452
estimates 565
    of covariance 565
    of expected return 565
    of residual variance 565
    of variance 565
estimation 119
    of eps 452
estimation leads 495
ETF (Exchange Traded Fund) 7, 26, 60
Euro bonds 310
Euro Yen bond 310
event study test 285
eventual return
    of principal at maturity 13
ex-ante model 255
excess return on security 572
excess return
    mutual fund 169
excess return-to-beta 574, 581
excess risk 569
exchange rate 264, 405, 491
exchange traded funds (ETFs) 7, 26
exchanges 27
ex-date 63
exempt from tax 244

exhaustion gaps 522
EXIM Bank (Export-import Bank of India) 16
existing barriers 428
expansion 414, 452
expansion phase 429
expansion plans 441
expansion stage 423, 443
expected earnings 104
expected future spot rate 357
expected growth 456
expected growth rate 461
expected market return 637
expected measure 86
expected outcome 85, 180
expected prices 255
expected rate of return 81, 82, 105
expected return 10, 71, 85-86, 103-106, 119, 135, 162, 180, 199, 222, 232-236, 245, 250, 267, 357, 422, 534, 536, 566
expected return of portfolio 114
    calculation of 568
expected return
    degree of risk 599
    estimates of 565
    minimum risk 599
expected returns 199
expected returns and risks 222
expected return-standard deviation pairs 197
expected return-standard deviation plane 201
expected risk 103, 199, 235, 245
expected value 85, 118
expenditure 413
expenses 4, 5, 8
exploration 454
exponential moving average (EMA) 514
export order 285
exports 456
ex-post alpha 624
ex-post average return 617
ex-post data 255
ex-post period 632
ex-right 56
extensive distribution 455
external commercial borrowings (ECB) 31
external environment 431
extrapolation 205
extreme volatility 455

face value 13, 16, 306, 344
factor specific risks (beta) 266
factor specific risks 266
fair market return 324
fair prices 7

fair rate of return 324
fair return 286
fair value 255
Fama 279
FCCBs 34, 43
FD certificate 18
FDI 29, 51
feasible combinations 221
feasible risk-return combinations 221
feasible set 197, 201, 203, 597, 598, 599
    construction 197
feasible set and efficient set 197
feasible set boundary 598
feasible set of portfolios 135
filter level 278
filter point 278
filter size 278
filter test 278
final equilibrium 273
final portfolio 226, 227, 229, 236, slope 228
finance 411
finance companies 16, 24
financial accounting depreciation methods 443
financial analyst 438, 451
financial assets 5
financial condition 441
financial data 444, 459
financial discipline 455
Financial Express Indices 42
financial gain 178
financial health 438
financial implications 440
financial index 48
financial information 436
financial institution 16, 43, 452
financial instruments 262
financial investment 3
financial leverage 178, 440, 444, 452, 453
financial leverage ratio 443
financial markets 272
financial parameters 436, 444, 449
financial potential 435
financial products 263
financial risk 104, 178, 431, 435, 436
financial statement 433, 436, 444, 495
financial strength 403, 438
financing 16, 413, 444
financing activities 441
firm-specific factors 269
firm-specific risks 266
fiscal deficit 161, 275
fiscal exit 409

fiscal policies 491, 566
fiscal policy 413
fiscal stimulus measures 412
Fitch 336
fixed assets 441, 443, 447, 449, 453
fixed assets turnover ratio 447
fixed charges 452
fixed costs 58, 175, 430
fixed coupon rate 308
fixed deposit account 18
fixed deposits 7
fixed expenses 431
fixed income holding 14
fixed income securities 12-13, 305, 343
    valuation 343
fixed income security 196, 306
fixed periodic payment 13
fixed rate bonds 308
fixed stream of income 305
fixed value 306
fixed interest rate 13
fixed-income asset 196
flag 526
flag pattern 507
flat cross 501
flat yield curve 353
flexibility 373
floating bar chart 618
floating rate bonds 308
floating stock 60
flow of information 275
fluctuation 55, 73, 456
    in prices of security 161
FMCG 414
food industry 429
food security 409
forecasted return 322
foreign bonds 309
foreign company 285
foreign currency 31
foreign currency convertible bonds (FCCBs) 34
foreign exchange rate 456
foreign exchange risk 265
forestry 408
Forex market 522
Forex rate 265
Forex reserves 262
forward integration 426, 427
forward rate 343, 348, 355, 358
founders 50
free cash flow 478
    to equity 476

INDEX 677

free float 60
free float factor 51-53, 55
free float market capitalization 49, 54, 56, 60, 61
free float market capitalization methodology 59
free float method 50, 55
free float methodology 50, 51, 55
free float shares 51, 55
FTSE 55
full corpus 62
functionality of portfolio 221
fund 229, 234
fund flow statement 436, 441
fund generating capacity 441
fund inflow 62
fund manager 55
fund outflow 62
fundamental analysis 255, 403, 421, 433, 489
fundamental analyst 459
fundamental of company 14
fundamentalists 292
funds 11
       employment 4
       surplus 8
future cash flow 494
future expectation 470
future spot rate 343, 356, 358
future trends 276
future value annuity 321
future value interest factor annuity (FVIFA) 321
futures 489
FVIFA 321

gap 521
       types of 522
GDP 265, 404, 414
GDRs 31, 43
generated funds 443
generating capacity 443
geometric average 351
geometric mean 76
geometric mean return 614
global crisis 407
global depository receipt (GDR) 30, 31
global economic environment 404
global economy recession 74
global expansion 404
global investment 637
global market 453
global output expansion 404
global recession 566
globalization 430
GNP 262

gold 26
gold certificates 26
gold mutual funds 26
gold options and futures 26
gold price 26
gold, negative correlation 26
government 13, 15, 21, 50, 196, 229
government debt 413
government expenditure 413
government of India 15, 17, 23
government policies 161, 175
government regulation 426
government securities 196
grievances 8
gross book value 443
gross profit margin 438, 444
gross value 443
gross world product 406
growth 6, 11, 25, 104, 164, 220, 265, 414, 423
       and dividend schemes 25
       in dividend 465
       in total expenditure 438
       of sectors 429
       value of 476
growth companies 434
growth expectation 469
growth industries 428-429
growth option 25
growth period 409
growth phase 407
growth prospects 449
growth rate 77, 406, 427, 473
       normal 466
       supernormal 466
growth share 472
growth stage 81, 423
growth stock 8, 434

head and shoulders pattern 504
head and shoulders reverse pattern 505
hedge 6
       against inflation 6
high fixed cost 426
high growth 81
high P/B value 292
high P/E ratio 286, 288
high P/E value 288
high price 489, 499
high return 118, 224
higher risk 118, 222
highest value 221
Hindu undivided families 17

historical costs 451
holding period 9, 75, 77, 196, 225, 244, 325, 462
       of bond 30
holding period return 75-78, 325
homogenous expectation 244
horizon analysis 322, 390
horizontal distance 630
horizontal trend line 506
horticulture 408
hospitality sector 411
HPR 75
hundis 12
hydro-power generation 409

ICICI Bank 20
ICRA 336
identical risky portfolios 244
IDFC 34
idiosyncratic random shock 266
idle fund 62
IFCI 16
IIP 262, 265
IL&FS 34
immunization 385-389
       issues 388
       of portfolio 387
impact cost 41, 59
implicit gain 327
implicit interest income 327
implicit yield 308
import parity price 456
inactive accounts 20
income 4, 6, 438
       from interest 17
income share 472
income tax 244
Income tax act, 1961 21, 22
income tax deduction 306
increased investment 438
incremental return 201, 203, 211
incremental return-risk 133
incremental return-risk ratio 135
incremental risk 201, 203, 211, 262
independent variables 170
index 8, 44, 53, 61-63, 167
       of inflation 309
       of return 262
       of risk 164
index based derivatives 60
index calculation 51, 55
index closure algorithm 55
index fund 60, 62
       return 62

index fund manager 59
index funds and futures 42
index futures 60, 63
index maintenance 55
index movement 61
index of industrial production (IIP) 409
index options 60
index portfolio 62
index schemes 25
indexing 381
India Index Services and Products Ltd. (IISL) 60
Indian Stamp Act 1899 (Central Act) 312
indices 41-43, 60, 175, 489
indifference curve 197, 205, 213, 234-238, 248, 606
       derivation 220
indifference curves 592-600
       for neutral investors 596
       for risk-averse investors 596
       for risk-takers 596
       implications 593
       intersection 594
       selection of 595
       theory of 592
       zone of eligibility 597
individual asset
       risk and return 534
individual securities 42, 103-106, 110, 114, 117, 158, 243-245, 269, 286, 534
       risk and return 291
individual security risk 184
individual stock risk quotient 253
individuals 34, 274
Industrial Finance Corporation of India (IFCI) 16
industrial goods 410
industrial growth 407, 409
industrial policies 161, 491, 566
industrial production growth rate 406
industrial revival 410
industrial sector 34, 407
industrial unit 453
industry 26, 42, 104, 406
       cost structure 430
industry analysis 421-431
industry average 445
industry life cycle 421
       assessment of 424
       decline stage 424
       expansion stage 423
       pioneering stage 422
       stabilization stage 423
industry life cycle curve 423
industry performance 425
       factors affecting 430

INDEX 679

industry structure 425
industry weightages 61
inefficient frontier 535
inefficient portfolio 603, 605
inefficient stock 117
inferior portfolios 254
inflation 4-8, 104, 244, 264, 265, 309, 343
       impact of 357
inflation rate 5, 256, 357, 491
inflation risk 262
Inflation, hedge against 6
inflow 24
       of fund 62, 441
information 273
         announcements 273
         financial statements 273
infrastructural activity 409
infrastructure 29, 410
infrastructure sector 34
initial investment 206
initial public offerings 57
initial yield 325
initiation phase 422
innovation 466
insecurity 71
insolvency 449
installments 21, 23
institutional borrowers 229
institutional investors 8, 43, 267
institutions 274
instrument 12
instruments 7, 11, 13, 17
insurance 104
insurance companies 8, 29
insurance group 23
insurance services 411
intangible assets 289
intercept 169, 184, 201, 249
intercept term 179, 634
interest 6, 14, 21, 273
       accrued 21
       taxable 14
interest bearing liabilities 444
interest coverage 453
interest coverage ratio 445
interest earned 21
interest expenses 438
interest rate 13-14, 18, 21, 196, 306, 345, 383, 491
       calculation 343
       fluctuations 313, 377
       movement 387
       term structure 265, 355

interest rate risk 21, 196, 262, 332, 373, 380, 385, 456
interest rate sensitivity 334
interest rate subsidies 430
inter-market spread swap 383
intermediate cash flows 307, 373
internal cash flow 371
internal environment 431
internal rate of return (IRR) 443, 614, 615
international monetary fund (IMF) 405
interpolation 320
interpolation method 345
intersection point 594
intraday movement 491
intraday trader 490
intrinsic value 6, 9, 254, 273, 292, 382, 433, 477
       of company 459
introduction stage 422
inventory management 445
inventory turnover 445-447
inventory turnover ratio 445
inverse floaters 311
inverse relation 369
inverted yield curve 354
invested fund 220
investible fund 206
investing 5
investment 3-9, 11, 14, 72, 103, 206, 220, 225, 244, 442
       diversification 104
investment activities 441
investment alternative 11, 538
investment assets 221
investment banking 443
investment company 8, 23
investment decision 71, 87, 103, 220, 224, 255, 403, 433, 473, 519, 534, 569
investment horizon 196, 256, 356, 381
investment management 263
investment manager 381, 614
investment objectives 71
investment options 71, 434
investment plans 19
investment proceeds 615
investment proposition 459
investment research 421
investment risk analyses 255
investment volumes 8
investments 29, 103, 273, 441
       holding period 244
investor 6, 14, 24, 43, 103, 221, 224, 231, 243, 244, 264
investor
       risk-averse 86, 87, 104, 204, 211, 221, 223, 236
       risk-loving 87, 204, 213, 224
       risk-neutral 87, 204, 223

investor's confidence 264
invests 5
IPO 60
irredeemable preference shares 15
issuance stamp duty 312
issuance
       of security 442
       of shares 441
       of warrants 441
IT stocks 61

Jenson's differential return measure 632
Jenson's performance measure 634
       superiority of 635
joint venture 60, 454

key personnel 276, 285
Kisan Vikas Patra (KVP) 12-13, 17-18
       low return 17
       low liquidity 17

large cap 49, 285
large cap companies 285, 286
large cap company 50
large company 49
large market capitalization 55
large scale diversification 161
leading indices 60
left shoulder 505
legal 8
legal and regulatory framework 7
legal immunity 21
legal terms 29
lending 206, 564
lending and borrowing rate 256
level of risk 634
leverage 208, 210, 229, 238
leverage analysis 451
levered firm 178
liabilities 25, 289
liberalization 430
LIC (Life Insurance Corporation) 23
life cycle, study of 424
lifetime annuity 29
line chart 498
line of best fit 170
linear efficient set 205, 248, 250
linear function 379, 635
linear regression 264
linear relationship 128, 178, 264
liquid investment 15
liquidation 58, 62

liquidation provision 358
liquidation value 464
liquidity 6-7, 15, 18, 29, 43, 58, 60, 63, 358, 444
liquidity position 440
liquidity preference theory 358
liquidity premium 359
listing of security 43
live stock 408
loan funds 442
loan repayment 442
loans and advances 441
locked in share 50
logging 408
logistics 426
London Stock Exchange 31
long position 278
long-term debt security 305, 312
long-term fixed income securities 104
long-term investment 414
long-term investor 414
long-term moving averages 517
long-term solvency 444
low cost 452
low liquidity 17, 22
low P/B value 292
low P/E ratio 287
low P/E stocks 288
low P/E value 288
low price 489
low return 17, 22
low risk 60
lower return 118
lower risk 118
lower trend line 506, 507
lower variable costs 175
lowest risk 122, 536
lump sum 23
Luxemburg Stock Exchange 31

M 248, 249 250
Macaulay duration 371, 376
Macaulay model 377
MACD 527
macroeconomic factors 8, 119, 161-163, 262-265, 268, 421
macroeconomic influences 264
macroeconomic variables 436, 491
magical effect 431
maharatnas 23
main portfolio 210
maintenance of index 55
major determinants 465

mall 454
management 445
management attitude 452
manufacturing processes 428
manufacturing sector 409
margin 263, 427
margin account 231
margin of safety 6, 449
marginal gap 595
market 9, 41-42, 55, 81, 220, 234, 245, 273
    fundamental principle 251
    standard deviation of 572
    variance of 568
market action 495
market analysis 84, 404
market analyst 272, 459
market anomalies 285
market benchmark 175
market beta 175
market breadth theory 495
market cap 49-50
market capitalization 41, 46-56, 60, 448, 456
market capitalization method 60
market condition 363
market demand 455
market discount function 347
market efficiency 272-293
    forms of 276
    strong form 292
    tests 277
    weak form 276
market equilibrium 244
market exchange rate 406
market factors 269
market fluctuations 278
market forms, characteristics 277
market functioning 403
market hypothesis, weak form 278
market index 42, 179-182, 254, 537, 627, 631, 634
    movement of 571
market indices 41-43, 264, 631
market inefficiencies 285
market leadership 455
market liquidity 58
market model 158, 170, 179, 180
market model equation 181
market momentum 490
market movement 10, 23, 42, 492
market participants 274
market portfolio 167, 175, 247-251, 256, 637
    excess return of 620
    location of 629
    symbol M 248

market price 263, 273, 286, 364, 433, 450, 477
market price data 290
market price per share 450
market prices 243, 275, 285
market related risk 565
market return 158, 164, 167-168, 173-175, 179-182, 245, 253, 566-567, 622, 623
market risk 8, 161-164, 183, 250, 373, 567, 616, 631
market risk premium 633
market segmentation theory 359
market share 425, 447
market strength 496
market time 635
market trend 55
market value 289, 306
    of firm 452
    of portfolio 225
    weighted index 46
market value of beta 164
    negative 164
    positive 164
market value
    growth 614
    loss 614
market variance 165, 167, 253, 579
marketable securities 264
Markowitz 103, 564, 601
Markowitz analysis 565
Markowitz Model 254, 533, 552-557
Markowitz Portfolio Theory (MPT) 136, 195, 243-244, 564
Markowitz theory 103
Markowitz's efficient set 606
mature industry 428
maturity 21, 25, 373, 423
maturity amount 386
maturity date 306
maturity of bonds 334
maturity period 24, 196, 345
maturity phase 425
maturity stage 423
maturity value 345
maximum benefit of diversification 127
maximum expected return 197
maximum possible return 114
maximum return 197
mean 84, 85, 284
mean return 567
mean-variance criterion 124
measure
    of risk 137
    of valuation 289
measured return 634
measurement errors 637

measurement parameters 631
medical expenses 4
medium cap company 50
medium company 49
mergers 57, 273, 434
mergers and acquisitions 424
MF (Mutual Fund) 7
mid cap 49, 285
mid cap companies 285, 286
mid cap index
    of BSE 623
    of NSE 623
minimum possible risk 115
minimum risk 103, 197, 305
minimum variance portfolio 115, 125, 534
mining sector 409
miniratnas 23
Ministry of Finance 18, 273
minority interest 448
miscellaneous expenses 25
mis-priced securities 274, 459
modern portfolio theory (MPT) 533, 535
    foundation of 564
modernization 452
modified duration 377
    formula 378
momentum 9
monetary policies 566
money 3, 4
money market 15
money market instrument 15, 103
money market scheme 25
money order 17
monthly income schemes 18
Moody 336
Moore 279
movement 44
    of share prices 490
moving average 497
moving average convergence divergence (MACD) 527
moving average line 508
moving averages 507, 518
MPT 244
    framework 534
MSCI 55
multi-period investment 614
multi-period relation 462
multi-period valuation 464
multi-period valuation model 462
multiple risk sources 262
mutual fund 21, 24, 629
    growth option 25
    dividend option 25

mutual fund companies 537
mutual fund company 25
mutual fund industry 537
mutual fund managers 42, 292
mutual fund performance 169
mutual funds 7, 8, 274

N portfolios (feasible set) 197
N securities 197
    possible combinations 197
NABARD (National Bank for Agricultural and Rural Development) 307
naïve diversification 122
NASDAQ 30
NASDAQ-*100* 55
National Housing Bank 21
National Sample Survey Organization 407
National Savings Certificate 7, 13, 17-19, 21
National Savings Schemes 13, 17, 22
National Spot Exchange Limited (NSEL) 28
natural calamities 161
natural gas 453
natural resources 427
nature of competition 430
nature of diversification 104
nature of product 452
NAV (net assets value) 25
NBFC (non-banking financial companies) 7, 18
    deposits 13
neckline 505
negative alpha 629
negative beta 254
negative beta portfolio 636
negative correlation 26, 113, 116, 122, 138
negative covariance 109
negative deviation 85, 86
negative price-earnings ratios 286
negative return probability 111
negative value 126
negatively correlated scrip 160
negotiable 29
negotiable instrument 11, 22
    characteristics 12
negotiable securities 30
net cash flow 441
net current assets 440
net present value (NPV) 475
net profit margin 447
net profit margin analysis 452
net risk of the portfolio 158
net worth 440
new base market capitalization 57
new index value 47

INDEX 683

new issues 56, 57
new market capitalization 57
new offerings 57
NHB (National Housing Bank) 16
Nifty 42, 164, 179
Nifty 50 41, 175, 565
Nifty index 60
Nifty Junior 42
Nikkie (Tokyo Stock Exchange) 44
no-arbitrage 268
noise 508
nominal 8
nominal rate 343, 357
non-adjacent portfolio
    hypothetical ratio 603
    standard deviation 603
non-banking companies 8
non-banking financial corporation (NBFC) 18
non-banking financial institutions (NBFIs) 18
non-consumer durables 409
non-convertible debentures (NCD) 14
non-convertible preference shares 15
non-diversifiable risk 263
non-government borrowers 236
non-linear 369
non-negotiable 17
non-negotiable instruments 17
non-negotiable securities 17
non-profit making organizations 34
normal curve 85, 284
normal distribution 78, 83-85
normal distribution table 85
normal growth rate 466
normal market condition 352
normal positive slope 353
normal probability distribution 84
    bell-shaped 84
    skewed 84
    smooth 84
    symmetric 84
normal probability table 85
normal yield curve 352
normally distributed pattern 84
north-western region 533, 556
notion of dominance 117
novel bonds 311
NPV 475
NSC 21
NSC scheme 21
NSE 58, 60, 61
NSE S&P CNX Nifty 456
NSE-50 42

NSEL 28
n-year maturity 359
NYSE 30

obligations 440
old market capitalization 57
open interest 489
open market 50, 51, 53, 55
open-ended schemes 24, 25
opening price 6, 489
operating activities 441
operating efficiency 443
operating leverage 431, 438
operating profit 438
operating rate 456
operating risk 431
operational inefficiency 409
opportunity set 197, 203, 597
opposite (negative) sign 281
optimal allocation 221
optimal distribution 221
optimal diversification 243
optimal portfolio 204, 231-236, 533-537, 557, 601, 606
    focal point 248
    identification 243
    location of 606
    selection 213
optimal weight 130, 234
optimism 415
optimum policy 474
optimum portfolio 114, 234, 238, 247
    with short sales 584
optimum return 103
optimum weight of securities 115
optimum weights 114, 133
order book 58
ordinary (equity) shareholder 15
ordinary share 13, 15
    valuation 459
OTC 30
other income 438
outcome 82
outflow 24
    of fund 62, 441
output 414
outstanding balance 318
outstanding debt 440
outstanding shares 25
overall market 60
overall momentum 519
overall portfolio return 162
overall return on investment 615

over-bought condition 519
over-priced bond 363, 382
over-priced stock 169, 436
over-valued share 477
over-valued stock 436
owner 445, 452

P & L account 436
P/B ratio 285, 286, 289
P/B value 289, 291
P/E ratio 285, 286, 289, 449
P/E value 289
paid-up share capital 452
PAN 23
panic situation 522
par value 14, 329
par value of bond 385
passive bond management strategies
       buy and hold 381
       indexing 381
passive portfolio 538, 539
passively managed portfolio 618
past data 277
past prices 284
past trends 495
patent 276, 426
patent application 455
patterns 490
payout ratio 450, 473
pennants 526
pension plan 29
per capita consumption 457
per capita income 457
percentage change 377
percentage payout ratio 450
percentile 619
perfect competitive market 324
perfect market 292
perfect negative correlation 125, 127
perfect substitute 428
perfectly positive correlation 117, 127
performance 42, 48, 280, 407, 430, 444
    of industry 409
    of mutual funds 169
    of sectors 429
performance indicator 618
perpetual bond 307, 323
perpetual earnings, value of 476
perpetual growth model 469
perpetual growth rate 474
perpetuity, present value 465
per-share earnings 286, 289

pessimism 415
pioneering phase 425
pioneering stage 422
pivotal role 456
planned expenditure 410
point and figure chart 498, 500
point of tangency 238
policy decision 465
political factors 161
politics 42
population 414
portfolio (ex-post) 621
portfolio
    beta of 568
    construction 114, 117, 199, 221, 247, 289, 533, 565, 584, 604
    efficient set 195
    evaluation of 556
    excess return of 620
    expected return of 568
    functionality 221
    Jenson's evaluation 632
    market value 224
    non-diversifiable risk 263
    of assets 440
    of equities 618
    of investment 103
    of liabilities 440
    performance measurement 618
    rate of return 569
    risk and return 125, 201
    risk-free 220
    risky 220
    standard deviation 116
    systematic risk of 245, 568
    total risk 158
    two-asset 113
    unsystematic risk of 568
    variance 113
    variance of 568
portfolio beta 627
portfolio characteristics 201
portfolio configuration 135
portfolio fund 386
portfolio management 3
    active strategy 363, 618
    passive strategy 363
portfolio management strategy 382
portfolio manager 103, 254, 272, 378, 433, 537, 637
portfolio measurement, limitations 637
portfolio opportunity set 135, 136, 597
portfolio P 268

portfolio performance measurement 613
    conventional methods 613
    risk-adjusted 616, 622
portfolio performance
    comparative study 636
    evaluation of 613-638
portfolio return 105, 114, 121, 201, 623
portfolio risk 110, 113, 116, 121, 158-159, 201, 266, 538
portfolio selection 213, 592-607, 635
portfolio selection model
    theoretical framework 534
portfolio study 285, 289
portfolio theory 78, 104, 221, 243
portfolio variance 538
portfolios 42, 197, 222, 286
    of risky securities 202, 250
    possible combinations 203
positive alpha 168, 629
positive beta 435
positive beta portfolio 636
positive correlation 116, 122, 131, 138
positive deviation 85, 86
positive risk premium 221, 227
positive sign 281
positive value 169
possible outcomes 83, 85, 105, 118
post office 7, 18
    savings account 19
    savings schemes 7
    schemes 17
    time deposit account 19
post offices 20, 21
post reform period 406
postal department 18
postal order 17
potential investor 597
potential returns 428
potential risk 71
    and reward 572
potential scrips 538
power of diversification 130
Power, Finance and Shipping Corporation 23
PPF account 20
PPP theory 405
predicted outcome 490
preference dividend 460
preference shareholders 15
preference shares 12-14, 438
preferential issue 43
premature redemption 330
premium 14, 23-24, 306
premium bonds 329

premium price 447
premium share price 470
present value interest factor (PVIF) 316
pre-tax income 438
price 6, 13, 244, 278
price appreciation 383, 473
price changes 280
price chart 490, 495
price earnings (P/E) ratio 104, 286, 289, 436
price fluctuation 9
price matrix 391
price movement 279-280, 490, 495
price multiple 449
price of bond 344
price patterns 524
price risk 358, 373, 568
price sensitivity 332, 374
price stability 409
price swing 519
price takers 274
price
    random nature 494
    sentiment 494
    valuation 494
price-earnings ratio 286, 449
price-equity ratio 289
price-to-book (P/B) ratio 286
    calculation 289
price-to-book-value 451
price-weighted index 46
price-weighted series 47
price-yield relationship 330
pricing 430
pricing strategy 443
primary bear market 493
primary movement 492
primary shares 57
primary trend 491
primary upward trend 493
principal amount 14
principal repayment 371
private (corporate) sector 14
private corporation 430
private data 277
privatization 430
privileged information 293
probabilities 81, 85
probability 82, 84, 108
    negative return 111
probability distribution 85, 86, 121, 180, 226
probability of occurrence 108, 121
probability theory 284

probable deviation 110
probable future trend 452
processing capacity 455
procurement of funds 453
product 428
product innovation 424
production 455
production capacity 430
production cost 430
production measures 264
professionals 292
profit 263, 445
profit and loss account 436
profit and loss statement 438
profit margin 425, 443
profit maximizing investor 274
profitability 427, 430, 441, 447, 448
profitable 7
profitable business integration 455
profitable investments 273
profitable patterns 279
profitable security 112
profits 23
project execution 455
projected return 322, 380
promised cash flow 460
promised cash outflow 389
promissory notes 11-12
promoter 51
promotion 452
proportion
    of debt 453
    of funds 199, 580
    of investment 105
    of securities 129, 538
    of wealth 122
protection 104
public data 277
public investment 409
public provident fund (PPF) 13, 17-19
    schemes 18
public sector bank (PSB) 7, 430
public sector undertakings 13, 23
pull-back 502
purchasing power 343, 414
purchasing power parity (PPP) 404
pure discount bond 307, 374
pure expectations theory 355
pure yield curve 351
pure yield pick-up swap 384
puttable bonds 309
PVIF 316

Q value 451
qualified institutional placements 43
qualified securities 571
qualitative analyses 421
qualitative aspect 433
quality complex asset 456
quality spread 354
quality spread index 355
quantitative analyses 421, 444
quarrying sector 409
quarterly report 285
question mark 422
quoted bond price 312

rainfall deficit 415
Rajiv Gandhi Equity Savings Schemes (RGESS) 22
random error 180
random error term 179-180, 247
    of portfolio 184
    standard deviation 181, 625
random movement 275
random number 284
random phenomena 495
random residual error 566
random walk hypothesis 81, 275
random walk theory 275, 277, 495
    assumptions 275
    of EMH 276
rank, of portfolio 632
rate anticipation swap 384
rate
    of dividend 460
    of return 71, 74, 79, 81, 234, 245, 254
    risk-free 226
rating 14
rating agencies 382
ratio analyses 443, 444
ratios
    beta squared 574
    beta to unsystematic risk 581
    excess return-to-beta 581, 584
    of standard deviation to mean return 118
    reward-to-systematic risk 630
    reward-to-variability 630
    reward-to-volatility 627
    squared beta to unsystematic risk 579
    systematic risk to unsystematic risk 571
rational investor 198, 264, 273, 274
rational product planning 455
raw material 429
RBI 13, 15, 21
RBI indices 42

INDEX 687

reaction rallies 493
real assets 5
real estate 5, 7, 29, 411
real estate sector 34
real market 255, 292
real output 414
real rate 343, 357
realistic borrowing 230
realized compound yield 322
realized return 21
realized yield 321
reallocation of assets 226
rebalancing 388
recession 26, 81, 112, 161, 164, 176, 414, 428, 436-438
recurring deposit schemes 18
redeemable preference shares 15
redemption, of debt 453
redemption value 306
reduction, in ROCE 447
reference point 537
refineries 455
regional disparity 407
regression analysis 245
regression equation 179
regression fit 158
regression line 169-170
regression line intercept 246
regular income 473
regular investment 14
regulatory 8
reinvestment earning 469
reinvestment method 356
reinvestment rate 322
reinvestment risk 196, 373
related index 619
    performance of 619
    variance of 619
related market index 619
relationship
    convexity and duration 378
    economy and stock price 403
    fixed assets and sales 447
relative strength chart 518
relative strength index (RSI) 518
rental yield 29
repayment 206
repayment, of capital 14
replacement cost 451
repurchase price 25
required rate of return 243, 253, 460, 472
    calculation 254
required yield 382

research 279
research and development 423
researchers 292
reserve and surplus 452
Reserve Bank of India 18
residual variance 567
    estimates of 565
resistance 502
resistance level 501, 502
resistance line 507
resources 440
retail investor 22
retained earnings 450, 452, 468, 474, 476
retention 473
retention rate 470
retention ratio 472, 473
retirement-planning tool 19
return 6, 9, 13, 60, 71, 112, 118, 221, 244, 285
return
    covariance of 567
    index funds 62
    variance of 567
    variation in 568
return and risk 286, 287
    of portfolio 207
    of securities 288
return and variances 537
return
    of bond 390
    of individual securities 110-111
    of portfolio 112, 114, 183, 201, 208, 265
    of security 164, 201
    of the market 247
    of whole market 250
return on assets (ROA) 175, 447
return on capital employed 447
return on equity (ROE) 443, 452, 471
return on investment (ROI) 452
return on market index 179
return on net worth (RONW) 448
return on portfolio 263
return on security 173, 175, 179, 182, 246, 253, 263, 265
return realized 435
return to risk ratio (slope) 203
return-risk 540
return-risk profile 133, 231, 263
return-risk trade off 228
returns 4, 84, 198
    of portfolio 103, 105
    of risky assets 244
    on assets 158
return-to-risk ratio 569

revenue 413, 415, 443
revenue deficit 413
revenue growth 477
reverse pattern 505
revised yield 325
reward-to-systematic risk ratio 630
reward-to-variability ratio 630
reward-to-volatility ratio 201, 203, 228, 234, 537, 552, 627
    Sharpe's measure 629
    Treynor's performance index 627
RGESS 23
right shares 56
right shoulder 505
rights issue 43, 55, 56
risk (standard deviation) 247
risk (â) 235
risk 6, 71, 78, 81, 85, 104, 106, 169, 173, 220-222, 250, 286
risk adjustments 285
risk analysis 616
risk and return 42, 117, 197, 263, 285-286, 290, 425, 556
    companies 289
    of individual securities 289, 291
    of portfolio 210, 288, 289, 292
    of stocks 289
risk and return profile 552
risk aversion 136, 225, 231, 236
    degree of 209, 223, 234, 537
risk aversion index 223
risk bearing capacity 599, 606
risk diversification 160
risk estimation 569
risk factor 5
risk level 125
risk of portfolio 110-111, 114-115, 137, 160, 184, 201
risk preferences 86, 104
risk premium 221, 226-227, 233, 245, 253, 262-265, 269, 358, 472, 633
risk quotient 71, 158, 221, 253, 533
risk return trade off 118-119
risk taker 211
risk tolerance 135, 597
risk
    components of 569
    correlation with return 78
risk-adjusted measure 169
risk-adjusted performance 569, 629
risk-adjusted performance measures
    issues in 631
risk-adjusted rate of return 434
risk-adjusted return 168, 245
risk-averse 87, 104, 534

risk-averse investor 204-205, 211, 213, 221, 223, 236
risk-free asset 196, 199, 201, 204-205, 221, 227, 250, 537
    characteristics 195
    investment in 198
    variance of 227
risk-free borrowing 195, 206-209, 212, 229, 232, 630
    characteristics 209
risk-free interest rate 244, 250
risk-free lending 195, 201, 204, 206, 209, 212, 630
    unique attribute 198
    and borrowing 250
risk-free lending portfolio 204
risk-free lending rate 206
risk-free payoff 268
risk-free portfolio 220
risk-free profit 268
risk-free rate 201, 206, 234, 429, 564
    summation of 633
risk-free rate of return 226
risk-free return 199, 266
risk-free securities 225, 343
risk-free security 196, 199, 201, 206, 221, 234, 243, 268
    allocation of funds 224
    selection of 221
Risk-less security 569
risk-loving investor 87, 204, 209, 213, 224
risk-neutral investor 87, 204, 223
risk-return 126, 197
risk-return category 164
risk-return ratio 115, 597
risk-return relationship 71, 251
risk-return trade-off 136, 170, 223, 244, 249, 262, 593
risk-return values 118
risk-return
    characteristics 205, 224, 534
    combinations 201, 236
    parameter 363
    performance 203
    preferences 213, 248
    profile 131, 201, 209, 211
risks of individual assets 158
risky 9, 24
risky asset 198, 201, 204, 210, 233, 533
    efficient frontier 564
    rate of return 196
risky constituent portfolio
    variance of 227
risky marketable securities 250
risky portfolio 201-205, 210, 220-221, 225-229, 232-233, 238, 249, 630
    allocation of funds 224
risky portfolio CAL 210

risky securities 203, 221, 225, 243, 533
risky security 112, 114, 196, 198, 202, 206, 221, 630
    selection of 221
risky stock 199, 205
ROA 447
ROA ratio 452
ROE 471
RONW 448
Ross, Stephen 263
rounding bottom 507, 509
RSI
    analysis 518
    chart formation 519
rules of dominance 117
runaway gaps 522
runs test 281
rupees-weighted average 616
rupees-weighted return 614, 615
rural market 414

S&P 45, 55
S&P CNX *500* 61
S&P CNX Nifty 58, 60
safe investment option 17
safety 7-9
    index 8
    principal amount 9
sale of shares 72
sales 445
sample 43
sample company 56
sample distribution 85
sample size 84, 282
sample stocks 279
save money 4
saving 4, 220
savings 5
savings account 18
savings account schemes 18
savings-cum-tax-saving instrument 19
scheduled bank 21
schemes 427
scrip 49, 53, 62
    in index 62
scrip issue 56
scrips 44, 45, 175
    S&P 45
    CNX 45
    from indices 538
    average returns 556
SEBI 63
secondary market 14, 306

secondary movement 491-493
    reactionary nature 493
secondary trend 494
section 80C 20, 21
section 80L 20
section 88 22
sector 175
sectors (industries) 104
sectors 43
securities 6, 14, 23, 62, 71, 86, 103, 112, 196, 220, 231, 273, 287
    diversification benefits 536
    market price 243, 273
    over-valued 459
    positive correlation 536
    profitable 112
    return-risk trade-off 243
    risky 112
    safety 8
    under-priced 6
    under-valued 459
    weighted average risk 113
    with negative returns 577
    with positive returns 578
securities market 23
security 57, 82, 104, 175, 245, 289
    intrinsic value 273
    unsystematic risk 571
security analyses 3, 255
security analyst 82, 119, 433, 449
security characteristics line (SCL) 169
security evaluation 71
security market line (SML) 243, 247, 250, 621, 624
security movement
    variance of 571
security prices 263, 273, 275, 277, 491
security return 158, 567
security, risk premium 564
selection
    of optimal portfolio 213
    of risk-free security 221
    of risky security 221
selection procedure 534
seller 502
selling 59
selling and administrative expenses 438
selling price 390
semi-annual duration 372
semi-strong efficient market 276
senior citizen savings schemes 18
Sensex 42, 48, 164, 179, 256, 414
sensitivity analysis 480

sensitivity measure of security 247
sensitivity of the return 182
sentiment 292, 505
separation principle 248, 249
serial correlation 279, 281
service fees 24
service sector 407
services 406
set of assets 197
share capital 13
share in the market
share premium 452
share price 460, 472
share valuation model 469
share value 465
share warrants 12
share
    fair value 478
    intrinsic value 478
shareholders 56
shareholders' earnings 452
shareholders' risk 452
shares 21, 70, 104
Sharpe, William 592
Sharpe's index model 575
Sharpe's measure 629
Sharpe's optimal portfolio 572
    construction of 569, 575
Sharpe's ratio 201, 228, 572
    formula for 569
    negative 569
Sharpe's single index model 565
    assumptions 566
    derivations 567
    limitations 567
short position 278
short sale 584
short-term debt instrument 15
short-term fixed income securities 104
short-term obligations 440
SIDBI (Small Industries Development Bank of India) 16
signals 495
silver ETFs 28
silver futures 27
simple annualized return 78
simple average 75
simple linear regression 624
simple moving averages (SMA) 508, 512
simple weighted average 111
single holding period 195
single index model, components 566
single investor 274

single period model 534
single period valuation model 460
single risky asset 203
single risky stock 210
size 452
skewed 84
slope 169, 182, 208, 210, 252
    characteristic line 245
    measure of systematic risk 170
    of CAL 201, 234
    of portfolio 184, 229
    positive value 252
slope coefficient of regression 175
SLR 161
slump 254
small cap company 49-50
small lot sizes 445
small market capitalization 285
small savings schemes 18
small scale companies 60, 285-286
SML 252, 263
smooth curve 84
solvency 449
sound capital base 426
sources of funds, analysis of 442
south-western region 136
special economic zone (SEZ) 29, 454
specific period of time 169
speculation 9, 292
speculative companies 436
speculative stocks 436
speculator 9
spending 4
spin-offs 57
spot contract 346
spot rate 346
stabilization stage 423
stamp duties 312
    issuance 312
    transfer 312
Standard & Poor (S&P) 60, 336
standard deviation 78-79, 84-86, 104-106, 110-113, 118, 135, 159, 196, 201, 223, 251, 282-284, 534-537, 540, 566, 617
    calculation 82
    measure of risk 163
    of portfolio 116-117
    of random error term 625
    square of 174
standard error
    of alpha 626
    of beta 625

standard normal variate 282
State Bank of India 20
static stage 81
statistics 78
statutory liquidity ratio 161
stock 13, 46, 206, 245, 292
    actual return 247
    closing price 614
    current closing price 289
    current price 273
    dividend 614
    fundamentals 292
    intrinsic value 459
    opening price 614
    over-priced 247, 436
    over-valued 436
    under-priced 247, 449
    upward movement 278
stock adjustment 438
stock beta 178
stock exchange 13, 24-25, 43, 57-58, 272-273, 292, 306
stock liquidity 58
stock market 58, 71, 103, 220, 272, 292, 403, 414
    analysis 404
stock market crash 521
stock market indices 41
stock market return 414
stock over-pricing 449
stock price 247, 273-274, 459, 472, 567
    random movement 275
    reversal 278
stock specific risk 23
stock split 46-47, 55, 273, 276, 285
stock volatility 490
Stock-outs 445
stocks 13, 60, 103, 117, 198, 288, 489
    with low P/B ratio 291
STOXX 55
straight bond 306
straight line 202, 208-209, 227-228, 379
straight line equation 250
straight line graph 201
stream of dividend 464
strong performance 433
structural change 407
structured pension plan 21
subsidies 414, 430
substitute product 428
substitute services 428
substitutes 427
substitution swap 383
superior product portfolio 455

superior return 285, 293
superior return on investment 277
superior risk-adjusted return 292
supernormal growth rate 466
supplier 427
supply 501
support 502
support and resistance levels 518
support level 501-502, 507
support line 507
surplus 8
sustainability 409
sustainable growth 423, 457
swaps 382
    types of 383-385
switching cost 427
symmetric 84
symmetrical triangle 506
synergistic effects 451
systematic component 173
systematic risk, measure of 632
systematic variance 363
systematic risk 160-164, 167, 245, 250, 253, 262, 267, 565, 575
    and expected return on individual security 269
    and expected return on portfolio 267
    assessment 164
systematic, undiversifiable risk 173

takeovers 273
tangency point 238, 606
tangency portfolio 564
tangent 213
tangent line 247, 379
target index 62
targeted expected return 536
targeted return 534
tax 4
tax benefits 20, 22
tax deduction at source (TDS) 17
tax exemption 21, 161
tax holidays 430
tax liability 19, 21, 385
tax management 438
tax rate 14, 273, 430
tax rebate 19, 20
tax saving instrument 22
tax savings scheme 25
tax sheltered instruments 17, 19
tax swap 385
taxable 17
taxable income 19, 327, 383

taxation policies 448
taxes 413
T-bill rate 637
T-bills 15, 196, 308
t-distribution 282
TDS 17
technical analysis 279, 403, 489-530
technical analysis indicators 501, 509
    exponential moving averages 514
    long-term moving averages 517
    moving averages 509
    simple moving averages 510
    support and resistance 501
    triangular moving averages 517
    variable moving averages 517
    weighted moving averages 511
technical analyst 278-279, 490
technical indicator tool 517
technology 273, 452
term deposits 18
term loans 452
term structure 355
    downward sloping 357
    upward sloping 357
term structure theories 343, 355
term to maturity 391
terminal value 307, 464
tests 277
    filter test 278
TFCI (Tourism Finance Corporation of India) 16
threat 452
time 7, 250
time change 391
time management 455
time period 14-15, 18, 75, 85, 173-175, 179, 287, 391, 489
time series data 281
time to maturity 391
time-weighted average 616
time-weighted concept 014
time-weighted rate of return 614
timing of cash flow 460
Tobin's q 451
top-down approach 403
total assets 289
total assets turnover 447
total assets/total shareholder equity 443
total cash 448
total expenditure 438
total fund 385
total market capitalization 50, 51
total outflow 615

total return 72
total return index (TR index) 61-63
total risk (variance) of security 162
total risk 158, 162, 252, 569, 575
    of portfolio 158
total variance 636
TR index 61-63
tracking error 41, 62-63
tradable commodity 27
tradable instruments 489
trade cycle 104
trade-off 136
trading 59, 71
trading day 522
trading distortion 508
trading gap 522
trading range 522
trading signal 518
transaction 9
transaction cost 58, 62, 244, 278, 389
transaction sizes 58
transfer stamp duty 312
transferability 22
transferor to transferee 12
transnational 448
transportation 411
treasury bill 7, 12, 196, 343
treasury bond 384
trend 292, 505
trend identification 518
trend line 491
trend reversal 514
Treynor's and Sharpe's method
    comparison of 631
Treynor's performance index 627-628
trial-and-error method 345
triangle pattern 506
triangles 524
triangular moving averages 517
trough 505
trusts 34
turnover ratio 445
two-asset portfolio 113

ULIP (Unit Linked Insurance Plan) 7
unavoidable risk 71
unbiased expectation theory 355
uncertainty 162, 206
under-priced 6
under-priced bond 363, 382
under-priced stock 169
under-valued stock 477

undiversifiable 245
undiversifiable risk 161
unique rate of return 71
unique risk 162, 183, 567, 616, 631
    of portfolio 163, 184
    of security 183
Unit Linked Insurance Plan (ULIP) 7
Unit Trust of India (UTI) 24
unlevered beta 178
unsystematic component 173
unsystematic risk 161-163, 169, 245, 269, 575
unsystematic variance 267
unsystematic, diversifiable risk 169
un-weighted index 48
up flag 507
upper trend line 506, 507
upside runaway gap 522
upward movement 501
    of stock 278
upward rating 382
upward sloping term structure 357
upward sloping yield curve 357
upward trend 446, 492
utility function 220-221, 224, 231-235
    calculation 222
utility industry 429
utility level 235
utility score 221-224
utility value 220-224, 235-236

validity, efficient market theory 292
valuation 255, 317
    equity 459
    of a company 289, 459
    ordinary share 459
valuation analysis 381, 382
Valuation model
    multi-period 462
    single period 460
value of alpha 247, 634
value of covariance 121
value stocks 436
variability
    of expenses 431
    of sales 431
variable cost 430
variable expenses 431
variable income securities 12
variable moving averages 517
variance 79, 112-113, 118, 162, 244, 540
    calculation 82
    estimates of 565

    of market 165
    of portfolio 159, 164, 184, 266
    of random error term 183
    of return of market index 183
    of risk-free asset 227
    of risky constituent portfolio 227
    of security 183
    of unsystematic risk 267
variance terms 159
variances 159, 198, 534
varying level of risk 197
varying levels of expected return 197
vertical distance 630
vertical integration 426, 451
vertical intercept 250, 252, 629
volatile market 508
volatile stocks 167
volatilities 125
volatility 119, 168, 176, 376, 428, 568
    measure of 568
volume 278, 279, 427, 497
volume data 284

WACC 434
warrants 441
weak inter-sector linkage 408
wealth 5
Wealth tax 21
wealth, of the economy 248
wedges 526
weight 540
weightage 456
weighted average 158, 266, 438
    alpha 184
    beta 266
    debt beta 178
    equity beta 178
    random error terms of individual securities 184
weighted average cost of capital (WACC) 434
weighted average cut-off yield 308
weighted average return 105, 252
    of individual securities 116, 183
    on securities 159
weighted average risk 110, 115
    of securities 113
weighted average standard deviation 116
    of assets 117
weighted moving averages 512
weights 105
    of securities 114
well-diversified portfolio 104, 160, 162, 264, 266-268
working capital 442

working capital management 449
world class assets 455
world class technology 455

yearly return 108
yield 29, 104, 306-307, 367, 373, 379
    percentage change 369, 377
yield change effect 391
yield constant effect 391
yield curve 343, 350, 388
    downward sloping 379, 381
    types of 352
yield debt instrument 312
yield rate 389
yield spread 383
yield structure 391
yield to call (YTC) 329

yield to maturity (YTM) 306, 318, 326, 343, 364, 379, 383, 388
    of bond 390

ZCB 307
zero beta 167
zero correlation 129, 131
zero coupon 374
zero coupon bond 13, 307, 326, 344, 371
    redemption 307
    yield 307
    face value 307
    duration 374
zero covariance 252
zero default risk 15
zero growth model 465
zero risk 234
zero value of alpha 168
Z-scores 85
Z-test 282